FROM
WILSON
TO
ROOSEVELT

FROM
WILSON
TO
ROOSEVELT

Foreign Policy of the United States

1913–1945

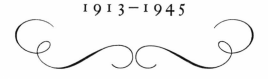

Jean-Baptiste Duroselle

Translated by Nancy Lyman Roelker

HARVARD UNIVERSITY PRESS

Cambridge, Massachusetts

1963

© Copyright 1963 by the President and Fellows of Harvard College

Library of Congress Catalog Card Number 63-17197

Printed in the United States of America

A translation of *De Wilson à Roosevelt: Politique extérieure des Etats-Unis, 1913–1945,* published by Librairie Armand Colin, Paris, 1960

Passages from *The Memoirs of Cordell Hull,* Copyright 1948 by Cordell Hull, are quoted by permission of The Macmillan Company; passages from *The Public Papers and Addresses of Franklin D. Roosevelt,* Copyright 1938, 1941, by Franklin Delano Roosevelt and Copyright 1950 by Samuel I. Rosenman, by permission of Random House, Inc.; and passages from Henry L. Stimson and McGeorge Bundy, *On Active Service in Peace and War,* Copyright 1947, 1948, by Henry L. Stimson, by permission of Harper and Row, Publishers, Inc.

TRANSLATOR'S FOREWORD

TRANSLATION often presents hazards beyond the basic problems of idiom and language, such as complicated style or technical vocabulary. In such cases the translator must attempt to work out a reasonable solution, apply it consistently, and justify it to the author, the publisher, and the reader. No such problems existed in this book, with its clarity of thought and lucidity of style.

It has been both a privilege and a pleasure to share in bringing to American readers an outstanding example of European scholarship in this study of our foreign policy in the twentieth century. I am confident that other American readers will find their understanding deepened by M. Duroselle's analysis, which combines the objectivity of a foreign observer with a profound knowledge of and sympathy with the United States.

Nancy Lyman Roelker

Cambridge, Massachusetts
May 1962

FOREWORD TO THE AMERICAN EDITION

I wish above all to thank Miss Nancy Roelker for translating this book. The intelligence and vigor of the translation, by an American historian who knows France well, are a source of satisfaction to me and should add to the value of the book. Nancy Roelker has been more than a translator; she has given me invaluable suggestions. With her help, and with the help of Professor Robert Ferrell of the University of Indiana, Professor Bernard Sinsheimer of the University of Maryland, and M. l'Inspecteur-General Gadrat, I have been able to correct the many errors in the French edition, and I wish to express my gratitude.

Jean-Baptiste Duroselle

Paris
May 1962

PREFACE

An author does not have to justify himself for having written a book; the reader is the only judge of whether he has found something valuable in it. I would, however, like to explain why I undertook the ambitious task of presenting the foreign policy of the United States in the dramatic period between 1913 and 1945. This ambition stems from theoretical, intellectual, considerations and also from a particular situation.

On the theoretical level, it seemed important to try to understand the complex process—made up of advances and retreats, of hesitations and leaps forward—by which the United States was brought to take an active part in world politics. The case of the United States is unique. In the early twentieth century, all the other major nations acted as if the essential objective of foreign action was to increase their real power in as many regions of the world as possible; in other words, they sought to have a *Weltpolitik*. The United States, however, seemed to consider that power was immoral. At least this was the attitude of a very great number of American citizens. At the same time, in the economic sphere, the United States had become the leading nation in the world, and its superiority, accelerated by two world wars, was to continue to increase. Its "potential" in political power was considerable.

Why did Americans tend to prevent this potential from being realized, to renounce the opportunities for action on a world scale which lay within their grasp? Why did Theodore Roosevelt's policy of expansion—really quite modest—meet with strong opposition? How can we account for the failure of Wilson, who had been gradually converted to the idea of American responsibility in world affairs? Why did the narrow concept of nationalism triumph in the 1920's—in contrast to Wilsonian internationalism—to be followed in the 1930's by isolationism, the refusal to participate? Why, finally, did Franklin D. Roosevelt and the majority of the American people become convinced that the policy of the United States could no longer be based on selfish withdrawal, but rather that it must be based on active participation in international affairs? Perhaps such irregular progress is inherent in the nature of things, perhaps the conversion of potentiality into active power is inevitable. In any case, Americans resigned themselves to it without enthusiasm. To attempt to describe and to explain this process seemed to me a task meriting the effort.

In such a vast undertaking it was impossible, except accidentally, to use unpublished sources. The published documents and memoirs and the extensive works of American historians on the most varied aspects of the subject are difficult enough to master. I have tried not to duplicate what American writers have already done. In particular I have avoided the approach of the textbooks by Samuel Flagg Bemis, Thomas A. Bailey, Julius W. Pratt, and Robert H. Ferrell. These excellent works emphasize the facts and devote much space to world events, even those in which the United States took little part, because they are geared primarily to the needs of students. Taking advantage of a number of works on the general history of international relations, I decided to assume that the major international events were known to the reader and to confine myself very specifically to American actions and reactions. I also judged it better to stress the motives behind the action more than factual detail.

Following Pierre Renouvin's already classic distinction between the role of statesmen and the role of profound impersonal forces which condition and explain a large part of international relations, I have tried to disentangle the perceptible elements of these different motivating forces. This has required an emphasis on individuals whose education, temperament, and ideas have greatly influenced certain events.

I have also tried to analyze economic forces and their relation to specific pressures exerted by various interest groups and movements, by psychological forces, and by public opinion. Finally, it seemed essential to analyze what I shall call the profound political forces—a will to power or a will to abstain from power—which often underlie prevailing strategic conceptions. I have naturally not arrived at a systematic, rigid formulation by this method, my prime concern being to explore, on the very imperfect level of the possible, all the kinds of motives and to show what seems to have been their relative importance at various times.

On the level of practical considerations, this book was inspired by an alarming fact which many visits to the United States in recent years helped me to discover: French historians have virtually turned their backs on the United States since World War I! This is an indifference which nothing can explain or justify, neither the object of research—American history is of exceptional interest—nor the opportunities for research, since American universities welcome French scholars. The situation is particularly painful when one realizes that the converse is not true; there exists in the United States a Society for French Historical Studies with more than 300 members.

Because of the high standards of the Institut d'Etudes Politiques de Paris and its director, Jacques Chapsal, since 1954 that institution has offered a course on the foreign policy of the United States. The course, which I am privileged to conduct, played a large part in my decision to write this book. I have been able to take advantage of several favorable circumstances: the seminar that Serge Hurtig and I have conducted in the graduate program of the Fondation National des Sciences Politiques; a grant from the Rockefeller Foundation which enabled me to specialize; the creation of a United States section in the Centre d'Etudes des Relations Internationales at the Fondation, and, more recently, a term as visiting lecturer at Harvard University, where I had at my disposal a very complete collection of materials related to American history.

I would not know how to list all those who have helped me with the conception of the book, but there are three men I must mention, as their influence on my thinking has been considerable: Pierre Renouvin and Raymond Aron in France, and Arnold Wolfers, director of the Washington Center of Foreign Policy Research, in the United States.

It is almost as difficult to acknowledge the aid of the many American experts I have had the privilege of meeting and of questioning, who have helped me with inexhaustible courtesy to gather information and to interpret events. I must first express my gratitude to my American colleagues: two brilliant young specialists of the Wilson period, Arno Mayer and Ernest R. May of Harvard; McGeorge Bundy, former Dean of the Faculty of Arts and Sciences at Harvard, who collaborated with Henry L. Stimson on that great statesman's memoirs; Elting Morison, of the Massachusetts Institute of Technology, who allowed me to consult the manuscript of his magnificent book on Stimson, since published; Frank Freidel and Arthur M. Schlesinger, Jr., of Harvard, two major specialists on Franklin D. Roosevelt and his era; Carl Friedrich of the government department at Harvard; Stanley Hoffmann of the same department, who was kind enough to read part of the manuscript and whose ever ready aid has been inestimable; Stephen Kertesz, chairman of the Committee on International Relations at the University of Notre Dame, distinguished expert on diplomacy; and Richard Monsen of the staff of the United States embassy in Paris, who read the manuscript and gave me infinitely valuable advice.

From the Fondation Nationale des Science Politiques I have had every imaginable support in the preparation of this book. Serge Hurtig, my fellow crusader for American studies in France, has also read the book and given me the benefit of his thorough knowledge of the United States; Nicole Deney, research assistant at our center, has been the most valuable possible collaborator; for more than two years she has worked, under my direction, with an enormous number of documents. Her perceptive criticism and her knowledge of the United States have been invaluable. Marina Cerné, also a research assistant at the center, gave me very valuable assistance in the last phases of the work.

Finally, I wish to express my appreciation to Kenneth Thompson of the Rockefeller Foundation, and to Shepard Stone of the Ford Foundation, because of whose interest considerable financial resources were placed at my disposal and made available to our center. Without their aid I would never have been able to take on such an enterprise. Because of their help and the help of the Fondation Nationale des Sciences Politiques and many friends and colleagues, I was able to complete this study.

Jean-Baptiste Duroselle

December 1960

CONTENTS

Contents

Part One

THE NEW DIPLOMACY AND
ITS DEFEAT

1913–1921

Chapter I

The Foundations of American Foreign Policy
before the Election of Wilson

American Intervention and Its Strategic Aspects

W<small>HEN</small> Woodrow Wilson became President on March 4, 1913, the
United States, twenty years behind Europe, was emerging from a
period of imperialism and colonial expansion. It would be impossible
to understand the Wilsonian era without first trying to define and
describe American "imperialism" in the early twentieth century.
There were both strategic and economic foundations to this movement which we shall examine in turn.

The United States had filled out its continental limits by 1848, if
one excepts small adjustments of frontiers and the acquisition of
Alaska in 1867. Partly as a result of the slavery controversy and the
Civil War, Manifest Destiny—according to which Providence, which
aids the virtuous, had set aside for the American people the whole of
North America—was hardly more than a memory of the past. For
thirty years the nation had been content to remain as it was. The
United States was isolationist because it was assured of safety and of
economic development, and because it felt strong enough, physically
and morally, to need neither conquests nor alliances.

Then suddenly the conflict with Great Britain and Germany over
the Samoan Islands, from 1886 to 1889, awakened anxiety and revived ambition. In rapid succession came the annexation of the
Hawaiian Islands (July 1898); the war with Spain which resulted
in the annexation of Puerto Rico, Guam, and the Philippines (December 1898); the establishment of United States influence in Wake
(January 1899) and a part of Samoa (1899–1904); the claim to a
sort of protectorate over Cuba (1901); the fostering of a revolution
in Panama to detach the region of the isthmus from Colombia in

3

order to be able to protect the future canal (November 1903); the extension of the quasi-protectorate system to include San Domingo (January 1905), and soon afterwards to include Nicaragua and Haiti.

Certain historians have tried to attribute this phenomenon to a simple cyclical process. Dexter Perkins[1] and Frank L. Klingberg[2] have tried to construct such cycles. Klingberg goes further than Perkins in the sense that he is not satisfied with a qualitative historical analysis but includes quantitative measurements such as budgetary credits allotted to the Navy, and the percentage of presidential speeches and messages devoted to foreign policy. Perkins and Klingberg agree in placing the very beginning of the century in the "extroversive" phase of the cycle, but disagreement appears over the period 1907–1915, which Klingberg places at the heart of the active phase, while Perkins sees it as a period of "relatively peaceful feeling." In general, one may be skeptical about the existence of real cycles in foreign policy, because by definition such policy depends as much on foreign attitudes as on internal factors. And foreigners have no reason to pay attention to the cycles even if they perceive some. One must, then, be resigned to explain American expansion at the opening of the century in terms of specific complex historical phenomena, rather than by a general dialectical law.

Despite certain resistances, the policy of expansion had the advantage of widespread public support. It was the era of the "rise of America to world power,"[3] the era of the "American Empire."[4] To put it concisely, and regardless of whatever connotations this word has since acquired, this is the epoch of American imperialism.

This imperialism had had its theorist, Admiral Mahan. The contribution of Mahan to political and strategic thought is considerable. But an analysis of his work here would not be justified if he had not had an impassioned, conscientious, and faithful disciple in President Theodore Roosevelt. One cannot understand strategic conceptions and American expansionism as they were formulated in 1913 without first trying to penetrate the thought of Admiral Mahan and also trying to measure his influence.

Alfred Thayer Mahan was born on September 27, 1840, at West Point, where his father, an Army officer, was professor of engineering. The son's tastes led him to another branch of the profession of arms, the Navy. He had an ordinary and uneventful career: midshipman in

1856, retired as captain in 1896, named rear admiral in the reserve in 1906. He died in Washington on December 1, 1914.

The most important event in his life was his appointment as professor, and in 1886 as president, of the Naval War College founded two years before. It was then that Mahan, an avid reader, had an inspiration like that of Newton and his apple tree, which was to make him justly famous. While reading Mommsen's *History of Rome* in 1885, he suddenly asked himself what would have become of the Roman Republic if Hannibal, instead of attacking by land, had been able to use the approach by sea. Mahan had found his ruling idea, the one that would permeate all his subsequent work, that of sea power. In order to re-create the atmosphere of the times we should note that the prevailing strategic theories of the nineteenth century—largely inspired by Napoleon—considered that the very essence of military power lay in land forces. Mahan's father was an admirer of Napoleon; the son was an admirer of England. Later, with Mackinder and Haushofer, there would be a revival of the conception of land supremacy, but between 1890 and the 1920's one can speak of "an era of Mahan."

Mahan published his first work, *The Influence of Sea Power upon History*, in 1890. There followed, in 1892, *The Influence of Sea Power upon the French Revolution and Empire, 1793–1812*, and in 1897, *The Life of Nelson*. During these years and afterwards he wrote more than one hundred and fifty articles, of which a number were collected into books, and several other works. His first book ran through fifteen editions in eight years; 29,000 copies had been sold by 1941. The book on the French Revolution sold 12,000 copies; the *Life of Nelson*, 24,000.[5] The salient points in Mahan's thought are his conceptions of sea power and of naval strategy.

For Mahan the enduring, essential power is sea power. In the long run, whoever dominates the seas always wins. The world supremacy of Great Britain, at its height in the Victorian era, was due to the fact that she was mistress of the seas. By "sea power" Mahan does not merely mean the superiority of the fighting navy. For him there is an indissoluble relationship between a powerful fighting navy, maritime commerce, and colonies. A nation acquires colonies if it has a strong navy. Colonies—bases or sources of economic wealth—stimulate maritime commerce, and the size of the merchant marine reinforces the fighting navy. Power and wealth are thus both derived from maritime strength. Sea power is not given to all, however. England, enclosed in its island, poor in natural resources, was forced to seek it; France, more prosperous, and too much lured by continental conquest, did not take the pains to acquire it.

Mahan thought as an American. He feared that the vast, rich United States was in danger of falling victim to a sort of "maritime laziness" which, if it continued for long, would be fatal for the country. All his works were written to convince his compatriots of this, for he considered that the reforms he wanted could not be permanently accomplished unless the public could be brought around to supporting them. Mahan had nothing of the incipient dictator about him, but he wanted greatness for his country, and he thought he had discovered the prescription for that greatness. "Self-interest is not only a legitimate, but a fundamental cause for national policy." [6] "It is futile to expect governments to act permanently on any other basis than that of national interest. They have no right to do otherwise." [7]

What is the basic interest of the United States? It is national growth. The frontier, which offered a virgin field to unused energies down to the 1880's, had disappeared. All the land was claimed. Should one take the position, as President Cleveland did, that the territorial limits had been reached and that one should not go beyond them? No. One must go further, according to Mahan, and revive the idea dear to Americans in the middle of the nineteenth century—Manifest Destiny. But the new expansion should not be continental; it should be overseas, in the acquisition of bases, even of colonies. Thus the cycle—strong navy, colonies, merchant marine—could work itself out. Let us imitate the Europeans: "The armaments of European states exist less for their protection against conquest than to assure them the greatest possible share in the regions of the world which are still unexploited, or only partially exploited." [8] Following their example, American expansion is "natural," necessary, inevitable. [9]

More than colonies Mahan wanted bases. One can imagine his joy at all the annexations between 1898 and 1903. Only the Philippines seemed to him of doubtful value, because for him a true base is one which protects an active commercial route, for example Cuba, or, lacking that, Puerto Rico, for the protection of the Straits of Florida. Because of the colonies, the fighting navy would grow stronger, and the merchant marine, and the cycle would go on. A powerful navy should be constructed. In 1911 he specified further, adding "a navy second to none, except the British," the qualification stemming from his realism rather than from his ambition.

Mahan is also, as was said earlier, the author of a new naval strategy. His essential idea is that of the concentration of a fleet composed largely of battleships. A war of movement is secondary for him, "linear" coastal defense a dangerous absurdity. What would protect the United States better than anything else would be to have the whole fleet concentrated in one ocean, whichever it might be. The naval disasters of the Russians in 1904–05 were for him a perfect illustration of his theory. The Russian Fleet was divided in two, part in the Pacific, part in the Baltic. The Japanese, with their Fleet concentrated, were thus able to destroy first the Pacific Fleet, later the Baltic, at Tsushima. If the Russian Fleet had been concentrated entirely in the Baltic, although it could not have succeeded without a long voyage, it would in the end have destroyed the Japanese Fleet and won the war. If the United States Fleet were concentrated in the Atlantic and the Japanese attacked, it would have to go all the way around Cape Horn (the Panama Canal opened in 1914, the year of Mahan's death), but in full strength it could be victorious.

This key idea was later adapted to fit varying geographical conditions, but it was never to disappear. Germany's rise as a naval power —von Tirpitz was to a great extent a disciple of Mahan, as were members of the British Admiralty—gave Britain no choice but to concentrate her Fleet in European waters. At that time Mahan saw an American-Japanese balance of power being established in the Pacific. Where he wanted absolute domination of the United States Fleet was in the Gulf of Mexico and the Caribbean. We should not tolerate a single foreign coaling station within 3000 miles of San Francisco, he said emphatically. "This should be an inviolable resolution of our foreign policy." [10]

What makes Mahan so important is the direct and specific influence he exerted. One certainly cannot attribute to him the entire responsibility for the acquisition of bases or the growth of the navy. He was part of a movement, of a new trend in national thinking. But the new ideas were vague; Mahan rationalized them by his dialectic and justified them by a profound study of history. He was their living and ardent spokesman.

The turning point of American naval policy in favor of a powerful navy came in 1889–90 after the controversy over the Samoan Islands. The United States Fleet was then the sixth in the world, with 122,000 tons, trailing Britain, with 802,000; France, with 515,000; Russia, with 246,000; Italy, with 203,000; and Germany, with 188,000.[11]

The Secretary of the Navy, Benjamin F. Tracy, proposed a vast plan of construction in 1889, which shows that he was familiar with Mahan's thought, even before Mahan had published his first book. Tracy must have read some of Mahan's lectures at the Naval War College.[12] Mahan's first book brought him other admirers: Henry Cabot Lodge, then member of the Naval Affairs Committee of the House of Representatives, and his friend Theodore Roosevelt. As early as 1890 Roosevelt wrote to Mahan to congratulate him. Later, as an ardent disciple, he was to spread the theorist's ideas as much as he could. More important, he put the ideas into practice, modestly at first, when in 1897 he was appointed assistant secretary of the navy under President McKinley—due to Lodge's influence—then on a grand scale, as President of the United States from 1901 to 1909. The voyage of the United States Fleet to the Pacific, 1907–1909, which was destined to arouse the Japanese, was ordered by Roosevelt after consultation with Mahan. On March 3, 1909, the very eve of leaving the presidency, Roosevelt wrote to Taft, his successor, to pass on to him Mahan's advice that the Fleet should not be divided. And the retiring President could report to his friend, "I am certain that the fleet will never be divided." [13] Roosevelt went so far as to advise the senators and representatives, in an official message, to read Mahan's books.

Roosevelt had a more active temperament than Mahan, however. Influenced by neo-Darwinian theories, according to which selection operates among nations in favor of the more powerful, he was more consciously imperialistic. Roosevelt praised war. Granted, for him war was not the bloody horror soon to be experienced: the former officer of the Rough Riders had a romantic notion derived from the "splendid little war" of 1898 against Spain. His conception fell far short of the "brisk happy war" or swaggering in the style of Mussolini. But as Chief Executive Roosevelt fostered the big navy.

In 1900 the United States Navy moved from sixth to fourth place, after France and Russia, ahead of Germany. Despite the formidable German naval effort, the American Fleet, because of Roosevelt's efforts, moved to third place in 1906 and to second place in 1907, with 611,000 tons to Germany's 529,000 tons. She held this position only until 1911, when Germany had 837,000 tons and the United States, 773,000.[14] German superiority increased gradually during the Taft administration, although the American naval budget went from 21 million dollars in 1885 to 31 million in 1891, 79 million in 1902, 104 million in 1906, and 137 million in 1909. Wilson's first naval budget dropped to 127 million dollars.

On August 5, 1914, Wilson decided to forbid all officers, active or retired, to express any opinions on the military or political consequences of events in Europe. This was to stifle Mahan—the propagandist of an idea. The Navy, down to third place, was no longer, according to the wishes of the great theorist, second to none but the British. Mahan could no longer make himself heard. All this is thought to have hastened his death.

It is curious to note that there existed already a minority, represented in Congress by Hobson, in the Navy by Admiral Fiske, which went further than Mahan. Since the United States held the first place economically, they wanted their country to have a fleet second to none, that is, at least equal to that of England. When Wilson, a university professor, came to power, he gave little thought to the Navy. The irony of events was to make him take up the idea of a fleet second to none beginning in 1916, and to bring the Navy's budget in 1919 to 2.2 billion dollars, or eighteen times the largest budget of Theodore Roosevelt.

If the country felt itself more and more protected by its powerful Navy, there was a temptation to neglect the Army. Who could attack the United States—so far away—over the obstacle of the Fleet? There would always be time to train soldiers, if Germany should some day defeat England. (There were some, like Theodore Roosevelt, who believed that there would, inevitably, be trouble with Germany.) The idea that the United States, complacent because of its wealth, might, on its own initiative, launch a war against a European adversary or Japan seemed absurd.

No doubt there were some moments of irrational panic—despite Spanish weakness—along the coasts when the United States declared war on Spain in 1898, and in 1907 when difficulties arose with Japan. But if one excepts a few thousand Marines necessary for debarking in the Caribbean, no one was seriously concerned with land troops.

Military doctrine since the Civil War had remained close to that of Jomini and Dennis Hart Mahan, father of the admiral. According to their doctrine the army would be concerned only with the theater of war, battle was an end in itself, and no connections were established between the concerns of the military chiefs and the political objectives of the nation. In the words of General Smith, this was a period of "military darkness." "The neglect of the army . . . can be explained . . . in large part by the security we enjoy thanks to our policy of isolation." [15] In this period, only Emory Upton, who had been a young officer in the Civil War and who committed suicide in 1881, had understood the necessity of preparing military forces in peacetime. His words had fallen on deaf ears.

The war with Spain in 1898 had naturally produced a national effort. The Federal Army, based on volunteers, reached the figure of 253,000 men (a small permanent Army of 28,000 plus 225,000 new soldiers).[16] But by February 1901 Elihu Root, Secretary of War under McKinley since June 1899, had a great deal of trouble getting approved a measure that provided for an effective Army of between 60,000 and 100,000 men (the exact figure to be set at the discretion of the President). Although the War College, a center for discussion and development of doctrine, was founded in November 1901, the General Staff remained only a skeleton.

In 1907 the United States Army consisted of 62,398 men and officers, of whom 16,000 were in the Philippines and 4000 in Cuba. This figure included 3400 men in the health services. This left less than 40,000 men to defend 3,022,387 square miles of territory.[17] Each state had its militia or national guard, to be sure, but these were not equipped to operate outside its own territory. In 1912 the regular Army comprised 75,000 men; the militia, 120,000.[18] It was thought that in case of conflict a grand total of 460,000 could be mustered, plus 43,000 in the artillery for coastal defense. But these forces were largely untried. If we think of the armies of France and Germany at the time, with their hundreds of thousands of men on active duty and their powerful reserves, the contrast is striking. To remedy this American poverty, which derived from exaggerated optimism, was the aim of General Leonard Wood (formerly surgeon general) when he was appointed chief of the general staff on April 22, 1910. We shall see later the direction of his efforts. "Wood saw, with an admirable shrewdness, that the key to his problem . . . lay, not in military planning, but in public opinion . . . Unless the psychology of 'defense' and 'preparedness' could be instilled into the nation as a whole, one was unlikely to draw from it in peacetime a great military organization capable of mobilizing for major land war." [19]

Thus, if there was any defense of the United States, it was on the seas. If there was any American imperialism, it was strategically limited. One could undertake punitive operations, police Central America, or occupy some colonies with a few thousand men, but a nation with a regular Army of 62,398 soldiers could hardly be classed with the great conquerors of empires. The defensive aspect of security prevailed over the offensive aspect. The United States lived in the illusion that this situation could last. There were other objectives in foreign policy, more immediate and more tempting than those proposed to the nation by Admiral Alfred Thayer Mahan.

Even Theodore Roosevelt, as much a disciple of Kipling as of Mahan, was more aggressive in his words than in his actions. On April 2, 1903, in Chicago, he pronounced the famous words—he said it was an African proverb—"Talk softly and carry a big stick, and you will go far." At the time he was brandishing the big stick as a reply to a campaign in the German press apropos of incidents between the two nations concerning a blockade of Venezuela.[20] It has become customary to describe the various interventions of the United States in Central America as applications of this policy of the Big Stick, and we will return to this subject later. But already we can establish that the stick was a threat only in a confined geographical area, and that American imperialism had narrow limits if we examine it from the point of view of military conquest.

American Interventionism and Dollar Diplomacy

There is another form of imperialism, more subtle and more effective, that of the dollar. President Taft, Roosevelt's successor, following approximately his predecessor's line although with less bluster, seems to have had a special predilection for "dollar diplomacy." This expression began to be used during his administration, for instance in the brochure of James Leets published in December 1912 and entitled, *The United States and Latin America: Dollar Diplomacy*.[21] Of what does this relatively new form of foreign policy consist?

Before analyzing its sources and manifestations one should recall the prodigious increase of wealth in the United States in the first years of the century. The country profited from abundant and well-situated natural resources in a territory of 3,022,387 square miles, and from an inexhaustible labor supply resulting from immigration. The United States, relatively poor in capital since the end of the Civil War, had been able to borrow in Europe without too much difficulty; foreign investments in the United States were valued at 4.5 to 5 billion dollars by 1914.[22] More than thirty million European immigrants crossed the Atlantic between 1830 and 1920—8,800,000 between 1830 and 1870; 10,700,000 between 1870 and 1900; 12,500,000 between 1900 and 1920. This extraordinary conjunction of the three factors essential to wealth—natural resources, labor, and capital—had enormously stimulated the national economy.

In the first place, national wealth was growing at an accelerated rate, estimated as: 7 billion dollars in 1850, 30 billion in 1870, 88 billion in 1900, and 186.3 billion in 1912. By contrast, in 1912 the national wealth of the United Kingdom was 79.3 billion dollars; that of Germany, 77.8 billion; that of France, 57.1 billion.[23]

This wealth permitted savings of about 5 billion dollars per year in the United States by 1914. The result was the possibility not only of large investment at home but also abroad. In 1900 American investments abroad are estimated to have been 500 million dollars; in 1913, 2.5 billion, of which half was in Latin America, one fourth in Canada. The net American indebtedness abroad was thus about 2.5 billion dollars at the outbreak of war; the war was to reverse the situation completely. But the important feature for the study of international relations is not the net balance, it is the fact that American holdings abroad had quintupled in 13 years, and that Latin America was the chief beneficiary, with all the complications this might involve.

The overall growth of the nation's wealth contributed to the creation of an optimistic attitude; Americans, despite their small army, felt strong. But a qualification must immediately be added: those who profited most from this increase of wealth were the capitalists, and especially the great monopolies, trusts, holding companies, and so forth. We cannot outline here, even briefly, the study of this complex situation. We can only assert that there was a cleavage, difficult to define or to place exactly, between the "national interest" as a whole and the "special interests," which were those of the great banks and monopolies, always adept at influencing legislation. The traditional structure of the two major parties, Republican and Democratic, persisted in 1912, but more important was the schism between the defenders of the special interests, the "old guard" of both parties, and those who claimed to defend (without being able to define it very precisely) the national interest.

These points established, one can attempt to give a historical definition of "dollar diplomacy." Let us say at once that the term does not mean exerting diplomatic pressure by paying out considerable bribes here and there. Real dollar diplomacy is very different. It can be defined in a broad and in a narrow sense.

In the broad sense, dollar diplomacy is the use by American interests abroad of the political support of their government, support which they solicit and try to obtain by every imaginable means. Instances of this would be diplomatic efforts to obtain certain modifications in customs laws, taxation, and regulation of concessions. A more extreme form would be protection of American interests by the threat or the use of force. The example of Panama in 1903 is that of a revolution incited by capitalist interests with the almost public support of the American government. In San Domingo it was to be a military occupation designed largely to protect American capital invested in the island. "Throughout this whole process economic interests worked hand in hand with the United States government. In the course of this cooperation a technique of imperialism has been developed which is now well advanced and which is accepted and practised alike by Democratic and Republican administrations." [24]

In 1908 Secretary of State Elihu Root recognized this method of operating. Citing the United States interventions in Cuba and San Domingo, he declared that a similar action in Haiti or Nicaragua could be expected if American interests in those countries reached comparable dimensions. He added that American investments in Mexico were so important that the government would certainly not stand by inactive if they were threatened.[25] The intervention in Nicaragua in 1912, for example, was clearly undertaken to protect two banks, Brown Brothers and Company, and J. and W. Seligman and Company.[26]

The narrow definition of "dollar diplomacy," which is more exact for the policy of Taft, could perhaps be formulated thus: an action of the American government in relation to foreign countries the purpose of which is to open such countries to American capital or to increase American capital already invested in them. A word on the theoretical origin of this attitude is required for real understanding. It is related to the writings of a British economist, John Atkinson Hobson (1858–1940), himself profoundly anti-imperialist.

Probably inspired by an article by an American financial expert, Charles A. Conant,[27] Hobson, who was a pacifist, a believer in free trade (he had written a biography of Cobden), and a declared opponent of colonial conquest, published his principal work, *Imperialism, A Study*, in 1902. Many Marxists, including Rudolf Hilferding, Rosa Luxemburg, and especially Lenin, were to be influenced by his essential idea. For him imperialism "is the undertaking by which the captains of industry enlarge the canal through which their excess wealth flows, seeking foreign markets and investments abroad, in such a way as to use goods and capital which they cannot sell or use at home."[28] Without question Hobson stated the idea in a more qualified way than Lenin was to do, and he admitted that there were other ingredients of imperialism—the primitive will to dominate, in particular. It is nevertheless true that he explains colonial expansion primarily by the determination of big capitalists to find territories which offer more profitable returns on investments than those to be expected at home. Hobson criticizes this situation and sees the dangers clearly.

The American imperialists, however, overlooked the criticism and retained mainly the aspect of Hobson's thesis that seemed useful to them: the tendency of excess capital to seek the possibility of investment outside its own national frontiers. It is not our concern here to argue either for or against this theory—historically very controversial [29] —but to show its effects on the diplomacy of Roosevelt and Taft, especially the latter.

For Roosevelt Hobson's reasoning carried little weight in itself. Roosevelt was primarily concerned about the "prestige" of the United States everywhere, and he saw this prestige threatened wherever foreign capital was invested in places where American capital could have been invested instead. He energetically supported the American China Development Company, a group of financiers that included Edward H. Harriman and J. P. Morgan, among others. When this group gave up its enterprise—the construction of railroads—because of the opposition of the Chinese government and rivalry with other foreign groups, Roosevelt deplored it loudly.

The group was reorganized at the beginning of the Taft administration and the State Department took active measures to protect it and to assure its admission to an international consortium of bankers recognized by the Chinese government. "The consistent aim of the present government," Taft told Congress on December 3, 1912, "has been to encourage the use of American capital in the development of China." As to Central America and the Caribbean, "the United States has been happy to support and to encourage American bankers who are willing to lend a helping hand to these countries, to aid in their financial rehabilitation." [30] Taft gave the following definition to his system: "While our foreign policy should not turn a hair's breadth from the straight path of justice, it may be well to include active intervention to secure for our merchandise and our capitalists opportunity for profitable investment which shall inure to the benefit of both countries concerned." [31]

It is to be noted that Taft always attributes a moral significance to dollar diplomacy. But the important point is that he practiced it on a grand scale. Diplomatic pressures and military interventions are the consequences to be expected of such a method. The beginnings of expansionism—the desire to acquire bases to aid in the achievement of sea power—is thus combined in a complex way with the desire for political control of territories suited to the absorption of excess American capital. The methods of control may be either direct or indirect.

We have now defined two of the basic elements of American foreign policy in 1913. But the picture would be very incomplete if we failed to examine in addition the psychological forces of the tradition, especially because these forces, although they favored expansionism, also produced the most effective restraints on the movement.

The Moral Tradition in Foreign Policy

We cannot in a few pages make a profound study of American traditions in foreign policy as they appeared in 1913, but we can try to point out their essential aspects. One would expect that this nation, long isolated by distances that could not be covered rapidly, would have developed new and original traditions. Everything contributed to this tendency, the make-up of the population, the geography and development of the country, the particulars of the nation's history. Before examining the outstanding characteristics of the tradition, we should recall what had been the principal elements in its formation: Anglo-American culture, the frontier, and the successive waves of immigration.

The white population of the United States is of European origin, English at first and then mixed. The English elements had given the country the most solid of all traditions, the language. There is an entire culture derived from the language which the United States shares with Great Britain. Arnold Wolfers and Laurence Martin could entitle a collection of British and American texts *The Anglo-American Tradition in Foreign Affairs*.[32] According to them, this tradition consisted of three elements:

> The first is the persistent impact of what until quite recently could be called the strategic insularity of both the British Isles and the American continent; the second is the striking contrast that exists for both countries between the internal and the external political scene; the third is a difference in the degree of moral opportunity offered by the domestic and the foreign field of political activity . . .
> In these countries domestic political conditions stand in striking contrast to the conditions these nations face in their external relations: the domestic conditions are characterized by order, lawfulness, and peace arising from popular consensus on principles—a consensus so marked that some believe coercion has practically ceased to play a role here; but the external relations continue to be full of bitter struggle, violence, and Machiavellian practices.[33]

Other elements were added to this truly English element, stemming, in a general way, from immigration. Oscar Handlin has made the best analysis of the effects of immigration as such. "One day," he says, "I thought of writing a history of American immigrants. Then I discovered that the immigrants *are* American history." [34] The immigrant is a displaced person who finds the structure of a new life already established. Though he can enjoy full American citizenship within five years, including political rights, he cannot always understand his new country. He suffers from his displacement, and for the first generation the result is a real alienation. Between the first and second generations there is a contrast in which the cultural anthropologists, especially Geoffrey Gorer,[35] have found the essential substance of American "national character."

Although it is true that Americans originally received their traditions from Europe, the other side of the coin is that the immigrants were absorbed in the "Melting Pot"—they became Americans. This can be explained in terms of political conditions, the economic advantages of the country, its system of public education; and certainly all these have played a part. But the most original interpretation of the phenomenon was given by Frederick Jackson Turner in a lecture to the American Historical Association in 1893, entitled "The Significance of the Frontier in American History." [36]

The frontier is here defined as the farthest point west that American colonization has reached at a certain moment, the meeting point of wilderness and civilization. It is also, for Turner, "the most rapid and effective avenue to Americanization" which "creates the dominant features of the American character." The advancement of the frontier meant a constant movement away from European influences.[37] The frontier diminished dependence on England, on Europe. It was the most important factor in overcoming the forces of separatism or "sectionalism." Because of the individualism of the pioneers, the frontier fostered the rapid growth of democracy. The Europeanized East had tried to control the frontier and to vest it with moral principles. In return the East received the influences which have given the American "crudeness and force combined with shrewdness and perspicacity . . . a practical and inventive turn of mind . . . mastery of material things . . . energy without repose." [38]

This theory has been disputed by various writers and it cannot be taken as an absolute and sufficient explanation by itself, but it does account for many aspects of American "national character." Many men in public life have adhered to this thesis, including Wilson, who knew Turner at Johns Hopkins, the whole generation of the 1920's, and even Franklin Delano Roosevelt.[39] In the light of this theory one can understand the foundations of American traditions as they are affected by the dynamic West, by the constantly moving frontier made up of waves of humanity starting from Europe and breaking all the way across the continent.

By 1913 these forces were no longer operating in the same way. There was no longer any frontier. There had not been since about 1890, and the later expansion to the islands was not at all like the formative battle against the wilderness with its contact between barbarism and the crude vanguards of civilization. Immigration had also taken a new form, so that it began to be a disturbing factor to Americans.

Let us examine a bit the new characteristics of immigration which are essential to the understanding of certain aspects of the American tradition. From 1820 to 1912, 29,611,052 immigrants entered the United States.[40] In the first decade of the twentieth century alone the number was 8,795,386. Even when the number of people who left the country is taken into account, for certain years we see a considerable population increase owing to immigration: 839,134 in 1910; 889,702 in 1913; 915,152 in 1914, the record year. As a general rule, the new immigration was not made up of those persecuted for political or religious reasons; it had become a matter of economics. People emigrated to the country of hope and plenty because they were poor and without hope in Europe. Specialized agencies for encouraging immigration, which disseminated propaganda for that purpose, grew up in the United States. This immigration coincided with the shrinkage of available land: for each immigrant to the United States in 1820 there were 20,927 square miles; in 1860, 1,205; in 1900, 824; in 1910, 347. At the same time, with industry expanding rapidly, the unions began to feel threatened by the arrival of newcomers with a lower standard of living who would work for lower wages.

But, more important, the new immigration was differently constituted. In the decade from 1861 to 1870, 35 percent of the immigrants came from Germany, 38 percent from England and Ireland, 0.33 percent from Austria-Hungary, 0.51 percent from Italy, 0.2 percent from Russia. Between 1881 and 1890 there was an increase in the number of Jews, Slavs, and Italians. In the decade from 1901 to 1910 only 3.9 percent of the immigrants were Germans, 4.4 percent were English, and 3.9 percent were Irish, while 24.4 percent came from Austria-Hungary, 23.3 percent from Italy, 18.2 percent from Russia. This meant that the new wave was much more difficult to assimilate, not only linguistically, but also from the point of view of their attitudes and ideas. The Jews and Slavs constituted new religious communities. The Roman Catholic Italians had difficulty, even friction, with the previously established Roman Catholic Irish and French Canadians. The Protestant churches were disturbed by the invasion of the country by large numbers of people they could not absorb.

It might have been easier if the new groups had been more evenly spread throughout the country. But, in contrast to the British, Irish, Scandinavians, and Germans of the old immigration, who settled by preference in rural areas, the new immigration stayed in the cities, especially those on the east coast and Chicago. Chicago had more Czechs than any other city except Prague and Vienna; in 1910 New

York had the largest Jewish population of any city in the world and the largest Italian population except for Naples. The immigrants had their own sections of the city, "little Italy," "the Ghetto," where they continued to speak their own language, where the signs in the stores were seldom in English. This was a further obstacle to assimilation. The new immigration was poorer, with a lower literacy rate, was less well trained vocationally, than the old.

Henry Pratt Fairchild entitles one of his chapters in *Immigration* (published 1913) "The New Problem of Immigration." Weighing the pros and cons, he did not dare to come out for restrictive legislation. In 1926, however, he called his new book *The Melting-Pot Mistake*.[41] A fervent nationalist, he considered that "the highest service rendered to humanity by America is to point the way, to show what opportunities exist, to lead the way to human happiness. Any force which tends to diminish our capacity for leadership is a threat to humanity and a flagrant violation of the spirit of liberalism. Unrestricted immigration is such a force; it would slowly, insidiously, irresistibly, devour the very heart of the United States."[42]

The year 1913 represents only the stage of anxiety; the defensive, restrictive stage was to come later. Limitations had already been placed on the immigration of Chinese and Japanese. Starting in the Pacific states, restrictive measures were gradually adopted by the whole United States. The first act excluding the Chinese was passed in California in 1852. After a treaty with China signed in 1880, a series of federal laws, culminating in the law of 1884, closed immigration to Chinese laborers for ten years. Since the law was subsequently extended, there were only 61,639 Chinese in the United States in 1920.[43]

The first protests against Japanese immigration came from the unions. In contrast to the Chinese, the Japanese came with their wives, which added anxiety on a racial basis to the economic anxiety. In 1900 there were about 25,000 Japanese in the United States. A campaign was launched that year to extend to the Japanese the restrictions applying to the Chinese. Japan was a major power, however, as China was not, and she would not accept discrimination against her nationals. In 1906 the School Committee of San Francisco excluded Japanese children from white schools. This caused serious tension, which was partially relieved by the Gentlemen's Agreement of 1907. Japan agreed not to issue passports to laborers who wished to go to the United States, except those returning, whether or not they were qualified. Nevertheless, in 1913 there were 77,625 Japanese in the United States and 87,561 in the Hawaiian Islands. More general restrictive measures were passed after the war, especially in 1924.

Let us now consider the most striking aspects of the American traditions which grew out of these elements. Even at the opening of the twentieth century, in the era of imperialist expansion, there existed a profound American "moralism"; this does not mean that American foreign policy was essentially "moral," but that the public thought it should be, and that the government always expressed moral concern in the declarations by which it justified its acts. In a general way everyone was convinced that American foreign policy was more just, more generous, than the foreign policy of other nations.

There was much speculation on and reappraisal of this problem after World War II when Hans Morgenthau in an influential work, *In Defense of the National Interest*,[44] attacked this pious and somewhat hypocritical moralism. Morgenthau tried to show that American foreign policy had been right and successful when it was geared to concrete national interests and that it had been unfortunate and wrong when these interests were sacrificed to moralism, idealism, or legalism. Morgenthau's book started a "great debate" which brought the question into clearer focus and gave an opportunity to various writers to express their opinions.

The extreme view was supported by Frank Tannenbaum: "Our history is so different from that of other nations that we see reality in a special light."[45] The American attitude is derived from a unique experience. The absence of feudal tradition, the repudiation of European domination early in the life of the nation, and above all the creation of a federal government gave to American policy its special character. Many things can be cited as consequences of this experience: belief in the equality of all men; belief in the cooperative method of action; racial tolerance; democratic, unstratified society; political and judicial equality of the states. "The projection of America abroad is, therefore, described within the broad conception of a world containing individuals endowed with fundamental rights and of governments possessed of limited sovereignty, operating in states that are equal to each other."[46] The result, according to Tannenbaum, is that American tradition is more moral than that of Europeans.

Dexter Perkins shares this opinion, although he is less extreme, has fewer illusions, and puts it in a more qualified way. He believes that domestic democracy has produced a moralistic attitude in foreign affairs. He sees and analyzes abuses, but he concludes that when one examines American imperialism, "there is one essential generalization with which we ought to begin. American rule over other peoples has always been rule with an uneasy conscience." Americans have always believed "that it was the duty of an imperial power to prepare the way to self-government for the peoples over whom it exercised control." [47]

The most thorough study of this conflict, or alleged conflict, between idealism and the national interest is that of Robert Osgood.[48] The key idea of his analysis is that the United States became aware, at the opening of the twentieth century, of the fact that it was becoming a world power and felt that a new era was beginning. Because it was still relatively isolated, however, it did not have to adapt the moral tradition to daily practice. "As a result [Americans] were encouraged to believe that reality was completely adaptable to their ideals." [49] Like all nations, the United States committed acts from egotism and self-interest, but Americans always thought that they could "reconcile their ideal with their own special national interest." [50]

It is not surprising that this should have given rise to a foreign policy which was ineffectual, impulsive, lacking in stability. When the United States declared war on Spain (Osgood calls it the "first crusade") it was to free Cuba from hateful Spanish domination; when it established a quasi-protectorate over Cuba it was to bring civilization to that island. Roosevelt intervened to assure law and order; Taft's dollar diplomacy was justified because American investments would benefit the unfortunate people. For Wilson, the "civilizing mission" of the United States was to give democracy to backward countries even if it had to be imposed on them by force. Osgood says that there has been no act, however realistic or cynical its purposes, which has not been justified in moral terms by its author, often in good faith. If there were some dissident voices against imperialism, the country as a whole was for it because the people sincerely believed that the goals sought were above all moral. Bismarckian realism is foreign to American thinking. The transformation of a conquest into a "mission," an intervention into "punishment of the wicked," a war into a "crusade," is sufficient to reconcile the irreconcilable and to assure complacency.

One could carry much further the analysis of opposition to imperialism, of the primacy of moral considerations, of the idea that the mission of the nation is not to defend its own selfish national interests but to work for the welfare of mankind. We shall find all these again in Wilson, and we see them already in the opponents of Theodore Roosevelt. As Beale says, "Imperialist sentiment was powerful but ineffective, because it lacked a positive and compelling program." [51] Former President Harrison, future Secretary of State Bryan, speaker of the House of Representatives Tom Reed, President Eliot of Harvard, the philosopher William James, were leaders of the anti-imperialist movement in 1900, which was financed by some of the richest industrial potentates, like Andrew Carnegie. It can be said that at the time of Wilson's election the moralist forces traditionally opposed to imperialism may have been momentarily submerged, but they remained intact.

Under the vague general heading of American moralism, which is the essence of American tradition in foreign policy, one can easily discern more concrete elements, which are simpler, few in number, and reducible to familiar classic formulation. The first is nonentanglement, or the refusal to form permanent alliances, especially with European powers. This dates from Washington's Farewell Address and Americans have always been faithful to it. It is, so to speak, the traditional isolationism.

The second element is the Monroe Doctrine, that is, a certain number of principles embedded in the message of President Monroe to Congress in December 1823. (These were not thought to constitute a permanent "doctrine" until later.) The Monroe Doctrine states that the United States (1) will not permit European intervention in the affairs of the American continents; (2) will not permit European nations to add any new colonies to those they already hold in the Western hemisphere; (3) will not meddle in European affairs. This doctrine has two possible interpretations: it can mean that the United States considers itself the natural protector of the Western hemisphere, but it can also mean that the Western hemisphere is really a zone of American influence. The first sense fits the "moralist" view, the second the realistic view based on national interests.

At the opening of the twentieth century the Monroe Doctrine was bent further in the second direction. This was the work of Theodore Roosevelt. From the idea that Europeans should not interfere in Latin American affairs Roosevelt drew a corollary: a situation could arise which necessitated intervention in the domestic affairs of a Latin American nation. As Europeans were excluded, only the United States could step in. This transformed the Monroe Doctrine into an instrument of the right of the United States to intervene. Curiously, it was the British who pushed Roosevelt in this direction. Knowing that they could not protect their interests in this guarded zone themselves without arousing American anger, and desiring that these interests—which were often threatened by revolutions, financial disorders, and the poor administration of the Latin republics—be protected somehow, the British were willing to see the region policed by the United States.

Roosevelt, like Wilson later, was sincerely convinced that the United States had a civilizing mission. Former commissioner of police in New York City (1895–1897), he conceived this mission in terms of maintaining or re-establishing order, whence his use of the expression "the Big Stick," already mentioned. Roosevelt saw himself very clearly as "policeman of the west," as Dexter Perkins puts it.[52]

In May 1904, when Roosevelt was asked to intervene in San Domingo, he declared that if a nation shows "that it knows how to act with decency in industrial and political matters, if it keeps order and pays its obligations, then it need fear no interference from the United States. Brutal wrong-doing, or an impotence which results in general loosening of the ties of civilized society, may finally require intervention by some civilized nation, and in the Western Hemisphere the United States cannot ignore this duty."[53] Elected President in November of that year, Roosevelt stated the corollary even more explicitly in his annual message to Congress. It was evident that these were not mere words when the United States intervened in San Domingo.

It is interesting that in order to justify this policy of intervention Roosevelt thought it necessary to place himself under the wing of the Monroe Doctrine. As Perkins says, "It is the habit of statesmen to justify innovations by stoutly maintaining that they are no innovations at all."[54] Here again the moralist tradition and the national interest meet, and it was possible to create a practical situation which public opinion in general would accept.

It is in this general context that Wilson, without training in diplomatic affairs but solidly attached to his principles, assumed, on March 4, 1913, the highest office in the land.

Chapter II

The Early Stages of President Wilson's Career

SOMETIMES a series of fortunate events gives the impression of a miracle. Possibly this was the case when Woodrow Wilson was elected President of the United States. At 56 he was new to political life, having entered it only two years earlier by the main door, thanks to his election as governor of New Jersey. What chance did there then seem for him to win the Democratic nomination? He was opposed by party regulars like Champ Clark and Oscar Underwood of Alabama. Clark, congressman since 1890, speaker of the House, was supported by the uncontested leader of the party, William Jennings Bryan, and by the Hearst press. Nevertheless, the Democratic convention in Baltimore nominated Wilson on the forty-sixth ballot of a hectic session with the support of Bryan and Underwood.

There remained the ultimate test: the verdict of a country the majority of whose voters were clearly Republican. Wilson benefited from the unusual fact that the Republican party had just split into two distinct wings: the "Old Guard," which nominated President Taft as candidate of the official Republican party, and the Progressive party of Senator La Follette, which presented former President Theodore Roosevelt, who had returned from lion hunting in 1910 more dynamic than ever. On November 4, Wilson received 6,293,000 votes, only 42 percent of the votes cast; Roosevelt had 4,119,000; Taft, 3,484,000, and the Socialist candidate, Eugene V. Debs, 901,000. This gave Wilson 435 electoral votes, against 88 for Roosevelt and 8 for Taft, and meant that in the election, Wilson had carried every state except California, Washington, South Dakota, Minnesota, Michigan, and Pennsylvania (carried by Roosevelt), and Vermont and Utah (carried by Taft). We must now explain this miracle.

Woodrow Wilson before His Entrance into Politics

Thomas Woodrow Wilson was born on December 28, 1856, at Staunton, Virginia. His father was a Presbyterian minister of Scottish extraction, his mother's background was Irish. Both sides of the family for many generations had been deeply religious. After he was elected to the presidency, Wilson wrote to his secretary, James P. Tumulty: "There are two natures combined in me that every day fight for supremacy and control . . . On the one side, there is the Irish in me, quick, generous, impulsive, passionate, anxious always to help and to sympathize with those in distress . . . Then, on the other side, there is the Scotch-canny, tenacious, cold and perhaps a little exclusive." [1] Wilson had inherited a tradition that everything should be sacrificed to principles and that one should hold to them tenaciously.

Since we are merely trying to bring out certain character traits, we will stress only a few aspects of Wilson's childhood. His family was a very closely knit one—Wilson refers to his "incomparable father"—in modest circumstances. At school in Augusta, Georgia, Wilson did not do particularly well and was often at the bottom of his class; his development was slow but promising. When he was fourteen his family moved to Columbia, South Carolina. He entered Princeton in September 1875. It is said that at the age of sixteen he had told one of his cousins that he wanted to be a statesman. Although an average student, he was passionately interested in politics and had done some important reading. These interests led him to publish his first article, "Cabinet Government," in a student paper, *The Princetonian*. He was graduated in 1879 and went on to study law at the University of Virginia, where he was elected president of the Democratic Club, the Jefferson Society, and proved to be an excellent debater.

In June 1882 he and a colleague opened a law office in Atlanta, but there were no clients, and after a year it became obvious that they had failed. One wonders whether Wilson felt bitter toward lawyers who succeeded; some people find in this an explanation of his future personal animosity toward Henry Cabot Lodge. The need to choose a new career was especially pressing because he wished to marry Ellen Louise Axson, a pious, intelligent, and affectionate person. He decided to do graduate work at Johns Hopkins University in preparation for college teaching. What a comedown! A successful lawyer may have a very high income; a professor, as far as financial status goes, is condemned to a middling position, and is in a poorer position to launch a political career.

From intensive work in his chosen fields of history and political science would come a famous book which ran to twenty-five editions—*Congressional Government* (published in January 1885)—in which he proposed modifications of the American Constitution in the direction of English parliamentarianism. At this point in his life he reluctantly abandoned his political ambitions. His marriage (June 24, 1885) [2] was rapidly followed by an appointment to the faculty of Bryn Mawr. He was not happy at the prospect of a life term teaching history to young women for a mediocre salary, and he consoled himself by writing.

The State was published in the autumn of 1889 after his appointment to Wesleyan University. He was invited to give lectures elsewhere with increasing frequency and finally, in September 1890, as a result of the good offices of a friend, he got what he wanted, a professorship in political science at Princeton. He expected to spend the rest of his life in this celebrated university.

In fact, he stayed twenty years, the last eight as president. His teaching talent was further recognized and his courses in constitutional and international law were well attended. He was interested in the details of Princeton's administrative problems. Six universities offered him their presidency and he was tempted by them. "I am tired of a purely verbal profession. I want to do something." In 1900 he began his *History of the American People;* but his books and articles no longer satisfied him. He dreamed of great reforms for Princeton, and he was eager for action. The trustees of the university, conscious of his energy and intelligence, elected him unanimously to the presidency on June 9, 1902; he was the first layman to hold the position. He accepted it gladly.

University presidents are often concerned more with relations with the rest of the community and financial affairs than with internal administration, but Wilson was not the man to follow this pattern. In fact, he soon showed his inclination to exercise authority and whispered references were made to his "dictatorship." It was a benevolent despotism, to be sure. In the first years, convinced that a university worthy of the name should not provide the students with a "career" but with "intellectual training," that students should not be confined merely to the facts but should think for themselves, he reformed the curriculum and introduced a variation of the British system of tutors. Fifty well-qualified young men were appointed to hold intermediate rank between the faculty and students. This development was followed with great interest in educational circles around the country. No one can doubt that Wilson's reputation and his consequent rise in politics was due in part to his imaginative administration.

But his setbacks played an even more important part. Beginning in 1906 he threw all his authority and energy into two problems that may seem of minor importance. He tried to replace the expensive and exclusive clubs in which students lived with quadrangles or colleges in which all students would live and eat together regardless of differences in financial resources. This would change the social life of the students to fit their academic life and make it genuinely democratic. Despite his great effort in this direction, he met resistance from the alumni, and the board of trustees refused to back him up. To others, and to himself if he had ever doubted it, Wilson appeared to be the "stubborn fighter," [3] the champion of the movement to make the colleges democratic.

The second problem, that of the graduate school, arose two years later, in 1909. Princeton's graduate school had been founded in 1900 and it lacked adequate space and buildings. Dean Andrew Fleming West, a linguist with a worldwide reputation, was instrumental in bringing about an offer of $500,000 from a rich industrialist for a new building on condition that it be located outside the college grounds. This led to a clash with Wilson, not only because this arrangement would make West independent of Wilson, a personal matter, but also on a point of principle. Wilson thought that the graduate school, the apex of university life, should be in the midst of the college so that undergraduates and graduates could mingle with mutual advantage, and he demanded that the gift be refused.

The university was divided into two camps. The press reported the course of the conflict which attracted national interest. Henry B. Brougham declared in the New York *Times*, on February 3, 1910, that the president of Princeton was fighting for the cause of democracy. (We now know that Wilson had collaborated with him in this article.) In Pittsburgh, Wilson made a violent speech in which he attacked "snobbism, reaction and obscurantism." The board of trustees hesitated, but when another donor left more than $2,000,000 in his will for the graduate school, provided that the wishes of West be carried out, the hesitation ceased. The trustees, who had resisted the temptation of a half million, gave in when offered four times as much. Wilson had to bow and he resigned, having given proof of his incredible tenacity, even stubbornness, but also of his moral courage, his passion, and his

ability as a manipulator. The witticism according to which Wilson
became President of the United States because he had failed as president of Princeton should be ignored. Wilson was a great university
president, but an individual cannot always control the outcome of
events. Later, he would have an even more bitter experience; as Arthur
Link says, the Princeton period was "the microcosm of the later macrocosm." [4]

The Rise to Power

Wilson's intransigence was not a constant factor. At times, especially
near the beginning of his career, his flexibility, one might even say his
deviousness, showed the other side of his character—a gift for maneu-
vering, a somewhat tortuous realism. In 1906 the abandoned dream of
a political career came to life again. Oddly, Wilson was to profit from
the reaction of the bosses of the Democratic party against the progressive tendencies of William Jennings Bryan, who appeared to be the
national leader of the party. Bryan had been the party's candidate for
president three times, in 1896, 1900, and 1908, and had been defeated
successively by the Republicans McKinley and Taft. He was an indi-
vidualist who would not take advice, a defender of certain oversimplified political panaceas: free silver and the prohibition of alcoholic beverages. The progressive wing which had formed in the Republican
party and had undertaken a program of reform in opposition to the
Old Guard, had its counterpart in the liberal group in the Democratic
party, a group which Bryan represented. Bryan had become to some
extent an institution. The conservatives of the party sought to find a
counter influence, and in 1906 they thought of Wilson, not because he
was opposed to progress, but because they thought they could control
this apparently naïve man. What an illusion!

In February 1906 Colonel George Harvey, publisher of *Harper's
Weekly*, which was financed by J. P. Morgan, began to advocate Wilson's candidacy for president and this attracted much notice. Wilson
was urged to run for the post of senator from New Jersey in 1906, a
purely symbolic gesture, because senators were at that time chosen by
the state legislature rather than popular election, and the legislature
of New Jersey had a Republican majority. In the end, Wilson refused
to run. It would have been premature for him to try for the presidential nomination in 1908. Bryan was nominated easily and as usual

was defeated, this time by Taft. Wilson, ironically appearing as the man of the bosses against the progressives, fought Taft with his usual energy.

The matter came up again in January 1910, when Harvey, Wilson's faithful supporter, in the course of a luncheon, persuaded James Smith, Jr., Democratic boss of New Jersey, to support Wilson for the office of governor. Wilson showed his credentials by writing an article in which he praised politicians. It was "unjust to scorn them," he said. He even promised not to change the party organization in New Jersey if he were elected. This was in July 1910. His defeat on the Graduate College issue at Princeton was certain, and Smith's offer came at the right time. On July 12, 1910, Wilson agreed to run as Democratic candidate. While the party convention's decision was pending Wilson talked like a conservative (the progressives were attacking him strongly at the time). He attacked the unions and was denounced by them as an enemy. He seemed to admit the painful necessity of corruption in politics. But as soon as the convention in Trenton made him its candidate (largely a result of the efforts of Smith and Harvey) Wilson declared, to the great joy of the progressives, that his only desire was to make the Democratic party "an instrument of justice for the state and for the nation," that he wished to serve the people, and that he was not committed to the bosses.[5] This set the tone of his forceful campaign. He defeated the Republican candidate by 50,000 votes on November 8, 1910.

Immediately upon election Wilson's progressive tendencies became even more pronounced. The new legislature of New Jersey was Democratic and Smith demanded Wilson's support for his own candidacy for the Senate as recompense for his aid in Wilson's campaign. Wilson refused and instead gave his full support to Smith's opponent, who won by forty-seven votes to three. It is said that the old boss wept at his defeat. Smith was to become the mortal enemy of the new governor. But Wilson had chosen the only possible way: if the Democrats were to defeat the Republicans they had to have the support of the liberals. From then on Wilson directed all his actions toward a precise goal: his designation as the Democratic candidate for the presidency in 1912.

At this time two unusual men appeared in his life, Edward Mandell House and Louis D. Brandeis. The former, the seventh son of a rich Texas landowner, was two years younger than Wilson. After a violent and uproarious childhood much affected by the aftermath of the Civil War, an accident had forced him to more quiet ways. He had left college at his father's death to manage his inheritance and to take up politics in Texas. He acquired a great deal of power there by staying in the background and playing the role of gray eminence—a role that is characteristic of his whole life. The man who was to be called "the silent partner" was the influential adviser of four successive governors of Texas. One of them, Hogg, called him "Colonel" of his personal general staff. This politician, who had never commanded even a small troop, was to go down in history as "Colonel House" or just "Colonel," a fact that seems to have annoyed him to some extent.

House was not satisfied to be merely the mysterious adviser of governors, he wished to play this role on the national level. He made no move as long as Bryan was the Democratic candidate, because Bryan would accept no adviser. But hope reappeared in 1908. He must get a president elected who would suit his purpose. After some groping he finally decided upon Wilson. The two men met for the first time in New York, on November 24, 1911, following an exchange of letters.

They became friends at once. It was a friendship based on wholehearted mutual understanding, a common political outlook and common interests. "Never before have I found both the man and the opportunity," said House.[6] "Mr. House is my second self," said Wilson. "He is myself independent of me, his thoughts and mine are one."[7] House was to bring to Wilson the votes of Texas and many other elements of success in the Democratic convention. After the election, he became, as he wished, the most influential of all Americans except the President, especially in foreign policy, and remained so until 1919, although without holding office.

The other important man was Louis D. Brandeis. After the Democratic convention in Baltimore had chosen Wilson, with the vicissitudes we have noted at the beginning of the chapter, Wilson realized that he lacked a platform. The old Democratic themes—like low tariffs—were worn out and unsuited to draw votes in opposition to the impressive campaign being waged by Theodore Roosevelt as the Progressive candidate under the slogan of the "New Nationalism." Inspired by the New York journalist Herbert Croly, author of the successful book *The Promise of American Life*, published in 1909, Roosevelt was trying to combine Hamilton's idea of a strong Federal government with the Jeffersonian liberal idea opposing the "special interests of the monied class." Roosevelt recognized the superior efficiency of trusts over small industry, but he wanted them to be under Federal control. The Federal government was to make great social reforms.

Brandeis provided Wilson with a means to offset this ideology so tempting to the majority of the people. Louis D. Brandeis was one of the strongest American personalities of the early twentieth century. Son of a Bohemian who had come to the United States as a refugee in 1848, Brandeis was born in Louisville, Kentucky, on November 13, 1856. From a precocious, spectacular career at the Harvard Law School, he became one of the great judges of the United States while still very young. As a leading member of the Boston bar, he was a prominent defender of citizens against trusts and played an important part in Boston affairs. He devoted his energies to the defense of the "general interest" versus the "special interests" of the financiers and businessmen—the identical position of La Follette and the progressives. Brandeis had voted Republican in 1908. Later he supported the formation of the Progressive party and the candidacy of the senator from Wisconsin, but the party chose Roosevelt instead. Brandeis considered Roosevelt too closely allied to the steel trust to wage the desired battle and he turned toward Wilson, the Democratic candidate.

Wilson met Brandeis at Sea Girt, New Jersey, on August 28, 1912, and was immediately drawn to him. Brandeis was the champion of economic freedom for small business, the determined opponent of monopoly and privilege. Instead of placing monopolies under government control, as Roosevelt advocated, would it not be better still to destroy the monopolies? "If America cannot have free enterprise, then she will not be able to preserve any kind of liberty," said Wilson in one of his speeches.[8] In doing this he declared that he was fighting for the American way of life. This platform was called the New Freedom.

To sum it up, Wilson's success is explained by his freeing himself from the bosses, because he preferred to appeal directly to the people. "Wilson had, to an exceptional degree," says Baker, "the gift of coming into intimate contact immediately . . . with his audience. He was even confidential. He was at ease, human, courteous, he had the gift of liking his listeners." [9]

Wilson's Collaborators

After the November election, Wilson went to Bermuda with his family where he worked out the composition of his cabinet with the aid of House, whose choice was reflected in seven of the ten members. Certain men in this cabinet are of special interest to us, especially the Secretary of State. Bryan had supported Wilson at the convention in the end, and the President could not avoid giving him a major post. Wilson respected and liked the man, but at the same time he feared his ideas and his great influence in the Democratic party. Moreover, though Bryan had been in Congress, in the 1890's, he had never had experience in administration and diplomacy. He would not be satisfied with an appointment as ambassador and Wilson resigned himself to giving him the State Department. Bryan pompously made a condition that no intoxicating liquors would be served at official functions [10] thus opening the era that foreign diplomats have called the era of "grape-juice diplomacy."

Bryan had in his favor a limitless capacity for work, but it can be held against him that he applied the "spoils system" on a grand scale by replacing Republicans in the diplomatic service with Democrats. This was natural in the veteran politician avid for power after so many years. James W. Gerard, a Tammany Hall politician, was appointed ambassador to Berlin; Walter Hines Page, a friend of Wilson's, to London; McCombs, one of the Democratic leaders who had supported Wilson, was offered the appointment to Paris, but he refused to "go to St. Helena." Wilson did not concern himself much with these details. In House, "he had a complete diplomatic service at his disposal." [11] In general, Bryan's ambassadors were inexperienced, and the information they were able to send to Washington in 1914 was of little value.

Another major idea of Bryan's was theoretical and doctrinaire pacifism: he thought that all wars were wrong. From this stemmed the naïve conclusion that war could be avoided by signing treaties of conciliation on all sides. This was the object of the "President's Peace Plan," of April 24, 1914, which really came from Bryan. Thirty such pacts, agreeing that questions that could not be resolved through normal diplomatic channels would be submitted to permanent investigating commissions, were signed. In addition arbitration treaties were negotiated with Italy, Spain, and Japan. England accepted the formula but Germany did not. This policy was a good example of beating the air. Thomas Bailey has described the foreign policy of Bryan as "an outburst of idealism." [12]

One should mention also, in relation to foreign policy, the Secretary of War, Garrison, a New Jersey judge who was merely a good administrator and was replaced in 1916 by Newton D. Baker, mayor of Cleveland; and the Secretary of the Navy, Josephus Daniels. Daniels, publisher of the *News and Observer* of Raleigh, North Carolina, and chief of the progressive movement within the Democratic party, was an unusual person. He wrote two very interesting volumes entitled *The Era of Wilson* which have little to say about the Navy. He was fortunately aided by a young man of thirty with a distinguished name, a distant cousin and nephew by marriage of the former President who was Wilson's rival in the election—Franklin Delano Roosevelt.[13]

Taken all in all, Colonel House was the only really strong influence in foreign affairs. He alone at first understood their overriding importance. We shall see him influencing foreign policy at Wilson's side.

Wilson's Political Philosophy in 1913

We must now examine briefly the new President's ideas about foreign problems. There is no question that they were only secondary to him. He had talked little about them in the campaign. "It would be an ironic destiny for me if my administration had to be principally concerned with foreign affairs." [14] "In my opinion," wrote House on June 24, 1915, "the President has never appreciated the importance of our foreign policy, and has wrongly stressed domestic matters." [15] As House had been passionately interested in international affairs since the days of his youth in Texas, Wilson constantly asked his advice and ambassadors sometimes wrote directly to him. Wilson kept the power in his own hands, however, and his ideas, as far as we can discern them at the beginning of his administration, are thus of capital importance. All the more so, because toward the end of his career foreign policy would swallow up everything else. Fortunately, we have at our disposition, aside from his own writings, two excellent studies, that of Harley Notter, *The Origins of the Foreign Policy of Woodrow Wilson*,[16] and that of Arthur Link in the collection *Wilson the Diplomatist*.[17]

Wilson was totally indifferent to foreign affairs at the start of his career, but in the 1880's was this attitude not shared by the majority of the American people? It was a period of "introversion" if ever there was one, when economic development took precedence over everything. There is one allusion to foreign affairs in Wilson's *Congressional Government*, one page in a hundred in *The State*, nothing more. In the late 1890's American nationalism, indeed imperialism, crystallized. Wilson approved of Cleveland's imposing his arbitration on England in her conflict with Venezuela. After some hesitation he approved the war of 1898 with Spain as justified by the vitality of American industrial power. He thought it was the duty of the United States to keep the Philippines, to teach them order and self-government, even if it meant the use of force. He adopted the imperialistic view of Alfred T. Mahan and Albert J. Beveridge that the flag should protect commerce, and he approved the acquisition of colonies.

More important because of its future potentiality was Wilson's idea that the war with Spain meant a definite end to isolationism and opened a new era in which the United States, long absorbed in domestic affairs, would play more and more of a world role. He had thus a lively prophetic sense of the inevitable necessities of the future. Even in 1887 he dreamed of a worldwide union of states of which the United States would be the "pilot." [18]

In short, before 1913 Wilson had thought very little about the problem of foreign policy and he had had no experience in that field. He did not know—and did not try to learn—the main facts of twentieth century diplomacy, American or European. As Link says, in his election campaign, "he never mentioned a problem in foreign policy which did not imply an underlying domestic policy." [19] Nevertheless, when he took office, he held certain idealistic principles in which he believed wholeheartedly.

According to Link, they came from his Presbyterian background, which gave him a very rigorous sense of the moral universe—the origin of the idea that moral principles apply equally to nations and to individuals. In addition to this, influenced by Bagehot and Burke, Wilson was a great admirer of the British Constitution and traditions. From Burke he takes over the vocabulary in which the words, "humanity," "voice of humanity," "human race," are constantly used. One wonders whether he had not also read Kant's *Plan for Perpetual Peace*, because some of his major themes, "making the world safe for democracy," "a single morality for all," "necessity of an international organization," are to be found also in the writings of the great German philosopher.

What are these principles which were so important? First, that material interests should be subordinated to moral principles. Morality is even above the law. Foreign policy, he said, should concern itself more with the rights of man than with property rights. Here we see again his opposition to what he called "special interests," big financial interests, and his support of the national interest of all, inherently connected with the ideal of America.

Thus Wilson, temporarily overlooking the doctrine of original sin, came to believe that man was sufficiently good so that democracy was the most humane and most Christian form of government. It follows that every people must be capable of self-government. If they do not achieve it by persuasion, it may sometimes be necessary to impose it on them by force. Finally, the American people, a new people grown out of the fusion of various nationalities, which more than any other had achieved an advanced form of democracy, of equality, had a mission to fulfill: to be guardian of the spirit of justice and of progress. The mission of the United States in the world was not to acquire wealth or power, but "to realize the ideal of liberty, to furnish a model of democracy, to defend moral principles." [20] Moreover, its history proves that it has always done so: America's "greatest victories have been victories of peace and humanity." This is the reason that the United States should "lead the world." [21]

It has been too often believed that these words prove that Wilson was a pure idealist, unable to grasp reality. This is certainly not so. At Princeton and in New Jersey he demonstrated his flexibility, even astuteness. As we shall see, he was to prove a remarkable negotiator. But he did hold certain illusions, and he oversimplified at times. He allowed himself to be too easily comforted by historical analogies. There was always a tendency toward pharisaism in his policy which was extremely irritating to Europeans. His ambition and his idea that he was the instrument of Providence (despite his own doubts and inner conflicts) gave him an unusual energy, but they also isolated him dangerously. With the exception of House, he had little confidence in others. He had an exaggerated notion of the presidential powers and scorned Congress too openly.

The New Foreign Policy

It is not surprising that Wilson's first acts in foreign policy were applications of his abstract principles to concrete situations. This holds for Latin America and the Far East, dollar diplomacy and customs policy.

A few days after his inauguration, on March 11, 1913, he made a declaration on Latin America in which he repudiated dollar diplomacy and tried to quell the suspicion which the attitudes of Roosevelt and Taft had aroused in Latin Americans. A just government, he said, rests always on the consent of the governed. "Therefore, throughout the world the United States must always support constitutional regimes. The United States has nothing to gain in Central or South America except the permanent interests of the people of those two continents." He set himself apart from the "special interests" and expressed the belief that commercial relations should be conducted for the mutual benefit of both parties.[22]

What did this mean? Henry Lane Wilson, ambassador to Mexico, was enthusiastically encouraging American capitalists to gain concessions. He seems to have contributed to the success of the great Mexican Revolution in November 1911, which ousted dictator Porfirio Diaz who had ruled Mexico for more than thirty years, but the revolution did not fulfill the desires of the ambassador when Madero, a radical who did not favor businessmen, rose to power. Madero was overthrown and assassinated in February 1913 by a military clique which brought to power Victoriano Huerta, and the American ambassador was suspected of having aided the coup d'état. At all events, he worked hard to get Huerta recognized by the United States.

The traditional policy was to recognize governments once they were well established, but Wilson did not follow that tradition. "I will not recognize a government of butchers," he said in a private conversation.[23] The question was discussed at a cabinet meeting on March 11. The "big interests" favored recognition on condition that Huerta promise to hold elections. If recognition were refused, House said in a memorandum, American influence in Mexico would be replaced by that of England and Germany. Wilson hesitated to adopt these views. On May 23 he decided, with the support of Bryan, to refuse recognition and on August 4 he recalled Ambassador Wilson. We shall see that this idealistic policy caused a three-year crisis in Mexico and greatly embarrassed the United States. On August 27, 1913, the President explained to Congress that he was following a policy of "wait and see."

Wilson's idealism led him to negotiate a treaty with Colombia, to make up to that country the harm done by Theodore Roosevelt. Negotiations began on May 3, 1913, in Washington, and led to the Treaty of Bogota, signed on April 6, 1914. The United States expressed "sincere regrets," and promised to pay $25,000,000 to Colombia. This was a long-range policy suited to reassuring the Latins, but it offended the narrow nationalism of the Senate and provided fuel for Republican propaganda. Roosevelt spoke of a "crime against the United States" and "an attack on the honor of the United States." This treaty was not ratified until the end of World War I, with modifications.

Wilson was also responsive to British protests against the lowering of passage duties through the Panama Canal for American vessels exclusively. This seemed to violate the Hay-Pauncefote Treaty of 1901 which proclaimed equality for all users of the canal. Wilson decided that honesty came first, and in spite of campaign promises, he told the Senate Committee on Foreign Relations on January 26, 1914, that he proposed to end these discriminatory measures because it was necessary to remain on good terms with Great Britain.

Wilson's South American policy was outlined in a speech full of promises made in Mobile, Alabama, on October 27, 1913. Interests sometimes separate nations, he said, but sympathy unites them. Therefore one should not build foreign policy in terms of material interests. "I want to take this occasion to say that the United States will never again seek one additional foot of territory by conquest . . . We dare not turn from the principle that morality and not expediency is the thing that must guide us, and that we will never condone iniquity because it is most convenient to do so." [24]

In the Far East, his policy was marked by the same moralism. There too, dollar diplomacy must cease; there too, the government must stop protecting the special interests. In 1911, as we have seen, the Taft administration had exerted political pressure to get a syndicate of American bankers admitted to an international consortium which the Chinese government had commissioned to build railroads. Wilson, who was much interested in China and had favored the Revolution of 1912,[25] was opposed to the consortium, which seemed to him to create an illegal regime in China. Bryan, for his part, knew a bit about China, Japan, and Korea. In 1907 he had proposed a toast—in water of course —to Admiral Togo, hero of the Russo-Japanese War. What bothered Wilson and Bryan were the onerous conditions on which the consortium was prepared to make a loan to China. Despite State Department opposition, on March 18, 1913, Wilson decided to make a declaration opposing the consortium, whose loan, he said, "threatened to touch very nearly the administrative independence of China itself . . .

just now awakening to a consciousness of its power and of its obligations to its people . . . Our interests are those of the Open Door—a door of friendship and mutual advantage. This is the only door we care to enter." [26]

This sensational declaration was generally well received. It appeared to be full of anti-imperialism and antimonopolism. It was generous if not realistic. In fact the withdrawal of the United States from the consortium did not stop the other foreigners from making the loan, and it discouraged American bankers from making others. Despite internal disorders, Wilson also decided to recognize the republican government of China as soon as the National Assembly met, which took place on March 2, 1913. The United States was the first great power to recognize the new government.

Relations with Japan were of an entirely different nature, but here again they were based on the generous intentions of the President. As early as March 5, 1913, the Japanese ambassador in Washington was complaining of discriminatory legislation in California with regard to agricultural workers. We have seen that there was a great deal of anti-Oriental feeling in that state, especially in the unions, and that in 1907 President Roosevelt had fought against segregation in the schools of San Francisco. Wilson favored a clause excluding the Japanese, who were considered impossible to assimilate. The Japanese protested, out of national pride, at being treated as inferior. Furthermore, an American-Japanese rivalry was growing in the Pacific and mutual suspicion rising. The annexation of Korea by Japan in 1910 had increased this tension.

On April 8, 1913, Wilson called the attention of the cabinet to the problem in California, and Bryan proposed a referendum in that state. Meetings were held in Tokyo. California was putting the Federal government in a difficult position and it was decided that Bryan should go there in person. In a speech to the state legislature he declared that the law containing the words "aliens ineligible for citizenship" should not be passed because the Chinese as well as the Japanese would be humiliated. In spite of this the legislature passed the Webb Bill, containing this phrase, on May 2. The Japanese ambassador protested energetically in a threatening note. Was Japan about to attack the Philippines? Admiral Fiske, in a report on naval operations, recalled that Japan had attacked Russia in 1904 without warning. Since the Panama Canal was nearing completion, might not Japan be tempted to start hostilities at once before the Atlantic fleet could come to the rescue? Wilson responded to Japan in a moderate tone, explaining that the Constitution forbade the Federal government to override state laws. The question was not resolved but it became less tense.

The last important act before 1914 was the lowering of tariffs. Democratic tradition demanded this, as did Wilson's belief in economic liberalism. The rise in the cost of living since the Dingley Tariff of 1897 and the astounding progress of business reinforced arguments in favor of greater flexibility. Was not the tariff favorable mostly to the trusts? The Payne-Aldrich Tariff of 1909 had not affected the protective system in any practical way.

The party was ill at ease. The Democrats of the East, of whom there were many in Congress, were hostile to the lowering of certain customs duties. Wilson decided, even before his inauguration, to assign to his old opponent, then supporter, representative Oscar W. Underwood of Alabama, the responsibility of preparing a general tariff bill. On May 8, 1913, the House of Representatives passed the Underwood Bill by a vote of 281 to 139. To compensate for the loss to the Treasury, representative Cordell Hull of Tennessee proposed a federal income tax yielding $100,000,000, which was enacted. The Senate debate was more heated. They fought especially over the free entry of wool and sugar and lowered duties on cotton textiles. Some of the future adversaries of the Treaty of Versailles, like Borah, took an active part. The bill was passed, nevertheless, by a vote of 44 to 37 on September 9, and in final form, after agreement with the House, on October 2. This was an enormous personal success for Wilson. He said on September 10: "A battle for the people and for free enterprise, a battle which has lasted for a whole generation, has finally been won, magnificently and completely." [27]

Chapter III

The European War and American Neutrality

Neutrality

Wᴵᴸꜱᴏɴ had every reason in the world to keep the United States out of the war which broke out on August 4, 1914, as the United States had no direct interests at stake, and the Monroe Doctrine forbade meddling in European affairs. Without doubt the President and a large part of the populace were shocked by the Austrian attack on Serbia, and even more by the violation of Belgian neutrality. Madame Tassier, in *La Belgique et l'entrée en guerre des Etats-Unis, 1914–1917,*[1] has given a good description of this attitude. The war had nothing of a crusade of good against evil, however. The Allied camp was not that of democracy, including as it did tsarist Russia, little admired in the United States.

American public opinion and the President were in agreement that the United States was not really concerned either through principles or because of interests.

In addition, Wilson had a more specific reason to stand aside. As we know, he believed that the United States, for him the new nation produced by the Melting Pot, had a mission ordained by Providence. He was a racist in a way, because he thought the nation should for the most part be white. "The whole question is one of assimilating different races. We cannot have a homogeneous population and include people who cannot mix with the Caucasian race,"[2] he wrote in October 1912. Even with regard to Caucasians, the several national traditions had not been wholly fused in the Melting Pot, and Wilson feared that they would flare up more powerful than ever and destroy the fragile cohesion of the new mixture.

Out of a population of 95,000,000 inhabitants there were 13,345,000 Americans who had been born abroad and 12,916,000 who were born in the United States of foreign-born parents. Of this total of more than 26,000,000, there were 6,400,000 Germans and 3,400,000 Irish, who for various reasons were favorable to the Central Powers, or opposed to England. There were 2,000,000 English and 2,000,000 Italians favorable to the Entente, and there were 2,500,000 from different parts of the Austro-Hungarian Empire, who according to their national diversity were for one camp or the other.[3] Therefore, on August 18, 1914, Wilson made a solemn appeal in favor of neutrality in thought as well as in deed.

Bryan, the only member of the cabinet who inclined to be pro-German, was a pacifist doctrinaire. Wilson had an increasingly more qualified attitude for which *neutralist* is a more exact term. For him, neutrality should not consist only in "keeping apart from difficulties." It was a positive asset, permitting him, for example, to mediate between the belligerents. Wilson also believed firmly in the sacred rights of neutrals, and he was to come gradually to the idea that the defense of these rights might justify the awesome decision to wage war.

In the beginning, the idea of using neutrality as a basis for a mediating role was more Colonel House's than Wilson's own, and it was the reason for the Colonel's trip to Europe, May–July 1914. As early as 1913 House envisioned a policy of rapprochement between England, Germany, and the United States, to be based on stopping the naval race and on cooperation for foreign investment of excess capital. Edward Grey, for his part, had since 1906 favored closer ties between Britain and the United States, and wished nothing more than to lessen tension between his country and Germany. Wilson approved the plan in December 1913, and House began to organize his "great adventure," as he called his first official trip to Europe.

In late May House arrived in Berlin, where he first met with Admiral von Tirpitz, who seemed to him the most aggressive of the Germans. Then on June 1 he had a personal interview with Wilhelm II, who reminded him somewhat of Theodore Roosevelt. While the Kaiser embroidered the theme of a Germany isolated and encircled, and called for an alliance between Germany, England, and the United States against other "half-savage nations," House patiently explained his ideas and talked about naval disarmament, naturally without success.

House went from Berlin to Paris, where a cabinet crisis following the elections of 1914 prevented his accomplishing much, and then to

London on June 10. He talked at length with Edward Grey, who was much more interested in House's plans than was the Kaiser. But Grey did not believe that war was coming and he did not wish to arouse apprehension among his French and Russian friends. The idea of a plan of joint investments seemed to please the British.[4]

In the course of the London talks, the shooting at Sarajevo took place, and the European diplomatic mechanism which was to lead to war was set in motion. The Colonel's trip was forced into the background. On July 7 House sent a letter to Wilhelm II which Undersecretary of State Zimmermann answered on August 1, after House had returned to the United States. "The Emperor has taken note of your letter with the greatest interest. Alas! all his strenuous efforts to preserve the peace have completely failed."[5] The only result of the "great adventure" was a letter Wilson wrote to the belligerent leaders on August 5 in which he proposed his own eventual mediation. This letter had no effect.

The First Phase: The British Blockade and American Protests, August 1914–February 1915

The immediate and temporary reaction of the United States was a sentimental one: Anger over the violation of Belgium, sympathy with the old ally France.

> Forget us God,
> If we forget
> The sacred sword
> Of Lafayette

wrote the poet Robert Underwood Johnson.[6] Wilson estimated that 90 percent of all Americans were for the Allies.[7] But attention shifted quickly to practical considerations, especially to the foreign commerce of the United States. There were to be three principal phases of reaction to the war before January 31, 1917, which show a sort of oscillation between these two viewpoints.

The first phase, which lasted until February–March 1915, was marked by difficulties with Great Britain. In the first place, the British cabinet decided, on August 20, not to regard as valid the Declaration of London of 1909 which stated some principles of maritime rights in time of war. Above all, there were the British orders in council which placed a blockade on Germany. For technical reasons this blockade, contrary to long-established custom, could not be a "linear blockade" of enemy coasts. For one thing, with a linear blockade neutral ports like Rotterdam and Genoa could receive goods in transit destined for the enemy. The French and the British therefore decided to search neutral vessels on the high seas to determine whether they were carrying contraband goods. Such a search, which could only take place in Allied ports, resulted in loss of time and money, and infinite controversies over the nature and destination of cargoes. There was the further problem of defining what goods were contraband. The orders in council of August 20 contained a long list of such goods, including foodstuffs. On September 21 a number of raw materials were added, including copper, a major American export. Oil and rubber were later added. To appease the United States cotton was not included (the financial losses of the South early in the war were catastrophic), but it was added to the list on August 20, 1915. Furthermore, on November 4, 1914, the North Sea was declared a theater of war and it was mined. On March 15, 1915, the British made known that they would forbid all neutral maritime commerce with Germany.

Pressed by German and Irish groups, by merchants, by agricultural producers in the West and the South, the American government protested continuously in the name of the Hague Convention and the Declaration of London, which had not been ratified by England. The United States did not, however, go so far as to declare reprisals, which could only have been an embargo on goods such as arms and munitions destined for Great Britain. Some bills to this effect were proposed in Congress, but such an embargo would have aggravated the growing number of businessmen dealing with the Allies, and would have arrested a boom that was developing in the United States, especially in the industrial East.

Wilson, and even Bryan, were also affected by the argument that the Allies, less well prepared than the enemy, would find themselves punished for not having prepared deliberately for war. Counselor Robert Lansing, judicial in temperament, defender by training of international law, often interpreted cases in favor of the Allied cause. For instance, he refused permission for German ships that could play the role of auxiliary cruisers to leave American ports although similar British ships might do so under the pretext that their arms were merely defensive.

Edward Grey made a point of conforming to the specific aspects of the blockade. He knew exactly how to balance two imperative needs: waging of economic war and maintenance of Anglo-American friendship. He was greatly aided by the American ambassador in London, Walter Hines Page, a determined Anglophile—in the end Wilson did not trust his dispatches—and by the British ambassador in Washington, Sir Cecil Spring-Rice. Moreover, European news reached America by trans-Atlantic cables owned by the British and this allowed a coordination of propaganda which the German radio stations could not offset.[8]

Neither Wilson nor House thought the problem insoluble. The best solution to all problems would be to restore peace, and Wilson's ambition was to do so. After the conversation between Bryan and the German ambassador, Bernstorff, in September during the Battle of the Marne, the President began to think that it would soon be possible to achieve a cease-fire. At the end of the year he approved a new trip planned by House. The Colonel went to Europe this time to try to define the terms of peace: the evacuation of Belgium and France, the former with an indemnity. This would essentially have been a restoration of the status quo ante bellum, but with the addition of general disarmament. Bryan was somewhat disappointed not to be chosen for this mission.

House left the United States on January 30 on the *Lusitania* and remained in Europe until June 5. His plan disturbed Grey who thought it necessary to defeat the Germans. From London House went to Paris, where he talked especially with Foreign Minister Delcassé. The expected invitation to Berlin finally arrived from Undersecretary of State Zimmermann. He went to Germany via Switzerland, and passed within a dozen miles of the front. In Paris he had become convinced that his peace plan was insufficient; the French wanted the restoration of Alsace-Lorraine, and Russia was demanding Constantinople (which the French and British were secretly conceding at the time). In Berlin, between March 20 and 26, he realized that the Germans would never accept such terms, that the annexationists had the majority behind them, and that the military, especially von Tirpitz, dominated the government. Whereas in Paris Wilson was accused of being pro-German, in Berlin he was accused of furnishing arms to the Allies. House wrote to the President on March 26: "I leave [Berlin] sadly disappointed that we were misled into believing that peace parleys might be begun upon a basis of evacuation of France and Belgium." [9]

House was not discouraged, however, and produced another plan on March 27, more limited but more directly affecting his country: to get both sides to accept what he called "freedom of the seas." Contraband would be defined only as arms and munitions; neutral ships would circulate freely outside of territorial waters and might even enter belligerent ports if there were no effective blockade. This meant that England would allow food and other products to go into Germany in exchange for cessation of submarine warfare. There was no doubt that this plan was advantageous to the neutrals and especially to the United States. It was also certain that it could be useful to Germany. House's illusion was to believe it equally advantageous to Great Britain, even supposing she could trust German promises. As a matter of principle, Great Britain, as a great naval power, had been opposed to the idea of freedom of the seas since the Congress of Vienna, 1814–1815. Furthermore, German propaganda interfered by making the plan public and declaring that if England accepted the idea of freedom of the seas, Germany would evacuate Belgium. This underlined the advantage to the Central Powers and House's plan came to nothing. The idea of freedom of the seas remained an article of American political faith and was to reappear as the second of President Wilson's Fourteen Points.

Second Phase: The Danger of War with Germany, February–December 1915

Already the balance had swung the other way and the second phase, of tension with Germany, began in February 1915. This was to last until the end of the year. The Germans declared the waters surrounding the British Isles to be a theater of war on February 4, 1915, which meant that German submarines would sink enemy ships without giving notice, and that neutral ships would enter that zone at their own risk. The success of small German submarines against British cruisers as early as September 1914 explained the decision to resort to this kind of warfare on a big scale. German propaganda cited, in justification, the danger of famine among the civilian population arising from the English blockade.

The United States protested at once, on February 10, and Chancellor Bethmann-Hollweg tried in vain to obtain special conditions for American ships. American protests became more strenuous when "overt acts" followed the declaration. To begin with, some American cargo ships were attacked by mistake of the German commanders, for instance the tanker *Gulflight* on May 1. This was a grave threat to the flourishing American commerce. More serious was the fact that American citizens were lost in the sinking of British passenger ships, for instance, the *Falaba* on March 28, in which one American was lost. Then on May 7, 1915, the liner *Lusitania*, on which Colonel House had gone to Europe, was torpedoed off the coast of Ireland by the submarine U-20. The German captain, Schwieger, seems not to have known until the last moment whether it was the *Lusitania* or the *Mauretania*, a sister ship which was being used as a troop transport. This was a serious matter. Of the 1959 passengers, 1198 were lost, including 128 American citizens. The *Lusitania* did have some models of weapons in her cargo, but the taking of so many civilian lives, including women and children, seemed inexcusable, and American opinion was inflamed.[10] "The torpedo which sank the *Lusitania*," said the *Nation*, "also sank Germany in the opinion of mankind."

In government circles there were three types of reaction. Some, like House, who was then in Europe, thought that war was now inevitable. On May 9 he wrote to Wilson from London: "America has come to the parting of the ways, when she must determine whether she stands for civilized or uncivilized warfare. We can no longer remain neutral spectators."[11] This opinion was loudly supported by many important people, like former President Theodore Roosevelt.

At the other extreme, more and more isolated and increasingly separated from Lansing, was Secretary of State Bryan. As a pacifist, Bryan wished above all to avoid war. In his opinion the Germans were not entirely in the wrong. He accepted the idea of a firm protest on condition that a simultaneous and equally strong protest be made to Great Britain about the blockade. He proposed that the problem of indemnity to American citizens be handled by the method of arbitration he had introduced in his conciliation treaties of 1913.[12] He suggested that American citizens not undertake the great risk of traveling on belligerent ships.

Between these two attitudes, Wilson's own took shape gradually but firmly. The President wanted to avoid war but thought that the public as a whole was not ready to follow Bryan's extreme measures. He wished to protest energetically and to use the threat of force to obtain a promise from the German government that no ships would be sunk without warning. He refused in the name of liberty to prohibit travel by American citizens on belligerent ships. At the same time it was not certain that Germany would accept the solution Wilson proposed. If she did not, the danger of war was considerable. Wilson did not hesitate to take this narrow path, and he did it ably, with conviction and realism. Bryan was to be the principal victim in this matter.

The first American note, written by Wilson, amended by Lansing, and signed by the President himself, was limited to demands for German disavowal of intention to torpedo passenger ships, and damages for American victims. The German response of May 28 justified the torpedoing of the *Lusitania* on the pretext that it was in fact an auxiliary armed cruiser. The American cabinet on June 1 discussed what should be done. Wilson proposed a note which would give the impression of an ultimatum. Bryan, on the other hand, proposed the ideas we have noted, and went so far as to accuse his colleagues of being pro-Ally. Furthermore it became known, by a telegram from House to the President on May 24, that Bryan had told the Austrian ambassador Dumba that the first American note was not to be taken too seriously.[13] Bryan refused to sign the second note. He offered his resignation June 8 and was immediately replaced by Robert Lansing, son of a great lawyer and himself an expert in international law. "Colonel House," Bryan told Wilson, "has been the real Secretary of State, not I, and I have never enjoyed your full confidence." [14]

The real meaning of these events was that Wilson, after having hesitated between Bryan's pacifism and isolationism and a firmer policy which would risk war, had, under the influence of House, opted for the latter. Bryan could no longer remain in the government.

The second note, of June 9, was a very firm one, rejecting the German arguments. The German response of July 8 seemed partially to give way: Germany would accept the principle of freedom of the seas and considered that if it had been violated the blame lay with the British. While Wilson was preparing for war, as we shall see, a third note, on which Wilson and Lansing collaborated, insisted that the sinking of the *Lusitania* was both "illegal and inhuman." War seemed all the more likely when, on August 19, another British liner, *The Arabic*, was sunk off Fastnet. This time the peace was saved by the German ambassador Bernstorff, who undertook to obtain a reply from his government which would satisfy Wilson, although it would be unofficial. He succeeded with some difficulty and could notify Lansing on September 1 that: "Liners will not be sunk by our submarines without warning, and without assuring the safety of the lives of non-combatants, provided that the liners do not try to escape or to offer resistance." [15]

In effect, these incidents on the sea ceased, except for the attacks of Austro-Hungarian submarines in the Mediterranean. Germany had renounced nothing, but in fact she was committed not to do it again. Wilson could obtain no more, not even indemnities for the families of the *Lusitania* victims, despite Lansing's efforts in the following months. When the unarmed French liner *Sussex* was attacked in the English Channel on March 24, 1916, Germany, after many hesitations, expressed regrets.

Tension again reached a high pitch when it was discovered (through the British Information Services) that two members of the German embassy in Washington—Captain Franz von Papen, military attaché, and Captain Karl Boy-Ed, naval attaché—and the Austrian consul-general in New York, Franz von Nuber, were engaged in sabotage. The British had been able to seize correspondence which contained plans to sabotage factories and bridges. Proof of the activities of the German secret agent Rintelen in Mexico was also included. Moreover, Boy-Ed had referred in a letter to "stupid Yankees." The Austro-Hungarian ambassador, Dumba, who was also compromised, was declared persona non grata and recalled in September 1915. Von Papen and Boy-Ed were urged to leave the United States in December. Germany had alienated sympathies important to her by the very zeal and organization of her agents. The propaganda line was that ambassador Bernstorff had not known of the subversive activities of his staff—we now know this to be untrue. Bernstorff also made blunders. He tried, for example, to bring pressure on House on September 28, 1915, by referring to the votes of Americans of German origin in the coming presidential election. This showed a lack of tact, certainly, to which the Colonel reacted strongly; it also displayed political naïveté as the German-Americans usually voted Republican.

Third Phase: Hardening of Feeling against the Allies,
December 1915–January 1917

After relations with Germany, so strained in the summer, had somewhat improved, the Entente, or at least Great Britain, again caused
anxiety to the United States government, if not to the public. Early
in 1916 a movie was shown in the United States ("The War Cry of
Peace") in which fictional "Raritanians," decked out in pointed hel-
mets, burned New York and massacred the civilian population. At the
same time the British war cabinet intensified the economic war. As
soon as the matter of the *Sussex* was settled in May 1916, the problems with England were more clearly seen. This became much more
important because 1916 was a presidential election year. On many
points Wilson stiffened his position to attract votes. The Irish revolt
of April 24, 1916, which had been followed by severe repression and
executions, made the Irish-Americans furious. Bainbridge Colby, future Secretary of State and a member of the progressive wing of the
Democratic party, denounced the repression in Ireland at a meeting
in New York attended by 2300 delegates of The Irish Race in America.
Many newspapers, even those favoring the Allies, demanded strong
measures against the blockade. It became a national question. The reaction was "more a sentiment than a movement," writes May, which
shows clearly its limitations.[16]

France, in the midst of the grim Battle of Verdun, had not aroused
similar hostility. "The United States is pro-Ally but anti-British,"
wrote the British ambassador.[17] Wilson had invited the French ambassador, Jusserand, to help him inaugurate the new lighting system
in the Statue of Liberty. On this occasion the Marseillaise was played
and a toast proposed to Poincaré. Wilson declared, "I do not think
that any peace can last as long as there exist countries whose behavior
depends on the selfish combinations of a few individuals." [18] This was
tantamount to a departure from neutrality, on the level of sentiment.

The refusal by the Allies of Wilson's offer of mediation was what
roused in him a new and profound resentment toward them. In October 1915 House had produced a new plan, compulsory mediation:
the United States threatened to use military force against whichever
belligerent refused American mediation. House favored the Allies,
and thought they would accept this scheme and thus assure their vic-

tory. If Germany did likewise, it would be "a master stroke of diplomacy." If she refused, the United States could break off diplomatic relations with her and even use force by drawing all neutrals to the side of the United States. Wilson was "stunned" at first, and then agreed. Lansing also approved,[19] but the Allies had yet to be convinced.

On October 17, 1915, House wrote to his friend Grey about this proposal. He prepared to go to Europe to get the approval of the Allied governments, first, and then that of Germany. Wilson supported House's plan, but with the intention to limit the action to moral pressure only.

When House arrived in London, on January 5, 1916, he learned that Grey's political position was considerably weakened. In his two-week stay he merely explored the lay of the land. He was struck by the confidence of various political leaders, especially Lloyd George, who was to become Prime Minister in October, in a final Allied victory. As he wrote on January 19: "I wish Lloyd George was Prime Minister, with Sir Edward Grey as Foreign Minister, for I believe we could then do something." [20]

House went next to Paris and from there, on January 26, to Berlin. He was well aware that a great controversy was raging in Germany between the advocates and opponents of unlimited submarine warfare. He spent a longer time in Paris on the way back, where he got along well with Briand, then Premier, who appeared to have a great admiration for Wilson. In the course of the conversation with Briand an important decision was made. "It was finally understood that in the event the Allies had some notable victories during the spring and summer, you would not intervene; and in the event that the tide of war went against them or remained stationary, you would intervene." [21] Only Briand and Jules Cambon, the highest official of the Quai d'Orsay, took part in this discussion.

Returning to London, the Colonel explained the details of his plan to Grey. Receiving a favorable response as early as February 10, he expected that it would succeed. On February 22 an unofficial agreement was signed by Grey and House to call a conference at the request of the Entente. If the Germans refused, "the United States would probably enter the war against Germany." [22] The conference might be held in the Hague and Wilson would attend in person. The project was submitted to Paul Cambon, French ambassador in London, who expressed immediate doubts about House's sincerity and the implications of his proposition. House returned to Washington on March 6, 1916, and Wilson accepted everything, underlining the word *probably*. There remained only to wait for general acceptance by the Allies, especially France. What a success it would have been for Wilson had it worked, and what effective campaign material for the coming elections!

The fact is that it did not succeed. The British, who were convinced that the Germans would not make an acceptable proposition, and who were receiving little encouragement from the French government, took a long time to reply. A majority of the British cabinet thought it absurd to call a conference "without a single indication of the basis on which a peace could be made," [23] as Grey wrote to House on May 12. On August 28 came a blank refusal. One can imagine Wilson's disappointment. This refusal not only dashed his ambition in terms of the election, but shocked him in terms of his mission. As early as May, in fact, Wilson, had decided to take a firmer stand toward the Allies.

Another incident which added to the hardening of his attitude was the publication by the British, on July 19, 1916, of a "black list" of 87 United States firms and 350 Latin American firms which had aided the Central Powers. British subjects were forced to forego trade with them. Was this not an intolerable interference in American affairs? "I am seriously considering asking the Congress to authorize me to prohibit loans to the Allies and to restrict exports destined for them," Wilson wrote to House.[24] But the British refused to respond to the American protests or to retract the black list. The only result was a law, passed September 7, permitting the President to cancel the sailing of any ship which refused to carry goods purchased from black-listed firms. Tension mounted between the two countries.

In this atmosphere the election campaign of 1916 took place. The Democratic party was divided; it included many pacifists and people opposed to the measures of military preparedness taken by Wilson, to which we will return. Wilson, lacking success in foreign policy, had to fall back on domestic affairs. He took further steps against the trusts and practically adopted Roosevelt's New Nationalism.

The Republican party inclined for its part to choose Roosevelt as its candidate. This would insure defeat, however, as Roosevelt had declared himself in favor of war. So the party chose instead Charles Evans Hughes,[25] Associate Justice of the Supreme Court, known for his integrity, his authority, and his keen intelligence. Hughes had the support of the traditionally Republican German-Americans who would not touch Roosevelt at any price.

For once—an exception in American history—the election was to turn largely on a matter of foreign policy. Both parties declared themselves neutralists. The Republicans claimed that Wilson had not been sufficiently energetic as a patriot; the Democrats praised the fact that he had known how to keep peace with honor. Wilson fiercely accused the Republicans of really being a war party and he stressed the idea that after the war there should be created a vast community of nations organized to keep the peace jointly. This would be the end of American isolationism. The Democratic slogan, "He Kept Us Out of War," quickly became popular throughout the country. This formula, doubtful logic but effective politics, can be seen in many newspapers.

> The lesson is clear
> If you want war, vote for Hughes
> If you want peace with honor
> Vote for Wilson.[26]

The election was so close that the Democrats on November 7 thought that they had lost, but in the end Wilson won with 9,129,606 popular votes against 8,538,221 for Hughes, and 277 electoral votes against 254 for his opponent.

Once re-elected, Wilson could return to his recurring ambition to mediate peace. Since the system of enforced mediation imagined by House had proved impossible, another formula must be found. When House suggested resumption of the original plan, Wilson replied "We cannot go back to those old plans. We must develop new ones." [27] But it was not possible to propose peace without being asked to do so by the belligerents, as Bryan had wished. If a unilateral initiative by the United States was rejected it would be a national humiliation. Then, through Ambassador Bernstorff, Chancellor Bethmann-Hollweg approached Wilson secretly and asked him to take some action toward the end of hostilities. In spite of American anger at the deportation of 300,000 Belgians to Germany, Wilson drafted a note between the fourteenth and twenty-fifth of November. Since war was futile and destructive to all nations, the position of the neutrals had become intolerable. The worst was that the war aims of the two sides were not known. Wilson was therefore taking the step of demanding firmly that the belligerents declare their aims.

Before Wilson's note was published, the Germans cut the ground out from under his feet. On December 12 Bethmann-Hollweg, in a speech to the Reichstag, announced that his government was ready to discuss a cease-fire. The tone of the proposal was particularly unacceptable to the Entente because the Chancellor spoke as a victor—six days before Bucharest had fallen to the Central Powers—and he breathed no word about German war aims. The Entente rejected such offers with indignation.

Wilson must have known that if he unveiled his project then it would cause a rift in relations with the Allies, but this did not stop him. On December 18 the American note, having been revised to avoid all reference to eventual intervention, was sent to both sides. It was painstakingly neutral in tone and it appeared—although this was misleading—to be a concerted action of Germany and the United States.

Germany did not wish to state her war aims or to accept a peace conference where Wilson—considered too favorable to the Entente—would be present. So she refused Wilson's proposal on December 29. This reassured the Allies and allowed them to declare themselves in favor of the American proposal and to set forth on January 12, 1917, in the vaguest possible way, their own war aims: the evacuation of occupied territory, the liberation of national minorities (which could mean almost anything), the autonomy of Poland, the restoration of Alsace-Lorraine to France, and a League of Nations to police the world after the war.

Wilson then decided to make known his own vision of the peace. House was again at Wilson's side, since only the Allies had responded to the President's appeal. (He had disapproved the December 18 note because of his pro-Allied feelings.) He helped Wilson a great deal in the preparation of the message sent to the Senate on January 22. Wilson wished to take part in the peace conference; he knew that there lay his mission. What had hurt him most in the German note was the suggestion that he might be excluded. He proposed that the United States would guarantee the future peace, which would be founded on justice, although it would not take part in negotiations of details. It would be "a peace without victory," a peace among equals, which was the only kind of settlement that would last. It would be founded on the right of peoples to rule themselves, freedom of the seas, and disarmament. These were "American principles." Finally Wilson declared that he was confident that he spoke for humanity.

But on January 22 the German decision which was to bring the United States into the war had already been made. Nine days after the speech on the "peace without victory" Wilson learned the shattering news.

Economic Strains on Neutrality

If one asks how real was this neutrality which Wilson was defending against opposition from all sides, the answer is that it was real in purely political matters but not in terms of economic reality. Wilson could not resist, in the name of abstract principles, the will of the great majority of Americans to take advantage of business opportunities, which meant business with the Allies, since Britain controlled the seas. The following figures are revealing.[28]

	Commerce with the Allies	*Commerce with the Central Powers*	*Commerce with the neutrals (Denmark, Holland, Norway, Sweden)*
1914	$ 824,000,000	$169,000,000	$187,000,000
1915	$1,991,000,000	11,000,000	$330,000,000
1916	$3,214,000,000	1,159,000	$279,000,000

It is understandable that Germany thought she had grounds for complaint. But more than the overall figures the details of the commerce are significant.

At the beginning of the war, Wilson, pressed by Bryan, considered that a policy of neutrality meant prohibiting extension of credit to belligerents. Early in the war when France asked for a loan from J. P. Morgan and Company, the State Department, in a note of August 15, 1914, which was published in the press, declared that banks should not extend such loans. It is true that in mid-1914 the Allied need for credit was not urgent, they could use some of their capital invested in the United States to pay for their purchases.[29] This would also have the result of lowering the market values on Wall Street.

Beginning in October 1914, it began to be clear that this would be a long war, and that the Allies could no longer pay for American goods by exports to the United States. In addition, the State Department, that is, Lansing with Bryan's approval, had told the National City Bank of New York that credits could in future be extended to *citizens* of nations at war but loans to belligerent *governments* were forbidden. This note was not made public until March 31, 1915.

J. P. Morgan and Company took advantage of this authorization as early as November 1914. In January 1915 it had become the intermediary between the French government and American businessmen. A contract was signed for a secured loan of $450,000,000, the security being American stocks mobilized by the French government. (The French owners were reimbursed in francs.) As time went on such French holdings of American stocks naturally became much more difficult to find. In March 1915 another system was adopted, the creation of bonds renewable in 90 days, but the Federal Reserve Board was reluctant. England and France began to cancel orders because of lack of funds. Another step had to be taken; on August 10, 1915, the Federal Reserve Board organized a general system of credit. McAdoo, Secretary of the Treasury, urged upon Wilson and Lansing the necessity of maintaining American prosperity through a flexible system of credit. The only solution was to allow the Entente to float government loans on the American market.[30] Otherwise there was risk of depression. Wilson let himself be convinced, and Lansing let the banks know that foreign loans would henceforth be permitted.

On September 25, Morgan announced the creation of a banking syndicate which would float a loan of $500,000,000 to France and Great Britain. One of his aims was to stabilize the exchange; the pound sterling was fluctuating dangerously. Banks and industrial suppliers of the Entente were the principal subscribers to this loan. Thus was the final step taken: on the financial level it could no longer be said that the American government was neutral. To maintain domestic prosperity the United States government had, in fact, given support to the Entente, in the form of loans. Perhaps it also secretly wished to help England and France in a difficult time. Perhaps these very favorable measures to the Entente were affected by German-American tension arising from the incidents of the *Lusitania* and the *Arabic*.

A year later, at the time of the worst tension with Great Britain, on November 28, 1916, the Federal Reserve Board demanded a return to a system of loans with guarantees. This step backward coincided with the growing effort of the United States to rearm. Wilson, always suspicious of "special interests," feared that too much prosperity would injure the United States in the long run, by stimulating certain sectors of the economy abnormally. Moreover, if members of the Entente were not supported too much, would it not help to bring them to accept that "peace without victory" which was Wilson's ideal at the end of 1916 and the beginning of 1917? For the moment, the Entente was in a difficult situation. Its members were supposed to pay for their purchases in gold. The Federal Reserve Board in December 1916 issued a statement adjusting the system. Circumstances were quickly to end this temporary hardening toward the Allies.

In all, according to Bailey,[31] by April 1917 the United States had loaned 2.3 billion dollars to the Entente [32] and 27 million to Germany. In German eyes this was a profound injustice and the advocates of unlimited submarine warfare could use it as a powerful argument.

Military and Naval Preparedness

How adequate were American military and naval forces during the course of the terrible European war? This question can be put in two different ways: (1) In case of American intervention, could the United States send to Europe an army worthy of the name? (2) In the event of victory of either side in Europe, could the United States resist possible future aggression by the victor? House wrote to Wilson on August 22, 1914: "If the Allies win, it means largely the domination of Russia on the continent of Europe; and if Germany wins, it means the unspeakable tyranny of militarism for generations to come . . . Germany's success would in the end bring us many enemies." [33]

The Navy was in better shape than the Army. Theodore Roosevelt had brought the total strength to 25,000 men in 1900 and 45,000 in 1909. In 1905 the Navy had twenty-eight armored ships and twelve armored cruisers. Armored ships were being built at the rate of two a year. The first submarine was built in 1900; by 1914 there were thirty-eight. The construction of cruisers and destroyers was not pursued as actively. From second place in naval power in 1909 the United States had dropped to third by 1914, far behind Germany. At that time, the number of heavy units (battleships, dreadnoughts, and battle cruisers) was thirty-four for the United Kingdom, twenty-one for Germany, eight for the United States, and four each for Japan and France.

If the Fleet was worthy of a great power, the same could not be said of the Army, despite the efforts of Henry L. Stimson, Taft's

Secretary of War, and General Leonard Wood, chief of the general staff from 1910 to April 1914. Wood was an active, ambitious man with a profound political sense, convinced, as we have seen, that only the support of public opinion would permit the United States to have an adequate army. "Wood [became a] military evangelist. His name is associated with few contributions in military strategy or technology, but is imperishably linked with the great campaign for preparedness which was to convert the American people from their free-born . . . ways to acceptance of the conscript army." [34]

When the European war broke out certain people had demanded the reinforcement of the Army, among them Theodore Roosevelt, Gardner, chairman of the Military Affairs Committee in the House of Representatives, General Wood, and Secretary of War Garrison. House was also in favor of it, but Wilson believed more in moral declarations than in arms, and in December 1914 he came out against any substantial increase. In March 1915 Wilson accepted the increase of the Navy, but declined to go along with the aim to make it first in the world. Josephus Daniels, Secretary of the Navy, had little competence, but he was passionately interested in his department, in a curious way: ships interested him little but he saw the Navy as a great instrument of popular education.[35] Fortunately, his undersecretary, Franklin Delano Roosevelt, who was an enthusiastic yachtsman and collector of ship models and books pertaining to the sea, was there to help him, and the department was well managed. Roosevelt got on very well with Daniels who spoke of their partnership as "friendship at first sight." [36]

Nevertheless, it was not until June 1915, under the impact of the *Lusitania* incident, that Wilson resigned himself to ask Garrison and Daniels, Secretaries of War and Navy, to elaborate plans for rearmament which were being called for with a great clamor by the National Security League—an organization headed by General Wood and sponsored by Roosevelt—and by the Navy League.

In September 1915 the Army General Staff submitted to Garrison a plan for a regular army of 281,000 men which could reach 500,000 with its reserves; a "continental army" of 500,000 which would be a National Guard under Federal control; and finally a reserve of 500,000 for the continental army—in all, 1,500,000 men. It is curious that no thought was given to the possibility of an American intervention in Europe, but only to the possibility of an attack against the United

States. Garrison, a realist, wanted to reduce this proposal to a regular army of 142,000 men with a Federal army which would reach 400,000 men in three years. The Navy General Board proposed to Daniels a plan for a fleet which would be as strong as the British Fleet by 1925.

The plan for the Army was violently attacked in the House of Representatives by the chairman of the Military Affairs Committee, the Virginian James Hay, an influential, able man. He thought that the substitution of a Federal army for the National Guard of the states would raise a storm of objections. Why not use the National Guard as the reserve? Its training could be at the expense of the Federal government and in return it would pass under Federal control in time of war. Wilson approved this plan despite the objections of Garrison. Wilson, newly converted to the idea of preparedness, had toured the country from New York to St. Louis to spread the idea. In St. Louis he let slip that the United States should have "without question the largest Navy in the world." Garrison, defeated, resigned and was replaced by Newton D. Baker. Hay's plan was made law on June 3, 1916. It provided for a regular army which would reach 175,000 men in five years, a National Guard of 475,000, a reserve, and an "army of volunteers" which would be called to duty only in wartime. The only concession to the pacifists was the limitation of the General Staff (under the direction of Hugh Scott) to 55 officers.

The plan for the Navy was to build in five years ten dreadnoughts, six battle cruisers, six light cruisers, fifty destroyers, fifteen submarines for the high seas, eighty-five submarines for coastal defense, and various small ships. Two dreadnoughts and two battle cruisers were to be built in the first year. The opponents of the "big Navy," especially the Democrats, hated on principle the words "dreadnought" and "battleship" and they succeeded in imposing on the House of Representatives, on June 2, a bill providing for the construction of five cruisers but not one dreadnought. Only two days before, in the Battle of Jutland, not one dreadnought had been destroyed, while battle cruisers had been decimated. Though the cruisers were just as big as dreadnoughts, and faster, they were less easily defended because of their heavy machinery.

The Battle of Jutland, with the help of a formidable campaign of public meetings and parades, turned the tide in favor of the big Navy. The Senate restored the original figures and speeded up the timetable of construction. The great majority of Representatives followed suit, and on August 29, 1916, the new Naval Act became law. It was with the forces provided by these two laws that the United States would enter the World War—with one previous experience, the "punitive expedition" in Mexico.

The Mexican Affair

Wilson's talents as a diplomat and negotiator were formed and developed in relation to Europe at war. Curiously, behind this chief concern the embarrassing matter of Mexico was taking shape. We must not make the mistake of thinking this a secondary matter. Europe remained far off even if she irritated the United States on the seas; Mexico is the closest southern neighbor. If one American tradition was not to interfere in European affairs directly, another tradition, derived from the Monroe Doctrine and Pan-Americanism, allowed for intervention in Latin America. Roosevelt had given to this tradition a positive content, even an offensive one. As we have seen, Wilson sought to avoid its offensive character. But the President could not control the daily actions of the State Department based on the Roosevelt Corollary, nor did Wilson himself exclude the use of diplomatic intervention, or even the use of force, when it came to establishing in Latin America the democratic regimes of which he dreamed. As a result there is a contradiction in Wilson's Latin American policy. Wilson's initial ignorance of diplomacy, combined with this contradiction, was to make relations with the southern neighbor very troublesome.

Wilson liked the idea of Pan-Americanism. This expression, used for the first time in the New York *Evening Post* on June 27, 1882,[37] had become very popular, and in 1889 Secretary of State Blaine had called the first Pan-American Conference. There, the principle had been established that political and military problems would be excluded from its competence, and that attention would be given only to harmonizing economic, social, and judicial policy of the several nations. This limitation had enabled the Pan-American movement to continue despite United States expansionism, the Roosevelt Corollary, and the subsequent growth of "Yankeephobia" among the Latin American peoples.

Wilson was certainly influenced by Herbert Croly's well-known book, *The Promise of American Life*, published in 1909. The fact that

Croly had been a leading advocate of Theodore Roosevelt's New Nationalism, when Roosevelt as the Progressive candidate was opposing Wilson in 1912, did not prevent Wilson from adopting the essence of the idea. This was a synthesis of the notion that the Western Hemisphere constituted in a sense a political unit with the idea of Manifest Destiny. The synthesis might be formulated as follows: The United States has a "civilizing mission" in relation to its neighbors to the south; therefore, the United States has a duty, by means of inter-American cooperation, to preserve the peace in Latin American countries and to make them democratic. It was a powerful moral justification for continuous intervention. Every possible form of imperialism could be camouflaged behind great liberal principles. This is a concept directly inherited from the British "White Man's Burden."

Wilson, having denounced imperialism in his speech in Mobile on October 1913, sought to embody the civilizing mission of the United States in a Pan-American pact. There is a similarity between the idea of a multinational pact and a proposition made by Luis Maria Drago, the Argentine Minister of Foreign Affairs, in December 1902. Drago's doctrine was that the American republics should jointly forbid Europeans to use force to collect what was owed to them in the Americas. This was a sort of corollary to the Monroe Doctrine which would extend to all twenty-one republics instead of being confined to North America. Theodore Roosevelt had rejected this proposal, but Wilson, without saying so, took it over. He and House drew up a Pan-American Pact in December 1914, which he proposed to the Latin American republics in January 1915. The aim of the pact was to transpose Pan-Americanism from the nonpolitical to the political sphere. Its essence was a "common and mutual guarantee of the territorial integrity and political independence of governments republican in form." Thus a hemisphere at peace would be created in contrast to a Europe torn apart. The pact was accepted by six small American states, but refused by Chile, which was having a territorial dispute with Peru, and by Brazil, which did not wish to oppose Chile. Argentina, though favoring it at first, rejected it in 1916. At the time Wilson was already looking further; he had begun to plan the League of Nations and wished territorial integrity and political independence to be guaranteed on a worldwide scale. In the meantime, in the absence of collective action, he had to resort to unilateral intervention, principally in Mexico.

We have seen that Wilson, in the summer of 1913, had refused to recognize the government of Huerta and was following a policy of waiting, waiting for Huerta to accept the principle of free elections. But on October 10, out of a kind of defiance, Huerta arrested 110 deputies and set up a military dictatorship. The next day Sir Lionel Carden, Britain's new ambassador, presented his credentials. Carden represented the British oil interests. It must be remembered that the Royal Navy had just converted to petroleum-powered ships and had therefore, an imperative need for Mexican oil. The other European nations, following diplomatic tradition, had also recognized the Huerta regime.

This was more than Wilson could stand, and the policy of waiting gave way to an ardent desire to overthrow the abhorred dictator. All the diplomatic machinery of the United States was put into action. The speech in Mobile in October was not only a condemnation of American imperialism, says Link,[38] it was also an attack, ardent though veiled, against the immoral realism of the British in Mexico. American efforts were first aimed at Europe, and pressure was put on to withdraw recognition from Huerta. Germany accepted and England recalled Carden, because for Edward Grey, as Link says, "American friendship was more vital than Mexican oil." [39]

Then action was directed to Mexico itself. A provisional government was established in the north by Venustiano Carranza, friend of Madero, ardent constitutionalist, social reformer, anticlerical, and uncompromising nationalist. Wilson offered him arms and advice on ways to make the country democratic. Carranza accepted the arms but refused the advice. Then, after the temporary arrests of some American sailors by Huerta officials in Tampico, Wilson demanded apologies and a 21-gun salute to the American flag. No apologies were forthcoming, and when the President learned that a German ship laden with arms for Huerta was about to arrive, he ordered the Marines to land on April 22, 1914, in Vera Cruz, which was occupied by Huerta forces and was being besieged by Carranza. Finally, Wilson appealed to Latin America as a whole. Pan-American mediation would be welcomed if it succeeded in ousting Huerta. Argentina, Brazil, and Chile —known as the ABC powers—agreed to send delegates to Niagara Falls, Canada, to act as mediators. But events came too thick and fast for this course of action. In fact, Huerta abdicated on July 15, 1914, and on August 20 Carranza triumphantly entered Mexico City. At the moment, it looked as if order were about to be restored. Wilson had succeeded in eliminating Huerta, and Carranza, a liberal, should have been well received by the United States government.

This is not the way it worked out, and here the responsibility of Wilson becomes very clear. The concept of a civilizing mission implied that the United States would help Mexico to become democratic, but Carranza, capitalizing on the Yankeephobia of his people and placing a high value on independence, categorically refused any American interference. He had protested the occupation of Vera Cruz, he had rejected the mediation of the ABC powers, he did not wish to be the "protégé" of the United States. Then one of Carranza's subordinates, Francisco Villa (called Pancho), an illiterate peon who was an able leader of men, defected from Carranza and secretly notified the government of the United States that he would accept democracy, as they wished. This was only a maneuver to satisfy his own unlimited ambition, but Wilson and Bryan were foolish enough to be taken in. American Roman Catholics, very hostile to Carranza, urged the government to support Villa. Wilson therefore decided to wait until Carranza had established civilian government by democratic elections before extending recognition.

Villa, with the aid of a guerrilla leader of the south, Emiliano Zapata, declared war on Carranza. Carranza was taken by surprise and fled to Vera Cruz. Civil war, which could without doubt have been avoided by immediate recognition of Carranza, burst out again more violently than ever. Wilson's conduct is partly to be explained by the fact that he was fully aware of the Mexican problem: 80 percent of the population were ignorant poverty-stricken peons. He looked upon Villa as the natural representative of the oppressed, who were the only ones to whom he could bring the benefits of democracy. He did not seem to realize the real strength of Carranza, founded on the will of the Mexican people to be independent and equal. Villa was defeated, in April 1915, and fled to the north. He reverted to what he had been at the outset, a guerrilla leader. Wilson, now plunged into difficulties with Germany, resumed the policy of waiting. Lansing, more in touch with Mexican affairs than Bryan, proposed mediation between Carranza and Villa under the auspices of the Pan-American Union. Both Mexican leaders refused, but on October 19 the United States and six Latin American nations agreed to grant de facto recognition to Carranza's government.

The calm was to be destroyed once again, but this time the fault was not Wilson's. German intrigues in Mexico, aimed at provoking a break with the United States, and the campaign put on by Americans who wanted to "clean it up by military intervention" explained the recurrence of crises. Theodore Roosevelt was loudly demanding a campaign in Mexico and the Hearst press favored it. So did advocates of intervention in the Senate, especially the Republicans. Senator Fall of Arizona and Senator Hayden of Texas demanded the occupation of Mexico by an army of 500,000 men. Fall, who upheld the oil interests, declared that Carranza was "more despotic than Peter the Great," and in the course of one speech called him a bandit and a thief.[40] Hugh Scott, chief of the general staff, and leading Roman Catholics also passionately desired Carranza's fall.

It was Pancho Villa who finally set off the explosion. Furious at foreign de facto recognition of his rival, he retaliated by killing United States citizens. He stopped a train at St. Ysabel on January 11, 1916, and shot sixteen Americans aboard. On March 9 he invaded New Mexico, burned the town of Columbus and killed nineteen citizens.

This time public opinion, boiling with righteous indignation, backed the advocates of intervention and a "punitive expedition" commanded by General John J. Pershing invaded Mexican territory on March 15 in an attempt to seize Villa. This was unilateral military intervention by the United States, unmistakable and on a grand scale. It was not war, but it was the next thing to it. At first the expedition consisted of 5000 men, by June it numbered 11,000. As early as April it had penetrated about 300 miles into the interior, but Villa could not be seized. Carranza, placing national pride above his rivalry with Villa, indignantly demanded the departure of American troops. One hundred thousand men of the National Guard were drawn up along the frontier, and on June 21 Americans found their passage barred by the Carranza troops. A cavalry captain named Boyd decided to attack. He was defeated with a loss of ten lives and twenty-four of his men were taken prisoners. The United States was then ready to risk a general war with Mexico.

War was avoided largely because of the efforts of the militant union leader Samuel Gompers, with the support of many Protestant churches, leaders of the Jewish community, and peace associations. Gompers managed to persuade Carranza to release the prisoners and tension was somewhat eased. Wilson, moved by the peace campaign, accepted the idea of a commission to be composed of three Americans and three Mexicans to discuss the conditions under which the "punitive expedition" might retreat. The discussion was a long one, as Mexico demanded evacuation with no conditions, while the United States wished to obtain certain guarantees, especially for investors in oil. An agreement was signed on November 24, but was rejected on December 27 by Carranza, and the commission ceased functioning on January 15, 1917.

At this time, however, growing apprehension about the European situation encouraged moderation. Moreover, one of Wilson's aims had been fulfilled: a constitutional convention in Mexico (elected October 22, 1916) meeting in Querétaro voted for a democratic constitution. Wilson decided to withdraw the expedition on January 18, and on March 13 he recognized Carranza's government de jure. The World War subsequently put the Mexican problem in the shade, but the big financial interests were far from satisfied, and several times in 1918 and afterwards they attempted to revive the policy of intervention.

To attempt to assure the welfare of Latin Americans by using force to end their civil wars was a moral policy, and Wilson felt he had the right to pursue it. He followed it elsewhere on a smaller scale than in Mexico. Marines landed in Haiti, after a massacre of leaders somewhat comparable to Huerta's on July 28, 1915. A veritable protectorate was established; and the same was true in Nicaragua. These were not protectorates in the legal sense, to be sure. When the Almanach de Gotha of 1924 listed as American "protectorates" Cuba, the Dominican Republic, Haiti, Panama, and Liberia,[41] there was a storm of protests, but in fact that's what they were. Wilson, who had begun by denouncing imperialism, dollar diplomacy, and intervention, "went on to more armed interventions in Latin America than Roosevelt and Taft put together, revived and developed dollar diplomacy and even invented a new form of intervention by transforming the American policy with regard to the recognition of governments." [42]

Chapter IV

Wilson and the War

United States Entry into the War

THE entry of the United States into the war was the result of a dramatic event. Wilson reported the meager results of his attempts to achieve peace to the Senate on January 22, while he was still hostile to the Entente. He took advantage of the occasion to set forth his views of a possible peace, "a peace without victory," with a League of Nations to guarantee it. Exactly nine days later, the German government announced to the United States its decision to wage unlimited submarine warfare. Ambassador Bernstorff had learned of it on January 19, and he did everything he could—in vain—to get the measure modified or at least delayed, but he did not breathe a word of it to the Americans.[1]

This decision, taken January 9, 1917, but discussed in German government circles since the previous summer, marked the triumph of the military—Hindenburg and Ludendorff—over Chancellor Bethmann-Hollweg. It was based on the proposition that if 600,000 tons of Allied merchant shipping could be destroyed every month, in six months the Entente would be strangled, asphyxiated, and would have to surrender. There was, to be sure, the great risk that the United States would enter the war. But given their lack of preparation, by the time the Americans had enough active forces to redress the balance it would be too late. The note of January 31, therefore, declared that all ships, belligerent or neutral, in European waters would be attacked by German submarines without notice. This would offer a double advantage, first, because almost all neutral ships were by then transporting goods destined for the Entente, and second, because the obligation of German submarine commanders to ascertain whether a ship was neutral or enemy greatly increased their vulnerability, and gave the target advance notice to escape or to shoot back. Between October 1916 and January 1917, German submarines had sunk an average of 350,000 tons a month. The new decision would make it possible to raise this to 600,000 tons.

It is true that two reservations were made in favor of the United States. First, every Sunday one American ship, carrying no contraband and very clearly marked with red and white stripes, was authorized to enter Falmouth. Second, Bethmann-Hollweg, in a secret letter to Colonel House, said that the German government would renounce submarine warfare as soon as Wilson proposed bases for peace that were acceptable to Germany.[2]

Wilson's reaction, after a few hours of hesitation, was very harsh. The abstract system he had erected—rights of neutrals, freedom of the seas, freedom of American citizens to travel and to trade—went down before the realism of the German militarists. But was it even realism? The future would show that, even if the goal of 600,000 tons were reached, it would not be enough to defeat the Allies. In any case, if any relenting of the United States position had been expected, that expectation was clearly in vain. In the meetings of the cabinet at the White House on February 1 and 2, Lansing started drafting a note to break off relations with Germany. He was supported by all members except two—William B. Wilson, Secretary of Labor, and Albert S. Burleson, Postmaster General. On February 3 it was decided that the note would be sent immediately instead of waiting for an "overt act"—meaning the destruction of an American ship by German submarines. Otherwise, it might be thought that the United States accepted the ultimatum. At this moment, House was convinced that war was becoming inevitable.

For Lansing the break with Germany was the realization of his firmest conviction; he had always thought that war on the side of the Allies was a necessity for the United States. Some weeks before the German decision he had written

I am most unhappy over the situation, because on no account must we range ourselves even indirectly on the side of Germany . . . What astonishes me is that the President doesn't see this. In fact, he doesn't seem to grasp the plain meaning of this war nor the principles at stake. I have talked to him about it constantly but the violation of American rights by both sides seems to interest him more . . . The fact that German imperialist ambition threatens free institutions everywhere doesn't seem to have penetrated his thinking. For six months I have talked about the struggle between Autocracy and Democracy but I do not see that I have made any great impression.[3]

Wilson himself hesitated up to the end. During the period which followed House and Lansing never stopped pushing him toward a more resolute attitude. "Peace and civilization depended on the establishment of democratic institutions throughout the world, and this would be impossible if, after the war, Prussian militarism controlled Germany." [4]

On February 3 Wilson finally announced to Congress his decision to break off diplomatic relations, but to wait for an overt act before declaring war. "I refuse to believe that it is the intention of the German authorities to do in fact what they have warned us they will feel at liberty to do . . . Only actual overt acts on their part can make me believe it even now." [5] While the government multiplied preparations—protection against sabotage, acceleration of arms production, propaganda directed at the German-Americans—everyone waited anxiously for the overt act.

In this feverish interval two events occurred which were particularly helpful in preparing public opinion for war. The first was the affair of the "Zimmermann Telegram." The American government was notified by the British on February 24 that the Naval Intelligence Service had captured and deciphered a telegram from the German Foreign Minister to Eckhardt, German minister in Mexico, which had been sent on January 16. This document advised Eckhardt of the decision to wage unlimited submarine warfare, and instructed him to try to negotiate an alliance with Mexico if the United States should declare war on Germany. Reannexation of Texas, New Mexico, and Arizona by Mexico were to be included in the agreement. The telegram was published March 1 by the United Press. The American reaction was a great explosion of anger. Not only was Germany proposing to dismember the country, but this perfidious telegram had been sent over State Department cables which had been made available to the Germans—an abuse of exceptional courtesy.[6] Few voices were raised to dispute the authenticity of the telegram. The British declared that the telegram had been found in Mexico. It was no longer a question of the great crusade for freedom of the seas—a bit vague for the average American. The safety of the country itself was at stake. Despite the resistance of a few pacifist senators, like La Follette, the Senate on March 4 approved the arming of American cargo ships (put into effect March 12).

The other important event was the first Russian Revolution, the March Revolution which led to the abdication of the Tsar and the creation of a democratic republic. The conscience of Americans could now be clear. It was indeed the camp of democracy without compromise that they were about to enter. This idea of a new "crusade" picked up converts from the peace camp, like Herbert Croly, the historian Charles Beard, Ray Stannard Baker, the future editor of Wilson's papers, even Bryan himself. All the same, Wilson was troubled by the strife in Russia. In May he was to send an American mission, headed by the former Secretary of State, Elihu Root, to the provisional government. This mission accomplished nothing as a new revolution was then brewing.

Overt acts had been delayed by the fact that the American shippers charged with transporting arms had kept their ships in port. Then on February 27 two American citizens were lost in the sinking of the steamer *Laconia*. It was like the situation of 1915 all over again, and public sentiment was much aroused. On March 12 the American cargo ship *Algonquin*, carrying foodstuffs from New York to London, was sunk without warning. On March 19 it was learned that three American ships had been sunk, and many factions of public opinion urged Wilson to act. On March 20, after a cabinet meeting— this time unanimous—Wilson called a special session of Congress for April 2. The delay was explained by his desire not to give in to panic or pressure.

On the evening of April 2 a shattered Wilson appeared before Congress to ask for a declaration of War on Germany:

The present German submarine warfare against commerce is a warfare against mankind . . . against all nations . . . Our goal should not be to avenge ourselves, nor to affirm in victory the physical power of the nation, but solely the defense of human law . . . There is a choice that we are incapable of making, we will not choose the way of submission . . . With a deep sense of the solemn and even the tragic nature of the step I am taking . . . I advise that the Congress declare the recent course of the Imperial German Government to be in fact nothing less than war against the Government and people of the United States.[7]

On April 6, 1917, the House of Representatives voted for war by 373 votes to 50, and the Senate 82 to 6. War was not immediately declared on Austria-Hungary, Bulgaria, and Turkey. Wilson justified this on June 14, saying that "The war had been undertaken by the military masters of Germany who happened also to be the masters of Austria-Hungary." [8] The distinction made for Germany between the people—not responsible—and the guilty leaders, was not made in relation to Austria-Hungary. The German rulers were guilty of all in Wilson's eyes, even of the Austro-Hungarian attack on Serbia. It was only after the Italian defeat of Caporetto that war was declared by the United States on Austria-Hungary. The intervention of various organizations concerned with relief for Bulgaria and Turkey was strong enough to protect them from being treated as enemies of the United States.

"Right is more precious than peace," Wilson said. It was to defend the right that he was willing to take the United States into the war. Can one claim, as did the committee headed by Senator Nye in 1934, that the decision was taken because of pressure from bankers who had made great loans to the Entente and wished to insure their eventual reimbursement? It seems difficult to support this thesis. On the one hand, between January 31 and April 2 Wilson did not seem to be under such pressure—there was even some evidence of pressure to the contrary—for example from Durant, president of General Motors.[9] On the other hand, the enormous power of the presidency in the United States justifies crediting Wilson's own actions with some importance. Wilson had always been opposed to the protection of the "special interests." His stubbornness on this point and the exalted idea he had of his own moral obligations, make it impossible to think that he could have knowingly accepted war to protect such interests.

It cannot be doubted that the industrialists and bankers had helped to make the atmosphere in some quarters favorable to war, but Wilson to the end wished to defend himself against the pressure of opinion,[10] against the irrational, against sentiment: "We must put excited feeling away," he said. Nye's one-sided thesis is really without foundation. But though for Wilson the war became immediately the "crusade for democracy" against German militarism, for his old opponent, Theodore Roosevelt, it was a matter of national interest: "It is our war, America's war." [11] The American people could thus feel at ease; once again morality and the national interests were clearly combined.

Wilson's willingness—too slowly arrived at in the view of Lansing and House—was the real cause of the United States entry into the war. Naturally, he could not have acted had Congress or public opinion in general been really opposed. To say with Walter Lippmann [12] that the war broke out because the American people condemned German goals is going too far. Was opinion really set on war?

There was nothing in 1917 comparable to the national explosion of 1898. Such an explosion did not take place until after the start of the war, and it often took unpleasant forms, notably in hysterical persecution of pacifist elements. Though the American Federation of Labor sent its leader, Samuel Gompers, to the Council of National Defense, the left wing Industrial Workers of the World and many socialists were persecuted, sometimes even lynched.[13]

Wilson's ideas on public opinion seemed to exclude the possibility of his being carried away by it. "One should not be wholly dominated by it, but one can learn from it what is feasible and what is not," he said.[14] When the public was opposed to a decision that was essential it must be educated, "mobilized." No power in the United States, he thought, could resist a President who had the "confidence" of the nation. We will see the consequences of this idea in 1919 and 1920. Wilson considered himself the ideal educator of the public. He was hostile to the lobbies because they represented the special interests. "It is of serious interest to the country that the people at large should be . . . voiceless, while great bodies of astute men seek to create an artificial opinion for their private profit . . . Only public opinion can check and destroy [this attempt]." [15]

Joseph Tumulty and Colonel House made an effort to establish contacts with the press, industrialists, and political leaders which would enable them to direct opinion. Wilson, breaking a tradition of 115 years, delivered messages to Congress in person to strengthen his control, and up to 1918 he succeeded. We should not minimize Wilson's personal role in the entry of the United States into the war by reference to economic arguments and public opinion. It was a preponderant role because of his well-developed ideology and his vision of the future.

The Conduct of the War and Diplomacy

Once the war was launched, there arose the problem of how to conduct it. By virtue of the two laws passed in 1916, there were 200,000 men under arms in April 1917 and a Fleet in the process of renovation, of which 65 percent of the units needed repairs. The naval program stressed big ships. As the British and French Fleets held the corresponding German units in port, the armored ships, the dreadnoughts and battle cruisers, were of no use, while destroyers were badly needed. We must remember that the 1916 laws were based on plans to defend the United States in a future war against the European victor, rather than on participation in the present war.

Everything had to be revised. This was quickly done. Six weeks after the Declaration of War, on May 18, Congress passed a law "for the temporary increase of the military forces." This law repealed that of August 1916 and created (1) a regular army of 488,000 men; (2) a National Guard of 470,000 men; (3) a "National Army" of 500,000 men at first, but capable of infinite expansion because it was to be recruited by the new system of "selective military service." [16] Between May 8, 1917, and the end of the year 365,000 men had crossed the Atlantic. On November 11, 1918, there were 2,079,000 American soldiers in Europe, 1,100,000 of them having been transported by the British.[17]

Following a tradition begun under Lincoln by which Congress granted enormous wartime powers to the President in his capacity as commander-in-chief of the Army and Navy, several laws were then passed: the Selective Service Act, the Espionage Act, the Trading with the Enemy Act, the Priority Shipment Act and above all the Food and Fuel Control Act of August 17, 1917. The Food and Fuel Control Act, proposed by representative Ashbury F. Lever of South Carolina, gave the President almost dictatorial control of the wartime economy, with power to purchase goods, to requisition stocks, and to alter the level of taxation. The President delegated these enormous powers to various organizations, principally the Council of National Defense, created in August 1916 and directed by Newton D. Baker, and the General Munitions Board, which in July 1917 became the War Industries Board. A Committee on Public Information, created on April 14, 1917, and directed by the newspaperman George Creel, gave the President control of propaganda.

It was easy to find financial resources in this rich country. On May 2, 1917, Secretary of the Treasury McAdoo announced the floating of a loan of 2 billion dollars, the Liberty Loan. It was in fact subscribed by June 15 with more than 83 billion dollars.[18] J. P. Morgan and Company alone had underwritten 850 million dollars. In June and July the Army Appropriations Bill was passed, making available 12 billion dollars in credit. In all, during the fiscal years 1918–1920 expenses averaged 12 billion dollars a year, of which 41 percent came from taxes.[19]

The most difficult problem by far was to increase the production of arms. We must avoid the anachronism of comparing the "conversion" of industry in 1917–1918 with the prodigious conversion of 1940–1944. With its many shipyards the United States could build 300 destroyers and 2,000,000 tons of commercial ships. Neutral ships, especially those of the Dutch, which were immobilized in American ports were requisitioned. But the attempt to assure sufficient airplane production failed completely. American machine guns were not produced on a large scale until the end of the war. In the artillery, the French 75 and short 155, which France produced in abundance and which were also made in America, were used. The small industrial nation furnished arms to the big one.[20] This also had the advantage of avoiding problems of differing calibers in the guns and of saving precious tonnage. In all, the effective entry of the United States into the land war was very slow.

In early May 1917 the first division was sent to Europe as a symbol. Then long months went by. The initial plan had called for 42 divisions; in the end 60 were trained and equipped. Two hundred thousand men a month were easily transported, especially to the base at Pauillac on the Gironde and in lesser numbers to La Pallice, Saint-Nazaire, and Brest. Great stocks of provisions were also created. There were four American divisions in the trenches on March 21, 1918, when the great German offensive began. General Pershing, commander-in-chief, placed his forces at the disposal of Marshal Foch on March 28, in spite of his instructions "that the United States forces were a distinctive, separate unit and their identity must be preserved." [21] American troops, initially included in the British and French Armies, played an independent role for the first time on September 12, 1918, when the American First Army overcame the enemy salient at Saint-Mihiel.

The fact that the French and British had already succeeded in stopping the Germans on the Marne and then at Verdun, and that they were to "plug up the holes" in the spring of 1918, should not cause the historian to minimize the role of the United States. The American divisions brought not just additional strength, but the certainty of growing overall superiority. The entry of the American Fleet was decisive in spoiling the effectiveness of unlimited submarine warfare—a fact which Ludendorff had not foreseen. The Fleet also made possible the decision of May 1917 to assure protection of ships by the convoy system, and it played the principal role in the laying of great mine fields in the North Sea, which made navigation in the vicinity of their bases exceedingly dangerous for German submarines. Finally, it solved the problem of shipping.

Colonel House, now accustomed to traveling in Europe, continued to make trips—this time to perfect the coordination of the war effort. The Allies had groped a great deal in their efforts to coordinate their several strategies. Only after the Italian defeat at Caporetto (October 24–27, 1917) and the Bolshevik Revolution of November was a conference held at Rapallo, where it was decided to create a Supreme War Council. The council was to consist of a president and one government member from each interested state, and was to meet every month. The first meeting, held December 1, was attended by Colonel House and the American General Bliss. There was protracted debate. House refused to involve the United States in controversies between the Allies, and the Allies hesitated to go along with House's suggestion to make a statement of war aims. General Bliss, who was pessimistic about the military situation, pressed for a unified command which was urged by Clemenceau but refused by Lloyd George.[22] After this first meeting of the Supreme War Council, Wilson decided not to send a political representative, but General Bliss took an active part in the meetings of the military chiefs at Versailles.

In all, House's mission had one result: it enabled him to understand the attitude of the Allies at the moment when Wilson was preparing to announce his program for peace. Fortunately this understanding caused him to modify the program in some ways.

The Fourteen Points

Wilson was preoccupied with the coming peace. He wished it to be based on solid foundations and refused to be diverted from this objective by other contingencies. Slowly the great themes of what he was to call the New Diplomacy took shape in his mind. Let us recall certain main points of this long and complex development.

First, there was a continuation of the old idea that the United States, a nation of exceptional origin, had a special mission to fulfill. As it was not seeking anything for itself, it could speak in the name of justice. On May 10, 1915, speaking at a naturalization ceremony in Philadelphia, Wilson said, "America does not consist of groups. A man who thinks of himself as belonging to a particular national group in America has not yet become an American . . . Americans must have a consciousness different from the consciousness of every other nation in the world." In his War Message he repeated this idea: "Our object . . . is to defend the principles of peace and justice throughout the world against selfish and autocratic powers."

This mission in itself implies being and remaining impartial. For this reason Wilson, as early as the United States entry into the war, refused to consider the United States an ally of the Entente. He would not renounce the possibility of a separate peace as France, Russia, and the United Kingdom had done by the treaty of September 5, 1914. In this matter he wished to keep his hands free and he had at his disposal a useful weapon of diplomatic pressure—the threat to withdraw. Above all he did not wish to be bound by the secret treaties which held the Entente together, laying the foundation for future conquests. He would, however, be an "associate." As early as May 10, 1917, Balfour sent the text of some of the secret treaties, though with some omissions: nothing on the agreements about the Cameroons, Togoland, and German colonies in the Pacific; nothing about the Franco-Russian agreements concerning German frontiers; nothing about the agreements with Italy made at Saint-Jean-de-Maurienne. But what did it matter? Wilson wanted his hands to be free, and even more he wished to have the means to impose his will. As he wrote House on July 21, 1917, "France and England do not share our views on the peace, far from it. When the war is over we can bring them around to our way of thinking, because then, among other things, they will be dependent on us financially." [23]

The keystone of the arch of the future system was to be the League of Nations. Without describing all the steps of his thinking we must note that he repudiated the European balance of power as a cause of wars, and that he wanted an association of nations founded on the right of self-determination of peoples.

On May 27, 1916, in a speech before the League to Enforce Peace, he said:

The peace of the world must henceforth depend upon a new and more wholesome diplomacy . . . The principles of public law from now on should prevail over the particular interests of such and such a nation. All the nations of the world should organize a sort of league to ensure that right and law will prevail against all selfish aggressions, to make it impossible for one alliance to be drawn up against another alliance . . .

We believe these fundamental things: First, that every people has the right to choose the sovereignty under which they live. Second, that the small states of the world have a right to enjoy the same respect for their sovereignty and for their territorial integrity that great and powerful nations expect and insist upon. Third, that the world has a right to be free from every disturbance of its peace that has its origin in aggression and the disregard of the rights of peoples and nations.

On January 22, 1917, still advocating "peace without victory," he took up these themes again:

The question on which depends the peace and the future political life of the world is this: is the present war a fight for a just and lasting peace or only [a fight] for a new balance of power? If it is only a war for a new balance of power, who can guarantee the stability of the new arrangements? . . . There must be not a mere balance of power but a league of powers, a universal, organized peace instead of organized rivalries.

On March 5, 1917, in his second Inaugural Address, he said: "Peace cannot rest securely and justly upon a balance of armed forces."

If one asks whether there was not a contradiction between these principles and the refusal of the peace proposals of Pope Benedict XV, on August 17, 1917, the answer is No, because what Wilson could not accept was "to take the word of the present rulers of Germany as a guarantee of a lasting settlement." From "peace without victory" he passed to what Arno Mayer called "war enthusiasm," because he wanted to base the peace on the democratization of Germany, which presupposed victory.[24]

Starting with these general ideas, how did Wilson come to formulate the more specific program of the Fourteen Points? It was the result of a slow evolution from April 1917 to January 1918. Wilson, on the advice of House, had refused to acknowledge the secret treaties *officially*. Precisely because he was not an official, House could discuss them with his British friends. Balfour came to the United States in late April 1917 and had a long conversation with the Colonel on the twenty-eighth in which all the cards were laid on the table. Balfour mentioned the return to France of Alsace-Lorraine, complete reconstruction of France and Belgium, and the reconstitution of an independent Poland. To give that country an outlet on the sea, however, raised difficulties. "Would it not create a new ulcer like Alsace-Lorraine? Could not Danzig be made a free port instead?" Austria would cede Bosnia and Herzegovina to Serbia, which would in turn give part of Macedonia to Bulgaria. Rumania would get some Russian territory and part of Transylvania. Three states would be formed from the Austro-Hungarian Empire: Bohemia, Hungary, and Austria. Constantinople was to be internationalized. No mention was made of the German colonies, nor of Dalmatia, nor of Trieste. Later, on January 30, 1918, Balfour, in a letter to Wilson, tried to justify allowing Italy to have strategic frontiers: "strong frontiers help peace."

Another important mission was that of Tardieu, who was named high commissioner to the United States. He arrived in April 1917 and stayed until the end of the war. In his book, *L'Amerique en Armes*,[25] he claimed to be responsible for the agreement of American leaders to the restoration of Alsace-Lorraine to France without a plebiscite.

Further progress was made in September 1917, when House persuaded Wilson to create a commission of experts, The Peace Inquiry Bureau, to study political and geographical problems of the peace. Among its members were: S. F. Mezes, president of the City College of New York, chairman; David Hunter Miller, Walter Lippmann, Isaiah Bowman, director of the American Geographical Society, and Professor J. T. Shotwell, a specialist in historical geography.

While the Inquiry Bureau worked quietly, House, as we have seen, went to Europe in October-November, 1917. As he could not obtain a common declaration of aims from the Allies—especially France and Italy—Wilson decided to formulate the United States war aims unilaterally.[26] Another forceful argument for doing so was the Bolshevik Revolution. The Bolsheviks published a striking declaration on November 8 in favor of a new type of peace, based on renunciation of conquest and the legitimate desire of peoples to rule themselves. This was Wilson's "peace without victory," but now Wilson wanted a victorious peace. He was put in the position of having to reply to an appeal which could have a disastrous effect, all the more so as the Bolsheviks made public the secret treaties, exposing them to worldwide condemnation. Thus the announcement of American war aims had an "eminently realistic origin" as Arno Mayer rightly points out. When House returned, on December 18, 1917, and conferred with Wilson, the Inquiry Bureau was charged with the harassing job of preparing a report. This report was inspired by the double necessity to encourage liberal elements in Allied countries and to make precise propositions concerning various geographic regions. The bureau's report stated that in addition to "the universal desire for peace," there was "a feeling generally held by the ordinary people of the world that the old diplomacy was bankrupt and that the system of armed peace should not be revived."

From this derived great hopes for a League of Nations.[27] Beginning in the evening of January 4, 1918, armed with this report and comments and maps provided on January 2, Wilson and House drew up a list of war aims that Wilson set forth in his speech to Congress on January 9. The President did not want to consult the Allies. He talked only to the ambassador of tsarist Russia, Bakhmetieff, and the Serb diplomat Vesnitch, who favored dismemberment of Austria-Hungary. Alsace-Lorraine caused a great deal of discussion. House at first wanted to omit all mention of it, but, on the President's insistence, he suggested a provisional wording: "If Alsace and Lorraine are returned to France, Germany should receive economic compensation." Wilson remained preoccupied with this problem and finally decided in favor of a firm, positive formula: "The wrong done to France by Prussia concerning Alsace-Lorraine, which has made the peace of the world uncertain for nearly 50 years, must be redressed."

Finally, the peace proposal was divided into fourteen points. The first four are general ones—open diplomacy, freedom of the seas, lowering of tariffs, disarmament—as is the fourteenth, which calls for the creation of the League of Nations. The others are "geographical," although Point Five, about colonies, does no more than set forth the principle that "The interests of peoples should have equal weight with the interests of governments." This does not condemn colonialism in principle, and is restricted to condemnation of the exploitation of natives by the colonial power.

In his remarkable book, *The Political Origins of the New Diplomacy*, Arno Mayer shows that in setting forth these general principles, Wilson, inspired by House, wanted to arouse the enthusiasm of liberals and progressives in Europe and to use them as a leverage to appeal to the people over the heads of their governments. Mayer also shows that these European liberals had greatly contributed to the elaboration of the New Diplomacy by their influence on Wilson through House. This was especially true of a group in the House of Commons, left-wing liberals such as Trevelyan and Ponsonby as well as members of the Labour party, including Ramsay MacDonald, Snowden, and Lansbury. This group called itself The Union for Democratic Control.

Point Six concerned Russia and suggested that after the evacuation of her territory Russia should choose her own institutions freely. All possible aid was also promised. Wilson and House had already succeeded in preventing the Entente from adopting a policy of force toward the Bolsheviks as Clemenceau and Sonnino had wished. The President did not, however, follow completely the advice of Ambassador Francis, who was still advocating "peace without victory" in January 1918. Point Seven dealt with the evacuation and restoration of Belgium, the test case of the effectiveness of international law. Point Eight concerned France: reparations for damages and the return of Alsace-Lorraine. Point Nine, on Italy, was vague; it said that the Italian frontiers should be fixed "along clearly recognizable (in the first draft, "recognized") national lines." Point Ten, on Austria-Hungary, promised autonomy to the national groups which made up the empire and seemed to indicate that Wilson did not want to break up its federal unity so as to "Balkanize" Central Europe. In this Wilson was following the opinion of the experts of the Inquiry Bureau, who felt strongly that Austria-Hungary should be maintained whole and stressed the economic necessities which they thought required this solution. They did not want Trieste to be given to Italy; they thought that "the abandonment of her imperial claims could be obtained from Italy in exchange for the assurance that her territory would be evacuated, and that her urgent economic needs would be satisfied at once and after the war." [28] Point Eleven put forth some vague propositions about the Balkans, in contrast to the much more specific report of the Inquiry Bureau. Wilson proposed that the frontiers should be established according to nationalities, economic interests, and historic rights—which is obscure at the least and could cover almost anything. Point Twelve dealt with Turkey, whose native peoples he wished to liberate. Point Thirteen said that the Polish frontiers should follow national lines but should *also* provide access to the sea.

This plan naturally made an immense impression on the world. Wilson was to develop it further by adding four points on February 11, 1918, four others on July 4, and five more on September 27, but all these new points were very general and did nothing more than paraphrase the ideas already set forth. People have often believed that Wilson was affected exclusively by the principle of national determination, but the Fourteen Points show much greater flexibility and prove that other considerations were very important to him. As he wrote to Lansing, January 29, 1918, "While, as you know, I am strongly inclined to nationality as the basis for territorial limits I believe that it cannot be invariably adopted, but that in certain cases physical boundaries and strategic boundaries must be considered and must modify boundaries based on nationality." [29]

The very great importance of the Fourteen Points is related to the fact that the United States increasingly appeared to be the potential arbiter between nations. They also stated the new political philosophy which Wilson was already calling the New Diplomacy. Finally, on the concrete level, it was on the basis of the Fourteen Points that Germany was to ask for the armistice.

The Far East and the Bolsheviks

In relation to the European war, the Far Eastern problem was growing more serious. American relations with Japan grew steadily worse. The fact that the Japanese had conquered the Pacific islands held by Germany and Tsingtao in the Shantung Peninsula in 1914 was in no way agreeable to the United States. Furthermore, Japan was sending arms to Mexico and was suspected of stirring up the Philippines, whose independence Wilson had promised. The Twenty-One Demands made on China on January 18, 1915, which virtually established a Japanese protectorate in China, had deeply disturbed Washington. So had the Russo-Japanese treaty of July 3, 1916, which in effect excluded the United States from northern China. It happened that the Entente, even before the United States entry into the war, had promised to support Japan at the peace conference in her claims to the islands and rights in Shantung formerly held by Germany. The problems for the future peace conference were further complicated by China's declaration of war on Germany, on August 14, 1917. Finally, the war, with its considerable replacement of armored ships by destroyers, left the United States dangerously exposed in the Pacific. There were periodic rumors in the United States that a shift in alliances might take place which would put Japan on the side of Germany.

Some kind of an agreement became necessary. It was facilitated by a Japanese mission to the United States headed by Kikujiro Ishii, former Minister of Foreign Affairs. Its purpose was to express Japanese gratitude for United States participation in the war and to urge this occasion to "exchange views with responsible Americans, views which should be frank concerning the problems of China and [also] to obtain in some form an accord and a solution for these problems." [30] The Ishii mission arrived September 1, 1917, and was welcomed with great ceremony. Talks followed with Wilson and Lansing on November 2, and the American government conceded that because of territorial proximity Japan had "special interests in China." The two governments committed themselves not to destroy either the independence or the territorial integrity of China and to observe the Open Door Policy. Finally, they declared themselves opposed to all acquisitions of special rights which would affect either the independence or the territorial integrity of China. This agreement was futile because each signatory interpreted it in a different way. We shall see the results in the peace negotiations.

For nearly two years attention was to be diverted from the problem of Shantung by a much more serious matter—the consequences of the Bolshevik Revolution in the Far East. The first result was an attempt of the Bolsheviks in December 1917 to take over control of the railroads belonging to the Chinese government in Manchuria. At the request of the Allied ministers in Peking—the American minister, Reinsch, abstaining—Chinese troops forced the Reds to depart. General Dimitri L. Horvat, commander of the Russian forces not won over to the Soviets, organized a resistance movement and under his orders Cossack captain Gregori Semenov invaded Transbaikalia to cut the Trans-Siberian Railroad. There he organized a reign of terror which discredited him completely.

From this time on the problem became even more complicated, and it is especially important to analyze Wilson's hesitations, because they throw light on his personality and on certain fundamental tendencies of American foreign policy.

As early as December 1917 the French government was convinced that the Bolsheviks were working hand in hand with the Germans. The armistice of that month and the negotiations which led to the Treaty of Brest-Litovsk on March 3, 1918, seemed to prove it beyond question. The Germans could now move more troops to the Western front, and the French lived in dread of a German offensive in the spring. Furthermore there were 1,600,000 prisoners of the Central Powers in Russia of which 150,000 were Germans. These prisoners were to be released and repatriated. It was more and more frequently rumored that some of them would be armed at once by the Bolsheviks. There was at the time a stock of more than 600,000 tons of war materials in Vladivostok which the inefficiency of the Trans-Siberian Railroad had prevented from arriving on the eastern European front. What would happen if the Germans got hold of them? The same problem, on a smaller scale, was caused by the stocks in Archangel and Murmansk, threatened by the Finnish *Läger* of Mannerheim, who seemed in French eyes to be German satellites. We should add that on February 12, 1918, the Soviets repudiated the debts of the Russian state which were mostly owed to France. The French government, convinced by its ambassador, Noulens, of the weakness of the Soviets, wanted to organize a great expedition in Siberia, partly to create a second front and partly to aid the White Russians to destroy the Bolshevik regime.

Great Britain shared the French views, and insisted that Japan, her ally since 1902, should undertake the major responsibility for the vast undertaking. From January and February on, Jusserand and the new British ambassador to the United States, Lord Reading, besieged the State Department with requests pertaining to this matter.

But Wilson did not agree. Without favoring Bolshevism—about which he knew little—he had been very much impressed by the second Russian Revolution, not just because of Lenin's plans for peace, which we have seen, but also because he thought it fulfilled the wishes of the majority of the Russian people. This was at first the position of Ambassador Francis, who had fled to Vologda, and especially of Raymond Robbins, diplomatic envoy to the new capital, Moscow. As a result, intervention against the Bolsheviks seemed to Wilson equivalent to intervention against the Russian people. To eliminate Bolshevism he envisioned quite a different method: aid to the population in the form of foodstuffs, technicians, and doctors. In 1917 he had sent a group of engineers, headed by John F. Stevens, to deal with the problems of the Trans-Siberian Railway. In February and March several other missions had reported to him that the German danger in Siberia was nonexistent: the establishment of an eastern front seemed impossible. Therefore he turned a deaf ear to Franco-British proposals for intervention.

All this was still further complicated by the Japanese problem. For their part, the Japanese wished nothing more than to intervene in Siberia, but for their own reasons: to create a base in Vladivostok, develop their fisheries, obtain free navigation on the Amur River, and above all to extend their politico-military domination over the South Manchurian Railway (which they had secured in 1905) to the railroad in northern Manchuria, called the Chinese Eastern Railway. The Chinese Eastern Railway was more or less held by General Horvat and it served as a southern branch of the Trans-Siberian. If this ambition could be realized it would be a serious attack on the Open Door Policy in China, so dear to the Americans. But could Japan be prevented from carrying out her aims? Certainly not, because the means were not at hand and there was the continuing risk that a shift of alliances or rapprochement between Germany and Japan would create a sort of "axis," as it was later to be called. The French ambassador, Jusserand, foresaw this possibility with keen clairvoyance. But if Japan were not stopped the Russians would be very much antagonized, as Bakhmetieff, the ambassador of the former regime in Washington, testified. There was a further risk of an alliance between the Bolsheviks and Germany. The French and British advocated dealing with this problem by substituting an inter-Allied expedition for the probable Japanese expedition. Since France and Great Britain could provide only symbolic forces, however, it would be up to the Americans to play the role of brake on Japan, which meant compromising with her and losing the friendship of the Russian people—so dear to the President's heart. Wilson's two principal collaborators, House and Lansing, with minor differences, shared his attitude.

These hesitations tore Wilson apart and caused him to be inconsistent and then to take half measures. At first, in January 1918, the Japanese sent four warships to Vladivostok, the British sent one, and Wilson consented reluctantly to send one. On March 1 Wilson, under pressure from France and Britain, appeared to approve a Japanese landing on condition that "they act as Russia's allies, without attempting to save Siberia from German invasion or intrigues." [31] House protested, declaring that the United States "would lose the fine moral position you have given to the cause of the Entente." The young diplomat William Bullitt stressed the same point: "If we stand aside while Japan invades Siberia with the assent of the Governments of England and France, the President's moral position as leader of the common people of the world will be fatally compromised . . . The President must oppose invasion of Siberia by Japan in the name of democracy and liberalism." [32]

At the beginning of March there was a rumor that the Bolsheviks would not sign the peace treaty and would resume the war against Germany. Trotsky wrote to Wilson asking him to prevent the "German-Japanese plot." All this made a deep impression on Wilson, and as early as March 5 he withdrew the vague approval he had given to the Japanese landings. On the eleventh he sent a message "to the Soviets" (not to the Soviet government) couched in a sentimental tone. "The whole heart of the people of the United States is with the people of Russia in their attempt to free themselves forever from autocratic government and become the masters of their own life." [33]

For four months—the most anguished of the war on the western front—Wilson followed the policy of deliberately standing aloof in Siberia. When the Japanese put some troops ashore at Vladivostok on April 5, Wilson said nothing. To the repeated appeals of the Allies for intervention he replied that such an act would be inconceivable for the United States unless requested by the Soviets. He was not pleased by the news of a military accord between China and Japan, signed May 16, for the common defense of the frontiers against "the enemy" because he saw in it a means by which Japan would increase her hold in Manchuria.

Not until the beginning of July did Wilson change his mind, owing to a new factor in the situation, the entry on the scene of the Czech Legion. As early as 1917 a Czechoslovak force, made up of prisoners captured from the Austro-Hungarian Army and Czechs in Russia, had been created. It numbered 70,000 men. The Treaty of Brest-Litovsk convinced the Czech National Council that the only practical solution was to evacuate these forces to Vladivostok so as to send them from there to the western front. We cannot tell the story of this extraordinary and complex odyssey here, but two facts should be noted: the Czechs who reached Vladivostok decided on June 20 to take control of the stock of arms already mentioned, and on June 29 they decided to drive out the local Bolshevik authorities. As a result, in both European Russia and Siberia the other Czech groups found themselves in a more and more dangerous position. How could they be protected? How could the arms of Vladivostok be returned to Allied control? While the Japanese and the British set new forces ashore, Wilson decided—regretfully—that he must act. Ambassador Francis had now become a hot partisan of intervention. Thomas Masaryk, who had Wilson's ear, and who up to this time been opposed to the Allied operation in Siberia, changed his opinion. The President, with the approval of Lansing and even of House, undertook secret negotiations with the Japanese on July 8—to land 7000 Japanese and 7000 Americans to protect the Czechs against the German and Austrian prisoners, without intervening in Russian domestic affairs. This was immediately accepted by the Japanese, tolerated by the British, greeted enthusiastically by the French. The landings began August 3; the American contingents were under the command of General William S. Graves.

This expedition was a complete disappointment for the United States. For one thing it was discovered that it was virtually impossible to protect the Czechs the whole length of the Trans-Siberian Railway. Moreover, Japan's intentions became clear when she extended her actions to northern Manchuria and constantly landed new troops— there were 72,000 instead of 7000 on November 11, 1918—which prevented the Americans from protecting the railroad east of Irkutsk.

The consequence was a completely ambiguous situation which irritated American opinion more and more after November 11. Should the troops be taken out—thus giving the Japanese a free hand? Or should they stay to act as a check on the Japanese—thus compromising the United States more and more in the eyes of the Bolsheviks? It was not until the beginning of 1920 that Wilson ordered the troops to retreat. This was carried out on April 1 leaving the Japanese troops in possession. We shall see later the results of this situation.

In Murmansk and Archangel, where there were similar problems but where the Japanese could not intervene, it is noteworthy that Wilson's position was more flexible. As early as May 11, 1918, Lansing, in a note to the President, tried to separate the problem of the Arctic Ocean from the Siberian problem. On July 17 Wilson approved an Allied expedition if Foch judged it to be necessary. A small contingent of American Marines, followed in early September by a few battalions, joined the British and French. Kennan has shown that the presence in northern Russia of these "forgotten men," in whom the United States government took little interest, made Wilson's policy self-contradictory and contributed to the Bolsheviks' growing distrust of him.[34]

The Armistice

On October 6 the Swiss delegation delivered to the State Department a German note, dated October 3, asking for the opening of negotiations for an armistice based on President Wilson's Fourteen

Points. The Swedish legation delivered a similar note from Austria-Hungary. It is easy to understand the fact that both the Central Powers preferred to approach Wilson rather than the other Allies. First, the Fourteen Points seemed to them less to be feared than the ambitions—declared or secret—of the Entente. Second, the United States being "associated" rather than "allied," Wilson might be persuaded to act as a mediator between the two camps. It was even possible to dream of a separate peace.

Lansing made a report on these two notes as early as October 7. He concluded that Germany and Austria-Hungary should not be treated alike. In Germany the population could be convinced that if they adopted a democratic form of government they could escape invasion and total ruin. But Austria-Hungary must give way to new nations. Wilson followed this advice. The first response to Germany (October 9) and also the subsequent American notes (October 14 and 23) insisted firmly on four conditions: unconditional acceptance of the Fourteen Points; evacuation of Allied territory; the end of illegal practices on land and on sea; assurance that the government that signed the Armistice would represent the German people and "not the military masters and the monarchical autocrats of Germany." [35] To Austria, on the other hand, Wilson gave notice that Point Ten—favoring the autonomy of various nationalities of the double monarchy but in a Federal framework—had been abandoned. The United States, impressed by the Rome meeting (April 9 and 11) of the Congress of Repressed Nationalities of Austria-Hungary, had given de facto recognition to the Czech Council and had decided to support the national aspirations of the Yugoslavs. As early as May 10, 1918, Wilson had authorized Lansing to support The Slav Movement in Austria. [36]

There remained the problem of obtaining Allied acceptance of the Fourteen Points. The European leaders, meeting at Versailles on October 9—there was no American representative as it was a "political" meeting of the Supreme War Council—had not been entirely satisfied with Wilson's note. They wished to insert in the Armistice military conditions which would make it technically impossible for Germany to resume hostilities. Wilson was both furious and deeply troubled, as he explained to France's Ambassador Jusserand. Then on October 14 he called a meeting of House, Lansing, Baker, and Daniels, at which a second and stronger note was drawn up. Colonel House was immediately sent to Paris.

In Paris House encountered great difficulties. Pershing, the American commander-in-chief, and Poincaré, President of the French Republic, were both against the Armistice. Nevertheless on October 26 the Allied governments gave it their support. The Fourteen Points contradicted the secret treaties in many ways and up to this time Wilson had never asked the Allies to accept them. They blocked the victorious peace Clemenceau wanted and, besides, the Allies did not want to push Wilson into the position of being a mediator, as the Germans wished, but wished him instead to act as a victor in concert with the other victors. Then, on October 20, the German Chancellor, Prince Max of Baden, replied—in spite of the resistance of Hindenburg and Ludendorff—that he would accept the American conditions in their entirety. House acted with great ability in this. At his request, two of his colleagues, Walter Lippmann, secretary of the Inquiry Bureau, and Frank Cobb, editor of the New York *World*, drew up an interpretation of the Fourteen Points which was cabled to Wilson in Washington and approved by him. House also deliberately used the specter of a separate peace in the sometimes violent discussions of the Allied leaders held in Paris between October 26 and November 4. As House said, "The opinion generally held by all American correspondents in Paris is that the only definite policy of the Allies at this moment is to remove control of the peace negotiations from the hands of President Wilson." [37]

The Allies then resigned themselves to accept the Fourteen Points —with a British reservation on the freedom of the seas,[38] and a French commentary to the effect that the Germans should pay for damages done to the civilian population, an idea suggested in various of Wilson's points. At the same time, Foch obtained general approval of a series of military measures designed to break the military power of the enemy and deprive Germany of the possibility of resuming the war after a period of reorganization, as Ludendorff had dreamed. In contrast to the American General Bliss, who would have wished immediate demobilization of German troops, Foch demanded their retreat across the Rhine and the surrender of an enormous quantity of arms. The naval conditions, elaborated by the British Naval Council, were adopted on November 4.

On November 5, Wilson, in the name of the Allied and Associated Powers, sent the joint note to the Germans.

Up to the last moment, the British—sometimes with House's support—had thought the terms of the Armistice too harsh, apt to bring forth a German refusal. But the Austrian Armistice of Villa Giusti on November 3 convinced them that from then on Germany could not continue the war.

On these terms, two days after the abdication of the Kaiser, a German delegation signed the Armistice of Rethondes which went into effect at eleven o'clock in the morning (November 11, 1918). In a proclamation to the American people, Wilson expressed his feelings: "Everything for which America fought has been accomplished. It will now be our fortunate duty to assist by example, by sober and friendly counsel and material aid in the establishment of a just democracy thoughout the world." [39] And Lippmann could write to House on November 7: "The President and you have more than justified the faith of those who affirmed that your leadership marked a turning-point in modern history." [40]

Chapter V

Wilson and the Peace

The Trip to Europe

ONE week after the Armistice, on November 18, 1918, Wilson announced to an astonished public his intention to go to Europe personally as head of the American delegation. There were a few scattered precedents of presidents in office leaving United States territory, but only for some place in the Western hemisphere. No president had ever gone to Europe. It was to become usual beginning with Franklin Delano Roosevelt, but at a time of much faster communications and always for rather short periods. Wilson was to be absent for long months, paralyzing the American process of government, for the actual functioning of which the president's physical presence is required. He was assailed by criticism from all sides. He was accused of inordinate vanity, of having a "Messiah complex," of thinking himself a "world prophet." It was thought that he would be a very bad diplomat; he hardly knew Europe, having been only twice to England, and once each to France and Italy. He spoke no foreign language; he did not even read French and German well. There was the risk that the astute and clever European politicians would take advantage of him, or, on the other hand, that he would impose too idealistic a peace, too little suited to harsh realities. In short, he would put all his moral leadership at stake. He would cut himself off from the American people at the very moment when his role should be to shape public opinion in his country while directing the important matters of reconversion and demobilization.

For their part, the European political leaders awaited without enthusiasm the arrival of this man who was so difficult to handle, and who was technically their superior, as he combined the functions of chief of state and head of the government, which are separate in Europe.

There was still another disadvantage in Wilson's going to Europe. House's idea, shared by Clemenceau, was to follow the established practice of European diplomacy to quickly make a preliminary treaty, which would later be followed by a permanent, definitive treaty. But Wilson was not willing to come until after his annual message on December 2. Clemenceau, warned of this by House, took cognizance of the problem in a telegram to House on November 15. "The coming of President Wilson naturally changes some of our plans in preparing the conference. It seems to me that we cannot begin work until the President arrives." [1] This would result in the lumping together in a single treaty of the proposed "preliminary" and the "final" treaty which would make the procedures much more rigid.

All of these arguments together could not change Wilson's mind. The summer before he was still planning to delegate his powers to Colonel House, but by October he had decided to go himself. As one keen observer says, "He was as excited as a debutante before her first ball." [2] On October 28 he announced his plan to House, who was not in favor of it. House wished to be the head of the delegation himself and to include McAdoo, Secretary of the Treasury, and Herbert Hoover. [3] Lansing and Wilson's secretary, Tumulty, were also opposed to Wilson's going. The majority of the cabinet, on the other hand, approved the President's plan. Wilson, however, was not inclined to ask advice of anyone. This is one of those cases, recurrent in his career, where he was convinced of the rightness of an idea and was ready to carry it through to the end with absolute stubbornness. Wilson's idea was that only he could impose on the world the new diplomatic order he considered essential. He cherished also a great illusion—that public opinion all over the world was with him, above the sordid practices of governments. "I am going to Europe because the Allied governments don't want me to," he explained to Professor Rappard on November 20. [4] On July 5 he had said in a private conversation: "Europe is still governed by the same reactionary forces which controlled this country until a few years ago. But I am satisfied that if necessary I can reach the people of Europe over the heads of their rulers." And again October 23: "It is astonishing how utterly out of sympathy with the sentiments of their own people the leaders of some of the foreign governments sometimes seem." [5]

But Lloyd George won the general election in Great Britain in December 1918 by an enormous majority. In the same month Clemenceau won a vote of confidence in the French Chamber by 380 to 134 votes. On the other hand Wilson, who had taken an active part in the Democratic campaign in October, had seen his party meet a grave setback. He had asked for a vote of confidence and the American people had responded by sending to the House of Representatives 237 Republicans and only 190 Democrats. The Republicans also acquired a majority of two in the Senate, and the chairmanship of the powerful Senate Committee on Foreign Relations had passed into the hands of Henry Cabot Lodge, a personal opponent of Wilson's. This seemed to matter little, and it slid off him without apparently affecting him. "It is universally expected and generally desired here that I attend the conference." [6]

Having made this decision without allowing any discussion, would Wilson maintain a bipartisan spirit by including in the delegation members of both parties? Would he take several senators to handle the treaty's future in the Senate? This was far from his thinking: the peace he wanted would be imposed on the world, and therefore on the Senate, by the irresistible pressure of peoples filled with enthusiasm for it. Senators could not be members of the delegation, he said, because the treaty should not be negotiated by the same men who were to vote on it. As for the chief Republican leaders, Lodge was a personal enemy, former Secretary of State Elihu Root was a "hopeless reactionary," former President Taft lacked ability, and in general all Republicans were "impossible." When Masaryk, President of the new Czech Republic, reproached him for not having any Republican advisers, Wilson replied, "I am descended from Scotch Presbyterians and therefore I am wholly stubborn." [7] It is a curious facet of his personality that this man whose flexibility and realism we have seen, who had a gift for negotiating, lost these traits when he had determined on an idea. He would defend it against men, against facts, against the evidence of reality, straight to the end, without relenting.

The delegation therefore consisted of men in whom he had confidence. Secretary of State Lansing was included, naturally; and Colonel House, an even more natural choice as he was the President's friend, had his full confidence, and above all because he was so accustomed by his many trips to dealing with the disturbing Europeans. As a personal friend of Grey, Lloyd George, and Clemenceau, House could certainly not have been excluded from the delegation. But the two other members were not very well known: General Tasker H. Bliss, American representative on the Supreme War Council, well liked by the Allied leaders, intelligent, able, but unknown to the public; Henry White, the only Republican, former diplomat, affable and tactful, who was the only delegate to speak French well and whose daughter had married a German nobleman, but who counted for little in the higher circles of the Republican party.

About 1300 American experts accompanied the American delegation; a century before Great Britain had taken 14 to the Congress of Vienna. The quality of these men was generally excellent. There were men like Herbert Hoover, Bernard Baruch, Norman Davis, Vance C. McCormick, all of whom were destined for brilliant careers. Hoover was to take charge of aid to devastated Europe with striking results. Baruch was chairman of the War Industries Board, then in the process of dissolution.

After having organized these matters, Wilson left his country on the *George Washington*, with many experts, especially the members of the Inquiry Bureau, and the ambassadors of the principal Allied countries. He said to Joseph Tumulty, as he was departing, that this trip "would either be the greatest success in history, or the supreme tragedy."

The Phase of the League

Wilson landed at Brest on Friday, December 13 to the salutes of the French Navy. For the next month—the peace conference opened January 12—he was to hear other salutes, those of popular acclaim. Wilson was at the height of his glory, in his element. As head of the great country whose role had been decisive, and symbol of the great principles which alone could change the face of the world, he was to be received with the most sincere enthusiasm and he was deeply moved by it. It may be that this enthusiasm made him forget too easily that the other victorious peoples also had national aspirations, which seemed legitimate to them. How much weight would his moral leadership have when it ran head-on into such aspirations?

In Paris first of all, where Wilson and his wife were received by Poincaré and Clemenceau, it was a real "honeymoon." Clemenceau, who had spent four years in America and had married a young American—although he had divorced her several decades back—was welcoming, understanding, and charming. But a little cloud appeared when the President refused to go to visit the still warm trenches. "The French want me to see red, but I do not want to despise the Germans anymore than I already do." This was a psychological error. He committed another at Reims, on January 26, by saying that the cathedral was less damaged than he had thought.[8] Clemenceau took subtle revenge by referring to Wilson's "noble candor" in a session of the Chamber of Deputies on December 29th. In English *candor* means *honesty;* the slightly pejorative sense of the word in French escaped no one.*

In London his reception was much cooler. British capacity to demonstrate enthusiasm had already been used up by the visits of Foch and Clemenceau. Wilson, in proposing a toast, forgot to congratulate the British on their victory; he was entirely absorbed in the League of Nations and in talking about it with Lord Robert Cecil, its foremost British advocate. While in England he went to Carlisle, near the Scottish border, the home of his ancestors. After he spoke in the church where his grandfather had officiated, the Bishop of Carlisle closed with the words: "God save you and guide you, sir."

He returned to Paris in late December and on January 1 left for Rome. There the welcome was triumphal. In a speech to the Chamber of Deputies he did not hesitate to raise the dangerous problem of the Slav countries—"which should now be independent"—an allusion to the Istrian frontier. He redeemed himself by promising Italy the South Tyrol although it was partially inhabited by German-speaking people. He even called on the Pope, whose wartime attempts at negotiation he had not appreciated, because he saw in him a possible defender of his dear League of Nations. All the same, he was not sympathetic with Roman Catholics and one of the reasons for his hostility to the *Anschluss* was the fear of increasing the number of Catholics in Germany. In Genoa he hailed the memories of Columbus and Mazzini; in Milan he shook the hands of a thousand mayors of North Italian towns; in Modena he learned of the death of his old rival, Theodore Roosevelt. On January 7 he returned to France for the start of the conference, full of confidence.

During this hectic month all his energies were directed toward making the League succeed. During the next month, even more hectic, Wilson was to guide the conference toward this goal which

* The French has implications of naïveté or ingenuousness, perhaps even gullibility.

seemed so essential to him. He thought that the pact or Covenant of the League of Nations should be worked out first, because it was the keystone of the building. It should not be "added on to the treaty, but incorporated into it." Going even further, he thought that it should be covered in the first articles.

Wilson's ideas were now fully developed. He had confided them on the *George Washington*, on December 10, to Isaiah Bowman.[9] In his mind the League of Nations was tied to the necessity to assure the territorial integrity of nations, by allowing them to keep frontiers which were just. He contrasted this notion with the balance of power, by which small nations were ruled by large, "which had never produced anything but aggression, egotism and war." He visualized the location of the world organization in The Hague or Berne, with a council which could impose discipline in the form of sanctions against aggressors. The German colonies as a group could be placed under the League of Nations with the small nations as administrators. This would be a way of proclaiming the truth to the world. It is to be noted that this idea of "mandates," so clearly expressed, came before the proposal of the South African General Smuts on this matter, which was published December 16. Wilson developed his ideas in the following weeks; by December 16 he had proposed an international labor office. When he returned from Italy on January 8 he worked out a new text, in collaboration with House, and submitted it to Lord Robert Cecil, to harmonize his own plan with the British plan. This was virtually accomplished by January 20.

Meanwhile the conference opened. The plenary sessions, including the delegates of twenty-six nations and four British Dominions, were purely formal occasions. The working sessions, following Clemenceau's suggestion, were to take place in a Council of Ten—chiefs of governments and foreign ministers of the United States, France, the United Kingdom, Italy, and Japan. Sixteen commissions of experts were created—they were to hold an average of a hundred sessions each. It was suspected that in all this activity only the highest organization was really important. In spite of this, in order to push his favorite project through, Wilson had himself named chairman of the Commission on the League of Nations. In the plenary session of January 25 he gained his first great success—a resolution in favor of the creation of the League of Nations as "an integral part of the general treaty." Thus he won out over Clemenceau, who wanted to postpone this type of discussion, and Lloyd George, who asked that only the main outlines be worked out at this time.

The commission over which Wilson presided met in extra sessions in Room 315 of the Hotel Crillon, House's room, in addition to its regular sessions. This schedule increased the strain on the President —ten meetings, thirty hours, in all. He had to fight against Lansing, who opposed a positive guarantee against all aggression; against the French, who suggested a League of Allies with an international army (this went against the Constitution of the United States which gives the exclusive power of declaring war to Congress); against France, Great Britain, and above all Australia, who were opposed to the mandate system. The intervention of the South African generals Smuts and Botha was to prove decisive in this matter, although the large nations rather than the small were to become the mandate powers. Finally, he defeated the proposals of the French delegate Léon Bourgeois, who advocated the creation of an international army. This "would accomplish nothing but the substitution of international militarism for national militarism," Wilson said. In the end he was able to get the essence of the Anglo-American plan adopted. On February 13, at seven in the evening, the "pact" was adopted by the commission, and the next day Wilson presented it in a plenary session. It was his hour of triumph, "the hour," says his biographer Walworth, "for which Wilson had been born." This college teacher, who had given much thought to constitutions, had put through a world constitution. He said, with deep feeling, "I think I can say of this document that it is at one and the same time a practical and humane document. There is a pulse of sympathy in it. There is a compulsion of conscience throughout it. It is practical, and yet it is intended to purify, to rectify, to elevate." [10]

The next day, February 15th, Wilson sailed from Brest for the United States.

The Interlude in the United States

Wilson returned to the United States to close the session of Congress. He had to resume contact with the American people and its elected representatives. Not for an instant did he dream that the Senate would one day refuse to approve this pact that he had put through so masterfully, and he wished to reassure the British and

French on this point before his departure. House was to work out the details during Wilson's absence but was not supposed to make decisions either on territorial questions or on reparations.

Wilson landed in Boston on February 24, where he was greeted by Calvin Coolidge, then governor of Massachusetts, and an enthusiastic crowd. This was a point scored against those senators who had already shown violent opposition to the Covenant. Wilson said that the nation would adhere to the text, because if it did not, "America's whole reputation would be lost and her power dissipated." Lodge thought it insulting of Wilson to make his views public before telling them to the Senate. Wilson's reception in Washington was equally enthusiastic. On the evening of the twenty-sixth he invited thirty-four members of Congress—members of the two committees on foreign relations—to the White House. Senators Borah and Fall, the "irreconcilables," refused to come. Henry Cabot Lodge came but said nothing. For two hours, after dinner, Wilson answered questions in a frank, friendly manner. Two days later, Lodge said in a speech that the Covenant threatened precious traditions: isolationism, the Monroe Doctrine, the right to control immigration; and he asked if there was not a risk, under Article 10, that some day American soldiers would be called upon to fight in Europe again. Would not it be better to make a peace treaty quickly and discuss the League of Nations later? Could not the plan for the League be amended?

On March 2, thirty-nine Republican senators signed a resolution saying that the Covenant was not acceptable in its present form. Besides, the Senate absolutely refused to vote for funds to aid the German people. Wilson told the Democratic leaders that when he retired to private life in 1921 he would take up his pen "to describe the fatuity of these gentlemen with their poor little minds that never get anywhere but run round in a circle and think they are going somewhere." [11] His indignation was great. On the eve of his departure he spoke in the Metropolitan Opera House in New York—with former President Taft at his side. He defended the League of Nations warmly, "I will not come back until all is accomplished over there. I pray God, for the sake of the peace of the world, that it will be soon." And he added, "you cannot dissect the Covenant from the Treaty without destroying the whole vital structure. The structure of peace will not be vital without the League of Nations, and no man is going to bring back a cadaver with him." On February 27 he was still optimistic, however, "The people of the United States are undoubtedly in favor of the League of Nations by an overwhelming majority . . . but there are many forces, particularly those prejudiced against Great Britain, which are exercising a considerable influence against it." [12]

In general the press supported Wilson, except for some Republican newspapers and the Hearst press. The *Literary Digest* in April published results of a vast poll: 718 newspapers representing 9,886,449 readers were favorable to the League of Nations; 181 newspapers representing 4,326,882 readers were hostile; 478 newspapers representing 6,792,461 readers were favorable under certain conditions. [13] All the South was in favor; the Irish-Americans were opposed.

When he arrived at Brest on March 13 Wilson was met by House, who gave him a report on his actions during the President's absence. Wilson was appalled. House had conceded much too much to the French; Bliss and White agreed. For instance, he had allowed the plan to prevail by which there would be a preliminary treaty—without the Covenant—to regulate the territorial questions as well as a final treaty with the Covenant. Was this not to admit that the League was powerless? "Thank God," said Wilson to his wife, "I can still fight and I will win." But it was the beginning of a break between the two friends. "He seemed to have aged ten years," Mrs. Wilson wrote, "and his jaw was set as it is when he makes a superhuman effort to control himself." He said to her with a bitter smile: "House has given away everything I had won before we left Paris. He has compromised on very side, and so I have to start all over again and this time it will be harder, as he has given the impression that my delegates are not in sympathy with me." [14]

True or false, this does not at all mean that House had tried to sabotage the League of Nations, as Baker has claimed. [15] As Alexander and Juliette George conclude, it was an unfortunate combination of circumstances—Wilson's resentment of House as a possible rival and House's insuperable desire to act on his own—that contributed so much to the gradual disappearance of the President's enthusiasm for his closest collaborator. [16]

The Quarrels of the Big Four in March and April

Wilson arrived at the Gare des Invalides in Paris on March 14. Although he had yet to do battle for the League of Nations, he knew that the difficult territorial questions, hardly considered up to then, would constitute the heart of the debates. French and British opinion held him responsible for the delays. Ray Stannard Baker, the future editor of his speeches and letters, acted as public relations agent and tried to reverse the tide of his rising unpopularity by every possible means.

The first days were devoted to the reconstruction of the League. Wilson invited House and Lord Robert Cecil to dinner on March 18 to discuss possible revisions. Wilson refused "with his usual stubbornness," wrote House, "every amendment, even though the only aim was to facilitate the passage of the treaty in the Senate." Even so, four changes were made: affirmation that each nation has exclusive control of its domestic affairs; a statement implying that the Monroe Doctrine would not be modified by the Covenant; the right of each member to withdraw from the League; and the right to refuse a mandate. On March 22 the Commission on the League of Nations came out against the French proposal which would have strengthened the organization by providing for coordinated military action and an international general staff. Finally, on March 27 the original plan was adopted, with the above-mentioned amendments.

As early as March 24 Wilson, influenced by Clemenceau, asked his colleagues to substitute as the working body a Council of Four (five when Japan was present to deal with Far Eastern affairs) for the clumsy Council of Ten. The foreign ministers would meet separately. This proposal was immediately adopted. As a result, Wilson, Clemenceau, Lloyd George, Orlando, and Captain Paul Mantoux, the interpreter, met almost every day at 11 Place des Etats-Unis, Wilson's residence (occasionally they met at Lloyd George's residence or at the Ministry of War or at the Quai d'Orsay). Thus they could discuss freely and in secret, call experts as they needed them, make major decisions. (Lieutenant Colonel Sir Maurice Hankey, acting as secretary, joined them on April 19.) Between March 24 and June 29 there were 148 meetings of the Big Four, one or two a day.

Paul Mantoux's notes on these meetings, in which he has taken pains to preserve the actual style and words of the members, make it possible to correct many of the judgments of John Maynard Keynes on Wilson. It is not a prophet, a "theologian" of more or less feeble spirit, a victim of European guile, that we will see in action, but an excellent negotiator, realistic although attached to high ideals, flexible despite his passion for them.

On March 24 Wilson opened what he called "the great debate" with these words:

> At this moment there is a real race between peace and anarchy, and the public is beginning to show its impatience . . . I am of the opinion that we should take up the most difficult and most urgent questions first—such as reparations, the protection of France against aggression, the Italian frontier on the Adriatic—so that the four of us can discuss them. Once the most important and difficult questions are settled the way will be cleared and the rest will go fast.[17]

I will not try to analyze the discussion on these delicate points in detail, but I hope to show in connection with them the main line of Wilson's policy and the imagination with which he proposed solutions.

In Wilson's thinking—which determined that of the American delegation—we must distinguish three kinds of cases: (1) those in which he finally gave in to his European colleagues, for example, reparations; (2) those in which he refused to give in on the substance but accepted some compromise, such as the questions of the Saar and the Rhineland; (3) those in which he remained intransigent to the end, such as the questions of Fiume and Dalmatia. We will discuss in a later section his attitude toward the Soviet Union and the Far East.

Wilson was not directly interested in the matter of reparations because the United States had no need of them. "Germany must pay" was a slogan without psychological appeal across the Atlantic. This detachment allowed Wilson to have a much broader approach than that of his European colleagues, driven by public opinion crying for vengeance. For instance, he accepted the British proposition—which did not fit the stipulations of the Armistice—to include in the total of reparations not only the damage to the civilian population but also military pensions, which practically doubled the amount. But he warned his colleagues: "I hope you are agreed . . . that it is necessary to show moderation to Germany . . . Our greatest mistake would be to give her powerful reasons to take revenge . . . We must avoid giving the enemy even the impression of injustice. It is not war prepared by the secret plots of governments that I fear in the future, but rather conflicts caused by the dissatisfaction of peoples." [18]

Wilson fought every step of the way to get an overall total amount fixed for reparations. He opposed the solution finally adopted, saying, "This would be to ask Germany to put everything she has at our disposal, indefinitely . . . Germany would think that it was worse for her to accept an unlimited obligation than to agree to pay a given amount, even a very considerable one." [19] He also tried to arrange to have reparations based on Germany's ability to pay—a realistic view —and not on the total of damages, and he insisted, in vain, on the idea that this ability was lessened by Germany's defeat and her territorial amputations. "It will not be possible to get the sums we are asking unless we can do it without crushing Germany for thirty-five years." [20]

But Wilson's reasonable attitude had to bow before the passion of his opponents. The same was true of the notorious Article 231 which placed in the treaty a declaration of German guilt.

He took a similar stand on the matter of a trial for the Kaiser. Legally, he said, such a procedure had no basis: "I have grave doubts about our right to set up a tribunal composed only of belligerents. The accusers would also be judges . . . It would create a dangerous precedent to have our enemies judged by judges who represent us." [21] Besides, would it not antagonize the Germans unnecessarily? Nonetheless, he gave in.

His attitude was entirely different toward the problems of the Saar and the Rhineland, problems raised by the French. Clemenceau and Tardieu were demanding in addition to reparations for the losses of 1871—Alsace-Lorraine—reparations for the losses of 1815: they desired the annexation of Saarlouis and Sarrebruck. They also wanted, and here Wilson had no objection, the transfer to France of the Saar mines in compensation for the destruction of the pits in the *départments* Nord and Pas-de-Calais. The discussion was heated, not only with Clemenceau, who wanted annexation, but with Lloyd George, who dreamed for a time of a Saar not only politically detached from Germany but independent, like another Luxembourg.

Wilson's first objection was that the claims on the Saar had not been mentioned in France's statement of her war aims. But above all, he thought it an injustice: "If you try to establish frontiers on historical and strategic considerations—and I would add economic— there will be no end to claims . . . There is not a sufficient historical basis for the annexation of these regions to France." Clemenceau's response to this was: "I recognize the words and the excellent intentions of President Wilson. He eliminates emotion and memory. The President of the United States does not understand the basic workings of human nature." [22] Wilson countered: "There is today throughout the world a passion for justice . . . The feeling which brought together peoples from all corners of the earth in the war is the feeling with which they will fight together for peace and justice. This is why I have been able to say several times that we here represent world opinion rather than states. This enthusiastic aspiration . . . will be changed to disillusioned skepticism if people get the impression that we do not ourselves apply the rules of justice we announced." [23] And he concluded: "I think that one violates the principle of the right of self-determination of peoples as much by giving people independence they do not want as in forcing them to accept foreign sovereignty." [24]

Finally, on April 8, recovered from a short illness, Wilson proposed the compromise that was accepted: "not to remove the Saar from German sovereignty" but to have it administered by a commission of five members for fifteen years, at the end of which a plebiscite would be held.[25] To gain Clemenceau's consent he resorted to moving words. "I am searching with all my might for a solution which will satisfy you and will satisfy me. I cannot see that the abolition of German sovereignty is acceptable . . . I ask you to help me to go in your direction. I have taken many steps to meet you; do not make it impossible for me to help you as much as I can." [26]

The other serious problem in the Franco-American crisis of late March and early April was that of the Rhineland. On Foch's advice, Clemenceau wanted to detach it from Germany and have it permanently occupied by Allied troops. The proposition was submitted to France's colleagues in a memorandum on March 10. Lloyd George, who was much opposed, hoped to substitute an Anglo-American guarantee for France in case of unprovoked German aggression. On March 12 he discussed this with House—Wilson had not yet returned—who tried to put the plan in a form that would be more acceptable to American public opinion. Wilson was taken by this plan and fully approved it, on condition that there would be two treaties, one Franco-American and the other Anglo-French, instead of a single tripartite treaty. But how would Clemenceau react? On March 31, Foch came to present his views to the Big Four. On the following days, while Wilson was sick (April 4–8), discussion became very heated. House represented Wilson in these Big Four meetings held near Wilson's sickroom. In addition to the meetings, there were private talks, but with poor results. On April 7 Wilson was completely discouraged and was considering a separate peace. He telegraphed the captain of the

George Washington to prepare to depart.[27] Maybe one should not exaggerate the importance of this; still, the Allies, aware of their danger, gave in. Already on April 6 the compromise on reparations had been adopted. On the tenth, compromise was reached on the Saar; on the fourteenth, on the Rhineland. The agreement on the Rhineland provided for military occupation for fifteen years and British and American guarantee treaties against future German aggression.

Some American historians, especially Bailey,[28] have always wondered how Wilson could have believed that the Senate would approve a guarantee treaty. Lansing had raised the objection as had the Republican White, but Wilson had paid no attention. As for Clemenceau, perhaps he counted on nonratification of the treaty by the United States to enable him to continue the occupation, following Article 429 of the treaty.

Wilson showed himself least flexible on the subject of Italy. As early as January he had granted that the frontier in the province of Trento should go to the Brenner Pass, in Istria to the watershed. What he absolutely refused, without compromise, was Italian annexation of Fiume, which Italy had not claimed at the time of the Treaty of London signed with the Entente in April 1915, or of Dalmatia, which had been promised Italy by France, England, and Russia. The problem was complicated by the fact that House, discussing the future Austrian treaty with the Allies on October 31, 1918, had admitted that Austrian troops would retreat to a certain line, which was exactly the line of the Treaty of London, and that the evacuated zone had been occupied at once by Italian troops. Wilson had refused to give in to the Serb request that this zone be taken over by American troops.

The discussion on Fiume and Dalmatia took up much time in the meetings. In no other problem can we see Wilson's views more clearly. After the Franco-American crisis of March 24–April 8 came the Italo-American crisis, April 14–May 5. Wilson sought at first to have a meeting of the German parliament *before* an agreement in principle on the Italian questions, which Orlando, head of the Italian government refused.[29] Orlando explained the substance of his complaint: "Italy thinks she is within her rights in claiming frontiers which God has given her." [30] Beyond this geographical consideration, he claimed Fiume "in the name of the right of self-determination of peoples" and Dalmatia for strategic and historical reasons. Wilson's reply was carefully worked out and is of the greatest importance: "We are agreed on very definite principles which should provide a basis for our peace with Germany. It is not possible for us to say that . . . we will invoke others to make peace with Turkey, Bulgaria, and Austria . . . We are trying to do something that has never been done before: we want to build a foundation for a new system of international relations." Fiume could be internationalized, Dalmatia would remain with Yugoslavia.

One of the great objects of this conference is to liberate the Balkan peninsula from interventions of the great powers . . . The strategic argument was used in 1815. It was used again in 1871. Military advisers who have imposed strategic frontiers bear the responsibility of some of the most serious wrongs which have been committed in the history of the world. I believe that it would endanger the peace of Europe if Italy insists on establishing herself on the east coast of the Adriatic Sea. We are creating a great League of Nations in which a leading role is reserved for Italy. If that is not enough, if we must have recourse to strategic measures at the same time, we are trying to combine two irreconcilable systems.[31]

By April 20 Orlando was reacting by threatening to break the alliance if the Treaty of London was not applied, to which Wilson replied: "This world conference in which we are taking part has the duty to express world sentiment and not to execute a pact made by a small group only." [32] A break with Italy would be "the supreme tragedy of this war." From April 21 on Orlando ceased to attend the meetings of the Big Four.

That same day, Wilson read a document in which he explained his attitude. He sought to publicize this document to put across his ideas to the Italian people. Lloyd George and Clemenceau approved, with some reservations. Wilson decided to make this gesture for, as he said on April 22, "If the Slavs feel they have been unjustly treated . . . that will open the way to Russian influence and the formation of a Slav bloc hostile to Western Europe." [33] On April 23 the American document was published and on the twenty-fourth Orlando came to the Council of Four to protest. Publication, he said, "gives the impression that this is an appeal to peoples in general. The consequence— even if unintended—is to cast doubt on my authority as representative of the Italian people." [34] Then he announced his departure for Rome. Was this the break? A message drawn up jointly by Wilson, Clemenceau, and Lloyd George finally persuaded him to return—if he did not, France and England would consider the Treaty of London broken.

On May 7, Orlando, back from Rome, where the crowds and the Parliament had acclaimed him, returned to the Council of Four. This time Wilson would not lend himself at all to compromise. Certain that he was representing American opinion, he had prevented what had appeared to him the most serious blow to the New Diplomacy of which he was the leader. Not without emotion he said to those who questioned him, "You think me insensible, but I fight constantly against emotion and I must put pressure on myself to keep my judgment sane." [35]

The Bolsheviks, the Japanese, and the Chinese

In the foreground of the drama of the Council of Four was Europe, but further behind, ever more troublesome, were the serious problems of Soviet Russia and the Far East.

Wilson did not like the Bolsheviks any more than Clemenceau did. He had, however, a sort of sentimental affection for the Russian people and wanted to help to bring them peace. In January 1919 Wilson took the initiative in calling a conference of representatives of the two Russian governments—Red and White. It was to be held on the Princes Islands in the Sea of Marmara. When the Whites refused, Wilson sent William Bullitt to Moscow with a mission to enter into relations with the Bolsheviks. Lansing did not favor "even the idea of investigating these assassins." [36] This attitude was shared by Ambassador Francis. Bullitt's mission came to nothing. When Wilson returned to the United States in March he learned that Winston Churchill had suggested a general intervention in Russia, a suggestion he totally disapproved of. He was also opposed to the recognition, advocated by France, of the White Russian government headed by Admiral Kolchak.

On March 24 the Communist rebellion under Béla Kun triumphed in Hungary. The next day Wilson, remarking that the people in Odessa were hostile to the French troops, said, "This indicates that my policy is right: to leave Russia to the Bolsheviks—they will stew in their own juice until circumstances make the Russians wiser—and to limit ourselves to preventing the spread of Bolshevism to other parts of Europe." [37] He agreed that it was necessary to use the Rumanian Army against the threat and therefore to evacuate Odessa. Marshal Foch suggested establishing a "barrier": "Against an epidemic disease we should erect a protective zone to safeguard health [*cordon sani-*

taire]." He proposed the occupation of Vienna to accomplish this. General Bliss, on the contrary, thought that a *"cordon sanitaire* could stop the Bolsheviks but not Bolshevism itself." Wilson elaborated this theme: "The word Bolshevism covers many different things. In my opinion, to try to stop a revolutionary movement by massed armies is to use a broom to stop a great tide . . . The only way to act against Bolshevism is to attack its causes so that they will disappear." This was a formidable enterprise. He concluded: "The only way to kill Bolshevism is to establish frontiers and open all ports to commerce." [38]

Wilson categorically refused to consider the occupation of Vienna. His policy stemmed from a certain liberalism and a consistent desire to avoid intervention. Of course he had the example of the Siberian affair. One wonders whether it was the ideal of nonintervention which had led him to participate so reluctantly in the Siberian expedition— or whether, on the contrary, the confusion with which that expedition was carried out had strengthened his leaning toward nonintervention. On April 2, 1919, Lansing sent Wilson's instructions on Siberia: promote the raising of economic standards; support the most moderate factions; insure the functioning of the railroads. Then Wilson agreed to have the Big Four send a letter to Kolchak, listing the conditions under which the Allied and Associated Powers would recognize him: the calling of a freely elected assembly as soon as he reached Moscow; a promise not to restore the privileges of the tsarist era; and a promise that the new democratic Russia would join the League of Nations. Kolchak's affirmative response arrived on June 4, but it was already too late: his defeat was near. Kolchak's defeat took place in November and in January 1920 the United States decided to withdraw its troops from Siberia. This was carried out on April 1, 1920.

The Siberian affair was already involved in the increasing tension between the United States and Japan. Even more than for the Russian people Wilson felt friendship for the Chinese people. In this he was strongly supported by two other members of the American delegation, White, who was a friend of former Secretary of State John Hay, creator of the Open Door Policy, and General Bliss, who had been stationed in the Philippines. The objective was to help China and block Japanese ambitions; but it is one thing to have an objective and another to realize it. The Japanese had two powerful means of exerting pressure in Paris. They could try to get the principle of "equality of races" embodied in the Covenant, which would have made impossible American legislation against the immigration of Orientals and would also meet with opposition from the British Dominions. They could also leave the conference. In late April, when Italy was making the same threat, this could be decisive. The whole future of the peace was at stake.

China was asking for an end to foreign privileges: discriminatory treaties, bases, control of railroads. Japan wanted to take over Germany's sphere of influence in the Shantung Peninsula and to exercise the privileges which the Germans had exercised. On April 11 a Japanese motion on "the equality of nations and just treatment of all nationals" was passed by eleven out of seventeen votes in the Commission for the League of Nations. As unanimity was required, this amounted to a defeat. But would Japan consent to enter the League under these conditions? The only way to assure this was to give in to her on Shantung. Japan had already acquired the mandate over most of the Pacific islands. Wilson had refused to follow the advice of the Navy and State departments to annex some of these islands to the United States. This would have been contrary to the Wilsonian policy of "no material gain."

Regarding Shantung, Baron Makino, the Japanese delegate, had demanded the former German rights as early as January 27, 1919, in the Council of Ten. The next day Wellington Koo, the young delegate who had studied at Columbia University, protested in the name of China. The substance of his argument was that the native province of Confucius, with a population of 36,000,000, which was strategically essential to north China, should be wholly returned to Chinese sovereignty. He said that the war had canceled the German-Chinese agreements. The Chinese trusted Wilson's New Diplomacy to satisfy their just demands.

But the facts had to be reckoned with, and in April 1919 the facts were that the Japanese would not join the League unless they could keep Shantung. Besides, how could one get them out? On April 21 Wilson and Lansing proposed the abolition of all spheres of influence in China. The two Japanese delegates, Makino and Chinda, accepted, knowing that neither France nor England would. (In 1917 a secret treaty on this point had been signed by Japan, France, Great Britain, and Italy.) After the defeat of Wilson's appeal to the Japanese delegates on April 22, it was decided to accept the articles the Japanese wanted to include in the treaty. In other words, the Japanese got what they wanted. China could not help either submitting to these articles or continuing the agreements with Japan, signed under Japanese pressure in 1915 and 1918. China wanted neither solution. Wilson could not convince Wellington Koo that once a member of the League, China would have nothing to fear.

On April 28, the President gave in. He was not willing to risk weakening the League of Nations by taking a strong stand like the one he had taken toward Italy, as House, Lansing, and Bliss advised. The general wrote him a letter of protest, saying that the agreement was immoral and unjust to China; "It cannot be right to act wrongly, even to secure peace." [39] Wilson's only response was to refuse to recognize the validity of the Sino-Japanese agreements signed during the war. In all, the whole question produced a deplorable effect in the United States and did no little damage to the defenders of the treaty. Secretary of State Lansing thought that the League of Nations was becoming a handicap, if under pretext of strengthening it the President was willing to give in on the substance of the treaty. The Chinese protested in early May, and on June 28 they refused to sign the Treaty of Versailles.

The Cooperation of Wilson and Clemenceau and the Signing of the Treaty of Versailles

The first official session with the German plenipotentiaries took place May 7 at Versailles in a tense atmosphere. Clemenceau presided, with Wilson on his right hand and Lloyd George on his left. The head of the German delegation was Brockdorff-Rantzau, who made an ill-tempered speech, without rising, which irritated Wilson profoundly. Had he not dared to say that the treaty did not conform to the President's principles? On leaving, Wilson commented: "What abominable manners! . . . The Germans are really a stupid people. They always do the wrong thing. They did everything wrong during the war—and that's why I am here. They don't understand human nature. This is the most tactless speech I have ever heard. It will set the whole world against them." [40] His irritation increased when he learned that the German Chancellor Scheidemann had said, "Wilson is a hypocrite and the Treaty of Versailles the vilest crime in all history."

Thomas Bailey has given an explanation of the intensity with which in the following weeks Wilson defended the proposed treaty against the Germans and against Lloyd George. The British Prime Minister, under pressure of public opinion, and in contrast to Clemenceau, now wished to soften the conditions, while the President was increasingly convinced that the treaty was satisfactory. According to Bailey, Wilson's vanity, his faith in his role of prophet, had led him to believe that what he had finally accepted could not be bad. He who had fought so hard against French "imperialism," was now to support Clemenceau energetically. This explanation does not seem correct. Wilson, irritated with Germany, thought it was necessary to "punish" that country, but he had far fewer illusions than people have believed concerning the value of the plan in itself. He had voluntarily made concessions and compromises to assure the entry of all powers into the League. It seemed to him that the future of the world would be secured by the League of Nations; with it all necessary adjustments could be made. The proposed treaty was the only means to satisfy his colleagues enough to make them enter "his" League of Nations. He was aware that German opinion was resigned; he believed in the possibility of Allied conquest of Weimar and Berlin, if necessary.

On May 10 Foch said in a meeting of the Big Four: "There are still 450,000 men in Germany nominally in the Army . . . but they are disorganized and disarmed. The military force of Germany, at the moment, does not exist." [41] To put pressure on Germany, Wilson declared: "What would be most effective in case the Germans refuse to sign would be military occupation. The German people must not be reduced to despair by famine." [42] On June 13 when Clemenceau and Lloyd George proposed to use the threat of blockade, Wilson still opposed it. "The immediate renewal of the blockade would create a painful impression throughout the world . . . the only result of a blockade would be Bolshevism." [43] But Wilson naturally visualized the strong hand only as a way of bringing pressure to make Germany sign. When Foch, on June 16, explained his plan to combine military action with political—that is, to recognize the independence of the South German states and make a separate peace with them—Wilson opposed it firmly, as did Clemenceau and Lloyd George.[44]

After some preliminary skirmishes, the great debate on the eventual concessions to be made to Germany was begun on June 2 by Lloyd George. "Our public opinion . . . will not support a government which would resume the war without overriding reasons"; therefore, "it is absolutely necessary to make some serious modifications in the treaty." These concessions should relate to a plebiscite in Upper Silesia, a substantial softening of reparations, and the abandonment of the occupation of the Rhineland. Germany should also be admitted to the League of Nations almost immediately. Clemenceau's reply is not surprising. "I too am aware of public opinion in my country and must reckon with it. I think everyone is anxious to get things settled. In England they think the way to do it is by making concessions. In France we think that we must stand firm. Unfortunately, we know the Germans better than anyone else; we think that the more concessions we make, the more they will demand." [45]

Wilson did not reply at once. He announced that he would see his colleagues the next day at the Hotel Crillon. House has left us an account of this meeting.[46] The Colonel thought it was too late to change, although he would have preferred a more liberal treaty. He thought Clemenceau would not give in and would get his way. This was Wilson's opinion too. "The great problem of the moment," said Wilson, "is the problem of agreement" among the allies. "We should not make changes in the treaty in order to get the Germans to sign, if these changes concern the things we fought for." On June 2 Wilson replied to Lloyd George, "It is a bit late to say all that. The question is, were our previous decisions right or not? . . . I am not moved by the argument that Germany will not sign—unless anyone can show that we have violated our own principles in our stipulations." [47]

The only concession that Wilson accepted was the plebiscite in Upper Silesia. On the rest he held his ground. He would nevertheless have liked to see the Germans join the League quickly: "My opinion has always been that we will control the Germans better when they are in the League than when they are outside." [48]

He clung to his views on German responsibility for the war; he defended the idea of occupation. Having been an advocate of fixing the total amount of reparations from the beginning, he gave it up in order to protect the understanding among the Allies and to achieve peace sooner. "If peace is not made or if it is not settled soon, my financial advisers fear the gravest consequences." [49] When the Germans scuttled their fleet at Scapa Flow on June 21 Wilson was indignant and wanted repayment. Nevertheless, he opposed the idea that this should be made a pretext to resume the war.

On June 22 Brockdorff-Rantzau was replaced as head of the German delegation by von Haniel, and later by Hermann Müller. Scheidemann's government fell and a government ready to sign the treaty took its place. Wilson's note in answer to the German reservations is as follows: "The Allied and Associated Governments have replied fully and clearly to the observations of the German delegation in making all concessions which are known to be just and possible . . . They declare that the time for discussion is past and they cannot admit any modification or reservation. The German Government must accept or refuse to sign the Treaty in the time allotted without any possible equivocation." [50] This text was adopted by Clemenceau and Lloyd George. The firm point of view had prevailed, thanks to Wilson.

The ceremony took place June 28 in the Hall of Mirrors at Versailles. Wilson was satisfied. The day before he had said at a press conference, "All things considered, I think a wonderful success has been achieved . . . It's a long job that I'm glad to see finished, and it is a good job." [51] The Germans were asked to sign first, to forestall any dramatic gesture. The ceremony lasted an hour. The huge crowds outside cried, "Vive Wilson! Vive Clemenceau! Vive Lloyd George!" Wilson left Paris in the afternoon, and the old Tiger, Clemenceau, standing beside his train with tears in his eyes, said, "I feel as though I were losing one of the best friends I ever had." [52]

Chapter VI

The Defeat of Wilsonian Internationalism

The First Skirmishes

WILSON left Brest on the *George Washington* on June 29, 1919, the day after the treaty was signed. He landed in Hoboken, New Jersey, on July 8 amid the salutes of a powerful American squadron, to be greeted by the members of the cabinet and many senators and representatives. After a very vague speech at Carnegie Hall, the President went to Washington. On July 10 he took the official text of the Treaty of Versailles to the Senate in person. The great debate was about to begin.

Before following its various stages, it is useful to note that the senators, whose approval of any treaty by a two-thirds vote is required by the Constitution, already knew the main provisions unofficially, and that a number of them had taken a stand. Wilson had made an agreement with his colleagues in Europe to keep the treaty strictly secret, and he had kept his side of the bargain, but after the submission of the treaty to the Germans in May the German leaders had revealed it and the European press had featured paraphrases of the text. The House of Morgan had succeeded in getting hold of an almost exact text and had shown it to certain senators.

Let us remember that the Senate then consisted of forty-seven Democrats and forty-nine Republicans. To understand the sequence of events, so important because of their international consequences, we must make a careful analysis of senatorial attitudes. Of the forty-seven Democrats, four were "irreconcilables"; for one reason or another, the treaty seemed hateful to them. Senator Walsh of Massachusetts, for instance, an Irish-American, would not approve of a peace that ignored the independence of Ireland. Reed of Missouri was a die-hard Anglophobe. The other forty-three Democrats respected party discipline; they were led by Senator Martin of Virginia, who was fading in powers and was to die during the course of the debate. These forty-three would follow Wilson's policy to approve the treaty without amendment. Martin's second in command was Gilbert Hitchcock of Nebraska, who was somewhat suspect in Wilson's eyes because he had once studied for two years in Germany. There was no striking personality among the forty-three reliable Democrats.

On the Republican side, the bloc of irreconcilables was more integrated and was, above all, more influential. There were fourteen of them, often called the "battalion of death." The most original figure was that of William E. Borah, the "Lion of Idaho"—a nickname which referred both to his manelike hair and to his fighting spirit. Borah was an eccentric with the irritating trait of contentiousness, and an excellent orator. He regarded the League as an absolute evil and had been fighting it with all his might since February 1919. Beside him there was a remarkable group of men. McCormick of Illinois, former publisher of the powerful Chicago *Daily Tribune;* Philander Knox of Pennsylvania, an able lawyer and Secretary of State under Taft; Hiram Johnson of California, a great popular speaker, respected by all for his fight against political corruption in his state. It can be said that the "battalion of death," despite its small numbers, attracted more attention than all the other factions.

Among the Republicans there were no ardent partisans of the treaty as it stood, without amendments. The twelve or fifteen Republican senators who were disposed to accept it with some improving amendments were called the "mild reservationists," led by the future Secretary of State Frank Kellogg. Twenty to twenty-five others demanded substantial amendments, some directed at the very spirit of the Treaty of Versailles and especially of the League of Nations. These were the "strong reservationists." The leaders of this group were future President Harding, then senator from Ohio, and especially Henry Cabot Lodge, chairman of the Senate Committee on Foreign Relations.

Before taking a further look at this important man, we should examine the probable results implied by this division of opinion: two thirds of ninety-six senators was sixty-four and there were only eighteen irreconcilables who would vote "no" under any circumstances. On the other hand, there were only forty-three senators inclined to support the treaty without reservations. Even if one added the fifteen mild reservationists to this number, the total was only fifty-eight. The inescapable conclusion was that a two-thirds majority could not be obtained without giving in to some amendments, more or less substantial. (Amendments are voted by a simple majority in the Senate.) Since the treaty was an international agreement, the executive, in accepting amendments, would have to reopen negotiations with the other powers. It remained to be seen if the Allies, after some soul searching, would not prefer some modifications of the treaty to its brutal rejection by the United States. It seems—theoretically—that Wilson could have envisaged this solution. By accepting without a fight the least harmful amendments, and by bargaining over the more serious ones to win over some of the strong reservationists, he could have assured himself a comfortable majority.

But from the beginning, Wilson's attitude was quite opposed to such a course. His personality, his attitude once he had taken a stand, would not tolerate any retreat or compromise. As formerly at Princeton, he was to prove his extreme stubbornness. He refused to consider even the possibility of amendment. He believed firmly that the large majority of public opinion favored the New Diplomacy and the League of Nations. He did not want to discard the treaty which he had achieved so painfully with the Allies, a treaty which he considered satisfactory. The only way, therefore, was to make the senators give in. Wilson thought that a sufficient number of them would rally to a favorable vote in the end—either by being carried by popular enthusiasm or through awareness of the immense international difficulties a defeat of the treaty would involve. "The Senate will ratify the treaty," he said, at a press conference in July. This was proof of his great optimism. Perhaps he counted too much on popular pressure. It must be recalled that one third of the senate is re-elected every two years. One third, elected in 1918, would be in office until 1925. Only one third had to face the voters in 1920. Was this enough to make concern with re-election affect the vote? As early as July, the French ambassador, Jusserand, was disturbed about this and let the President know that certain amendments would be acceptable to the Allies. Wilson's reply was, "*Monsieur* Ambassador, I will not consent to a single concession. The Senate must take its medicine." [1]

Henry Cabot Lodge was to take advantage of this stubbornness. Lodge had several reasons to prevent "Wilson's treaty" from passing in its original form. As Republican leader of the Senate he opposed anything that would appear to be a great Democratic success. Furthermore, he disliked Wilson—a mutual feeling. A member of the Foreign Relations Committee for twenty-three years, he had had a much longer political career than Wilson. Armed with a doctorate in history from Harvard, rich, cultivated, widely traveled, up to the time of the spectacular arrival of Wilson on the scene he was the only American politician with a reputation as a specialist in political science. Since then, Wilson had eclipsed him and he was upset by this. For Wilson, Lodge was a successful lawyer and the great man remembered with bitterness his own unsuccessful attempt to practice law. Finally, mere jealousy had degenerated into a feud between them when, in 1916, Lodge had accused Wilson of keeping secret certain details of the *Lusitania* affair and the President had called him a liar. Naturally Lodge always denied that he had opposed the treaty out of personal bitterness. "My opposition to Mr. Wilson over the war and the League was entirely in the realm of public affairs." [2] One cannot help feeling, however, that the enmity of these two men contributed not a little to the further complications of a situation already insoluble in itself.

Henry Cabot Lodge was not opposed to the idea of a League of Nations as such. Several times during the war he had defended the idea, notably in March and June, 1915.

In differences between nations which go beyond the limited range of arbitrable questions peace can only be maintained by putting behind it the force of united nations determined to uphold it and to prevent war. No one is more conscious than I of the enormous difficulties which beset such a solution or such a scheme, but I am certain that it is in this direction alone that we can find hope for the maintenance of the world's peace.[3]

But Theodore Roosevelt had convinced him: (1) that under no circumstances should the United States agree to police the Old World; and (2) that the United States should not abandon the Monroe Doctrine, that is, to allow non-American nations to interfere in the Western Hemisphere in the name of an international organization.

Lodge launched his campaign in late April 1919. For this purpose he met with Borah and told him, "personally I could not accept the League as it stood under any circumstances, but that I thought the interest and safety of the United States might be so protected by amendments or reservations that a large majority of the Republicans could vote for it." [4] Borah declared that for his part, he would vote against the treaty in any case, but he understood that one could not hope to defeat it by voting "no" so he would accept all the amendments and reservations Lodge proposed.

Lodge's great strength lay in the Committee on Foreign Relations of the Senate, of which he was chairman. Given the coming debate on the Treaty of Versailles, membership in this committee had unusual importance. There were ten Republicans and seven Democrats, and only one of the Republicans, McCumber of North Dakota, generally voted with the Democrats. Six Republicans, including Lodge, Borah, and Knox, and five Democrats had been members of the committee for some time. Harding and Johnson were among the new members. In all there were four irreconcilables out of seventeen members—a much greater proportion than in the Senate as a whole.

The committee received the treaty on July 10 and had it published by the fourteenth. Lodge wanted to gain time, sensing that public opinion, which had seemed very favorable, was crumbling bit by bit. His first maneuver was to read all 268 pages of the treaty aloud to the committee, most of whose members were not present because they resented this tiring and futile operation. This went on for two weeks. On July 26 the guarantee treaty with France, which Wilson had not yet sent to the Senate, was submitted. No one has ever been able to explain this delay. No doubt Wilson was embarrassed by the contradiction between the idea of a universal League of Nations and this specific alliance. On July 31 the hearings, in which any American citizen may take part, began.[5] Several outstanding men testified, including Secretary of State Lansing, Bernard Baruch, Daniel H. Miller, speaking as experts. In general, Lodge called on Anglophobes, the Irish, and representatives of national groups, like La Guardia, future mayor of New York City. Lansing provided grist to the mill of the enemies of the treaty when he complained discreetly of having been ignored by the President. He gave the committee to understand that the President had not had to sacrifice China's rights in Shantung. The committee gradually prepared its chief weapon for the fight: a report voted on September 10 and published September 12, whose text will be analyzed below.

In July and August Wilson was trying to win over Republican senators by direct means—especially the mild reservationists. He invited about twenty of them to the White House, including McCumber, Harding, and Kellogg, and spent about an hour talking to each. Almost all of them said that the Senate would not approve the treaty without reservations.

On August 19, at the request of Lodge, Wilson had lunch with the committee. Of the seventeen members the Democrat Shields was the only one not attending. Wilson defended his treaty inch by inch and would agree only to "separate" reservations to be voted independently of the text of the treaty, so as not to have to reopen negotiations with Germany and the Allies.[6] He also defended the guarantee treaty with France. He came up against the general lack of understanding of the Republican members of the committee. The situation grew worse. Was not an appeal to public opinion his only recourse? This was the object of the President's important decision at the end of August—to undertake a grand tour around the country.

Wilson's Campaign and Illness

What picture can we get of this American public opinion which Wilson wanted to use as a political instrument? The historian Thomas Bailey has made a detailed analysis which can only be taken as approximate because of the lack of public opinion polls at the time. On April 5, 1919, the *Literary Digest* had published the results of an inquiry into the stand of 1377 daily newspapers. The great majority were favorable to the League. This was especially true in the South, from Texas to the Atlantic, and from Virginia and Delaware to Florida. Everywhere else opinion was more mixed, but in July it really seemed that the people generally did favor the League. Innumerable clergymen, philanthropists, and idealists saw in it the means finally to achieve that universal peace which would satisfy all their longings. From another quarter, the great banking interests, anxious to have the situation clarified in order to settle the question of repayment of war debts, were urging prompt ratification.

But one can also discern organized groups which were resolutely opposed to the treaty. First, national groups: 7,000,000 German-Americans, generally Republican, deplored the fact that the treaty had been dictated to Germany. The agitator George Viereck—who would be imprisoned as a Nazi sympathizer during World War II—organized meetings against what he called the "League of Damnation." The Irish-Americans, influenced by troubles in Ireland in 1919, were irreconcilables, though generally Democrats. Their leader was Senator

Walsh of Massachusetts. The Irish nationalist leader Eamon de Valera spent the spring and summer of 1919 in America and reproached Wilson in his speeches for not supporting self-determination for Ireland at the conference in Paris. Some Italo-Americans, among them La Guardia, held it against Wilson that he had not accepted the Italian claims on Fiume and Dalmatia.

In addition to national groups were ideological ones. It is striking that many irreconcilable senators were former progressives, liberals —Johnson, Borah, and La Follette, for example. Some liberal publications, like the *New Republic* and the *Nation,* were hostile to this "victor's peace." They were much influenced by John Maynard Keynes, the argument of whose book, *The Economic Consequences of the Peace*—not published until November—was already known to the British and American press.

The so-called "nationalists" constituted another ideological group. They were always ready to brandish the advice of Washington and Jefferson to avoid permanent alliances and any obligations outside the American continent. To this was added the notion that the European nations were ungrateful; not satisfied with having called American boys to Europe, they constantly demanded more food, more money. They seemed little inclined to pay their debts and did not hesitate to criticize the United States in their newspapers. Since November 1918 many American journalists and experts had constantly expressed indignation at the hostile attitude of the press in France.

We must add to these groups those whom Bailey calls "professional British haters": the Chicago *Daily Tribune,* and especially William Randolph Hearst, owner of a powerful chain of newspapers with a circulation of 3,000,000, who was hostile to British and Japanese imperialism and to the British origins of the Covenant. They spent their time attacking a League in which the British Empire, including four Dominions and India, was to be given six votes.

It would be useful to be able to measure the intensity of public sentiment in favor of the League. Unfortunately, one can only make estimates on this point. It is certain that the large majority of citizens had not read the text of the treaty. It is equally certain that opinion was more occupied with direct and disturbing concerns such as the demobilization of 4,000,000 men, and difficulties involved in industrial reconversion, in the return of the soldiers, and in an economic crisis which came about in 1919. Great strikes occurred in the steel mills in Gary, among the miners, and even in the Boston police department. People were worried about the "Bolshevik menace." The race problem produced riots in Washington, Chicago, and Omaha. The problems of life at the moment interested the public more than international politics. As Bailey says, "People were more interested in the National League than in the League of Nations." It was in the summer of 1919 that Jack Dempsey first became heavyweight champion of the world by defeating Jess Willard. Could Wilson compete with these down-to-earth attractions and create the enthusiastic movement on which he was counting?

He believed he could and as he was by nature a fighter he decided to take up the challenge. He was running a colossal risk from the standpoint of his health and he knew it. He had always had a frail constitution. He suffered from gastritis and from neuritis in his arm. For long stretches he consumed only raw eggs and orange juice. In April 1919, in Paris, he had had an attack of influenza and in July he suffered from dysentery. He had constant headaches. In short, his personal physician, Dr. Grayson, did not conceal from him that the proposed trip would be suicidal. Wilson was too set in his ideas not to accept the idea of sacrificing his life. His enemies have said that he had a "martyr complex," but it is wrong to make light of this form of courage. It is better to say, with Bailey, that this immense effort would not have been necessary twenty years later. At that time Wilson could have reached an audience ten or twenty times greater by radio, from his office in the White House, without risking his health. This dramatic gamble, which he was to lose, was to have incalculable results.

Wilson left Washington on September 3 in a special train, with an apartment for him, a car for the staff, a restaurant, and a car for newspapermen and photographers. The tour would not include New England, too Republican and too determinedly hostile to be persuaded, nor the South, too favorable to make it necessary. The decisive regions were the Middle West (avoiding the unassailable bastions of Chicago and Milwaukee) and the Far West, especially California, the home ground of the irreconcilable Hiram Johnson. The first speech, in Columbus, Ohio, was warmly applauded by a crowd of 4000 despite the rain—but Columbus was a city of 300,000 inhabitants! It was the same elsewhere, especially in Indianapolis, St. Louis, Kansas City,

Des Moines, Omaha, St. Paul, Minneapolis, and in the mountain states, especially Idaho, Borah's territory. From there the President went to the West Coast where he was triumphantly welcomed in Seattle. On September 17 and 18 he spoke in northern California, in San Francisco, where there were more Irish-Americans. The high point of the trip was in California, especially in San Diego, Los Angeles, and even Sacramento, Johnson's home town.

This gave Wilson the idea—at first not considered—of storming another enemy stronghold, Massachusetts, whose two senators were Lodge and the irreconcilable Walsh. But the President was exhausted, he was living on nerve. Despite the success of the return trip through Nevada, Utah, and Colorado, he felt that he could not continue. On September 29 in Pueblo, he gave a last speech with difficulty. It was imperative to cancel the other planned stops and to return at once to Washington, after a tour of 3000 miles and thirty-six speeches averaging an hour apiece, not counting short ones given from the rear platform of the train.

The President had adopted a moving tone in these speeches. He had referred to American graves in France and declared that the League of Nations would avoid a repetition of that. He had expressed his confidence that the treaty would be ratified. He had said that it was a great and just peace profoundly suited to American ideals. He had insisted on American obligations more than on the advantages of the treaty for the United States. He had highlighted the League and asked his audiences to read the Covenant, saying that it was "the greatest human document of all time." He had fought against prejudice and attempted to take his inspiration from the people who were listening to him.

But had he won? During the trip the disagreement between Wilson and Lansing in Paris was revealed. William Bullitt,[7] brilliant young diplomat who had been among the American experts at the peace conference, and had later been sent to Russia, was furious at having his opinion disregarded; he had resigned and had testified at the committee hearings. Bullitt had revealed the content of confidential notes on what had happened in Paris, especially the fact that Lansing had told him that most of the treaty was bad. Lansing was much embarrassed by this indiscretion and sent a telegram to Wilson on September 16 offering to make a public explanation. In despair at what he thought to be a blow below the belt, the President refused. Did not this matter, deliberately manipulated by Bullitt, cancel out his enormous effort by undermining public confidence? The disagreement between the President and the Secretary of State was not a myth. Lansing explained his side of the story in a book published in 1921.[8] The presence of Wilson in Paris was described as "one of the greatest mistakes of his career."[9] Disagreement on the League, on the mandate system, on the guarantee treaty to France, on concessions to Japan in Shantung, and on secret diplomacy were also revealed as points of friction.

Moreover, in Wilson's wake came irreconcilables McCormick, Borah, and Johnson, making speeches in the cities where the President had been to destroy the results he had achieved. Johnson, who aspired to the presidency, attracted much attention by asking his audiences whether American boys should take on "policing the world." Wilson returned sick after an effort which was more wearing than productive. His illness was to play a vital role in the history of the whole world.

At first it seemed that Wilson was only suffering from exhaustion. But on the fourth morning Mrs. Wilson found him in bed complaining of numbness in his left arm. Between her going to call Dr. Grayson and her return, the blow fell—the President was lying unconscious on the floor. He had had an attack which had paralyzed the whole left side of his body. It was difficult to lift him up. At his request the state of his health was at first kept secret, but complications followed. On October 17 a swelling of the prostate gland brought him very near death. Then the crisis passed and Wilson, still in bed, began slowly to get better. His mind and memory were clear, and he had his old intellectual energy, but the problem remained of how to carry on the fight in his enfeebled state.

The consequences of this crisis were incalculable. Mrs. Wilson and Dr. Grayson were the only people to see the President; even his private secretary Tumulty was excluded. This paralyzed the political life of the United States because the Constitution does not provide for such a situation. Among other things, bills not signed by the President automatically become law in ten days. He did not sign four on October 24, and on the twenty-seventh he vetoed the Volstead Act, which prohibited the manufacture and sale of alcoholic beverages. On October 30 he received for a few minutes the King of the Belgians, who was on an official visit to the United States. On November 17 he was taken into the White House garden in a wheelchair. The cabinet, meanwhile, met informally, with Lansing presiding, but it could do little other than continue existing policies. The Democratic party, whose Senate leader was now Hitchcock, was at a loss without its powerful chief.

Rumor had it that Wilson had lost his mind. On December 5 the Senate Committee on Foreign Relations sent two of its members to see the President on the pretext of discussing the Mexican affair, but really to see if there was any foundation to these rumors—which was emphatically not the case.

The paralysis of the executive power was not the most serious consequence of this tragedy. Much worse was Wilson's increased determination that the treaty should be approved without amendment. This hardened attitude was connected with the merciless screening which Mrs. Wilson, as a good wife but a poor politician, exercised in relation to her husband. The barrier which she put up against anything which might disturb the sick man has been compared to the great wall of China. She not only kept men from coming to talk to the President, she also stopped any bad news. If there seemed to be anything favorable, on the other hand, such as a rumor that the Senate would give in to Wilson's will, she told him at once. As a result Wilson, instead of negotiating or bargaining on the amendments, was more and more persuaded that it was a test of strength and that he would win if he did not weaken.

When the former chief of the British Foreign Office, Sir Edward Grey, was sent to the United States by his government to inform Wilson that England preferred an amended treaty to a defeat, he was not received at the White House. When Colonel House, who had returned from Europe in bad health, sent one of his friends, Colonel Bonsal, to negotiate with Lodge on a possible compromise in October, Lodge lent himself to the maneuver. A Lodge-Bonsal memorandum was drawn up which House wished to take to the White House in person. But he was not admitted and the document was not answered. We do not know if Wilson ever saw it. If he did, his silence must be attributed to his stubbornness. If he did not, it was because Mrs. Wilson deliberately prevented it. In this case, which is the more probable, Mrs. Wilson's responsibility is considerable. By her screening she had prevented the last possible compromise. Lodge, furious, decided then to wage outright war and to bargain no further. He drew near to the irreconcilables.

The Two Senate Votes

The general discussion in the Senate was supposed to be based on the report of the Committee on Foreign Relations voted by the nine Republicans on September 10. In addition to this majority report there were two others, one drawn up by six Democrats in favor of rapid approval without amendments or reservations, and another by the Republican senator McCumber, favoring the treaty with six small reservations.

Let us analyze in detail the majority report, which was essentially the work of Lodge. The text begins by attempting to justify delay. The discussion had gone on for only forty-five days, not much compared to the six-month conference in Paris. Besides, Wilson, in failing to send the text promptly to the Senate, and in postponing or refusing to divulge certain details, bore a good part of the responsibility for the delays. The majority report listed the proposed amendments and reservations. Amendments would involve a modification of the text of the treaty—thus new negotiations with the Allies; a reservation was an interpretation of the text by the United States which did not require modification. Even for amendments there should be no difficulty, according to the report, because the conference was still meeting in Paris and it would not be hard to recall the German delegates.

There were forty-five amendments but they applied to just four problems. Amendments 1 and 2 dealt with the six votes the British Empire was to have in the League—the United States should also have six votes. Also it should be understood that if any of the six voting members of the Empire were party to a dispute none of the other five should take part in the vote. Amendments 3 through 38 forbade all American representation on commissions created by the League to handle matters that did not concern the United States. Amendments 39 through 44 transferred the former German rights in Shantung, not to Japan, but to China. This inevitably reopened the whole question of Far Eastern policy.[10] Finally, Amendment 45 declared that the American delegate on the Reparations Commission should abstain from voting except on explicit orders from his government.

The reservations were four in number and all concerned the League of Nations. (1) The Covenant said that a member state could leave the League on condition that it had fulfilled all its international obligations. The committee report proposed that the United States should be the only judge—if it should decide to quit the League—of whether it had fulfilled the said obligations. (2) The United States should not be obliged by Article 10 to apply military sanctions or economic boycott to another state merely by a declaration of the Council of the League of Nations, but only by a vote of Congress. The same should hold in the case of the acceptance or refusal of a mandate. We see here the reaction of the legislative power against infringements by the executive necessary in wartime. (3) The League of Nations could not interfere in domestic matters of member states. The report declared that only the United States could make decisions about matters it considered domestic and therefore not under League jurisdiction. Examples of such affairs were immigration, customs, commerce, and coastal traffic. (4) The United States refused to allow the League of Nations the right to investigate or arbitrate in regions to which the Monroe Doctrine applied.

The report ended with an attack on the very idea of the "pact."

The Committee believe that the League as it stands will breed wars instead of securing peace. They also believe that the Covenant of the League demands sacrifices of American independence and sovereignty . . . The amendments and reservations alike are governed by a single purpose and that is to guard American rights and sovereignty . . . The other nations will take us on our own terms, for without us their League is a wreck and all their gains from a victorious peace are imperiled.[11]

This text is absolutely clear. The only territorial clause the United States was rejecting was that concerning Shantung. For the rest, the Committee was raising a barrier against everything which could create permanent obligations or which would risk breaching the absolute sovereignty of the United States, that is, against all the innovations which Wilson accepted with enthusiasm and which threatened the sacrosanct traditions of isolationism and the Monroe Doctrine.

Before voting on the treaty as a whole, the Senate had first to vote on amendments and reservations by a simple majority. The bloc of Wilsonian Democrats and the 12 mild reservationists, that is fifty-five senators out of ninety-six, permitted all the amendments to be defeated on the grounds that they would entail long negotiations with the Allies. Then Lodge, after the failure of his negotiations with Wilson through

House and Bonsal, decided to include all his points in a list of fourteen reservations. The document he prepared November 5 is known as the "Lodge Reservations." He hoped by this not only to have his point of view prevail, but also to re-establish the unity of the Republican party, split on the amendments. He succeeded completely. On November 7, by forty-eight votes to forty, Lodge's fourteen reservations were adopted with some modifications of detail. Forty-four Republicans and the four Democratic irreconcilables voted for them; thirty-nine Democrats and the Republican McCumber voted against. The fourteen reservations took up the points of the committee report exactly, with several adjustments. For example, regarding Shantung the United States would be satisfied not to recognize the Japanese power. On the question of six votes for the British Empire, the United States would not demand six votes also, but the United States would not recognize itself as bound by any decision of the League in which any member had more than one vote.

Wilson, in his sick room, rejected in anger all the reservations except for the one on the Monroe Doctrine. According to him, they "annulled" the treaty in its entirety, and especially the Covenant. It was a betrayal of the Allies and of the soldiers who had died in Europe. Badly informed, convinced that public opinion was overwhelmingly in favor of the League and that the Senate would give in, the President sent to the newspapers a letter in which he asked for a negative vote on the treaty, accompanied as it was by reservations, and he asked his friends, the Democratic senators, to vote against it in this form.

On the afternoon of November 19, 1919, the decisive vote was taken on the whole—that is the treaty and the fourteen reservations. There were thirty-nine ayes and fifty-five nays. Thirty-four Republicans and five Democrats voted in favor—the Republicans who followed Lodge, whether mild or strong reservationists, and some Democrats who, though favoring the treaty, preferred to see it ratified with reservations rather than rejected, and who had refused to follow Wilson's directions. All the Wilsonians and all the irreconcilables, Republicans or Democrats, voted against. Wilson had preferred rejection pure and simple to a modified treaty. A two-thirds vote was necessary but even a simple majority was far from achieved. This was a paradoxical vote: ratification had failed because of a coalition of Wilson's partisans and the irreconcilables. By a second vote, sixty-three to thirty, it was decided to re-examine the treaty. Was it possible to vote on the treaty without reservations? Lodge accepted this procedure to make clear the weakness of the President's stubborn position. This solution was rejected—with forty-one votes for accepting the treaty without reservations (Wilsonian Democrats) and fifty against (Republicans and irreconcilable Democrats).

The Senate adjourned until the new session which would begin on the first Tuesday in December. While Mrs. Wilson carefully conveyed the distressing news to her husband, Lodge visited his constituency in Massachusetts and found out that the public was anxious. The vote was being explained by party politics and the public wished the treaty to be re-examined. On the Democratic side further attempts were made to get Wilson to be more flexible. Herbert Hoover, Bernard Baruch, and Colonel House sent letters and telegrams to the President asking him to accept at least a part of Lodge's reservations, but the President remained resolute. On December 14 he declared publicly that he refused all compromise. He still believed that public opinion would force the Senate to accept the treaty. It must be noted that he continued to be protected by Mrs. Wilson and that he did not know how little interest the public was taking in the League of Nations.

In January, Senator Hitchcock, the Democratic leader, agreed with Lodge to hold a bipartisan conference of nine members who would try to reach an agreement on the reservations. This committee worked for two weeks. Of the fourteen reservations some were modified so that both parties could accept them, but they were deadlocked on Article 10 of the League and the matter of the six British votes. Wilson congratulated himself on this defeat and appealed to the country by proposing an unprecedented procedure—a referendum which would be in the form of new senatorial elections, with all present members having resigned. This had no chance of being accepted. In another message he proposed "to give to the next election the form of a great and solemn referendum." Thus, more and more he tried to set the country against the Senate instead of turning to compromise, as an increasing number of both Republicans and Democrats were doing.

Then in March the process of October and November was repeated. The Senate voted anew the Lodge reservations slightly modified. This time the majorities were larger, because many Democrats declined to follow Wilson. On March 18, in a surprise move, Demo-

cratic Senator Gerry of Rhode Island proposed a fifteenth reservation
—in favor of the independence of Ireland. This passed by 38 votes
to 36. This meant that the new vote would be on the whole package,
that is, the treaty, the fourteen reservations and the new reservation
on Ireland. The vote took place March 19, 1920. This time about
one half of the Democrats abandoned Wilson and voted for Lodge's
proposal—forty-nine (including twenty-one Democrats) voting for
and thirty-five against (twenty-three Wilsonian Democrats and the
irreconcilables). In contrast to the November vote, the Lodge proposal had a substantial majority, but was still seven votes short of
two-thirds. The treaty was therefore rejected. It was rejected because
twenty-three Democrats (almost all Southerners) had faithfully followed Wilson's orders. This time the rejection was final. It is to be
noted that the guarantee treaty with France was never even submitted
to Senate vote by the Committee on Foreign Relations.

The President's health had greatly improved and this made him
more pugnacious than ever. Under the pretext that Lansing had held
unofficial cabinet meetings during his illness, Wilson claimed that the
Secretary of State had overstepped his powers. He forced him to
resign and replaced him—to the general surprise—by a New York
lawyer, Bainbridge Colby, who was brilliant but inexperienced. When
Congress passed a joint resolution to make a separate peace with
Germany in May, Wilson vetoed it, saying that it would be a stain
on the honor of the United States. It was not until the next administration (Republican) that the state of war between the United States
and Germany was legally abolished.

The Democratic Defeat in the Elections of 1920

Wilson had now only one hope left: the elections of 1920. Could
he be a candidate himself? It would have been an innovation in American politics but constitutionally there was nothing to prevent it;
Attorney General A. Mitchell Palmer had declared so officially in
1919. In February of that year rumor had it that he would refuse, but
the White House denied the rumor. As early as January 1920, as we
have seen, Wilson declared that he considered the presidential elections a "great and solemn referendum" on the treaty.[12]

It appears certain that Wilson wanted very much to be elected to
a third term. He said nothing about it and we have no direct proof.

But his son-in-law, William G. McAdoo, who was a possible candidate, announced that he was withdrawing on June 18, six days after the nomination of Harding by the Republican convention and ten days before the opening of the Democratic convention in San Francisco. On the same day Louis Siebold published an interview with Wilson in the New York *World*. Without mentioning his candidacy, Wilson stressed his recovery and asked anew that the election be a referendum in favor of the League of Nations.

When the convention opened Wilson had still said nothing, but it was clear that though he still had many supporters among the people the party leaders would have no more of him. His illness had affected him a great deal. He had trouble following the discussion in the cabinet meetings; he could not dictate for longer than five minutes; he had lapses of memory; he was irritable and incapable of controlling his feelings.

Secretary of State Bainbridge Colby tried to have Wilson nominated by acclamation, but he failed and had to telegraph the President that the opposition was too strong. The most likely candidates were men of the second rank: McAdoo, Attorney General Palmer, Governor James M. Cox of Ohio. It had been hoped that a man of greater stature, Herbert Hoover, would be available, but he had let it be known that he was a Republican. The old Bryan, little interested in the League of Nations, had declared that the essential plank in the party platform was prohibition.

It took forty-four ballots before Cox was nominated. The only consolation for the outgoing administration was the nomination of Franklin Delano Roosevelt as vice president. Cox was set on supporting United States membership in the League but he was much too pale a figure to symbolize the great referendum desired by Wilson. His Republican opponent was a strong reservationist. In fact, the election did not turn on the problem of the League as Wilson had wished. Harding's campaign slogan—Back to Normalcy—seduced the public. Since the New Diplomacy had failed, why not return to the old ways which Wilson had seemed to condemn? Harding defeated Cox by 7,000,000 votes, an unprecedented margin. Wilson was irrevocably defeated.

This defeat has distorted historical judgment of Wilson. The prophetic importance of his actions has been forgotten and only his failure remembered. People have remembered the stubbornness of the final period—though related to his illness and to Mrs. Wilson's subsequent control—and forgotten the gifts of the Paris negotiator. Too many French historians have seen in Wilson only a dangerous dreamer whose idealism defeated the practical plans of Clemenceau. Too many American historians—like Bailey—have stressed the alleged naïveté of the President, always victimized by his Machiavellian partners, Lloyd George and Clemenceau. Keynes has drawn an exceptionally cruel portrait of Wilson—neither a philosopher nor a trail-blazer, but a narrow theologian, a "blind and deaf prophet." Wilson's great adversary, Henry Cabot Lodge, rejoiced afterwards that he had been "beaten" (it was the treaty with the Lodge reservations that had failed of ratification). Having ascertained the impotence of the League, Lodge said, Americans should rejoice that they had not joined.

Lodge's portrait of Wilson is consistently deformed by deep bitterness. How can one say that "the key to his actions should always be sought in the fact that he thought of all problems in terms of his own personal interest?" [13] Is this compatible with the sacrifice of his health? Lodge says "There are those still extant who speak of Mr. Wilson as a 'very great man.' An able man in certain ways, an ambitious man in all ways he certainly was; by no means a commonplace man. But 'very great men' are extremely rare. Mr. Wilson was not one of them." [14]

With hindsight one can think he was a great man, he who, ahead of his time, was to break the forms of a diplomacy which had led to the massacre of millions of men and who tried to create a new order. Compared with Lodge, who represents American complacency, faithfully and clearly, Wilson was one who believed in the humanitarian mission of the United States. Would not the face of the earth have been changed if that great country, instead of withdrawing into herself from 1920–1940, had taken the lead in that revolutionary institution—the "League of Wilson"?

Part Two

THE ERA OF NATIONALISM
1921–1933

Chapter VII

Hughes and the Postwar Problems

Isolationism or Nationalism

THE Republican tidal wave of November 1920 is to be explained by the expressed will of the people to "return to normalcy." As Thomas Bailey has shown, the election did not and could not turn on the League of Nations—the people had too little interest in it. They had a more pressing concern: how to resolve the immense problems left by the war. These problems included the effects of demobilization, the reconversion of certain industries, the recovery of European war debts, the reduction of the budget, and the continuation of social progress. The crusading spirit could not last indefinitely and the crusaders wanted to return to normal life. Wilson's mistake had been to think he could mobilize opinion in favor of his grand scheme, which seemed too far off, too Utopian, too incomprehensible, to receive more than passive acceptance. Arthur S. Link has passed a stern judgment on the new era: "The 1920's were a period made almost unique by an extraordinary reaction against idealism and reform . . . The surging tides of nationalism and mass hatreds generated by World War I continued to engulf the land and were manifested, among other things, by the fear of communism, the suppression of civil liberties, the revival of nativism and anti-Semitism . . . and the triumph of racism and prejudice in immigration legislation."[1] History never goes backward; if the "normal" meant the past, Americans were under an illusion in thinking it could be recalled. The postwar United States was no longer, and could not be, the United States of 1913.

Let us pause over this phenomenon and observe first the most profound elements of change, which are related, directly or indirectly, to the future foreign policy of the country.

Between 1910 and 1920 the population had risen from 91,972,000 to 105,711,000 inhabitants,[2] an increase of more than 13,000,000.[3] Although more than 10,000,000 are accounted for by an increase in births over deaths, immigration was also a factor. Only in 1918 and 1919 was there any notable decrease in immigration. In 1921 the number by which arrivals exceeded departures reached a new high, 557,000, about the same as in 1911 and 1912. As in the preceding decade, though a bit less clearly, people of Southern and Eastern Europe constituted the majority, 58.9 percent. The "old immigration" had decreased even more and provided only 17.4 percent. A new phenomenon was the arrival of 12.9 percent of the total number from Canada and Newfoundland and 3.8 percent from Mexico.[4]

At the very time when immigration—only slowed down by the war —was reaching a new high, came the economic crisis of 1920–1921. In 1921 alone 20,000 business failures were registered and 4,750,000 workers lost their jobs.[5] In these circumstances it is understandable that unlimited access to the Melting Pot came to be viewed as a potential danger, and that the unions took the lead in demanding measures to restrict immigration. By the middle of 1921, to be sure, prosperity was restored, but the seed of restriction had been planted and in 1921 the first law establishing quotas had been passed, limiting the annual total of immigrants from a given country to 3 percent of the number of foreign-born of such nationality living in the United States in 1910. This quantitative restriction was also qualitative in that it favored the "old immigration" at the expense of Mediterraneans and Slavs. The Johnson Act of 1924 reduced the percentage to 2 percent and took 1891 instead of 1910 as the year to be used as the criterion. This would reduce the number of newcomers of the "new immigration," which were deemed undesirable, to 21,847 per year. This is certainly far from a "return to normalcy."

The increase in population was not the most important change, however. Economic progress entailed even more profound transformations. The national wealth, estimated at 186.3 billion dollars in 1921, reached 320.8 billion in 1922.[6] The national income, 33 billion dollars in 1914, rose to 45 billion in 1916, to 61 billion in 1918, and to 72 billion in 1920—that is, it was more than doubled by the war. During the four years of the war the excess of exports over imports had reached 11 billion dollars.[7]

Another economic phenomenon related to the war and fraught with political consequences was the complete reversal of the balance of foreign investments. In 1914 whereas Europeans had investments in the United States of between 4.5 and 5 billion dollars, Americans had invested only 2.5 billion abroad. But since the war foreign capital in the United States had been greatly reduced and, on the other hand, American investments abroad had greatly increased—reaching to 3.9 billion by 1920, according to Ingall. The Department of Commerce estimates are much higher: 9 billion dollars in 1924, of which 4 billion were in Latin America, 2.5 billion in Canada and Newfoundland, and 1.9 billion in Europe.[8] The total figure by the end of 1927 was between 11.5 and 13.5 billion dollars, as compared with 3.7 billion dollars of foreign investments in the United States.[9] A country having such huge investments abroad would certainly be influenced by that fact in developing its foreign policy.

In addition to investments—almost all private—economic concern with the rest of the world had another and more complicated aspect. The war debts of the Entente had to be dealt with. This was no longer a private question causing certain pressure groups to try to influence the State Department, but a national problem. Counting loans properly so called made before and after the Armistice, the furnishing of arms, and aid to civilian populations, the debt owed to America was enormous—10.3 billion dollars in 1929. The principal debtor nations were Great Britain (4.3 billion), France (3.4 billion), and Italy (1.6 billion).[10]

The very size of these sums created a problem of which certain men in public office were very much aware. Senator Cummings of Iowa declared shortly after the United States entry into the war: "I am perfectly willing to give to any of the Allied Nations the money which they need to carry on our war, for it is now our war . . . [but] I do not want the United States to become the bond creditor of Great Britain or of France or of Russia or of Italy: I do not want to enter the entangling alliance which the possession of these evidences of indebtedness will inevitably create." [11]

Under these conditions what does "back to normalcy" mean? Does it mean to behave like a good shopkeeper as in the past, and to demand repayment? But in that case, as Senator Cummings pointed out, non-entanglement is no longer possible. The United States could no longer remain faithful to the tradition in George Washington's Farewell Address. As it appeared that the United States would indeed demand repayment—by 1919 it was established government policy and it was not to be changed—there could be no return to normalcy. A policy of repayment was to be launched, and it remained a permanent source of tension and irritation. The war debts blocked isolationism. Unilateral repudiation, if it occurred, risked the danger of plunging the United States into extreme isolationism.

This is the essence of the problem. Did the return to normalcy mean that from Wilsonian internationalism the United States would pass to "splendid isolation" as in the decades following the Civil War? This situation is fundamental and must be seriously considered.

What is isolationism? It is hard to give a precise definition of something which is more an emotion than a concept, but one can show its general configuration by referring to some of its simpler elements. Isolationism is first and foremost nonentanglement: the United States should not enter into any direct alliance nor participate in any political system like the League of Nations. The associations of which it was a member, like the Pan-American Union, were in principle or in practice nonpolitical. The refusal to enter into specific alliances was a policy followed by Wilson himself, he who wished to be an Associate and not an Ally of the Entente. It would take another world war to make the United States abandon this stand. The refusal to take part in an organization like the League of Nations under the pretext that it infringed American national sovereignty was the rejection of Wilsonian internationalism.

Isolationism, in the second place, is reluctance to have any relations with foreign nations. As this is impossible in a world growing ever more interdependent, isolationism became a systematic effort to limit such relations. The laws of 1921 and 1924 restricting immigration are clearly isolationist, for instance. The same is true of protectionist measures relative to tariffs, and of prohibition. Alcoholic beverages were regarded as foreign in their influence; many were in fact imported.

Isolationism, finally, is a conviction of moral superiority. If we feel ourselves better than others, others have nothing to give us and we are not disposed to accept their teaching. This is complacency, a widespread sentiment in the United States, which we discussed in the first chapter.

By analyzing isolationism in this way, we can see that it is very difficult, at least in the Republican era, to answer the question, "was the United States isolationist or not?" The question has nevertheless been debated with vigor. Professor William Appleman Williams, then at the University of Oregon, started the debate in 1954 in an article in *Science and Society*,[12] a magazine of Marxist tendency. Williams notes that the majority of historians of this period, beginning with Arthur M. Schlesinger, Dexter Perkins, and Samuel Flagg Bemis, have called the Republican era an isolationist period. In a detailed analysis, he shows that most of them do not hesitate to equate isolationism with expansionist tendencies. As he seems to follow the second definition made above—isolationism is reluctance to have relations with foreign countries—he concludes that the idea of isolationism in the 1920's is simply a legend. But if we are right in thinking that isolationism is a complex, emotional attitude the only problem is to find out if the politicians of the 1920's thought they were isolationists. The texts show that they did not. Harding, as we shall see, declared himself opposed to isolationism but firmly nationalist. Hughes certainly did not consider himself an isolationist. Perry Belmont, in his book, *National Isolation: An Illusion*, published in 1925, reflects this attitude exactly: "This book was written to prove the proposition that the United States has never been isolated and that there has never been any break in the interdependence of the United States and Europe." [13]

The key word which determined the choosing of sides, the cleavage in American politics at this time, is the word "nationalist." People were nationalists if they opposed the entry of the United States into the League; they were internationalists if they favored it.

One cannot determine whether this generation was or was not isolationist without reference to a definition, which, as we have seen, can only be arbitrary and hypothetical. What is certain is that most of the Republicans in power, despite individual variations, were nationalists. They believed in restricting immigration, and in "keeping a free hand" in relation to the League of Nations, but they took an active part in discussions on war debts, German reparations, Japanese ambitions, the continuation of dollar diplomacy, investments abroad, renewed intervention in Latin America, and so forth. One might perhaps say that this nationalism is one aspect of isolationism—the aspect of complacency, the feeling of moral superiority, well meaning, to be sure, but slightly irritating to foreigners. As Philip Dexter and John Hunter Sedgwick put it in 1928, "Americans would do better to stop preaching to Europe and attempting to teach the rest of the world about our moral superiority, our magnificent ideas, and the excellence of our ways of solving human problems. British and French lack of friendliness to us is more the result of our superior attitude than of our [financial] exactions. If we are superior, let us keep it to ourselves instead of proclaiming it to the entire world." [14]

Finally, the Republican era was essentially empirical in relation to foreign policy. The emphasis was on resolving the problems of the present. There was nothing comparable to Wilson's thinking—no coherent system of thought or doctrine. The return to normalcy was the return to the absence of doctrine. It is appropriate to mediocre statesmen like President Harding. It is appropriate also for the man who left his mark, who dominated the first four of these twelve years, Secretary of State Hughes.

The Leaders: Hughes, Harding, Coolidge

The new President of the United States, Warren G. Harding, presented an astonishing contrast to his predecessor. As little a theorist or doctrinaire as can be imagined, he was first of all a politician. Harding was born in Blooming Grove, Ohio, on November 2, 1865. From the age of seventeen he had concerned himself with politics. He was, successively, state senator (1898) and lieutenant governor of Ohio under Governor Myron T. Herrick, future ambassador to France. He was defeated in the gubernatorial race of 1910 but was elected to the United States Senate in 1914, and his influence in Ohio continued to grow. In 1920 the Republican convention had to choose between him, Senator Hiram Johnson of California, Governor Lowden of Illinois, General Leonard Wood, former chief of staff, Nicholas Murray Butler, president of Columbia University, and others. None of them was a man of stature and none very well known to the American people as a whole. On the first ballot Harding had only 65 votes. (There were 984 delegates.) Gradually it became evident that, as a result of political bargains, Harding would be in first place after Lowden and Wood, the leading contenders. The convention delegates, after numerous ballots, abandoned both the leading rivals and nominated Harding.

The Democratic candidate, Cox, was also from Ohio, in fact governor of the state. Harding was almost unknown, but the American people wanted to go back to normalcy, a definite reaction against Wilson's disturbing innovations. Accordingly they voted Republican by an enormous majority, with secret satisfaction at electing an average man—"an American like any other." Harding received 16,152,000 votes to Cox's 9,147,353.

Compared with Wilson's speeches, Harding's, one must admit, are mediocre. His thought is couched in vague and superficial formulas. He claimed to be a nationalist. In his speech on January 10, 1920, after having declared that he did not stand for a policy of isolation, he added:

> But I have confidence in our America that requires no council of foreign powers to point the way to American duty . . .
> Call it the selfishness of nationality if you will, I think it an inspiration to patriotic devotion—
> To safeguard American first . . .
> To think of America first,
> To exalt America first.[15]

America First—this slogan embodies isolationist sentiment. It expresses the profound desire of a whole people, tired of civilizing missions and firmly resolved to go on no more crusades, to sacrifice no longer its own interests to those of humanity. To the ardent prophet of the New Diplomacy there had succeeded a Candide who invited Americans to cultivate their own gardens. Americans were more than ready to listen. In his acceptance speech of July 22, 1920, Harding set forth his platform, which included cooperation with industry, a building program for railroads and highways, some changes of policy toward the treasury and agriculture, and protective tariffs. As for foreign policy, it was very simple: to preserve American independence while maintaining friendly cooperation with all nations, to restore peace with Germany (since the Treaty of Versailles had not been ratified), and support "world justice." As for armaments, "I believe in a large Navy . . . I believe in a small Army, but the best in the world." The only really interesting point was: "I believe in establishing standards for immigration, which are concerned with the future citizenship of the Republic, not with mere man-power in industry." [16]

Chance and the necessity of American politics decreed that this mediocrity had as Secretary of State a man of quite different stature, Charles Evans Hughes.

Charles Evans Hughes was born on April 11, 1862, in Glens Falls, New York. His father was a Baptist minister who had emigrated to the United States from England in 1855 in accordance with what he thought was a providential call. He was an ardent preacher; his only son's deeply religious spirit reflects this influence. Charles was of delicate health and did his early studies at home, under his mother's direction. He entered Madison University (now Colgate) very young, and in two years made a brilliant record in languages—Greek, Latin, and French. Then he transferred to Brown University. In the relatively free and lively atmosphere there he gave up the idea of the ministry and chose the law as his profession. Perkins says,

> Hughes had reasons for this strength and self-confidence. He had superb intellectual equipment. At school he was always near the top of the class. At college he was graduated with high distinction. His memory was almost photographic, and his capacity for rapid reasoning phenomenal. In later life he could come very near to repeating *verbatim* a speech of substantial length which he had dictated to his stenographer . . . To these qualities he joined prodigious industry.[17]

Intelligent, even brilliant, endowed with an attractive personality and unquestioned moral integrity, he had everything required for a spectacular career.

After two years at Columbia Law School, Hughes passed the New York Bar examination in June 1884 with very high marks. He entered a law firm and began to earn a substantial living. In 1888 he married the daughter of the senior partner of the firm, Antoinette Carter. From 1891 to 1893 he left his practice to teach law at Cornell University. Why did he leave the profession in which he was so successful? In part because of nervous tension and poor health resulting from overwork, but also because all his life he held it as a fixed principle that a man worthy of the name should be able to change his profession if he felt his calling lay elsewhere. Cornell was a place to relax. His father-in-law was furious, especially as it was necessary for him to help finance the young couple, and Hughes resigned himself to returning to the firm. This was a major step in his career, because it was as a judge that Hughes was to shine and a successful practising lawyer is more likely to reach the bench than a college professor. His success as a lawyer helped to make Hughes one of the leading political figures in the country. His ability and his great reputation for integrity caused him to be appointed to a commission investigating the cost of gas and electricity in New York in 1904 and 1905 and then to another commission on insurance. These activities gave him national standing and brought him to the attention of Theodore Roosevelt.

In 1906 Hughes became the Republican nominee for governor of

New York. His Democratic opponent was none other than William Randolph Hearst. The campaign was brilliant and eventful. To the general surprise, the serious lawyer showed that he had the gift of pleasing crowds, of being entertaining, and Hearst could not hold his own with Hughes's lively, quick mind. Hughes was elected by 749,000 votes to 691,000 for Hearst, who had spent $500,000 of his personal fortune on the campaign. It was one of the biggest defeats of Hearst's extraordinary career.

Like Wilson in New Jersey two years later, Hughes had appeal because of his consistent hostility to the party bosses, his fight against the trusts, his democratic and progressive way of thinking. In his book *Conditions of Progress in Democratic Government*, he says "Under certain forms of government stability has been maintained by force, exercised for the benefit of a privileged minority . . . in a democracy stability depends on the rule of reason." The people must therefore have "the truth, the whole truth and nothing but the truth." [18] Hughes was a determined optimist, like Wilson, whom he resembles in more ways than one.

In 1907, when he was forty-five years old, he was considered the best qualified Republican candidate for the presidential nomination in 1908. Roosevelt made the mistake of supporting Taft's candidacy instead. If Hughes had been the Republican candidate in 1908 and had been elected, as Taft was, there is little doubt that there would not have been a split between Republicans and Progressives in 1912. In fact, Hughes had the support of both wings of the party: the conservatives admired his moderation, the progressives his desire for reform. In 1908 he was elected not to the presidency, but to a second term as governor of New York. He was a bit tired of politics and had planned to retire from public life in 1910. In April of that year, however, Taft appointed him to the Supreme Court. Hughes accepted without hesitation, although the salary was only $14,500 a year, and if he had returned to the bar he would have earned $100,000 or more. But did not this post offer the means to work toward the perfection of American democracy? This was the ambition of his life. The Senate confirmed his appointment unanimously on May 2, 1910. There was talk of making him Chief Justice that autumn, but Taft decided against it. If Hughes had been Chief Justice he would certainly not have run for the presidency in 1916 nor would he have been Secretary of State in 1921.

Hughes and Wilson had great respect for each other, but politics made them rivals for the presidency in 1916. Hughes was chosen by the Republican convention because he was really the only possible candidate among the party leaders. Taft had been defeated in 1912; Roosevelt and Elihu Root were the founders and leaders of the progressive schism.

Hughes did not wish to take such a responsibility. "I am entirely out of politics," he wrote on February 9, 1916.[19] He made no campaign to be elected at the convention in Chicago, but he was leading on the first ballot, and on the third he was nominated. He accepted because he thought it his duty and he resigned his seat on the Court. In his acceptance speech he said, "I did not want the nomination. I would rather have remained on the Court. But in this critical period of our national history, I recognize that it is your right to call upon me and it is my absolute duty to respond to your call." [20]

The campaign of 1916 is not one of the most interesting in American history. Hughes was a man of outstanding intelligence and of proven character, but he was not, says Perkins, a political organizer. He did not have the gift of surrounding himself with able advisers; he did not know how to handle the press; he wasted much time speaking in small towns. Above all his campaign was necessarily negative, critical of the policy of Wilson, more as to methods than as to goals, a subtlety the public did not grasp very well. Finally, Theodore Roosevelt, fervent advocate of United States entry into the war, a hateful idea to the majority, spent his time noisily undermining Hughes. Hughes favored a League of Nations: "No national isolation is possible in the world of the 20th century. If at the end of the present war the nations are ready to take steps in the common interest to assure justice among nations, we cannot fail to accept our international duty." [21]

The issue which excited the voters was the war. Like Wilson, Hughes favored the increase of military forces. He could only attack Wilson on the technical aspects and methods of rearmament. Here again the difference between the two platforms was a little too subtle for the public. The Democrats accused Hughes of secret understandings with the German-Americans. Their great theme, was "He kept us out of war," and that the choice was between "Wilson with peace and honor or Hughes with Roosevelt and war." Hughes responded that if the Republicans had been in power, "The *Lusitania* would never have been sunk."

The election was very close; the Republicans were strong throughout the country and had only been defeated in 1912 because of the split in the party. For a few hours it was thought that Hughes was the victor. But Wilson won with 9,129,606 popular votes and 277 electoral votes to 8,538,221 popular votes and 254 electoral votes for Hughes. Hughes accepted his defeat philosophically and retired to his law practice.

Wilson has often been reproached for not having included a prominent Republican in his delegation in Paris. Hughes would have been a good choice—was he not an advocate of the League? During the great debate, Hughes took the side of the mild reservationists and supported the amendments—especially that concerning Article 10. As a private citizen, of course, he took only a small part in the battle. At the Republican convention in Chicago in 1920 the party turned away from him to Harding. Hughes campaigned for Harding while also fighting for United States membership in the League. It appears that he was coauthor with Elihu Root of the appeal which thirty-one Republican leaders published in favor of the League on October 15, 1920.

Harding was aware of his inexperience, and on December 10, 1920, he called on Hughes for advice. Hughes thought the newly elected President was simply calling on him as a judge, seeking consultation. To his great surprise, Harding offered him the post of Secretary of State. Hughes accepted without hesitation. "I am sure," Harding said to him, "that the country will be pleased and will greet your return to public service in this capacity with pleasure." The advantage of this combination, in addition to Hughes's ability, was that he was capable of resisting the obvious ambitions of Republican senators who—intoxicated by their double victory over Wilson and the Democrats—were planning to have the Senate take over the direction of foreign policy. George Washington had had to deal with this pretension as early as 1793; Hughes was to deal with it in his turn. As Harding was content to leave his Secretary of State the entire responsibility for foreign policy, it was Hughes who would dominate American diplomacy. Almost all American historians agree that he is among the greatest secretaries of state.

When Harding died, on August 2, 1923, he was succeeded by his Vice President, Calvin Coolidge. Harding's last months were darkened by a series of scandals in his administration. With the exception of some cabinet members, especially Hughes and Hoover, the executive branch consisted of a group of professional politicians, some of dubious character. Harding could not say No. Gambling and, despite prohibition, alcohol were casually tolerated on the second floor of the White House. The actions of certain cabinet members were quite frankly dishonest. Most compromised was the Secretary of the Interior, former senator Albert B. Fall, who, burdened with debts, took advantage of his office to yield to the oil interests rich concessions belonging to the United States Navy in exchange for a "loan" of $100,000.

Calvin Coolidge was just the man to send a purifying current of fresh air over these evil-smelling swamps. Coolidge was a Vermonter, a real Yankee, whose family had arrived in the seventeenth century. His grandfather had been a farmer; his father a shopkeeper in Plymouth, the small town where the future President was born on July 4, 1872.

At Amherst College he was a serious and hard-working student, though very reserved and for the most part without charm and personal warmth. These qualities were always lacking in this worthy, but cold and careful man. Lacking in "magnetism," says his principal biographer,[22] he was timid and a bit standoffish.

Coolidge began to practice law in 1895 in Northampton, Massachusetts. Attracted to politics, he had become a member of the Republican committee of the town by 1897; in 1906 he was elected to the Massachusetts legislature. He probably would never have gone any further without the support of a Boston politician, Frank Stearns, who discerned his hidden potentiality. With Stearns's help, Coolidge was elected lieutenant governor of Massachusetts in 1916 and was reelected in 1918. When Governor McCall became a candidate for the Senate, Coolidge took his place. "I thought I had reached the summit," he wrote, "and I was entirely satisfied to end my public career as Governor of Massachusetts."[23] The Republican convention of 1920, which had nominated Harding, was dominated by a group of senators. To offset this monopoly the party delegates nominated Coolidge as vice president, a bit in spite of himself. Although he was not a national figure, he was known for his handling of the Boston police strike in

1920. The death of Harding took him by surprise when he was visiting his father in Vermont. He took the oath of office at once and went to Washington.

When this modest and retiring man became President it could be said that his inexperience in international affairs was total, and that he was little interested in them. In his autobiography he mentions the problems he considered urgent—there is not a word about foreign policy. As different as he was from the free-and-easy Harding, they had in common that the importance of foreign affairs escaped them both completely. As a result, he decided to keep Hughes, for as he said, "The most important rule for Presidential action consists in doing nothing that someone else can do for you," given that the other person is "competent." [24] Hughes more than filled this elementary requirement. Coolidge considered himself merely a good and faithful servant of the Constitution and the law, "an instrument in the hand of God." [25] He knew how to restore to the White House a dignity it had lost under Harding, and Hughes could have a free hand.

Relations between the President and the Secretary of State were good but cool. Could it have been otherwise? When Coolidge ran for re-election in 1924, Hughes campaigned vigorously for him against the Democratic candidate John W. Davis of New York, and the Progressive candidate La Follette. Coolidge won 15,718,789 popular votes and 379 electoral votes, as against 8,378,962 popular votes and 139 electoral votes for Davis, and 4,822,319 popular votes and 13 electoral votes for La Follette. But Coolidge showed little gratitude to Hughes, who had already decided to resign. He did so in January 1925 in order to make his resignation effective as of March 4. He noted with some bitterness that Coolidge accepted it without protest. Thus ended the "era of Hughes," for in matters which concern us, one cannot speak of an "era of Harding" or of an "era of Coolidge."

The United States, the League of Nations, and Europe

Not often does a statesman find such a situation as Hughes faced when he came to power. Since the framework of Wilson's construction had collapsed, Hughes had to start from the beginning. The Democratic President had certainly done nothing in his last year of the presidency to smooth the way for his successor. Since for him everything was subordinated to the League, he made no attempt to find another solution to the pressing problems of foreign policy. After the Senate vote in March 1920 correspondence between the United States and the League of Nations was conspicuously broken off on the American side and messages from the League remained unanswered. Wilson had vetoed Knox's proposal of a separate peace with Germany, and nothing had been done in relation to Japan, except for the withdrawal of American troops from Siberia and a protest when the Japanese occupied Sakhalin.

The few actions undertaken were rather negative. For example, when Congress passed the Jones Merchant Shipping Act—whose object was to improve the Merchant Marine—it asked the Executive to revise existing commercial treaties. Wilson and his Secretary of State, Bainbridge Colby, decided to ignore this injunction under the pretext that it was unconstitutional. In August 1920 the administration decided not to recognize the Soviet government. As Colby said, "With the rejection of the Treaty, the hope perished of our honorable entry into the League of Nations, which our leading statesmen, regardless of party, had advocated for a generation. From that moment we sank into the category of nations which mean well feebly." He adds that Wilson was neither bitter nor rebellious. He seldom mentioned the subject, saying only that it would take thirty years before "we return to the real basis of our security and of our international duty." Wilson awaited the "verdict of humanity." [26]

As a result everything had to be done over again. Hughes tackled the job with vigor. To help him he had three undersecretaries in succession: Henry P. Fletcher, who became ambassador to Belgium in 1922, William Phillips, and finally Joseph C. Grew, who had been secretary of the American delegation in Paris. The most urgent problem to be resolved was obviously that of peace with Germany and her allies. The continued legal state of war blocked the resumption of diplomatic relations and, above all, created serious uncertainty in Germany about what claims might be made by the United States.

The first solution Hughes tried was to get the Treaty of Versailles ratified without the paragraphs concerning the League of Nations. But on July 2, 1921, Congress passed a joint resolution—as it had done the year before—declaring the war with Germany at an end, reserving "the rights, privileges, indemnities, reparations and advantages" to which the United States government and citizens had a right.

This meant that the United States would have nothing to do with the Treaty of Versailles; the senators, victorious over Wilson, hated even its name. A new treaty must be drawn up. Hughes sounded out opinion and came to the conclusion that his solution was politically impractical. A treaty was required, however; a joint resolution of Congress was not binding on Germany. The Secretary of State then took up a more modest plan. He worked out a new text in which he incorporated the articles from the Treaty of Versailles that stipulated American rights and certain passages of the joint resolution. Such a treaty would give to the United States all the privileges of the signatories of the Treaty of Versailles without any of the obligations. Germany, wanting above everything to re-establish a normal situation, accepted it without hesitation. The treaty was signed in Berlin on August 25, 1921, and approved by the Senate in October. Similar treaties were signed with Austria (August 24) and with Hungary (August 29).

There remained the task of arranging for a commission to draw up in detail the American claims and demands. Senator Underwood proposed that this commission consist exclusively of Americans. Hughes fought this proposition effectively by winning over Senator Borah to his side. On August 10, 1922, he succeeded in gaining acceptance of a commission composed of Germans and Americans. Hughes, more faithful than Wilson himself to the Fourteen Points, ruled out of American claims the whole matter of military pensions, which reduced reparations to an insignificant figure.

A problem less urgent but more charged with emotion was the matter of the League of Nations. As we have seen, Hughes was a warm supporter of the League. During the election campaign of 1920 he had signed the declaration of thirty-one Republicans in favor of entry of the United States into the League with certain mild reservations. This solution was rendered impossible by Harding. Very sensitive to the influence of the irreconcilables, Harding rallied to their position in a message to Congress on April 2, 1921. "There will be no betrayal of the deliberate expression of the American people in the recent election . . . the League Covenant can have no sanction by us." [27] Let us note that the Secretary of Treasury, the multimillionaire Andrew Mellon, had contributed heavily to the propaganda campaign against the League. Hughes thought of resigning but decided against it. After all, he did not think American participation would insure world peace; he thought it rather a moral obligation. Was it not possible to find a solution which would assure effective cooperation while awaiting better days?

Such a solution could have been the establishment of a new league better adapted than Wilson's to American demands. It was obviously not possible to realize this project politically, so Hughes decided to make the best of the rejection of the Covenant by the Senate. The United States could not participate in any activity of the League on the political plane, but unofficial observers could be sent to all the organizations in Geneva that dealt with humanitarian problems— opium, public health, white slave trade, and so forth—or that dealt with any problem in which the United States had a direct interest. Instead of refusing to answer the League's messages, Hughes decided to resume the correspondence. The system was very flexible and enabled the United States to keep full freedom of action. When the Secretary-General of the League, Sir Eric Drummond, asked the United States in 1921 if it would join a convention on the sale of arms, Hughes refused, because that would have hindered the furnishing of American arms to various Latin American nations.

Though not a member of the League of Nations, perhaps the United States could join the World Court. Hughes was a determined defender of the Court. In this he was following a Republican tradition, that of Hay, Root, and Theodore Roosevelt. Root had been one of the authors of the statute for a permanent court of international justice approved by the League Assembly on December 13, 1920. Hughes succeeded in persuading Harding that America should join. On October 30, 1922, in a speech in Boston, the Secretary of State declared that he supported the Court and hoped that the American government could take part in the election of justices. There was an American already on the bench, John Bassett Moore. The difficulty lay in the fact that the Court depended on the League of Nations; it was the *League* Court not the *World* Court. This was enough to make it an emotional issue, so Hughes tried to free it from emotion. On February 24, 1923, Harding sent to the Senate a letter from Hughes setting forth conditions for American membership: (1) acceptance of the statute did not in any way imply that the United States was entering into official relations with the League of Nations; (2) the United States would take part as an equal in meetings of the Assembly and Council of the League of Nations which concerned the Court; (3) the financial responsibility of the United States would be fixed by Congress;

(4) the statute dealing with the Court could not be amended without the consent of the United States.

Would the Senate accept? The matter dragged on for three months in the Committee on Foreign Relations. Henry Cabot Lodge, chairman until his death in 1924, feared that the World Court would become a tribunal whose decisions would be binding. This was excluded by the statutes except for nations which had voluntarily accepted the clause making acceptance of decisions obligatory. Hughes desired to avoid any infringement, however slight, of the sacrosanct principle of nonentanglement. Hughes said: "If you are to treat participation in a permanent court of international justice as an entanglement foreign to our institutions, you must rewrite American history." [28] Even Judge Bassett Moore was skeptical of the effectiveness of the Court. He feared that it would be forced to multiply "advisory opinions." Finally, the Court still bore the stain of the original sin of being the Court of the League. Therefore the text which was passed, on January 26, 1926, after Hughes resigned, contained so many reservations that the members of the League of Nations refused to accept it.

But nonentanglement became a subject for passion only in relation to the League of Nations. Otherwise the United States could easily take part in European affairs. This can be proved by a study of the problems of reparations and war debts. Although the United States had strongly contradictory attitudes regarding these two matters, it can be said that they are logically as well as historically connected.

What was the major interest of the United States on the economic plane? It lay certainly in maintaining a large foreign commerce. Of course the 11 billion dollar excess of exports over imports in the war years could not be maintained in peacetime; the crisis of 1920–21 had shown the harsh effects—for the United States—of European recovery. But in the long run advantageous markets must be assured, especially in Europe, markets for goods first of all—whatever the importance of the domestic market—and then markets for investments. The businessmen's thinking, even if they had not read Hobson, was dominated by the importance of investments abroad and geared to the principles of Dollar Diplomacy. Europe must prosper for such markets to exist, however. It was easy enough to build up a market for American goods in Germany, where the United States was asking almost no reparations and where it was opposing German reparations to the Allies, which were considered "intolerable." By using its good offices, the United States intervened in favor of reducing the German burden. It might also have seemed logical to favor the victors, and therefore to pursue a comparable policy in relation to the war debts and those acquired since by the Allies. But in this case the United States was the principal creditor, and the old Wilsonian idea, according to which right and wrong between states was identical to right and wrong between individuals, reappeared with éclat. An individual has a moral obligation to pay his debts; the debtor nations, from the moral point of view, should do likewise.

Let us look first at the problem of reparations. In 1921 Germany had appealed to the United States to play the role of mediator in this matter. Hughes felt strongly about this: "The prosperity of the United States . . . depends largely upon the economic settlements which may be made in Europe." [29] In September 1922 Hughes informed the American ambassador in Paris, Myron T. Herrick, that he had a plan to create a committee of leading financiers which would prepare a report on Germany's ability to pay. The French ambassador, Jusserand, was informed of this plan on November 7. But Poincaré had already decided to occupy the Ruhr as a "productive guarantee" and he was not receptive to any suggestion whose inevitable consequence would be a reduction of German payments. Hughes made his plan public on December 29 in a speech which he considered a solemn announcement: "We should view with disfavor measures which instead of producing reparations would threaten disaster." [30] Hughes spoke in vain —Poincaré carried out the occupation of the Ruhr in January 1923.

A possible response to the occupation could be financial reprisals which would weaken the French franc. This was seriously discussed in the State Department during the summer, but Hughes preferred a more prudent attitude. He took advantage of the visit of Stanley Baldwin, Chancellor of the Exchequer, to Washington in January to organize a common Anglo-American "front" in favor of his plan of a commission of experts. This plan also had the support of President Coolidge. Belgium and Italy then gave their support. Poincaré—for reasons which do not concern us here—yielded on November 30, 1923. On that day the Reparations Commission, which included an unofficial observer from the United States, decided unanimously to create two committees of experts, one to deal with stabilizing the German currency and the other to study reparations from the standpoint of German ability to pay. On December 7 Hughes named

General Charles G. Dawes United States delegate to the Reparations Commission. The other delegate was Owen D. Young.

Dawes, elected chairman of the commission, has left an account of the discussions in Paris, which began on January 8, and ended on April 9 with the presentation of a report—the Dawes Plan.[31] The details do not concern us here. What is interesting, though, is the general attitude in the United States.

When the Dawes Plan was submitted to a conference in London, Hughes attended in person. He was not a member of an American delegation of course; there was no American delegation—that would have been entanglement and the United States must limit itself to "good offices." Hughes wanted the good offices to succeed, and he sought a pretext to attend the conferences. As president of the American Bar Association he decided to join the trip that organization was making to Europe. In London, the American ambassador, Kellogg, gave a dinner where Hughes could talk for two hours with Herriot, new Premier of France. It is not impossible that this conversation was instrumental in Hughes's decision to make his famous lightning trip to Paris where he convinced the French cabinet of the necessity to adopt the Dawes Plan. "I give in, I give in," Herriot is supposed to have said at the end of the talk.[32] Hughes went to Paris and Berlin with the same ends in mind. This was a spectacular success for diplomacy by unofficial participation.

Left to himself Hughes would no doubt have dealt with the problem of war debts in just as liberal a manner, but there was the Senate to deal with, and the Senate let no occasion go by without showing what little account it took of foreign opinions and feelings. The tragicomic example of prohibition shows this clearly.

The Eighteenth Amendment, forbidding the manufacture, transport, and sale of alcoholic beverages, had been passed by Congress in December 1917. Schlesinger points out that its passage is to be explained at least in part by the fact that the majority of breweries and distilleries in the United States belonged to German-Americans.[33] However that may be, the amendment went into effect on January 16, 1919. It forbade the transport of alcoholic beverages into American ports and even into American territorial waters. There was naturally a great deal of smuggling, so much that Congress, in 1922, passed a law authorizing American customs officials to search for and seize liquor on foreign ships even beyond the three-mile limit. This was a curious breach of international law. The right of search, which had been recognized with difficulty for the slave trade, became especially ridiculous when applied to alcohol and seemed offensive to Europeans. When some ships were actually seized Lord Curzon declared that the situation was "very serious." Hughes set himself to deal with these difficulties and in 1924 signed a treaty with Great Britain and six other countries which regulated the transport of alcohol. Here one can see that Congress pursued a policy of narrow nationalism. The affair throws light on the congressional attitude toward the war debts.

The Bolsheviks, as early as January 1918, had solemnly repudiated the debts of the former "capitalist" government of Russia, which included 192 million dollars owed to the United States. This was the original cause of the policy of nonrecognition. President Coolidge clearly stated the American position in his message to Congress on December 9, 1923: "Our government does not propose to enter into relations with a regime which refuses to recognize the sanctity of international obligations." [34]

There was certainly a basis for this position in principle, but did not practical considerations and self-interest require that the United States show a tolerance toward Russia comparable to the tolerance she was demanding for Germany? Such was the attitude of the Allies. Balfour declared on August 1, 1922, that England would renounce her share of reparations if all inter-Allied war debts were canceled. Poincaré put the matter a bit differently: he would not consider a settlement of war debts until Germany had paid reparations. The French position was, then, to establish a direct connection between war debts and reparations. On this matter Europeans generally invoked different moral principles from Americans: we made our contribution to the common cause in blood; the Americans, late arrivals on the battlefield and enriched by the war, have a duty to be generous.

Two moral concepts were in conflict on this point and therefore, once again, an emotional problem arose. Clemenceau came out of retirement to write a letter to President Coolidge in 1926, in which he said,

If nations were only business firms, bank notes would determine the fate of the world. You ask us to pay a debt incurred not in commerce, but in war, and you know as well as we do that our till is empty . . . Three mortal years we waited to hear America say "France is the frontier of freedom." Three years of blood as well as money flowing out of our pores. Come see the endless lists of dead in our villages . . . Is the life force of lost youth not a bank note? [35]

On the American side this manner of reasoning raised some echoes, for instance, from congressman A. Pratt Andrew of Massachusetts. Professors at Princeton and Columbia universities passed motions advising at least that the question be reopened.[36] Benjamin H. Williams, in 1928, stressed the futility of asking repayment, not only because there would be an economic advantage to wiping out the debt but also because the transfer of money to the United States was technically impossible without further large American loans, which would set up a vicious circle. He added that France could not be taxed any more; 20 percent of French national income went for taxes in 1924 as opposed to 11.5 percent in the United States.[37] The only way for Europe to pay would be to increase her exports to the American market and how could this be done with the existing high tariffs? Ever since the war, tariffs had mounted steadily. The Emergency Tariff Act of May 27, 1921, was followed and strengthened by the Fordney-McCumber Tariff of September 21, 1922. Far from increasing economic disadvantages, Williams concludes, the cancellation of the debts would have nothing but advantages for the United States. Politically it would improve the situation. As Keynes said, "a debtor nation does not love its creditor."

There are few responsible Americans who believe that the debts should be cancelled forthwith . . . It seems, however, that wise statesmanship would stand ready to participate in a general readjustment in which the debts, reparations, and any other economic disabilities would be subject to such revision as would appear calculated to advance the best interests of the world.[38]

Williams was right on one point at least: few Americans would accept it. Although he was aware of the problem, Hughes felt himself to be powerless in the face of Congress, the President, and popular opinion. Hughes, a realist, knew that in such a case one must limit oneself to the possible. What was possible was to negotiate agreements about payment with the debtor nations. This was what Great Britain wanted, if France did not. Baldwin went to Washington on January 8, 1923, and entered into conversations with Secretary of the Treasury Andrew Mellon, chairman of the American Commission on War Debts, of which Hughes and Hoover were also members.

The great difficulty was that the Americans wanted not only repayment of the principal, but also interest at 4.5 percent. An agreement was finally reached on June 18, 1923. After various fruitless attempts to avoid it, France signed a similar agreement on April 29, 1926: she would pay back the debt—with the principal reduced by 52.8 percent—in sixty-two annual payments on which interest was fixed at between 1 and 3.5 percent. The lack of realism of American policy in this matter was to be demonstrated several years later. For the moment Hughes had coped with the immediate danger.

Once more Republican foreign policy showed its essential characteristic—empiricism. Empiricism permits short-term success but the absence of continuity and of theory of which it is the expression makes such success fragile. In this connection we might note the judgment of Dexter Perkins. Perkins reports the results of a poll among American historians on the relative rank of the secretaries of state in which Hughes was rated the third greatest, after John Quincy Adams and William H. Seward. He adds: "There are few people whose results are more admirable and successful if compared to the objectives set. Almost everything Hughes attempted to do he did, and did well . . . but it was not his fate to construct a long-term policy destined to last a long time." Perkins blames the circumstances. This is partly true, but a factor even more important than circumstances was the empirical nature of his policy. It is the absence of theory which will no doubt keep historians of the future from placing Hughes on the level of Wilson.

The Washington Conference and the Far East

If Hughes's policy in Europe was cautious, even sometimes incoherent, it was not the same with the two great problems of the Washington Conference—those of naval disarmament and the situation in the Far East. The two matters are interrelated. The power of the American Fleet could be used as a diplomatic weapon in relation to Great Britain, but certainly not as a military one. In relation to Japan, however, this was a possibility. In 1919 the American Fleet had 900,000 tons and there were 1,100,000 tons under construction. Great Britain had 2,400,000 tons in service, but only 500,000 under construction. The United States had 16 dreadnoughts; Britain, 33 armored ships and 9 battle cruisers. But the United States had under construction 3 dreadnoughts, 10 superdreadnoughts, and 6 large battle cruisers,[39] which would mean in the near future the achievement of the "Navy second to none" announced by Wilson in 1916. It is true that the war had hindered the construction of heavy ships, but 100 destroyers had been built and 200 more were under construction.

The prevailing doctrine, set forth before the House Naval Affairs Committee by Admiral James J. Badger, was still that of Mahan. Badger stressed that there should be a large merchant marine and that the fighting navy's purpose was "to keep the trade routes open." Many American naval officers, wanting the United States to reach first place, demanded that advantage be taken of Great Britain's war-time setback to attain this goal. The British were quite conscious of this and Lloyd George had declared firmly to Colonel House that Great Britain would fight to keep its lead. At the time of the Treaty of Versailles it seemed that a new naval race was about to begin, this time between the United States and Britain. But Secretary of Navy Daniels considered a Fleet equal to that of Great Britain to be sufficient.

There had been a military aspect to Wilson's campaign in favor of the League of Nations. Wilson and Daniels tried to arouse public opinion by making it appear that the choice lay between the League of Nations and military power—meaning especially the big navy. To join the League would certainly be less expensive. Franklin D. Roosevelt, undersecretary of the navy, announced on January 31, 1920, that if the United States were to return to the old diplomacy, the Navy would cost 1 billion dollars a year—seven times more than under Theodore Roosevelt. As soon as the treaty was definitely rejected, the administration decided to continue the large naval program already begun, because, as Daniels said, "The world today is in chaos, nobody knows what will happen next year." [40]

When Harding became President he came out for a strong navy, as we have seen, but the choice still had to be made between the solution of the Navy Board—a navy equal to Great Britain's—and a "naval holiday," that is, a temporary suspension of naval construction, which was advocated by Senator Borah. The partisans of the former alternative used the Anglo-Japanese alliance of 1902 as an argument. When friction mounted between the United States and Great Britain and Britain announced in March 1921 that she would resume naval construction, it strengthened the case even more.

The American-Japanese crisis was much more serious than the tension with Britain. The clauses of the Treaty of Versailles concerning Shantung and Japanese occupation of the former German islands— which included the Island of Jaluit 2000 miles southwest of Hawaii— greatly irritated the Americans. When in Saipan the Japanese Fleet was only a few hours from Guam. The Japanese held Yap, on the route of the American (formerly German) cable, and the Marshall Islands were on the sea route from Hawaii to the Philippines. Finally, the Japanese continued to occupy eastern Siberia and Sakhalin. The Japanese Navy consisted of 5 dreadnoughts and 4 battle cruisers, and in 1920 the Japanese parliament voted for a program which would provide 8 superdreadnoughts and 8 large battle cruisers by 1927. By that year the Japanese would have a total of 25 capital ships, as well as 25 light cruisers, 102 destroyers, and 116 submarines. Would Japan not fortify the Pacific islands and make them into submarine bases? A war against German submarines was just over; the general fear of a renewed threat was assuming a specific and extremely unpleasant form. In late 1919 the United States transferred 800,000 tons to the Pacific. In 1921 Harding decided to send almost the whole Atlantic Fleet to the Pacific. The quarrel focused on Yap, which had become a Japanese mandate without United States consent.

Hughes decided to take up the matter and he did it masterfully. On July 17, 1921, there was a rumor that Lloyd George was about to propose a naval conference. Hughes, having convinced Harding to take the initiative, invited Great Britain, Japan, France, and Italy to join the United States in a conference in Washington to discuss limitations of naval armaments. How is this sudden decision to be explained?

It is related to what Harold and Margaret Sprout call "the popular revolt against navalism." [41] The public was tired of enormous military budgets. The war was over and people did not believe in a continuing danger. From this stemmed the idea that the big interests—of steel and shipbuilding—were artificially stimulating a fear psychosis. Congress, pressed by the voters, began to cut down the program of the executive branch. After all, the United States Navy was bigger than the Japanese and it was "grotesque" to speak of British aggression. This was a very effective point for all those who were crying for disarmament: peace groups like the World Peace Foundation and the Carnegie Endowment for International Peace, women's clubs—women had obtained the vote by the Nineteenth Amendment—churches, the American Federation of Labor, and even many industrialists and bankers. Senator Borah had become the spokesman of this great movement; the recession of 1920–21 further strengthened it. Even General Pershing, the national hero, declared himself much in favor of it. Many people were demanding a conference and, following the suggestion of General Bliss, they wanted it held in Washington where the representatives of other nations would understand better what to expect if they forced the United States to compete with them in an arms race.[42] Besides, Congress had cut the naval budget to less than 500 million dollars, a considerable contrast to the billion announced by Franklin D. Roosevelt. Finally, by proposing a naval conference Hughes was cutting the ground from under the feet of Borah, the consistent and dangerous opponent.

The conference could have another advantage: Britain was ready to renew her alliance with Japan, but it became clear at a meeting of prime ministers of the United Kingdom and the Dominions in June 1921 that the Dominions, especially Canada, were hostile to that alliance. The United States could widen the breach which was becoming apparent and in this way discourage the renewal. On July 11, 1921, the public learned with satisfaction that an American invitation had been issued three days earlier. England had proposed a preliminary conference on problems in the Pacific to be held in London, but Hughes had firmly declined. He feared an Anglo-Japanese agreement which would block American claims to equality. He preferred to have the Washington Conference take up the problems of the Pacific and the Far East in addition to the problem of naval limitations. The Japanese accepted in the end because they thought an Anglo-American agreement impossible. It was decided to ask China, the Netherlands, Portugal, and Belgium, who were also naval powers, to join the others for discussions dealing with China. The Soviet Union—not recognized by the United States—was not invited. The opening was set for November 12. The United States delegation, led by Hughes, included Elihu Root, former secretary of war and of state, Henry Cabot Lodge, chairman of the Senate Committee on Foreign Relations, and a Democratic member of the same committee, Oscar W. Underwood. The intransigent Borah was deliberately not included.

Hughes approached the conference with trumps in his hand: the United States had then or was in the process of building sixteen ultramodern armored ships which benefited from the lessons learned at the Battle of Jutland. They were enormous for the time, 32,000 to 43,500 tons. Given the rapidity with which ships became obsolete, these would give the United States by far the most powerful fighting fleet in the world. The other members of the conference would thus have a real interest in limiting naval armaments.

Nor was this all. Japan's great hope was that as a result of some sort of prior understanding with Great Britain in regard to naval armaments, discussion on the Far East could be kept on a purely theoretical plane. The "Black Chamber" or Bureau of Cryptography of the State Department was deciphering the Japanese codes and had even succeeded in breaking within forty days a new code, first used in July 1921. As a result Hughes had followed the development of Japanese policy from day to day. He knew of the Japanese efforts to make a prior agreement with the British and he could maneuver effectively to prevent it.[43]

Moreover, an understanding with Britain on disarmament was possible because the British were now resigned to equality with the American Fleet. Hughes was also certain of the wholehearted support of Britain in the Far East. Instead of an Anglo-Japanese front which would have blocked everything, there would be an Anglo-American front which was to hand Japan a major diplomatic defeat. The Americans were not certain of being able to establish this front at the start of the conference, which explains their decision to hold in reserve their diplomatic offensive concerning China and the Pacific, and to start with the question of disarmament. It was decided to offer on the first day a concrete plan which had been carefully worked out in collaboration with the Navy General Board. It fixed a ratio for the fleets of the major powers at 5, 5, and 3, respectively for the United States, Great Britain, and Japan. It remained to specify the categories to which this ratio would apply. At first it was planned that the United States and Great Britain would each have one million tons in ships of the line and Japan would have 600,000. Later the figure was lowered to a little more than 500,000 tons for Britain and the United States and approximately 300,000 for Japan.

But this system was only the second American proposal; the first was the declaration of a naval holiday, effective immediately, prohibiting all construction of armored ships for ten years. As proof of their good faith, the United States would stop construction and destroy a total of 845,740 tons. After the naval holiday the armored ships of the three countries would be limited to 500,000 and 300,000 tons respectively.

Hughes's proposal was received by the American public with an enthusiasm which was only equaled by the reserve of the British and the Japanese. France and Italy were not mentioned in Hughes's speech. Balfour and Baron Kato expressed polite but firm objections. Briand, in an eloquent speech, let it be clearly understood that the question of land armaments should be excluded from consideration at the conference and that France must restore her naval losses sustained during the war. He secured the support of Japan on the first point and Hughes did not object. For Hughes, land armaments were not the real problem.

Negotiations primarily concerned the ratio. Japan proposed 5, 5, and 3.5, and during the first weeks seemed unwilling to modify her position. She also asked that the armored ship *Matsu*—just launched —should not be included in the list of ships whose construction was to be abandoned. Hughes replied that the United States would sacrifice three armored ships. But in early December the Black Chamber intercepted a telegram from Tokyo dated November 28, indicating that Japan might give in to 5, 5, and 3 if an agreement could be reached to maintain the status quo concerning fortifications of the Pacific islands.[44] Hughes therefore knew that he did not have to give in to the Japanese.

Finally, on December 12 Kato made the offer the United States was expecting, and on December 15 agreement was reached between the three major naval powers: a ratio of 5, 5, and 3 and a ten-year naval holiday except for the *Matsu* and two armored ships each for Great Britain and the United States. The status quo in the Pacific islands would be maintained (Article 19 of the final treaty). Hawaii was not included. It was difficult to include France and Italy in the naval agreement, but it was finally accomplished by setting a ratio of 1.75 for each of them. This was only achieved by agreeing not to limit the construction of small ships and submarines. The Five-Power Treaty was signed on February 6, 1922. Hughes, with an optimism not justified by history, said at the time:

> This Treaty ends, absolutely ends, the race in competition in naval armament. At the same time it leaves the relative security of the great naval powers unimpaired.

The significance of the Treaty is far more than that. In this Treaty we are talking of arms in the language of peace . . . In other words, we are taking perhaps the greatest forward step in history to establish the reign of peace.[45]

This statement, which expresses exactly Hughes's views and those of the American people, should not make us forget that at the same time Hughes was preparing a much more important diplomatic victory over Japan. Once more we see how American policy mixed grand idealistic views with concrete national interests.

Hughes knew very well how to take advantage of the Japanese request for the status quo in the Pacific islands to break the Anglo-Japanese alliance. Because of inaccurate information from the American ambassador in London, Harvey, Lord Curzon thought Hughes was indifferent on this subject. He soon found out otherwise, especially when Hughes threatened that if the Anglo-Japanese treaty were renewed, the United States might well recognize the new Republic of Ireland. Pressed also by the Dominions, Lord Curzon decided that the alliance should be given up. But how could it be done without hurting Japanese feelings and without losing the control over Japanese action which this alliance had permitted? Balfour suggested inclusion of the United States in the alliance, but this was counter to established tradition and to American opinion. There was one way of solving the problem, to include France. This would flatter French vanity, and eliminate the stigma of alliance. "A general and safe agreement was substituted for the defensive Anglo-Japanese alliance." [46] Lodge let it be known that he would not object if the guarantee of security did not include the territory of the continental United States. Viviani, chief of the French delegation, showed his satisfaction by kissing Hughes on both cheeks when he was asked to join. Root wanted the Netherlands included also but Hughes refused, in order not to enlarge the guaranteed zone. Japan was offered a four power agreement which she decided to accept, because of her eagerness to advance her plans concerning the fortifications.

The Four-Power Treaty was worked out by Hughes and signed on December 13, 1921. It was agreed that not only the Japanese possessions but also the Japanese islands themselves would be guaranteed. This put Japan in an ambiguous position, as there was no such provision for the United States. A tragicomic episode occurred in relation to this situation which nearly ruined the whole agreement. Harding, informed by Hughes but not very gifted at grasping such subtleties, replied to a reporter's question in a press conference, on December 20, that the treaty did not apply to Japan itself any more than to the territory of the continental United States. The opponents of the administration took hold of this incident with delight. Japan protested and finally obtained the omission of the Japanese islands from the guarantee treaty. As for Harding, he explained pathetically to Hughes, "I shouldn't have said anything about it to the press, but when they asked me about it I didn't want to appear to be a dud." [47] The clause excluding Japan was signed on December 31. The four powers mutually guaranteed their Pacific possessions and promised to consult one another in case of differences. Not only was there no longer an Anglo-Japanese alliance, there was no alliance at all. This was not clear to the Senate irreconcilables, Borah and Hiram Johnson, who found traces of entanglement in it and did their best to delay approval. The defeat of the treaty, Hughes said, "Would be nothing less than a national calamity." [48] In the end the Senate gave its approval.

There remained the various problems relating to China. American policy since 1900 had been that of the Open Door. It seemed difficult to dislodge the European powers from their concessions, but there was hope in Washington of putting an end to Japanese claims to Shantung and the Japanese occupation of Siberia. An Anglo-American agreement, together with the economic difficulties of Japan, could help to bring about a solution which suited the United States. After long negotiations the Nine-Power Treaty on China was signed, on February 26, 1922. This treaty guaranteed the sovereignty, independence, and integrity of China. Article 3 constituted virtually international acceptance of the American policy of the Open Door. Spheres of influence were explicitly condemned. Hughes, with great skill, had Elihu Root incorporate into the treaty a sentence from a secret agreement of 1917 between Lansing and Ishii, by which Japan promised not to seek "special rights or privileges" in China.

The Nine-Power Treaty gave Hughes a sound theoretical basis from which to approach the problem of Shantung. "The only yellow peril," said Hughes, "lies in the exploitation of China by the Japanese Imperial Government." [49] He avoided this problem in the discussions of the nine signatory nations, six of whom had signed and ratified the Treaty of Versailles, which yielded former German rights in that province to Japan. The best tactic was for the United States to offer its good offices to both China and Japan and for them to enter into direct negotiations at the same time as the Washington Conference. Balfour joined Hughes in advocating this procedure, which isolated the Japanese even more. The greatest difficulty was to persuade the Chinese representative to negotiate with the Japanese. Strong Anglo-American pressure and the skill of the Japanese ambassador in Washington, Shidehara, were required to accomplish this. Bilateral conversations began on December 1, and thirty-six meetings were held before agreement was finally reached on a compromise text submitted by Hughes and Balfour. The treaty, signed on January 31, 1922, provided that Japanese troops would evacuate Shantung and that the railroad would be returned to China. To save face, Japan kept certain vague economic rights. In this whole affair, writes Fifield, "Charles Evans Hughes was the leading force, the catalytic agent." [50]

The Japanese evacuation of Siberia was not accomplished by a treaty. Hughes had demanded withdrawal in a note to Tokyo on May 31, 1921. The United States had all sorts of reasons to desire it, and one of the main ones was connected with the principle of nonintervention. Though Hughes refused to recognize the Soviet government despite various pressures, notably from Senator Borah, he thought Japanese military intervention in Soviet affairs inadmissible. He wanted to write the principle of the integrity of Russia into the agenda of the Washington Conference, though he ignored the protest of the People's Commissar for Foreign Affairs over not having been invited to the conference. Feeling herself isolated and needing American economic aid, Japan decided to give in. On January 23, 1922, in the course of a debate, Shidehara announced that Japan would withdraw her troops. Siberia was evacuated several months later; North Sakhalin, in 1925.

The American public received the news of this series of successes with enthusiasm—an enthusiasm generally not shared abroad. In France and Japan the news was met with frank hostility. Even in America there were dissenting voices. Some, like the socialists and the Wilsonian senators Walsh of Montana and Hitchcock of Nebraska, deplored the fact that disarmament was not more general, and that the question of land forces had been excluded. Others, on the contrary, like the Hearst press, deplored the sight of the United States "tied hand and foot" to the war machine of foreign imperialism. The most violent reaction came from the Navy, which was almost unanimous in deploring the treaty. It did not really assure equality with Great

Britain, said Admiral Fiske. It destroyed the dream of having the strongest navy in the world. According to Admiral Knapp, it allowed Japan to dominate the Pacific and dealt a fearful blow to the power of the United States. Captain D. W. Knox published a little book in 1922, *The Eclipse of American Sea Power*, in which he said that the treaty had made Japan "entirely free from American intervention in the Orient." This was prophetic.

The era of Mahan was indeed at an end, but the Washington Conference was more the symbol than the cause of this. Submarines and airplanes were about to upset strategic principles and relegate the admiral's doctrines to the world of ghosts.

The Washington Conference, even in the respect in which it seemed a success in American eyes, contained the seeds of new troubles. Hughes's diplomatic victory over Japan was total and all inclusive. The result was the illusion that Japan would give in every time. Anti-Japanese sentiment could have a free rein. By the Johnson Act of 1924, which placed major restrictions on immigration, Japanese immigration, which we have seen restricted by the Gentlemen's Agreement in 1907—was now totally forbidden. The Japanese, like the Chinese, were now aliens ineligible for citizenship. The law forbade immigration of Japanese wives for the first time, and the effects were immediately felt. Departures exceeded arrivals by 5081 in 1925 and by 4613 in 1926.[51]

The Japanese ambassador Hanihara protested on April 10, 1924. "For Japan it is not a question of convenience but one of principle . . . The important thing is to determine whether Japan, as a nation, has or has not a right to the respect and consideration of other nations." [52] Hughes agreed with Hanihara. Before the law was passed, he wrote to its author, Albert Johnson, chairman of the House Committee on Immigration and Naturalization, "I regret to have to say that in my opinion such legislation would largely destroy the effects of the Washington conference." [53] Hughes proposed that the quota system be applied to Japan. This would have limited Japanese immigration to 246 persons per year. The nationalism of the congressional majority would not permit such a modification, and the Johnson Act was passed by 325 to 71 votes in the House, 76 to 2 in the Senate. An amendment proposed by Hughes, which would have recognized the Gentlemen's Agreement of 1907, was rejected. Hughes considered resigning and Hanihara actually did so.

In this affair, small in itself, there is something very characteristic of American thinking in the 1920's—which sheds light on Japanese-American relations in the 1930's. We shall see later how the seeds sown so thoughtlessly were to grow.

The Underlying Origins of the Good Neighbor Policy

Compared to this nationalist policy, active and offensive, in Europe, in the Far East, and in naval disarmament, Hughes's accomplishment in Latin America was more modest. It is nevertheless an area in which his work seems most fruitful to historians in the long run. Hughes was certainly very much opposed to the policy of the Big Stick. He wanted to "liquidate the interventions of the United States in the Caribbean and Central America" as soon as political stability was restored.[54] He was very much helped, up to 1922, by a remarkable man who was chief of the Latin American division of the State Department, Sumner Welles.

Hughes's Latin American policy had two aspects, which are connected though distinct: on the one hand, he multiplied his efforts to arrive at settlements, and on the other, he tried to purify the Monroe Doctrine, to make it clearer, more acceptable, firmer.

Hughes's policy of settlement took various forms. Honduras, Nicaragua, and San Salvador were accusing each other of encouraging invasions of the others' territories by revolutionary elements. In August 1922 Hughes succeeded in bringing about a meeting of the presidents of the three countries on the American ship *Tacoma* in the Gulf of Fonseca. When Guatemala and Honduras had a frontier dispute, Hughes tried to get them to accept arbitration, this time in vain. The formula of arbitration was not to succeed until 1930. It was the same story concerning the differences between Chile and Peru over the Tacna-Arica region. Hughes persuaded Harding to call a conference of the Central American states in Washington in December 1922, a Conference in which Hughes and Welles took part without the right to vote. From this meeting came a treaty of peace and friendship and various other agreements.

In October 1923 the Secretary of State refused to send Marines to Honduras, then having a revolution. Going even further, he tried to withdraw American troops from countries where they had formerly been sent. He succeeded in the case of San Domingo, not without difficulty. He would have done likewise in Haiti, but he feared bloody consequences. He paved the way for a similar action in Nicaragua; and troops were withdrawn in 1925, though Coolidge reoccupied the country in 1926, following troubles which broke out almost immediately. Hughes went to Rio de Janeiro in 1922 to celebrate the centennial of Brazilian independence.

He had more difficulty with Mexico. Carranza, soon after achieving stability and recognition for his government in 1917, took legislative measures which injured American interests. These roused violent protests and even calls for war in certain American circles after the Armistice of 1918. Later, Carranza was overthrown and replaced by Alvaro Obregón, who was legally elected in 1920. Hughes decided to recognize the government of Obregón on condition that a treaty be signed guaranteeing the property of American citizens, and restoring property which had been confiscated or providing a fair indemnity. Obregón refused these conditions and as a result recognition was withheld—on the same principle which had been applied to the Soviet Union. For a year and a half there was a deadlock. Hughes wanted to break it, because he was sympathetic to Obregón's colossal efforts to improve social conditions in the country. In May 1923 he sent two commissioners to work out a compromise, Charles Beecher Warren, former ambassador to Japan, and Judge John Barton Payne, former secretary of the interior. Meetings took place in Bucareli between May and August 1923 and produced an agreement (published August 31) set forth in two parallel declarations. Obregón was then recognized and the American government even agreed to send him arms for defense against a rival. The election in the summer of 1924 of Obregón's friend Plutarco Elias Calles was to reopen the quarrel in June 1925.

More interesting is Hughes's theoretical position, because in matters concerned with the Monroe Doctrine he was his most consistent and least empirical. His position was made especially clear in speeches in Brazil in 1922, in Boston on October 30, 1922, in Minneapolis in 1923, and in Philadelphia on the occasion of the centennial of the Monroe Doctrine. Its substance was to free the Monroe Doctrine from the Roosevelt Corollary. Hughes did not renounce the United States' right to intervene, as Franklin Delano Roosevelt was to do in 1933; but, if interventions were permissible they did not, in his opinion, derive from the Monroe Doctrine. "The Monroe Doctrine as a particular declaration in no way exhausts [North] American rights or policy; the United States has rights and obligations which that doctrine does not define." [55]

Hughes carefully limited these rights and obligations to intervene to the region of the Caribbean "which is of particular interest to us, not with the object of trying to control others, but to be sure that our security cannot be threatened." Thus he excluded any zones outside the Caribbean and Central America from the sphere in which the United States might intervene. For the rest, in language no different from that of Theodore Roosevelt, he stuck by the affirmation that the United States had no territorial ambitions, did not want to set up protectorates and recognized the equality of all American republics and their right to be treated as equals.

Had not the time come to abandon this century-old doctrine? Was it not outmoded? To be sure there was no immediate threat to Latin America, but as Hughes said, "The future holds infinite possibilities, and the doctrine remains as an essential policy to be applied whenever any exigency may arise requiring its application. To withdraw it, or to weaken it, would aid no just interest . . . but would simply invite trouble by removing an established safeguard of the peace of the American continents." [56]

The menace was not slow to appear, indirect at first, but fearful in American eyes: It was the Protocol of Geneva developed by member nations of the League of Nations in 1924. This Protocol provided for compulsory arbitration in international disputes and declared that whichever party refused to comply would automatically be considered the aggressor. Sanctions would also be applied to the aggressor automatically. What would happen if one or more Latin American countries became involved in this procedure? From another angle, the Protocol anticipated a disarmament conference. This aspect interested Hughes, but he had to separate it effectively from the Protocol—in which he saw a new Holy Alliance taking shape, "the protocol derives from a concerted movement against the United States." [57] (Originally, the Monroe Doctrine had been a unilateral position taken by the United States faced with the possibility of a collective intervention of the Holy Alliance in Latin America.*)

* Proposed at the Congress of Vienna in 1815 by Tsar Alexander I, the Holy Alliance was supposed to be the basis for joint action of legitimate monarchs to suppress nationalist and liberal movements. When Spain's Latin American colonies revolted

Hughes decided to do everything he could in secret to prevent ratification of the Protocol. He first proposed to Briand, via the American ambassador in Rome, Fletcher, to limit the Protocol to Europe. This was impossible: Chile, Brazil, and Uruguay had already joined. Then he tried to prevent the British from joining. At that moment (November 7, 1924) the replacement of the Labour cabinet of MacDonald by that of the Conservative Baldwin brought to power men reluctant to accept an agreement worked out by their predecessors. Moreover it was unwelcome to some of the Dominions. Hughes did his best to transform these British hesitations into a refusal. Through either American ambassador Kellogg in London or British ambassador Howard in Washington, he let it be known that, League or no League, the United States would not tolerate any intervention in Latin America, especially in the Caribbean area. Who would undertake such interventions in the name of the League of Nations if not Great Britain, the great naval power? This meant that Great Britain had to choose between the Protocol and American friendship. She did not hesitate. Austen Chamberlain, Foreign Secretary, announced that his government could not accept the Protocol on grounds that the United States was not a member of the League of Nations, and therefore would never accept any compulsory arbitration which affected her interests. The "Holy Alliance"—but was Hughes not exaggerating?—was stillborn. Britain's rejection of the Protocol occurred on March 12, 1925, exactly eight days after Hughes had left the State Department. He finished his term in office with a final victory.

---

and claimed independence in 1821, the monarchs of Russia and Austria, evoking this concept, threatened to intervene and repress them.

Chapter VIII

Prosperity and the Great Illusion, 1925-1929

Prosperity and the Diplomacy of "Big Business"

Because of the Kellogg-Briand Pact, Kellogg is probably better known in Europe than other secretaries of state. It must be said that this is an injustice, as Frank Kellogg was only continuing the policy of Hughes, without contributing anything original. Hughes sought to dominate events; Kellogg let himself be carried along by them. He had submitted to the views of big business in the matter of the export of capital and he had been very much influenced by the pacifists. It was only after a certain resistance that he allowed himself to get involved in negotiations of the pact which bears his name. His Latin American policy was a continuation of Hughes's policy to such an extent that at the Havana conference—its main achievement—Hughes was recalled from private life to head the United States delegation.

If Kellogg has any distinction, it is his career in itself, for he began at the bottom of the social ladder and rose almost to the top. Born in New York State in 1857, he moved to Minnesota with his family after the Civil War. He did not attend either secondary school or college but studied law in an office in Rochester, Minnesota. This enabled him to become a lawyer, another on the list of American leaders in this profession. This irascible man showed considerable ability at the bar. He gained renown by fighting the trusts under Theodore Roosevelt and he acquired wealth by subsequently becoming a lawyer for one of those trusts. In 1916 he was elected to the Senate. He was not re-elected in 1922, but Hughes secured his nomination as ambassador to London shortly afterwards. Rather uncultivated, irritable, always sensitive to remarks by newspapermen, he played a lively but rather ineffective role in Washington. The great economic and moral forces agitating the country could range at will without having to reckon with him.

The period of Kellogg—March 1925 to March 1929—is above all the period of prosperity, of the incredible economic expansion which appeared to be fundamentally changing the material basis of American civilization. A phenomenon of such scope, combined with the ideological reactions analyzed in the preceding chapter, could not but exercise a great influence on foreign policy. There was an indirect influence because prosperity created an atmosphere of confidence, contributed to the desire for peace and led to overflowing optimism. There was also a direct influence, because the increase in capital which led its possessors to look for foreign markets would oblige the government to formulate a policy in relation to foreign investments.

It is not necessary for us to analyze here the prosperity as such. Some figures will suffice to indicate its scope. The slump began in 1920 and ended in July 1921. Between 1923 and 1929, while the population increased by 9 percent, the national income increased by more than 30 percent (from 60.7 billion dollars in 1923 to 87.2 billion dollars in 1929). The average real income per capita went from $634 to $716 a year, a 13 percent increase in the standard of living. The index of wholesale prices stayed relatively stable; productivity, on the contrary increased. If one takes 100 as the number of man-hours required to produce a given commodity in 1899, for 1919 the figure would be 74 and for 1929, 42. In agriculture, if one takes 100 as the number of men necessary for a given product in 1900, the number would be 84 for 1919 and 67 for 1929. The external signs of prosperity are striking: construction of housing, which attained a record in 1926; purchase of radio sets (there were 7,500,000 in 1928 compared to 60,000 in 1922); and above all the number of automobiles, whose production doubled in seven years and reached the figure of 5,300,000 in 1929. At that time there was one private automobile for every six inhabitants. In short, there was an unprecedented boom of which we will speak more in the following chapter.[1]

This picture would be very incomplete if we did not see in it an essential point: although the entire population benefited from the economic expansion, it was primarily to the advantage of big business, as a result of a variety of technical factors with which we are not concerned here. This was really the age of business as Arthur M. Schlesinger, Jr., says.[2] James Warren Prothro called his study of this era *The Dollar Decade*, with the subtitle, *Business Ideas in the 1920's*.[3] Describing "the spirit of the new era," Joseph Dorfmann, author of a recent monumental work on this period, characterizes it principally by the phrases "concentration of economic power," "development of a market system," "extension of scientific methods in managing business," "rise of the engineer," "progress of planning," and finally, "optimism." [4]

The age of business means much more than the age of manufacture and trade; it means the age of government by business. Herbert Feis proposes the substitution of the expression Diplomacy of the Dollar for Dollar Diplomacy to describe the foreign policy of the time.[5] In this change Feis is suggesting that everything about Dollar Diplomacy derived from the imperialist tradition—with its emotional overtones —was eliminated, leaving only the idea of government by the great interests. President Coolidge, speaking to the Chamber of Commerce in January 1926, expressed it very succinctly:

Business and Government might have had a better understanding of each other.

The general welfare of our country could be very much advanced through a better knowledge by both parties of the multifold problems with which each has to deal.

I should put an even stronger emphasis on the desirability of the largest possible independence between Government and Business. Each ought to be sovereign in its own sphere.[6]

This is a new adaptation of the medieval theory of the two swords, Prothro says humorously.* But it goes much further. The president of the Chamber of Commerce, Julius H. Barnes, said quite crudely, "The government must learn that the opinion of business, developed and ripened after careful study, observation and experience, must be respected by government policy." [7] And Coolidge virtually agreed: "I have been greatly pleased to observe the many evidences which come here, indicating that the attitude of the Chamber of Commerce very accurately reflects that of public opinion generally." [8]

The President's impression was correct. The historians of the period reveal that the "cult of business" together with a sort of democratic Darwinism, the idea that the humblest citizen could reach the heights, was very widespread even among people at the bottom of the economic ladder. Schlesinger and Prothro have quoted a theologian of the new doctrine as saying: "Jesus chose twelve men from the lowest

* In the middle ages there was a theory that the temporal power and the spiritual power constituted "two swords."

ranks of Business and with them he built an organization that conquered the world." [9] Jesus Christ was thus the prototype of the American businessman, and among other things he was a public relations man
of the first rank.

Schlesinger considers that although the farmers and some sections
of the working class did not go over to this "religion," the only real
revolt against business came from intellectual circles. In general, optimism held sway. Coolidge, in his State of the Union Message, December 4, 1928, expressed it thus:

No Congress of the United States ever assembled in surveying the state
of the Union, has met with a more pleasing prospect than that which appears at the present time . . . The great wealth created by our enterprise
and industry and saved by our economy, has had the widest distribution
among our own people, and has gone out in a steady stream to serve the
charity and the business of the world . . . The country can regard the
present with satisfaction and the future with optimism.[10]

Prosperity also had very direct effects on the foreign policy of the
United States. Herbert Hoover, Secretary of Commerce from 1921 to
1929, Secretary of the Treasury Andrew Mellon, one of the two or
three richest men in the country, and Secretaries of State Hughes and
Kellogg developed a policy which was carefully followed up to the
crash of 1929. Let us try to define its main aspects.

First, the United States government, as a government, should not
make foreign loans. Hughes said in August 1923, "It is not the
policy of our Government to make loans to other governments, and
the needed capital if it is to be supplied at all, must be furnished by private organizations." [11] Private enterprises which exported capital must
do so entirely at their own risk; nevertheless, the government had a
right to supervise and guide these operations. As early as the summer
of 1921, the directors of J. P. Morgan and Company and some other
big banks were summoned by Harding to discuss this question with
Hughes, Mellon, and Hoover. On June 6, the head of J. P. Morgan
wrote a letter to Harding in which he committed himself, in the name
of the bankers, not to undertake foreign investments without consulting the State Department. Thus the principle of supervision was established. Hoover would have preferred supervision by the Department
of Commerce, but Hughes and Kellogg supported the prerogative of
the State Department in this matter.

The aim of this half-control ("half" because sometimes the banks disregarded it or protested energetically in the name of free enterprise) was to avoid loans harmful to general government policy, while retaining as a diplomatic weapon the powerful pressure afforded by the power to grant or refuse a large sum to a foreign country.

In addition to supervising it was necessary for the government to guide investments. Bit by bit a doctrine was developed, according to which loans were to be avoided in the following circumstances: [12] (1) Loans to a foreign government to balance its budget when it was not taxing its own people sufficiently; (2) Loans for military equipment; (3) Loans to aid foreign trusts that kept their prices too high for American consumers; (4) Loans to governments not recognized by the United States; (5) Loans to governments or citizens of nations that had not discharged their obligations to the United States.

This last principle, clearly formulated in 1921, had by far the most important consequences. There was a kind of irony in the fact that it led the United States to favor Germany—and its former allies Austria and Hungary—to the detriment of the Entente nations, France, Belgium, Greece, Rumania, Yugoslavia, and Italy. Unlike Great Britain, these nations had not signed agreements about payments of their war debts when Kellogg took office. Having not met their obligations they were not eligible for loans from American banks. Mellon was very firm on this point. Hoover thought that the precedent of nonpayment of former debts was unpromising for repayment of further loans. American citizens must be put on guard. When the French government attempted to negotiate an important loan with J. P. Morgan and Company in November 1921—a period when the franc was in danger—the State Department came out against it. In order to obtain a loan, France would have to use a substantial part of what she had received as reparations from Germany to pay a part of her American war debt—$400 million owed for American military surplus.

But the dollar door was not opened for long. In December 1924, Minister of Finance Clementel invoked the principle of "strict justice"—that the Allies should pay the expenses of the war according to their ability. Louis Marin gave forthright expression to current French opinion: "In the common cause some gave ships, others arms, others the lives of their children, others, finally, their money, and today those who gave only their money say to us 'pay back what we loaned you.'" [13] We have seen that this type of reasoning made no impression on Congress or the State Department, and the latter, indeed, virtually prohibited private loans to France.

Negotiations were reopened in September 1925 and a French delegation went to the United States to hold talks with "The American
Commission for Foreign Debts of the World War." Despite the commission's cooperative attitude, no agreement could be reached. Only
in April 1926 was a treaty on payments signed—the Mellon-Beranger
agreement. If it were ratified quickly American loans could be resumed. The position of the franc was so desperate that it seemed
likely that France would ratify the agreement quickly. But as there
was a sure majority in the Chamber of Deputies against the agreement,
successive French governments did not dare to propose it, and Poincaré, returned to power in July 1926, saved the franc without American aid. Toward the end of 1927 the State Department, responding to
the rising tension between the two nations, was disposed to take a
more indulgent attitude, but the Treasury prevented it as far as loans
to the French government were concerned. The channels could be
reopened for French industry. Besides, French government and industry had managed by devious means, for example through the owner
of the Swedish Match Company, the famous Kruger, to take advantage of the flood of dollars. Only in July 1929, after the adoption of
the Young Plan on reparations, did France ratify the agreement of
1926. Then the door opened wide—just too late to do any good. The
economic crisis was to come in October.

The case of Italy was about the same, with the slight difference that
the difficulties were more rapidly resolved. The Italian government,
considering a loan from the House of Morgan to be essential in 1925,
hastened to sign an agreement on the war debts on November 14. On
the eighteenth Morgan agreed to make the loan, on the twenty-third
the State Department announced that it had no objection.

Germany had no war debts—for good reason—so there was no
obstacle to loans from American banks. Also, American industry
favored the growth of the German market. Moreover, it seemed right
and just to help an exhausted country to recover. One hundred and
eighty different loans contracted by the German government were
financed by American savings, amounting to 2.4 billion dollars, not
counting innumerable loans to private persons totaling 1.5 billion
dollars. The first big loan to the German government was the "Dawes
loan," in October 1924. To carry out the Dawes Plan, it was decided
to stimulate the German payment of reparations by granting a loan of
200 million dollars to Germany—of which the American share was
110 million. J. P. Morgan and Company was asked by France and

England to provide this money (the American government was not officially a partner in the Dawes Plan). One of its directors, Dwight Morrow, went to Washington to consult Hughes. Morrow was not enthusiastic because he feared that it would be a first step toward a system which would mean in fact that reparations would be paid by American banks. Hughes, on the other hand, insisted on it and in the end he convinced Morrow. "I believe that in all countries the great mass of people want peace. I do not think that the people of Germany constitute an exception . . . I believe that the execution of the Dawes Plan is necessary . . . If it failed because American bankers would not aid, I think it would be most unfortunate." [14]

When the loan was floated on the American market the 110 million dollars was oversubscribed by 1 billion. This proved that, for various reasons, the American public at least was willing to loan money to Germany. The trend continued despite growing State Department anxiety, and the misgivings of the general agent of reparations S. Parker Gilbert, an American citizen. The State Department attempted to have loans—at least those granted to local authorities or private business—controlled by the government in Berlin, but in fact this control was very uncertain.

Thus was created a technically absurd situation: Germany paid its reparations to the Allies and the Allies their debts to the United States, while the Americans furnished money to Germany which in the long run paid the reparations. Feis, underlining the disparity in the treatment of Germany and France, draws the following conclusion: "We did not do enough after the end of the war to chasten and reform the German people; or later to encourage the Republic; or after Hitler appeared to demand his head; or give enough support to those nations that resisted him." [15]

This policy, largely imposed on the government by business, in no way justified the optimism of its promoters. One can make a similar judgment of the refusal of loans to the Soviet Union—the unrecognized, unreliable debtor. The principle was clearly announced by Hughes on March 21, 1923, and repeated by Kellogg on January 21, 1928: only certain short-term credits were authorized—contracts by which large American firms (General Electric, General Motors, American Locomotive Company) sold goods on credit to the Soviet Union. This was a shortsighted policy and bred resentment.

Similarly Japan, which was not sharing in world prosperity and which had harbored a lively resentment against the United States since 1922 for reasons we have noted, might perhaps have been able to reduce the pressure of the imperialist elements if she had been able to profit from American loans to a significant extent. But the State Department took pains to block the loan (by the Oriental Development Company, with the guarantee of the National City Company) which might have been used in Manchuria. Japan had sovereign rights in the area of the South Manchurian Railway and her troops were occupying the railroad zone. Was this not a breach of the Open Door Policy in China? The problem grew in importance in 1927. The cabinet discussed the prospect of a loan requested by the South Manchurian Railway from the National City Company and J. P. Morgan. Coolidge and Kellogg favored it but Marshal Chang Tso-lin, who controlled Manchuria, and the Chinese Minister of Foreign Affairs protested (November 30–December 4, 1927) and the State Department modified its attitude. The banks were advised that the plan was inopportune and they abandoned it.

In all, the United States, "becoming bankers to the world," exported an average of 733 million dollars per year between 1922 and 1929—a minimum of 454 million in 1926, a maximum of 1 billion in 1929. This export of capital was much encouraged by the investment banking community which solicited potential borrowers through many active agents. A Bavarian village which needed $125,000, for example, was persuaded to accept a loan of 3 million.[16] For the period 1922 to 1929 private credits granted in the form of subscriptions to foreign government bonds can be estimated at 5 billion dollars, and direct investments abroad, either through the creation of affiliates, or through American companies operating exclusively abroad, or through American participation in foreign enterprises, at 3.5 billion.[17]

On August 20, 1932, Franklin Delano Roosevelt, candidate for the presidency, vividly put forth his objections to such a policy. It was a new chapter of *Alice in Wonderland*, he said, and he imagined the following dialogue between little Alice and the Republican leader, Humpty Dumpty:

"What if we produce a surplus?" she asked.
"Oh, we can sell it to foreign consumers."
"How can the foreigners pay for it?"
"Why, we will lend them the money."
"I see," said little Alice, "they will buy our surplus with our money. Of course, they will pay us back by selling us their goods?"
"Oh, not at all," said Humpty-Dumpty. "We set up a high wall called the tariff."

"And," said Alice at last, "how will the foreigners pay off these loans?"
"That is easy," said Humpty-Dumpty, "did you ever heard of a mora-
    torium?" [18]

The Crusade for Peace and the Kellogg-Briand Pact

Parallel to the policy of big business the peace movement was also
developing in the United States. It would be a serious error to believe
that there was an inherent opposition between these two tendencies
of business leadership and pacifism, or even to associate them with
different social groups. Whereas in Europe pacifism was almost exclusively an ideal of the Left, in the United States a great number of
businessmen took an active part in the movement. In 1910 Andrew
Carnegie gave 10 million dollars to establish the Endowment for International Peace—at the suggestion of Nicholas Murray Butler, president of Columbia. In 1913 the Peace Palace in The Hague, also given
by Carnegie, was opened. Henry Ford devoted some of his boundless
energy to propaganda for peace. Thousands of men in key business
positions contributed to or took part in certain peace groups. Big
business was not alone in desiring peace, but businessmen generally
considered it to be the essential condition of expansion.

It would also be a mistake to equate the peace movement with advocates of United States membership in the League of Nations. The
"nationalists" and "America firsters"—Senator Borah in the lead—
were often convinced and active pacifists. The peace movement was a
popular ideal, a collective undertaking dominated by a ruling idea,
regardless of party and social class. It was brought about by innumerable efforts, sometimes in competition with or in contradiction to each
other, which all tended toward action to block the renewal of the
horrors of the World War. There is no doubt that it was aided by
prosperity, which created general optimism and made the realization
of the noble ideal of peace seem less utopian. Conversely, it was the
disappearance of prosperity which permitted the skeptics and realists
to see that pacifism was loaded with illusions.

One can distinguish two main types of peace organizations in the
United States—conservative and radical. The conservative organizations were all located in the East and so were most of their members.
These organizations were generally endowed with substantial funds
from the beginning. Let us note the leading ones. The Carnegie En-

dowment for International Peace, already mentioned, founded in 1910, favored close cooperation with the League of Nations. Five hundred thousand dollars a year was spent in publications, including a monthly, *International Conciliation,* and a monumental *Economic and Social History of the World War* in over one hundred volumes. The endowment, among other things, set up libraries, subsidized small local peace organizations, and rebuilt the library at the University of Louvain. The World Peace Foundation, founded in 1910 with an endowment of $500,000, favored the League of Nations and distributed its publications. It especially favored United States membership in the World Court. The Woodrow Wilson Foundation, which was founded in 1923 with about 1 million dollars, kept the flame of Wilsonianism burning by aiding scholars who were studying Wilson. The League of Nations Association, also created in 1923, sought to attract members, but never gained more than 50,000.

The radical organizations were much more numerous and much less rich—drawing support chiefly from the dues of their members. Most of them were not much in favor of the League of Nations, and in a sense were isolationist. They preached disarmament and the outlawry of war, and believed in the possibility of the effectiveness of arbitration by the World Court. Their names, which changed often, are very interesting: American Committee for the Cause and Cure of War, Committee on Militarism in Education, Fellowship of Reconciliation (4500 members), Parliament of Peace and Universal Brotherhood, Peace Heroes Memorial Society, War Resisters' League (400 members), Women's Peace Association.

Three of these came to predominate over the others because of the personality of their leaders. The Women's Peace Party, which became after the war the Women's International League for Peace and Freedom, had been founded by Jane Addams, aided by Emily Balch, who was director of the American branch. Mrs. Carrie Chapman Catt broke with Jane Addams to found the American Committee for the Cause and Cure of War in 1921. This impressive person, an ardent feminist, proposed an ambitious program to women, who had just won the vote: to substitute the slogan "Go out and abolish war" for "Go home and wash the dishes." Jane Addams succeeded in gaining 6000 followers and she played an active role at the time of the Kellogg-Briand Pact.

The National Council for the Prevention of War, whose director was Frederick J. Libby, had its offices in Washington facing the building which housed the Departments of War, Navy, and State. Libby was a former Congregational minister turned Quaker. His goal was to coordinate the activities of organizations of many different kinds to get them to participate in the peace movement. He was able to raise enough money—$113,000 in 1927—to distribute peace literature—430,000 documents in January 1927. In 1932, at the start of the Disarmament Conference, the National Council published bimonthly manifestos in 2500 daily newspapers and 5000 weeklies. Its members gave 3000 lectures, participated in 4000 meetings on disarmament, and published 2,615,000 copies of antiwar documents. The National Council was most active in propaganda for disarmament.

Special mention must be made of the American Committee for the Outlawry of War and its founder Salmon O. Levinson, because to outlaw war was the specific intention of the Kellogg-Briand Pact. Levinson was the grandson of a Jewish refugee who had fled Prussia in 1848 and settled in Indiana. There was a strong antimilitarist tradition in the family. Levinson became a successful lawyer and belonged to the progressive wing of the Republican party. The outbreak of war in Europe led him to formulate a doctrine which might be summarized thus: International law recognizes war as an "institution," and forbids only certain practices. All institutions exist under law. Slavery and the family are institutions; slavery has been abolished by law, and war can also be abolished, declared "outside the law," by law—international and national. This doctrine assumes the existence of an international instrument with the power of compulsory arbitration. The decisions of such a court would not result in "collective sanctions" which really amount to war, but in individual sanctions, under the laws of his own country, against the statesman guilty of starting a war. There was a weakness in the system: one can easily imagine a case where a country, following its leader in the path of war, would refuse to condemn him by applying international or even national law.

These ideas—partly inspired by Charles W. Eliot, president-emeritus of Harvard, and Herbert Croly—were first set forth in the *New Republic* on March 19, 1918, in an article entitled "The Legal Status of War," and later embodied in a pamphlet of December 25, 1921, "The Plan to Outlaw War." In the meantime, Levinson had turned against the League of Nations, "a compromise . . . a system without force, a court without power, a body without a head . . . more an alliance than a league." [19] Levinson struggled to get the Republican party to choose as candidate Senator Knox, whom he had converted to his views, at the time Harding was chosen, and he tried in vain to get his plan included in the Republican platform. The plan to outlaw war was drawn up on the same day, December 9, 1921, that Levinson created the American Committee for the Outlawry of War. From then on Levinson, with the support of the American Committee, tried to put his ideas across by action and by propaganda, which he generally financed himself. With the help of Borah, the plan was inserted in the *Congressional Record* and approximately a million copies were distributed.

The illustrious Senator Borah was Levinson's chief disciple. They met for the first time in December 1919. Levinson thought him a choice recruit—Borah the opponent of the League of Nations, Borah the champion of disarmament, Borah the successful spokesman of a point of view. Levinson, on the other hand, could be useful to Borah's political career. Since Harding and Hughes had refused to declare war outlawed, Levinson suggested to Borah that it be done in a Senate resolution. (Levinson was deeply opposed to Hughes whom he considered too much in favor of the League of Nations.) After much hesitation, Borah decided to propose such a resolution in February 1923, but he put little energy into supporting it, preoccupied as he was with other causes. Borah became chairman of the Senate Committee on Foreign Relations at Lodge's death in 1924.

The peace groups—conservative or radical, supporting or opposing the League, excited or not by the World Court and the outlawry of war—represented a deep current of American opinion. Even with remarkably few members they succeeded through influencing other organizations in reaching between forty and sixty million Americans, according to Masland.[20] They lobbied in Washington also. All this was to be transferred to the political plane, but in a curious way, because Coolidge and Kellogg were not much in favor of the outlawry of war. "People are not interested in this proposition," said Coolidge in 1927, "they probably think it is impractical."

The initiative on the political plane came from Aristide Briand. On April 6, 1927, the tenth anniversary of the American entry in the war, Briand addressed a message to the American people—not to the government—proposing that the two nations, France and the United States, forever renounce war as a means of resolving national differences. Briand's initiative and the developments which followed are closely related to the actions of certain American pacifists, and the process is interesting to study.

Briand, who was not naïve, knew that his message had no significance in itself. For France and the United States to renounce war would be an empty gesture because such a contingency was very improbable. But Briand seems to have been working for two results (beyond personal glory). First, he wanted to counteract the current American criticism of France for her militarism, her policy of alliances (with Rumania in June 1926, and with Yugoslavia in November 1927), her failure to pay her debts, and her refusal to take part in a conference on naval disarmament proposed by Coolidge for the following summer in Geneva. The second object was to sign a treaty with the United States, if possible, which would assure France of American neutrality in all circumstances—what Borah and Levinson called a "negative alliance."

Two eminent American scholars, conservative advocates of peace connected with the Carnegie Endowment, had given Briand the idea. Nicholas Murray Butler first advised Briand, in June 1926, to read Clausewitz' chapter "War as an Instrument of Policy." Why did not civilized governments try to abolish this instrument? [21] The historian James T. Shotwell, professor at Columbia, former member of the Inquiry Bureau, who had been sent by the Carnegie Endowment to the University of Berlin as visiting professor of international relations, met Briand on March 22, 1927, and according to his own account, drew up what was to become Briand's message almost word for word. There were two key sentences which drew reactions from both the partisans and the opponents of the League of Nations. The first said that the two nations should conclude an agreement "tending to outlaw war, to borrow an American expression." This flattered the American peace groups. The second sentence spoke of the "renunciation of war," meaning that war would only be allowable in "international form," the sanctions of the League of Nations.[22]

By a happy coincidence, Levinson was on the ocean en route to France for a vacation with his family on April 6, 1927. He greeted the news of Briand's message enthusiastically and called on Briand to congratulate him immediately on arrival in France. Briand, knowing that he was caught between the pro-League and anti-League factions, let Levinson understand that he found Butler and Shotwell burdensome. At the same time he told Shotwell that Levinson seemed to him dangerous. This maneuver succeeded. American newspapers, after some hesitation, gave a great deal of favorable coverage to Briand's proposal. The French, for their part, saved their enthusiasm for Charles Lindbergh, who landed at Le Bourget on May 21, 1927, after the first successful trans-Atlantic flight. Briand took the occasion of a luncheon he gave in Lindbergh's honor to propose to ambassador Myron T. Herrick a plan for a treaty to carry out his message, addressing himself this time to the United States government.

Kellogg was not pleased. He scorned, and he feared, this private and meddling diplomacy of Butler, Shotwell, and Levinson. Furthermore, his main objective at the time was the signing of bilateral arbitration treaties, like Bryan's in 1913 but even less effective because they excluded arbitration of conflicts involving the internal affairs of signatories, of conflicts with third parties, of conflicts involving the Monroe Doctrine, and of conflicts which would bring about action in the League of Nations. (A Franco-American treaty of this type was signed in Washington on February 6, 1928, by the French ambassador, Paul Claudel.) Moreover, Kellogg took a very dim view of a bilateral treaty with France, which would antagonize other countries and raise objections in the Senate. All during the summer Kellogg, by agreement with Coolidge, remained silent, despite the mounting pressure of the peace groups and the discreet advances of Claudel.

Kellogg was saved by Borah, who had not reacted very well to the idea of the renunciation of war as an instrument of policy, which was too reminiscent of Geneva. On the other hand, briefed by his friend Levinson, he praised the outlawry of war. Why not outlaw war for *all* nations and not just for the United States and France? This idea made its appearance in the press as early as May. On December 22 when Kellogg went to a meeting of the Senate Committee on Foreign Relations with his arbitration treaty under his arm, Borah told him that war should be outlawed for all the nations of the world. Kellogg leapt at this idea. Thus this man who never pronounced the word "pacifist" without pejorative adjectives became the champion of outlawing war, to the great surprise of his staff. He finally sent a reply to Claudel on December 28.

The rest of the negotiations do not concern American foreign policy. Briand, who had already won the Nobel Peace Prize—Kellogg was soon to get it—no longer needed to make futile gestures. His bilateral treaty would have been infinitely more popular in France just because it seemed a little like an alliance, but one by one the great powers, led by Germany, acclaimed Kellogg's proposition and showed a desire to go along with it. Briand gave way in March. It remained only to harmonize the proposal with the League of Nations, specifically to reintroduce the condemnation of war "as an instrument of national policy." This was a matter of diplomatic routine. On August 18 Kellogg and his staff sailed on the *Ile de France* to sign the pact in Paris— partly to flatter Briand's somewhat wounded vanity. On August 27 fifteen nations signed the pact which condemned war as a means "to solve international conflicts" and bound the signatories solemnly to "renounce [war] as an instrument of national policy in their mutual relations."

One cannot understand this development, nor the Senate's approval by 85 votes to 1 (January 15, 1929) without understanding the atmosphere which had prevailed since Briand's proposal. The peace movements had been unleashed. Levinson and Jane Addams multiplied their calls on Kellogg and his subordinates. The indomitable Mrs. Catt organized 12,533 meetings, mostly of women, at which resolutions were passed. She called on each senator, declaring that if these resolutions were laid end to end they would stretch for a mile. Tens of thousands of people signed the petitions; one of them had 180,000 signatures. The National Council for the Prevention of War sent out 18,000 letters between November 5 and January 14. In December 1928 the White House received 200 letters a day and the State Department, 600. Without doubt this great agitation swayed Kellogg, encouraged Borah, and was responsible for the Senate decision.

This effective enthusiasm was the determining factor; there was no political activity involved. Public opinion acted directly through many small but well-organized pressure groups. Public opinion is naïve. Levinson thought himself responsible for a great historical event, but he was forgetting human inertia and man's tendency not to carry out his promises when there is no agency with power to make him do so. Any arrangement which might involve a possible resort to war (to enforce peace) was discredited in American eyes. It would merely introduce the old evils. War was abolished by denying its existence.

It was one thing for this idea to be held by noble idealists and quite another for Kellogg to be suddenly converted after having declared himself hostile. This is no longer even "open diplomacy," formulated by statesmen and presented to the public; it is diplomacy of the public adopted by statesmen. Such a situation is only possible if the statesmen are weak or lacking in force. Kellogg was explosive in temperament, but his anger would simmer down and he did not know how to hold a firm line. The episode is another instance of the policy of illusion—dangerous illusion—because it created an artificial sense of psychological security, with no shadow of effective guarantee. Kellogg, who died in 1937, could see by 1931 what his pact was worth. He said then he felt he was living in another epoch. As for Levinson, his consolation was near. War was outlawed but a tribunal with the power of compulsory arbitration was still lacking. Without the court the whole edifice would crumble. "Public ignorance [hence] created a serious problem in the conduct of American diplomacy. American diplomats were capable men, well-intentioned, as full of good will as the peace leaders and workers who bothered them. But they had to cope with a public opinion whose only virtue often was that it was public and opinionated." [23]

The Havana Conference

Under Kellogg Latin American policy continued in the general direction given it by Hughes. Without changing any principles or abandoning the right of intervention, an attempt was made to limit their application as much as possible. This was done so systematically that the period can be considered the dawn of the "Good Neighbor Policy."

In the first place, Latin America received its share of the dollar flood described above. From the point of view of the American government, this was the way, Hughes said, "not to exploit but to aid in laying the foundations for a sane, stable and independent government." [24] From the standpoint of the banks making loans, the picture was less bright: they wanted the government to help them (by force if necessary) to realize the substantial profits they had expected from their loans to Latin America and in any case to recover what was owed them.

As the Latin American nations saw it, this was nothing but the continuation of the old dollar diplomacy with all its disagreeable consequences for them. Nevertheless one can hardly doubt that they benefited from it. The State Department exercised over private loans to Latin America a control similar to its control over loans to Europe. Indeed, in the case of three countries, Cuba, Haiti, and San Domingo, the treaties in force—treaties which virtually made them protectorates —gave the United States power to approve or reject loans. Everywhere else the State Department tried to prevent loans which would favor corrupt regimes or which were destined for the purchase of arms. Thus in October 1924 it blocked a Peruvian request for a loan which would have antagonized Chile because of the continued conflict over Tacna-Arica.

Coolidge's own attitude evolved in a liberal direction. In April 1925 Coolidge was still defending the principle of intervention: "There is a clear and simple obligation for self-respecting governments to protect the persons and property of their citizens wherever they may be." [25] Three years later, at the Havana conference, the American attitude was much more moderate. It was the Sixth Pan-American Conference (the Fifth had taken place in Santiago in 1923). Coolidge decided to attend in person, with a particularly brilliant delegation, including Kellogg, Hughes, Ambassador Fletcher, Dwight Morrow— formerly of J. P. Morgan, now ambassador to Mexico—and former Senator Underwood, among others. Cuba's President Machado received Coolidge on January 15, 1928. Hughes, presiding over the American delegation, had been instructed to bear in mind the "vigorous anti-American propaganda" which Argentina was aiming at the Yankees, to avoid dangerous subjects, and not to accept the doctrine of nonintervention.

It is in relation to this last point that the conference was important. The decisions concerning the reorganization of the Pan-American Union and the acceptance of a Mexican resolution denouncing aggression have little significance compared to the challenging problem of nonintervention. As it happened, the Marines who had been withdrawn from Nicaragua in 1925 had landed there again at the end of 1926 to protect American citizens from the effects of a bitter civil war. Henry L. Stimson, Secretary of War under Taft, had been sent on a special mission to reach an agreement with President Diaz, who was conservative and pro-American. Stimson had succeeded in achieving a cease-fire. But the return of the Marines, which took place before the Havana Conference, violently aroused Latin American opinion against the Colossus of the North.

The problem was first approached indirectly. A commission of jurists meeting in Rio de Janeiro had worked out a code of international law for the use of the American republics. They had inserted the following formula: "No state may intervene in the domestic affairs of another." This wording was in itself quite innocuous as there was no definition of the word "intervene" nor of "domestic affairs." On the other hand, prevailing international law recognized cases where intervention would be legitimate. Nevertheless this text was submitted to the conference by Puyrredón, Argentine ambassador to the United States, and Gustave Guerrero, Minister of Foreign Affairs of San Salvador. Hughes maneuvered with great ability and succeeded in obtaining agreement that the question would not be discussed until the next Pan-American Conference, scheduled to be held in Montevideo in 1933. Everything seemed to be under control.

But the problem soon reappeared. On February 18 in the final plenary session, Guerrero, at the request of Cuba's Bustamente, chairman of the conference, brought up again the proposition of the jurists. There was a violent debate. Would the United States be isolated and put in an untenable moral position? Hughes saved the situation in a speech outstanding for its logic, which was translated verbatim into Spanish. He began by proclaiming his country's concern for the independence of all nations and especially of all American nations: "We do not wish the territory of any American Republic. We do not wish to govern any American Republic. We do not wish to intervene in the affairs of any American Republic. We simply wish peace and order and stability and recognition of honest rights properly acquired." And he faced the problem squarely, "What are we to do when government breaks down and American citizens are in danger of their lives? Are we to stand by and see them butchered in the jungle because a government in circumstances which it cannot control and for which it may not be responsible can no longer afford reasonable protection? . . . Of course the United States cannot forego its right to protect its citizens . . . International law cannot be changed by the resolutions of this conference." [26]

Hughes had shown that the Latin Americans—often bedeviled by bloody revolutions—had their own share of responsibility in this matter. The result was that Guerrero had to withdraw his proposal. The conference could close on a more friendly note.

Coolidge and Kellogg were to go even further. Without yet renouncing the right of intervention, the United States could at least officially renounce the Roosevelt Corollary. We have seen that Hughes had already made a move in this direction in 1923, when he tried to disassociate the right of intervention from the Monroe Doctrine. Kellogg asked Undersecretary of State Reuben J. Clark to prepare a memorandum on the Monroe Doctrine which was submitted to Kellogg on December 17, 1928. Clark defended the thesis that the Monroe Doctrine—aimed at possible infringements from Europe and founded on the principle of New World security—did not apply to purely inter-American relations. "The so-called Roosevelt Corollary was to the effect, as generally understood, that in case of financial or other difficulties in weak Latin American countries, the United States should attempt an adjustment thereof lest European governments should intervene . . . an act which would be contrary to the Monroe Doctrine . . . It is not believed that this Corollary is justified by the terms of the Monroe Doctrine." [27] The Clark memorandum was not published until June 1930, under Stimson, Kellogg's successor, but it indicates that United States policy toward Latin America was taking a more flexible and moderate form as early as 1928.

Further proof of this lies in the relations between the United States and Mexico. It will be remembered that Plutarco Elias Calles had been elected president in 1924. Up to June 1925 relations remained good, but many difficulties concerned with American property in Mexico continued to arise. Kellogg at this time published a strong declaration of protest: "The Mexican government is now being tested in the eyes of the world. We have the greatest interest in the stability, prosperity and independence of Mexico. We have been patient and we understand that it takes time to establish a stable government, but we cannot tolerate the violation of [the government's] obligations and the lack of protection of American citizens."

Calles replied that Kellogg's words threatened Mexican sovereignty and two laws were quickly passed by the Mexican legislature which were not of a kind to clear the air. The first (December 31, 1925) declared that since oil was a national resource, only Mexicans could exploit it. The law limited to fifty years concessions granted before May 1, 1917. The second law (January 21, 1926) forbade foreigners to purchase land within fifty miles of the coasts and frontiers. In February 1926 persecution of Roman Catholics began. Violent protests were made by Americans owning property in Mexico and by American Roman Catholics. They demanded that Coolidge withdraw recognition. The landing of the Marines in Nicaragua further poisoned the atmosphere.

Kellogg, however, wanted to establish good relations. His choice of the financier Dwight D. Morrow as ambassador to Mexico—October 27—was a fortunate one. Morrow, trying to change the atmosphere from suspicion to confidence and cooperation, decided that it would be more effective to deal with concrete problems rather than continue to exchange mutual protests. He succeeded in reaching an agreement on oil and on some indemnities for American property owners. He also succeeded in persuading the Mexican government to adopt a less hostile attitude toward the clergy. When he left Mexico on September 17, 1930, President Ortiz Rubio could say that relations between the two countries had reached "the height of cordiality." Morrow had followed Coolidge's advice, which can be considered as an expression of a new attitude toward Latin America in the United States: "A firm adherence to our rights and a scrupulous respect for the sovereignty of Mexico . . . coupled with patience and forbearance, it is hoped, will resolve all our difficulties." [28]

Chapter IX

Hoover, Stimson, and the Great Depression

The New Team

THERE is a striking contrast between the mediocre, dull, uninspired diplomacy of Kellogg and the positive—at least temporarily—nature of American foreign policy when the new team came to power in March 1929. For the first time in many years there was in fact a "team." Wilson's personality had to some extent overwhelmed his three successive secretaries of state and Roosevelt would do the same, except at first when he left foreign policy to Cordell Hull. Colonel House under Wilson, and Raymond Moley and later Harry Hopkins under Roosevelt, had a much more important place—although without holding office—than the secretaries of state. In contrast, Hughes, as we have seen, had played the leading part in foreign policy and kept President Harding virtually on the sidelines. The association of Coolidge and Kellogg had not been a very close one, nor had they followed a dynamic policy.

First let us look at the new President. He was, as Schlesinger says, "The American who, more and more, emerges as the man who might bridge the gap between ideals and the realities of the new era." [1] Herbert Clark Hoover had been born in 1874 in West Branch, Iowa, of a middle-class family strongly attached to Quaker ideals. At the age of eight, after his parents died, he went to live with cousins in Oregon. He was an outstanding student of engineering in newly founded Stanford University, and in 1897 he took a job with a British mining firm as a specialist in gold mines. From then on he was to lead a life rich in travel and in experience. He spent two years in western Australia and at the age of twenty-five he became chief engineer of the Chinese Bureau of Mines. At twenty-seven, he was codirector of the large British firm Bervick-Moreing and made his headquarters in London, but he continued to travel to Burma, Transvaal, Egypt, Malaya, and elsewhere.

A determined, forceful, and objective worker, Hoover's special gift was for organization. He was cold and reserved, however, and completely lacked a sense of humor. "I never remember hearing him laugh out loud" wrote one of his college friends in 1928.[2] He had that Quaker quality that can be described as "unemotional stoicism." [3] Although living in England, he took an active interest in American politics. In 1908 he decided to work on his own as a consulting engineer. In addition he became politically active and in 1909 he joined the National Republican Club. In 1912 he campaigned for Theodore Roosevelt, candidate of the Progressive party. He had acquired a large fortune from his various mining ventures throughout the world.

When the war broke out, Wilson—on whom Hoover had made a great impression—appointed him to take charge of aid to Belgium. This was very much in line with his Quaker ideals: to help the unfortunate without taking sides and to combine generosity and systematic organization—a technique of which the Quakers are past masters. Thus diplomatic experience was added to his experience as a businessman. When the United States entered the war he became administrator of supply. At the end of 1918 he was put in charge of aid to Europe. When he returned to the United States in September 1919, he was, as Schlesinger puts it, "a political figure on the national level." Louis Brandeis said in 1920, "I am one hundred per cent for him . . . High public spirit, extraordinary intelligence, knowledge, sympathy with youth and a rare perception of what is really worthwhile for the country, would, with his organizing ability and power of inspiring loyalty, do wonderful things in the presidency." [4]

At that time he had the support of many Democrats; we have quoted Brandeis. Franklin D. Roosevelt hoped also to win him over to the party. He had known him during the war and said "There could not be a better President." [5] Hoover, however, decided in favor of the Republican party to which he had formerly adhered. Although favoring the League of Nations, he campaigned for Harding, who appointed him Secretary of Commerce. In 1922 he published a book, *American Individualism*, in which he set forth his political philosophy. He rejected equally socialism and selfish individualism, both of European origin. America should adopt what he called "progressive individualism," based on equality of opportunity and equality of responsibility. He believed in a society with a hierarchy based on merit and characterized by cooperation between its component parts. He optimistically believed that the concentrated power of big business favored this cooperation. In his position as Secretary of Commerce he tried to apply this doctrine: to encourage exports, especially those of the major companies; to encourage foreign investment of capital to develop prosperity. He favored the continuation of high tariffs and was one of the most active creators of the economic boom—the prosperity which was to end so suddenly during his presidency.

In 1928, Hoover—still Secretary of Commerce under Coolidge—was the obvious Republican candidate. Only Coolidge, had he decided to run, could have opposed him successfully. When Coolidge refused, the Republican convention in Chicago nominated Hoover, who easily defeated his Democratic opponent, Alfred E. Smith. The astonishing American prosperity was a factor in his favor. As he said during the campaign, "Without the wise policies which the Republican Party has made effective during the past seven and one-half years the great prosperity we now enjoy would not have been possible." [6]

On January 26, 1929, Henry L. Stimson, governor general of the Philippines, received a telegram from the President asking him to join the cabinet either as Attorney General or as Secretary of State. Hoover had suggested to Kellogg that he stay on, but Kellogg was too weary. The President had then approached Borah, but the senator had preferred to remain chairman of the Committee on Foreign Relations. Hoover then thought of Stimson, who had the strong support of Root, Hughes, and Taft. "I appreciate deeply Mr. Hoover's confidence and personal association with him would be very agreeable," he said. He chose the State Department: "Foreign affairs are now our most important national concern." [7]

Henry L. Stimson was seven years older than Hoover. He was born in New York on September 21, 1867, of a New England family. In contrast to Hoover, associated with Iowa and Oregon, he represented the East. His family had migrated to Massachusetts in the seventeenth century and he had some Huguenot ancestry. His grandparents were still country dwellers but his father, preferring life in the city, had moved to New York and had had an unusual career. After becoming established as a banker, he decided to study medicine; he studied under Pasteur in Paris and became a practicing and teaching physician. His son Henry attended Phillips Academy at Andover, Yale (1884–1888), and Harvard Law School. In 1893 he joined one of the largest law firms in New York, Root and Clark. Elihu Root,

McKinley's Secretary of War and Theodore Roosevelt's Secretary of State, influenced Stimson to a great extent. Indeed, Stimson said that Root was his model.

Stimson took part in local politics in his New York district, but his career was to be spent for the most part in positions outside the party machinery. Theodore Roosevelt, his neighbor on Long Island, started him on the longest and richest political career of any American statesman in the twentieth century when he appointed him district attorney for the southern district of New York in December 1905—an office which he took over on February 1, 1906. From then until September 21, 1946—his seventy-eighth birthday—he was to hold many positions and be four times a cabinet member, three times under Republican presidents and once under Franklin D. Roosevelt.

Let us review the main phases of his long career prior to 1929. He remained district attorney until April 1, 1909. In May 1911 Taft offered him the post of Secretary of War, which he accepted, not without some soul-searching. The rift between the Progressives, led by his old friend Theodore Roosevelt, and the Republican conservatives under Taft was taking shape at the time. Stimson wished to support the program of General Wood, chief of the general staff, to strengthen the Army. He was also responsible for the administration of the Philippines and Puerto Rico and had to see that the Panama Canal was completed. When the rupture between the two Republican factions occurred in 1912, he supported Taft. "I entered into public life under the inspiration of Theodore Roosevelt. I am a firm believer in the great national policies for which he has fought. And I now remain his sincere friend. But I believe that those who are forcing him, contrary to his original intention, into the arena against Mr. Taft, are jeopardizing instead of helping the real cause of progress in the nation." [8] For three years he was to be at odds with "Teddy." Stimson, known up to this time as a progressive, was to appear—wrongly—a determined conservative from then on.

The outbreak of war found him back in private life, as a result of the victory of the Democrats under Wilson. We must remember that he was a warm supporter of France, where he had lived as a child when his father studied medicine in Paris. Well before Wilson's conversion, Stimson was a militant advocate of "preparedness" in the Army and Navy. Nevertheless he strongly opposed Wilson's methods for implementing it. Once the war broke out, he went back into the

Army as lieutenant colonel and then as colonel in the artillery. He went to the front for several weeks with a British division, took a specialized artillery course, spent some more weeks in the trenches —this time with an American regiment—and on August 2 was recalled to the United States. If he had fought little, he had nevertheless gained great practical experience which would be useful in June 1940.

Returned to civilian life, he was, along with Hoover whom he didn't yet know, one of the warmest Republican supporters of the League of Nations. He agreed with Root about the necessary amendments and would have preferred a less rigid Covenant, allowing the organization to be perfected gradually. In 1920, again like Hoover, he supported Harding, whom he wrongly considered to be in favor of membership in the League. He was to say in 1948 that this was one of the greatest mistakes of his life. All this shows that he was in no way an isolationist. He wrote in his diary for November 26, 1919, "if the situation ever came to a point where the Republican Party stood for a selfish isolation of America as against a participation in the burdens of the world at the present time by this country, I should certainly vote against the Republican Party." [9]

This explains the frankly "internationalist" attitude that he was to take under Hoover. Up to 1926 he held no Federal office but pursued a brilliant career at the bar, very closely intertwined with political life. In the spring of 1927 Coolidge appointed him special envoy to the President of Nicaragua, which had just been reoccupied by the Marines and was torn by civil war. Stimson succeeded in bringing this war to an end, which explains why Coolidge appointed him to succeed General Leonard Wood as governor general of the Philippines early in 1928. It was in the Philippines that he received Hoover's telegram calling him to the cabinet.

Hoover the engineer and Stimson the lawyer had much in common. Like Hoover, Stimson was cold, reserved, austere. "He was dignity incarnate, a fanatic about punctuality and protocol." One of his subordinates said he was "a man under whom it was very difficult to work." [10] This judgment must be weighed against all the affection he inspired in his other associates. From a firm self-confidence stemmed a strong will, amazing tenacity, and a sense of duty and of honor which was consistently rigid. He had something of the theorist in him but also something of the soldier. The harshest of his biographers, Richard Current, has drawn attention to his decision to entitle his memoirs *On Active Service*. It is not surprising that he was sympathetic to the slightly flamboyant imperialism of Theodore Roosevelt, that he favored colonial expansion in the sense implied by the idea of "the White Man's Burden." All told, his was an unusual personality. Although he had great business experience, in 1929 he was not trained in foreign policy, and he applied to it the characteristics of thought developed in other spheres. Never popular, especially disliking press conferences, he preferred to write his own articles and books.

Hoover and Stimson respected each other, but between these two authoritarian personalities there were frequent clashes, especially after 1931. While Stimson liked a certain ceremony, Hoover had simple tastes. Furthermore they did not see problems in the same way.

One was by nature and training an advocate and a fighter; the other was an organizer and a planner. Mr. Hoover liked to calculate his moves as he would the building of a bridge, while Stimson preferred to choose his main objective and then charge ahead without worrying . . . Mr. Hoover was a worker, capable of more intense and prolonged intellectual effort than any other man [Stimson ever met] . . . Stimson was not made that way; his strength depended on regular rest, substantial vacations, and constant physical exercise.[11]

"Their mental habits were fundamentally incompatible." [12]

The Depression

Hoover's presidency is above all dominated by the economic crisis which cost him a political career that might have been one of the most brilliant in American history. Hoover's career was ended in the election of 1932 because of the depression. Public reaction was harsher than Hoover deserved. His attitude, compared to Roosevelt's, has and still does cause passionate controversy among economists and historians. Perhaps after thirty years one can do him greater justice.

Our task is not to describe the depression as a whole, nor to go into detail, but to try to measure its importance on the international plane. A rapid survey of the facts is nevertheless necessary.

The prosperity of the 1920's had been characterized by an enormous growth of the national income and of industrial production— as distinct from agricultural production—and above all by an extraordinary expansion of credit. The index of industrial production had gone from 73 in 1922 to 110 in 1928 and to 126 in July 1929.[13] The national income, as we have seen, had risen from 60.7 billion dollars to 87.2 billion. The index of wholesale prices had slightly declined; that of wages had gone up 13 percent. The overall value of shares on the stock market had risen from 27 billion dollars in January 1925 to 67 billion in January 1929. Whereas the expansion of production had tapered off since 1927, and especially since 1929, the total value of shares went from 67 to 87 billion dollars between January and October 1929.

It is not surprising, therefore, that the crisis broke in the form of a crash in the stock market. Since 1927 the increase in the number of stocks quoted on the market was a result not of industrial expansion but of pure speculation. On Black Thursday, October 24, 1929, a wind of panic blew through the stock exchange and 13 billion shares were dumped on the market, whence a formidable fall of 32 percent in industrial stocks between September and December 1929. This crash of the market was not the *cause* of the crisis, which was related to the excess in production and the abnormal growth of credit, it was merely a sign of it, but it acted also as a psychological factor, in the sense that it immediately paralyzed the will to fight of the great credit organizations, caused the shutdown of many large industries, and thus led to unemployment. The domestic market shrank in an unprecedented manner. Salaries and wages fell 40 percent and rural revenue—the hardest hit—fell from 5.1 billion dollars in 1929 to 1.5 billion in 1932. Production fell 45 percent in these same three years. Prices fell; so did the cost of living, by 20 percent. The total wages of those who continued to be employed—for longer hours and lower wages—fell 32 percent, which proved a severe blow to the standard of living. Nevertheless, those who were still employed were fortunate. In 1929 there were between 1.5 and 2.5 million unemployed, by 1932 the number had risen to between 11.4 and 14.7 million.

On the international level, which interests us here, we know that prosperity had coincided with an enormous export of capital. The "rugged individualism" of the Republican leaders, which Hoover called "American individualism," had prevented complete and strict government control of the movement of capital, and had resulted in a wild expansion. During the era of prosperity the excess of exports over imports had averaged 733 million dollars a year, rising from 454 million dollars in 1926 to over 1 billion in 1929. A large part of the resulting profits were used in the form of credit abroad and we have seen in the last chapter how this phenomenon had worked. Direct investments were much healthier than private credits; they at least permitted American personnel to control the management of the undertakings, and private credits represented the same type of specu-lation—on a smaller scale—as the increasing issue of stock certificates at home. Appeals were made to the holders of American savings either to buy stock certificates or to buy foreign stocks. For the latter pur-pose every organization capable of borrowing was solicited with a barrage of propaganda. Banking houses saw in this the possibility of considerable profits.

To this very understandable desire for profits was added a kind of conscious effort on the part of the big bankers to assure the United States world supremacy in commercial, financial, and monetary mat-ters. Testifying before an investigating commission, the banker Otto Kahn said, "In 1929, we thought that we were greater and stronger than we were in reality. We wished to control the entire world, we wished to be the monetary center of the world; we wished to be the greatest country from the industrial point of view, the greatest ex-porter of goods, the greatest lender of money." [14]

This is a characteristic attitude of Republican foreign policy: let industry and the banks act for the greater glory of the United States. On December 4, 1928, in the message so full of optimism and pride that we have already quoted, President Coolidge said, evoking pros-perity and universal peace, "The principal source of these unprece-dented blessings lies in the integrity and character of the American people." [15] Thus it was not so much foreign *policy*—as the govern-ment imposed laissez faire on itself—as foreign *affairs*. There was an immense effort, if not of the whole nation, at least of its great bankers and businessmen, to control the world economy. American finance, in a special and original way, was strongly internationalist.

When the crisis broke, this structure foundered and with it the financial leadership of the nation. Foreign commerce declined first. Imports—raw materials above all—dropped from 4.4 billion dollars in 1929 to 1.3 billion in 1933. Exports fell from 5.2 billion dollars in 1929 to 1.6 billion in 1933. The balance of payments remained favor-able but fell to 175 million dollars in 1931 and to 160 million in 1932; in 1933 it climbed back to 287 million.

Investments abroad continued in the first months of 1930, but later ceased almost entirely. By 1939 subscription to foreign issues had fallen to an annual average of 60 million dollars as against about 1.2 billion in 1927. Direct investments disappeared: they totaled 294 million dollars in 1930, 222 million in 1931, almost none in 1932. In 1931 and 1932 American holdings abroad were largely brought home, which affected Germany and Latin America especially, and contributed to the rapid spread of the crisis in Europe and the Western Hemisphere. Naturally the nations which suffered from the stoppage of credit reacted violently, usually in the traditional manner: abandonment of the gold standard and devaluation; sharp rises in tariffs—the most spectacular was the Import Duties Act of March 1932 which put an end to British free trade—the establishment of exchange control, and clearing and compensation agreements. As we shall see below, the annulment of German reparations and the refusal of debtor nations—"brave little Finland" excepted—to continue payment on the war debts were reactions of major importance, as was the development of economic autarchy, especially in Germany. Not only had the United States lost its financial hegemony, but a kind of economic warfare broke out to which the United States responded, at least under Roosevelt, by economic isolationism in perfect harmony with its increasing political isolationism.

This enormous shake-up had an obvious psychological aspect. Because of its balanced and flexible constitution, the United States did not experience, as a result of the crisis, either a fascist revolution as in Germany, or a disintegration of power as in France, or a tidal wave of conservatism as in Great Britain. Still it must be noted that in the darkest year, 1932, the multiplication of strikes and agitation was sometimes interpreted as threatening civil war. (History has proved this to have been an exaggeration, of course.) American reaction in the direction of isolationism was very strong, however, so that if one can question the application of this term to the period 1921–1932, in the 1930's the isolationist attitude was clearly dominant.

Isolationism, then, was but one manifestation of the general loss of confidence and bitter pessimism which overcame the country. The birth rate was another manifestation; it fell 17 percent from 1921 to 1931. The political and economic leaders of the period of prosperity had lost all their standing. Former President Coolidge said in December 1932, "We are in a new era to which I do not belong." [16] And

Walter Lippmann said, "The industrial and financial leaders of America have fallen from one of the highest positions of influence and power in American history to one of the lowest." [17] Similarly, Europeans, already considered by Americans to be imperialists and troublemakers, became targets of widespread anger. Their refusal to pay the war debts appeared really to be betrayal of the alliance. In Congress the influence of the die-hard isolationists like Borah and Pittman grew stronger because public opinion was known to support them. The result was one of the most important phenomena in the history of the world at the time: While Nazism was gaining strength and the first blows were struck against democracy by the Fascists and the Japanese militarists, the United States, the leading democratic power, disassociated itself from world affairs systematically, out of disillusionment. This dramatic consequence of the crisis was not immediately apparent, however. Hoover and Stimson tried, in their way, to pursue an internationalist policy.

Efforts at International Cooperation

From the start Hoover and Stimson showed a will to modify the American attitude toward international conferences. Instead of attempting to have them held in Washington or sending unofficial observers, as Hughes had, the United States would thenceforth take part in and even initiate conferences—regardless of whether they were more or less connected with the League of Nations. In contrast to the opinion of the nationalist senators, the League was not regarded as evil in itself by the Hoover administration, which desired to cooperate with it as much as possible. The system of "unofficial observers" was to be replaced by that of parallel action, even joint action in certain cases. Disarmament on land and sea, international economic questions, results of the depression, all these would be dealt with by conferences.

The first two problems to be resolved during the month of euphoria which preceded the crisis were those of the tariff—Hoover had promised revision in his presidential campaign—and naval disarmament. The Fordney-McCumber Tariff, passed in September 1922, raised the average rate from 26 percent (under the Underwood Act) to 38 percent, and provided for much greater flexibility. The tariff commission could raise any given tariff by 50 percent in cases where the American cost of production was greater than that of foreign goods.[18]

The discussions of a new law begun in 1929 were submerged by the crisis, creating a reaction of panic—shortsighted of course—with which Hoover associated himself in spite of Stimson. The old American Tariff League, a powerful pressure group of conservative interests, took the lead under Senator Joseph R. Grundy, a spokesman of the manufacturers, who has been called "the prince of Lobbyists." [19] Congress passed the Hawley-Smoot Tariff on June 17, 1930, despite the resistance of certain senators and especially of the Democrat Cordell Hull. This raised to 59 percent the average duty on protected goods and was the highest tariff since those of Dingley and McKinley. The fact that the United States was the chief creditor of the world and should thus favor the entrance of foreign goods to increase the chances of getting her money back, completely escaped the authors of the law. Hoover approved unreservedly the construction of this protectionist wall. There is a flagrant contradiction between his attitude on this point and the economic internationalism he otherwise defended.

The idea that a high tariff was a healthy and useful tradition was certainly shared by a majority of Americans. Today's judgments are somewhat more severe; Harris Gaylord Warren says it was a "political disaster." [20] Foreign nations responded at once with discriminatory measures of all sorts and Americans lost many markets. In 1937 the foreign commerce of the United States had fallen to the level of 1915. Among the consequences was to be the refusal of Europeans to pay the war debts. But the problem of debts came up later and it is better to follow events chronologically since their timing was often very important.

In his first sixteen months in the State Department, Stimson was chiefly busy with naval disarmament, which was, at least since 1921, a constant concern of Republican policy. Hughes had succeeded in obtaining a limitation in relation to warships over 10,000 tons, but the problem of smaller units remained. In the summer of 1927, Kellogg, less fortunate than his predecessor, had seen his efforts along this line fail. The Geneva Conference, in which France refused to participate, was a complete fiasco: the British, having a network of naval bases throughout the world, wanted many small cruisers; the Americans preferred a smaller number of large cruisers because they had few bases. The Japanese had watched this quarrel with amusement. The failure of Kellogg's attempt to limit the number of smaller ships caused a resurgence of the naval arms race. American legislation of February 13, 1929, provided for the construction of 15 cruisers of 10,000 tons each in the next three years.

Hoover considered the arms race to be absurd. Borah's proposed remedy was to include in the naval law a paragraph about the rights of neutrals, which he thought the only possible means to make a war with England impossible. Hoover, who knew Great Britain well, preferred to reopen discussions on disarmament. In this he was in agreement with Stimson. "It was the President who gave the real impulse to the effort to overcome the impasse of 1927." [21] As early as March 1929 he took the initiative. The assumption of power by the Labour party under MacDonald in Great Britain in June made things easier, and Charles Dawes, former Vice President and new ambassador to Great Britain, showed great ability.

Negotiations were held, therefore, primarily between the United States and Great Britain. The first attempt was to reconcile through a common formula the British idea of many cruisers with the American idea of big cruisers. Instead of measuring in tons and numbers of units, the negotiators resorted to an idea Hughes had had in 1921— that of a "yardstick" with which to measure existing armaments and which could also be used in any general plan for reduction.[22] Ambassador Hugh S. Gibson officially proposed this method in Geneva on April 22, 1929. The Naval War College and the Navy General Board worked actively on the problem and ended by proposing a formula in which E (fighting efficiency) $= D$ (tonnage displacement) $\times A$ (relative age) $\times G$ (firepower). Charles Francis Adams, Secretary of the Navy, defended this formula only halfheartedly. Many American experts claimed that there were too many qualitative elements involved to measure all types of vessels by a single formula. On July 15 the British rejected the yardstick. In October the negotiations concerning tonnage were well advanced and MacDonald came to the United States. This was the first time a British Prime Minister in office had visited the great republic. He had enormous personal success; the American administration felt on an equal plane with this "gentleman risen from the people." Agreement was reached on a tonnage of 339,000 for cruisers and small British ships, 315,000 for the United

States,[23] but with a larger number of heavy cruisers. As early as October 7 Hoover and MacDonald sent an invitation to the other naval powers to come to London to discuss naval disarmament.

The London Naval Conference was opened January 17, 1930, by King George V; it lasted until April 22. Stimson was chairman of the American delegation, which included also Secretary Adams and ambassadors Dawes, Morrow, and Gibson. There were three phases of the negotiations. The first consisted in completing the existing Anglo-American agreement; this was accomplished February 4 by a slight reduction (from 21 to 18) of the number of American heavy cruisers. The second consisted in obtaining Japan's adherence to the agreement. To achieve this the Japanese had to be granted a ratio of 3.5 (and not 3 as at the Washington Conference) to 5. The British wanted to reduce the maximum tonnage of each armored ship from 35,000 to 25,000 tons and also the number of aircraft carriers. The Americans—perhaps under the influence of Mahan's doctrine—refused. The third phase concerned France and Italy, but both countries refused to sign numerous clauses of the treaty. The Franco-Italian disagreement in London "was Stimson's introduction to the complexities of post-war Europe . . . it was the French intransigence that he found particularly annoying; but he was never able to forget the great part France had played in 1914–1918, and his friendship for the French people . . . never wavered." [24] Hoover on the contrary, disconcerted by the impulsiveness and the subtlety of Briand, showed a total incomprehension of the French attitude. We should note that the naval holiday for armored ships was extended to 1936 and that rules against unlimited submarine warfare were adopted, to Stimson's great satisfaction.

In all, at least in appearance, the conference was a great success for the United States, because the Treaty of London (April 22) insured real naval parity with Great Britain—which at the Washington Conference had only been established for heavy units. Officers of the United States Navy naturally thought it had been sacrificed and protested the reduction of heavy cruisers to 18.

Because of naval parity with Great Britain and a clear supremacy over Japan, the United States felt secure. The problem of land disarmament became of less interest. The American peacetime Army, fixed in 1929 at a maximum of 288,000 men, was soon reduced to 150,000 and even, after 1927, to 119,000.[25] This was barely the skeleton of an army. During the period when Douglas MacArthur was chief of the general staff (1930–1935) the American Army was extremely weak. In aviation the situation was the same, although in this sphere concern for national defense should have made Congress more flexible. Had not Lindbergh's flight across the Atlantic marked the dawn of a new era?

In aviation the United States had a farsighted theorist—Brigadier General William Mitchell, who had commanded the American Air Forces in France. As early as 1918, Mitchell, who thought the airplane "an offensive and not a defensive weapon," had conceived the singularly prophetic idea of a division of airborne paratroops. Anticipating the Italian General Douhet, he foresaw the possibility of bombardment not only of factories but of cities, as the surest way to destroy the moral and economic force of an enemy. He advocated the creation of a separate branch of the services under a new department of aviation. From then on, for Mitchell, air power was distinct from land power and from sea power. Douhet has been called the "Mahan of the air," but Mitchell deserves the title.

Mitchell came on the scene at an inopportune moment. The proposal to create a Department of Aeronautics, put forward in 1920 by Senator Harry S. New of Indiana, did not succeed. Mitchell undertook a fight in behalf of his ideas during which, in 1925, he used such a violent tone against his superiors that he was court-martialed and suspended for five years. He resigned and intensified the propaganda offensive to which his trial had given great publicity. Coolidge appointed a commission, under Dwight Morrow, to study the problem of air power, but its conclusions were contrary to Mitchell's ideas. This meant that in 1930, the air force—divided between the Army and the Navy—was as much a skeleton as the Army.

Hoover, however, was interested in disarmament for more general reasons, the idea of a sort of balance of power (he especially wanted to see revised the clauses of the Treaty of Versailles which kept Germany in a state of inferiority) and the moral ideal which derived from his Quaker tradition. On May 4, 1931, speaking to the International Chamber of Commerce in Washington, he declared that since success in naval disarmament had been achieved, success in disarmament of land forces should also be sought. On December 10, 1931, in a message to Congress, he announced that the United States would take part in a disarmament conference called by the League of Nations for

February 2, 1932, in Geneva. The American ambassador to Belgium, Hugh S. Gibson, who had already taken part in a preliminary conference, was designated head of the American delegation.

Stimson did not share Hoover's views on land disarmament. Here we see one of the first difficulties which were to separate these two remarkable men. Stimson's "own conviction was that armaments were less a cause than a result of international insecurity, and he was not optimistic about the prospects for disarmament unless and until the major political differences of Europe should have been materially eased." [26] For Stimson the problem of land disarmament was a European problem and above all a Franco-German problem. What he advised therefore, was that the United States should stand aside at Geneva, play the role of "honest broker," but attempt to reassure France on the problem most important to her—that is, her security. "Thus in Stimson's eyes, the disarmament problem was secondary to political problems." [27]

Stimson went to France in 1931; Premier Laval came to the United States in October of the same year. Stimson suggested greater flexibility concerning the eventual revision of Germany's eastern frontier. To apply the Treaty of Versailles strictly, he said, would be sure to revive the situation of 1806, after Jena, when France completely dominated a crushed Prussia. But seven years after Jena occurred the Battle of Leipzig.* Despite this line of reasoning Stimson had little chance of success. On the other hand, when Laval asked for a guarantee in the form of a Franco-American treaty by which the two countries would promise to consult each other—nothing more—if the Kellogg-Briand Pact was violated, Stimson was very tempted to agree. Hoover, however, harshly rejected the idea: "A political impossibility," he said.[28]

Hoover wanted to succeed in the matter of disarmament. He followed the conference closely. He personally drew up a memorandum which he read at a cabinet meeting on May 24, 1932, announcing that after a phase in which the United States had played a subordinate role at the conference, American policy should be changed; a "bold and constructive suggestion" should be formulated which would help to pull the world out of the mire.[29] To accomplish this he proposed

* The Battle of Leipzig, or Battle of the Nations, in October 1813, was the first general nationalist uprising in the Germanies against Napoleon.

a great plan: reduce by one third the number of armored ships, cruisers, and destroyers; abolish aircraft carriers, submarines, military aviation (except for purposes of observation), heavy artillery, tanks, poison gas; reduce the size of armies by one third. This proposition met with no success. Hoover attempted to save it by making it public on June 22 in a slightly different form, but public opinion was too weak or too much opposed to accept it, and nothing more came of it.

It was the same with another plan, which showed Hoover the Quaker and the organizer of aid to Europe, the adversary of blockading Germany in 1919. In a speech on November 1, 1929, Hoover proposed that the nations agree to assure complete liberty of movement to all ships carrying food in wartime. France and England opposed this, saying that it would deprive the League of Nations of one of its weapons against aggression. They were probably thinking that the blockade against Germany had been one of the reasons for their victory.

While these debates were going on, American foreign policy was faced with the very difficult problem of Europe's war debts, naturally connected with that of German reparations. The American crisis of 1929 soon engulfed Europe. The failure of the Credit-Anstalt in Vienna is generally considered the first serious manifestation of the European crisis. We could say in any case that it set off a catastrophic panic. Hoover was very optimistic about the American crisis and called it a "recession." At the Sixth Congress of the International Chamber of Commerce in Washington, May 4–9, 1931, he did not even refer to it in his speech to the 800 delegates from 35 nations, but confined himself to the subject of the reduction of armaments. Nevertheless he followed the European crisis closely and it appears that the idea of a moratorium came to him on May 6 in a conversation with the ambassador to Germany, Frederic M. Sackett. He discussed it with the financiers Dawes, Mellon, and Morrow, and on June 5 with certain members of the cabinet. Following an appeal from President Hindenburg, he decided on June 20 to make the plan public: payment on all intergovernmental debts would be suspended for a year.

A financial conference, initiated by Hoover, opened in London on July 20, 1931. It accepted the Hoover moratorium, not without some resistance, especially on the part of France, which was less hard hit by the depression than the other countries. Congress ratified the moratorium in December, in spite of the opposition of certain isolationist senators like Hiram Johnson. It remained to decide what to do next.

The United States had remained very firm on maintaining the distinction between German reparations and Allied war and postwar debts, which had been reduced and consolidated. The United States was not directly concerned with reparations but was highly favorable to a large reduction of this political debt. It was an American, Owen D. Young, who had been chairman of the Commission of Experts which had produced the Young Plan in 1928–29. The Young Plan had brought about a considerable further reduction of reparations. On the Allied war debts American policy was firm and consistent—they must be paid, regardless of what happened about reparations. On June 8, 1931, Hoover still hesitated to propose a moratorium because it might appear to establish a connection—which he absolutely refused to admit—between these two large categories of intergovernmental debts.

Stimson, who had applauded the moratorium vigorously, decided to go to Europe in the summer to study the situation in a series of personal conversations with the statesmen of the Old World. He went to Italy and to Paris and took part in a conference on finances in London. With his new financial and economic adviser, Harvey H. Bundy, a Boston lawyer, and Herbert Feis, he tried to form a clear idea of the problems to be resolved. His first idea was to propose an extension of the moratorium for another year, and in his conversations with Laval—this time in the United States in early October 1931—his words seemed to fall on fertile ground. He also supported the Europeans when they practically abolished German reparations at a conference in Lausanne in June 1932. All the same, and without any agreement having been reached, it looked as if, as a result of the conversations between Hoover and Laval, the end of war debts should correspond to the end of reparations. By a sort of Gentleman's Agreement the signatories of the Lausanne agreement promised that they would not ratify it before satisfactory arrangements had been concluded with the United States. This Gentleman's Agreement was made known to the American public and created a considerable impression. It appeared to be a new "European conspiracy" to reduce the sacred debts.

Stimson had finally concluded that the only reasonable solution was to cancel the debts. Hoover absoultely refused. Stimson wrote on July 11, "He told me that he entirely differed with me, in fundamentals . . . he thought that the debts to us could and should be paid . . . I replied that if he felt that way we were indeed on such different grounds that I couldn't give him much good advice, and that I oughtn't to be his adviser." [30] Hoover knew that he had the support of the great majority of public opinion and of Congress. Only certain economists and bankers and—suprisingly—Senator Borah supported Stimson's point of view. It was a conflict between moral principle and a policy which accommodated itself to reality. Stimson, against his will, had to carry out the President's instructions faithfully. His private notes show his own personal attitude.

We know the result of this policy: the great pressure of public opinion in Europe on the governments to stop payment. Most of the nations did not honor the payment due December 15, 1932. In France, the Herriot government, which wanted to pay, was overthrown on this question. England and five other nations paid, with the exception of Finland, for the last time. The system of "symbolic payments" was refused by the United States Attorney General. American public opinion, already turned to isolationism by the depression, found in this default one more reason for Americans to detach themselves from the immoral and corrupt Europeans. This was one and a half months before Hitler came to power in Germany.

The Manchurian Affair

For two reasons special attention must be given to the policy of Hoover and Stimson in the Far East. First, because it is during this period that the policy of sudden attacks which was to shake the world was begun by the Japanese. And second, because many American isolationists applied their doctrine primarily to Europe. The doctrine of the Open Door in China, the widespread sympathy for the Chinese, and the threat of the Japanese Fleet made American public opinion much more sensitive to the problems of the Pacific and the Far East than to those of Europe. Hoover had been in China at the time of the Boxer Rebellion in 1900, and Stimson had been governor general of the Philippines. The new undersecretary of state, William Castle, had been ambassador to Japan. [31]

The Far Eastern question did not become the major concern of the United States government until September 1931. Shidehara, Japanese Minister of Foreign Affairs from 1924 to 1927 and again from 1929 to 1931, was a liberal, convinced that the serious economic difficulties of his country—Japan had not shared in the great boom—should be resolved by peaceful means. The Japanese Prime Minister, Yuko Hamaguchi, had advised the Emperor to ratify the London Naval Treaty in 1930, in spite of the opposition of Admiral Kato, chief of staff of the Navy. Everything seemed to indicate that Japan would continue to observe the rules of international life and especially of the Nine-Power Treaty on China signed in Washington in 1922. This treaty proclaimed solemnly that the "sovereignty, independence and administrative integrity of China" would be respected.

Nevertheless, on September 19, 1931—the day Great Britain abandoned the gold standard—Japanese troops began the occupation of Mukden and other cities of southern Manchuria. Manchuria was legally a part of China. During the period of troubles following the Chinese Revolution of 1912 it had been under the dictatorship of Marshal Chang Tso-lin. When the marshal died in June 1928, after an attack on the train in which he was traveling, his son Chang Hsueh-liang rallied to the support of Chiang Kai-shek. Chiang was, in that year, 1928, in the process of re-establishing the unity of China. Chang Hsueh-liang was given command of the Nationalist troops and the administration of Manchuria and Jehol, a section of Inner Mongolia. Chinese colonization in Manchuria reinforced Chinese rights, (the Manchurians accounted for only 10 percent of the total population of Manchuria) and the Chinese had begun to invest capital to build new railroads and to bring under cultivation lands formerly neglected.

The Japanese, however, were already established in Manchuria and challenging Chinese power. Victorious over the Russians in 1905, by the Treaty of Portsmouth they had gained not only the lease of the base at Port Arthur in the south, but also control of the South Manchurian Railway, a control that permitted occupation of the "railway zone" by Japanese troops with the powers of local administration and police. The Chinese naturally accepted these extensive rights less and less willingly and demanded the liquidation of the "unequal treaties." Not only did Japan not accede to this demand, but there was in Japan a strong current in the opposite direction—for a "positive policy," that is for the conquest of Manchuria as an indispensable safety zone between Japanese Korea and Soviet Russia. General Baron

Tanaka, leader of this movement, advocated the establishment of Japanese sovereignty over all Manchuria.

The pretext for Japanese intervention on September 19, 1931, had been the alleged sabotage of the railway by the Chinese. The promptness of the Japanese reaction and the perfect coordination of operations showed, however, that there had been a carefully prepared plan and that the militarists had won out over Shidehara. The Chinese Army, inefficient and scattered, could not put up any resistance. The Japanese militarists were convinced that the only way to resolve the chronic economic crisis—made twice as bad by the world depression —was to conquer their markets and sources of raw materials, that force was the only way to save their country. Had not the policy of "commercial expansion and political neighborliness" of Shidehara failed? Thus the Manchurian affair was directly tied to the world crisis as well as to the extreme imperialism of the Japanese militarists.

What would the American reaction be? Would the United States act alone or in cooperation with the League of Nations? As early as September 21, Alfred Sze, representing China in Geneva, had appealed to the League. Stimson thought that his country should associate itself with the League. For one thing, the League had at its disposal a variety of political instruments designed to assure conciliation and the solution of conflicts, which could be used to advantage. Furthermore, an isolated American reaction would give the appearance of conflict between two imperialisms; cooperation with the League of Nations, on the contrary, would make American policy appear to be an aspect of a world effort supported by universal public opinion. All this, wrote the Secretary of State, "would indicate that our most useful role would be to provide the League with independent aid rather than to play a leading role." [32] This role derived from the Nine-Power Treaty and also from the Kellogg-Briand Pact. Such was the gist of the response Stimson sent Sir Eric Drummond, who had asked him in the name of the League on September 21 what the intentions of Washington were.

One cannot say that the first American reaction was very strong. When the League of Nations asked that an American representative participate in the Commission of Enquiry sent to Manchuria—the Lytton Commission—Stimson declined. He said that he did not want to give the impression of acting against the will of Japan. The shaky authority of Shidehara should be reinforced. He proposed instead a commission of neutrals to be named with the agreement of China and Japan. "I think that such an inquiry imposed on Japan at this time would accelerate the unleashing of nationalist passions." [33] He confined himself to asking Shidehara for authorization to send two American diplomats to the scene. Shidehara accepted this offer with alacrity.

There is no doubt that Stimson, much attracted to Japan and preferring that modern nation to a China in upheaval, wished to try to maintain an atmosphere of friendship as long as possible. He was supported in his views by his aides, Undersecretary Castle and Stanley Hornbeck, chief of the Far Eastern Division of the State Department, who had taught history in China. Besides, Japanese troops seemed to have begun the affair on their own initiative, without government orders. This was a good pretext not to accuse the government of having violated the Kellogg-Briand Pact. Hoover was in full agreement. Hornbeck and Castle privately accepted Japanese sovereignty in Manchuria.

On September 22 the president of the League sent identical telegrams to China and Japan asking them to stop hostilities and to withdraw their troops. On the twenty-fourth the United States joined in this request. Japan replied that she was sending troops to the railroad zone only, had no territorial ambitions in Manchuria, and only wanted to protect her nationals in their efforts toward economic development. All was thus for the best: "It seemed," Stimson said, "that Baron Shidehara could succeed in maintaining his authority and his former policy." [34]

This complacent opinion of the Secretary of State did not last. On October 8, eleven Japanese planes bombarded the city of Chinchow without warning. At the end of that month Japanese troops advanced again toward northern Manchuria, entirely beyond the zone of the South Manchuria Railway, following a purely Chinese railroad and crossing another which connected western Siberia with Vladivostok. The latter, the Chinese Eastern Railway, was under Russian influence. Chinchow, the last important town held by the young Marshal Chang Hsueh-liang, fell on January 3, 1932. The Japanese were masters of Manchuria.

In October Stimson changed his mind. Japan had lied. She spoke of treaties as "scraps of paper." "I fear," said Stimson in his memoirs, "that we should have taken a firm position and an attitude of force towards Japan." [35] Stimson thought more and more about intervention, at least by diplomatic pressure and economic sanctions. Was the United States to pursue an interventionist policy? No, because this time President Hoover opposed it and Stimson confined himself to continued cooperation with the League of Nations. At least his initial action was definite. When an invitation was issued on October 16 by Briand—then president of the Council of the League—Stimson authorized the American consul in Geneva to take part in the meetings of the Council studying the question of whether the Kellogg-Briand Pact had been violated, and if so to what extent. This was little enough, but S. Parker Gilbert soon received orders not to attend any further meetings. When the Council voted a resolution on October 24 asking the Japanese to evacuate Chinese territory by November 16, Stimson hesitated to send a similar note and waited two weeks to send a text which had been made "inoffensive."

During this time Japanese opinion became inflamed. The government lost more authority each day and resigned on December 11. The new government, which naturally did not include Shidehara, aligned its policy with that of the Army. In the United States the press, and without doubt a great part of the populace, became more excited, but the isolationism of Congress—Borah had been chairman of the Senate Foreign Relations Committee since 1924—would not permit the prospect of even economic sanctions and Hoover was unwilling to follow the lead of the League. "He wants to get completely out of the League," said Castle.[36] How were these divergent tendencies to be reconciled? Little by little Hoover and Stimson worked out a solution which was to lead to the "Stimson doctrine": moral condemnation and nonrecognition of conquests. Hoover said to the cabinet, "We have a moral obligation to use every influence short of war to have the treaties upheld . . . and we should 'cooperate' with the rest of the world in using 'moral pressures' to these ends. But that is the limit. We will not go along on any of the sanctions, either economic or military, for these are roads to war." [37]

This explains the note sent to China and Japan on January 7, 1932, announcing that the United States would recognize no de facto political arrangement which violated the rights of Americans in China or the Kellogg-Briand Pact. England, more deeply pacifist even than the United States, absolutely refused to adopt a similar attitude. Thus in January 1932, the United States, torn between two conflicting tendencies, confined itself to formulating a policy of nonrecognition of annexations founded on force. The three preceding months had led only to a rather confused position unlikely to cause serious anxiety to the Japanese.

Japan took advantage of the situation to go on with her conquest. At the end of January 1932, using as a pretext the boycott of Japanese products by the Chinese, Japanese troops landed at Shanghai and occupied the city and its surrounding territory. This was too much; what remained of pro-Japanese sentiment in the State Department was transformed into fury. For Stimson it was a personal outrage. "The Secretary is in a high state of excitement about the situation in Shanghai," wrote Castle.[38] He hoped for a joint Anglo-American naval action. This was to be Stimson's attitude from then on. American ships did indeed arrive in Shanghai and bases in Hawaii and the Philippines were strengthened. But here again Hoover exercised a moderating influence. For the President the ships had as their only object protection of American citizens; in no case would they be used as a means of pressure against Japan. The bombardment of Shanghai by Japanese planes on January 29 did not change his views.

From then on, during the last year of Hoover's presidency, a growing divergence between his point of view and Stimson's can be seen. The note of January 7, 1932, on nonrecognition of a fait accompli sets forth what is usually called a "doctrine," that is, an overall policy. But was it the "Hoover doctrine" or the "Stimson doctrine"? It was much debated at the time. It was not only a question of personal vanity. For Hoover nonrecognition with moral condemnation of aggression was a *sufficient* policy. Founded on law and world opinion, it would put pressure on the Japanese to give in. This was the way Hoover interpreted the Armistice of May 5, 1932, between China and Japan, in which the Japanese promised to evacuate Shanghai. Hoover repeatedly made it clear that the United States would certainly not resort to force, would refuse to play the role of international policeman and would reject all economic sanctions.

If the doctrine of January 7 was the Stimson doctrine, on the other hand, nonrecognition and moral condemnation was only the first step. Recourse to force must be adjudged a possibility, as must joint action with the League of Nations in the direction of economic sanctions and cooperation with Anglo-French intervention in the Far East. In any case Japan should not be told that the United States would not resort to force—in short, the United States should bluff. The Navy in the Far East must be strengthened and it must be prepared against the eventuality—in which Stimson came to believe—of a Japanese attack against American possessions in the Pacific. The Stimson doctrine was thus nonisolationist because it supported intervention in concert with the League of Nations. Stimson interpreted the evacuation of Shanghai by the Japanese as a result of the bluff and not of moral pressure.

The Japanese, little aware of this domestic quarrel and ready to consider the United States their chief enemy, continued to go ahead by creating the satellite state of Manchukuo (March 1932), granting it recognition (August 24), claiming for itself the right of occupation (September 2). For Stimson disappointment followed disappointment. He was disappointed first by the British: Sir John Simon, Foreign Secretary in the MacDonald cabinet, let it be clearly understood in February that his country was little disposed to go to war in so remote a country. His second disappointment was with the League of Nations. Stimson went to Geneva in April for the disarmament conference. To the general surprise, he took part in the meetings of the League Council. There he attempted to introduce the idea of cooperation in the Far East. The subject was politely avoided and only disarmament was discussed. Later the Lytton Report, drawn up by the League's Commission of Inquiry (October 2, 1932), proposed that Manchuria be declared autonomous under Chinese sovereignty. The Assembly, whose meetings began on December 2, 1932, did nothing more in its final report of February 24, 1933, than proclaim Chinese sovereignty in Manchuria and declare that Manchukuo should not be recognized. It refused to declare Japan an aggressor. This was simple moral condemnation. And, finally, Stimson was disappointed by Hoover himself. Not only did Hoover let it be said openly that the United States would not resort to force, though Stimson thought silence at least should be maintained on this point, but further, on June 22, 1932, he proposed to the Disarmament Conference the reduction of all existing armaments by one third. The "Hoover plan" came as a sharp blow, for at the moment Stimson was preaching the necessity of strengthening the Navy with eventual intervention in view.

Abandoned by Hoover, Stimson had only one hope left—to see Hoover's successor, Franklin D. Roosevelt, adopt the Stimson doctrine instead of the Hoover doctrine. He wrote in his diary, "I can see countless matters in which it will be important for me to have an interview with him in regard to such matters as Manchuria, the conferences and situations in Europe, about which I personally know so much and he so little . . . I think it most important for the United States and her foreign policy during the next four years that we should give this man as fair a chance as possible." [39]

The Beginnings of the Good Neighbor Policy

Relations with Latin America constitute a sort of domain apart in the policy of Hoover and Stimson. Far from showing differences, on this subject they were always in perfect agreement. Furthermore, the depression, though it affected the Latin American states, had no direct influence on the policy of the United States toward them.

Everything stemmed from the Havana Conference of 1928, which had shown the extent of Yankeephobia and how nearly at the breaking point relations between United States and Latin America were. Kellogg had been deeply impressed by this fact and his final acts had shown a deliberate effort to reduce friction. Hoover the Quaker felt even more strongly than Kellogg.

The main thing was to re-establish confidence. This was a long-term policy because as confidence had been destroyed by actions, mere words could not re-establish it. Words are nevertheless an indispensable preliminary and Hoover knew this so well that he decided, after his election and before taking office, to make a good-will tour to Latin America. Coolidge and Kellogg approved and Hoover was accompanied by a representative of the State Department, Henry P. Fletcher. The trip began on November 19, 1928, when Hoover left San Pedro on the armored ship *Maryland*. He went to Honduras, San Salvador, Nicaragua, Costa Rica, Ecuador, Peru, Chile, Argentina, Uruguay, and Brazil. He made twenty-five speeches during the six-week trip.

This tour was generally well received by the Latin Americans, especially as the President talked constantly of "good neighborliness." "We desire to maintain not only cordial relations between governments, but relations of good neighbors." [40] At Buenos Aires he went further and tried to destroy the concept of the United States as the North American "big brother," supervising with good will the little Latin brothers. "There has long been a notion that among nations as in families there are older and younger brothers. From this has stemmed the notion that the right to act as a tutor at least in spiritual ways, and often also in disciplinary ways, belongs to the older brothers. I absolutely disapprove of this idea, in sentiment and in policy. Among the sovereign and independent states of the American continents there are no older or younger brothers." [41]

Having begun, Hoover continued to develop these ideas. As we have seen, he decided to publish the Clark Memorandum which detached the Roosevelt Corollary from the Monroe Doctrine (June 1930). But the most certain proof of this "good neighbor policy" was the concrete, active, and constant evidence of American good will. Hoover took pains to multiply its manifestations. He did it in circumstances made especially difficult by the depression. Never had agitations, civil wars, military coups d'état, and revolutionary explosions related to poverty been more frequent in Latin America. Everywhere North American interests were injured. Everywhere payment of debts was delayed or suspended, to the point that in 1933 the default was estimated at 1 billion dollars.

Even so, Hoover refused to send the Marines again either for the recovery of debts or for the protection of American citizens, who, in his opinion, did business in Latin American countries at their own risk and peril. They were only protected, eventually, in part, by warships sent for the purpose. The policy of nonintervention was deliberately followed, even in the Caribbean zone. When Hoover accepted the idea of a Pan-American Conference in Montevideo in 1933, he did it knowing that—as at Havana—certain Latin Americans, especially the Argentine Minister of Foreign Affairs Saavedra Lamas, would bring up the principle of nonintervention again. The matter was to be settled by the new administration. Hoover, for his part, in contrast to Coolidge in 1928, was ready to accept this principle.

The United States in 1929 still occupied the republics of Nicaragua and Haiti with 1600 Marines in the former and 700 in the latter. On December 3, 1929, in his first message to Congress, Hoover announced that he was "anxious to withdraw them as soon as the situation permitted." [42] In Nicaragua a civil war did not permit the first withdrawal until June 1932. The elections of November 1932, giving power to a liberal, Sacasa, who was quite hostile to the United States, allowed evacuation to take place January 2, 1933, with the certainty that the vote had not been tampered with.

The situation in Haiti, occupied since 1915, was still more complex. Hoover sent several commissions of inquiry there after great pressure was brought by the National Association for the Advancement of Colored People. One, headed by W. Cameron Forbes, former governor general of the Philippines, found that the immediate withdrawal of the Marines was not desirable. Another commission, headed by Robert E. Moton, Negro president of Tuskegee Institute, found that American occupation had not favored the social and educational advancement of the country. A treaty of friendship was signed between the United States and Haiti, on November 3, 1932, which envisaged the end of the occupation in December 1934. This treaty, which sanctioned the retention of certain financial controls by the United States, was unanimously rejected by the Haitian parliament. It was nevertheless applied by the United States.

Let us add that the policy by which governments were recognized was deliberately transformed. With the exception of five governments of Central America which had signed an agreement according to which no government established by force would be recognized, Hoover's policy marked a return to the so-called Jeffersonian tradition. This consisted in recognizing any government which in fact controlled the country. The United States confined itself to an embargo of arms and munitions destined for insurgent factions which was a serious handicap only in the case of Brazil when the revolution of October 30 brought to power a "strong man," Dr. Getulio Vargas, but even Vargas was recognized two weeks after coming to power.

The only exception to the abandonment of the policy of the Big Stick was the maintenance in Cuba of strict control established by the Platt Amendment of 1901. But at no moment did Hoover envision use of the rights conferred by the Platt Amendment, which included recourse to force.

The President's method consisted of playing the role of peacemaker here and there, in close collaboration if necessary with the League of Nations. Thus he succeeded in bringing to an end the conflict over Tacna-Arica between Chile and Peru on June 3, 1929, by getting both nations to accept his arbitration. It was the same when the frontier dispute between Guatemala and Honduras, which had lasted for years, was ended by the treaty of July 16, 1930. The treaty provided for the creation of a special court for frontier problems. Presiding over this court was Hughes, then Chief Justice, who handed down a decision January 23 which was subsequently accepted by both parties.

Hoover was less successful in settling the conflict over the Chaco between Bolivia and Paraguay, and the conflict over Leticia between Colombia and Peru. It is not necessary here to go into the complex details of these affairs, in which Stimson used all his ingenuity to get the Pan-American Union and the League of Nations to intervene, because his efforts were more or less futile.

If Hoover's efforts in Latin America were not entirely successful it was not on the political plane, where the consistent will to avoid intervention—direct or indirect—had finally gained support, but on the plane of economic relationships. As great producers of raw materials, the Latin Americans suffered most from the contraction of their chief market, in the United States. The enormous wall of the Hawley-Smoot Tariff added to the adverse effect of the depression—already sufficiently serious in itself. As for the temporary easing of the economic situation connected with Hoover's moratorium, Latin American countries could not profit from it because the moratorium concerned only payments between governments and the Latin American debts were owed to private capitalists. Grave dissatisfaction resulted, especially in Argentina and Uruguay, whose products were more in competition with those of the United States. Everywhere defaults of payments occurred which naturally aroused violent resentment in the United States. Hoover never followed the advice of the creditors who wanted to use force. He was content to follow—with a combination of firmness and flexibility—the policy he had already developed before 1922 with Hughes and Mellon. This policy placed limits upon the granting of new private credits to countries which had failed to pay their debts.

Once again we see the embarrassment the depression caused Hoover, and the contradiction which he never could resolve between increased internationalism and the raising of tariff barriers. He left to his successor not only the good neighbor policy, but also an atmosphere of reciprocal bitterness, which if one judges by his good will, was really not deserved. This is the opinion of an expert whom his successor, Roosevelt, was to use in his Latin American relations from the start, Sumner Welles.[43] Welles explains the relative setback in the good neighbor policy not only by the Smoot-Hawley Tariff, but also by the fact that Hoover, having been eight years Secretary of Commerce before being President, was compromised in the eyes of the Latin Americans by the tradition of dollar diplomacy. His chief biographer,

Alexander De Conde, thinks this judgment too harsh, and with him one can concede that he "helped to eliminate some of the hate and fear aroused by preceeding governments;" and that "he established the foundations of a Latin-American policy which was to pay rich dividends in the crisis of the Second World War." [44]

Part Three

THE ROOSEVELT ERA
1933–1945

Chapter X
Roosevelt and Isolationism, 1933-1937

The Preparation

DESPITE the excellent studies devoted to Franklin Delano Roosevelt and his time, notably by Frank Freidel, Arthur M. Schlesinger, Jr., William L. Langer, S. Everett Gleason, and Herbert Feis, he remains one of the great enigmas of our era. Was he another Wilson, benefiting from the experience of his distinguished predecessor and perhaps more able? Was he an opportunist of unlimited ambition who donned an ideological halo? Or was he rather an empiricist on principle, who subtly adapted himself to reality? Did his death at a time of intense disagreement with the Soviet Union heighten the tension or did it save what the West could still save? What is certain is that he was an incredibly complex personality, as his Secretary of Labor Frances Perkins has said. Without pretending to unravel this tangled skein in a few chapters, we will try to form a clearer picture of this President —exceptional in so many ways—by a close look at his development. We must first consider how his life had prepared him for the task of diplomatic leader of the United States.

Franklin Delano Roosevelt was born on January 30, 1882, in Hyde Park, New York, on the Hudson Valley estate of his father, James Roosevelt. The Roosevelt family, of Dutch extraction, had emigrated to North America in the seventeenth century. By the third generation the family had separated into two branches, so that the two Roosevelt presidents were only distant cousins. Franklin's mother, Sara Delano, who was the second wife of James, came from an old American family of French origin. Franklin's father, after a brief campaign in the Garibaldi Legion and a short tour of diplomatic duty, had chosen to live as a gentleman farmer on his estate of 1400 acres in Hyde Park. Without being really rich, James and Sara were extremely comfortable, and their income provided an environment quite different from the modest circumstances of the Wilsons. Franklin was able to spend much time with his family, who moved in high circles, and to travel to Europe every year with his parents. His way was made easy and he had every opportunity to broaden his horizon through a wide acquaintance at home and abroad. As a child he learned French and German; on this point the contrast with Wilson is striking. His father taught him the joys of sailing and he developed early in life the love of ships which was to influence his career profoundly.

In September 1896 he was sent to Groton School, which, though rather recently founded, had quickly become an outstanding preparatory school attended by boys of prominent New York families. Sumner Welles, Dean Acheson, Averell Harriman, and the Alsop brothers were also to be educated there. Franklin was only an average student at Groton, and had an equally undistinguished academic career at Harvard College from 1900 to 1904, where he studied American history and government. Although he enjoyed reading he was decidedly not an intellectual; he did not have much interest in a subject for its own sake. He undoubtedly attached too much importance to the social side of college life and he enjoyed taking a leading part in extracurricular activities. He was elected president of the Harvard *Crimson,* for instance, and always claimed that this had been his best preparation for public life.[1] His failure to make the exclusive Porcellian Club seemed a catastrophe. In short there was much of the snob in this outstanding, bright young man.

Young Franklin frequently saw his distant cousin Eleanor, niece of Theodore Roosevelt and daughter of Franklin's godfather. He fell in love with her in the winter of 1903–04, but had to convince his mother to accept the idea of marriage. For James Roosevelt had died in 1901, and Sara Roosevelt was a very demanding mother—right up to the time of her death in 1941—to whom Franklin deferred.

In October 1904, after graduation from Harvard, Franklin went to Columbia Law School with the object of becoming a member of the New York bar. During his first year he married Eleanor, on March 17, 1905. President Theodore Roosevelt came to New York for the wedding which was as important a social event as Franklin could have wished. The young couple went to Europe on their honeymoon. In Paris a fortune teller is supposed to have told Franklin that he would be President of the United States—which did not displease him—and Eleanor, that she would live 105 years. They had six children between 1906 and 1916, one of whom died very young, and 17 grandchildren.

In 1907 the young Roosevelt joined the well-known law firm of Carter, Ledyard, and Milburn which handled the legal business of J. P. Morgan and Company, but he did not like the life. He could distract himself with golf, hunting, and sailing, but they were not enough. He was attracted to politics by the example of Theodore Roosevelt. In 1910 the Democrats of Poughkeepsie, delighted to have a Roosevelt in their party, suggested that he run as their candidate for the New York Senate. He accepted eagerly and was elected despite the strength of the Republican party in New York State. His name, his personality, and his innate gift of informal eloquence contributed to this success.

Roosevelt's first piece of good luck was his name. The second was Wilson's triumph in 1912. As a member of a state Senate he knew how to put himself in the limelight and he became well known in Albany. Throughout the 1912 campaign he supported Wilson's progressive ideas, which he shared. Like Wilson he was opposed to the domination of the party machine, represented in New York City by the notorious Tammany Hall. He went to see Wilson when the latter was governor of New Jersey and Wilson was very much taken with him: "He is the handsomest young giant I have ever seen." He made many other friends in Democratic circles, including Alfred E. Smith, future candidate for the presidency, Josephus Daniels, and Cordell Hull. He took an active part in the 1912 convention in Baltimore which nominated Wilson. It was therefore natural that when Wilson was forming his cabinet in March 1913 he should think of Roosevelt as a possible assistant secretary. Roosevelt refused a post in the Treasury Department, but when Josephus Daniels, now Secretary of the Navy, suggested that he be his assistant, Roosevelt, lover of ships and collector of ship models and books about the sea, could not refuse. "His face beamed with pleasure," wrote Daniels.

From 1913 to 1920 Roosevelt was to hold this important position. Although he lived in Washington, he did not neglect New York politics. We need not concern ourselves with his activity in the Navy Department, except to note that in addition to acquiring administrative and technical experience he made useful contacts in labor circles, via the shipyards. He had an important share in the building of a powerful Navy capable of dealing with any eventuality. During the

period of neutrality he was one of the warmest advocates of preparedness. As early as 1915 he had joined those who thought that the
United States should defend its principles as well as its territory, and
he was convinced that sooner or later his country would enter the
war. Finally, he had to concern himself directly with political intervention in Latin America, especially in Haiti. During the war years
he was very active. As Freidel says, "The pressure of war work
ripened Roosevelt and made him grow; it shaped his mind; it not
only increased the probability that he would one day rise to the
supreme leadership, but it in large measure determined the methods
he would adopt in the handling of crises." [2] In 1918 he was sent to
Europe where he visited the front.

At the time of the Paris Peace Conference Roosevelt accompanied
Wilson. His assignment was to supervise the disposition of naval supplies and other matters resulting from the war. He was an active
supporter of the League of Nations but did not understand Wilson's
refusal to accept any amendment of the Covenant. For him the important thing was to assure American participation in the League;
he was never a doctrinaire supporter of the organization. The Democratic defeat in the election of 1920 brought the first phase of his
political career to an end. It concluded on a high note—when the
Democratic convention in San Francisco nominated him for the vice
presidency. He was 38 years old. The temporary and not unexpected
setback of his party at this time left the door open for a brilliant future.

Then he was struck by illness, poliomyelitis, which threatened to
cost him everything but which in the end changed his personality and
perhaps enabled him to win everything. After leaving public life
Roosevelt had become vice president of an important banking firm,
the Fidelity and Deposit Company of Maryland. In the summer of
1921 he felt very tired and went to Campobello, New Brunswick,
for a vacation of fishing and sailing. On August 10 he fought a forest
fire with his sons. He went for a swim, and walked back to the house
and sat down to read the mail in his bathing suit. That night at dinner
he complained of lumbago and went to bed early. The next morning
one of his legs was paralyzed and he had a high fever. Then the other
leg became paralyzed. On August 25 a Boston specialist diagnosed
poliomyelitis.

Every indication was that if he recovered at all it would take a
long time. At this point Eleanor Roosevelt's influence was decisive.

While Roosevelt's mother urged him to come to Hyde Park and spend the rest of his life in comfortable idleness—as his father had—his wife encouraged him to continue in active political life. On September 12, 1922, he accepted membership on the executive committee of the Democratic party in New York, to give at least the illusion of activity. He moved to New York City and began his relentless fight against illness. He was naturally strong and the muscles of his arms and back regained their full strength. Despite spells when his condition seemed worse he began to walk with crutches and a heavy steel brace. His health improved slowly, beginning in the spring of 1922, but the muscles of his legs were never to recover. Never would he be able to stand without support or braces; never would he be able to stand up or sit down by himself; never would he really be able to walk again. In the autumn of 1924 he became familiar with the beneficial effects of a treatment (very little used up to that time) that he was to make famous, in Warm Springs, Georgia. From then on he returned to Warm Springs every year, often several times, and other victims of the disease followed his example. He was to die there in April 1945.

Franklin Roosevelt was naturally energetic; his illness made him indomitable. He viewed his handicap with scorn. He hated to use a wheel chair; he wanted to be treated as a normal person. His staff knew that no allusion should ever be made to his infirmity. His handicap cut him off from many of his former activities and he concentrated his energies on a tremendous drive for power. With the help of his friend Louis Howe, who had been his assistant in the Navy Department, he decided which activities were indispensable and which could be sacrificed. Forced to stay at home most of the time, he entertained a great deal, with his wife's able assistance. His social contacts began to broaden little by little. Acquaintances who hunted and played golf gave way to Democratic politicians and representatives of the labor movement. The snobbism of his youth disappeared; class consciousness gave way to personal pride. The prejudices of the rich man faded and his mind turned more to the Left as his attitude became less conservative. He read a great deal and meditated on suffering. From this relentless trial a virtually new man was to be born.

Only in 1924 can one properly speak of Roosevelt's re-entry into political life. He had known the extraordinary Alfred E. Smith ever since 1911. A Roman Catholic of Irish extraction, Smith possessed an unusual talent as a leader of men and a politician despite a very sketchy education. He had been elected governor of New York in 1918, and although defeated in 1920 he was re-elected in 1922 despite the determined opposition of his opponent within the Democratic party, William Randolph Hearst. Roosevelt had supported Smith in 1922 and in 1924 he worked for his nomination as Democratic candidate for the presidency. Smith was a liberal in foreign policy and favored United States membership in the League of Nations, but Roosevelt's choice is to be explained more by his personal sympathy for Smith and their agreement on domestic policy. He presented Smith to the Democratic convention as the "happy warrior." Smith's opponent was W. G. McAdoo, Wilson's son-in-law. After 103 ballots the Democratic convention finally chose a dark horse candidate, John W. Davis.

The Republican President Calvin Coolidge was elected in November. The important thing is what Freidel calls the "personal triumph" [3] of Roosevelt in this episode. From this time on he was recognized as one of the principal leaders in the Democratic party. He had become a possible candidate for the presidency, his secret ambition. To realize this ambition a Democratic victory was needed, however. "I did not think that the Nation would elect a Democrat again until the Republicans had led us into a serious period of depression and unemployment," he wrote in 1924.[4]

Neither a Democratic victory nor Roosevelt's candidacy for the presidency was possible in 1928. Roosevelt was fighting for his health and he preferred to support his friend Al Smith, who had been elected and re-elected governor of New York. While Smith focused his attention on his job as governor, Roosevelt tried to reform the Democratic National Committee and to give the party a progressive although not a radical program. He continued to promote a Wilsonian foreign policy. If he no longer advocated the entry of the United States into the League, at least he wanted the country to join the World Court. "The isolation of individual nations will be as difficult in the future as would be the isolation of New England or the South today." [5]

The Democratic convention of 1928, in Houston, nominated Smith for the presidency. He was to be defeated by the Republican Hoover, but at this time a significant episode in Roosevelt's career occurred. Because he needed to carry the State of New York, Smith urged

Roosevelt to run for governor of the state. Roosevelt did not think that this was a necessary step to achieve the presidency, and as his health was still far from good, he declined. When the state Democratic convention met, Roosevelt went to Warm Springs. His wife had to bring pressure on him before he would accept the nomination. The result was not what Smith expected—out of more than 4,200,000 votes Roosevelt won by a majority of only 25,000, but the Republicans carried the state in the presidential election. Smith, defeated, thought he could continue to control New York from behind the scenes, but in this he misjudged the newly elected governor. From this time on relations were strained between the two men; in 1932 they would be open rivals.

This is not the place to discuss Roosevelt's career as governor, but it should be noted that after the crash of October 1929 he became the progressive and humanitarian governor that he had aspired to be. As he had foreseen, the depression brought about a Democratic tidal wave; in 1930 he was re-elected by the enormous majority of 725,000 votes. His duties, necessarily concentrated on domestic policy, distracted him substantially from his former Wilsonian attitude, and his staff urged him in this direction. During the campaign of 1928 he met Judge Samuel Rosenman, who was to help him write his speeches and later to publish them. At this time also he began to collaborate with Frances Perkins, an expert in labor questions, and with Henry Morgenthau, Jr., an expert in agriculture. He also discovered, through his wife, the chairman of the New York Emergency Relief Commission, Harry Hopkins, who was later to become his confidant in all matters.

In January 1932 Roosevelt announced his intention to present himself as candidate to the Democratic convention. His health—aside from the paralysis—was good. His reputation as a progressive and his effectiveness in the fight against unemployment had brought him immense popularity. Against him were the conservative elements of the party, the bosses of the big cities, Tammany Hall, William Randolph Hearst and his chain of newspapers, and the chairman of the Democratic National Committee, Raskob. For him, on the other hand, were former Wilsonians like Colonel House, idealists like Senators Cordell Hull of Tennessee, Wheeler of Montana, and Walsh of Massachusetts, the Irishman who had fought so hard against the

Treaty of Versailles. His friends Ed Flynn, Jim Farley, and Louis Howe campaigned throughout the country, aided by leading members of the party.

When the convention met in June in Chicago, aside from Roosevelt, the leading candidates were John N. Garner, a Democrat from Texas, who was supported by W. G. McAdoo and the California delegation, and Al Smith. Two thirds of the votes, 770, were necessary for nomination. On the first ballot Roosevelt received 666; on the third, 682. Was this the maximum? It often happens in conventions that the candidate who leads in the beginning loses ground and that finally an outsider, a compromise candidate or "dark horse," is nominated. This had been the case in 1924. But in 1932 there was a depression. Only a progressive had any chance of defeating the Republicans. Hearst, the most influential man of the right wing of the party, was persuaded of this by a telephone call from Jim Farley, the ablest of Roosevelt's agents. Hearst did not like Roosevelt, dangerously suspect in his eyes because of his Wilsonianism, but he hated Smith, his former opponent in New York. Hearst persuaded McAdoo to give Roosevelt the support of California and persuaded Garner to retire from the race—in return for nomination as vice president. On the fourth ballot, therefore, Roosevelt was nominated by 945 votes; Smith had only 190. Roosevelt, who had remained in Albany—in communication with his friends by telephone—then flew to Chicago and made his acceptance speech on the spot.

We will examine below the foreign policy plank of his platform, but it was not very important. The central issue was the depression. Roosevelt's brief but substantial platform announced the New Deal: an extensive public works program, federal aid to the unemployed, old age pensions, price controls, reform of the banks, repeal of prohibition, subsidies for agriculture, a balanced budget, and reduction of government expenses by 25 percent. This program of social democracy and government regulation pleased the public. Roosevelt made a superb campaign, covering 30,000 miles to show himself to the people and to give the lie to rumors circulating about his health. The election was a triumph: Roosevelt received 22,813,000 popular votes (57 percent) against 15,759,000 for Hoover and 472 electoral votes against 59 for his opponent. Only 6 of the 48 states had been carried by the Republicans.

The Program

What was Roosevelt's foreign policy when he was elected President of the United States in November 1932? We have seen that Wilson became President without having concerned himself much with foreign policy and that only circumstances had eventually made him attach prime importance to it. It was quite different with the new Democratic President. He had traveled widely and he had dealt with foreign problems for eight years in the Navy Department. He had campaigned enthusiastically for the League of Nations, advocating only slight reservations on the part of the United States. As candidate for the vice presidency in 1920 he had defended the "internationalist" platform of his party. In 1924 and 1928 we have seen him opposing a narrow nationalism. He was both well prepared and well qualified to deal with foreign policy, and yet in the first months and even years of his administration he seemed to neglect it. As we shall show, he even encouraged isolationism.

This fact can be explained primarily by the situation. Not only did the depression which had begun in October 1929 continue, but it deepened to such a point that Arthur M. Schlesinger, Jr., can speak of "the crisis of 1932." [6] The national income had fallen from 87.9 billion dollars in 1929 to 41.7 billion dollars in 1932. There were four million unemployed in 1930, and twelve million in 1932—one worker out of every four. Anxiety was very great and the general discontent seemed to favor radical movements. Hoover's optimism and his use of laissez-faire methods had failed. In his inaugural address of March 4, 1933, Roosevelt expressed very well the necessity to direct all the Federal government's attention to domestic affairs, social and economic. "I will ask the Congress . . . to grant to the Executive broad power to wage war against the depression as great as the power that would be granted to me if we were in fact invaded by a foreign foe." [7]

The situation demanded immediate action and Roosevelt was temperamentally suited to it. Addressing the Democratic convention of 1932, he said, "I believe that we are at the threshold of a fundamental change in our popular economic thought . . . We need to correct, by drastic means if necessary, the faults in our economic system from which we now suffer . . . The country needs and, unless I mistake its temper, the country demands bold, persistent experimentation . . . Above all, try something." [8]

It is a little harsh to say, as Walter Lippmann did in 1932, that Roosevelt was not a progressive in theory, that he only wanted to please, that he was "not a crusader." But Lippmann nevertheless puts his finger on the man's essential characteristic—with all his flexibility and imagination, he was better suited to solving problems than if he were governed by a theoretical system. What was needed was ingenuity and action. This applies equally to foreign policy. There are few more revealing texts than his speech to the Democratic convention of June 1928.

If the vision of world peace, of the abolition of war, ever comes true, it will not be through the mere mathematical calculations of a reduction of armaments program, nor the platitudes of multilateral treaties piously deprecating armed conflict. It will be because this nation will select as its head a leader who understands the human side of life, who has the force of character and the keenness of brain to take, instinctively, the right course.[9]

Of course this speech was intended as an answer to the Kellogg-Briand Pact—the product of a Republican administration. It was an appeal to the people to support Alfred E. Smith. But did not Roosevelt consider himself to be the man who had this ability to grasp the human aspect of things, this imagination, this force of character? He certainly did! He reveals his empirical approach here and also the force of his will.

In 1932 Walter Lippmann perceived the empiricism but not the tenacious will.

Roosevelt's attitude toward the League of Nations is proof of this empiricism. The historian Charles Beard, a great supporter of Roosevelt's progressivism and an equally great adversary when, after 1937, Roosevelt repudiated isolationism, has written an admirable chapter —admirable despite its partisan emotion—called "Roosevelt Repudiates the League of Nations in 1932." [10] William Randolph Hearst, right-wing Democrat, was a supporter of John Nance Garner's candidacy for the presidency. The other possible candidates, Roosevelt, Newton D. Baker, and Al Smith, all followed Wilson's "visionary" policy of meddling in European conflicts and complications. Only Garner, a Southerner, was an isolationist. It became obvious that Hearst's support was needed for the nomination. Garner, in fact, did not have a chance. After several ballots his votes would go to another candidate with Hearst's consent—but to which candidate? Roosevelt, with the support of former Wilsonians like Colonel House and in contrast to his attitude in 1924, had given up demanding United States membership in the League of Nations but he still advocated cooperation with the League. "Let us not raise this question," said Senator Clarence Dill. "The economic problem seriously affects the great masses of our people who are unemployed and it should not be obscured by other problems."

Roosevelt's negative attitude did not satisfy Hearst, who demanded an outright repudiation of the League of Nations in the name of "America first." Jim Farley undertook to negotiate with the powerful publisher, more or less in secret. In an open letter published on January 21, 1932, Hearst declared that Roosevelt should make a public declaration—not just a private one—in favor of "national independence."

Roosevelt did not hesitate. In a speech on February 2, he explained first, that he had been in favor of the League in 1920, like many of his fellow citizens, and that he would still be in favor of it today, "But the League of Nations today is not the League conceived by Woodrow Wilson. It might have been, had the United States joined. Too often through these years its major function has been not the broad overwhelming purpose of world peace, but rather a mere meeting place for the political discussion of strictly European national difficulties. In these the United States should have no part." He added that Europe owed money to the United States and that the Europeans must pay, despite adjustments necessitated by the depression. The United States should not belong to the League of Nations. It should follow the principles of George Washington and "preserve our international freedom." Finally, in a part of the speech which Beard quotes [11] but which is omitted from the *Public Papers and Addresses of Franklin D. Roosevelt*, he declares that United States participation in a world economic conference—prepared by Hoover—should not lead the country to get mixed up in foreign difficulties.

On the central point the text was clear. It was a public declaration in favor of staying out of the League. Roosevelt had yielded to Hearst's demands, but he had done it very skillfully so as not to antagonize the former Wilsonians. He had said that he remained faithful to Wilson's League. In what way was the League no longer

Wilson's League? This he was careful not to specify. The episode shows that Roosevelt was not a doctrinaire. To be elected president one could make concessions. In contrast to Wilson, he thought that it was the man and not the theory that solved problems, and he was sure that he was the man best able to solve the problems.

As early as 1932 it was clear that this speech did not constitute a foreign policy. Roosevelt, according to his adviser Raymond Moley,[12] had decided not to concern himself with foreign policy during the election campaign. He confined himself to saluting the memory of "our great leader Woodrow Wilson" from time to time. The only point at which he touched upon foreign affairs concerned tariffs. In contrast to certain Democrats—especially Senator Hull—he did not advocate immediate reduction of the Hawley-Smoot tariff then in effect. He limited himself to proposing a flexibility in tariffs which would allow the Executive to bargain with other nations on a reciprocal basis. The Reciprocal Trade Agreement Act of 1934 would result from this proposal. Hearst approved this part of the program also. Hearst favored a strong Navy, directed especially at Japan. The former undersecretary of the navy could not fail to agree.

Roosevelt's only specific foreign policies in the first term were recognition de jure of the Soviet Union, the development of the good neighbor policy toward Latin American states, a policy of relative firmness toward Japan in the Far East, and recognition of the independence of the Philippines. None of these matters was dealt with in his campaign speeches, however. We shall limit ourselves here to an analysis of his attitude toward the Far East.

We have seen that the opinions of President Hoover and his Secretary of State Henry L. Stimson were not identical. Stimson supported an active policy and wanted to collaborate with the League of Nations in the Far East. He had gone to Geneva in April 1932 for this purpose. Hoover favored a mere moral condemnation of Japan, as is shown in his speech of January 7, 1932; this is sometimes called the "Hoover Doctrine" and sometimes the "Stimson Doctrine." Which of these two policies would Roosevelt adopt, that of Hoover or that of Stimson? He waited until after he was elected to declare himself. On January 9, 1933, he invited Stimson to lunch at Hyde Park, without including his adviser Raymond Moley who had been discussing the Far Eastern problem with Hoover. This indicated the direction that he would take.

Moley was an ardent neutralist and considered that even the Hoover Doctrine went too far, that even simple moral condemnation was dangerous and that it made the United States take sides. He thought it would lead to a future war with Japan. Stimson, on the other hand, would have liked to strengthen the statement of condemnation and accompany it with economic sanctions. Without really knowing what was said in the five-hour conversation between the two men, we can guess that Roosevelt declared himself in favor of nonrecognition of Manchukuo and of eventual sanctions against Japan, with the support of a strong Navy. Stimson left the interview very much pleased. In a press conference on January 17, 1933, Roosevelt merely said that there would be no change in the Far Eastern policy of the United States. When Moley demanded an explanation the next day, Roosevelt replied that he had always had a special sympathy for the Chinese, with whom his ancestors had traded. He had really only made a declaration of principle, however. In fact he paid no attention to Japan in 1933.

All of this adds up to a very slight program because Roosevelt's attention was concentrated entirely on domestic problems. For more than four years he would leave a large part of the initiative in foreign affairs to his Secretary of State, Cordell Hull. Even so, concerning the heart of the matter—that is, isolationism—he kept a tight rein on his Secretary of State.

The Early Stages of the Roosevelt Administration

Cordell Hull was undoubtedly the leader of American diplomacy in 1933 and 1934. The senator from Tennessee was born on October 2, 1871, in a family of poor farmers who had supported the Confederacy. At the age of seventeen he began the study of law and, at the same time, entered political life. In 1892 he was elected to the Tennessee legislature at the minimum age of 21. He fought in the war against Spain in 1898, then practiced law until his election to the House of Representatives in November 1906. The election of Wilson, an idealist and progressive like Hull himself, was in his eyes "the opening of a new era." [13] In 1930 he was elected to the United States Senate. As an influential member of the Democratic National Committee he gave his active support to Roosevelt. He had considerable influence in both houses of Congress owing to his integrity, his admirable character, and his experience. For these reasons Roosevelt, after long hesitation, decided to offer him the post of secretary of state.

Cordell Hull's ideas were very simple. "Economic and military disarmament seemed to me the two most vital and outstanding factors for peace and business recovery." [14] As a result, he asked for a 10 percent reduction in tariffs and a less stringent attitude toward the war debts. He proposed that the debts should be reduced in "exchange" for tariff reductions on the part of the debtor nations.

"If I accept the Secretaryship of State," he said to Roosevelt, "I do not have in mind the mere carrying on of correspondence with foreign governments." [15] Roosevelt agreed and Hull thought that he would play a leading role, that he would bring about the triumph of his free trade policy. We shall see that he deceived himself. William Phillips, former assistant secretary of state under Wilson, was named undersecretary. Raymond Moley and Wilbur Carr, both friends of Roosevelt's, were named assistant secretaries. Was Roosevelt not seeking to place his own men in the department? This was increasingly to be his policy.

Hull, whether because of blindness or because of magnanimity, was not disturbed, however. "Never an unfriendly word passed between the President and me during my twelve years in the Department of State . . . he and I entertained in most respects the same philosophy in international relations." [16] Is this really true? Certainly in the first years, we have said, and Hull himself bears this out. "During his first term in office President Roosevelt was so immersed in an avalanche of domestic questions that he left me in almost full charge of foreign affairs . . . It was not until the beginning of 1936 that he made a major address on foreign affairs, this being his address to Congress on January 3 . . . Beginning with his second term, his interest and participation in foreign affairs greatly increased." [17] Hull praises in Roosevelt an excellent knowledge of foreign nations, great personal charm, rare psychological judgment, and a gift of expressing his ideas vividly and effectively.

If we examine the international events of 1933 to 1935, we will find only one main thread which determined United States policy, otherwise rather negative—isolationism. It was not theoretical isolation, certainly, but rather the firm conviction that the depression could only be dealt with internally.

In relation to Europe there were three major problems: disarmament, the war debts, and economic problems. The disarmament conference, in which the United States and the Soviet Union participated, although they were not members of the League of Nations, met in Geneva on February 2, 1932. By 1933 it had made little progress despite the efforts of Hoover, who was internationalist in this sphere. The European nations were not much concerned with eventual American disarmament, but they wished that the United States would agree to be available for consultation and would not hinder sanctions passed by the League of Nations in situations where peace was threatened.

At first it seemed that Roosevelt favored such minimal cooperation with the League. In fact he nominated Norman Davis as American delegate in Geneva. Davis, a Tennessean like Hull, was a champion of disarmament and of the League of Nations. He believed in the policy of American consultation with the League and in frank recognition of aggressor nations as a threat to peace. British Prime Minister MacDonald had gone to Washington after proposing in Geneva a plan which would reduce the armies of the great powers to 200,000 men. Roosevelt agreed to give moral support to the plan, as well as to the principles of consultation and agreement not to aid aggressors. But the Senate Committee on Foreign Relations rejected the latter point. Senator Key Pittman, Democratic chairman of the committee, who had succeeded the Republican Borah, proposed instead to place an embargo on all arms and munitions to aggressors and victims alike. This was the seed of the future neutrality laws. Even without going so far, the administration refused to equate the principle of consultation with United States adherence to a comprehensive policy of collective security. This was clearly demonstrated at Roosevelt's press conference on May 10, when the President told newspapermen that the consultation agreement "does not tie the hands of the United States . . . we in no way—in *no* way—are limiting our own right to determine our own action." [18] On May 11, in an "appeal to the nations," Roosevelt made it clear that the United States would agree to nothing but consultation. In this we see that he took a clear stand on isolationist ground.

The world financial conference, convoked by the League of Nations in 1932 to meet in London in the spring of 1933, had been welcomed by Hoover, who saw in international collaboration a means of mitigating the depression. Cordell Hull headed the United States delegation to the conference, which opened in London on June 12. There were two schools of thought in the United States. One consisted of internationalists who expected to find a solution to the depression in general agreements on trade and prices in addition to the lowering of tariff barriers. This was the position of the Secretary of State. The other school of thought was that of the nationalists, who thought that the solution to the depression was purely domestic and that the United States should remain absolutely free to defend its economic system and its currency. This was the position of Raymond Moley, one of Roosevelt's advisers. As early as May 20 he declared in a radio speech that he was skeptical about the possible outcome of the conference and that international trade was unimportant. "The heart of the program for recovery . . . should be domestic." The "Brain Trust" and in particular Rexford Tugwell and Adolph Berle, shared this opinion. Roosevelt deliberately chose the second of these views. He telegraphed Hull to limit himself to bilateral reciprocal trade treaties and instructed him that there should be no question of a general lowering of tariffs. This was a "terrific blow," Hull said.[19]

The conference accomplished nothing and Roosevelt was largely responsible. He sent Moley to London as his personal envoy in the middle of negotiations, much to Hull's annoyance. In early July he sent a message to the conference in which he declared that it would be a "world tragedy" if the conference undertook to regulate monetary exchanges between the leading nations. Roosevelt thus torpedoed any possible attempt to solve the depression on an international basis. MacDonald complained bitterly on July 4 and proposed adjournment. This did not occur until three weeks later, but the failure was total.

Roosevelt's isolationism was demonstrated again in relation to the war debts. The Europeans had been very outspoken in their criticism of United States policy at the London Conference. The Americans, on their side, had been exasperated by the attitude of the European debtors, who at the end of 1932 when the Hoover moratorium was running out had either refused to resume payments—as in the case of France, despite the efforts of Herriot—or had proposed "symbolic payments," as in the case of Britain.

In the United States the internationalists thought that an important gesture should be made, that is, the debts should either be reduced or abolished. American high tariffs made payments virtually impossible in time of depression. Would it not be just to admit, finally, that the Entente had paid in blood and that the common victory should result in a certain generosity? Some powerful American economic interests supported this view because a healthier European economy —made possible by canceling the debts—would be much more advantageous for the United States. The government and therefore the taxpayers would take over the debts and the banks would lose nothing. Naturally these ideas were not popular with the taxpayers, nor in general with Congress.

Roosevelt delegated responsibility in this matter not to Hull but to Moley, whose nationalist sentiments we have already noted. Hoover, at the very end of his administration, leaned toward cancellation of the debts and he had written to his successor to propose this solution, with an expansion of American markets in Europe as a compensating factor. Hoover thus tried to enlist the support of the incoming Democratic administration for the relatively internationalist policy which he himself had developed. Roosevelt and Moley had gone to the White House to meet with Hoover and his Secretary of the Treasury, Ogden Mills. Roosevelt declined to follow the path suggested by Hoover, and when Congress refused to cancel the debts Roosevelt did nothing to modify its attitude. Even more, Roosevelt did not hesitate to sign the Johnson Act of April 13, 1934. This law, initiated by Congress, forbade Americans to make loans to nations which had not paid their war debts. Nevertheless the Federal government could grant credits in certain cases, through the Export-Import Bank.

Such were the manifestations of the empirical isolationism which Roosevelt had adopted and which he was to continue for several years. His other actions in foreign policy were not in contradiction to these views.

One of these actions was de jure recognition of the Soviet Union. The United States was the only major power not to have done so before 1933. The moral argument dear to Wilson had prevailed: governments which were established by violence and which fostered world revolution should not be recognized. In addition, Communist propaganda in the United States aroused public opinion, and there were American citizens in Soviet prisons. The debts of the tsarist government to the United States had been repudiated and American property had been confiscated.[20] Finally, the lack of religious freedom in Russia deeply offended American religious sentiment. On the other hand, there were important arguments in favor of recognition, especially a common attitude toward Japanese aggression. Would not Soviet-American collaboration contribute to the establishment of world peace? Russia needed American credits and technicians; it was necessary for the United States government to be in a position to protect its interests and to develop trade.

In London Hull had met Maxim Litvinov, People's Commissar for Foreign Affairs, and when he returned to Washington, Hull prepared a long memorandum which he submitted to Roosevelt on September 21, 1933. In contrast to his predecessor, Hull was in favor of recognition. He thought that the United States could use the loans to Russia which would follow recognition to bring pressure on the Soviets and thus obtain satisfaction on several points. William Bullitt, whom Wilson had sent on a mission to Moscow in 1919, had become a special assistant to the Secretary of State. He advocated three conditions preliminary to recognition: the prohibition of Communist propaganda in the United States; the protection of the religious and civil rights of Americans in Russia; and the stipulation that recognition should not be retroactive, so as to avoid various lawsuits concerning damages and accrued interest.[21]

Roosevelt decided to follow the advice of Hull and Bullitt. On October 10, 1933, he sent a letter to the President of the Central Executive Committee, Kalinin, asking that a special envoy be sent. Kalinin's answer on October 17 announced that he was sending Litvinov himself. The text of recognition was based on twenty-six treaties Russia had signed with other nations and Litvinov gave his assent. The essence lay in Bullitt's conditions. The Soviet government also agreed to pay a total sum of between 75 and a 150 million dollars, a portion of her debt to the United States.

Recognition was accomplished through an exchange of letters on November 16. Bullitt was appointed the first United States ambassador to Moscow. Relations between the two nations, concerned with Russia's industrial development, immediately assumed a very friendly tone. Stalin had a long conversation with Bullitt on December 20, 1933, in which he promised that he would receive Bullitt whenever the latter wished, "day or night"—unlike other ambassadors. Stalin said, "President Roosevelt is today one of the most popular men in the U.S.S.R., even though he is the leader of a capitalist nation."[22] It is possible that Roosevelt developed certain serious illusions about his potential influence with Stalin from these early expressions of friendship. We shall see the consequences later.

Simultaneously, at the beginning of the administration, Roosevelt established the good neighbor policy between the United States and Latin America. In this there was no break with Hoover's conciliatory policy. It was a question of formalizing the existing situation and of giving it a legalized character.

The United States had stopped military intervention in Central America and in the Caribbean. The next logical step would be a commitment not to resume intervention and the development of an atmosphere of confidence. In his inaugural speech Roosevelt had invoked the idea of "good neighborliness." In this sphere Cordell Hull felt comfortable and he was charged with the task of carrying out the new doctrine. The past weighed heavily and the depression had exacerbated friction between the United States and Latin America. From a high of one billion dollars in 1929, trade—in both directions—had fallen to only one fourth of that sum. Between July 1932 and June 30, 1933, the United States had imported only 212 million dollars' worth of goods from Latin America and had exported 291 million dollars' worth. Everywhere there were complaints of high American tariffs. There was also a conflict between Paraguay and Bolivia over the Chaco and another between Columbia and Peru over Leticia.

The Inter-American Conference planned for Montevideo in 1932 had been postponed until 1933. Cordell Hull prepared the ground carefully to insure its success. The Democratic platform of 1932 had included the principle of nonintervention in the domestic affairs of other states. Furthermore Roosevelt and Hull had decided in March 1933 to collaborate with the League of Nations on the solution of the Leticia conflict. A commission consisting of representatives of Spain, the United States, and Brazil went to Leticia and succeeded in avoiding war by bringing about the withdrawal of Colombian and Peruvian troops. Immediately after his return from London, Hull persuaded Roosevelt to sign an Executive Agreement with Haiti by which the Marines, who had been stationed there since 1915, were withdrawn. In Cuba, where a revolution against the dictator Machado was brewing, the Platt Amendment gave the United States a legal right to intervene, but Hull refused to take advantage of it. Sumner Welles, who had just been appointed assistant secretary of state, was immediately sent as a mediator "between independent and equal sovereign powers." In August Machado withdrew and Roosevelt sent two destroyers into Cuban waters, but with express instructions not to land troops. Welles favored a landing, but Roosevelt followed Hull's advice and absolutely opposed it. Hull's opinion was shared by Josephus Daniels, Roosevelt's former chief, now ambassador to Mexico.

The Montevideo Conference opened on December 3, 1933, under the most favorable conditions, but there was great skepticism. Other conferences, notably the economic conference in London, had recently failed. Argentine Prime Minister Saavedra Lamas even proposed a new adjournment.

Hull would have liked to bring about multilateral economic agreements—the idea dear to his heart—but Roosevelt opposed it. "It was thus manifest," wrote Hull, "that the old struggle between the nationalist philosophy of the New Deal group around the President and my international philosophy of economics was still acute." [23]

At Montevideo Hull made many gestures. He took the initiative in calling on his Latin American colleagues. To Saavedra Lamas he announced that the United States was ready to join the pact against war that the Argentine had proposed and which had been signed by six Latin American nations on October 6, 1932. In exchange Hull asked the support of Saavedra Lamas for his plan of economic collaboration.

The most important accomplishment, however, was the signing of a convention on rights and duties of states. Article Eight of this convention read, "No State has the right to intervene in the domestic or foreign affairs of another State." Because of Hull's attitude and because of the adoption of the principle of nonintervention, Latin American hostility to the United States tended to disappear.

The other results of the conference seem slightly academic by comparison. The good neighbor policy was to be developed from then on. The Platt Amendment was repealed and replaced by a treaty (on May 29, 1934) which left the United States only the right to a naval base at Guantanamo. Economic aid in the form of a substantial reduction in the tariff on sugar was offered to Cuba. Evacuation of Haiti took place two months earlier than planned. The United States, with the consent of Congress, was a member of a neutral commission to arbitrate the Chaco dispute. Paraguay had refused to accept arbitration and the League of Nations decided to apply an arms embargo. The

United States did not follow suit on this point because Congress believed that in case of war an embargo should be applied to all belligerents. Here again we see the beginnings of the policy of neutrality.

Roosevelt and the Neutrality Laws

At the time when Roosevelt was putting all his energies into the development and launching of a vast plan for economic recovery, the New Deal, everything tended to reinforce the isolationist attitude of the American people. The clouds were gathering over Europe: Hitler's rise to power on January 30, 1933; the first Nazi anti-Semitic measures; the assassination of Chancellor Dolfuss in July 1934; the announcement of German rearmament on March 17, 1935; the outbreak of the Ethiopian war on October 3, 1935; the remilitarization of the Rhineland on March 7, 1936; and the outbreak of Civil War in Spain, July 1936. In his annual message to Congress on January 3, 1934, Roosevelt said in his brief reference to foreign policy, "Unfortunately I cannot present to you a picture of complete optimism regarding world affairs." If the good neighbor policy characterizes the western hemisphere, "In other parts of the world, however, fear of immediate or future aggression and with it the spending of vast sums on armament and the continued building up of defensive trade barriers prevent any great progress in peace or trade agreements." [24]

The same somber description occurred in the annual message of January 4, 1935, with another firm declaration of American neutrality. "America shall and must remain . . . unentangled and free" he said on October 2, 1935, the eve of the Italian attack on Ethiopia. [25] If one remembers the fact that the Europeans had refused to pay their debts, one can understand the defensive reaction of a nation which, having no ambition but domestic recovery, refused to become involved in a cruel war. The weakness of the League of Nations was obvious and there was satisfaction that the United States was not a member. In 1935 the new technique of opinion testing, public opinion polls, like the Gallup Poll, began to be used. Their reputation arose from the fact that in the presidential election of 1936, while the newspapers and the *Literary Digest* predicted the victory of the Republican Landon, the Gallup and Fortune polls predicted the amazing victory of Roosevelt with a margin of error of only two to three percent. From this time on we can form a much more precise estimate of American public opinion, with the help of these polls. It suffices to say here that in 1937 the public opinion polls revealed that a large majority of Americans thought that the entry of the United States into the war in 1917 had been a fatal error.

This leads us to speak of the Nye Committee. In February 1934 Republican Senator Gerald P. Nye of North Dakota introduced a motion in the Senate to create a "committee to study the munitions industry." The idea was supported by the American Legion and in April the committee was established. In addition to Nye—to whom Senator Pittman, chairman of the Committee on Foreign Relations, left the chairmanship—the committee included Senators Barbour, Bone, Clark, George, Pope, and Vandenberg. It appointed investigators and began methodically but with no discretion to study the profits of the war industries. The committee commandeered many documents from the government, including those of the State Department. Cordell Hull, reticent at first, became frankly hostile to this investigation, especially when the committee—in complete disregard of the international custom which forbids the publication of diplomatic correspondence without the agreement of the other party—made public dispatches of the French, the British, the Italians, and the Latin Americans. Flooded with indignant protests from the ambassadors of these nations, Hull hardly knew in which direction to look.

But the most serious result of the investigation in the eyes of the Secretary of State, as in those of all internationalists, was the encouragement it gave to American isolationism. "The Committee made undoubtedly useful disclosures concerning the traffic in arms, but its effect was to throw the country into the deepest isolationism at the very moment when our influence was so vitally needed to help ward off the approaching threats of war abroad." [26] Indeed the committee, quite carried away by its subject, was not satisfied to study the profits of the munitions makers; it went on to study the origins of the World War and arrived at the simple but explosive conclusion that the United States had been plunged into the war by the bankers and munitions makers.

The defense of the principle of freedom of the seas, Wilson's main —even sole—motive for going to war, disappeared. The bankers had forced the United States into the war to assure the victory of the Entente and thus the repayment of money owed to them. Naturally all this was accompanied by equally oversimplified and severe judgment of the sordid imperialism of France and England and a consistent indulgence toward Germany. We have previously discussed the theory; let us now look at its consequences.

To conclude that the United States entry into the war in 1917 had come about in this way was to believe in the existence of a simple mechanism which appropriate measures would eliminate: since the United States had gone to war to obtain the repayment of credits, it would suffice not to grant credits to any belligerent, aggressor or victim. If one consistently put an embargo on all shipments of arms and munitions to belligerents there would be no cause for the arms industry to be interested in the success of either camp, and especially not one with naval power—which would be the only one in a position to buy arms in the United States.

This was specious reasoning, as arms and munitions had constituted only about 10 percent of the goods delivered to the Entente. To be logical, the United States would have had to put an embargo on *all* trade with belligerents, but in that case she would have deprived herself of a magnificent opportunity to make profits. The economic superiority of the United States in the world, already established by 1914, had been immensely increased by the deliveries made to the Entente, who in turn had multiplied their investments in the United States (investments later used up to cover their purchases of war materials). Since such a possible advantage could not be sacrificed, the result was a compromise: an embargo on arms and munitions only, the producers of these dangerous goods being considered particularly evil.

The Nye Committee thus took a position against the principle of freedom of the seas so dear to Wilson. Furthermore the entire investigation tended to present Wilson as a dishonest person, the conscious tool of the trusts—to such an extent that Cordell Hull thought it necessary to defend the former President in public. The committee's point of view was supported on May 8, 1935, by Admiral William S. Sims, who energetically opposed the doctrine of Admiral Mahan and Theodore Roosevelt that the nation should have a strong Navy to defend the freedom of the seas.

We cannot keep out of a war and at the same time enforce the freedom of the seas . . . If a war arises, we must therefore choose between two courses: between great profits, with grave risks of war, on the one hand; or smaller profits and less risk, on the other . . . We, as a people, must come to understand that peace is priceless; that it is worth any reasonable sacrifice of war profits; that a decent regard for humanity must be placed ahead of gold . . . Our trade as a neutral must be at the risk of the traders; our Army and Navy must not be used to protect this trade. It is a choice of profits or peace.[27]

The neutrality laws of 1935, 1936, and 1937 stemmed directly from the findings of the Nye Committee. Faced with the threat of war between Italy and Ethiopia in the spring of 1935, many senators and representatives, especially Nye and Clark, drew up bills aimed to make neutrality automatic, that is, to take from the Executive all freedom to maneuver with regard to any distinction between aggressors and victims. To avoid this limitation on Executive action, the State Department itself devised a plan (July 20, 1935) which would give the President power to decree an embargo on arms, to forbid their transport in American ships, to forbid all loans to belligerents, and to prohibit American citizens from traveling on belligerent ships. This was to underestimate the strength of the isolationist majority in Congress. Despite Hull, Roosevelt, carried along by public opinion, resigned himself to accept Senator Pittman's bill, which provided for an automatic embargo. It was passed by the Senate on August 21 and by the House of Representatives on August 23. Roosevelt signed it on August 31.

This first neutrality law was temporary, in force only until February 29, 1936. It stipulated that in case of war the President should immediately proclaim an embargo on arms and munitions destined for any belligerent. A National Munitions Control Board was established on September 24 under the chairmanship of Cordell Hull. In fact— Roosevelt understood this well—not too much harm was done: the war that threatened was that which Italy was about to unleash against Ethiopia. Italy, the aggressor, who had superiority on the sea, would be much more affected than the victim; and the law was temporary in any case. Roosevelt appeared to be pleased with it, and declared at the same time that too rigid legislation would risk dragging the United States into war, in certain circumstances.

When all attempts of the League of Nations to mediate between the two nations had failed and the United States had refused to take part in the League's efforts (September 12) Mussolini attacked Ethiopia, on October 3, 1935. Curiously enough, Roosevelt had a fairly good opinion of Mussolini up to this time. On June 16, 1933, he wrote, "I am very much interested and deeply impressed by what he has accomplished and by his obviously honest intention to build up Italy and to oppose general trouble in Europe." [28] This was the time of the Four-Power Pact which Mussolini had conceived as a way of revising the 1918 treaties. Later, on January 19, 1937, Mussolini told the reporter Anne O'Hare McCormick, "I admire Roosevelt . . . because he is bold, because he is a sort of dictator, not—he smiled—in the sense in which I am a dictator. He is what I would call a social dictator. He concentrates in his own hands as much power as possible under your system, in order to impose social justice." [29] Roosevelt was not impervious to flattery; nevertheless the Ethiopian war seemed inexcusable to him.

Since the United States did not intend to ally itself with the League or to apply economic sanctions, what would its attitude be? The neutrality law forbade the furnishing of arms and the Johnson Act forbade extending credits, as Italy had not paid her war debts. Roosevelt also decided not to authorize the Export-Import Bank to make loans to Italy. It was, however, still possible for Mussolini to buy quantities of supplies in the United States which the League of Nations' invocation of sanctions would prevent him from purchasing from member nations. Cordell Hull tried to find a way to prevent such purchases, because although the trade would be profitable it would also, in his eyes, be immoral. He called his method the moral embargo. In a proclamation of November 15—which preceded by three days the League's note applying sanctions—he said,

The American people are entitled to know that there are certain commodities such as oil, copper, trucks, tractors, scrap iron and scrap steel, which are essential war materials, although not actually "arms, ammunition" . . . and that, according to recent Government trade reports, a considerably increased amount of these is being exported for war purposes. This class of trade is directly contrary to the policy of this Government . . . as it is also contrary to the general spirit of the recent Neutrality Act.[30]

Mussolini protested in the name of strict neutrality, but Hull held to his program, in which he had a slightly naïve pride. Had he not included oil in his embargo, which the League of Nations had left out —at least in the first months of the war? Hull recognized that exports continued to increase but by substantially less than they would have without his moral embargo, he said. A moral embargo is only effective in the last analysis with moral people. One cannot expect the moral argument to prevail with those who place personal profit above such considerations as prolonging a war, aiding an aggressor, or increasing the number of dead and wounded.[31] The trouble is that business often involves such an attitude.

Should the moral embargo be transformed into a law against abnormal exports? This was Hull's opinion, but not that of Congress. Congress was not opposed to anything which would favor prosperity as long as it did not risk war. On the other hand, Congress did not wish to increase the power of the Executive by giving the President the right to decide what were "abnormal exports." Also, Roosevelt preferred to allow Senator Pittman and Representative McReynolds to propose a new neutrality law intended to extend the old one beyond the six months' deadline. The Pittman bill contained a clause on abnormal exports. The ardent isolationists like Nye and Clark, aided by Borah and Johnson, proposed another bill without such a clause.

The second neutrality law, which went into effect on February 29, 1936, and was to remain in force until May 1, 1937, did not go beyond the terms of the 1935 law. It did, however, establish an exception in favor of an American state at war with a non-American state and it expressly forbade all loans or credit to belligerents. Finally, it slightly increased the power of the President; instead of stating that the embargo would be applied "in case . . . of war" it read "when the President considers that a state of war exists." In 1937 this permitted Roosevelt to continue to send arms to China against Japan, under pretext that a real state of war did not exist between the two countries.

The Spanish Civil War, which began on July 17, 1936, posed new problems to American neutralists. The neutrality law did not apply, since it was a question of civil war. At first, Cordell Hull proclaimed a new kind of moral embargo. American policy toward all nations conformed rigorously to the principle of nonintervention, but the United States was not a member of the Committee of Non-Intervention proposed by France on July 31. (Membership would have meant involvement in European affairs.) Roosevelt insisted on independent action by the United States in an important speech at Chautauqua, New York, on August 14. "We are not isolationist except in so far as we seek to isolate ourselves completely from war. Yet we must remember that so long as war exists on earth there will be some danger that even the nation which most ardently desires peace may be drawn into war."[32]

No new step was taken before Roosevelt's triumphal re-election in

November 1936. Let us note in passing that considerations of foreign policy—hardly mentioned in the Democratic platform—seem not to have played any part in the outcome, the New Deal having absorbed all the interest and attention of the voters. In January 1937, however, Congress passed almost unanimously a special law of neutrality applying to the war in Spain, putting an embargo on all arms and munitions to either side. In this case the executive and the legislative branches were in perfect accord; Roosevelt had asked for this legislation in his annual message to Congress on January 6. It may be said to have marked the high point of American neutralism.

Roosevelt and Hull favored the extension of such neutralism to the whole western hemisphere. In 1935 they suggested an extraordinary inter-American conference to be held in Buenos Aires at the end of 1936, with the aim of studying means to maintain peace in the Americas. Bolivia and Paraguay had ended the Chaco War by an agreement on January 21, 1936, so there was nothing to prevent such a conference. Cordell Hull headed the United States delegation, which arrived on November 25—the day Hitler announced the signature of the anti-Comintern pact with Japan. Roosevelt himself went to Buenos Aires on the cruiser *Indianapolis*, which was unprecedented. He was enthusiastically welcomed.

Roosevelt proposed an agreement according to which all twenty-one American republics would consult in case of a threat to any one of them. This was not purely academic: as a result of extensive German and Italian emigration to Argentina and Brazil there was a real network of Nazi subversion in South America and many Americans were suspicious of the role the German airline Lufthansa might eventually play. The German airline had succeeded in monopolizing a large part of Latin American traffic.

Roosevelt left after three days, but the conference reached agreement, following Hull's proposal on what he called the "eight pillars of peace": popular education for peace; frequent international conferences; application of treaties (the Kellogg-Briand pact and the antiwar pact of Saavedra Lamas); a joint policy of neutrality in the hemisphere; the coordination of commercial policies; practical international cooperation; reinforcement of international law; faithful adherence to treaties. One must not attach too much importance to these solemn abstractions, very much in line with the idealism of the Secretary of State. Hull would have liked to create an international commission to coordinate the neutrality policies of the American states, but he met opposition from Saavedra Lamas, who saw in it an expression of mistrust in the League of Nations. Nevertheless, a fruitful decision was taken—to organize a procedure of consultation in case of a threat of war against any of the members. Furthermore, no mention was made of Spain, which meant that the whole hemisphere was in fact rallying to the principle of nonintervention.

Thus at the end of 1936 and the beginning of 1937, Roosevelt and Congress were agreed on a rigorous policy of neutrality—backed up by laws. This agreement was not to last. Congress wanted to make the neutrality law permanent instead of allowing it to expire on May 1, 1937. From January to April of that year Congress was constantly concerned with this question. The State Department prudently took no stand. Two similar plans proposed by Pittman in the Senate and McReynolds in the House were passed by enormous majorities: 63 to 6, and 376 to 12. It was easy to reconcile them and Roosevelt signed the new law on May 1. The third neutrality law continued the embargo provisions of the second but it added two important clauses: the first forbade American citizens to travel on belligerent ships; the second concerned goods other than arms and munitions for which the famous "cash and carry" clause was introduced. This clause was very popular throughout the country. When a belligerent nation bought supplies in the United States it must pay cash (there were some possible exceptions of purchases with three months' credit). The buyer must also have the goods transported in non-American ships. The third neutrality law had no time limit.

This was as much limitation as the Executive could tolerate if it wished to keep a small margin of initiative, for which it had greater and greater need, and it explains the energy with which Roosevelt opposed two new initiatives by the neutralists. The first, emanating from Senator Nye, proposed the extension of the arms embargo to Germany and Italy, since these two nations were increasingly taking open sides with the rebels in Spain. American sympathy was with the Loyalists—1700 American citizens had enlisted on their side despite the American laws. Roosevelt thought that such a measure would not serve the interests of his policy of peace.

Also in February 1937, Louis Ludlow, Democratic representative from Indiana, had proposed a new constitutional amendment. According to the Constitution Congress has the sole right to declare war.

Ludlow wanted to make the process still more cumbersome: except in the case of invasion of American territory, he proposed that a declaration of war should first be approved by a popular referendum. Hull wrote that enactment of this amendment would "most seriously handicap the Government in the conduct of our foreign affairs generally, and would thus impair disastrously its ability to safeguard the peace." [33] The Ludlow Amendment, which had first to get a two-thirds majority in both houses of Congress, was defeated by a narrow margin on January 10, 1938, in the House of Representatives: 208 in favor, 188 opposed.

Already Roosevelt's shift toward a new attitude—in the direction of the abandonment of isolation—had begun to manifest itself. The "quarantine speech" of October 4, 1937, was the obvious sign of this change.

Chapter XI

Roosevelt Abandons Neutrality, October 1937-June 1940

The Quarantine Speech and the Peace Plans

In 1937 the New Deal was virtually completed, despite certain adverse decisions of the Supreme Court and their effects, which began to be felt early in that year. In comparison with 1933, the national income had increased by 70 percent, production by 64 percent and employment by 48 percent. Unemployment had dropped from 13 million to 7.5 million. Optimism was reasserting itself on the American scene. Nevertheless a new recession came about between the spring of 1937 and June 1938. This was caused by a sudden and premature cut in government spending, restrictions on credit and intense social agitation which coincided with a rise in union membership. The number of unemployed rose again to 10 million. Roosevelt checked this new fall in the economy by adopting Keynesian methods, stimulus of the economy by increased government spending. At the same time it is clear that his immediate concern was with problems of foreign policy. The public in general remained firmly isolationist. The special characteristic of this period is that the President, instead of letting himself be carried along on the current of opinion as he had formerly, clearly detached himself from it. From 1937 on he was to guide the American people toward a less neutral policy and to advocate increasingly the defense of democracy, which was seriously threatened in Europe and Asia. He did this with great caution and dexterity.

The "quarantine" speech of October 5, 1937, marked the beginning of this development. There had been some foreshadowings of this speech, whose most significant passage we shall analyze below. Without abandoning isolationism Roosevelt had let it be known that it was not a universal remedy. At the National Cemetery in Arlington,

Virginia, on November 11, 1935, he had said, "We cannot build walls around ourselves and hide our heads in the sand." He had not drawn any practical conclusion, however, and had gone on to say, "the fundamental aim of the United States of America is above all to avoid being drawn into war." [1] In his message to Congress on January 3, 1936, instead of keeping silent on foreign policy as in former years, he spoke of it at length, but his conclusion was still an isolationist one: "But if face it [an era of European crises] we must, then the United States and the rest of the Americas can play but one role; through a well-ordered neutrality to do naught to encourage the contest, through adequate defense to save ourselves from embroilment and attack, and through example and all legitimate encouragement and assistance to persuade other nations to return to the ways of peace and good will." [2] The United States would limit itself to "moral aid," as he said a little later. In other words, it would do nothing.

The new feature of the quarantine speech is that he proposed to do something, although in vague and obscure terms. The speech had been drafted by the State Department and by Norman Davis, the President's friend and adviser, but the President added the significant passages on his own initiative at the last minute. In Chicago on October 5, 1937, he described at length the "international reign of terror," which he called a regular epidemic. If this epidemic should spread, "let us not imagine that America will escape . . . that the western hemisphere will not be attacked, that it could continue tranquilly and peacefully to carry on the ethics and arts of civilization."

The peace-loving nations must make a concerted effort in opposition to those violations of treaties and those ignorings of human instincts which today are creating a state of international anarchy and instability from which there is no escape through mere isolation or neutrality.

Those who cherish their freedom and recognize and respect the equal right of their neighbors to be free and to live in peace, must work together for the triumph of law and moral principles . . .

There is a solidarity and interdependence about the modern world, both technically and morally, which makes it impossible for any nation completely to isolate itself from economic and political upheavals in the rest of the world . . .

The peace, the freedom and the security of ninety percent of the world is being jeopardized by the remaining ten percent who are threatening a breakdown of all international order and law. Surely the ninety percent can and must find some way to make their will prevail . . .

When an epidemic of physical disease starts to spread, the community approves and joins in a quarantine of the patients in order to protect the health of the community against the spread of the disease.

It is my determination to pursue a policy of peace . . .

America hates war. America hopes for peace. America actively engages in the search for peace.[3]

This long excerpt shows us clearly the revolution which had occurred in Roosevelt's thought: (1) isolation and neutrality are no longer enough to protect America; (2) "a concerted effort," a "positive undertaking" of peaceful nations is required; (3) the undertaking should take the form of quarantining the aggressors. This meant that for the first time a distinction would be made between the aggressors and their victims. Of course this spectacular declaration came on the heels of Japan's new aggression against China, which we will discuss later. Nevertheless there had been no warning and as the isolationist historian Charles Beard has said, it was "like a bolt from the blue." [4]

The problem was to know what Roosevelt meant by a "concerted effort." Confronted by a storm of protests from the isolationists, his answers to newspapermen at a press conference in Chicago on October 6 were extremely vague, and he asked that they be withheld from publication. For instance,

Question: . . . you were speaking of something more than moral indignation. That is preparing the way for collaborative—
The President: Yes?
Question: Is anything contemplated? Have you moved?
The President: No, just the speech itself.
Question: Yes, but how do you reconcile that? Do you accept the fact that it is a repudiation of neutrality—
The President: Not for a minute. It may be an expansion.

This is not clear. When he was asked if this meant the participation of the United States in economic sanctions, he said "no." Was there to be a conference of peaceful nations? No again. Ernest Lindley then asked him:

Wouldn't it be almost inevitable, if any program is reached, that our present Neutrality Act will have to be overhauled?
The President: Not necessarily . . .
Question: You say that there isn't any conflict between what you outline and the Neutrality Act. They seem to be at opposite poles to me and your assertion does not enlighten me.
The President: Put on your thinking cap, Ernest.

Finally, Roosevelt refused to give the slightest indication of what he meant by the word "quarantine," but he asserted clearly that he had a "program," a "plan" which he would not reveal.[5]

Let us try to discover the President's mysterious plan about which the entire press was guessing. One essential fact was the appointment of Sumner Welles as undersecretary of state on May 20, 1937. His predecessor William Phillips, a friend of Cordell Hull, had been named ambassador to Italy in September 1936 at his own request. Welles's appointment, accepted by Hull without enthusiasm, had a clear meaning: the President wanted to take a more and more active part in foreign policy and wanted to find a way of doing so which would bypass consultation with Hull. Naturally this was not immediately obvious, but it was increasingly demonstrated. Roosevelt, who really valued Welles more than Hull, habitually consulted Welles on vital matters. Welles was a born diplomat, highly cultivated, with intense energy. Hull was important because of his excellent relations with Congress but he was a hesitant man, cautious, little suited to revolutionary decisions. Roosevelt respected Hull and leaned on Welles—not a bad solution.

It was Welles who drew up the President's plan, to hold a meeting with diplomatic representatives of the whole world and to reach an agreement on a certain number of principles. At first the idea was to hold this conference in mid-ocean, and then it was planned to hold it at the White House on November 11. Welles's memorandum of October 6 suggested that the world conference should aim for agreement on five points: (1) The basic principles which should be observed in international relations (as, for example, noninterference in the affairs of other nations); (2) the laws and customs of land warfare; (3) the laws and customs of naval warfare; (4) the rights and obligations of neutrals both on land and at sea, except in so far as they may be restricted by existing international agreements; (5) the right of freedom of access on the part of all peoples to raw materials. Welles added: "On this basis I should assume that the nondictatorial governments would be willing to cooperate. I should likewise assume that Germany and Italy would find it to their advantage to cooperate. Under present circumstances it would appear unlikely that Japan would take part." [6]

The conventional nature of most of this plan is self-evident. In the first four points the illusion persists that peace is furthered by condemning war in a solemn treaty, and that the application of international law is furthered by signing agreements. The characteristic of aggressors is precisely that they pay slight attention to signed documents. The fifth point is newer and more interesting. Roosevelt, who had caused the economic conference of 1933 to fail, was discovering that war involved economic factors. The "have nots" thought it unjust that there should be "haves." If the "haves" would make the raw materials available to the "have nots," war would no longer be necessary. Without discussing this immense problem here, it is evident that the ideas of Welles and Roosevelt were extremely naïve. Political imperialism, the will to power and conquest, disappeared in their conception. Also, there is no reference to Hitler's racist theory, with all it implies about the will for virtual domination by the superior race. Cordell Hull, who was very much disturbed by the quarantine speech because of the wave of isolationist protest and who was annoyed that the plan was developed without him, pointed out that the Axis would find the proposition ironic. Italy, Germany, and Japan were at the time arming to the teeth.

Roosevelt, still attracted to the idea of a meeting on November 11, slightly amended Welles's suggestions. He retained four points to be submitted to the conference: (1) The fundamental principles of international law; (2) methods which would assure equal access to raw materials; (3) means of peaceful revision of international agreements; (4) the rights and obligations of neutrals in case of war.

The novelty is in point three. The idea of revision was similar to Mussolini's when he suggested the re-establishment of the Concert of Europe, or leadership of the great powers, as a way to approach revision. This was the Four-Power Pact of June 1933 which died before it was signed. Roosevelt appears to have brought up the idea of peaceful revision following a conversation between Welles and German ambassador Dieckhoff on October 11, 1937.

Although very modest, this was at least a plan. It was still kept secret. Would it be carried out on November 11? Hull feared a violent reaction in Congress, then at the height of its isolationist sentiment. Roosevelt intended to educate the American public and to bring it to accept the idea to which he had been recently converted himself, that is, that the United States could no longer follow a policy of isolationism consistently. It seemed wise to move cautiously and to feel out Great Britain and France as a preliminary.

On January 11, 1938, Roosevelt therefore decided to submit the plan to British Prime Minister Neville Chamberlain in a confidential message. Chamberlain was convinced that appeasement was the only possible policy. He proposed to negotiate directly with Germany and Italy and give them satisfaction on the points which seemed legitimate so as to prevent them from resorting to force. He was also convinced that Roosevelt could not act because of isolationist pressures. He therefore thanked Roosevelt for his "courageous initiative" but made it clear that it would do more harm than good by hindering the negotiations he had already undertaken. In particular he was prepared to recognize the Italian conquest of Ethiopia.

This was a cruel disillusionment for Roosevelt. England, upon being consulted, had rejected the plan and was abandoning the attitude of nonrecognition of conquests by force. Roosevelt wrote to Chamberlain on January 17, 1938, that this would have a very bad effect on United States public opinion. In any case the plan of "concerted effort" could not be carried out.

The Crisis in the Far East

American public opinion and Congress were less isolationist in relation to the Far East than they were in relation to Europe. In 1933, as we have seen, Roosevelt was inclined toward the Stimson Doctrine, that is toward eventual economic sanctions against Japan, but in his preoccupation with domestic problems he had not followed out this policy. The continued advance of Japanese forces in 1935 had aroused practically no American reaction. (Japan had occupied Jehol in May, Chahar in June, and the regions of Peiping and Tientsin in November.) Roosevelt was much more concerned with the Japanese attitude toward naval armaments. A conference of the five great naval powers was scheduled to take place in London in December 1935. On the pretext that the United States had announced its intention of building a fleet as big as the Washington Conference of 1922 permitted—in 1933 it had only 65 percent of the tonnage allowed—the Japanese decided to denounce the agreement and to claim naval parity. Although Roosevelt had transferred part of the Pacific Fleet to the Atlantic in April 1934—as a gesture of good will—the Japanese Minister for Foreign Affairs, Hirota, unofficially announced the new policy of his government on September 18. Roosevelt then sent the

Fleet back to the Pacific and Japan declared on December 29, 1935, this time officially, that as of December 31, 1936, when the agreements of Washington (1922) and London (1930) would come to an end, it would no longer observe the limits it had accepted at the Washington Conference.

The London Naval Conference can be considered an unfortunate phase of American diplomacy. It opened on the heels of new Japanese aggressions in North China and in the midst of the Italo-Ethiopian War. We should add that China resented the fact that the United States was regularly buying silver without regard to the economic situation in China. Much of the silver on which China's currency was based was flowing to the United States. The Chinese economic situation was adversely affected and China had to go off the silver standard in November 1935.

The American delegation in London, headed by Norman Davis, was instructed to maintain the limits of the Japanese fleet at a ratio of six to ten for armored ships (according to the Washington Treaty) and at a ratio of seven to ten for cruisers (specified in the Treaty of London of 1930). They were also instructed to fight a naval arms race. But how could they convince the Japanese? Even the wholehearted support of the British would not have been sufficient, but Great Britain was more concerned at the time with Europe than with the Far East and did not wish to take too firm a stand. The Japanese delegation refused to discuss anything until the principle of parity had been conceded. This, naturally, did not occur and Japan withdrew from the conference leaving only an observer. As a final blow, Hitler remilitarized the Rhineland in March 1936 just as the conference was concluding.

The agreement was confined to four powers, the United States, Great Britain, France, and Italy. The signatories agreed to limit armored ships to 35,000 tons with 14-inch guns. At the same time Japan undertook the construction of three cruisers of 46,000 tons with heavier guns. This was to prove a serious matter in 1941 and 1942. In 1936 Japan had 200 warships displacing 756,800 tons; by 1941 it would have 289, including 12 armored ships and 11 carriers, displacing 1,109,130 tons. Japanese superiority was growing in the Pacific. In the Treaty of London there was an escape clause which allowed the signatories to exceed the limits if certain other powers—not signatories—could be assumed to be doing so. This led the Japanese to keep absolute secrecy about their naval construction, which was a threat understood by Roosevelt, an expert in naval affairs. Perhaps this was the cause of the development in his policy described above.

In this atmosphere and without declaring war, on July 26, 1937, Japan launched a military attack against China on a scale much greater than those of 1931, 1932, and 1935. It was, in fact, war. Would Roosevelt adopt the solution he appeared to favor in 1933, that is, concerted action with Great Britain? As early as July 20 the British government suggested this to him, but he did not dare to go so far. Cordell Hull favored "parallel and simultaneous" rather than "joint" action.[7] On the other hand, Roosevelt made maximum use of a device afforded by the neutrality act of the preceding May: the embargo and the cash and carry clause would go into effect if the President considered that a state of war existed. To the great indignation of the extreme isolationists he decided that a state of war did not exist. Charles A. Beard, pro-Roosevelt up to this time, wrote in the magazine *Events:* "the American people may well prepare themselves to see President Roosevelt plunge the country into the European War, when it comes, far more quickly than did President Wilson." [8] But American opinion was pro-China and gladly accepted the idea that arms would continue to be sent to that nation.

Aside from this decision, the United States limited itself to participation in a few futile attempts at conciliation. The main attempt was a League of Nations resolution of October 6, 1937—the day after the quarantine speech. The League of Nations suggested a meeting of the signatories of the Nine-Power Treaty (signed in Washington in 1922), which dealt with China. The meeting, in which the United States took part and to which Germany and the Soviet Union were invited, accomplished nothing. There was much talk of eventual economic sanctions. Japan and Germany refused to attend; Italy, which was about to join the Anti-Comintern Pact, energetically defended her Japanese partner. The conference lasted three weeks and closed on November 24, with a declaration, "reaffirming energetically the principles of the Nine Power Treaty." Since that treaty had been openly violated, this was no more than lip service—a display of verbal activity—and Japan paid no attention.

On December 12, 1937, Japanese planes bombed and sank the American gunboat *Panay* in the Yangtze River and destroyed three American tankers. As the *Panay* was flying a huge American flag and had others painted on the bridge, it seemed to be a deliberate act of the Japanese militarists, if not of the government. The next day Cordell Hull sent a message to Tokyo: the American government, "deeply shocked," demanded apologies, an indemnity, and assurance that measures would be taken to avoid any further incidents of this kind. The opinion of Langer and Gleason that the *Panay* incident "brought the United States to the brink of war" seems an exaggeration.[9] Cordell Hull thinks that the country "generally took the incident calmly," [10] and by December 23 the Japanese government had offered the apologies, the indemnity, and the guarantees demanded, including punishment of the officers responsible. Significantly, the *Panay* incident did not bring about passage of the Ludlow Amendment, which, as mentioned above, would have made all declarations of war subject to popular referendum. If Roosevelt was deeply disturbed, the country remained solidly isolationist.

Until the defeat of France and the consequent Japanese invasion of Indochina, the United States government did not change its cautious attitude: nonrecognition, moral condemnation, but no real concerted action in the Far East and no sanctions of any kind. Cordell Hull calls it a "constructive attitude," which meant "maintaining friendly relations with both China and Japan so as to facilitate their resuming friendly relations between themselves." [11]

As the Japanese extended their sway throughout 1938, the quarrel took on the air of an academic debate. The United States talked of the Open Door policy in China and the Nine-Power Treaty. Japan retorted, for example in a note of December 1938, that in fact the Open Door no longer existed and that Japan, less favored by nature than the United States and the British Empire, should institute "economic cooperation" with Manchukuo and China in order to assure herself of a position comparable to that of those two more favored nations. Once this situation was established, naturally Japan would accept the Open Door. At the same time, on December 15, 1938, a credit of 25 million dollars was granted to Chiang Kai-shek. This was very limited aid, by comparison, for example, to that which the Soviet Union was sending to the Chinese.

The Crisis in Europe

United States action in the agitated Europe of 1937 to 1939 was even more timid—if possible—than its action in the Far East. Nevertheless, something was accomplished, on a level which, although less conspicuous, was singularly important—that of military reinforcement of the Western democracies. On January 28, 1938, Roosevelt, convinced by the British refusal to cooperate that he could not hold to the great peace conference for which he had hoped, turned to the most urgent matter, the strengthening of the Navy. In a special message to Congress he asked simultaneously for an increase in naval armaments and legislation to "prevent war profits." The second point—discussed constantly in Congress since the time of the Nye Committee —was slightly academic. The first point was presented one week after the House of Representatives had already voted the largest naval budget in history. Was this a trial balloon to increase the budget still more? Admiral Leahy, Roosevelt's friend who was responsible for defending the Navy budget in the House Committee on Naval Affairs, seemed to indicate that it was. Nevertheless, he refused to admit that there was any relation between the quarantine speech and the new plans for the Navy. Despite this, some isolationists—a minority—turned down a new increase, on the pretext that it revealed "the outlines of a policy of universal quarantine and of an intervention policy in Asia and that it was based on the outdated doctrines of the British and Mahan." They added that it was a "blank cheque." [12] The bill was passed, however. The law allowed only two additional armored ships to be constructed. American naval power did not keep pace with that of Japan.

Apart from this, the year 1938 was one of the least productive in American diplomatic history. There was almost no reaction to the *Anschluss*. At the time of the Czech crisis, September 8, Georges Bonnet, French Foreign Minister, suggested that Roosevelt play the role of arbitrator, an offer which was politely declined. Only on September 26 and 27, when war seemed imminent, did Roosevelt send a message to the European statesmen. On the twenty-sixth, he reminded Hitler, Beneš, Chamberlain, and Daladier of the principles of the Kellogg-Briand Pact—this was not going very far. On the twenty-seventh he suggested a meeting of responsible statesmen—including the representative of Czechoslovakia—in a neutral city, The Hague, for example. One cannot compare this proposition to that of Chamberlain of the next day, a proposition which, with Mussolini's help, led to the Munich Conference. Roosevelt had added, "The United States has no interest in Europe and will assume no obligation in the present negotiations." After Munich he sent Chamberlain a brief but flattering message—"Good Man." On October 5 Roosevelt wrote to Chamberlain offering to use his supposed influence with Hitler to achieve an abatement of the Nazi anti-Jewish persecutions. He seems to have been carried away by Chamberlain's optimism. "I wholly share your hope and your belief that today there is the greatest opportunity in recent years to establish a new order based on justice and right."

American opinion grew more indignant each day at Hitler's excesses, but it had not yet begun to undergo a dramatic change. A Gallup poll at the end of 1938 shows that 95 percent of the American people were opposed to participation in another war, and two thirds thought that the embargo on arms and munitions should be maintained. Chamberlain's optimism was not shared by French Premier Daladier, who saw in the results of Munich "an immense diplomatic defeat for France and England."

Beginning in late 1938, Roosevelt's conviction that the danger was near grew stronger. From then on—history will bear us out—step by step, Roosevelt was ahead of the public, but he wanted to educate and to lead it. What had been an inclination became a determination. The storm loosed abroad, he said in his message to Congress, on January 4, 1939, directly challenged three institutions indispensable to Americans: "The first is religion. It is the source of the other two—democracy and international good faith. From this we can conclude, on the one hand, that legislation for neutrality could be harmful, and on the other hand, that the strength of the nation and that of the democracies must be increased." [13]

As early as November 14, 1938, at a military conference, Roosevelt showed that while Germany was producing 12,000 planes a year, England was producing only 4000 and France only 3600. The United States must therefore prepare itself to have a force of 20,000 planes and an annual production of 24,000. Since January 1938, France had made a point of signing contracts with American manufacturers, especially manufacturers of airplanes. Such contracts were only legal if France were at peace, according to the neutrality law. On December 17, 1938, Roosevelt told Henry Morgenthau, Secretary of the Treasury, to concern himself with foreign orders, with the clear intention of facilitating aid to the democracies by every possible means. The military budget was substantially increased so that the Army might be raised from 180,000 to 220,000 men.

Would the neutrality law be revised immediately? One incident made this impossible. On January 23, 1939, a new type of airplane with secret equipment crashed in California. The public learned in amazement that one of the victims was an officer of the French Air Force. Did this mean that military secrets were being turned over to other nations? There was even a rumor—energetically denied by Roosevelt—that he had said that the frontier of the United States was on the Rhine. The isolationists became alarmed and declared that an alliance with France was secretly being prepared. Former Secretary of State Stimson openly advocated such a policy. In any case, Roosevelt more and more sought to distinguish between aggressors and victims. Langer and Gleason,[14] whose excellent analysis of this affair I am following closely, stress the fact that public opinion was less isolationist than Congress. According to Gallup polls 65 percent of the people approved the sale of airplanes to England and France, and 44 percent approved legislation which discriminated against Germany.

In May 1939, Sol Bloom, chairman of the House Committee on Foreign Affairs, at the suggestion of Hull, proposed a resolution to revise the neutrality law and to eliminate from the new text the embargo on arms and munitions. He was unsuccessful in his attempt despite support from his colleagues, including some Republicans, and the Senate committee rejected any revision of the neutrality law then in force.

Hull had fought vigorously for Bloom's resolution, because William Bullitt, ambassador in Paris, in a report of May 10, had persuaded him that the only fear of the Western powers was that Hitler would go to war because he knew that it would put a stop to American aid to the democracies. When the House voted against revision, Bullitt spoke of "tragedy" and "disorder." On July 14, the Secretary of State made a clear declaration that the embargo on arms "works directly against the interests of the peace-loving nations, especially those which do not possess their own munitions plants. It means that if a country is disposed toward conquest . . . that country may be more tempted to try the fortunes of war if it knows that its less well-prepared opponents would be shut off from these supplies which, under international law, they should be able to buy in neutral countries." [15]

Discussing this problem with the President and a group of senators, Hull heard Borah say that in his opinion there would be no war in the near future. The Secretary replied that all the reports he was receiving indicated war to be imminent. Borah, imperturbable, assured Hull that he also had confidential information which confirmed his opinion. "Never," says the worthy Hull, "had I found it nearly so difficult to restrain myself, and to refrain from an explosion of spontaneous anger." [16] Should one conclude with Hull that the rejection of the proposition to revise the embargo played a determining role in Hitler's decision? It hardly seems probable. Today we know that the decision to attack Poland on September 1 had been made in May.

Confronted with the increasingly clear decision of the President to put an end to the neutrality law, how should we interpret Roosevelt's solemn move in favor of peace on April 14, 1939? On that day (Pan-American Day), one month after the Nazi invasion of Bohemia and several days after the Fascist occupation of Albania, Roosevelt made a speech to the Pan-American Union in which he said, "We are prepared to maintain [peace] and to defend it to the fullest extent of our strength, matching force with force if any attempt is made to subvert our institutions or to impair the independence of any of our group." A few hours later the President sent messages to Hitler and Mussolini. After remarking that four independent nations had disappeared from the map, Austria, Czechoslovakia, Albania and Ethiopia, the note went on to say that according to reports, "which we trust are not true" further aggression against independent nations was to be expected. The President asked the two dictators to give assurance that their armed forces would not attack any of 30 nations on a list which accompanied the letter. "I hope that your answer will make it possible for humanity to lose fear." [17] If the assurance requested were forthcoming, Roosevelt proposed that discussions be held with the United States participating, on the followiing points: (1) means to end the arms race; and (2) means to assure all peoples of a chance to buy and sell on the world market on an equal basis and with sufficient access to raw materials.

Did Roosevelt sincerely think that this would make the dictators pause for a single instant? If so, the harsh and ironic replies of the dictators must have been a bitter blow. It is infinitely more probable that the President, while recognizing the futility of his gesture, wished to make a strong impression on world opinion and especially on opinion in the United States. To address the dictators directly was to revive the idea of a quarantine. This move belongs, therefore, in my opinion, in the category of steps toward the education of the American people which Roosevelt had undertaken. But there is no better teacher than catastrophe, and it was a great catastrophe that was needed to break the vicious circle of an isolationism which was indeed very appealing.

The European War and American Aid

The first dramatic event which upset American public opinion was, of course, the outbreak of the war in Europe at the beginning of September 1939. The public followed events with passionate interest and Roosevelt was very well informed, especially by Joseph P. Kennedy, ambassador to Britain—who followed Chamberlain in the policy of appeasement and later in the British policy of guarantee to threatened nations—and by William Bullitt, ambassador to France, who was more inclined to the idea of effective American intervention.

Relations with the Soviet Union were relatively good, even after the departure in 1938 of Ambassador Davies, a warm supporter of Soviet-American rapprochement. On August 4, 1939, Roosevelt used all his influence to assure the success of negotiations between England, France, and the Soviet Union. Sumner Welles sent a confidential letter to the new American ambassador in Moscow, Steinhardt:

> The President said that if war were now to break out in Europe and the Far East, and were the Axis powers to gain a victory, the position of both the United States and the Soviet Union would inevitably be immediately and materially affected thereby. In such event, the position of the Soviet Union would be affected more rapidly than the position of the United States. For these reasons, while he was, of course, in no position either to accept any responsibility or to give any assurances as to the possible course which Great Britain and France might undertake in connection with their present negotiations with the Soviet Union, the President could not help but feel that if a satisfactory agreement against aggression . . . were reached, it would prove to have a decidedly stabilizing effect in the interest of world peace.[18]

The message arrived too late to influence Soviet policy; whether it would have made any difference is problematical.

The Nazi-Soviet Pact of August 23 freed Hitler's hands. On August 24, Roosevelt appealed to Hitler and Poland's President Mościcki to keep the peace. Hitler's reply of August 31 was confined to the statement that he had "greatly appreciated" the President's message; the next day at dawn his troops invaded Poland. Roosevelt learned about it in a telephone call from William Bullitt.

The initial effects of war on American public opinion are clear.

In contrast to 1914, opinion was not divided, it was resolutely and clearly against Nazi Germany. Even the German-Americans hated Hitler and all that he represented. Of course, in general their German origins were farther removed than in the First World War, owing to the virtual cessation of immigration since 1924, but the deep revulsion against Hitler was unmistakable .

Nevertheless, public opinion was opposed to war; in general, isolationism persisted. It was certainly receding, but it could not be ignored. At the end of August, 61 percent of the people favored an economic boycott against aggressors. In early September a significant poll revealed that 44 percent of the American people would be willing to send arms to Europe if England and France were in danger of being defeated. Whereas in 1914 Wilson had asked Americans to be neutral even in their thinking, Roosevelt declared in a fireside chat: "This nation will remain a neutral nation, but I cannot ask that every American remain neutral in thought as well. Even a neutral has a right to take account of facts. Even a neutral cannot be asked to close his mind or his conscience." [19]

A second effect of the outbreak of war was obviously to bring the neutrality law into operation. Since arms (planes and tanks) destined for England and France were immobilized in port, Roosevelt and Hull, at the urging of Chamberlain and Daladier, undertook to get Congress to revise the law. Conditions were now more favorable to such change than they had been in the spring.

As early as September 13, Roosevelt called Congress into special session, which opened on the twenty-first. He encountered opposition from ardent isolationists like Borah and Charles Lindbergh, but he had the support of a considerable number of Republicans such as Alfred M. Landon, his opponent in the election of 1936, Colonel Frank Knox, and Henry L. Stimson. Taking advantage of his experience in the spring, Roosevelt this time did not ask for repeal of the neutrality law, but proposed that another law be substituted for it. The word "neutrality" would be kept because it was useful politically, but the technique would become more flexible.

The plan, which was proposed by Senator Pittman on October 2, was harshly attacked by Borah, Hiram Johnson, Nye, and La Follette. We find again the "battalion of irreconcilables" of 1919–1920. Their main argument was that France and England, as European nations guilty of "power politics," did not in any way deserve to be aided.

Curiously enough, former President Hoover provided grist for their mill by voicing throughout the country an idea tragically contradicted by events, that the democracies were so sure to win that lifting the arms embargo was not necessary. Lindbergh, for his part, proposed the seizure of French and British holdings in the Americas as payment of their debts in the First World War! Nevertheless, on October 27 the Senate passed the Pitmann Bill by 63 votes to 30, and on November 2 the House followed suit with a vote of 243 to 181. The President signed the new neutrality act on November 4.

The new law abolished the embargo on arms and munitions and put them in the same category as other supplies—cash and carry. France and England must pay cash or purchase on short-term credits (three months) and be responsible for transporting the goods themselves. Naturally, England and France were not mentioned in the law, but as they had great naval superiority the result was, in fact, to prevent shipments to Germany only. Neutrality became clearly discriminatory, even more than it had been from 1914 to 1917. This was in conformity with the wishes of the President and with public opinion. The President obtained the power to define war zones which American ships and citizens might not legally enter. Contrary to the idea of freedom of the seas—with which nobody was concerned any longer—American citizens could not travel on the ships of belligerent nations. On the economic level, the law favored American production but hit one sector of the economy very hard, the Merchant Marine. Its annual losses were estimated to be 52 million dollars.

From this time on, American policy took the form of a sort of "contemplation" of events in Europe. There was no question of an offer of mediation. On September 11, 1939, Roosevelt cabled Kennedy: "The people of the United States would not support any move for peace initiated by this Government that would consolidate or make possible a survival of a regime of force and aggression." [20] For this reason, Roosevelt refused to associate himself with the peacemaking attempt of the King of the Belgians and the Queen of Holland in early November 1939. He also refused to lead a sort of "League of Neutrals." He refused to protest against the rigorous blockade established by the British—an attitude strikingly different from Wilson's. He did nothing when Soviet forces invaded Poland, or when the Soviet Union demanded bases in the Baltic countries in accordance with secret treaties with Germany.

As for "brave little Finland," the only nation which had paid its previous war debts, he confined himself to sending a message to Kalinin (October 11) to draw his attention to "the deep and lasting friendship between the United States and Finland." This, too, was a feeble gesture. When the Soviet Union attacked Finland on November 30, 1939, Roosevelt publicly condemned the aggression. Real reprisal was weak, however, and the United States confined itself to a moral embargo which scarcely interfered with Soviet purchases of aluminum, molybdenum, nickel, tungsten, and machines. The furnishing of war materials to Finland was difficult because of the cash and carry clause. A loan of 50 to 60 million dollars was discussed at length in Congress and a new law was passed to make it possible. It was passed in the Senate on February 13, and in the House on February 28, a few days before the defeat of Finland. The same situation prevailed in relation to the sale of American military surplus. Cordell Hull, fearing the isolationist reactions of Congress, seems to have contributed substantially to the delay of these measures.

The only positive actions Roosevelt took during the "phony war" were the appointment of Myron C. Taylor as his personal envoy to the Vatican, and the sending of Undersecretary of State Sumner Welles to Europe to gather information on February 9, 1940. Roosevelt declared that this trip was for the "sole purpose of informing the President and the Secretary of State of present conditions in Europe." He was much too concerned with the war and its effects not to feel the need of direct information. This was established United States practice. Had not Wilson done likewise, in sending Colonel House on frequent trips to acquire information? It was also necessary to dispel the clouds which were threatening Anglo-American relations, clouds resulting from the British blockade. The British were stopping American ships, tampering with mail, and holding up American cargoes in the Mediterranean. In early 1940 there were many protests. In any case, Welles's mission, which he suggested himself, was undertaken without serious consultation with Hull.

Welles took with him J. Pierrepont Moffat, chief of the European Division of the State Department, and both men have left records of the trip. They sailed on the liner *Rex*, stopped at Gibraltar on February 23, and arrived in Naples two days later. On February 26, in Rome, Foreign Minister Ciano revealed to Welles his hostility to Germany and to the Nazi-Soviet Pact, but Mussolini, who was still hesitant as to which policy to follow, spoke of the "just claims" of Germany in Central Europe. It was already clear that tension existed between the Duce and his son-in-law.

On March 1, Welles arrived in Berlin where the Führer's orders were to refuse to discuss peace with him. Ribbentrop made him a long speech on British responsibility, as did Hitler himself on March 2. Welles drew the conclusion—justified by events—that it had already been decided to launch a great offensive.

Welles went to France via Switzerland and met President Lebrun and Premier Daladier in Paris on March 7. Daladier pointed out that peace was impossible as long as Hitler wanted to dominate the continent of Europe. Welles was struck by the pessimism of some of the French leaders, such as Herriot and Blum.

Quite different was his impression in London, where he found, on the contrary, especially in Winston Churchill, a very determined attitude, a set determination to destroy the Nazi system. Moffat wrote, "The Government is determined not only that it will not make peace with the present 'gang' in Germany, but will not make peace on any terms that would enable any German Government or the German people to say they had won the war." [21]

All told, Welles returned convinced that peace could not be made with Hitler but with the fragile hope that Italy would stay out of the war. He sailed from Naples on March 20. His confidential report to Roosevelt and Hull was of inestimable value because it anticipated the great upheavals in the offing.

The first upheaval was caused by the German attack on Denmark and Norway, to which Roosevelt responded on April 13 by a solemn reproach. The danger was coming closer. What would become of the Danish possessions, the Faroe Islands, Iceland, and Greenland? The United States was willing to have the British defend the first two. Defense meant occupation, and this was carried out on May 10. The same was not true of Greenland, however. Hull told Lord Lothian on April 12 that for this vast subcontinent, which was clearly in the western hemisphere, there could be no question of British occupation. The ambassador accepted this point of view and thought that the responsibility could be taken on in the name of Canada. Canada protested to Great Britain and let the United States know that it would be useful to send Canadian contingents to Greenland, but only after the United States had clarified its position. The anti-Nazi coalition, including the Danish minister in Washington, really wished the establishment of an American "protectorate" in Greenland, as the best way to prevent the Germans from setting up bases there, but Roosevelt refused to do anything more than send a small contingent to guard the coasts and establish a consulate. A consulate was also set up in Reykjavik, Iceland.

The second crisis—on a much larger scale—was the German offensive of May 10 and its results: the penetration of the Ardennes region as early as May 15, Dunkirk, Italy's entry into the war on June 10, the formation of Pétain's government on June 16 and finally the Franco-German Armistice of June 22, carried out on June 25. Roosevelt played the part of an interested spectator in all of these events. He made a considerable effort, however, to prevent Italy's entry into the war. As early as April 29, the American ambassador in Rome, Phillips, was instructed to read Mussolini a long message. Roosevelt, in the usual friendly tone of his correspondence with the Duce, asked the dictator to help in preventing the spread of war to the Mediterranean. Mussolini's reply was moderate but nevertheless stressed Germany's invincibility, and stated that it was intolerable for Italy to be "a prisoner in the Mediterranean." In fact, he had already decided to go to war, and Count Ciano says in his diary that he was much displeased by Roosevelt's intervention. When Roosevelt was informed on May 14 that Italy's entrance into the war was imminent, he sent a new and solemn message to the Duce:

I do not know what Your Excellency plans or proposes, but reports reaching me from many sources, to the effect that you may be contemplating early entry into the war, have given me great concern . . .

I have sent word to Your Excellency before that I am a realist. As a realist, you also will, I know, recognize that if this war should extend throughout the world it would pass beyond the control of heads of states, would encompass the destruction of millions of lives and the best of what we call the liberty and culture of civilization. And no man, no matter how omniscient, how powerful, can foretell the result either to himself or to his own people.

To these prophetic words Mussolini replied:

I understand perfectly the motives by which [your message] was inspired . . . but there are two fundamental motives which cannot escape your spirit of political realism, and those are that Italy is and intends to remain allied with Germany and that Italy cannot remain absent at a moment in which the fate of Europe is at stake.[22]

At this time the Battle of France was already lost. As early as May 16 Bullitt had cabled that only a miracle could save the French Army. Roosevelt then decided to send a third message to Mussolini, on May 26. This time he asked him to state his "legitimate aspirations." Roosevelt would communicate them to England and France and do his best to secure their agreement to them. If they agreed, the United States would guarantee execution in the treaty to come. There is evidence that he was trying to avoid a repetition of what had happened in 1919. Italy had a bitter memory of the Treaty of London of 1915 with England and France and of Wilson's attitude at the peace conference. Under the pretext that the United States had not signed the Treaty of London, Wilson had prevented it from being fully executed. But, as Ciano said, "It would take more than this to stop Mussolini. In fact what he wants is not to obtain this or that, what he wants is war." Winston Churchill, Prime Minister of Great Britain since May 10, began his famous correspondence with Roosevelt. On the twenty-ninth he wrote him, "Al Capone is about to enter the war . . . unless you can arouse in him sufficient fear of the United States."

Aside from these gestures the only aid the United States could provide the democracies was in the production of arms, which was far from satisfactory despite the creation of a War Resources Board under Edward Stettinius, Jr., on August 4, 1939, and the arrival of a Franco-British Purchasing Commission under A. B. Purvis in Washington on December 6. (The Purchasing Commission was a subsidiary of the Franco-British Coordination Commission in London, whose chairman was Jean Monnet.) In the overoptimistic expectation that there would be a long period of defensive fighting, the Allies geared their purchases primarily to raw materials, food, and machine tools, while reducing their purchases of tobacco and fruit.

By January 1, 1940, France had ordered 2095 airplanes of which 617 had been delivered, Great Britain had ordered 1450 of which 650 had been delivered. The two nations planned to buy 10,000 planes and 20,000 engines in 1940, one third of the planes to be fighters and two thirds, bombers. In the period immediately prior to the Battle of France, between January 1 and April 26, 1940, the Allies ordered only 1280 fighters and 1980 bombers, of which 140 fighters and 352 bombers were delivered. The situation was no better in the American Army itself. In May 1940 it comprised 14,000 officers and 227,000 men, with only five divisions ready for immediate action.

Immediately after the attack of May 10, a great effort was launched with the support of the great majority of the American public. General Marshall, chief of the general staff since September 1939, thought that the Army should not be increased too much in advance of the production of arms required. He envisaged an army of 400,000 men. As early as May 16, 1940, Roosevelt, in a special message to Congress, requested that the production of airplanes be raised to 50,000 a year—the number necessary to have 50,000 planes in service in the Army and the Navy. He asked for an additional billion dollars for military purposes. Before the end of May, Congress voted one and a half billion. The extensive war effort of the United States had begun. In early June, General Marshall was planning an Army of 500,000 men by July 1941; 1,000,000 men by January 1942; 2,000,000 men by July 1942. This time three billion dollars more was needed.

These few oversimplified examples are characteristic, in my opinion, of the American national temperament. After a long period of hesitation, of holding back, faced with bitter necessity, there was a dramatic reversal. As soon as the danger became clear, the immense majority of the nation, the legislative power, and the Executive were all united in agreement to make the effort that seemed necessary and to take the long-range view.

One thing remained to be done—to mobilize industry and create a War Industries Board. In this, Roosevelt, always careful to keep the control in his own hands, hesitated a long time. He agreed to the creation of an Office of Emergency Management on May 25, which was responsible for the coordination of different agencies, and at the end of the month he set up the National Defense Advisory Commission, but the latter had only advisory power. Not until October did he resign himself to create an effective agency. "There is no reason for panic," he said, "but there is reason for haste." Langer and Gleason write that the President "was extremely sensitive to such waves of popular feeling." [23]

This vast program was begun too late in relation to France. England, protected temporarily by the Channel, could hope for some benefit from a long-range plan. In his letter of May 15 to Roosevelt—signed like those which followed, "Former Naval Person"—Churchill sketched a broad picture of the situation and of Britain's needs. At this time he mentioned the need for 40 or 50 old American destroyers to protect the Atlantic transports, as well as hundreds of planes and antiaircraft artillery. He also expressed the wish that the United States would renounce neutrality entirely and adopt a position of nonbelligerency. Finally, he wished that American pressure could be brought to bear on neutral Ireland. Roosevelt replied on May 16, that he was "very happy to continue our private correspondence as in the past." He told the Prime Minister, as was expected, that it would take a long time to give England satisfaction. The immediate aid available, in view of the Army's slight equipment, was limited to a few hundred guns. He was also not sure that he had a legal right to transfer to a foreign nation equipment belonging to the United States Armed Forces.

The Battle of France and the French defeat had considerable effect on American diplomacy. In Paris, Ambassador Bullitt was frenetically active. On May 18 he let Washington know that French Premier Paul Reynaud had decided to ask Roosevelt to declare war on Germany. This was obviously impossible, since the Constitution gives Congress the exclusive right to declare war, and besides, public opinion was very much opposed to it. It is difficult to assess the real intentions of the French Premier and in any case it is not relevant to the purpose of this book. Despite Bullitt's objections, Reynaud said on May 22 that he hoped that "you can convince the Senators and Representatives that a Declaration of War and the cooperation of the [United States] fleet and Air Force is a necessity for the protection of the United States." [24]

Reynaud put the United States in a very difficult position, but Roosevelt handled the matter skillfully. On May 23, speaking before the Business Advisory Council, he proclaimed, "The buffer [between Nazism and the Americas] has been the British Fleet and the French Army. If those are removed, there is nothing between the Americas and those new forces in Europe. And so we have to think in terms of the Americas more and more and infinitely faster." [25] He warned Reynaud and Daladier about the fate of the French Fleet if the worst should happen. At all costs the French Fleet must not fall into German hands or be bottled up in the Mediterranean. The future of France herself depended on it. Finally Roosevelt and Hull let it be known that United States intervention in the war was "unthinkable."

At Charlottesville, in a speech to students at the University of Virginia on June 10, Roosevelt condemned Italy's entrance into the war and declared that the United States "could not . . . become a lone island isolated in a world dominated by the philosophy of force." [26] He drew the conclusion that American policy should be to aid the opponents of violence as soon as possible and at the same time to arm itself to resist force. It was another step away from isolationism, but there was no commitment to act along the lines suggested by Reynaud.

This did not discourage Reynaud. On June 10 he sent a message asking for an immediate increase in aid—without going so far as a declaration of war—to enable France to continue the fight, if only in North Africa. Churchill, returning from a meeting of the Supreme War Council at Briare on June 11, wrote to Roosevelt describing the struggle between the advocates and opponents of an armistice in France and he begged the President to send an immediate message to Reynaud to encourage him in his firm position. At Tours on June 13 Churchill suggested to Reynaud that he send another message, "very frank and bold," to the President of the United States. Reynaud did so on the morning of June 14.

I know that the declaration of war does not depend on you alone. I must tell you, however, in this critical hour for us and for you, that if you cannot, in the next few hours, give France the assurance that the United States will enter the war in the very near future, the fate of the world will be changed.[27]

Obviously Roosevelt's response to Reynaud's messages could not be what was desired. Roosevelt encouraged France to continue the war and not to yield the Fleet; he promised arms "in constantly increasing quantity," but he added, "I know that you will understand that these statements carry with them no implication of military commitments. Only the Congress can make such commitments." [28]

This second reply arrived in Bordeaux on the morning of Sunday June 16. That very evening Marshal Pétain replaced Reynaud as head of the French government. This meant the certainty of an armistice and affected the United States in that it meant a continuing threat to the French Fleet. It explains Secretary Hull's sharp message of June 17, which said, in part, that "should the French Government . . . fail to see that the fleet is kept out of the hands of [the Germans] . . . the French Government will permanently lose the friendship and goodwill of the Government of the United States." [29]

These tragic events were not enough to bring the United States into the war against its will, but there is no doubt that they had an important effect in the future. Roosevelt had decided a long time previously to abandon the policy of isolationism, but up to this time public opinion had followed him with extreme reluctance. The defeat of France was a turning point in that it suddenly brought the American people to face the bitter reality from which they had tried to shield themselves by denying its existence and by constructing fragile barriers against it.

Chapter XII

The United States Entry into the War

The Great Change in American Opinion

AFTER the defeat of France and the destruction of the rampart that her Army had seemed to provide, the American people realized how close war was coming to them. The result was a tremendous reversal in public opinion, despite the resistance of the isolationists and the neutralists.

We are in a position to study the change in some detail because of the many public opinion polls taken at this time, using the methods Gallup had originated in 1935.[1] We also know that the President studied the polls from week to week. Whatever reservations one may have about particular details of this method, it nevertheless gives us very important information about the development of public opinion.

There are two main questions: first, did Americans believe that the United States could really stay out of the war and second, did Americans favor the entry of their country into the war, at least under circumstances in which United States participation would be the only way to prevent the fall of Britain?

Before 1939 a majority of American citizens thought that under any circumstances the country *could* stay out of a European conflict, by 56 percent to 44 percent on April 4, 1939, and by 62 percent to 38 percent on August 20, 1939. But when they were asked if, in case of war in Europe, the United States *should* enter the conflict, an immense majority was opposed: 95 per cent to 5 percent on April 9, 1939, 84 percent to 16 percent on May 3, 1939. During the "phony war" there was undoubted sympathy for France and England but it did not cause opinion to become less cautious. A poll of November 1939 undertook to discern what Americans thought about various possible solutions. The replies were as follows: 1.7 percent thought that the United States should go to war at once on the side of England

and France and send armed forces to join those of the Allies; 10.1 percent thought that the United States should go to war only if the democracies were on the point of being defeated and in the meantime should supply them with food and arms; 12.2 percent thought that the United States should not go to war, but should provide supplies and arms to the democracies and refuse them to Germany; 36.9 percent thought that the United States should remain neutral and offer to sell arms and supplies to both sides with strict maintenance of the cash and carry clause; 6.4 percent thought that the United States should refuse to sell war materials to anyone but should provide products not needed for war; 23.7 percent thought that the United States should refuse all aid of whatever kind to both sides and sell them nothing; 0.1 percent thought the United States should find a way to aid Germany; 3 percent had other solutions; 5.9 percent had no opinion.

The small number of supporters of Germany (0.1 percent) is very interesting when compared to the attitude of the German-Americans in 1914. The horror of Nazism and the relative remoteness of their German origin seems to explain this. In public opinion as a whole caution prevailed. On March 8, 1940, the situation was more alarming and opinions had changed slightly. When asked what should be done if Germany appeared to be about to defeat the democracies, 8.7 percent thought that the United States should declare war and send troops; 52.1 percent thought the United States should give all possible aid short of war; 3.6 percent hesitated between these first two solutions; 25.8 percent thought the cash and carry system should be continued; 6 percent thought that aid to the democracies should be reduced; 3.8 percent had no opinion.

The defeat of France brought about profound changes, fluctuating to be sure, but consistent in their direction. Regarding the eventuality of United States participation in the war the following table is revealing:

	Believe U.S. will go to war (percent)	Believe U.S. can avoid war (percent)
June 11, 1940	65	35
September 17, 1940	67	33
October 24, 1940	59	41

	Believe U.S. will go to war (*percent*)	Believe U.S. can avoid war (*percent*)
January 9, 1941	72	28
March 29, 1941	80	20
April 8, 1941	82	18
May 29, 1941	83	17
October 22, 1941	85	15

Naturally the wish to go to war remained a minority opinion, but the minority was growing. When asked what would be their attitude if they had to vote in the near future to enter the war, the results were as follows:

	Favor going to war (*percent*)	Against going to war (*percent*)	No opinion (*percent*)
June 25, 1940	14	86	—
July 3, 1940	15	85	—
September 26, 1940	17	83	—
June 7, 1941	24	76	—
June 24, 1941 (after the German offensive against Russia)	21	79	—
July 29, 1941	20	75	5
August 5, 1941	20	75	5
August 19, 1941	20	74	6
August 27, 1941	21	74	5
September 9, 1941	26	69	5

Still more interesting are the answers to a less clear-cut question: "What is our main duty, to keep out of the war or to aid England even if it involves serious risk of war?"

	Stay out of war (*percent*)	Aid England (*percent*)	No opinion (*percent*)
May 23, 1940	64	36	—
December 11, 1940	37	60	3

	Stay out of war (percent)	Aid England (percent)	No opinion (percent)
March 29, 1941	27	70	3
May 6, 1941	41	54	5
May 29, 1941	39	58	3
July 10, 1941	33	61	6

We can see that in the spring of 1941 there was a substantial rise of neutral feeling, but it did not last. The sharp drop between May 23 and December 1940 is particularly revealing.

On September 17, 1941, to the question, "Which is more important, for the United States to stay out of war or for Germany to be defeated?" 70 percent replied that the latter was more important and only 30 percent supported the former. It is interesting to break down this particular poll by regions and by parties.

	Defeat of Germany more important (percent)	Stay out of war more important (percent)
National total	70	30
Democrats	77	23
Republicans	64	36
New England and Middle Atlantic states	70	30
Middle East	63	37
Middle West	64	36
South	88	12
West	69	31

It is clear that Democrats were more opposed to Germany than Republicans and that the South was by far the most aggressive region in desiring German defeat.

Americans soon had a feeling that they were, in fact, at war. When asked, on January 9, 1941, whether or not they thought the country was at war 48 percent replied "yes," 42 percent replied "no," and 10 percent were hesitant. To the same question on September 17, 1941, 56 percent replied "yes," 33 percent replied "no," and 11 percent did not commit themselves.

On November 5, 1941, Americans were asked, "If it were necessary for the United States to send a large army to Europe in order to defeat Germany would you favor doing so?" The answers were 47 percent "yes," 46 percent "no," and 2 percent "no opinion."

When the United States did in fact enter the war it met with virtually unanimous approval. On December 10, 1941, when asked "Do you approve or disapprove the Declaration of War on Japan?" 96 percent approved and only 2 percent disapproved. The belief that the decision was right persisted. On April 10, 1946, when asked "Do you think that it was a mistake for the United States to enter the Second World War?" 15 percent replied that it was a mistake and 77 percent approved United States participation.

These are very revealing figures. They show that the defeat of France had destroyed the popular myth that neutrality was possible. Thereafter events gradually strengthened the wish to defend democracy until the climactic attack on Pearl Harbor.

It is not enough to look at opinion in the raw, one must also study the pressure groups which acted upon it. On one side we find the peace movement, the doctrinaire isolationists, certain Protestant churches, some fanatical Catholics like Father Coughlin, publisher of the magazine *Social Justice*, and the almost insignificant Nazi sympathizers of the German-American Bund, under George Sylvester Viereck. This last organization had quite different motives from the others. On the other side were those who wished to defend Great Britain and who thought democracy was in danger. We shall confine ourselves to a few words about these two large pressure groups, which tried to influence the government in opposite directions.

Let us start with the groups which favored the Allies. A certain number of internationalists, members of The Union of Concerted Peace Efforts, an offshoot of the moribund League of Nations Non-Partisan Association, met in New York in September 1939. They thought it necessary to take action favoring the Allies and founded The Non-partisan Committee for Peace through the Revision of the Neutrality Law. The chairman of this committee was an unusual person, well known in the peace movement, William Allen White.

Born in 1868 in Emporia, Kansas, White belonged to a Quaker family. One of his biographers, David Hinshaw, who was also a Quaker, said of White that he was "an almost perfect mixture of provincialism and cosmopolitanism." [2] White was a newspaperman by profession and became in 1895 the publisher of the Emporia *Gazette*. He was to remain in this position the rest of his life and to put the stamp of his strong personality on the local newspaper. He wrote a life of Coolidge, whom he admired very much. He also devoted part of his energy to the fight against the Ku Klux Klan. The Fascist Black Shirts and the Nazi Brown Shirts seemed to him to be the same kind of secret society as the Ku Klux Klan, whose purposes and methods he hated: secrecy, violence, racism, inequality. In 1939 he thought the best way to help peace was to launch a great movement to aid Britain and France. Although White was an outspoken opponent of Roosevelt at the start—he was an old friend of Theodore Roosevelt's—he became sympathetic to the President after 1939 when Roosevelt seemed to share his views.

In June 1940, after Dunkirk, the committee changed its name to The Committee to Defend America by Aiding the Allies. This committee was often called the White Committee for short. The organization grew and established chapters throughout the United States —750 in all, with 10,000 active members. The chapters organized meetings and lectures, published articles and placed announcements in the press. The committee also developed a well-organized lobby in Washington and White was often received by the President, despite their former differences of opinion. White made a point of not accepting the financial support of businessmen who might have a direct stake in the war. The average contribution to his organization was $25. Besides White, the most prominent members were James B. Conant, president of Harvard, Henry R. Luce, editor of *Time* and *Fortune*, Mrs. Dwight Morrow—mother-in-law of Lindbergh, who was a prominent leader of the opposite camp—and Robert Sherwood, a friend of both Roosevelt and Hopkins.

There was a conflict in this powerful organization which soon became evident. Some—like White—were sincerely devoted to peace and thought that the best way to keep peace was for the United States to reinforce the British "shield." Others—a majority—thought the defense of democracy was more important than peace. When White became convinced that the committee was taking the latter direction he disassociated himself from his brainchild and in a letter published in the Scripps-Howard papers on December 23, 1940, he said, "War would destroy the supreme goal for which our Committee was founded, to defend America by aiding Great Britain." [3] On January 2, 1941, he resigned as chairman. This meant a victory for the militant wing of the movement. The Fight for Freedom Committee was then set up, which favored United States entry into the war.

Confronting the White Committee on the opposite side, was the America First Committee. It is interesting to note that the historian of the White Committee, Walter C. Johnson, calls his book *The Battle against Isolation*,[4] whereas the historian of the America First Committee, Wayne S. Cole, calls his book *The Battle against Intervention*.[5] Intervention was indeed the issue; the White Committee was no more interventionist than its rival, at least in theory, but America First, an expression used to some extent in World War I and then by Harding, evoked every nationalist and anti-internationalist tendency. The America First Committee could claim to be the heir of a venerable American tradition, although it may have deformed that tradition.

The America First Committee was founded in September 1940 by 24-year-old Douglas Stuart, Jr., son of the vice-president of the Quaker Oats Company of Chicago, and General Robert Wood, a veteran of the First World War. It is not surprising that the movement was born in Chicago because the Chicago *Daily Tribune*, a violently anti-British newspaper, proclaimed throughout the Middle West an extremely isolationist sentiment. Furthermore, in Illinois there was an important group of German-Americans. They were no longer pro-German, as in 1914, but many of them would have preferred a neutral policy. The argument of America Firsters was that keeping the peace was the supreme objective—more important even than the defense of democracy in Europe. Their thinking did not lack logic if one admits their premise—that war would destroy democracy in America because violence is antidemocratic by definition. Thus there was a risk of destroying the last stronghold of democracy in the world without being able thereby to stop the growth of Nazism and Communism in Europe and Asia.

The organization attracted members. There were 850,000 in all; only a small proportion of these were militant, however. The national committee, with Wood as president and Stuart as director and later secretary-general—a more modest title and more appropriate for his age—raised a total of $370,000 from 25,000 contributors. The greatest benefactor was William H. Regnerie, president of the Western Shade Cloth Company. The majority of the members were manufacturers and bankers, like Henry Ford. There were also politicians, for example, Senators Clark, Nye, and Wheeler, former governor Phillip La Follette of Wisconsin, and president Robert Hutchins of the University of Chicago, as well as bishops, Catholic priests and labor leaders —especially of the Chicago region. One of the most active and well known of the members was Charles A. Lindbergh, whose family was traditionally anti-British. It is significant that two thirds of the members lived within a radius of sixty miles of Chicago. The committee used the same methods as its rival: meetings, pamphlets, articles, and lobbying. We shall follow their activity at the time of lend-lease.

It would be a mistake to think that the America First Committee was connected with the small pro-Nazi groups—quite the contrary. It consisted of loyal Americans, mostly Republicans but including some Democrats. On the whole it was neither racist nor seriously anti-Semitic. It represented the old guard of nationalist isolationism at a moment when the majority of Americans were turning away from that tradition.

Despite the efforts of the America First Committee the presidential campaign of 1940 did not turn in the least on the issue of the war or increased aid to England. The Democrats had nominated President Roosevelt for a third term—unprecedented in American history— on the first ballot by 946 votes to 147 for his various opponents. It is difficult to be sure when Roosevelt had decided to break tradition and run for a third term. As early as June 1939 Hopkins urged him to run, but Roosevelt had seemed to oppose it. It was certainly the war in Europe, especially the Fall of France, which decided the question.

The Republican convention refused to nominate a known isolationist and chose Wendell Willkie, a Wall Street lawyer and president of the Commonwealth and Southern Corporation. Willkie was a former Democrat, an adversary of the New Deal, and very unpopular with the bosses of his party. He was on good terms with William Allen White and supported his policy of increased aid to England.

In his acceptance speech on July 19, Roosevelt announced that he would not campaign personally. He was to change his mind in October on the advice of his staff, who were more and more alarmed by Willkie's vigorous campaign. Willkie's program was similar to that of the President and so he had to resort to *ad hominem* argument; he said everywhere that Roosevelt's election would mean war. Would Roosevelt be defeated because of a great wave of fear among the people, clearly stimulated by his opponent? Willkie's campaign was full of exaggerated statements and Roosevelt replied in kind when, on October 23, he made up his mind to campaign personally. Not only did he multiply assurances that he was opposed to war but he did not hesitate to make some extremely equivocal declarations. The best known was in a speech in Boston on October 30. Since the Selective Military Service Act was in operation and 800,000 men were about to be drafted, Roosevelt said: "And while I am talking to you mothers and fathers, I give you one more assurance . . . Your boys are not going to be sent into any foreign wars. They are going into training to form a force so strong that, by its very existence, it will keep the threat of war far away from our shores. The purpose of our defense is defense." [6]

Roosevelt's victory was a clear-cut one but it is possible that only foreign policy gave him the necessary margin for success. He received 27,242,000 votes as opposed to 22,327,000 for Willkie. He had carried 38 states with 449 electoral votes against 82 electoral votes for his opponent. This election had a profound significance—both Roosevelt and Willkie wished to increase aid to England. The isolationists had not been able to find a spokesman for their views and if they voted for Willkie it was much more out of hate for Roosevelt than out of admiration for his opponent. From then on Roosevelt felt that he had the support of public opinion and could go forward with his policy. We shall soon see that he knew how to take advantage of these favorable circumstances.

Strategy and Economic Mobilization

Clearly, strategic considerations could not play a major role in United States foreign policy during the period of neutrality. To believe that war can be avoided by passing laws is to deny the possibility that there are other ways of avoiding war; even more, it is to deny the necessity of war. Preoccupied with the New Deal and with his great peace plans, President Roosevelt did not become interested in strategic problems until quite late in the game. There was, indeed, a joint Army-Navy Commission to formulate military plans—the so-called "Orange plans" based only on the possibility of war with Japan —in which the two services discussed whether it would be possible to defend the Philippines or whether the United States should limit itself to defend only a line from Alaska to Hawaii and Panama. Roosevelt paid little attention to this planning before the summer of 1939, however.

From that time on, and especially after the outbreak of war in September, the President concerned himself more and more with the problem of strategic planning and he asked that plans be drawn up with a view to the possibility of simultaneous war against Germany and Japan. These were the so-called "Rainbow plans," the most important of which was Rainbow V in 1939. At the time of the French defeat and after the appointment to the cabinet of two leading Republicans, Stimson as Secretary of War and Knox as Secretary of the Navy (June 1940), strategic planning became an important concern of the administration.

The problems raised by strategic planning were vast and complex. The first was to determine whether it was possible to aid Britain "short of war." If this had been a certain possibility it would not have been necessary to increase the United States Army to any great extent and all war production could have gone to bolster Great Britain. (The Army in September 1939 stood at the minimum of 190,000 men, feebly supported by a National Guard of 200,000 men). Since England's survival hung by a thread in the summer of 1940, however, it was necessary to plan for an enormous increase in United States armed forces. Under these circumstances, how should war materials be divided between Great Britain and the United States? A second problem, almost equally serious, was to determine whether public opinion would agree to make the effort necessary for production of war materials. At the start of the war a popular slogan was, "business as usual," that is, there was to be no lowering of the civilian standard of living. This assumed the production of consumer goods in great quantity. The questions now arose, should not consumer goods be subordinated to military production and should not government controls—in such forms as rationing and arbitrary power over labor—be introduced?

In case of entry into the war a third problem presented itself—how to coordinate the armaments and strategies of the United States and

Great Britain. Models of weapons were not the same in the two nations. The Army objected to building factories limited to the production of British models, which would not be of use to the American forces. Also, to reduce expense, weapons must be produced in great quantity.

On the level of strategy, Admiral Stark and Secretary Knox held important discussions in 1940 in which a plan was drawn up, in agreement with General George C. Marshall, chief of the General Staff of the Army since September 1, 1939. This plan, known as Plan Dog, completed on November 4, 1940, anticipated that in case of war the principal effort would be aimed against Germany, directly and on a large scale, with relatively limited operations against Japan. This was to be the American theory throughout the war. The British had quite different ideas. Having far-flung possessions, the British wished to reinforce their position in all parts of the world. Instead of a frontal attack on Germany they would have preferred a series of peripheral operations which would make it possible to land on the continent of Europe at various points from the Balkans to Scandinavia. They hoped that if the United States intervened she would aid them especially at Singapore and in the Mediterranean.

Roosevelt thus found himself faced with great difficulties. To resolve them he employed, at least until the Victory Plan of November 1941, a series of empirical, improvised measures, which suited his temperament. We shall trace his actions chronologically in order to illustrate his method, which might be described as hopping from one subject to another.

The most urgent problem was to aid Britain—left standing alone against the Axis. We recall that in May Churchill had earnestly requested 50 old American destroyers of the 300 in reserve. This appeared to be the sole means of assuring escort for the precious convoys, which were bringing to beleaguered England, from all over the world, the means to survive and hold firm. The difficulty was that the neutrality law of June 28, 1940, would permit only such material as was declared unessential for the national defense to be sent abroad. Congress would probably not vote in favor of yielding the 50 destroyers. Stimson, Knox, and Secretary of the Interior Ickes, backed by the White Committee and especially by the columnist Joseph Alsop, were urging Roosevelt to act.

A number of prominent New Yorkers on the White Committee

who favored the immediate entry of the United States into the war, proposed on July 11 that the 50 destroyers be exchanged for certain bases on the British islands in the western Atlantic. Among the advocates of this plan were Lewis Douglas, Robert Sherwood, Joseph Alsop, and Dean Acheson. In June 1940 they had formed a special group known as the Century Group. On August 1, representatives of this group proposed the destroyer-bases exchange plan to the President and also informed Willkie, the Republican candidate. After the President had ascertained—through White—that Willkie also favored it, the cabinet came out for the exchange, on August 2.

The British would have preferred to avoid the exchange aspect of the agreement, but Roosevelt felt that it was essential if American opinion was to accept the yielding of the destroyers. Aging General Pershing, hero of World War I, made a speech on August 4 at the request of the Century Group in which he said, "Today is perhaps the last time when we can still avoid war by means short of war." [7] William Bullitt, just home from Paris, made a similar statement on August 18: "I am sure that if Britain falls we will be attacked." [8] His words brought a strong response: in the next few days he received 22,000 letters and telegrams. On August 13 Roosevelt drew up the general outlines of the plan in a meeting with Morgenthau, Stimson, Knox, and Welles, overcoming some resistance on Hull's part. Stimson kept urging the President to faster and more positive action because he was convinced that if the President led opinion would follow. Churchill agreed to the plan at once.

The destroyer-bases agreement was accomplished in an exchange of letters between Hull and the British ambassador, Lord Lothian. Its form was that of an Executive Agreement which obviated the necessity for the President to submit it for Senate approval. There remained only to specify the bases, some of which would be in return for the destroyers. Others were offered beyond the original terms of the agreement. The exchange of letters took place on September 3, 1940, and was generally well received by the public, although it was recognized that this was a deliberate violation of neutrality.

The second great decision was embodied in the Selective Service Act. To recruit and train troops had become a national necessity. Stimson thought the best way to accomplish this was through selective military service, that is, the drafting of men from each of several categories which would be defined by law in terms of certain criteria.

Mobilization was carried out in two stages. On August 27 a joint resolution of Congress authorized the President to call up the National Guard and Reserves. And on September 16, after passage by both Houses, the President signed the Selective Service Act, which permitted the immediate drafting of 800,000 men (out of 16,000,000 available) for one year of military service. In fact, the Draft Extension Act of 1941 was to keep them in service longer. Thus the United States Army reached 1,400,000 men, 500,000 in the Regular Army (this was later increased), 270,000 in the National Guard, and 630,000 draftees. On October 29, in the midst of the election campaign, Roosevelt made a courageous speech on the subject, "worthy of a great statesman," wrote Stimson.[9] It was indeed more courageous than his "appeasement" speech in Boston the next day.

The recruitment of a big army made more acute the problem of aid to Great Britain and consequently threatened the policy of "business as usual." The respite of October, after the Battle of Britain, in no way excluded the possibility that England might be invaded in the following spring. It was necessary for the United States to be able to equip an Army of 1,400,000 men before the summer of 1941. A report of General George V. Strong, chief of the War Plans Division, on September 25, 1940, stressed the immense difficulties which would arise if Britain were attacked and Japan should attack the United States at the same time. In September 1940 there were only 55,000 men ready for combat. The Air Force—then a branch of the Navy—had only 49 daylight bombers and 140 modern fighter planes. The Air Force was demanding 13,000 planes, a number which could not be reached before the spring of 1942 according to the current schedule. The Army informed Roosevelt that it was not possible to arm the United States and Great Britain at the same time unless, as Walter Lippmann urged, all the labor, industry, and money of the nation were to be mobilized. As William L. Langer says, "It was a choice between guns and butter." [10]

At the beginning of October Sir Walter Layton, special envoy of the British Ministry of Supply, arrived in Washington. He had come to ask for all the equipment required to arm six more divisions with arms of British models. He asked that 12,000 airplanes be manufactured in the United States for the Royal Air Force, in addition to the 14,000 already on order. Less than 1600 had been delivered since September 1, 1939, and the total United States production of planes had not yet reached one thousand a month.

There was the further problem of payment, because the cash and carry clause was still in effect, but we will reserve discussion of this problem for a later section.

Secretaries Morgenthau and Stimson were determined to find a way to resolve the difficulty of fulfilling both the American needs outlined in the Strong memorandum and the British needs outlined by Layton. To do so meant the abandonment of "business as usual." Roosevelt refused to take such a step before the election. In October the only progress made was Layton's agreement to accept American models of arms instead of British for the six new divisions. On October 30, in the Boston speech, Roosevelt announced his intention to satisfy the British request for 26,000 planes and also to make the United States "the greatest air power in the world." [11] But how was it to be done?

Not until December, after a final moving appeal from Lord Lothian, British ambassador in Washington, who was fatally ill, did Roosevelt make his decision. In the December 29 speech, the theme—to which we will return—of which was "We must be the great arsenal of democracy" he came out clearly for the end of the policy of "business as usual."

I want to make it clear that it is the purpose of the nation to build now with all possible speed every machine, every arsenal, every factory that we need to manufacture our defense material. We have the men—the skill —the wealth—and above all, the will.

I am confident that if and when the production of consumer or luxury goods in certain industries requires the use of machines and raw materials that are essential for defense purposes, then such production must yield, and will gladly yield, to our primary and compelling purpose.[12]

The new policy required the establishment of powerful agencies of direction and coordination. The National Defense Advisory Commission, created in May 1941, did not have enough authority. Important new agencies were therefore created: The Office of Production Management (OPM) under the joint direction of labor leader Sydney Hillman and the industrialist William S. Knudsen, in January 1941; the Office of Price Administration and Civilian Supply (OPACS) directed by the New Dealer Leon Henderson, in April

1941. Finally, on August 28, 1941, the Supply Priorities and Allocation Board was established under the direction of Donald Nelson. At the same time the OPACS became the OPA. The President, very jealous of his powers, was reluctant to give exceptional, almost dictatorial, powers to the chairmen of these agencies.

Stimson thought that the President did not go far enough, that he should take more initiative and present the situation to the public frankly, instead of trying to influence opinion by roundabout means. On May 27, 1941, however, the President decided to proclaim "an unlimited state of national emergency."

Because the agencies lacked sufficient authority the cooperation of industrialists was all the more important. As a group the industrialists, far from having wanted war, had supported a somewhat pacifist and neutralist point of view in the 1930's. In various opinion polls in 1939 the richest groups in the population had been shown to be more opposed to war than the country as a whole. The industrialists also feared economic control by the government.

There had been a change of opinion in the business group, however, in accordance with that of the country as a whole. In late 1939, while the financial publications *Sphere* and the *Wall Street Journal* referred fearfully to the threat of Nazism, others like *Nation's Business* and the *Commercial and Financial Chronicle* took an extreme isolationist position. Roosevelt was violently hated by big business because of the New Deal, but as early as June 1940 the powerful National Association of Manufacturers had come out for increased national defense. "American sympathies are with the Allies and this country will do everything in its power to help them—armed intervention aside" said the *Banker and Tradesman*.[13] Some businessmen were also impressed by Henry R. Luce's argument, in his book *The American Century*, that war could open many more new markets to the United States. The idea that Hitler would exclude America from world markets and that the United States would be ruined and reduced to an inferior position in the competition, worried American businessmen very much. On the other hand, the businessmen would welcome a situation which permitted them to increase profits—Stimson thought this an indispensable incentive—without going to war. They were not enthusiastic about conversion. "The manufacturers remained cautious."[14] Labor struck repeatedly in the six months before Pearl Harbor. In November 1941 there was even a major strike in the coal mines led by John L. Lewis. Only war could put an end to such hesitations and unwillingness to take action.

Plans for war—more and more inevitable—were drawn up in co-operation with the British. Roosevelt approved joint discussions between the General Staff and the British in Washington between January 29 and March 29, 1941. There was already a Permanent Joint Board of Defense for Canada and the United States.

The differences between the Americans and the British, already mentioned, were most serious in relation to Singapore. The Americans declared that

> The objective of the war will be most effectively attained by the United States exerting its principal effort in the Atlantic or navally in the Mediterranean regions . . . [The United States General Staff agrees] that the retention of Singapore is very desirable. But it also believes that the diversion to the Asiatic theatre of sufficient forces to assure the retention of Singapore might jeopardize the success of the main effort [of the Associated Powers.][15]

The difficulty could not be completely eliminated. Further discussions were held through an exchange of military missions between Washington and London. It took the Atlantic meeting between Roosevelt and Churchill to arrive at a common line of thought. Despite the military men of both nations, Roosevelt decided to send reinforcements to United States possessions in the Pacific, thus moving in the direction of British theory. Churchill decided to disregard the request of his generals for American contributions to the defense of Singapore. The allies-to-be took the unequivocal stand that Germany was the prime target.

Little by little strategic problems were worked out. On the American side an overall program was drawn up by responsible military leaders, notably General Wedemeyer, at Roosevelt's request in July 1941. The Victory Program, as it was called, was adopted in November 1941. It rested on the following five principles:

1. The Monroe Doctrine: resist penetration of the western hemisphere by the Axis by all possible means.

2. Aid to Great Britain: aid to be limited only by United States needs and by the British capacity to use such aid. This included the assurance of delivery of the goods.

3. Aid to nations opposed to the Axis: aid to be limited only by needs of United States and Great Britain.

4. Far Eastern policy: express strong disapproval of Japanese aggression and prove to Japan that the United States had decided to act positively. Avoid for the time being any major engagements on land or sea in the Far East.

5. Freedom of the seas.[16]

The Victory Plan involved the mobilization of 8,795,000 men (or 215 divisions), 2,000,000 of them in the Air Force. Five million men would have to be transported overseas, requiring as many as 2500 ships at one time. Production of airplanes would reach 60,000 in 1942 and 125,000 in 1943; production of trucks, 45,000 in 1942 and 75,000 in 1943. The United States military budget rose from 13.1 billion dollars in 1939 to 71.3 billion dollars in 1944. Federal revenue increased sevenfold during this period, principally through the income tax. The national debt rose by 236 billion dollars because the public invested heavily in government bonds, although they bore only 3 percent interest.[17]

Thus gradually, not without ups and downs, the immense war machine got under way.

Lend-Lease

If strategy and industrial conversion developed slowly and without coordinated action because of Roosevelt's evident timidity, in the development of lend-lease, on the contrary, the President demonstrated his capacity for leadership. This is a matter of capital importance from every point of view. The Lend-Lease Act of March 11, 1941, was one of the most important decisions ever taken in the history of the world. Not only did it resolve in the President's favor the long-standing conflict between the Executive and Congress over foreign policy, which had been going on since Wilson's time, but it introduced for the first time the idea that large nations should aid smaller nations virtually without compensation because it was advantageous to both. This idea was to become increasingly important as the war went on. It eliminated in advance any question of war debts. Moreover, it removed the obligation of Great Britain to pay cash for the supplies she had already received. The Lend-Lease Act was not only, in Stettinius' words, the "weapon of victory," but a real revolution in world diplomacy.

The British, and the Greeks, who had been attacked by Mussolini in October 1940, needed not only the divisions and planes requested by Sir Walter Layton, but also means by which to pay for and transport these items. The cash and carry clause put them in an increasingly difficult situation on both counts. The British Merchant Marine —dangerously weakened by the Battle of the Atlantic—could no longer do the job. The reserves of gold and foreign currency for cash payments were almost exhausted. A large proportion of British investments in the United States had been used up; what remained was more difficult to liquidate rapidly and, in any event, would not last long. There was the additional complication that United States laws prevented the sale of any material essential to the national defense. Secretaries Stimson and Morgenthau attacked these problems, as did Arthur Purvis of the British Purchasing Commission.

During the month of November 1940 Roosevelt allowed his subordinates to prepare plans feverishly and appeared not to react to their increasing irritation with his vague generalizations. Stimson and Morgenthau tried hard to find devices for getting around the laws without having to risk congressional action. Everyone was surprised that the President did not seem willing to draw the logical conclusion from the election: to increase the war effort and to aid England by all possible means. The White Committee multiplied its efforts. Roosevelt responded by going for a vacation cruise in the Gulf of Mexico on the cruiser *Tuscaloosa*.

During this cruise he received a letter from Churchill dated December 8. It was a long letter explaining in detail all the aspects of Britain's position. The aim, the Prime Minister said, was now to hold firm and to increase British forces so as to make possible victory without the help of an American expeditionary force. The Battle of the Atlantic, between the convoys and German submarines, constituted the mortal danger. For this reason Churchill asked a revision of the cash and carry clause and thus of the neutrality law. He suggested that raw materials be transported partly in American ships escorted by the United States Fleet. There was only a slight chance that Germany would retaliate by a declaration of war. Churchill also besought Roosevelt to bring pressure on the Irish Prime Minister de Valera to allow bases to be established in his country. He urged greater effort in the delivery of weapons. Finally, he pointed out that soon American shipments could no longer be paid for in cash by the British. He stressed the fact that United States and British interests were identical.

The Treasury Department had established that while Britain's orders were already in excess of five billion dollars, available resources were less than two billion dollars. Lord Lothian addressed an urgent appeal to the American people on December 11. On December 14 Roosevelt landed in Charleston after his cruise and found his associates in an agitated state of mind.

On December 17, lunching with Morgenthau, Roosevelt suddenly said, "I've thought a great deal about what we should do for the British and I think the thing to do is to get rid of the dollar problem." To accomplish this, the United States could "lend" the material to the British. On the same day he held a press conference, the most famous of his career. He said first, that from a selfish point of view, America had a vital interest in aiding Great Britain, but that the old methods of aid—which would involve revising the Johnson Act and the neutrality laws, and the granting of loans—were "nonsense," worthy only of "narrow-minded men." What should be done was what a man who owned a hose would do when his neighbor's house was on fire. He would not say, "Neighbor, my hose cost $15, you must pay me $15 in order to use it." No, he would lend it to him, help put out the fire, and later retrieve the hose. In this homely way the President explained his new idea to the American people. He added that his method did not imply going to war but only the passage of new laws. Sherwood [18] and Langer and Gleason [19] consider that the metaphor of the hose was a most important factor in winning public support for Roosevelt's new plan.

It remained to organize the immense undertaking. We have already seen how the directing agencies had been created, culminating in the decision to establish the OPM. The President spelled out the terms of the necessary changes in law in two important speeches. In the first, on December 29, a "fireside chat," at which he excelled, Roosevelt showed that the policy of the dictators was radically opposed to American ideals and therefore that a negotiated peace—still advocated by Senator Vandenberg—had no chance of success. If the Nazis won, America would live through a "new and terrible era." Thinking in terms of today and tomorrow, "I make the direct statement to the American people that there is far less chance of the United States getting into war, if we do all we can now to support the nations defending themselves against attack by the Axis than if we acquiesce in their defeat." [20] "We should be the great arsenal of democracy," he added, in an expression admirably suited to the sentiments of his audience, as an arsenal produces but it does not fight. The "great" arsenal flattered the vanity of a nation that loved things on a big scale. The word "democracy" was there to add the moral tone for which Americans are always thirsty.

The second speech was his annual message on the State of the Union on January 6, a message "unique in our history," Roosevelt said. In it he repeated the idea and proposed certain principles to guide national policy, announcing that in the desperate situation prevailing, "the nation's hands should not be tied when its life is in danger." [21] He proposed legislation necessary to meet the problem. Finally, he proclaimed that the war aims of the democracies were related to what he called the four freedoms: freedom of speech, freedom of worship, freedom from want, freedom from fear.

As early as the beginning of January Morgenthau was put in charge of working out legislation for what was to be the lend-lease program. He did it with the help of the legal experts of the Treasury Department and representatives of the British Purchasing Commission. He then consulted other leaders, including Stimson. The plan provided that the President could "lend" arms, munitions, and other goods, within the limit of credits voted by Congress, to all nations whose defense he thought essential to the security of the United States. After the war, the goods could either be returned or paid for. On January 6 the plan was submitted to Roosevelt. Hull then studied it and made several criticisms, one of which was important and was embodied in the final text. Morgenthau's plan listed the nations which would profit from the aid, Hull proposed that it be left to the President's discretion as to which nations would be elegible.

On January 9 the plan was discussed at a White House meeting attended by Secretaries Hull, Stimson, and Morgenthau, Senators Connally, Harrison, and George, Representatives Rayburn, McCormack, Bloom, and Luther Johnson, and Knudsen, Director of the Office of Production Management. On January 10 the text was presented to both Houses of Congress. In order to impress the economic facts on Congress and the American people—who tended to think that Britain had unlimited wealth—it was decided to make public Britain's actual resources. The Treasury Department estimated the remaining British assets abroad (outside the United States) at ten billion dollars.

Hull thought it was eighteen billion dollars. Even if the situation were not desperate, Stimson thought Britain should not be asked to give her pound of flesh. Roosevelt thought the British holdings in the United States amounted to 1.5 billion dollars of which one billion could be liquidated.

The next step was to hold hearings in the committees on foreign affairs of both Houses. These were particularly interesting. The four Secretaries shared the task of presenting and defending the plan. In the hearings in the House, Hull spoke first on the international aspects. As a congressional veteran he did it well. "It has become increasingly apparent that mankind is today face to face, not with regional wars or isolated conflicts, but with an organized, ruthless and implacable movement of steadily expanding conquest . . . The most serious question today for this country is whether the control of the high seas shall pass into the hands of the powers bent on a program of unlimited conquest." [22]

Morgenthau confined himself to the financial aspects and produced documents on Britain's prospects. He met with some skepticism. Stimson followed. As a Republican "renegade" he was under fire from the isolationist opposition, but he defended himself with vigor. He showed how the plan would enable the production and synchronization of weapons with the British and thus would assure the defense of the United States better than in the past. As to Knox, he said that the British Fleet, which for more than a century had provided the best defense for the United States, remained essential to the nation's survival, because a victorious Axis could command a Fleet greater than that of the United States. Knudsen supported similar views.

The opposition, organized by the America First Committee, managed as best they could. Their choice witness was Joseph P. Kennedy, who had recently resigned as ambassador to Great Britain. Kennedy feared that the plan would involve the United States in war. Lindbergh thought that the only thing to do was to create a tremendous Air Force operating from bases which could defend the western hemisphere. For the rest of the world he preferred a negotiated peace. Claiming to be absolutely neutral, he said that a complete British victory would be almost as dangerous as that of the Axis. In addition, war would destroy democracy in America. This was also the theory of the socialist Norman Thomas. The jurists John Bassett Moore and Edwin Borchard explained that the law gave too much power to the President, an argument which was repeated by the representatives of the large peace organizations. Robert Hutchins, president of the University of Chicago, said that the plan was suicidal. The executive committee of the C.I.O. was divided on the bill: Henry Ford opposed it, William Bullitt favored it. On February 8, 1941, the House of Representatives passed the bill with some amendments, by 260 to 165 votes; 236 Democrats and 24 Republicans voted for it.

The hearings in the Senate Committee on Foreign Relations began on January 27. The arguments and their spokesmen were approximately the same, although one must add to the list of opponents General Wood, president of the America First Committee, the historian Charles A. Beard, and Colonel Robert McCormick, owner of the *Chicago Daily Tribune*. Herbert Wright, professor at the Catholic University of America, said that the bill would open the door to Communism. On the other hand, Wendell Willkie, Republican candidate in the recent election, returning from a trip to England, echoed enthusiastically the sentiments Churchill had just expressed in a radio speech (February 9): "Give us the tools and we will finish the job."

The Senate passed the bill on March 8 by 60 to 31 votes, after adding an amendment proposed by Democratic Senators Byrnes and Byrd, and supported by Republican Senator Robert A. Taft, to the effect that the President could not control the sums necessary for lend-lease but that Congress would have to vote an appropriation for each loan to a given nation. Although this reduced the leeway for presidential action, Roosevelt did not fight the restriction and when the House had accepted the Senate amendment, he signed the new law on March 11, 1941.

To measure the immediate impact of this action it suffices to realize that whereas up to October 1, 1941, seven billion dollars had gone to lend-lease, during that single month of October six billion dollars in additional aid was voted by Congress.

The War in the Atlantic

The Tripartite Pact of September 27, 1940, seemed to increase the solidarity of the Axis Powers and to open the door for the Soviet Union eventually to join in a vast division of the world into spheres of influence. After some hesitation the Soviets declined. If they had accepted, the United States influence might have been limited to the western hemisphere. In reality, the bonds between the two leading partners of the pact, Germany and Japan, remained more theoretical than real. The Nazi attack on the Soviet Union on June 22, 1941, isolated them completely from each other. The result of Japanese abstention from war with Russia was to impose upon the United States, in this period before American entry into the war, the necessity of two quite different policies, one for the Atlantic and one for the Pacific.

Until the autumn of 1941 the Atlantic had first priority and, surprisingly, was even more important in American strategy than in British strategy. Up to the invasion of Iran in September 1941 lend-lease was limited essentially to the European theater. The first meeting between Roosevelt and Churchill was to be called the Atlantic Meeting. The most important battle of 1941 was, more than ever, the Battle of the Atlantic. Since the destroyer-bases exchange, the United States was no longer truly neutral in the Atlantic, and the tone of American pronouncements reflected the change. The furious oratorical attacks of Hitler against the United States alternated with the scornful replies of Roosevelt and other American leaders. The President said in a fireside chat on December 29, "This nation cannot make peace with the Nazis except at the price of total surrender." The full force of American diplomatic pressure was brought to bear against Germany.

The British had persuaded the Americans that the best way to keep Franco's Spain from joining with Hitler was economic pressure and in October 1940 Roosevelt allowed the Red Cross to send food to Spain. The United States even offered to negotiate a loan of 100 million dollars for Spain in exchange for the assurance of Spanish neutrality. Ambassador Weddell said that aid to Spain should be based on "political considerations rather than humanitarian or commercial considerations." [23] American public opinion was resolutely hostile to Franco and caused Hull to suspend aid to Spain in November 1940. It was later resumed, with constant haggling.

In regard to Marshal Pétain there was a similar attitude. After the Montoire meeting between Pétain and Hitler, Stimson was convinced that France would hand over her fleet and her North African bases to the Germans. On October 25 Roosevelt sent a serious warning to the marshal: If Vichy gave aid to Hitler the United States would no longer guarantee the safety of French overseas possessions. The fear that Martinique and Guadeloupe would fall into German hands haunted the Americans, especially Undersecretary of State Welles, a specialist in Caribbean affairs. Discreet pressures were put on General Weygand, French commander in chief in North Africa. Finally it was decided to send an ambassador to Vichy. Roosevelt first offered the post to General Pershing, who had fought side by side with Pétain in 1918, but Pershing refused for reasons of health and Admiral William D. Leahy, then governor of Puerto Rico, was appointed. His instructions were to see to it that France did not yield her Fleet and her bases. In order to do so he must gain Pétain's confidence. Leahy arrived in Vichy in January 1941.

Of greatest importance to the United States, naturally, was Great Britain. On January 5, 1941, it was announced that Harry Hopkins, the President's personal adviser, would go to England immediately. Was this a "mission," newspapermen asked Roosevelt? "No," he replied, "he is going over just to say hello to a lot of my friends." [24] But what friends? On the advice of Jean Monnet, who had remained in Washington and who became intimate with Hopkins, Roosevelt decided to concentrate his efforts on Churchill. The Prime Minister had not dealt with Hopkins before, but the two men liked and understood each other at once. Hopkins, with his keen intellect and his remarkable intuition, went to inform himself of Great Britain's real needs at the time when lend-lease was under discussion. He also took Churchill an invitation to meet with the President personally. Already, through Hopkins, what Churchill called "a heart to heart contact with the President" had been established.[25]

Hopkins accompanied Churchill to Scotland when Lord Halifax was to sail for his new post as British ambassador to the United States. He spent three weekends and twelve evenings with the Prime Minister during his six-week visit, and was shown the most secret correspondence. Hopkins drew the following conclusion: "Your 'Former Naval Person' "—Churchill's signature in letters to Roosevelt—"is not only the Prime Minister, he is the directing force behind the strategy and conduct of the war." Hopkins added, "I am convinced that if we move audaciously and quickly on certain essential points we can find enough material to give Great Britain within a few weeks the additional power she needs to throw Hitler back." [26] Shortly after Hopkins' return, a new United States ambassador, John G. Winant, went to London. Hopkins was to become, without official title, the President's adviser and assistant in lend-lease, while Averell Harriman went to London with the rank of minister to put it into effect.

The chief problem was how to deliver the flood of goods which industry was turning out and which lend-lease permitted to be sent. As early as December 1940 Stimson, Knox, and General Marshall were convinced that there was only one solution—for the United States to escort the convoys at least part of the way. On December 19, in a conversation with the President, Stimson compared the problem with that of a leaking bathtub. Should one keep pouring in water? No! First the holes must be plugged up. In other words, the attacks of German submarines must be discouraged.

No doubt Stimson, Marshall, and Admiral Stark had already concluded that entry of the United States into the war was necessary, if not at once at least in the near future. Roosevelt himself did not want to move so fast, especially as in the spring of 1941 there seemed to be a slight decline in the public desire to aid Great Britain militarily in case of imminent danger. While Stimson advised the President to exercise active leadership, Roosevelt confined himself to a series of partial measures: the exchange of scientific information (President James B. Conant of Harvard was sent to England for this purpose); the exchange of military information (which resulted from the conversations between the general staffs mentioned above); cooperation in counterespionage; the sending of American technicians to England; the repair of British warships in American shipyards; and the training of pilots for the R.A.F. in the United States. On March 28, when Roosevelt learned of a plot to sabotage German ships immobilized in American ports, he ordered them to be seized.

On April 2 Roosevelt seemed converted to the idea of escorting the convoys and ordered a plan to be prepared which was known as Defense of the Hemisphere Number 1. But on April 13 he learned that Japan had signed a neutrality treaty with the Soviet Union. This aroused such fear of a possible attack that Roosevelt drew back. Furthermore, he was disturbed by the reaction in the Senate. Senator Charles W. Tobey of New Hampshire had introduced a resolution forbidding the use of American cargo ships for goods destined for belligerent nations and forbidding the escort of convoys. The plan known as Defense of the Hemisphere Number 2, which went into effect on April 24, replaced the system of convoys by that of "patrols." In the area west of 25° west longitude (halfway between Brazil and Africa) American ships and planes would inform convoys of the presence of German submarines. In contrast to the convoy system, American forces would not attack German submarines, however. They would attack them only within a radius of 25 miles of bases yielded by Great Britain to the United States, and after giving warning. This system provided only partial relief for the British difficulties of escort.

On May 27 Roosevelt proclaimed a "state of unlimited emergency" after urging from Secretaries Knox, Stimson, and Ickes and Attorney-General Jackson and in spite of Hull's more cautious attitude. This decision is to be explained by the sudden appearance of the German armored ship *Bismarck* on the high seas and the military disasters in Yugoslavia, Greece, and Crete. But on the following day at a press conference Roosevelt indicated that this did not mean that the American Fleet would escort convoys. On July 2 Stimson, discouraged, wrote in his diary, "Whether we are really powerful enough and sincere enough and devoted enough to meet the Germans is getting to be more and more of a real problem." [27] Roosevelt refused to extend the system of "patrols," in spite of urging from Hopkins, even after the first American cargo ship, the *Robin Moor*, was sunk by the Germans.

Another problem was that of the Atlantic bases. Since the end of 1940 the establishment of a United States military base in Greenland had been considered. On April 9, 1941, an agreement was made with the Danish minister in Washington placing Greenland under the temporary protection of the United States. Roosevelt preferred to see United States bases established rather than British or Canadian bases, a preference which represented an extension of the Monroe Doctrine to this northern territory.

The same system was applied to Iceland, another Danish colony, which declared itself independent on May 27, 1941. The British and Canadians had sent some forces to Iceland as early as May 1940, but the activity of German submarines and the concentration of German warships off Norway created great anxiety for the safety of the island. Iceland was to the east of the 25° line but it was in a vital strategic position. In April 1941 the United States sent the destroyer *Niblack* on a reconnaissance mission to Iceland, which resulted in a clash with a German submarine—the first fight in "the undeclared war."

Hopkins negotiated with the consul-general of Iceland in Washington at the insistence of Hull himself. If there were a United States base in Iceland, American cargo ships escorted by American warships could transport war material to the base, saving British tonnage and escorts. Iceland and Greenland could serve as intermediary airfields for planes being delivered to Great Britain. Churchill warmly approved this plan, which, in addition, freed a division for other purposes. There were two difficulties, one was a legal technicality—it was outside the western hemisphere as traditionally defined. Also, the Premier of Iceland, Jónasson, did not favor it. The British let Jónasson know that they needed their troops for other theaters of war. American forces landed in Iceland on July 7; on the eleventh the plan Defense of the Hemisphere Number 4 was put into effect, which permitted the escort of convoys between the United States and Iceland.

A long negotiation was undertaken with Portugal about the Cape Verde Islands and especially the Azores. Not until 1943 was it completed.

American diplomacy was feverishly active at this time in its attempts to prevent France from yielding essential bases, especially Dakar, to the Germans. We know that the notorious Protocols of Paris signed by Darlan in May 1941—which would have yielded the bases to the Germans—were finally rejected by the Vichy government. When news of the interview between Hitler and Darlan was received by Roosevelt the President declared: "The people of the United States can hardly believe that the present government of France could be brought to lend itself to a plan of voluntary alliance, implied or otherwise, which would apparently deliver up France and its colonial Empire, including French African colonies and their Atlantic coasts, with the menace which that involves to the peace and safety of the Western Hemisphere." [28]

Roosevelt then ordered that French ships in American ports be placed under surveillance. Admiral Leahy brought great pressure to bear on Marshal Pétain. High hopes were placed in General Weygand. The Murphy-Weygand Agreements on supply for North Africa had been signed between February 26 and March 10, 1941, and it was Weygand who played the decisive role in the rejection of the Protocols of Paris. The upshot of this is clear: the Americans, led by Cordell Hull, had entered into friendly relations with the Vichy government. Roosevelt had refused to receive General de Gaulle's envoy,

René Pleven, at the White House. Hull was in favor of increasing Red Cross supplies to France. The British, who had no confidence in Darlan, wanted, on the contrary, to stiffen the blockade. The crisis over the Protocols of Paris did not convert Hull to De Gaulle but United States policy did become more moderate after the anguish experienced in June. For example, Hull enthusiastically approved the action of the British and De Gaulle in Syria in June. Nevertheless, one must admit, as Hull said, that the United States, "exercised the strongest influence [of any foreign power] in Vichy." [29]

The German attack on Russia naturally had important results for American foreign policy. There was, of course, a moment of triumph for the isolationists—it proved that the Communists were not pro-Nazi and that to fight against Germany would be to aid the Reds. "The victory of Communism in the world," said Senator Taft, "would be much more dangerous for the United States than the victory of Fascism." [30] The administration was not unduly disturbed however, and a poll showed that 73 percent of the American people hoped for a Russian victory. Stimson wrote Roosevelt that the military chiefs

were unanimously of the belief that this precious and unforeseen period of respite should be used to push with the utmost vigor our movements in the Atlantic theatre of operations . . . As you know, Marshall and I have been troubled by the fear lest we be prematurely dragged into two major operations in the Atlantic, one in the northeast and the other in Brazil . . . By getting into this war with Russia, Germany has much relieved our anxiety, provided we act promptly.[31]

The War Department expected a German victory in Russia in a matter of one to three months. Churchill had immediately promised all possible British aid to Russia, despite his dislike for Communism. Roosevelt decided to follow suit. On June 26 he announced that the United States would offer aid to Russia. Soviet ambassador Oumansky opened negotiations with Undersecretary of State Welles on this point. To supply Russia would pose terrible problems of convoy, however. On July 11, Harry Hopkins flew to England to discuss the new situation with Churchill. Hope was dawning that Russia would be able to hold out. Hopkins, acting at Churchill's suggestion, suddenly decided to go to Russia and Roosevelt agreed at once. Churchill arranged his trip from Scotland to Archangel. Hopkins carried with him a message from Roosevelt to Stalin: "All possible aid will be given by the United States Government in obtaining munitions, armaments and other supplies needed to meet your most urgent requirements and which can be made available for actual use in the coming two months in your country . . . The visit now being made by Mr. Hopkins to Moscow, will, I feel, be invaluable." [32]

Hopkins stayed in Moscow from July 30 to August 1, 1941. Stalin explained his immediate needs, which were principally 20,000 coast artillery and one million machine guns. Aluminum was the raw material most needed. There was a long list of other products desired by the Russians, the total estimated to be worth 1.8 billion dollars. Up to October 9, only 29 million dollars' worth was provided, a small start for a contribution which would reach a total value of 10 billion by the end of the war. It was decided that Archangel was preferable to Vladivostok as a port for delivery. Hopkins talked at length with Stalin and was impressed by his tremendous confidence. Stalin quite simply asked that the United States enter the war against Germany. Hopkins reported that Stalin had said "the power of Germany is so great, that although Russian can defend herself, it would be very difficult for England and Russia to destroy the German military machine together. He said that the only thing that could defeat Hitler . . . would be the announcement that the United States would go to war against Germany." [33]

Hopkins' visit to London had had as its ultimate purpose to make arrangements for a meeting between Roosevelt and Churchill. He returned from Archangel in time to sail with the Prime Minister on the *Prince of Wales*.

The Atlantic meeting was held off the coast of Newfoundland, Roosevelt on the *Augusta* and Churchill on the *Prince of Wales*. The two men were meeting for the first time since World War I. Churchill had even forgotten that he had encountered the young undersecretary of the navy. The highest military and naval officers of both nations attended the meeting, with representatives of the State Department and the Foreign Office. Sumner Welles led the delegation of the State Department. The place and nature of this meeting, which lasted from August 9 to 12, was kept absolutely secret.

The first subject of discussion was general strategy, the outlines of which we have already discussed. Roosevelt conceded—an essential point—that in convoys bound for Iceland the United States Navy could escort British as well as American cargo ships. Churchill let it be clearly understood that he wished the United States to enter the war. A study was made of possible military operations. There was discussion of a Second Front, which Stalin was avidly demanding as early as his first letter to Churchill on July 19. A telegram was sent to Stalin to suggest a meeting in Moscow to develop long-term policies of aid. We shall discuss below the decisions taken about the Pacific theater.

In addition, Roosevelt and Churchill worked out a joint declaration, the Atlantic Charter, which seems to have been more or less improvised. The problem of a future peace seemed far off and the research division of the State Department under Leo Pasvolsky had hardly begun its job. In July, Roosevelt had warned Churchill that he opposed the drawing up of any plans for territorial settlements in the midst of the war. This meant that any peace plans made could only deal with principles. Roosevelt wanted to make a declaration which would prevent England from following a policy of secret agreements. He wanted to eliminate for the future the kind of difficulties which had hampered Wilson. He had such confidence in himself that he believed that he would be able personally to deal with all kinds of problems when the moment came. Let us remember the 1928 speech in which he expressed his faith in the part "the right man" could play in keeping the peace.

Churchill's interest in the matter was above all in its propaganda effect: the whole world would learn that the United States and Great Britain were in agreement. The only point which aroused any discussion on the British side was equal opportunity to obtain raw materials after the war, because it opposed the principle of imperial preference. Roosevelt did not wish to introduce any precise references to a future international organization out of fear of the reaction of the isolationists.

On the whole, the Atlantic Charter was cast in the moralistic style of the American tradition: repudiation of territorial aggrandizement, consent of peoples to all territorial changes, the right of peoples to choose their own government, equal access to raw materials, economic cooperation, freedom of the seas, guarantees of peace, and the renunciation of force. All of this couched in general terms might perhaps appeal to American public opinion. In fact, the immediate political significance was very limited, as later events showed. Cordell Hull, displeased to have his subordinate Welles playing the leading part in the preparation of the charter, felt that he discerned in it some obstacles to his cherished ideas of economic liberalism. One could, in fact, discover in the charter just about anything one was looking for. The isolationists denounced the "Secret Treaty of Intervention" which they said the charter implied. They were astonished to find no reference to freedom of worship and saw in this omission a concession to atheist Russia. As Langer says, "The American people had a notorious weakness for high-sounding principles and were definitely more willing to participate in the making of peace than in the waging of war." [34]

For Churchill the main point was that it was a *joint* declaration. In England people spoke of "pious platitudes" and would have preferred increased American aid. On September 30, Churchill summed up the situation admirably when he said: "Nothing is more dangerous in wartime than to live in the temperamental atmosphere of a Gallup poll, always feelings one's pulse and taking one's temperature . . . There is only one duty, only one safe course, and that is to try to be right and not to fear to do or say what you believe to be right." [35]

The War in the Pacific

In 1941, there was a striking contrast between the Atlantic and the Pacific. While the United States Fleet patrolled the Atlantic 24 hours a day with its lights out, under the command of the dynamic Admiral King, in the Pacific the Fleet was mostly in port, especially at Pearl Harbor, lights ablaze. There was a Battle of the Atlantic and there was no battle in the Pacific. This contrast did not conceal the fact that for the Americans the Sino-Japanese war (stemming from the "incident" of 1937) was almost as odious as the Nazi offensive in Europe.

Between 1937 and 1940, American reaction to the war in China was primarily one of moral condemnation couched in the theoretical terms of the Hoover Doctrine. The United States confined itself to the announcement, on July 29, 1939, that the commercial treaty between the United States and Japan would cease to be in effect within six months. This was a modest decision, but interesting in the light of later events. During the first two years the United States, with strategic plans based entirely on the premise that in case of war the main effort would be in Europe, used only the weapon of economic pressure against Japan. Only Joseph C. Grew, United States ambassador to Japan, seemed to understand the implications of the policy: "If we once start sanctions against Japan we must see them through to the end, and the end may conceivably be war . . . If we cut off Japanese supplies of oil and Japan then finds she cannot obtain sufficient oil from other commercial sources to ensure her national security, she will, in all probability, send her fleet down to take the Dutch East Indies." [36] As Japan had reacted unfavorably to the Nazi-Soviet Pact of August 23, 1939, and had announced on September 3 that she would remain neutral in the European war, American-Japanese relations remained cool but peaceful until the fall of France.

The German victories in Europe, combined with the increased power of Japan in China, stiffened the attitude of the Japanese government. Was this not the moment to settle two essential questions? First, could not the Dutch East Indies supply Japan with a large part of the raw materials she needed? Second, could not Japan cut the supply route of Chiang Kai-shek, whose government had fled to Chungking, capital of Szechwan province on the upper Yangtze River? Falls which separate the upper from the middle stretches of the Yangtze River made it impossible for the Japanese to make a frontal attack on Chungking. A possible solution was to cut the supply routes of the Chinese Nationalist leader. Two of these routes passed through Sinkiang and Inner Mongolia, connecting China with Russia. This was a matter for negotiation. The other route was the French railroad between Haiphong and Kunming. And the Burma Road was about to be completed.

The Japanese thus had a choice between three strategies. One was a frontal attack on China combined with the creation of a puppet government under Wang Ching-wei. This proved impractical. Another was to form an alliance with Germany against the Soviet Union. This was the policy of Matsuoka, Foreign Minister in the spring of 1941, but his government forced him to sign a nonaggression pact with the Soviets on April 13, 1941. The third possibility, more and more tempting, was a policy of threat and force in Southeast Asia. In that region lay the needed raw materials; conquest of northern Indochina and Burma would cut off Chinese supplies. The Navy objected to this policy because it might bring the United States into the war, and the Fleet, instead of fighting glorious battles, would have to use its

strength to protect huge convoys between the islands and the penin-
sulas. Nevertheless, between 1940 and July 1941, Japan slowly and
hesitantly took the measures necessary to assure this policy.

The British were more aware of this new danger than the Americans, which explains the importance of Singapore in their strategic
plans and their futile attempts to interest the Americans in them. Negotiations begun in January 1940 between Japan and the Netherlands
to increase Japanese trade with Indonesia caused little concern. There
was still the hope, expressed by Grew, that Japan's conflict with China
could be resolved and an extension of her power avoided. The conversations between Grew and Foreign Minister Arita in June 1940
accomplished nothing, however. This was the time Japan chose to
make her first advances in Southeast Asia. At the end of June the Yonai
cabinet asked France to admit a Japanese military mission to Tonkin,
asked Great Britain to close the Burma Road, and asked the Dutch
government-in-exile in London to increase Indonesian supplies to
Japan substantially.

The British, who were hostile to the policy of appeasement but
desperately threatened in Europe, asked the United States to help
them defend Singapore. Hull declined. On July 12, 1940, Lord
Lothian told him that, as a result, the British had resigned themselves
to close the Burma Road for three months. The National Defense Act,
passed by Congress on July 2, allowed Roosevelt to place the export of
certain key materials in a category requiring a special license, but
neither oil or scrap iron—both urgently needed by Japan—were included in this category. Effective reprisals against Japan were therefore not undertaken at this time.

On July 17, a more aggressive cabinet replaced the Yonai cabinet,
with Prince Konoye as Premier and Matsuoka, Japanese delegate to
the League of Nations at the time of the Manchurian affair, as Foreign Minister. This was a victory for the Army, which favored a
policy of force. The new cabinet's secret plan—decided at the Imperial Conference of July 26 and 27—was to pursue a much more aggressive policy in Indochina and the Dutch East Indies while still
trying to avoid war.

The Dutch government agreed to deliver a great quantity of material to the Japanese because it could not do otherwise, and the Vichy
government was subject to equally strong pressures. It was learned in
Washington on August 6 that the Japanese, with German backing,

had demanded permission to land troops in Tonkin. The agreement was signed on August 29. On September 19, finding the French authorities in Indochina too uncooperative, the Japanese issued an ultimatum, and on the twenty-fourth Japanese troops entered northern Indochina.

American policy between July and September had been hesitant. Hull, in keeping with his temperament, feared that Japan would react too strongly to new economic sanctions. Morgenthau, Stimson, and Knox, on the other hand, were pressing the President to act. Since July 25, oil and scrap iron had been added to the list of products requiring an export license; this made it possible to prohibit their export to Japan. On September 19, Roosevelt was persuaded to prohibit the export of steel and iron beginning September 25—the very time when Japan was to sign the tripartite pact with Germany and Italy. This was, finally, an effective reprisal against Japan, but only a reprisal, as Japan had built up stocks of these materials in advance. All the same, she would have to convert more factories and supply herself from overseas with her own ships. The British, more confident because they had been able to resist German pressure, decided to reopen the Burma Road. In the Dutch East Indies, Governor Van Mook, under pressure from the United States, haggled over every economic concession to Japan. Japan did no more than protest, in October, against these unfriendly acts.

In the following month the situation changed little. Once more the British proposed a joint plan for the defense of Singapore and once more the Americans declined. Aid to China was increased by 100 million dollars on November 30, and a few feeble reinforcements were sent to the Philippines. Cordell Hull's policy of extreme caution prevailed in the Pacific. Japan prepared to continue on her course by imposing herself as mediator in a conflict between Thailand and French Indochina. The United States government, after pushing Vichy to accept so as not to throw Thailand into Japan's arms, took no new diplomatic action between January and March 1941. This reserved attitude can be explained by the necessity not to create an international crisis in the middle of the debate on lend-lease, which would only have benefited the isolationists. Nevertheless, almost every week new categories were added to the list of goods requiring an export license and this cut down Japanese imports from the United States. Oil, the most vital of all, continued to flow freely to Japan however, despite minor restrictions.

After March 1941, the United States vacillated between two policies. The first was to try to stop Japan by threats—threats of economic sanctions or even of the use of force, as Chiang wanted. The second was to seek a formula for peace that would be acceptable to both China and Japan. The problem was whether there could be such a formula while the Japanese wanted to consolidate their control of China and the United States wanted to end it. Roosevelt and Hull both favored wide exploration of the possibilities of agreement and on March 8—at the suggestion of Catholic missionaries in Japan—Hull and the new Japanese ambassador, Admiral Nomura, opened discussions. The two men met about fifty times during the following months. It should be noted that, because of the deciphering of Japanese codes by the Americans, and of some American codes by the Japanese, the two negotiators sometimes were more aware of each other's real intentions than was evident in their conversations.

Up to May 12 it seemed possible that an agreement could be concluded on the following basis: in exchange for a Japanese promise not to expand further but to limit itself to a part of China, and not to aid Germany, the United States would lift the existing economic embargoes and cease to aid Chiang Kai-shek. On the one hand, the plan did not satisfy the Americans because it yielded a part of China to the Japanese, and on the other, the Japanese Army and Navy were urging their government to continue expansion to the south even at the risk of war. They were encouraged in this aggressive policy by Hitler's promise to aid Japan in case of war with the United States (made to Matsuoka in Berlin, between March 29 and April 4) and by a treaty of neutrality between Japan and the Soviet Union signed on April 13.

Ever since January, Admiral Yamamoto had been preparing plans for an attack on Pearl Harbor. There was, therefore, a continuing struggle in Japan between those who wished to negotiate and those who wished to pursue an aggressive policy. From April on the latter gained strength. Prince Konoye, who was aware of the country's serious economic difficulties and who thought that Japanese forces were not ready to go further in the south, favored negotiation. Matsuoka, leader of the pro-German faction, supported the opinion of the Army and the Navy. Because of these conflicting influences the American proposals were rejected. Japan accepted with reservations a series of general principles which Hull—in his devotion to great abstractions—had submitted to Nomura. These principles included respect for the territorial integrity and sovereignty of all nations, nonintervention, equality—especially in the commercial sphere—and the maintenance of the status quo in the Pacific.

The question was, would increased American reprisals combined with the concentration of the Fleet at Pearl Harbor provide a sufficient means of restraining the Japanese, or would they instead give the Japanese one more reason to adopt the solution of expansion? Stimson and Morgenthau advocated the repeal of the existing economic measures; Hull, and in the end Roosevelt, kept to a middle path, refusing to abandon those already established but refusing also to extend them, waiting for a gesture from the Japanese.

Such a gesture came but in an unexpected way. The German attack against Russia obliged the Japanese Emperor to discharge Matsuoka, who wanted Japan to attack Russia also. In the course of two important meetings on June 25 and July 2, it was decided that Japan would stay neutral, but would extend her military occupation throughout Indochina, as an excellent point of departure for further moves. On July 12, an ultimatum was sent to Vichy confirming the occupation of southern Indochina. On July 16, the Konoye cabinet resigned in order to eliminate Matsuoka. It was immediately reconstructed with no other changes, and General Tojo, champion of aggression, kept the war portfolio.

In Washington the text of the Japanese decision of July 2 and that of the ultimatum to Vichy had been intercepted. There was an immediate reaction, following on long months of discussion. On July 21 Japanese assets in the United States were frozen, permitting the government to cut down Japanese purchases as it wished. The import of silk was drastically reduced and the export of oil limited to "normal quantities" to prevent accumulation. The export of high-octane gas required for airplanes was prohibited. The administration of these operations was given to a committee of legal experts on which Dean Acheson represented the State Department. Roosevelt sent for Nomura and gave him a serious warning. "If Japan attempted to seize the oil supplies by force in the Netherlands East Indies, the Dutch would, without a shadow of doubt, resist; the British would immediately come to their assistance, war would result between Japan and the British and the Dutch, and in view of our own policy of aiding Great Britain, an exceedingly serious situation would immediately result." [37]

General Marshall and Admiral Stark, who knew better than anyone else the unprepared state of the United States, feared an imminent outbreak of war and were anxious about these measures, but Roosevelt, under the influence of Churchill, thought that Japan would not unleash war while Great Britain was still undefeated. "This conviction, shared by Roosevelt, was of enormous importance in the formulation of policy prior to Pearl Harbor." [38] Thus the United States came back to a policy of applying sanctions, but a clear choice between sanctions and negotiation was not definitely made. Great Britain, with the Dominions and to some extent the Dutch East Indies, had also frozen Japanese assets and was urging the United States toward a firmer policy. On the other hand, Ambassador Grew was uneasy, saying that "once the vicious circle of reprisals and counter-reprisals is established . . . the obvious outcome is eventual war." [39] Hull shared these views. On August 6, Nomura suggested to him that negotiations should be reopened by a meeting between Roosevelt and Prince Konoye.

The Japanese Premier wished to keep the peace. He wanted to diminish the increasing influence of General Tojo. Would not a meeting with Roosevelt save the peace and save face at the same time? Japan asked the United States to accept the principle of the Greater East Asia Co-Prosperity Sphere and to promise not to go to war. It was a last attempt.

The idea of a meeting was discussed by Roosevelt and Churchill at the Atlantic Conference. Churchill, strongly supported by the Dominions, personally wanted the United States to state publicly that it would intervene in the event of further Japanese expansion. On the American side this idea was not favorably received. Congress did not wish its hand to be forced and public opinion was reluctant. Roosevelt, admitting that negotiations would have little chance of success, nevertheless considered that a meeting would have the advantage of gaining time, which could be used to reinforce the Philippines. He rejected any idea of an Anglo-American warning and decided that the United States should act independently. On August 17 he called Nomura to the White House. If Japan took one more step, said the President, the United States, "would be forced immediately to take all measures required to safeguard the legitimate rights of the United States and of American citizens." [40] He did not use the phrase Churchill wanted him to include, "all measures including war." The warning remained a timid one.

Ambassador Grew, for his part, insisted that the meeting with

Konoye should take place. If it did not, he said, Japan's fate from then on would be in the hands of the Army and the Navy. But Hull and Stimson opposed it and thought that only a bad peace could result. Besides, was this not simply a Japanese maneuver? In short, Grew believed in Konoye's sincerity, and Hull, worn out by long and futile negotiations, no longer did. On August 28, the Prince addressed a message directly to the President. Roosevelt was tempted but finally replied that he could not meet Konoye until the situation had been clarified by negotiations. An imperial conference in Japan on September 6 decided that if "by the beginning of October, we do not have a reasonable hope of seeing our demands met . . . we will be in a state of mind which will prepare us to wage war against America, England and Holland." [41] These demands were the closing of the Burma Road, the end of aid to Chiang Kai-shek, the cessation of Anglo-American reinforcements in the Pacific, and re-establishment of normal commercial relations. In exchange, the Japanese would not use Indochina as a base from which to expand southward, would carry out the neutrality pact with the Soviet Union, and would promise to evacuate Indochina after the war.

There is naturally every reason to believe that Roosevelt would never have agreed to these conditions in a meeting with Konoye. At any rate, an American note to Japan on October 2, 1941, definitely rejected the idea of a meeting. On October 16 the Konoye cabinet resigned, having failed in its policy of negotiation. General Tojo, the man of war, became Premier of Japan.

Pearl Harbor

The imperial decision of September 6 and the failure of negotiations had brought about the triumph of the war party in Japan. Three months were to pass before war actually broke out; three months during which one of the most feverish diplomatic exchanges in the history of the world took place; three months during which the Japanese perfected their war machine while the Americans tried to make up for lost time; three months which ended in an attack which although expected, occurred in an unexpected place, the naval base at Pearl Harbor in the Hawaiian Islands.

The new Japanese cabinet, formed on October 18, developed a final plan for negotiations in early November. On November 5 two plans, called respectively A and B, were drawn up. They were to be submitted to the United States successively. If neither had been accepted by November 29 it was for the Emperor to decide whether or not to go to war. Plan A, the first alternative, looked toward a definitive settlement in the Far East. The principle of economic equality among nations in China would apply only if it were to be applied throughout the rest of the world, that is, if other nations would surrender their economic privileges in certain areas. Unwillingness on the part of the Allies to meet this condition would permit the maintenance of Japanese privileges in China. Japanese troops would continue to occupy north China, Mongolia, and Hainan for at least 25 years. They would evacuate the rest of China within two years of a peace settlement. The same would hold for Japanese bases in Indochina. This plan would establish Japanese sovereignty in China with the support of the United States, which would bring pressure on Chiang Kai-shek to this end.

Plan B constituted a temporary modus vivendi, capable of avoiding war by postponing a final settlement to better times. The two governments would commit themselves not to reinforce their troops in Southeast Asia and the South Pacific. Japan could withdraw its troops from south Indochina and, in the north, wait for a final settlement with China. Japan and the United States would cooperate to obtain from the Dutch East Indies all the materials they needed. Japanese-American commerce would be resumed under conditions which had prevailed before the freezing of Japanese assets. The United States would supply a given amount of oil to Japan. Finally, the United States would abstain from any action which would prejudice the restoration of Sino-Japanese peace.

One could say that Plan A rested on full United States recognition of Japanese sovereignty in China and Plan B allowed Japan to wage war in China until she won. It is to be noted that on November 3 Admiral Yamamoto had given orders for "Operation 1" (the attack on Pearl Harbor) to go into effect, without fixing D day, but in such a way that the Navy was ready for action.

Admiral Nomura's task was to stress the "final" nature of the Japanese proposal. On November 7 Nomura presented Plan A—already known by the decoding process. On November 10 Nomura was received by Roosevelt, who told him that the plan was unacceptable and that in any case Japan should show its good intentions by the evacuation of China and Indochina.

In presenting Plan B, Admiral Nomura, a convinced partisan of peace, had asked the help of a professional diplomat, Ambassador Kurusu. This was a very bad choice. Secretary Hull, who trusted Nomura, regarded Kurusu with the greatest suspicion. On November 29 Plan B was submitted to Hull, who already knew that Nomura's peaceful opinion and his desire to gain time were not in favor in Tokyo. Hull received Plan B unfavorably. It was not possible to betray China.

After consulting Churchill and soothing Chiang Kai-shek as much as possible, the United States government rejected Plan B on November 26, and made a counterproposal, obviously unacceptable to Tojo: the signing of nonaggression treaties which would apply throughout Southeast Asia. The proposal was couched in the form of a ten-point memorandum which mainly reaffirmed abstract principles, but also included the withdrawal of Japanese troops from China and Indochina. On November 27 the military chiefs, General MacArthur in the Philippines and Admiral Kimmel at Pearl Harbor, were warned that there was imminent danger of war. Reinforcements were arriving very slowly in the Philippines—there were at the time only nine B17 bombers. General Marshall and Admiral Stark were very much disturbed; they begged for delay and asked that no ultimatum be sent to Japan.

War was inevitable from this time on, because of the Japanese decision to attack. On November 29, D day was fixed for December 8, and the great Japanese fleet, concentrated in the Kuril Islands, went to sea. The message was not intercepted by the United States. Japan threw caution to the winds. Konoye himself, when asked by the Emperor, considered that war had become the only acceptable solution. A surprise attack was planned for the afternoon of December 7. It was decided that Nomura and Kurusu should continue to negotiate until the last moment and should notify Hull of the attack only 20 minutes before it took place.

The United States government was informed of important ship movements off Indochina and thought that war was imminent. It was also learned that Nomura was destroying his records and his codes in Washington. Although the possibility of an attack on Pearl Harbor had been mentioned several times in the preceding months, in early December 1941 it was thought to be improbable. Stimson and his aides foresaw a Japanese operation in Malaya or the Dutch East Indies. It was decided that Roosevelt should send a message to the Emperor saying that any attack on these territories would bring the United States into the war. This warning, which was supposed to be followed by a congressional resolution, was delayed for several days for reasons that are not clear. Grew received it on December 6 at 9:00 P.M. On the morning of December 7 a Japanese note was deciphered saying that: "The Japanese Government regrets to have to notify hereby the American Government that it cannot but consider that it is impossible to reach agreement through further negotiations." [42]

Kurusu and Nomura took a long time to decipher it with the result that instead of delivering the note to Hull at 1:00 o'clock—the attack on Pearl Harbor took place at 1:25 Washington time—they arrived at 2:00. They were received at 2:20. At that time Hull, but not Nomura, already knew of the attack. "I have never seen a document that was more crowded with infamous falsehoods and distortions," he said. [43]

In the evening Roosevelt composed a message to Congress. On December 8 Congress declared, with one dissenting vote, that a state of war existed. Stimson wanted to declare war on Germany also. Hitler anticipated this move by declaring war on the United States, honoring the tripartite pact. Roosevelt had known that Hitler would take this action by a cable intercepted October 29, which allowed him to avoid a last-ditch fight with the isolationists.

Thus it was as a result of events in the Pacific that the United States was eventually led to enter the war after two years in which it had moved from absolute neutrality to "undeclared war."

There are two schools of thought about Pearl Harbor. [44] For the "revisionists" opposed to Roosevelt the President's responsibility is enormous. They consider that the Axis Powers did not present a real threat to the western hemisphere. For them the Japanese attack on Pearl Harbor was provoked by the United States policy of sanctions. In this view the cause of war lay less in the world situation than in the actions of the United States itself. They think that the President followed a policy which he knew, or ought to have known, would lead to war. For them, Roosevelt deceived the nation in claiming to be working for peace when he was actually preparing for war. In the eyes of the revisionists peace was more precious than democracy and the Communist danger which would result from the war seemed greater than the Nazi danger. Some, like Tansill and Morgenstern, even see in Pearl Harbor a criminal act on the part of Roosevelt and his collaborators, especially Stimson, who they think more or less knew that an attack would occur but omitted to warn the commanders at Pearl Harbor.

The pro-Roosevelt historians, the internationalists, think, on the contrary, that the best means to avoid war would have been to discourage aggression by a firm policy. The isolationism of the 1930's had prevented the President from pursuing such a policy, however. For the internationalists the security of the United States depended on the final defeat of Nazism and Fascism. Roosevelt hoped for a long time to bring this about by measures short of war and his attitude was midway between Hull's caution and the attitude of Stimson, Knox, and Morgenthau, who very soon came to believe that anything short of war would not be enough. Roosevelt was really concerned not to be too much in advance of American public opinion. As to Japan, Roosevelt and Hull seriously wanted to avoid war in the Pacific, which seemed to them less vital than the war in Europe. For the internationalists, finally, United States avoidance of war was less related to American policy than to a situation in which, willy-nilly, the country would finally find itself involved. In the Pearl Harbor "surprise" there were technical failures but certainly not a perfidious plot of a warlike administration.

This is without doubt a matter of interpretation. History cannot consist of an analysis of what might have been; it studies and tries to explain what actually happened. Nevertheless the works of Rauch, Feis, and especially Langer and Gleason seem to us much more reliable than those of the revisionists, and any French historian has more than enough experience with the disastrous nature of the appeasement policy in recent decades and of the withdrawal of a nation into itself not to choose deliberately to side with the internationalist interpretation of American history.

Chapter XIII

The United States at War:
Initial Defeats and Recovery, 1942-1943

The Arcadia Conference

AFTER Pearl Harbor United States foreign policy was no longer confined to mere diplomatic negotiations. In fact, they moved down to second place. Diplomacy was in the background when military action was unsuccessful during this critical period; it became active with military success. The relationship of diplomacy to the course of the war can be illustrated in concrete detail.

Roosevelt had formerly bypassed Hull at moments of important decisions; now he excluded the Secretary of State even more consistently. "After Pearl Harbor I did not sit in on meetings concerned with military matters. This was because the President did not invite me to such meetings . . . The President did not take me with him to Casablanca, Cairo or Teheran . . . I learned from other sources than the President what had occurred." [1] With the State Department—except for Undersecretary Sumner Welles—in the background, the President's immediate entourage, especially Hopkins, became the important center of policy making. Secretary of War Stimson, more energetic and dynamic than ever, also played a leading part. For the first time the United States was to take the initative on a worldwide scale, much more than in Wilson's time.

The impressive potential resources of the nation were harnessed to the needs of the war and within three years the production of matériel and the training of a large army would give the United States unparalleled power. On December 7, 1941, this was a long way off, however. The situation was serious. As Roosevelt said to Congress on December 8, "it must not be denied that our people, our land and our interests are exposed to a grave danger." In a radio speech on

December 9 he said: "we must face the fact that modern warfare as conducted in the Nazi manner is a dirty business. We don't like it —we didn't want to get into it—but we are in it, and we're going to fight it with everything we've got." [2]

It was not a war with fanfare and flags flying, it was a huge and essential enterprise. Public opinion was never enthusiastic about the war, but neither was it really opposed. Americans thought that the job should be well done and they applied themselves to it with all the qualities they had demonstrated in business.

The first job was to coordinate Allied activity in fact and not just in theory, as in the past. In London it was feared—unnecessarily—that the United States would abandon the plan to attack and defeat Germany first. Churchill therefore hastened to America on December 22 for a series of conferences known by the code name "Arcadia." He stayed until January 14. In Washington he was in constant contact with Roosevelt and Hopkins, except for a trip to Canada over New Year's and a few days vacation in Florida between January 5 and 11. Maxim Litvinov, Soviet ambassador to the United States, attended a number of these meetings.

To really understand the Arcadia Conference it is necessary to recreate the atmosphere of the time, an atmosphere of defeat but also of hope. Every week brought news of new Japanese successes. The attack on Pearl Harbor was followed by the destruction of the two best British ships in the Indian Ocean, *The Prince of Wales*— aboard which some of the meetings of the Atlantic Conference had been held—and the *Repulse*. Then came the fall of Hong Kong. Japanese troops had invaded Malaya and Indonesia and they were advancing everywhere. Guam and Wake had fallen. Japanese propaganda asked ironically, "Where is the American fleet?" In the Philippines General MacArthur was preparing to defend the Bataan peninsula and then to retreat to Corregidor. Japanese landings in New Guinea, New Britain, and the Solomon Islands seriously threatened Australia. Singapore, so important in British strategy, fell on February 15, 1942. Burma was about to be invaded and the supply route to China, the Burma Road, cut off.

The situation was no better in the European theater. In the two months of January and February 1942 German submarines sank 132 ships in the Atlantic, which was worse than a major land defeat, as Samuel Eliot Morison points out. Rommel had reversed the tide of war in Libya and was advancing on Egypt and Suez. On January 9 German saboteurs set fire to the liner *Normandie* in the New York harbor. As a final humiliation, on February 12 the *Scharnhorst,* the *Gneisenau,* and the *Prinz Eugen* escaped from Brest and crossed the Channel without opposition.

Nevertheless, nothing would be more inaccurate than to conclude that the participants in the Arcadia Conference were pessimistic. Quite the contrary, reasoned optimism prevailed. There was confidence in the great potential power which must be brought to bear. Everyone was convinced that in time the situation would be reversed and that what was needed was to create the means of victory by continued determination and by effective organization.

The first thing on the agenda was to proclaim the determination to win of the associated or "united" nations, to use Roosevelt's expression, which was finally adopted to describe the alliance. A declaration was drawn up which was no longer based merely on the pious abstractions of the Atlantic Charter. The United Nations Declaration did subscribe to "the program of aims and principles . . . known as the Atlantic Charter," and included a statement on freedom of worship, which the Charter had omitted, but its main emphasis was on the necessity of "total victory." Each government committed itself "to use all military and economic resources against the members of the Tripartite Pact with which this government is at war" and promised "to cooperate with other signatory governments to continue the war and not to make peace or an armistice with the enemy or any one of the enemy."

The signing of the declaration raised various difficulties. The British proposed that the United States and Great Britain sign first, ahead of the other partners, to be followed by the Dominions and then by the rest of the nations—including the Soviet Union—in alphabetical order. The plan was carefully studied by Hopkins, who referred it to Roosevelt on December 27. The President proposed that China and the Soviet Union sign at the beginning along with Britain and the United States. He thought that the Free French forces should not be included for the time being. The problem of Saint Pierre and Miquelon, which we will discuss below, had just arisen and Hull was extremely angry with De Gaulle. Hull thought that the inclusion of India was desirable but left it to the British to decide. In addition, a way must be found to include the Latin American republics which had followed the United States in declaring war on the Axis. In fact, only nine small republics of Central America and the Caribbean had done so. Despite British opposition, Roosevelt held firm on the exclusion of the Free French and the British agreed to include India. The Dominions were listed alphabetically in the general list and not in a group apart. The document was signed on January 1, 1942, by twenty-six nations.

But the will to win the war was not enough. It was necessary to work out strategy and problems of command and to devise the means for winning the war. At the beginning of the conference General Marshall and Admiral Stark presented a proposal concerning "fundamental bases of joint strategy" in which they took up again the main idea of the Atlantic Conference: "Our opinion is still that Germany is the principal enemy and that her defeat is the key to victory. Once Germany is vaniquished, the fall of Italy and the defeat of Japan will follow." [3] Having reaffirmed the principle, it was necessary to decide on the nature of the operations and the distribution of equipment, given the limitations of the means at their disposal. In the Pacific the line to be held would be drawn from the Aleutian Islands to Hawaii, Samoa, and Fiji, for which a base would be established in New Caledonia. In Europe, the Anglo-American bombing would be stepped up and Russia aided by all possible means. The blockade would continue and steps would be taken to encourage "the spirit of revolt and the organization of subversive movements in occupied nations." It was not to be hoped that a large-scale attack on Germany could be mounted in 1942, but it was not impossible that in 1943 an offensive could be launched in the Balkans or in Western Europe. Finally, the leaders began to think of operations in North Africa, known by the code name "Gymnast."

The immediate problem was a choice between reducing lend-lease to Russia by 30 percent in order to reinforce the Far East, or to maintain the level of aid to Russia and risk having to retreat again in Southeast Asia. The latter alternative was adopted despite some resistance from Churchill, who still hoped to save Singapore, or failing that, Burma. Roosevelt could inform Stalin on February 13 that another billion dollars, the second, was being put at the disposal of the Soviet Union in the form of lend-lease.

Afterwards from time to time, especially in early March, Churchill again urged his "peripheral strategy." This was most energetically opposed by Stimson, with the support of the War Plans Division (which would soon become the Operations Division), then under the direction of Brigadier General Dwight D. Eisenhower. The Secretary of War said, "We must send an invincible force to the British Isles and threaten to attack the Germans in France"; that was, in his opinion, "the straight line." [4] Stimson disapproved of Gymnast and he advised on the contrary a plan called Bolero, which would put the main effort into landings in France.

Two essential decisions about command were made at the Arcadia Conference. The first was to create the combined chiefs of staff, composed of Generals Marshall and Arnold and Admiral King, representing the United States, and Field Marshal Sir John Dill and two other British officers. Roosevelt insisted that the combined chiefs' headquarters be located in Washington. Australians, New Zealanders, and Dutch were attached to this command but only in an advisory capacity.

Under the combined chiefs were specialized agencies for the allocation of arms, shipping adjustment, raw materials, and supply and production. Churchill opposed Roosevelt on two points. He wished Hopkins to head a production agency with full powers. He would also have liked the United States and Great Britain to divide up what he called the "protected zones," that is, those areas to which aid was being sent. Roosevelt refused to make Hopkins a "production czar" because he would not allow such a diminution of his own power. He also refused to allow Great Britain to have unilateral charge of lend-lease in Europe, Turkey, the Arab countries, and the British Empire.

Under the combined chiefs there were also regional commands for each theater of war. At first there were two commands, A.B.D.A. (American, British, Dutch, Australian) under the British General Wavell, and China under Chiang Kai-shek. But the A.B.D.A. command zone was practically annihilated by the Japanese by the end of February. The loss of Java and Singapore brought Roosevelt to a dramatic decision: to allow General MacArthur—then leading a desperate fight in Corregidor—to flee the island and go to Australia. Corregidor fell on May 5, 1942. It was decided that MacArthur would command operations in the South Pacific; the British, in the Mediterranean (except in the case of landings in North Africa) and in Singapore. The Atlantic and Western Europe would be the joint responsibility of the two nations.

On April 1 a Pacific War Council was set up, consisting of Roosevelt, Hopkins, Lord Halifax, T. V. Soong representing China, Herbert V. Evatt representing Australia, and representatives of the Netherlands, Canada, and New Zealand. Later representatives from the Philippines and India were added. In regard to the purely American command, the President, as commander-in-chief of the Army and Navy, declared in an Executive Order of March 4, 1942, that he would communicate directly with the military chiefs in the various zones, without going through Secretary of War Stimson, "in matters concerning strategy, tactics and operations." Stimson continued to play an important part, however, as a result of his excellent relations with General Marshall.

On the political plane, the thorniest problem was certainly that of the command in the Chinese theater. As early as December 8, a few hours after Pearl Harbor, Chiang had sent for the diplomatic representatives of the United States and Great Britain and presented them with a large-scale plan. In order not to sacrifice the war in the Far East to the European war, he proposed that China and the other Allies —including the Soviet Union—should establish a Council of War to coordinate operations in the Pacific, which he thought could be directed from Chungking.

The plan was blocked by Russia's refusal to go to war against Japan. Cordell Hull's discreet pressures on Litvinov were to no avail. The plan also met firm opposition from the British. Churchill deplored what he called "the extraordinary importance given to China in American thinking, even at the highest level, [and] totally out of proportion to the realities." [5] He thought it ridiculous to place Chinese strength on the same level with British strength and he thought it enough to be "always available and polite to the Chinese."

The Americans were inclined to encourage the Chinese actively without, of course, relinquishing the responsibility of the Pacific war. On December 14 Roosevelt sent a message to the Generalissimo suggesting that an inter-Allied conference be held immediately to formulate joint strategy. This conference opened on December 17. Chiang tried in vain to obtain the top command of the Pacific war for himself. The Allied representatives politely declined the proposal. Then Chiang asked that there be a joint Sino-British defense of Malaya and Burma in order to prevent dispersal of available resources and the weakening of the war effort itself. The British wanted to reinforce Singapore; the Dutch, Java; and the Chinese, China.

It was decided at the Arcadia meeting on December 31 to make

Chiang commander-in-chief of the Chinese theater with future Allied units under his command. The difficulty at the moment was that aside from airplanes, such units were virtually nonexistent. This meant that actually the Allies could not give Chiang anything more than he already had. Nevertheless, he accepted the command on January 5, 1942, and asked that an American general be sent to serve as chief of the inter-Allied staff under him. Roosevelt agreed and General Joseph Stilwell left for China on February 9.

To return to the Arcadia Conference and its major decisions concerning the organization of the war, Hopkins was named chairman of the Munitions Assignment Board under the combined chiefs, but he was not given control of production as such. The War Production Board, created by Roosevelt at the end of the Arcadia Conference, was a strictly American organization (replacing the Supply Priorities and Allocation Board) under the direction of Donald Nelson. Nelson succeeded as coordinator the industrialist Knudsen who went into the Army. A look at the basic figures in Roosevelt's directive of January 6, 1942, suffices to show the scale of the war effort:

	For 1942	*For 1943*
Aircraft	45,000	100,000
Tanks	45,000	75,000
Anti-aircraft guns	20,000	35,000
Merchant ships (tonnage)	8,000,000	10,000,000

"These figures," Roosevelt said, "and others like them . . . will give the Japanese and the Nazis a little idea of exactly what they accomplished by the attack on Pearl Harbor." [6]

The Landings in North Africa

The Arcadia Conference had maintained the priority of the war against Germany but had not officially chosen between possible strategies. One was Churchill's imperial and peripheral strategy. Churchill, who had been responsible for the Dardanelles campaign of 1915, could not help but believe in "diversions." The heartland of the enemy, Germany, should be attacked only in the end, to avoid big Allied losses. The other strategy, proposed by the American generals with the strong support of Secretary Stimson, was, on the contrary, based on the "concentration" theory derived from Napoleon and Clausewitz. We detect here the long-range influence of Mahan's ideas, applied to the fighting forces as a whole. The admiral's axiom had been, "the fleet should not be divided." Stimson said that the only right and appropriate strategy was that of concentration. This meant that everything else would be sacrificed to the most essential matter, that is, to the most direct and powerful attack possible on Germany. Stimson and the joint chiefs, Marshall, Arnold, and King, expected that the offensive would be carried out in four steps: first, a massive bombardment of Germany; then Bolero (transporting a million Americans to England); then Sledgehammer, a limited landing in 1942 to give some relief to the Russians; and finally Roundup, that is, massive landings in 1943. Stimson wrote in his diary, "We cannot make our offensive diversion this summer unless we have the courage, even the hardness of heart, to reject appeals for other good purposes." [7]

Only one man could arbitrate the differences between Churchill and the American generals—President Roosevelt. But Roosevelt vacillated between April and July 1942, adopting various positions in succession. First, on April 1, 1942, after a two-and-one-half-hour discussion with Hopkins, Stimson, and General Marshall, Roosevelt decided to subordinate all other concerns to the landings in France, a decision which, according to Stimson, "should mark this day as one of the most momentous of the war." [8] On April 4 Marshall and Hopkins left for London to persuade Churchill and the British military chiefs, especially Sir Alan Brooke, who seemed to yield. On April 14 the combined chiefs accepted the American theory. This gave priority to a frontal attack, with limited landings in 1942 and massive landings in 1943.

Was Churchill's acceptance of this plan sincere? We may doubt it. It would appear rather that he was trying to gain time to wear Roosevelt down. In early June, Admiral Lord Louis Mountbatten came to Washington, followed, later in the month, by Churchill himself. Tobruk had just fallen. On June 21 Churchill gave Roosevelt a careful criticism of Sledgehammer, which he thought impractical, as did all the British generals. This made a great impression on the President. Nevertheless, Bolero (transportation of troops) held its priority at the same time that the operation in North Africa, Gymnast, was being prepared. On July 8 it was learned in Washington that Churchill was not holding to this decision and that he had decided to give up Sledgehammer in favor of landings in North Africa or possibly in Norway. Stimson, Arnold, and King were much disturbed and addressed a memorandum to the President which described the British position as "disastrous." The American military chiefs proposed to react vigorously by turning the whole American effort to the Pacific. In this way the sacrosanct theory of "concentration" would be maintained.

Roosevelt's vision was larger, however. He felt that American opinion needed a success against Germany in 1942. If such success were associated with the peripheral theory rather than the American theory, that was too bad. In any case the priority of the European war over the Pacific war should be maintained. Nevertheless, Roosevelt made a final effort to secure British cooperation and on July 18 he sent Hopkins, Marshall, and King to London, but the British would not budge. The only decision was to plan operation Roundup —landings on the continent—for 1943. The combined chiefs could not agree and were split along national lines. This was "a critical test of the capacity of the Anglo-Americans to function as a military coalition." [9]

It required the arbitration of Roosevelt and Churchill to break the impasse. On July 23 the President told his envoys in England to accept the idea of landings in North Africa and on the twenty-fifth the decision was made. The operation was given the name Torch. The British had suggested that Marshall command it, but Roosevelt preferred to appoint Eisenhower, who thus began the important phase of his career which would lead to the presidency of the United States.

Beyond its strategic importance, the decision had significant political implications. An operation in North Africa reopened the whole question of American policy toward France. The renunciation of a continental operation necessarily created serious difficulties with Russia. We shall take up first the French problem as it appeared in Washington.

Since 1941 the United States was represented in Vichy by Admiral Leahy. His entire tour of duty could be described as a rear-guard action to hold Pétain back from more active collaboration with the Germans. It is possible that this policy contributed to the failure of the Paris Protocols—by which French bases were to be yielded to Germany—but it was increasingly unrewarding. In the first place, the overwhelming majority of American public opinion was opposed to Vichy. A poll in December 1941 showed that 75 percent of the American people questioned did not think that Pétain represented France and 65 percent thought that sooner or later he would turn over the Fleet and the North African bases to the Nazis. When the Free French National Committee came into being on September 24, 1941, a number of articles appeared in the American press urging that it be recognized and that diplomatic relations with Vichy be broken off.

The recall of General Weygand, who had been commander-in-chief in North Africa, on November 18, 1941, increased anxiety and criticism. Then in early 1942 Rommel's army was supplied with trucks and oil from Tunisia. In February 1942 Admiral Leahy, discouraged, suggested his own recall. He was kept at his post until April 15, 1942, when Laval returned to power. A whole series of warning notes to Pétain's ambassador in Washington, Henri Haye, had not been able to prevent what appeared to be the German take-over of command and Leahy was recalled. Only the illness and death of his wife kept him from leaving until several weeks later.

In opposition to Vichy there was General de Gaulle. Roosevelt and especially Hull certainly misjudged the capacity for leadership of the Free French commander and the depth of his patriotic and democratic convictions. By force of circumstances his movement was small and Roosevelt and Hull did not realize the magnetic attraction he held for the French. Hull even went so far as to say, "Our British friends seem to believe that the majority of the French people are overwhelmingly in favor of de Gaulle, whereas according to all my sources of information . . . although about 95% of the French are opposed to Hitler, more than 95% of these are not Gaullists and would not follow de Gaulle." [10]

One wonders what the Secretary's sources were. As far as Hull and De Gaulle are concerned, however, from what we know of the two men it is not surprising that there was not perfect understanding between them. It must be added that the general was hardly known in America. A poll in December 1941 showed that only 34 percent of the Americans questioned were able to identify De Gaulle while 63 percent could give no answer and 3 percent gave erroneous answers.

A tragicomic episode—Saint Pierre and Miquelon—shows the full extent of the administration's and particularly Hull's misunderstanding of De Gaulle. In December 1941 an agreement concerning the status of these two little islands had been signed with Admiral Robert, Vichy governor of the French Antilles, in whose jurisdiction they lay. The islands had no strategic value but they had a radio station, which posed a serious threat to the Allies in the Battle of the Atlantic, because it could broadcast weather reports which would be helpful to German submarine commanders. The Canadian government proposed to take control of the islands but when De Gaulle protested the British arranged that the Free French would undertake the operation, subject to United States approval. The agreement between the United States and Admiral Robert, however, was based on the maintenance of the status quo in French possessions in the western hemisphere. On December 17, therefore, Roosevelt let it be known that he did not favor the proposed Free French operation. De Gaulle seemed to accept this. Churchill, as we know, arrived in Washington on December 22 for the Arcadia Conference. On December 18, however, General de Gaulle gave orders to Admiral Muselier to override the President's orders, saying that he would "take the whole responsibility" for the decision. On December 24, without firing a shot, the Free French took over Saint Pierre and Miquelon, to the great joy of the populace.

American opinion reacted favorably. It was a piece of good news, although a minor one, in a period when each morning's paper announced a fresh disaster. The public did not really know where the islands were, but realized that at least they had escaped Vichy control and that this would be an asset in the Battle of the Atlantic. But Cordell Hull was seized with an inexpressible fury: "Our preliminary reports show that the action taken by the so-called Free French at St. Pierre-Miquelon was an arbitrary action contrary to the agreement of all parties concerned and certainly without the prior knowledge or consent in any sense of the United States Government. This Government has inquired of the Canadian Government as to the steps that Government is prepared to take to restore the *status quo* of those islands." [11]

This statement was designed to appease the Vichy government and Hull made a point of receiving Pétain's ambassador, Henri Haye, to notify him of his desire to re-establish the marshal's control of the islands. The American public was indignant. Some newspapers replied to Hull's reference to the "so-called Free French" by referring to the "so-called Department of State" and Hull received some letters addressed to the "so-called Secretary of State." Robert Sherwood comments on Hull's reaction,

[He] did not accept this indignant outburst in a spirit of amused indifference. It should be remembered that in his eight years of distinguished service as Secretary of State he had been virtually exempt from the criticism which had been heaped upon other members of the Cabinet— Morgenthau, Ickes, Hopkins, Frances Perkins, and certainly, on the President himself . . . Hull had establish for himself a position that was almost sacrosanct.[12]

Hull's anger took on "hurricane proportions" when Churchill, in an important speech on December 30 in Ottawa, passed rapidly over the question of Saint Pierre, praised the courage of the Free French, and severely criticized "the men of Vichy." As Roosevelt refused to take the matter seriously, Hull went so far as to write a letter of resignation, which the President, who cared a great deal about administration solidarity, absolutely refused to accept.

The consequences of the Saint Pierre and Miquelon affair were nonetheless considerable. This affair explains to a great extent the profound antagonism of the United States government to De Gaulle in the following years. De Gaulle, as Langer says, "had forgotten the old diplomatic adage that it is dangerous to play little tricks on great powers." [13] It seems probable that the American refusal to admit the Free French to the United Nations stems from this incident.

De Gaulle was thought to be too inflexible and the United States government did not understand when he said in a speech on April 1, 1942: "For 1500 years France has had the habit of being a great power. She feels strongly that everyone, but especially her friends, should not forget it." [14]

Americans did recognize the authority of the French National Committee in the French possessions in the Pacific when New Caledonia was occupied on March 1, and in Equatorial Africa on April 4. "Step by step and not without difficulty, we are narrowing the diplomatic gap which separates Washington and France," De Gaulle commented.[15] There was no question of official recognition, however. The nearest thing to it was an acknowledgement "of the contribution of General de Gaulle to the maintenance of the spirit of the

French tradition" and a promise of increased military aid, on July 9, 1942. Stimson found the State Department's attitude somewhat unreasonable, but it continued to prevail.

The most important result of the mounting American distrust of Vichy on the one hand and irritation with De Gaulle on the other was what could be called the search for a "third man." The idea was to find a leader who, when the moment came, could rally all the forces of the French Empire. The decision to make landings in North Africa made the question urgent. It is true that the attitude of the Army and a majority of the *colons* made the choice of De Gaulle as leader of an uprising impossible—at least for the time being. Nevertheless, the search for a third man was to create insuperable difficulties for both the United States and France.

The original idea, in 1941, was that it would be helpful to find a well-known personality like, for example, Edouard Herriot, to join De Gaulle, but as Herriot was in prison this was mere wishful thinking. Great hopes were subsequently placed in General Weygand, who had returned to France, and at the Arcadia Conference Roosevelt and Churchill decided to enter into secret negotiations with him. H. Freeman Matthews, first secretary of the United States embassy in Bordeaux and later in Vichy, happened to be on leave in the United States. He expressed the opinion that Weygand would refuse to act in North Africa against the orders of Marshal Pétain—to whom he was very loyal—but that he should be approached anyway. One of the secretaries of the United States legation in Lisbon was sent to Vichy with the necessary instructions. Admiral Leahy's chief aide, Douglas MacArthur (General MacArthur's nephew) held a secret talk with Weygand on January 20 in a hotel near Nice, in which he gave the general a written message from Roosevelt asking whether Weygand would agree to take over the administration of the French colonies under certain conditions. These were: (1) the death or removal of Pétain, (2) a German move toward North Africa—through Spain, for example, (3) the use of the French Fleet to aid the Germans, (4) German use of French bases in North Africa. The reply was very disappointing.

The General was courteous and agreeable, but he declined to give any consideration to the possibility of his taking any action in the African problem. He said that he is now a private citizen with no political status, that he is completely loyal to the Marshal, and that if France should be so unfortunate as to lose the services of the Marshal, he would have no opportunity to render service to the country under the legally designated successor of the Marshal.[16]

To solve the problem with Weygand thus proved to be impossible. Leahy concluded that the third man was not to be found in Vichy government circles.

In Washington, an attempt was made to interest Alexis Léger, former secretary-general of the French Foreign Office, in heading up a "Fighting France" movement. Henri Haye got wind of this; he suspected it to be a plot organized by William Bullitt and certain French political exiles, like Camille Chautemps and Pierre Cot. Léger refused to associate with De Gaulle.

Still another idea was to look for the third man in cooperation with the leaders of the Resistance movement in North Africa, especially Lemaigre-Dubreuil. This group was at the time working with United States consul-general Robert Murphy to bring North Africa back into the war. They considered General de Lattre de Tassigny and Yves Chatel, governor-general of Algeria. The Office of Coordination of Information (later called the Office of Strategic Services, or O.S.S.) under Colonel William J. Donovan was actively concerned with this problem. Lieutenant Colonel Solborg and William A. Eddy, then United States naval attaché in Tangiers, acted as intermediaries. Eddy had had a good deal of experience in the Near East and spoke Arabic fluently. Through Eddy, Murphy was in constant contact with the O.S.S. The North African Resistance leaders asked that substantial war matériel be secretly stocked in Liberia to re-equip the French Army when it resumed fighting. Eddy and Murphy favored the plan but Donovan thought it impractical. The only steps taken were to send money and to collaborate with the Resistance leaders in search for the indispensable leader.

On April 17, 1942, General Henri Giraud escaped from the chateau of Koenigstein; he arrived in Vichy on April 27. As early as May 2, the American chargé d'affaires in Vichy, S. Pinckney Tuck, reported that although Weygand had refused to lead a renewed fight against Germany, Giraud, "who combined the indispensable qualities necessary for command and the necessary prestige, with the Army as well as among civilians, could perhaps accomplish it." [17] The fact that Giraud had conspicuously joined Pétain was not taken very seriously by the State Department. Colonel Solborg was attracted to the plan and took it up with Murphy and Lemaigre-Dubreuil. The latter, who was continually going back and forth between France and Algeria, was commissioned to approach Giraud in June 1942. Solborg, in North Africa against the orders of his superior, Donovan, was discharged from the O.S.S. His idea, nevertheless, was soon to triumph.

On September 2, shortly before operation Torch received final approval, Roosevelt—who had been opposed to any Gaullist participation—came out for the maintenance of civilian government in North Africa because it was "indispensable to friendly relations." He said on September 16, "I consider it essential that de Gaulle be kept out of the affair and that he be given no information without making sure that he won't make it a pretext to get angry and make us angry." [18] On November 5 he again urged Churchill to exclude De Gaulle.

Thus, because the Americans did not understand that General de Gaulle was exercising increasing control of the Resistance in France and that more and more Frenchmen thought him their real leader, the United States became involved in an infinite series of complications. General de Gaulle learned of the proposed landings unofficially and criticized American policy as "wrongly inspired by the advice of Leahy, Bullitt and Donovan." [19] Neither did he have any use for Murphy, whom he describes as "able and determined, conditioned by years in good society so that he seemed to think that 'France' meant people whom he met at dinner." [20] When Walter Lippmann returned from London, on the contrary, he declared that "the evidence shows that . . . General de Gaulle and the French National Committee are the real leaders of the French nation." Instead of comparing him to Jeanne d'Arc, as Roosevelt and Willkie were ironically doing, Lippmann showed that De Gaulle was above all a leader in the cause of national independence, and should rather be compared with George Washington.

The Giraud affair was brewing on October 6, 1942, when Roosevelt, wishing to make a minor concession, ordered the delivery of lend-lease aid directly to the Free French instead of via the British, as formerly. Under the pretext of nonintervention in French domestic affairs, the United States was actually creating considerable political disturbance in France by attempting to raise up a new leader of doubtful political orientation—from the point of view of democracy

—and attached to certain aspects of the Vichy regime. Murphy planned to go to Washington to convince the administration to use Giraud. In fact Eddy made several trips to London and succeeded in obtaining official approval of the policy, notably from General Eisenhower. Eisenhower sent Giraud a message, approved by Roosevelt, suggesting that he assume the "leadership of the French effort."

Without going into the details of what followed, we should mention General Mark Clark's famous secret trip to Algeria, where he met Giraud's representative, General Mast, and Murphy. He arrived on October 22 in a British submarine and barely escaped arrest by the Vichy police. He left on the evening of the twenty-third. The interview made it possible to draw up a plan to transport Giraud from France to North Africa via Gibraltar. No commitment had been made by the Americans to meet Giraud's extraordinary demand to be placed in supreme command of the expedition, outranking Eisenhower. The agreement, embodied in a letter of November 2 from Giraud to Murphy, is known as the Murphy-Giraud agreement. It stipulated that France should be "re-established in all her greatness," including overseas territories where the French flag had flown in 1939. France was recognized to be an ally of the United States. The command would be turned over to the French as soon as possible. The United States would not intervene in French domestic affairs and promised to maintain a French administration.

Giraud was the cause of great embarrassment. First, he was not willing to leave France until November 20. Eisenhower naturally refused to follow Murphy's advice to postpone the landings. Troops had already left the United States and Great Britain. Lemaigre-Dubreuil succeeded in persuading Giraud, who arrived in Gibraltar on November 7, but even then he argued for six hours with Eisenhower about his claim to be commander-in-chief. Eisenhower wrote, "Giraud was deaf to all arguments. His firm position was that he must be Commander-in-Chief with no responsibility to the Anglo-American Combined Chiefs of Staff, and that [my] function should be to obtain the necessary re-inforcements and supplies from the Allied Governments." [21] Giraud's principal idea was to organize a landing in the south of France as soon as possible, to make contact with "the army of the armistice." Great Britain and the United States thought this impossible. As soon as Giraud resigned himself to command only the French forces, on November 8, the landings were made. When he reached Algiers on November 9, an unexpected "third man" had taken his place. This was Admiral Darlan, much more gifted in political matters and much harder to handle.

The landings of 100,000 men (initially) thus took place in Morocco and Algeria on November 8. It was the first expedition of the kind and was carried out in great disorder, partly caused by the violent sporadic resistance by French forces, especially in Morocco, who were confused by the stubborn policy of Vichy. The resistants, on the other hand, had been told that Giraud would broadcast a message, (which did not happen) and the Americans' arrival 13 hours behind schedule had allowed time for the Vichy police to arrest the patriots.

Darlan, who was in North Africa at the time and who had postponed his return to France for a day, was on the spot. He was already convinced of eventual Anglo-American victory and was making a complete about-face, which there is every reason to think was not prearranged with the Americans. His first reaction is characteristic. "I've always known that the British were stupid, but I thought the Americans were more intelligent. I am beginning to think that you make as many mistakes as they do," [22] he said to Murphy when the latter undertook to persuade him to cooperate. He began by reaffirming his oath of loyalty to Marshal Pétain, whom he addressed by radio. He was not sure that the message had been sent, however. Murphy was temporarily checked. Then Darlan was gradually won over to the Allied cause and suggested that Giraud be eliminated. "He is not your man; politically, he is a child. He is a good division commander, no more." [23] At the same time Roosevelt sent a message to Pétain, who replied, "You know that we will defend the Empire against any aggressor . . . we have been attacked and we will defend ourselves." [24]

We will not discuss what the marshal's true intentions were, as they lie outside our subject and in any case the results are more important. Laval, for his part, went to meet Hitler in Munich on November 9. He refused to enter an alliance, as Hitler proposed, and on November 11 German troops invaded the unoccupied (Vichy) zone of France.

When Giraud arrived in Algiers he was coldly received by the acting French authorities and only General Clark's intervention made him willing to meet Darlan and General Juin on November 11. On that same day Darlan decided to go over to the Allied side, now that it was possible to say that Pétain was a prisoner of the Germans.

The Americans, having mishandled the Giraud affair, had to resign themselves—on Eisenhower's advice—to cooperate with Admiral Darlan, whose antidemocratic sentiments were very distasteful to them. The whole matter was controlled by the generals, practically without the knowledge of the State Department; the solution was "dictated solely by considerations of military opportunity." [25] American opinion, in general as well as in the State Department, was deeply shocked, but Roosevelt came to the defense of Eisenhower and Clark. He thought that any agreement with Darlan should be merely temporary, however, and he suggested to Churchill that diplomats be assigned to Eisenhower's staff to supervise civilian affairs. Robert Murphy and Harold Macmillan took over these duties.

We know now that Darlan could not rally the French Fleet, contrary to the hopes of Britain's Admiral Cunningham. Darlan was assassinated in Algiers on December 24, and Giraud succeeded him, largely because of strong pressure from Eisenhower, who would not deal with General Noguès, considered too pro-Vichy, and who explicitly condemned Vichy legislation. On instructions from Washington Giraud was given the strange title "Commander-in-Chief for Military and Civilian Affairs."

The Problem of the Second Front in 1942

United States policy toward the Soviet Union was firm on two points: first, that Russia should receive considerable aid. Emergency aid was promised by Hopkins in early August 1941. And at the Atlantic Conference the United States and Great Britain agreed to send long-term aid on a big scale. Hopkins brought back from Moscow the impression that the Russians could hold out until winter, contrary to the predictions of the War Department. But it was necessary to put Russia in a position to wage an energetic campaign in the spring of 1942. Averell Harriman and Lord Beaverbrook were sent to Moscow, arriving on September 25, 1941. Initially they were treated somewhat harshly by Stalin, who reproached them on the grounds that the United States and Great Britain were doing nothing to relieve the Russians, but in the end they came to an understanding with him and signed the Protocol of October 1. This provided that up until July 1, 1942, the monthly supplies would increase to an impressive figure—400 planes, 500 tanks, large quantities of raw materials, and products of all sorts. In theory, the Soviet Union would transport them but the United States and Great Britain would "help" in their transport; in fact, the convoys were almost exclusively Anglo-American.

The second point on which American policy was firm was the desire to gain Russian agreement to a certain number of principles which it was thought would be helpful in the future peace settlement. This was a practice, as Feis says, "to which the American Government—and especially Secretary Hull—was very much given." [26] The principles had just been formulated in the Atlantic Charter; Roosevelt, therefore, desired Russian adherence to the charter.

This presented a major difficulty. Since 1939 the Soviet Union had annexed eastern Poland, part of Finland, Bessarabia, and the three Baltic nations. The charter bound its signatories not to claim any territory and not to recognize any territorial change without consent of the populations involved. Since the Soviet position was that the peoples involved were overjoyed to be included in a great socialist state, there was nothing to prevent the Soviets from signing. On September 24, 1941, Maisky, Soviet ambassador in London communicated his government's decision to sign, with the reservation that "the practical application of these principles would be adapted to historical circumstances and needs." [27]

This was the beginning of an ambiguous and confused situation which was to outlast the war itself. When Anthony Eden was preparing to go to Moscow in early December to try to clarify the question, Hull was disturbed and hastened to send him a warning. The "mistake" of making secret treaties like those of World War I must not be repeated. When Eden was in Moscow shortly after Pearl Harbor (December 16 to 28), he kept American ambassador Walter Thurston constantly informed. Stalin did not attempt to conceal from the British Foreign Secretary that he wanted a written agreement on Russia's western frontiers; he even offered in exchange Russian support for British acquisition of bases in France, Belgium, Holland, Norway, and Denmark after the war. Eden naturally refused and invoked the Atlantic Charter. Stalin replied that he had previously thought that the principles of this document were directed against the Axis but that now it appeared to be an instrument designed to dismember the Soviet Union. The United States and Great Britain had recognized the Polish government-in-exile headed by General Sikorski, who strenuously refused to accept the Curzon Line of 1919 as the eastern frontier of his country.

American policy was very firm on the two points of aid to Russia and adherence to the Atlantic Charter; it vacillated, however, on the problem of the Second Front.

Stalin, whose prime concern was the relief of Russian troops from German pressure, had asked Churchill as early as July 18 that a British attack on western Europe be made in the near future. This would have necessitated the diversion of 30 or 40 German divisions to the West. But it was technically impossible in 1941. Did the chances seem better for 1942? We have seen that the American military chiefs were not opposed to this idea, which fitted in with the notion of defeating Germany first.

On January 22, 1942, General Eisenhower expressed his views in a personal note. "We've got to go to Europe and fight—and we've got to quit wasting resources all over the world—and still worse—wasting time. If we're going to keep Russia in, save the Middle East, India and Burma, we've got to begin slugging with air-power at Western Europe, to be followed up by a land attack as soon as possible." [28]

We have seen that although in April 1942 the British had seemed to accept the idea of a landing in 1942 to help the Russians and a full-scale invasion in April 1943, in July Churchill had opposed the plan. In the meantime Molotov had gone to London and then to Washington, in late May 1942, as a result of an invitation from Roosevelt to Stalin. The main purpose of his mission was to hasten the establishment of a Second Front. Churchill was extremely cautious, but in Washington things were different. Roosevelt told Molotov on May 30 that he could inform Stalin that "we expect to establish a Second Front this year." [29] Roosevelt's feeling that he had a right to speak thus and to indicate clearly that the Second Front would be established in Western Europe, derived from the joint decisions of April 14. Whether he was well-advised to speak of it so openly is another question. General Marshall hastened to add that the President was making a prediction and not a promise.

If Roosevelt spoke out so clearly, it was because it seemed essential to him to maintain the solidarity of the coalition. Molotov had not mentioned the possibility of total defeat for Russia, but he had said that without the Second Front the Germans might well take Moscow, the wheat fields of the Ukraine, and the oil of the Caucasus, which would further strengthen the Germans and help them to resist landings in the West. Roosevelt was impressed, but he stressed the difficulty of transporting divisions to France. When he mentioned ten divisions, Molotov replied that at least thirty divisions of infantry and five armored divisions would be required to relieve the Russians substantially. Roosevelt also indicated that in order to provide the tonnage required for such an operation it might be necessary to reduce lend-lease to Russia from 4.1 million to 2.5 million tons. Molotov replied that the Second Front would be more easily established if the First Front were as strong as possible, and he did not modify his demands, either for lend-lease or for landings in France.

It is noteworthy that Roosevelt and Molotov discussed the future international organization. Roosevelt envisaged the concentration of power in any such organization in the hands of the major powers, the United States, Great Britain, the Soviet Union, and possibly China. He thought it would take from ten to twenty years for France to resume the position of a great power. Roosevelt also proposed to take colonial possessions from the "weaker nations" and to place them under a sort of international trusteeship. Molotov welcomed this suggestion. It was decided that it was too soon to discuss the future frontiers of the Soviet Union. The final communiqué, published on June 11, declared that "in the course of the discussions full agreement was reached about the urgent task of creating a Second Front in Europe in 1942." [30]

When Molotov went back to London, Churchill, more and more skeptical about a Second Front in 1942, did what he could to modify the scope of this communiqué. He thought it would be better not to undertake the operation than to risk a disastrous failure; "We can therefore promise nothing in this matter." Whatever personal doubts Molotov may have had, he professed to believe—as he said to the Supreme Soviet on June 18—that a Second Front in 1942 had been decided upon. He continually referred to the "Anglo-American promises," and American ambassador Admiral Standley expressed his anxiety: "If such a front does not materialize quickly and on a large scale, these people will be so deluded in their belief in our sincerity of purpose and will for concerted action that inestimable harm will be done to the cause of the United Nations." [31]

The British reversal about the Second Front on July 8 put Roosevelt in a very embarrassing position with the Russians. The decision to suspend the escort of convoys to Murmansk for the summer— because of the midnight sun—did not make the situation easier. On July 17 Churchill wrote to Stalin to explain it. Stalin's reply of July 23 was extremely harsh. "Our military and naval specialists do not accept the basis of the arguments of the British . . . as valid. I must say categorically that the Soviet Government cannot agree to see the opening of a Second Front postponed to 1943." [32]

On July 29 Roosevelt advised Churchill not to take this communication seriously, but the Prime Minister decided to go to Moscow himself to get a frank explanation. Roosevelt would have preferred not to get involved in this matter but he gave in to Churchill's desire to take Averell Harriman with him, to aid "in my talks with Uncle Joe." These talks (August 12 to 15) began in a somewhat hostile atmosphere. Stalin became calmer only when Churchill explained the plans for increased bombardment and for operation Torch. Even so, there were other outbursts of anger and only on the last evening did the atmosphere become more harmonious.

Roosevelt, a great believer in his own personal magnetism, wished to meet Stalin in person. He expressed this desire as early as the beginning of November 1941 and on April 12, 1942, he suggested a meeting of several days "in the region of our common frontier in Alaska." [33] Stalin suggested a three-power meeting during the visit of Churchill and Harriman.

Churchill tried to assure Stalin that a Second Front could be opened in 1943, thus repeating the dangerous prediction that Roosevelt had made in 1942. Roosevelt wrote to Stalin, "We are coming as quickly and as strongly to your assistance as we possibly can and I hope that you will believe me when I tell you this." [34] Stalin's reply of August 22 omitted to mention that he had confidence in the President.

The most serious problem was that of the convoys to Murmansk, which had been resumed in early September. Sometimes as many as one third of the ships were lost. In early October, at the height of the Battle of Stalingrad, Roosevelt and Churchill therefore decided to stop the convoys. Stalin was told on October 9 that the convoys would be resumed when the days were shorter and when operation Torch had been completed. Stalin sent a terse rely. The Americans and British tried to use other supply routes, especially the one through Iran, where American engineers were working to increase the capacity of the ports and railroads under the direction of Averell Harriman, son of a multimillionaire railroad magnate. There was also some talk of sending twenty British and American squadrons to the southern Russian front, but this project was never carried out.

Stalin was nevertheless impressed by the success of operation Torch in North Africa and his letter of November 13 to Roosevelt was couched in a more friendly tone. His realistic attitude led him to support wholeheartedly Eisenhower's policy toward Darlan, in particular. Churchill had written him on November 24, "Don't worry about that rascal Darlan." [35] On December 6, however, Stalin wrote that he could not come to meet Roosevelt and Churchill at Casablanca. Roosevelt replied "I am deeply disappointed that you cannot see your way to free yourself in January for a conference." [36] What Stalin hoped, it seems, was that the Americans and British would soon move their operations from North Africa to the European continent.

The Fight against Japan

The height of Japanese conquest in the Far East was reached about April 1942. In the south they had developed a string of bases in New Guinea and New Britain. The United States, in the midst of the war, had hastily sent an expedition of 30,000 men to New Caledonia, which was welcomed by Admiral Thierry d'Argenlieu, high commissioner for France in the Pacific. In late April a relatively important fleet appeared in these latitudes.

Let us rapidly survey the principal military operations in order to understand the context of United States foreign policy. Between April 1942 and September 1943 the main problem for the United States was to hold out while at the same time feverishly trying to find a way to take the offensive. The Americans were able to withstand two Japanese offensives, one after the other, in the two directions in which Japanese expansion might go even farther, in the south, toward the Solomon Islands, and in the east, toward the Hawaiian Islands.

In the south, between May 3 and 8, there occurred the first naval-air

battle of the war—the Battle of the Coral Sea. Although it was in-
decisive, it prevented the Japanese from pursuing their invasion of
the Solomon Islands. A month later, June 3 to 6, the Japanese launched
an attack on Midway Island, not far from the Hawaiian Islands.
Another naval-air battle took place, resulting this time in a decisive
American victory. Four Japanese aircraft carriers were sent to the
bottom. From then on it can be said that the attack on Pearl Harbor
was virtually avenged.

For about a year there was a rough balance between Japanese and
American power. There was to be furious fighting, of course, but
it was limited chiefly to the Solomon Islands and especially Guadalcanal, at the extreme south end of the archipelago. If the Japanese
were to dislodge the Americans from the Solomons they would break
Allied communications with Australia. For the Americans, therefore,
it was essential to hold these islands. The operations, which involved
small columns, fighting in the bush and in an unhealthy climate,
were very bitterly fought. The Americans were fighting on land and
sea to prevent construction of a large Japanese airfield. This has been
called an American Verdun. On February 7, 1943, the Japanese, after
substantial naval losses, had to evacuate Guadalcanal. The Americans
then concentrated on the conquest of the rest of the Solomon archipelago and by November 1, 1943, they had succeeded. During this
same period we should note that equally intense operations were going
on in New Guinea, between the Japanese and the Americans and
Australians.

The turning point in the Pacific war took place in the autumn of
1943. The underlying cause is more interesting than the tactical successes themselves. The cause was the superiority of American industry
over Japanese industry. The chief battles were not naval battles as
such—that is, with ships within gunshot of each other—but naval-air
battles. Armored ships became defensive weapons, especially against
aircraft, the offensive weapon was the fast heavy aircraft carrier.
American experts had foreseen the importance of carriers as early as
the summer of 1940. The large naval program, which was stepped
up after Pearl Harbor, bore fruit when the big carrier *Essex* (which
had been built since 1940) arrived in Pearl Harbor on May 13, 1943.
The Pacific Fleet had at the time only two carriers which had sur-
vived early battles more or less intact. The arrival of the *Essex*, there-

fore, became a symbol of a new "generation" of naval units. Two other carriers arrived a few weeks later and three more in September and October of that year.

In addition, there were improvements in logistics, so painfully inadequate in the first months of the war. In the summer of 1943 appeared the first landing craft—troop transports and tank carriers. In the autumn of 1943 Admiral Nimitz, commander-in-chief in the Central Pacific, had at his disposal a powerful offensive fleet, sufficient means of transport, and nine divisions. General MacArthur, commander-in-chief in the South Pacific, had four American divisions and six Australian divisions. Following upon the phase of overwhelming Japanese victories (Pearl Harbor to April 1942) and the stalemate phase (April 1942 to autumn 1943), the third phase of the Pacific war was about to open—that of giant American counteroffensives.

There were two other fronts in the Far East, if the word can be applied to small outposts separated from each other by great distances in difficult and hazardous natural conditions and, in the south, situated in a very unhealthy climate. These were the China front under Chiang, with headquarters in Chungking on the upper Yangtze River, and the Burma front, held by the Indian Army under British command and the Sino-American Army in Assam under General Stilwell. On October 9, 1943, Vice-Admiral Lord Louis Mountbatten, cousin of King George VI, took command in Southeast Asia with Stilwell as his subordinate. On both the China and Burma fronts the period from the spring to the fall of 1943 was a period of relative calm and stability with the principal activity taking place in the air, accompanied by a few patrol actions on the ground.

This general view of the military situation should enable us to study American foreign policy in the Far East. Although, of course, the prosecution of the war held highest priority, diplomatic action was needed to make the war as effective as possible. In order to be able eventually to resume the offensive on any one of the four fronts —Central Pacific, South Pacific, Burma, and China—it was necessary to stand firm politically. If the discouragement of any of the partners were to bring about the collapse of any one of the fronts it would be a disaster for all the others, despite the great distances between them and their diverse characteristics. Of the four fronts, the two in the Pacific did not cause any political anxiety. The United States, Australia, and New Zealand, with the support of the weak Free French forces of Admiral Thierry d'Argenlieu, had confidence in their combined strength. A small difficulty existed because the Australians and New Zealanders were a bit less committed to the war in Libya since Pearl Harbor and demanded anxiously the return of their divisions from the African theater. This was a matter in which the United States could not and did not wish to interfere, however.

In Roosevelt's eyes the important thing was to make it possible for the other two, more "sensitive," fronts to hold firm. The Indians must be encouraged to continue their considerable war effort against Japan and to resist the bait of independence offered by Tokyo, of which the Indian National Army of Chandra Bose was the symbol. It was also necessary to prevent the surrender of Chiang, or his defeat owing to lack of supplies. The United States therefore developed a firm policy with regard to India and, more important, China in 1942–1943.

Roosevelt would not have chosen to take responsibility in relation to India, but he was led to do so because his ideological conceptions differed markedly in this matter from Churchill's. The Japanese conquest of Burma was a serious threat to India. What would happen if the nationalist leaders of the Congress party were to follow Gandhi in his policy of peaceful resistance, that is, if they were to allow Japanese occupation of the country? Churchill decided to negotiate with the leaders who had not been imprisoned and sent Sir Stafford Cripps, a Labour member of the cabinet, on a mission to India on March 10, 1942. As early as March 9 Roosevelt sent Churchill a long cable in which, after admitting that he knew much less about the situation than the British and that he hated to make suggestions, he proceeded to make some, claiming not that they were based on experience, but rather on a philosophy of history.

In good American fashion, Roosevelt could not resist comparing the Indian situation to that of the revolt of the thirteen colonies in 1776. Since he favored immediate independence, he suggested that for the duration of the war, or for five or six years, a loose form of federation be adopted in India, like that of the colonies under the Continental Congress, in which each member was virtually sovereign. Afterwards, India could move gradually toward a federal constitution similar to that enjoyed by the United States since 1789. He added that he simply wished to offer his assistance, because "it is absolutely none of my business." [37]

Churchill was infuriated by this intervention and it became one of the chief clouds that troubled relations between the two men. Roosevelt's move was made in a context worth analyzing. Cordell Hull writes, "The President and I, both before and after Pearl Harbor, were convinced that the Indians would cooperate better with the British if they were assured of independence, at least after the war." [38]

The United States also brought constant pressure to bear on Great Britain "on as unofficial a basis as possible," without wishing to embarrass the British.[39] Hull mentioned the independence of India in a conversation with Lord Halifax on May 7, 1941. At the same time an Indian with the rank of minister was appointed to the British embassy in Washington. The United States had sent a quasi-diplomatic mission to New Delhi in October and had allowed a General Indian Agency to be established in the capital of the United States. The agent-general, Sir Girja Shankar Baypai, had been presented to Hull by Lord Halifax on November 25, shortly before Pearl Harbor.

Conversations concerning the granting of independence or dominion status to India were not conducted through these men, however. Sumner Welles suggested that the President discuss the matter directly with Churchill; once more Hull would be bypassed. The message quoted above seems to have been drawn up without consulting him.

American pressures on the British concerning India were of various kinds. After the fall of Singapore, for example, Roosevelt insisted that Chiang visit Burma and India to stiffen the spirit of resistance to the Japanese. The Chinese generalissimo tried in vain to convert Gandhi to the idea of organized military effort. Gandhi complained that the Asiatics were never treated as equals by the British and Americans. He asked Chiang "Why don't they even include your country in their high level talks?" At the time of the Cripps mission, the problem was narrowed down to the question of whether Indians would take over control of the Indian Army during the war or whether the British would keep it. Churchill thought the latter course a vital necessity. Roosevelt stressed with the Prime Minister the views of congressional leaders, who favored Indian autonomy. This greatly displeased Churchill. Colonel Louis Johnson, former assistant secretary of war under Secretary Woodring, was appointed as the personal representative of the President in New Delhi. He arrived at the time of the Cripps mission and it was all the British could do to keep him from playing the role of "mediator." [40]

After the failure of the mission, American predictions proved to be wrong. The Indian Army continued to fight without the granting of independence. American diplomatic intervention became more discreet. In August 1942, for example, when the British government decided to arrest Gandhi, the Americans let it be understood that they did not approve, but prudently. As Gandhi had written to Roosevelt, the President answered him. The letter arrived when Gandhi was in prison and Roosevelt, on Hull's advice, decided to hold up delivery until Gandhi was released. This happened two years later.

The anxiety created in the United States by the civil disobedience movement in India seems to have been somewhat exaggerated. William Phillips, former undersecretary of state and ambassador to Italy, was appointed to succeed Colonel Johnson as the President's personal representative in India. In his instructions, dated November 20, 1942, Hull explained that American policy favored independence of colonies as soon and as fully as possible but that the British should not be irritated by the exertion of obvious pressure. Gandhi was in the midst of a fast and Viceroy Lord Linlithgow forbade Phillips to visit him in prison. United States policy embarrassed the British and seems to have accomplished nothing. Cordell Hull sadly admits this, while blaming the vacillations of the President. "Our inability to influence British policy in India, coupled with the presence of our troops in that area, gradually gave rise, toward the end of 1943, to considerable anti-American feeling among the Indians, who felt that we were buttressing the British Empire." [41]

Did American policy meet with any greater success in China? American interest in China, which was both sentimental and practical, was only increased after Pearl Harbor. After all, China tied up a considerable number of Japanese soldiers and a large quantity of Japanese war materials. She should be helped in every possible way. As Owen Lattimore, distinguished American expert on China attached to the staff of Chiang, said, it was important that China should not be isolated and downgraded to second place. "There is a growing apprehension here that after the war the Chinese will not obtain equal standing and fair and equal treatment." [42] One result of this idea was Roosevelt's insistance on China's inclusion among the Big Four signatories of the United Nations Declaration—against Churchill's advice.

The problem of aid to China was fraught with immense difficulties. In February 1942 a loan of 500 million dollars was enthusiastically voted by Congress to help China combat inflation, but many experts feared that it would chiefly go to line the pockets of a few members of the Kuomintang. T. V. Soong, Chiang's ambassador in Washington, begged the United States to increase deliveries, in vain. There was a certain tendency, even before Pearl Harbor, to consider the Chinese theater secondary. We will cite only two examples. At the time of the lend-lease negotiations, Chiang had urgently requested 350 fighters and 150 bombers as well as a great deal of other equipment. In October, 100 fighters were delivered but still not one bomber, not a single antitank gun out of the 720 requested, only 44 of the 600 75 mm. guns requested, not a single light tank of the 120 requested. On the note Hopkins addressed to him on October 24 Roosevelt wrote, "Speed up!" Most of these arms had still not arrived when the Japanese cut the Burma Road.

The second example dates from June–July 1942. Rommel's great offensive in Libya had been successful and the Suez Canal was threatened. General Marshall let Roosevelt know that the Germans could reach Cairo in a week. The British desperately needed equipment to stop them. Roosevelt did not hesitate and ordered that certain lend-lease deliveries destined for Russia or China to be diverted to the Middle East. "Do the Allies want to keep the war in the Chinese theater going or not?" asked Chiang in an explosion of anger. Only a cable from Roosevelt explaining the situation could appease the generalissimo.

What matériel was sent to China could only get there by air transport. An aerial "bridge" across the Himalayas—called operation Hump by United States airmen—was established the length of the Brahmaputra Valley. The mountains had to be cleared at a height of more than 12,000 feet. It was—rather late—a technical success, in that the amount thus delivered went from a few dozen tons a month in 1942 to 10,000 tons a month in late 1943 and ended at 45,000 tons in February 1945. Even so, only supplies required for aerial warfare were delivered in this way. In fact, the Chinese theater was extremely disappointing, partly owing to the Nationalist government's incapacity to decide on a suitable strategy.

The situation was made more difficult by the rivalry of the two American generals working with Chiang. One was General Claire

Chennault, who had been sent even before Pearl Harbor to help Chiang establish a volunteer air force—the Flying Tigers. With the entry of the United States into the war, Chennault was reintegrated into the regular Air Force and was in Chungking as commander of the Tenth and Fourteenth United States Air Forces. Chennault was on excellent terms with the generalissimo. His opinion was that ground operations would not be very useful and that the war against the Japanese should consist primarily of bombing their bases and supply lines and gaining mastery of the sky.

The other general was Joseph Stilwell. After Pearl Harbor it seemed necessary to send a high ranking American officer to China to command American forces in the China-Burma-India theater. Secretary Stimson, at the suggestion of his aide John J. McCloy, first thought of Hugh Drum. Drum, however, who hoped for a more attractive post in Europe, quarreled with General Marshall and refused the assignment. Stilwell was a fine soldier and leader of men, an excellent organizer and a valuable tactician. But right from the start he did not get on with Chiang Kai-shek.

Stilwell's first job, in February and March, was to defend Burma at all costs. He realized that the Indian and British troops were demoralized and that the Chinese divisions he could obtain with difficulty were undisciplined and poorly equipped. He quickly understood the defects of the Nationalist government and the extent of its corruption. He naturally thought that, since winning the war was the main objective, greater reliance should be placed on the Chinese Communists, who were believed to have 500,000 men. He thought that Chiang should be obliged to come to an understanding with them, instead of keeping a part of his forces—perhaps 150,000 men—immobilized by the necessity to contain them. A special strategic conception accompanied this general point of view—the generalissimo's passive policy seemed disastrous to Stilwell.

Stilwell thought it necessary to prepare a vast operation against the Japanese in order to reopen the Burma Road. For this operation Chinese, British, and American forces would be needed and Stilwell constantly demanded reinforcements. He came to underestimate the needs of other fronts. He succeeded in having Chinese troops sent to Assam and trained for this offensive. Other troops, south of Yunnan, were also to be trained and given modern equipment. He was not able to put this plan into effect, however. Roosevelt, concerned with Chinese friendship, confused this with the friendship of Chiang Kai-shek to some extent, and Stilwell was a source of embarrassment to him. Chennault, whose point of view was defended by Alsop, was more popular in the United States. It should be noted that Stimson and Marshall supported Stilwell to the hilt.

During 1942 these difficulties were not overcome and American policy bogged down. In an attempt to improve the situation, Wendell Willkie, Roosevelt's former opponent in the election of 1940, was sent to China after a trip to Africa, the Middle East, and the Soviet Union (September and October 1942). It was an unofficial mission. Chiang, in Willkie's presence, violently criticized the Allies in general, especially the British, and above all the American ambassador, Clarence Gauss, and General Stilwell.

In 1943 tension increased. At the beginning of the year, nonetheless, there were a few favorable signs. On January 11, 1943, Hull signed a treaty with China by which all foreign extraterritorial rights in China would be abolished; he obtained British agreement on the same day. This treaty was the result of long negotiations of the kind at which Hull excelled—on the level of high principles. Chiang was delighted. "This day is the beginning of a new era in the history of China," he said.[43]

At the same time, at the Casablanca conference between Roosevelt and Churchill—to which the generalissimo had not been invited—the plan for a Burma campaign, called Anakim, was adopted, not for the spring as Stilwell wanted, but for the autumn, around November 15. A mission, directed on the American side by General Arnold, representative of the Air Force on the General Staff, went to India to meet General Stilwell and General Wavell, now viceroy, and then to China to meet Chiang Kai-shek. Chiang wrote to Roosevelt on February 7 to ask for major airplane reinforcements. He followed the theories of Chennault, defensive tactics on the ground and a stepped-up air offensive. Again Roosevelt had to choose. On one side, Stilwell and with him the War Department and Marshall, Arnold, and King wanted the Casablanca decisions carried out, that is, a land campaign by the British and Chinese in north Burma and British landings in the south. On the other side were the generalissimo and Chennault, supported by Hopkins and Madame Chiang Kai-shek— who was in the United States from November 1942 to February 1943—who were opposed to the Casablanca plan.

Roosevelt, who always exaggerated the fighting quality of the Chinese Nationalist Army and who wanted to please Chiang, decided in favor of the second view, to the great fury of Stilwell, whose relations with Chiang grew steadily worse. Stilwell thought that the generalisimo's—"Peanut," as he called him in his diary—main purpose was much less to fight the Japanese than to wait for an Allied victory on other fronts and keep his forces intact in order to triumph over his adversaries in China, especially the Communists. This necessitated staying on good terms with his generals, who were mostly rebellious, rapacious, and not interested in waging real war.

In June 1943 the United States ambassador in Chungking encouraged negotiations between the Nationalists and the Chinese Communists. As early as July the reports were pessimistic. Was the generalissimo trying to get the upper hand over the Communists, who were solidly in control in northwest China in the provinces of Shensi, Kansu, and Ningsia? Such a move would be fatal for the war against the Japanese. Furthermore, it disturbed and annoyed the Russians, who asked the United States to intervene. There was, therefore, a vigorous action by the State Department, and on September 13 Chiang declared that the Communist problem would be handled by "political means," which ruled out civil war, at least for the time being.

Stilwell thought the generalissimo's policy absurd and that his position would be perfectly secure if he would only favor what Stilwell increasingly urged, the training of 30 modern divisions, well equipped, disciplined, and regularly paid. In theory Chiang had 300 divisions. In the United States there was too great a tendency to think of these disorganized bands as real divisions. Chiang preferred these bands, which he thought he could control, to troops that were capable of real fighting.

Stilwell's trials were still not over. Even before the conference called Trident opened in May 1943, he and Chennault were summoned by Roosevelt and Churchill. Chennault's opinion triumphed. On May 3 Roosevelt ordered that operation Hump over the Himalayas be exclusively devoted in the next three months to preparation for Chennault's big aerial offensive. Despite the resistance of Marshall and King, the combined chiefs supported this priority on May 20. At the conference called Quadrant in August, the date for the Burma offensive was postponed until February 1944. It was at this time that Lord Louis Mountbatten took over command of the Southeast Asia theater. Stilwell stormed, "the command set-up is a Chinese puzzle, with Wavell [viceroy of India], Auk [Auchinleck, commander-in-chief in India], Mountbatten, Peanut [Chiang Kai-shek], Alexander and me interwoven and mixed beyond recognition." [44]

Encouraged by this success, Chiang let Roosevelt know that he wanted to get rid of Stilwell. The President replied that he would agree provided the generalissimo wrote him in person on the subject. The Chinese Nationalist leader drafted a letter but after a family quarrel in which Madame Chiang told her husband that the departure of Stilwell would end the good will of the United States War Department toward China, he did not dare to send it and Stilwell stayed at his post. A meeting was arranged between the two men. "Peanut did his best to be cooperative," wrote the fierce general.[45]

All told, American policy in China in the autumn of 1943 cannot be considered a success. To the observer, however, it seems that Stilwell, despite his stiffness, his excessive frankness and even his crudeness, saw the problem correctly. The trouble was that there were so many fronts and such pressure from the different commanders to obtain a greater share of equipment, such lack of understanding on the part of the Kuomintang and such illusions on Roosevelt's part, that Stilwell's good sense and wisdom could not prevail.

The Problem of the Second Front in 1943

The first seven months of 1943 saw the most serious crisis so far in the political relations between the British and Americans on one side and the Soviet Union on the other. The crisis concerned the opening of the Second Front. In 1943 there was no Second Front properly speaking, unless one counts the operations in southern Italy as such. Further delays were to be expected, because of the slowdown of the campaign in Tunisia. The political atmosphere of these months was, therefore, one of tension between the British and Americans and the Soviets. Under the circumstances, what part did United States diplomacy play?

Roosevelt's main idea was to hold a meeting with Churchill and Stalin. On November 21, 1942, after the landings in North Africa, Roosevelt proposed that such a meeting be held somewhere in Morocco. Churchill accepted but Stalin, as we know, refused on the grounds that he could not leave home because of military operations.

Churchill preferred a meeting with Roosevelt alone for the simple reason that the main question to be decided was whether there would be a Second Front in France in 1943 or whether the operations in the Mediterranean would be extended, a question which could not be discussed with the Russians. On the American side, General Marshall wanted the Second Front in France while Arnold and King preferred to pursue a course which would hasten the capitulation of Italy. Roosevelt pressed Stalin twice more but Stalin replied that he was interested in one thing only, the creation of a Second Front in the spring of 1943.

The conference, which was held in Casablanca, opened on January 12. Roosevelt was accompanied by Hopkins and his military advisers. Eisenhower, Murphy, and Macmillan were also present. The President had not wanted to take Hull with him, perhaps because he wanted to attempt a rapprochement with De Gaulle.

The Casablanca Conference produced results on various levels. On the strategic level, it was decided to invade Sicily without abandoning the idea of landings in France in 1943 or any of the other operations currently in progress. It should be noted that according to Admiral King, 85 percent of all resources were being used against Germany and only 15 percent in the Pacific.

On the political level, Roosevelt persuaded Churchill to accept the idea of "unconditional surrender" for Germany and Japan. The British cabinet decided that the same terms should apply to Italy. Contrary to the claim of Elliott Roosevelt, this idea did not come to the President suddenly in the midst of the discussions.[46] A subcommittee on problems of security, under Norman Davis, a friend of Hull's, had been set up in the State Department, and had advanced this idea as early as May 21, 1942. The aim was to avoid the complications which had arisen at the end of World War I because of an armistice loaded with conditions. Total surrender would allow any terms which seemed essential to be made at the time of the peace treaty. The advantages of the scheme seemed striking and the disadvantages were not evident at the time, because no opposition was voiced. The difficulty was that it put the Allies in a position where they could not negotiate with any opposing groups which might come to power in the Axis nations. The policy also postulated great confidence in the Allied coalition. If in making the peace the victors were to start from scratch without consultation with the vanquished, could the victorious Allies agree with each other? Roosevelt's confidence in his own powers of persuasion led him to view these difficulties with a somewhat naïve optimism. In the end it was a policy of withdrawing from the problem instead of tackling it. Roosevelt was so pleased with his idea that on January 24 he made a public declaration without even consulting Churchill, it would seem.

Peace will only be restored to the world by the total elimination of the warlike power of the Germans and the Japanese. The elimination of the power to make war of Germany, Italy and Japan implies the unconditional surrender of Germany, Italy and Japan . . . This does not mean the destruction of the people of Germany, Italy and Japan, but it does mean the destruction of their ideology, which is based on the conquest and domination of other peoples.[47]

Another problem which was much discussed was the future of France. First, there was a minor matter to be straightened out. When Darlan was assassinated Eisenhower and Murphy wanted to replace him with another Vichy minister, Marcel Peyrouton, a determined opponent of Laval. Peyrouton was in Argentina at the time and the State Department arranged for his transportation. Sumner Welles tried to stop him in Rio de Janeiro, because he feared that any solution which seemed to favor the antidemocratic regime of Vichy would be very unpopular. Cordell Hull, no doubt because of his opposition to De Gaulle and because he found it more and more difficult to tolerate the independent action of his subordinate, gave instructions for Peyrouton to proceed. Peyrouton reached Algiers shortly before Roosevelt arrived in Casablanca. The President, informed by Churchill, was displeased with this affair. Eisenhower recognized that his unfamiliarity with European affairs had led to the inopportune action and the matter was dropped.

Although the Peyrouton episode was insignificant in itself, it complicated a more important task which Roosevelt wanted to accomplish—the reconciliation of De Gaulle and Giraud. The two French leaders were summoned to meet Roosevelt and Churchill. De Gaulle was displeased not to have been informed in advance (Roosevelt was always fearful of possible indiscretion on the part of the French in London) and at first refused to come. He preferred a private meeting with Giraud to a meeting under the eyes of the Allied leaders. Roosevelt was irritated by this refusal and thought it a proof of De Gaulle's

unlimited ambition. Roosevelt thought France could only be represented effectively by one man, and a man whose determined will
would be able to make itself felt after the war. Roosevelt still did not
understand that this was precisely De Gaulle's objective—in contrast
to Giraud, who was a Royalist with little understanding of non-
military affairs. Giraud, therefore, came alone. On January 21 Eden
finally persuaded De Gaulle to join him.

The meeting of Roosevelt and De Gaulle was very cold. The
United States Secret Service had stationed armed men all over the
building, no doubt because they considered the general a dangerous
man. Hopkins, who was present, has explicitly denied the apocryphal
account according to which De Gaulle compared himself, first to
Clemenceau and then to Jeanne d'Arc. "The story is pure fiction—
although I have heard the President tell it myself—to show the impression that General de Gaulle made on him." [48]

De Gaulle held his ground firmly. He refused to serve under
Giraud and thought that the only viable solution was for Giraud
to agree to serve under Fighting France. Did not the Resistance support De Gaulle while Giraud was supported only by the governors
and residents-general appointed by Vichy? The awkward situation
was resolved on the surface by the issuance of a vague communiqué
and a photograph of the two men shaking hands on January 24. This
was Roosevelt's idea. Unity among the French had not taken a step
forward.

Roosevelt returned to Washington on January 31, the day the
Russians won the Battle of Stalingrad by obtaining the surrender of
Marshal von Paulus. As early as January 25 Roosevelt and Churchill
had sent Stalin a report on the Casablanca Conference. Stalin was
keenly disappointed that no date had been set for the landings in
Europe. There would certainly not be a Second Front in the spring,
but could he hope that there would be one before the end of 1943?
In February Churchill raised Stalin's hopes by telling him that he
expected a victory in Tunisia in April, the fall of Italy in July, and,
perhaps, a landing in France in August or September. It is true that
these predictions were accompanied by conditions, such as the number
of ships and landing craft available and the state of German defenses.
Nevertheless, Stalin could reasonably take it as a promise.

When it became clear that the promise would not be carried out, the correspondence between the three men took on an increasingly bitter tone. On February 16 Stalin did nothing more than ask that the landings be set for an earlier date than August 1943. He accused the British and Americans of deliberately slowing down operations in Tunisia so as to allow Hitler to transfer twenty-seven divisions to the Russian front. On March 9, the United States ambassador, Standley, told an American correspondent that although the Soviet Union was receiving enormous quantities of American supplies, the government was not informing the people and allowed them to believe that the country was fighting alone and unaided. This was undoubtedly true, but the ambassador's public statement obviously did not improve the atmosphere. On March 15 Stalin again accused his partners of delaying the end of the Tunisian campaign. He wrote harshly to Roosevelt, "The vagueness of your reply about the opening of a Second Front in France provokes anxiety which I cannot conceal." [49] On March 30 Churchill told Stalin that the convoys to Murmansk would again be suspended, as they had been the previous year, because of the short nights. Stalin complained of "this catastrophic reduction in deliveries to the U.S.S.R."

In the midst of these exchanges, Foreign Secretary Eden went to Washington (March 12 to 30), where he had long consultations with Hull. The American Secretary of State explained to him in no uncertain terms his aversion to General de Gaulle. Eden also saw Roosevelt and Hopkins at the White House. The main purpose of these talks was to discuss the problems of the future peace, without yet making any decisions about them. We shall examine their substance in the following chapter. It is important to note here that Roosevelt and Churchill firmly believed that the Soviets desired "a peaceful and friendly association with the United States and Great Britain" [50] after the war. Herbert Feis, having studied their attitude, has passed the following judgment.

Now, with our retrospective knowledge and chance to re-examine the whole past, the prevailing American optimism regarding the possibility of dealing with Stalin on friendly and frank terms in a spirit of good faith and in a belief in his moderation, is amazing. How did Roosevelt, how did most of the American nation, fail to grasp, or ignore, or overlook, the traits which had enabled Stalin to get and hold supreme power in the Soviet Union? . . . Roosevelt and those who shared his feelings and purposes were determined not to allow their hopeful belief in the possibility of cooperation with the Soviet Union to be destroyed.[51]

In any case, Eden showed great optimism in Washington. He even went so far as to interpret Russian insistence on a Second Front as a political gesture, because they did not want to have to concern themselves too much with German and European problems after the war!

Shortly after Eden's visit the Tunisian campaign ended in victory, and on May 7 American and French troops took Bizerte while the British took Tunis. It remained only to capture the rest of the Italian and German forces, an affair of a few days. Churchill then went to Washington for the conference called Trident, held May 12 to 25. From the beginning, Churchill undertook to convert the American military chiefs to the idea that the Allies should take advantage of the opportunity to pursue the Mediterranean war and especially to assure the defeat of Italy. Perhaps he was also planning a campaign in the Balkans. This policy eliminated the opening of a Second Front in France for 1943. Roosevelt, for his part, thought that the large-scale landings should be made in the spring of 1944 instead, but, unlike Churchill, he felt strongly that they should be made. It was decided to plan landings for May 1, 1944, and an Anglo-American group was appointed to draw up plans, under General Sir Frederick Morgan.

This decision was obviously of capital importance and it had to be communicated to Stalin. Even before Trident, on May 5, Roosevelt had sent former ambassador Joseph E. Davies to Moscow, bearing a letter which asked Stalin to meet the President. Roosevelt suggested "an unofficial meeting of just you and me" [52] without ceremony, for several days. He went on to suggest the coming summer as the time and a location off the American or Russian coast of the Bering Sea as the place. He preferred a meeting between the two of them to a tripartite meeting with Churchill. There was a rumor in the United States that the President was overshadowed by the Prime Minister, and this would be a good way to dispel it. Furthermore, as we know, Roosevelt was a great believer in his own power to act directly man to man. He also thought Stalin would trust him more than he trusted Churchill. It was a good sign that during Davies' visit, on May 22, Stalin announced the dissolution of the Comintern. Stalin agreed in principle to such a meeting as Roosevelt wished but refused to set a date.

On June 4—when Stalin received from Roosevelt the news of the decisions of the Trident Conference—the whole plan disintegrated. Stalin's reply of June 11 was furious. On June 24 he wrote:

The Soviet Government could not have imagined that the British and American Governments would revise the decision to invade Western Europe, which they had adopted early this year. In fact, the Soviet Government was fully entitled to expect that the Anglo-American decision would be carried out . . . [The plans had been changed without consulting the USSR.] I must tell you that the point here is not just the disappointment of the Soviet Government, but the preservation of its confidence in its Allies, a confidence which is being subjected to severe stress.[53]

Churchill replied to this epistle in a fairly stiff tone; Roosevelt preferred to keep silent. The situation did not improve.

There was another subject of disagreement, which also involved disagreement between the United States and Great Britain, the problem of the conflicting French authorities. After long negotiations whose details do not concern us, De Gaulle and Giraud had come to an agreement. On May 31, 1943, they had established the French Committee of National Liberation under their joint chairmanship. This solution, very favorable to French interests, was approved by the British with reservations but it did not please Roosevelt, nor, of course, Hull. The Secretary of State would have preferred to continue his system of negotiation with "local authorities" in the various parts of the French Empire.

Clearly, what had been done in Algiers could not be totally undone in Washington, but an attempt was made to limit its scope in two ways: first, by putting strong pressure on the British not to recognize the French Committee of National Liberation as a government, and second, by demanding that French forces—at least in North Africa—remain under the command of Giraud. The policy was explained fully and in as unfriendly a tone as possible in a message from Roosevelt to Eisenhower on June 17. General Eisenhower had instructions to inform De Gaulle and Giraud. "The position of this Government is that during our military occupation of North Africa we will not tolerate the control of the French Army by any agency which is not subject to the Allied Supreme Commander's direction. We must have someone whom we wholly and completely trust." [54] The Americans had at their disposal a powerful means of bringing pressure—the granting or withholding of arms.

By June 19 Eisenhower had carried out the disagreeable task of notifying De Gaulle that the Allies did not have confidence in him. On June 22 it was established that Giraud would remain commander-in-chief in West Africa and North Africa, De Gaulle would command everywhere else.

The Soviet government was very much opposed to this policy. As early as September 1941 it had received a representative of Fighting France in Moscow and the Communist Resistance in France had declared for General de Gaulle. Stalin wanted prompt recognition. Churchill wrote him on June 23 in the name of the two major Western Allies that "de Gaulle could endanger the bases and lines of communication" of the Sicilian expedition.[55] Stalin replied on the twenty-sixth that he still wished to recognize the French Committee of National Liberation but that as a matter of courtesy he would not do so unilaterally. He decided to send Ambassador Bogomolov to Algiers, but even this was delayed at the request of the Americans.

The Far East, the Mediterranean, the Second Front, France—at every point there was tension between the Soviet Union on the one hand and the British and Americans on the other in the summer of 1943. Did the United States government really fear a separate peace between the Soviet Union and Germany? No document seems to justify the idea that such a fear played any part in the political calculations. It would seem that the American military chiefs were more concerned about such an eventuality in 1942 than in 1943. General Eisenhower, then chief of the Operations Division, had written in 1942, "Russia's problem is to hold out through the coming summer." [56] By 1943, however, everyone knew that the Soviet Union could hold out.

The Surrender of Italy

During this period of tension with Russia, Anglo-American strategy and policy met with success in one respect, namely in Italy's unconditional surrender. Our interest here is in the part played by the United States in bringing about this important historic event.

On the strategic level, the decisions of the Trident Conference about the Mediterranean theater were successfully carried out in July 1943. Landings in Sicily occurred on July 9, Mussolini's abdication and arrest followed on the twenty-fifth. The most serious problem was how to proceed from then on. Churchill, who did not favor landings in France because he feared that they would fail and because he still preferred his "peripheral strategy," wrote to Field Marshal Smuts of South Africa on July 16, "not only must we take Rome and march as far north as possible in Italy, but our right hand must give succour to the Balkan patriots." [57] Stimson, who went to England in mid-July, thought, on the contrary, that the Allies should not go beyond Rome, because to do so would divert strength from the landings in France. Eisenhower's proposal, a compromise solution, was to land in September in the Gulf of Salerno and advance north as far as possible. Roosevelt agreed with this plan and authorized reinforcements of 66,000 men for the Italian campaign.

In spite of his vacillations, the President remained faithful to the overall plan of Stimson and Marshall. At the time, there was only one American division and 700 American heavy bombers in Great Britain. The President decided to send a good many more heavy bombers in order to have 2500 in Great Britain by April 1, 1944. Furthermore, seven divisions were to be transferred from the Mediterranean to England after November 1, 1943. Stimson returned from England with the idea that, as the British did not favor landings in France, the command of the expedition should be given to an American general. Stimson wanted Marshall to be chosen, as did Hopkins. Roosevelt took readily to the idea of an American commander but waited until December to make the appointment—and then appointed Eisenhower, not Marshall.

These matters, coinciding with the prospects of Italian surrender, made it necessary for Roosevelt and Churchill to hold another meeting on strategy and military matters. The British Prime Minister proposed to hold it in Quebec. The Quadrant Conference, as it was called, took place between August 14 and August 24. On the American side, the principal participants included Hopkins, the chiefs of the general staff and Secretaries Hull, Stimson, and Knox, who arrived a few days after the opening. Churchill remained in America some time after the conference and had another important meeting with Roosevelt at the White House on September 9, the day after Italy's unconditional surrender. At that time the first landings in the Gulf of Salerno were taking place.

The political problem raised by the Italian situation dominated the period between July 25 and the end of October 1943. As soon as Mussolini fell from power and was replaced by Badoglio, the United States government sought to formulate an Italian policy. There were two important matters to be settled: first, what conditions should be imposed on Italy when she surrendered, as everyone was expecting her to do? Second, how much confidence could be placed in the government of Victor Emmanuel III, which had accepted Mussolini's rise to power in October 1922 and had collaborated with the Duce for twenty years?

General Eisenhower took the initiative on the first point. He instructed his staff to draw up the text of a purely military surrender, in which the word "unconditional" did not appear, but which gave the Allied commander-in-chief the right to establish military government in Italy. It provided for what is called a "temporary armistice." After it had been revised by the American General Staff and by Churchill, the text anticipated any eventuality. Churchill, however, wished to elaborate a much longer and more precise text which would show the Italians what to expect. Roosevelt did not favor such a procedure; why not leave as much latitude as possible to Eisenhower, the President asked. Only at the Quadrant Conference did the Americans and British agree on a text for a "long armistice," which spelled out the political, administrative, and financial policies which would apply to Italy.

Let us examine the American part in the negotiations which led to Italy's surrender. Eisenhower and Roosevelt favored a quick signing of the "short armistice," after which the Italians would be obliged to agree to a "long armistice." The first contacts between the Italians and the Allies took place on August 4 at the British embassy in Lisbon and on August 6 at the British consulate in Tangiers, but real negotiations did not begin until the Quebec Conference. On August 15 General Castellano, armed with a letter from the British minister to the Vatican, attempted to make contact with Sir Samuel Hoare in Madrid and—to insure greater secrecy—with the British ambassador in Lisbon.

On August 18 the American point of view seemed to have won out and the terms of a short armistice were sent to Castellano in Lisbon by the American General Walter Bedell Smith and the British General Kenneth Strong. Castellano was to report the terms to Rome. On August 26 the British took the lead and General Zanessi found in Lisbon the terms of the long armistice, containing the words "unconditional surrender."

Eisenhower, however, understood that there was a risk of failure for the whole policy in this procedure and he obtained authority—

through the joint chiefs—not to present the long armistice until and unless the short armistice had been accepted, making quite clear that the latter was a provisional document. Several more days of negotiation were needed because the Germans had brought nine crack divisions into Italy which were threatening Rome, including the King and Badoglio. The Italian government therefore suggested that Castellano go to Sicily to sign the surrender terms, which he did on September 3. They also asked that the terms be kept secret until after the Allies had landed at Salerno and had penetrated further into the interior. Roosevelt and Churchill, strongly supported by Eisenhower, decided to overrule this condition and the Italian government, under strong pressure, accepted the publication of the armistice terms on September 8. They had to give in even more, in that the announcement made it clear that it was an unconditional surrender.

Further negotiations were required to make the Italians sign the long armistice on September 29. Finally, on October 13, Italy's claim to be admitted as a cobelligerent with the Allies against Germany was allowed and she declared war on Germany. On the same day Roosevelt, Churchill, and Stalin announced in a joint declaration that they would accept Italian cobelligerency.

The second problem concerned the government of Italy. The first American reaction, expressed by the Office of War Information after the fall of Mussolini, was that the Italian government was still essentially Fascist and that therefore it was too soon to rejoice. Roosevelt, however, expressed satisfaction as early as July 27. He saw more advantages than drawbacks in the situation, despite his aversion to compromise solutions of the type represented by dealings with Darlan and Badoglio. Even so, he did not consider that there was any definite commitment to maintain the House of Savoy, and wished rather to see a republic established in Italy. In any case his theory was that Italy, like any other nation, should be allowed to choose her own form of government after the war. Churchill, for his part, had a definite preference for the monarchy and thought it the most stable form of government. He was very much inclined to support the House of Savoy, if not Victor Emmanuel III himself. Roosevelt and Churchill were divided on this point, a foreshadowing of a more serious crisis in 1944. In the end, Roosevelt insisted that Italy's right to choose her own government by free elections be made clear in terms of the "long armistice" and Churchill had to give in.

The problem of Italy created another crisis with the Soviet Union. It was in itself of short duration, but it differed from earlier crises in that it finally brought about a more cooperative attitude on the part of the Russians. The crisis was caused by Stalin's wish to have his say about Italy.

United States ambassadors Winant in London and Standley in Moscow strongly advised the inclusion of the Soviets in political decisions about Italy. As Winant puts it, "When the tide turns, and the Russian armies are capable of advancing, we may well want then to influence their conditions of surrender and occupation in Allied and enemy territory." [58] After some hesitation, because it was a two-edged sword, Hull was convinced. On August 5 he informed Molotov that Eisenhower was authorized to accept the "short armistice," the text of which had just been sent to the Russians by the British. "All suggestions that the Soviet Government wishes to make, now or later, will be welcomed by the United States Government." [59]

Stalin did not reply at once. The Red Army was then winning important battles around Kursk, Orel, and Kharkov and he was too busy with his military duties. On August 11, when Stalin and Molotov received the British and American ambassadors bearing information about the first steps in the Italian negotiations, Stalin confined himself to an expression of suspicion of Badoglio and again brought up the question of the Second Front. The Russians accepted the conditions of the short armistice, however. The crisis arose over the long armistice. The provisional text Churchill had sent was incomplete, because of certain technical errors, and Stalin used this as a pretext to protest that he was not being told the truth and that information was being withheld from him. Since the Soviet ambassadors in London and Washington, Maisky and Litvinov, had just been called home for "consultations," it looked as if a break in diplomatic relations might be in the offing.

It was more in the nature of a maneuver, however. Stalin probably hoped that by vehemently expressing his displeasure he would improve the chances of a favorable answer to a request he was to make on August 22, when he asked that a "Military and Political Commission," consisting of representatives of the three nations, be created to direct negotiations with "governments disassociating themselves from Germany. Until now . . . the United States and Great Britain have made agreements but the Soviet Union received information about the results of the agreements just as a passive third observer. I have to tell you that it is impossible to tolerate this situation any longer. I propose that the Commission be established and that Sicily be assigned at the beginning as its place of residence." [60]

On August 24 Stalin showed a more conciliatory attitude and he accepted the long armistice. He was influenced especially by the provision for the Military and Political Commission. He allowed Eisenhower to sign the Italian surrender terms in the name of the Soviet Union. In the same message he excused himself again for not being able to arrange a meeting with Roosevelt. Several days later he agreed that a meeting of the three foreign ministers, which he himself had suggested on August 9, should be held in October, preferably in Moscow. On September 8 he finally agreed to meet Roosevelt and Churchill in Iran, between November 15 and December 15.

On the surface at least, it was a great success for Roosevelt. The President thought he could "win Stalin over" to a number of his ideas, especially to an organization for collective security and the dismemberment of Germany. Roosevelt did not dare to go as far as Stalin in regard to the Military and Political Commission. He did not wish Eisenhower, as commander-in-chief, to be subordinated to the commission. There was nothing to prevent its establishment as an advisory organ, however. Stalin hastened to accept and on September 12 he announced that Russia would be represented by Andrei Vishinsky, assistant commissar for foreign affairs, seconded by Bogomolov, whom he had formerly sent to Algiers. Discussion on the powers of the Military and Political Commission went on interminably and were never fully resolved, as we shall see, until the meeting of the foreign ministers in Moscow. This matter, which seems purely technical and even absurdly tortuous, is really of great importance. The months of August and September 1943 seem to have provided a key—a decision to hold Big Three meetings. In fact, all these conferences, as we now know, were to focus attention on a central point: who would possess real power in the reconquered territories?

Chapter XIV

Victory in Sight, Spring 1943-Autumn 1944

Preparation for Peace in 1943

THE Trident and Quadrant conferences had provided a resolution of the strategic difficulties between the Americans and the British. The decision not to prepare for operation Overlord (the invasion of France in May 1944) until after the surrender of Italy might be said to have marked the final concession by the United States to British peripheral strategy. In the future the American strategy of concentration would prevail. At the very time the strategic decisions were taken, however, several political problems arose which showed how difficult it would be to arrange a peace and caused a great deal of time and energy to be devoted to the matter.

Naturally, the problem had long been in the minds of the Allied leaders. Even before the United States' entry into the war, on September 3, 1939, Roosevelt had declared: "it seems to me clear, even at the outbreak of this great war, that the influence of America should be consistent in seeking for humanity a final peace which will eliminate, as far as it is possible to do so, the continued use of force between nations." [1]

Several private organizations, notably the Council on Foreign Relations in New York, had offered their services to the State Department. On September 16 Cordell Hull had appointed Leo Pasvolsky as his special assistant on problems related to the peace. Hull's idea was to have an agency whose business it would be to prepare peace terms within the State Department itself and not outside, as was the Inquiry Bureau under Colonel House during World War I. On December 27, 1939, Hull set up a Committee on Problems of Peace and Reconstruction, which included Sumner Welles, counselor Robert Watson Moore, assistant secretaries George S. Messersmith, Adolf A. Berle, Jr., Leo Pasvolsky, Henry F. Grady, and various officials, including Herbert Feis and J. Pierrepont Moffat. The name of this committee was changed on January 8, 1940, to Advisory Committee on Problems of Foreign Relations. It was subdivided into three committees, one to deal with political problems, a second with limitation and reduction of armaments, and a third with economic problems. Since all its members were burdened with other important jobs, it was essential to distribute the work.

On February 3, 1941, it was decided to reinforce the committee with a special research division under Pasvolsky, whose members would not concern themselves with current problems, but would devote themselves exclusively to providing documents for the Advisory Committee. The Four Freedoms proclaimed by Roosevelt on January 6, 1941, provided a framework for the work of the new division.

As this did not afford enough leeway, Hull proposed the establishment of an Advisory Committee on Post-War Foreign Policy on December 22, 1941. Under Hull as chairman, its members included Sumner Welles, Leo Pasvolsky, Dean Acheson (assistant secretary of state), Herbert Feis, Myron C. Taylor (the President's personal representative to Pope Pius XII) and several prominent men in private life such as Norman H. Davis, chairman of the Council on Foreign Relations, Hamilton Fish Armstrong, publisher of the magazine *Foreign Affairs*, Anne O'Hare McCormick, editorial writer for the New York *Times*, and a former prominent member of the Inquiry Bureau, Isaiah Bowman, then president of Johns Hopkins University. On December 28, 1941, Roosevelt enthusiastically endorsed the idea. The committee was enlarged to include, as unofficial members, five senators, three members of the House of Representatives, representatives of six government departments including those of War and the Navy, one from the joint chiefs and four from the war agencies. In the end there were eleven State Department members and ten from private life. James Shotwell was added to the committee in June 1942. Among the nongovernment members were two representatives of labor, one each from the A.F.L. and the C.I.O., the president of the United States Chamber of Commerce, and two economists, Percy W. Bidwell and Jacob Viner. The congressional representatives included Senator Tom Connally of Texas, Democratic chairman of the Senate Committee on Foreign Relations, and Senator Warren R. Austin of Vermont, Republican member of that committee.

The size of the Advisory Committee shifted slightly from time to time. The important point is that the membership was very well chosen. Under the chairmanship of Hull, it brought together leading members of other departments in collaboration with the State Department. It also brought together representatives of the executive and legislative branches of the government—the latter on a bipartisan basis—and outstandingly qualified private citizens. Ranking officials, academic specialists, legal experts, businessmen, financiers, writers, and newspapermen shared in its work. There were specialists on Europe, on the Far East, and on Latin America—Nelson A. Rockefeller, for example. The committee held its first meeting on February 12, 1942. It rarely met in plenary session but frequently in subcommittees on special problems including political and territorial problems, problems of economic reconstruction, and security problems. It was the Inquiry Bureau of 1917 highly perfected and formalized.

Before examining the results of the committee's work, we should form a picture of how the vast problems of the future peace looked and should consider the methods by which Roosevelt planned to deal with them. Wilson had tried to create an association of nations to assure world peace and under its aegis to resolve territorial problems by means of law and justice. Roosevelt shared these views. There was a new problem, however, which had hardly existed for Wilson: relations with the Soviet Union, a nation whose socio-economic theory and general ideology were fundamentally different from those of the United States. In Wilson's time the Soviets were very weak. In 1943, on the contrary, there was every indication that after the war their power would be considerable. There was a risk, therefore, that the problem of Soviet-American relations would overshadow the problems of international organization and territorial adjustments. The question was, whether those responsible were aware of this risk.

In regard to methods, Roosevelt, and especially Hull, shared Wilson's suspicion of secret treaties by which agreements about future territorial settlements were made in the midst of war. In December 1941, when Foreign Secretary Anthony Eden went to Moscow, Hull had thought it necessary to warn him against this practice. A point of capital importance is that Roosevelt did not believe, as Wilson did, that it was necessary to make a public declaration of American war aims. Although it was perfectly feasible to proclaim untiringly and later to refine a series of abstract principles, such as the Four Freedoms and the Atlantic Charter, any elaboration of concrete plans about frontiers and territories should at all costs be avoided. All such matters would be more easily handled at the end of the war if the victors were not burdened with definite plans to which they were committed in advance.

It is difficult to explain why Roosevelt followed this method because he never revealed his thinking on the subject. One can only hazard hypothetical explanations. The first possibility that suggests itself is that Roosevelt was primarily concerned with winning the war. He did not conceive of war as "the continuation of politics by other means" as Clausewitz did, but as a sort of illness which must be cured. Let us recall the quarantine metaphor used as early as 1937. Everything else must be subordinated to victory. After the war had been won things could be worked out, provided that the victory was complete—whence the prescription of unconditional surrender. Unconditional surrender of the enemy would assure that the victors could start from scratch and the principal Allies working together could impose conditions on the vanquished, free of any previous commitments. It had been embarrassing for Wilson to sign the Armistice on the basis of the Fourteen Points and more embarrassing still when he tried to make the Entente carry them out. Without "points" things would be easier to handle.

The second hypothesis is that the President had constantly minimized the difficulties of agreement with the Soviet Union, which alone would permit a unified front toward the vaniquished after their unconditional surrender. The subcommittee on political problems, mentioned above, was largely responsible for this viewpoint. The Soviet Union was expected to cooperate with the United States because it would be in the Soviets' national interest. We have seen that Eden shared this opinion, which he expressed in Washington in March 1943. Churchill was infinitely more skeptical, at least after the summer of 1943, and he personally sought to adapt strategy so as to take certain territories as "hostages" in relation to the Soviets. From this attitude stemmed his desire to penetrate the Balkans, which we have mentioned and which requires further discussion below. In this he clashed head on with Roosevelt's inveterate optimism.

Finally, we must repeat once more that Roosevelt had an imperturbable confidence in his own capacity to influence the minds of other men, even Stalin's. When he invited Stalin to meet him alone, he spoke of a "meeting of minds." This was to underestimate the man and to exaggerate the degree to which he could be influenced, even if one leaves aside his deep attachment to the dialectical theory that every expansion of Socialist power is part of the inevitable process of history and every resistance to that expansion, a manipulation of capitalist power politics. Roosevelt's knowledge of Marxism-Leninism seems to have been superficial. A psychological error about the man, Stalin, and an insufficient understanding of Soviet theory, would appear, therefore, to have been the sources of Roosevelt's optimism.

Let us now look at the principal results of the work of the sub-committee up to July 12, 1943, when Hull decided to suspend its activities and concentrate the preparation of peace plans within the State Department. He thought this method would provide a more flexible instrument during the Big Three meetings. It will suffice to summarize the most important suggestions, all of which were virtually incorporated into United States foreign policy for the postwar period. First, everyone was agreed on two closely related points: it was necessary to create an international organization in which nations would be equal. As early as 1942 the experts had concluded that the League of Nations could not be revived. In 1943 they thought of transforming the United Nations—at the time merely a coalition against the Axis—into the core of an international organization which other nations would subsequently be invited to join, according to certain criteria. At the same time they thought that the United States should undertake a great share of world responsibility after the war, as a member of the United Nations. It was understood that a return to isolationism was no longer possible.

A second important idea, stemming from Article 5 of the Atlantic Charter, which stated that members should renounce territorial conquest and intervention in the domestic affairs of other states, was that the vital interest of the United States required a "diplomacy of principle," of moral impartiality.[2] This meant that the United States should refuse to make any commitment about territorial settlements until the end of the war. This explains why the subcommittee on territorial problems, in contrast to the Inquiry Bureau of 1917, took pains never to make a single recommendation, even though it collected a considerable amount of material.

On the economic level, Cordell Hull naturally gained a hearing for his idea that postwar relations should be largely based on free trade.

The notion of equal access to raw materials was also brought up again. In 1939 Roosevelt had thought it could be used as a method for keeping the peace. The subcommittees did not prepare any specific formulas on these points, however. On the other hand, as early as 1942 plans were made for an organization of postwar aid, an agency concerned with agriculture and food, and an international monetary fund. These plans were made public in the spring of 1943.

The most original idea was certainly that which concerned the status of colonies and dependent territories after the war. Roosevelt had not always been "anticolonial." As assistant secretary of the navy, he had taken an active part in the policy of the Big Stick. Speaking of the Philippines, Puerto Rico, Haiti, and San Domingo on March 30, 1922, he could still say, "The vast majority of people in this country, I have always been certain, understand that complete independence for all of these people is not to be thought of for many years to come." [3]

During the 1920's, however, his ideas changed and he developed the position he was to maintain to the end of his life—favoring the independence of colonies. He set forth his new theory in an article in *Foreign Affairs* in July 1928. At the Atlantic Conference he secured Churchill's acceptance of a text which committed the two nations to "respect the right of all peoples to choose the form of government under which they wish to live." Churchill interpreted this text as excluding the peoples of the British Empire, but Roosevelt interpreted it as applying to all the peoples of the world. He was to argue this point at various times with Churchill, especially in relation to India. He discussed it with Molotov when the Soviet Foreign Minister came to Washington in June 1942. This seems to have been the first time that he proposed the system of international "trusteeship" for the colonial possessions of weaker nations, especially in southeast Asia. When Willkie returned from his trip around the world in late 1942, he made a speech favoring the adoption by the United States of a firmly anticolonial policy. The next day Roosevelt declared in a press conference: "I have already made it perfectly clear that we believed that the Atlantic Charter applied to all humanity." [4]

At Casablanca Roosevelt's position was even firmer, and if one believes his son Elliott—who is not wholly reliable—he even gave specific encouragement to the Sultan of Morocco. A few weeks later, on March 9, 1943, the political subcommittee and Secretary Hull submitted a memorandum on "national independence" to the President. This memorandum, invoking the Atlantic Charter, proposed not only that countries which were liberated from Japan be placed under international trusteeship, but also that the colonial powers (among the Allies) commit themselves to giving their own colonies independence by setting dates for their emancipation. Roosevelt approved this memorandum and from then on it was the foundation of American policy.[5] It should be understood that at the time Roosevelt visualized an international police force with strategically located bases from which to operate, such as Hong Kong, the Bonin Islands, the Kuril Islands, Truk, the Solomon Islands, Assumption Island, Dakar and a port in Liberia. It is, therefore, clear that American policy for the postwar world had solid and precise theoretical foundations as early as 1943.

When we leave the level of principle and look at specific problems we are reminded that Roosevelt always wanted to keep his hands absolutely free, especially in territorial questions. To understand what followed, however, it is indispensable to study the discussions concerning territories which took place, first with Britain alone, during Eden's Washington visit in March 1943, and then with the other two principal Allies at the conference of foreign ministers in Moscow in October of that year.

When Eden was in Washington the talks centered on postwar problems. Roosevelt had formulated his ideas about the future international organization. He suggested that it consist of a general assembly, an advisory council of the four great powers and six or eight other nations, and finally an executive council of four—the United States, Great Britain, the Soviet Union, and China. The idea of giving such a position to China was specifically American and met with lively resistance from the British and the Russians, who did not believe in the alleged power of China. Roosevelt also proposed his system of a police force and bases, mentioned above, without making clear whether the police force would really be international or would consist of national contingents furnished by the Big Four.

There was a long exchange about territories. In relation to Soviet frontiers, Roosevelt and Eden conceded that Russia could justifiably keep Bessarabia and the frontier with Finland established in March 1940. They did not seem to oppose the Curzon Line as Poland's eastern frontier, but in compensation they proposed that Poland annex East

Prussia and a part of Silesia. Roosevelt, however, wished to propose to the Russians a new plebiscite to determine the will of the population, although he did not have much expectation of success.

In regard to Eastern Europe, Roosevelt and Eden were agreed on the independence of Austria. Roosevelt envisaged the breakup of Yugoslavia into two parts, Serbia and Croatia, but Eden was very much opposed to this. Eden's discussions about the future of Germany were held primarily with Hull and Welles, rather than with the President. The idea was to dismember Germany; Prussia would be isolated and deprived of East Prussia, and the rest of the country would be divided into two or three independent states. Hull did not wish to make any definite commitment, however. In the Far East, Roosevelt confined himself to the suggestion that Manchuria and Formosa be returned to China, that Korea and Indochina be placed under trusteeship, and that the mandated Japanese islands be internationalized. In general, as Feis says, "the President's comments on frontier questions were cautious." [6]

In Moscow the American attitude remained equally prudent, and Hull rarely departed from the plane of principle, where he felt at home. Even so, between March and October 1943 several new difficulties arose, especially concerning Poland. On January 6, 1943, the Soviet government notified the Polish government-in-exile in London, headed by General Sikorski, that Russia would claim the territories in eastern Poland that the Soviets had occupied in 1939. Tension mounted seriously when the Nazis announced on the radio on April 13 that they had discovered in Katyn a mass grave of Polish officers massacred by the Russians. On the sixteenth the Polish government, without taking sufficient precautions, asked the International Red Cross to make an investigation at Katyn. The Soviets reacted violently and on April 24 Stalin told Roosevelt and Churchill that he was going to break off diplomatic relations with the Polish government-in-exile. He carried out this intention on April 26 without waiting for a reply. A Union of Polish Patriots, with Communist leanings, had been established in Moscow. For the British and Americans this was a serious threat—were the Russians trying to create a second Polish government-in-exile?

On October 7 Hull went to Moscow, well briefed on the position of the Polish government in London, presided over, since the accidental death of Sikorski, by the leader of the Peasant Party, Mikolajczyk. When the Polish problem came up, Eden took a strong position against Molotov's intransigence. Hull merely expressed the hope that things would work out. He wrote, "We wanted to see normal diplomatic relations restored between Russia and Poland . . . But we did not intend to insist on a wartime settlement of specific questions such as the determination of the future boundary between Poland and Russia." [7]

Hull was also cautious about Eden's attempt to dissuade the Soviets from signing a bilateral treaty with Czechoslovakia, President Beneš' plan, which Churchill thought extremely dangerous. Likewise, when Eden asked Molotov's approval of a fusion of the two resistance movements in Yugoslavia—those of Mihajlović and Tito—Hull remained silent. He also had nothing to say about Greece, where the Communist and non-Communist resistance movements were coming to blows. As Feis says, "The American Government was uncertain, sharing Churchill's desire that the peoples of these small countries should have freedom and order, but not sharing his inclination to rely on monarchies . . . Besides, it did not want to be drawn directly into these Balkan troubles, nor into taking sides between the British and the Russians." [8]

The worthy Secretary of State had something else on his mind. He thought that the "vital interest" of the United States was to follow a "diplomacy of principle," a policy "of moral impartiality instead of power politics." This was in line with the recommendation of the sub-committee on territorial problems, which had prepared the text of a Declaration to be proposed to the two main Allies. Roosevelt had approved the Declaration and the British had accepted it at the Quadrant Conference. It remained to obtain the adherence of the Soviets and the Chinese.

The Declaration's preamble, on which everyone was agreed, referred to the necessity of unconditional surrender by the enemy. Molotov's agreement to this preamble indicated for the first time that the Soviets were going along with the idea of unconditional surrender.

The American plan asked of the great powers a commitment (1) to act together in all matters relating to the surrender and disarmament of the enemy and occupation of territories belonging to or controlled by the enemy; (2) to create an international organization; (3) to consult together and act jointly in the name of the community of nations; (4) not to use their armed forces after the end of the war in other territories "except to achieve goals set forth in this Declaration, after having consulted each other and come to an agreement."

Molotov was brought to accept the inclusion of China by the Chinese ambassador in Moscow, but he weakened the effectiveness of the Declaration in two important ways. First, he would agree to common action with regard to surrender and disarmament of the enemy, but he refused to commit his government to common action concerning the occupation of territories. He used the situation in Italy as a pretext for this stand. In this way he opened the possibility for Russia to act alone in territories she was occupying. Accordingly, he agreed to the idea of consultation to maintain international peace, but rejected the expression "to act in common." This was another proof that he wanted to keep Soviet hands free. Second, he succeeded in changing the wording so that the phrase "come to an agreement" was omitted, leaving only "after having consulted each other." This meant that the Soviet Union would not agree to give up future interventions of which the other great powers might not approve. Molotov agreed throughout to the principle of "consultation," which did not tie his hands, but refused any precise commitment.

The Declaration of Four was adopted but it was couched in vague terms which opened the door to worse difficulties when it was necessary to move from abstractions to concrete situations. The only real accomplishments were the Soviet acceptance of unconditional surrender and the establishment of an international organization. In his memoirs, Cordell Hull calls the chapter on this conference "The Birth of the United Nations." At the end of the chapter he calls it "an historic event." [9] Historic it certainly was, but the Declaration was a two-edged sword.

Eden had given Hull strong support during the discussions of the Declaration. This was because he wanted to obtain adoption of another resolution, embodying the principle of "common responsibility in Europe in contrast to the principle of separate spheres of influence." If adopted, it would mean that the three governments promised not to set up spheres of influence. Molotov replied that the Soviet Union had no desire to cut out a sphere of influence for itself and Cordell Hull seemed to take this statement at face value. The Declaration of Four thus qualified was much sweetened by the fact that future territorial occupation only required consultation and not pre-established agreement. It really opened wide the door for the establishment of spheres of influence.

Was it nevertheless possible to go further in cooperation, regarding more specific regions in Europe? The British and Americans wished to keep the military commands over former enemy territories in their own hands for the duration of the war. The Russians, as we have seen, wanted to subordinate them to a political and military commission. Everyone was agreed that after the war "democratic" elements in these territories should be encouraged, but no definition of this term was included. The three foreign ministers confined themselves to proposing a European advisory commission. The Soviets would have liked territories liberated from the enemy to be subordinated also to the authority of this commission, but Hull thought he should avoid any such commitment for the United States and no decision was reached. In United States' administration circles the idea still persisted that American troops would not remain in Europe very long after the war. On the other hand, Hull would have liked an agreement to be reached on the fate of dependent nations, but Eden opposed it.

The Americans were more concerned with the case of Germany. Hull submitted to the conference a document entitled "Fundamental Principles Related to the Surrender of Germany," which listed five conditions to be imposed on defeated Germany: (1) Germany would admit total defeat; (2) Germany would be occupied by the forces of the three victorious powers; (3) the Nazis would be eliminated from the government; (4) political prisoners would be liberated and persons accused of war crimes would be turned over to the United Nations; (5) German armed forces would be demobilized. Hull recommended also the creation of a Democratic government in Germany, the maintenance of a reasonable standard of living, and the establishment of limited Allied control.

According to Hull, Stalin and Molotov were enthusiastic about his plan. Eden also agreed to it. It was decided that the European Advisory Commission should study the question. The rivalry between the British and Americans and the Soviets in Germany was already apparent. Should Germany be dismembered, thus allowing the Russians to appear as the champions of unity? Would it not be better to consider the problem in terms of security and dismember Germany in order to make further German aggression impossible? Roosevelt hesitated, as did Churchill, and Hull did not have instructions on this essential problem. There was no clear intention or prediction concerning the future frontiers of Germany.

Teheran

The first summit conference, at Teheran, was to use as a point of departure these rather loosely formulated political agreements of the three foreign ministers. The Teheran Conference would be supplemented by two less important conferences in Cairo.

In Moscow the atmosphere had been cordial, especially as Eden and Hull had been able to convince Molotov that the large-scale landings in France, operation Overlord, would really take place in the spring of 1944. This improvement in the atmosphere was certainly very important, but was it not founded on an excessive lack of precision in the decisions reached? Would the Big Three themselves be able to agree on the essential questions?

Roosevelt sailed on November 13 on the new battleship *Iowa*, accompanied by Hopkins, Marshall, Arnold, and Admirals King and Leahy. When the ship arrived in Oran, on November 20, General Eisenhower went to see the President, who then flew to Tunis and inspected the battlefields of Tunisia with Eisenhower. At this time the President told the general of his plan to appoint General Marshall as supreme commander of Overlord and to put Eisenhower in his place as chief of the general staff. "He has a right to make his name in history as a great general." [10] We know that this plan, strongly opposed by Arnold and King and a portion of the press, was not carried out. From Tunis the presidential party went to Cairo.

The first Cairo Conference, called Sextant, November 23 to 26, brought together Roosevelt, Churchill, and Chiang Kai-shek. On the strategic level, Roosevelt obtained agreement to the continuation of preparation for the vast operation in Burma called Anakim, which we have already discussed, combined with the Chinese offensive to the north. Churchill, however, was not enthusiastic about Anakim and Chiang was opposed to any land offensive for his army. General Stilwell, a great believer in these two operations, was to be disappointed over and over again.

Roosevelt and Churchill met separately to discuss military operations in the Mediterranean, where the Allies had just suffered two setbacks. They had not been able to take Rome and they had lost the recently occupied Dodecanese Islands as a result of an overwhelming counteroffensive by German dive bombers and parachutists. They also discussed Overlord, with Churchill opposing the appointment of Marshall as its commander because he thought him much more useful as chief of the general staff.

On the political plane, the main object of the Cairo Conference was to reassure Chiang Kai-shek who felt neglected and complained of insufficient Allied aid. Stalin, who had little use for the Kuomintang and was not at war with Japan, had refused to send Molotov to participate in the Cairo Conference. Churchill still thought that the Americans overestimated the power of China. It was, therefore, exclusively Roosevelt who was responsible for the meeting with the generalissimo. Roosevelt thought that China must be made a great power—at least in theory. He hoped that as a result China would put up a better fight and that she would contribute to the maintenance of peace in the Western Pacific. Moreover, at the time of the Quadrant Conference, Chinese Foreign Minister T. V. Soong had urgently requested Hull to include China in important conferences. We have seen how hard it was for Hull to obtain Molotov's acceptance of China as a cosignatory of the Declaration. On the last day of the Moscow Conference, Stalin told Hull that the Soviet Union would enter the war against Japan as soon as the Germans were defeated. "He didn't ask for anything in return," says Hull, in delighted surprise.[11] But would he not make demands for some compensation in the future? And what would be his attitude to Chiang? The problem was so troublesome that Hull did not inform the Chinese of Stalin's statement.

The situation made one thing clear—if the only point of the Cairo Conference was to build up Chinese morale it would not accomplish much. We do not know what was said in the long conversations between the President and the generalissimo. Madame Chiang acted as interpreter and no notes were taken on the American side. Churchill and Sherwood hardly mention it in their books. Stalin had to be consulted before any proclamation could be issued and none was issued until December 1, at the second Cairo Conference, after Teheran. We shall return to it later.

Roosevelt and Churchill took off from Cairo for Teheran at dawn on November 27 in separate planes following separate routes. The greatest secrecy had been preserved about the Big Three Conference in Teheran between November 28 and December 1, 1943. Nevertheless, the great concentration of Soviet and British sentries had attracted the attention of the Iranian people and Churchill complains in his memoirs that the security measures were not adequate. Roosevelt agreed to stay in the Soviet embassy, where the meetings were held, in order not to have to travel through the streets of the city.

Beyond the plenary sessions, at which the three statesmen were surrounded by all their advisers, there were three meetings between Roosevelt and Stalin, on November 28 after the President's arrival and again on November 29 and December 1. At these meetings only the interpreters Pavlov and Charles Bohlen were present. Churchill wanted to have a private meeting with the President but he was refused because Roosevelt did not want to give the Russians the impression of prior agreement between the United States and Great Britain. At meals the conversation was freer, more relaxed and accompanied by toasts, sometimes amusing in tone. Only one sharp exchange occurred, between Stalin and Churchill, when Stalin spoke of the necessity to shoot 50,000 German officers. Roosevelt calmed Churchill. The military experts met separately, but Stalin opposed the idea of meetings between the foreign ministers, Eden, Molotov, and, in Hull's absence, Hopkins.

On December 2 Roosevelt told American soldiers guarding a military base at Amirabad, Iran, which protected transports en route to the Soviet Union: "I came here . . . to try to do two things: the first was to lay the military plans for cooperation between the three nations looking toward the winning of the war just just as fast as we possibly can . . . The other purpose was to talk over world conditions after the war." [12] These were indeed the two most important aspects of the talks. Although strategic and political questions were constantly overlapping, it is better to analyze them separately.

On the strategic level, Stalin's only interest was in finding out if operation Overlord would surely take place in the spring of 1944 as planned. He was able to secure a formal commitment to this effect. He wanted to know who would command it and Roosevelt promised to let him know soon. Stalin committed himself to launching a simultaneous offensive on the eastern front.

The real dispute was between Churchill and Roosevelt. In his memoirs Churchill defends himself against the charge that he tried to avoid operation Overlord and there is no doubt that he is sincere. In fact, there was disagreement on two points. First, in the Far East, the Prime Minister did not favor the Burma operation, which included landings on the coast, and wanted instead to use the thirty or forty landing barges the Burma operation would require in the Mediterranean. Just at the moment when the battle of the Atlantic could be said to be won—the rate of the destruction of German submarines by the Allies had become overwhelming—the bottleneck was no longer tonnage but the number of landing craft, especially LST's, each of which could transport forty tanks.

Churchill had an excellent argument in that Stalin repeated in Teheran his Moscow statement of intention to enter the war against Japan as soon as Germany was defeated. Under the circumstances, why should the Allies commit themselves to a difficult operation in the jungles of Burma for the sole prospect—if the campaign succeeded —of reopening the not very effective Burma Road, when the Red Army could strike much more effective blows? Roosevelt, the champion of China, was determined to launch the Far Eastern operation, however, and American military men did not hesitate to imply that the British were much less interested in rapid victory than in the preservation of their empire after the war.

The second subject of disagreement was the Mediterranean. Everyone agreed that Overlord should be accompanied by simultaneous operations in southern Europe. One of these was to be an offensive in Italy as far north as a line from Pisa to Rimini—the illusion persisted that Rome would be taken in the near future—and the other operation would be either landings in the south of France (operation Anvil) or a breakthrough from northeastern Italy, using the gap from Ljubljana to Vienna. Churchill much preferred the second alternative, and Roosevelt had proposed this solution in Cairo even before the Prime Minister had mentioned it. Anvil and a breakthrough toward Vienna could not be carried out at the same time, however. Since their arrival in Teheran the American military chiefs had persuaded the President to favor Anvil for technical reasons and Stalin hoped really to convince him.

We still do not know whether there was an ulterior political motive behind Churchill's desire to advance into Central Europe, namely to get there before the Russians, and whether Stalin did not also have his own ulterior motives in opposing it. Roosevelt took it as a question of tactics and refused to believe that the Russians had

sinister intentions in the matter. Churchill, still faithful to his "peripheral" strategy, visualized other Mediterranean operations, such as the
reconquest of the Dodecanese and Aegean islands, with the use of landing craft brought from the Gulf of Bengal. Thus Turkey could be
brought into the war and landings could be made in the Balkans, with
or without the Turks, to help the Greek Resistance and Tito. Forces
not needed in the eastern Mediterranean could be used in this way.
The question was, however, could these plans be carried out without
weakening operation Anvil? Neither Stalin nor Roosevelt thought so
and neither favored the Balkan expedition. Churchill writes, "I could
have gained Stalin, but the President was oppressed by the prejudices
of his military advisers, and drifted to and fro in the argument, with
the result that the whole of these subsidiary but gleaming opportunities were cast aside unused." [13]

On the political plane the discussions were friendly, and this very
cordiality threatened to obscure the concrete problem. In any case, it
was primarily a matter of exchanging views rather than of making
important decisions. Roosevelt's tactics were to introduce the Russians as "new members of the family circle," as he put it in his opening speech.[14] It seemed to him worthwhile to make special concessions to the Russians in order to give them confidence and show that
the Western Allies understood their concerns and their need of security. Roosevelt himself, therefore, took the initiative in offering
them warm water ports—Dairen and Port Arthur in southern Manchuria—on lease. This would be to revert to the situation which had
prevailed before 1905. (It is possible that Roosevelt had obtained
prior agreement to this concession from Chiang Kai-shek at Cairo.)
The Russians were also offered completely free access to the Dardanelles and the internationalization of the Kiel Canal.

When Stalin asked for still further territorial concessions, saying
that he would submit a list of his claims later, Roosevelt granted
almost everything. In Finland, for example, Stalin announced that
he had no intention of annexing the whole country but that he
wanted to keep the frontiers of March 1940 and a base at Viipuri
and either Hangö in the south or Petsamo in the north. Roosevelt
conceded Petsamo without argument. The British and Americans
tried to offer their good offices to arrange the withdrawal of Finland
from the war. Stalin replied that discussions had already begun but
that since the Finns were claiming their 1939 frontiers there was no

point in continuing them. When he demanded that Finland pay reparations amounting to 50 percent of the damages, Roosevelt did no more than express some timid reservations on the subject.

Further south, Russia had designs on the northern part of East Prussia, especially the city of Königsberg, and Roosevelt did not object. On the other hand, Stalin's desire to keep the three Baltic countries, which he said had expressed their wish to be incorporated into the Soviet Union, did not meet with explicit approval. Roosevelt wanted a plebiscite held, although he recognized that there was little chance of obtaining it.

The Anglo-American attempt to re-establish diplomatic relations between the Soviet Union and the Polish government-in-exile in London met with a very firm rejection by Stalin, who claimed that he was friendly to the Poles and wanted to see a restored Poland which would be friendly to the Soviet Union. He did not, however, consider that the London Poles represented Poland. He thought, or pretended to think, that they were a sort of "gang of thieves" more or less allied to Nazi Germany. He wanted the Polish frontiers to be restored to the status of 1939. When he claimed that this coincided with the Curzon Line Eden protested, but Roosevelt was ready to make many concessions and especially to allow Russia to keep Lvov. No decision was made on this subject. Churchill brought pressure on the Americans to allow Poland to expand to the West, to the Oder-Neisse Line. It should be said that animosity toward Germany was so great that it was not easy to apply the principle of national self-determination to the Germans. This was far from the "just peace" of Wilson.

Roosevelt had a plan for Germany: to divide her into five states and two international zones. The five states would be: a reduced and isolated Prussia; Hanover and northwest Germany; Saxony; Hesse-Darmstadt, Hesse-Cassel, and the Rhineland; Bavaria, Baden, and Württemberg. The two internationalized zones would be the Kiel Canal and the Hanseatic ports, especially Hamburg; and the Ruhr and Saar. In place of Roosevelt's plan, Churchill proposed another. He agreed that Prussia should be isolated and reduced because he considered it the source of German nationalism. Prussia should be severely treated. South Germany, on the other hand, which was less warlike, could be attached to a sort of Danubian confederation.

Stalin expressed no opinion beyond supporting the necessity of dismembering Germany, which seemed to liberate the British and Americans from the fear that Russia would pose as the champion of German unification. As between the two plans Stalin leaned toward Roosevelt's. Obviously opposed to a large and powerful Danubian confederation and preferring a division which would give Russia an uncontested domination of the continent, he pretended to believe that the President's plan of dismemberment was viable. He said that the south Germans were just as eager on the fighting front as the Prussians; indeed, only the Austrians had shown themselves opposed to war. Roosevelt accepted the argument and the independence of Austria was agreed upon by all three statesmen.

There was much less discussion of other regions of the world. Stalin gave his consent to the declaration on China and Japan, which had been prepared at Cairo and published on December 2. This stated that the Allies would dismember the vast Japanese Empire. China, transformed into a great power, at least nominally, by Roosevelt, would recover all its former territories then occupied by the Japanese, including Manchuria, Formosa, and the Pescadores. Korea would become independent after the war. The Big Three issued another declaration about Iran, which they were occupying with military forces, and submitted it to the Shah. They promised to maintain Iran's territorial integrity and sovereignty after the war and to give her economic aid. They recognized Iran's contribution to the war.

In his first meeting with Stalin after his arrival, Roosevelt set forth his ideas about the independence of colonies and the establishment of United Nations' trusteeship. Stalin could not help but subscribe to a plan which supported Soviet theory and which also tended to extend Russian influence into many regions. The President suggested that these problems, especially in relation to India, not be discussed with Churchill. This was agreed upon.

It was indirectly referred to, however, in discussions of the future international organization. Here again Roosevelt took the initiative. He explained his plan of an association composed of a general assembly of all the member nations, a council of ten nations, and the four "policemen." Stalin did not like the idea. Like Churchill, he would have preferred regional councils, one for Europe, another for the Far East (Churchill proposed a third for the Americas), on which the Big Three would be represented. Stalin did not want China to be included among the great powers and he claimed that the smaller nations would not like the system. Without doubt the division of Europe to which he aspired would be easier to accomplish if the Soviets were freer to act.

Roosevelt opposed regional councils on the grounds that the Senate would never allow the United States to undertake such specific responsibilities in Europe. He conceived of any intervention by an American police force in Europe merely in terms of sea and air power. This presupposed bases, and the plan of a string of bases for the world police force was brought up again. Stalin pretended to believe that France would follow Pétain rather than De Gaulle and stressed the necessity of converting at least Dakar and Bizerte into international bases. The only precise point obtained by Roosevelt in this whole matter was Stalin's abandonment, at the end of the conference, of the plan of regional councils.

The communiqué published at the close of the conference reflects the atmosphere of relative confidence which had prevailed. "We express our determination that our nations shall work together in war and in the peace that will follow . . . We are sure that our concord will make an enduring peace. We came here in hope and determination. We leave here friends, in fact, in spirit and in purpose." All told, the nature of the discussions, which were overall surveys producing few specific decisions, had fostered the development of a real cordiality. "If there was a high point in Roosevelt's career," says Sherwood, "I think it occurred at the end of the Teheran Conference." [15] Faced with Churchill, the brilliant debater and Stalin, stubborn and crude, "Roosevelt sat in the middle, by common consent the moderator, arbitrator . . . His contributions to the conversation were infrequent and sometimes annoyingly irrelevant, but it appears time and again that it was he who spoke the last word." [16]

From Teheran, with the full agreement of the Russians, Roosevelt and Churchill went back to Cairo to meet the Turkish leaders, President Inönü and Foreign Minister Menemendjoglu. The meetings, which took place between December 4 and 6, achieved nothing. Churchill was obviously most eager to convert the Turks, because their participation in the war would lead to the execution of his plan in the eastern Mediterranean, but the British setback in the Dodecanese in September had convinced the Turks that Germany was still very dangerous. Neutrality still seemed advantageous to them. They preferred to hold their power in reserve for the postwar period because they feared possible Russian claims. The British promise of aid and the Soviet promise not to permit the Bulgarians to attack Turkey left them unconvinced, as did the Allied threat to treat them in the future not as allies but as neutrals. Were they not really neutral, in spite of their alliance with Great Britain? The second Cairo Conference was thus a total failure, but Roosevelt did not seem to be unduly troubled by the fact.

It was at Cairo that Roosevelt, disregarding the pressure of Stimson, Hopkins, and many military men, as well as Stalin's clearly expressed preference, decided to appoint Eisenhower instead of Marshall as commander-in-chief of operation Overlord.

Strategic and Political Aspects of the Invasion of France

Between the Teheran Conference in December 1943 and June 1944, after the landings in France, American diplomacy remained extremely cautious, in contrast to British diplomacy. For the Americans everything was subordinated to the preparations for the great enterprise; other matters seemed relatively unimportant. The correspondence between Roosevelt and Stalin, very friendly in tone, dealt, with few exceptions, with secondary matters, such as the transfer of some Italian ships to the Soviet Union and the Soviet refusal to take part in the conference of the International Labor Organization.

Two serious problems did arise in this period, however. One was created by the refusal of the Polish government-in-exile to accept territorial concessions in relation to Poland's eastern frontier. Stalin still refused to recognize this government of "reactionaries" and "Hitlerites," as he described them. The other was the problem of Greece, where Communist and non-Communist guerillas were fighting bitterly. A Greek fleet and a Greek brigade (stationed in Egypt) rose in mutiny against the King's authority. Churchill was feverishly concerned with both Poland and Greece, while Roosevelt remained virtually passive. When the Greek rebels were encircled, under instructions from Churchill, Roosevelt confined himself, in a letter of April 18, 1944, to a pious hope: "I join with you in a hope that your line of action toward the problem may succeed in bringing the Greeks back into the Allied camp and to participation against the barbarians that will be worthy of the traditions established by the heroes of Greek history." [17]

Great Britain redoubled its efforts, both in London and in Moscow, to reconcile the London Poles with the Soviets. Averell Harriman, representing the United States, was merely instructed to follow the negotiations and to encourage them. Of twenty-six letters from Roosevelt to Stalin between January 1 and June 19, only four dealt with the Polish question and two of these dealt with the visit of two Poles who were private citizens of the United States, Professor Oscar Lange and Father Orlemanski. The other two, while urging Stalin to take a conciliatory attitude, were full of reservations, almost excuses.

Roosevelt obviously wanted to maintain good Soviet-American relations at all costs and was not much bothered by a problem which was, nonetheless, capable of disrupting those relations in a very short time. On February 10 he wrote to Stalin, "I quite understand your desire to treat only with a Polish Government in which you can trust . . . but I hope with all my heart that nothing will be done while this problem is still unresolved which might transform this particular question into a source of difficulty on the more general plane of future international cooperation."[18] On June 18 the President wrote to Stalin to tell him that he had been obliged to receive Mikolajczyk, the President of the Polish government. "This visit is not a part of any attempt on my part to interfere in the settlement of the differences which separate the Polish Government-in-exile and the Soviet Government."[19] Roosevelt asked the Soviets to adopt a conciliatory attitude but carefully avoided taking sides himself.

At the same time, when General Eisenhower, who had arrived in London on January 14, was setting up the Supreme Headquarters, Allied Expeditionary Force in Europe (SHAEF), Roosevelt made an effort to prevent any modification of the invasion plans by Churchill, who was too active in his eyes. The Anzio landings, supposed to hasten the fall of Rome, were a failure partly because the Allied forces could not break through the German lines. Not until a new offensive, launched on May 11 under Field Marshal Alexander, were the German lines pierced. The Italian capital fell to the Allies on June 4. This was an appreciable delay. There was another delay caused by tactical and logistic considerations. Overlord was supposed to take place in May 1944. Eisenhower decided that five divisions, rather than three as planned, would be required on the first day. To have a real sufficiency of transport for the landings, an additional month of production seemed essential. This month would also make it possible "to bomb without limit the vital economic centers in France." [20] The combined chiefs of staff, therefore, accepted Eisenhower's proposal to fix D Day for the time of the new moon in June.

These delays caused Churchill to resume his attempt to have the Italian campaign extended by a penetration toward Ljubljana, which would require the cancellation of operation Anvil in southern France. It was indeed necessary, in the interests of Overlord, to commandeer certain supplementary equipment which had originally been assigned to Anvil. Churchill wanted to meet Roosevelt in early April in Bermuda to persuade him to his own point of view. Roosevelt refused; he was tired and did not want to have to cope with the Prime Minister's verbal gymnastics. Churchill then wrote to General Marshall on April 16 that the offensive which was soon to be launched in Italy must be pushed to the limit. "Do me the favor of allowing me to remind you that the situation has greatly changed since Teheran." [21] A compromise was finally agreed upon when it was decided to delay operation Anvil at least until July 15.

The invasion, which General Eisenhower delayed a day because of bad weather, took place on June 6, 1944. We shall not describe here what General Eisenhower himself has called "a whole host." [22] The Germans were taken completely by surprise, even as to the location of the operation. The Allies succeeded in giving them the impression that it would take place in the *département* of the Pas-de-Calais. In fact, the action was in three other places. The British landed to the east of Arromanches; and the Americans, to the west (Omaha Beach, where there was violent resistance) and on the southeast coast of the Cotentin Peninsula (Utah Beach). Parachutists had landed in the region of Sainte-Mère-Eglise. The first objective, after penetration of the German defenses on the beaches, was to capture the port of Cherbourg. This was accomplished on June 26, after hard fighting. The Germans had meanwhile sent the first V-1 attack against the British on June 12.

According to Eisenhower, by July 4 about one million men had landed (thirteen American divisions, eleven British, and one Canadian) as well as 566,648 tons of supplies and 171,532 vehicles. On July 25 the drive toward Avranches in the Cotentin began; by August 1 it had succeeded. Between August 1 and 12 Brittany was "cleaned up" with the exception of the "pockets" of Brest, Lorient, and Saint-Nazaire.

During the first two weeks in August Eisenhower had to argue every inch of the way for retention of operation Anvil.

Although I never heard him say so, I felt that the Prime Minister's real concern was possibly of a political rather than a military nature. He may have thought that a postwar situation which would see the Western Allies posted in great strength in the Balkans would be far more effective in producing a stable post-hostilities world than if the Russian armies should be the ones to occupy that region . . . I am quite certain that no experienced soldier would question the wisdom, strictly from the military viewpoint, of adhering to the plan for attacking southern France.[23]

Eisenhower suggested to Churchill that he discuss such political decisions with the President. Alexander, on the other hand, would have preferred the continuation of the Italian campaign. On June 29 Roosevelt officially came out for the retention of Anvil. "The exploitation of *Overlord*, our victorious advances in Italy, an early assault on southern France, combined with the Soviet drives to the west—all as envisaged at Teheran—will most surely serve to realize our object —the unconditional surrender of Germany." He added, in the same letter, "I agree that the political considerations you mention are important factors, but military operations based thereon must be definitely secondary to the primary operation of striking at the heart of Germany." [24]

This text is of incalculable importance in showing the point to which unconditional surrender overrode in the mind of the President Clausewitz's principle that war is the continuation of politics by other means. The future of the world might have been changed if Roosevelt had listened to the British Prime Minister instead of to Hopkins and his chiefs of staff. South African Field Marshal Smuts saw the problem clearly when he wrote to Churchill on August 30, "please do not let strategy absorb all your attention to the damage of the greater issue now looming up. From now on it would be wise to keep a very close eye on all matters bearing on the future settlement of Europe. This is the crucial issue on which the future of the world for generations will depend." [25]

On August 8 Roosevelt reiterated his point of view forcefully and on August 15 landings were made in southern France. On August 25 and 26 General De Gaulle made his triumphal entry into Paris. By autumn Belgium and France were almost entirely liberated.

The reconquest of Europe progressed by great strides. The Russian offensive, which began on June 21 against the Finns and on June 23 against the Germans, was successful everywhere. The Red Army invaded Poland, Rumania, then Bulgaria and Hungary; soon after that Germany itself. In Italy Marshal Alexander's troops were stopped at the "Gothic Line" (Pisa-Rimini) at the end of the summer.

This liberation of friendly countries and conquest of Axis satellites forced into the open the political problems which American diplomacy had so unwisely bypassed. In Western Europe—France and Italy—there was a certain degree of tension between the Americans and the British. In Eastern Europe new problems increasingly revealed the extent of the gulf which separated the United States and Britain from the Soviet Union. Let us examine this matter from the point of view of American policy up to October 1944.

In France the urgent problem was to decide whether to recognize the French Committee of National Liberation (which had become the Provisional Government of the French Republic on June 1, 1944) as a provisional civilian authority in liberated France. On November 8, 1943, De Gaulle had succeeded in eliminating Giraud—who had, incidently, been a disappointment to the Americans—and he had become the sole chairman. The British were more and more convinced that De Gaulle should be trusted. This was also the opinion of Eisenhower, who had tried in January 1944 to convince Roosevelt that it was necessary to reach an agreement with De Gaulle. Roosevelt had refused, but, even so, a certain evolution was taking place in United States policy. In March Eisenhower was authorized to consult with the committee. On April 9, Hull himself, with the agreement of the President, declared, "We are inclined to see the French Committee of National Liberation increase its leadership in establishing law and order under the Allied Commander-in-Chief." [26] De Gaulle was invited to London to be briefed on the eve of the invasion and he protested that the invitation came so late. On June 14 Stimson tried to convince Roosevelt that the provisional government should be recognized, but Roosevelt, Stimson says, "believes that de Gaulle will crumple and that the British supporters of de Gaulle will be confounded by the course of events." [27]

The general's visit to Washington between July 6 and 11 began to open the President's eyes, and the triumphal entry into Paris of the man who had launched the appeal of June 18, 1940, dramatically showed Roosevelt that he had been mistaken for four years. On

August 26 General Eisenhower said in a letter to General Koenig: "I have been authorized to deal with the French Committee of National Liberation as the *de facto* authority in France, which will assume the leadership and responsibility for the administration of the liberated areas of France." [28] Recognition de jure was delayed until October 23, 1944.

In Italy, on the previous November 10, General Eisenhower had announced the creation of a control commission, purely advisory, on which Vishinsky represented Russia. On March 14, 1944, without notifying the Western Allies, the Soviet Union announced that it was about to exchange diplomatic representatives with the Badoglio government. This obliged Great Britain and the United States to send diplomatic representatives to Rome. Alexander Kirk represented the United States.

Since October 1943 the Americans and the British had been disagreeing about Italian policy, with the Americans demanding the abdication of the King and the re-organization of the government and Churchill opposing it energetically. The slowness of the Allied military advance had allowed the resolution of this difficulty to be postponed. The Soviet initiative had in no way made Churchill modify his "royalist" inclination, which was a matter of principle. Roosevelt and Hull were averse to the maintenance of these "survivals of Fascism" and on April 11, 1944 Murphy was told to ask for the abdication of Victor Emmanuel. The King refused but he consented to retire and appoint his son, Umberto, as lieutenant general of the kingdom.

The Americans accepted the compromise and on April 24 Badoglio formed a new government, which included the Communist leader Togliatti, Count Sforza—an American protégé detested by Churchill —and the philosopher and historian Benedetto Croce. After the fall of Rome Bonomi succeeded Badoglio and Sforza became Foreign Minister. There is no doubt that this change was brought about by a unilateral initiative of the United States. Churchill complained of it to Stalin who, strangely, replied that he regretted Badoglio's departure.

Roosevelt and Churchill announced in Hyde Park on September 26 that they would gradually transfer civilian administration to the Italian government. The International Allied Control Commission became the Inter-Allied Commission. In Hull's words, finding that

Italy "after more than two decades of Fascist domination had made gratifying progress toward embracing . . . democracy," [29] the United States decided on October 26 to exchange ambassadors with Italy, three days after a similar decision with regard to France.

We will not examine separately the relations of the United States with the small states of Eastern and Southeastern Europe. The essential point is that between August and October the former Axis partners all asked for an armistice on the basis of previous negotiations and, with the exception of Hungary, were quickly granted it on terms proposed by the Soviets. In Allied or occupied countries, and especially in Germany, Yugoslavia, and Poland, the United States continued to take a less active part than the British, whose policy the Americans merely supported. Elsewhere a very serious question, which had been there right along but which Roosevelt and Hull had not taken seriously—despite warnings from their representatives in Moscow—broke into the open and could no longer be avoided, namely, what policy would the Soviet Union follow toward countries invaded by the Red Army, or even toward the Communist movements in Greece, Yugoslavia, and Italy?

Churchill posed the problem clearly on May 4, 1944. "Will we accept the Communization of the Balkans and perhaps of Italy?" Eden, the next day, suggested to Russian ambassador Gusev an agreement by which the British would settle the situation in Greece and the Soviet Union the situation in Rumania. Gusev had accepted on condition that the United States also agree. Hull, however, detecting in the plan the establishment of the detested spheres of influence, condemned in the Moscow Declaration, had protested indignantly. Churchill then put it to Roosevelt on May 31 that it was the only practical solution. Roosevelt took advantage of Hull's absence to agree, without consulting the Secretary of State, "on condition that it be clearly shown that we are not establishing spheres of influence for after the war." At the same time the State Department sent a message from Hull to the British saying exactly the opposite. This caused some confusion. Churchill, following Roosevelt's lead, in a letter to Stalin on July 11 stressed the temporary nature of the arrangement.

In the summer of 1944 the United States government maintained its inflexible position. "It refused," says Feis, "not only any agreement dividing the world or any part of it into separate spheres of influence, but also any military plans whose object was to influence the future balance of power or prestige." [30] We are reminded here of the discussions about Churchill's plan for an invasion of the Balkans. On the one hand, Roosevelt did not believe it was possible to stop the Russians if they really wanted to establish domination in Eastern Europe; on the other hand, he persisted in the idea that it was essential to trust the Soviets.

Even the Polish question did not convince Roosevelt that from then on a firmer attitude toward the Soviets was required. After Mikolajczyk's trip to Washington (June 7–14, 1944), Roosevelt had strongly urged the Polish leader to go to Moscow and he had taken diplomatic action, through Averell Harriman, to get Stalin to invite him. He also wrote a personal letter to Stalin on June 17 to this effect. Stalin showed great reluctance. Furthermore, on July 21 at Chelm, behind the front, the pro-Communist Polish National Council had established a Committee of National Liberation under the chairmanship of Boleslaw Bierut.

Churchill, who found the situation increasingly disturbing, finally succeeded in persuading Stalin to receive Mikolajczyk in Moscow. He arrived on July 30. The following day 35,000 members of the Polish Resistance in Warsaw rose against the Germans. The Red Army was near the city and the Poles expected it to help them. We know that the Red Army did not move and that the Poles fought alone until they were annihilated sixty-three days later. While Mikolajczyk negotiated in vain with the Polish Committee of Liberation, which had set up headquarters in Lublin, the British and Americans multiplied appeals to Stalin to help the embattled insurrectionists. They proposed to drop supplies by parachute, but it would be necessary for their planes to land behind Russian lines. Stalin refused, despite urgent requests from Harriman and Clark-Kerr to Molotov. Vishinsky declared that the Soviet government did not want to become involved in the "escapade" of Warsaw. Churchill convinced Roosevelt, who was very reluctant, to send a message on August 20, asking Stalin to reconsider. Upon receiving a negative response on the twenty-second, Roosevelt refused to send another message, as Churchill suggested, to find out what would be the Soviet attitude if Western planes were forced to land behind Russian lines. Once more, Roosevelt thought more in terms of military than political victory. He wrote the Prime Minister, "In my opinion it would not be useful to the general prosecution of the war for me to accept your proposition of a telegram to Stalin." [31]

The increasing difficulties made it necessary to have another conference, at least between Roosevelt and Churchill (on July 22 Stalin had refused for the time being Roosevelt's proposal for a meeting of the three leaders). This was the second Quebec meeting, called Octagon, which took place between September 13 and 16, 1944. It gave rise, said Churchill, to an "outburst of friendship." The two leaders congratulated each other on their superb success since the meetings at Teheran and Cairo. The discussions chiefly concerned the war against Germany—the difficulties involved were not to be minimized—and the "reconversion" of forces for the fight against Japan. Victory in the Pacific war was not expected to be achieved in less than 18 months after the defeat of Germany. We shall study these problems below. The worries created by the Soviet attitude were hardly mentioned. Churchill was satisfied to have the Americans accept the idea of a breakthrough toward Ljubljana and Vienna, "if the war lasts that long and if others don't get there before us." [32]

The Far East in 1944

The attention of the Russians and the British was almost entirely focused on Europe, as a result of their big strategic operations and the complexity of the political problems, but the Far East continued to draw considerable attention from the Americans in 1944.

Beginning in November 1943 a new phase of the Pacific war began, with a great American offensive, or rather with a double offensive: Admiral Nimitz' naval offensive in the Central Pacific against the Gilbert, Caroline, Mariana, and Bonin Islands and then against the Ryukyu Archipelago south of Japan, and the offensive of General MacArthur in the South Pacific, which, starting from the Solomon Islands and Australia, was directed at reconquest of all of New Guinea and then of the Philippines.

It had become possible to resume the offensive because the superiority of the United States on the sea and in the air was constantly growing. In two years the Americans had succeeded in preparing an impressive logistic operation. In the Pacific logistics became the key to the conduct of the war. For one thing, distances were three times as great as in the Atlantic. It was estimated that a cargo ship could make only three round trips a year, matériel from the west coast ports of the United States was transferred to Hawaii and from there to advanced bases which were farther away as the war progressed. "Bases" in this case meant very impressive installations—ports, airfields, encampments, storage facilities, radar facilities, and so forth —built from scratch by the Seabees on atolls or uninhabited islands.

The nature of these bases involved the transportation of a wide variety of goods, ranging from cement to pipes and from oil tanks to timber for construction, not just men and arms. During the first two years of the war the indispensable substructure had been created while the positions were being held. In a war of this kind improvisation will not do. Each operation required a long period of planning and perfect coordination between logistics and tactics. It can be said that it was a triumph of the American organizing genius. This type of war is like a colossal "business," in which the ability of a whole people showed itself in a striking manner. To describe it merely in these terms, however, would be to overlook the intensity of the fighting and the bravery and self-sacrifice of the troops involved. There were never very many of them, since the main land forces were concentrated in the European theater. Most of the Fleet was active in the Pacific, however.

It will suffice to suggest the outlines of the two major offensives. Admiral Nimitz' strategy was to proceed by jumps from island to island, to take one island in each archipelago by surprise attack, and then to establish the base required for the next jump, without taking time to clean up the rest of the archipelago.

The first jump put the Americans in a position to take Tarawa and Makin in the Gilbert Islands, a necessary base for the approach to the Marshalls and the Carolines. The second jump included taking over a large part of the Marshalls, especially Kwajalein and Eniwetok (January 30–February 20, 1944). In the same month of February Admiral Spruance, commander of the Fifth Fleet, who was in charge of these operations, made a surprise naval-air attack on the great base of Truk in the Carolines. It was a "Pearl Harbor" in reverse, with enormous Japanese losses. From this time on the United States naval superiority was incontestable.

The next objective was the Marianas. On June 11, three divisions landed on Saipan, which fell to the Americans on July 4 after fierce fighting. Simultaneously, a huge naval-air battle, the Battle of the

Philippine Sea, was taking place. A powerful Japanese fleet, leaving the Philippines to go to the aid of Japanese forces in the Marianas, was intercepted by Admiral Spruance's fleet and on June 19 and 20 the Japanese lost several hundred planes and suffered heavy naval losses: three carriers were sunk and three more damaged, along with many other ships. The Japanese defeats at Saipan and in the Philippine Sea had an important political result. On July 19 the Tojo cabinet, which was responsible for the war, had to resign. Between July and November two other islands in the Marianas, Guam and Tinian, were taken despite a very strong defense by the Japanese. Guam was a former United States possession lost after Pearl Harbor.

The next jump involved penetration of the Carolines and the Palaus and the conquest of the small islands of Angaur and Peleliu, so as to isolate Truk, which was the main Japanese base. Truk could then be kept under surveillance and neutralized.

In the South Pacific General MacArthur, with the Seventh Fleet of Admiral Kinkaid under his command, planned to attack the Philippines, beginning with the island of Leyte. Admiral Nimitz suggested instead an attack on Formosa to be followed by an attack on the mainland of China. At first Roosevelt leaned toward this plan, but when he went to Pearl Harbor on July 15 to confer with Nimitz and MacArthur, he found MacArthur's arguments persuasive and chose the reconquest of the Philippines. The plan was approved by the joint chiefs at the second Quebec Conference, and landings began on October 17, 1944. The Japanese, for whom the Philippines were essential, decided to stake their all. They hastily sent three squadrons, which were crippled one after another. The first, which had come from Singapore, was entirely destroyed between October 23 and 26, except for one destroyer. Two battleships, three cruisers, and several other ships were sunk, while the Americans suffered only the damage of one destroyer. The second squadron, which came from Indochina, was engaged between October 24 and 26. It managed to sink two American destroyers and two carrier escorts and to damage three others, but it lost a new battleship of 40,000 tons, and four others were hit by bombs. Three cruisers were also lost. The third squadron came from Formosa and was attacked on October 25. It destroyed one American light carrier but lost four of its own as well as a cruiser. This was not the end of the Japanese Fleet but the Fleet was reduced almost exclusively to small units, and a large proportion of Japanese air power had been destroyed.

The clean-up operations on Leyte lasted for several months, but as early as January 9, 1945, the Americans landed—to the complete surprise of the Japanese—on Luzon. The landing was protected by a tremendous concentration of 850 ships. Manila, the capital, fell on February 23. The Bataan peninsula and the island of Corregidor, scenes of the last American resistance in May 1943, were then reconquered. The Americans had accomplished in two months what the Japanese had taken four months to do at the start of the war.

The next steps were the reconquest of Iwo Jima, "the Japanese Gibraltar" in the Bonin Islands, in February 1945, and then of Okinawa in the southern Ryukyus, between April 1 and June 21, 1945. These steps made possible an attack on Japan itself, already under heavy daily bombardment.

It is clear that the Japanese were certain to be defeated without Russian intervention and without use of the terrifying weapon which was being secretly prepared, the atomic bomb. Nevertheless, no one knew how the enemy would react when attacked at home. Japan's resistance had been very fierce and her soldiers were apt to kill themselves rather than surrender. On Leyte, for example, the Americans counted 74,000 dead and only 684 prisoners; at Guam 17,238 dead and 438 prisoners. American losses were lighter, but still too high. The very nature of the war thus had political implications. If the Soviet Union could be persuaded to intervene, would it not save hundreds of thousands of American lives? This was the serious problem faced by the United States government. We shall see the outcome when we discuss the Yalta Conference.

From the Pacific theater let us now turn to China and Southeast Asia. It will be remembered that at the Cairo Conference the Burma operation, so strongly supported by General Stilwell, was decided upon, together with British landings in South Burma. Chiang Kai-shek was very keen on these landings but did not wish large numbers of Chinese troops to take part in the continental attack, although he ended by giving in. When Roosevelt and Churchill returned to Cairo, after the Teheran Conference, Churchill, who had always been skeptical of the Burma campaign, showed that the naval operation, which was supposed to take off from the Andaman Islands, was impossible because of insufficient landing craft. The annoying thing was that this gave Chiang an excellent pretext to avoid Chinese participation in the land operations. Roosevelt, nevertheless, agreed. The combined chiefs of staff decided on December 6, 1943, that the landings would be delayed until the autumn of 1944 and that the landing craft would be sent to Europe.

No decision was made about the land operations. Roosevelt and Churchill left to the generalissimo the choice between two alternatives, a land operation in North Burma (Stilwell's plan) or an increase of the airlift over the Himalayas and a huge air offensive (Chennault's plan). One or the other of these courses might be followed until November 1944, the date set for the resumption of the land offensive. Roosevelt instructed Stilwell to explain the situation to Chiang. The generalissimo began by protesting—to magnify his own position— against "this radical change in policy and strategy." [33] In reality he was delighted because it permitted him not to commit his troops and also to request a loan of one billion dollars to bolster his weak financial position. He agreed, nevertheless, that Stilwell might begin operations with the Chinese troops already stationed in Assam.

The loan was refused on January 5. Roosevelt had begun to be irritated by the delaying tactics of the generalissimo. Secretary of the Treasury Morgenthau and United States ambassador in China Gauss thought the loan futile and undesirable. In their opinion it would be money down the drain. Let the Chinese attack the Japanese and then bring up the question of a loan. Stimson and Marshall thought that the United States should take a much firmer tone with Chiang and force him to put up a real fight. Only Hull favored a more lenient attitude, because he feared the fall of Chiang's regime and the substitution of a government much less helpful to the Allied cause.

As a result of Stilwell's efforts, there was a campaign in Burma in 1944, in which the persistent problem was to obtain Chiang's approval of the use of Chinese forces in Yunnan. Mountbatten, on instructions from Churchill, used only a limited number of troops at the start, but he joined Stilwell in bringing pressure on the generalissimo. In fact, in January and February 1944, the Chinese in Assam and a few thousand Americans, under the command of Stilwell, were able to march from Ledo to Mytkina, an important airfield in North Burma, which was finally taken by an airborne Anglo-Indian division under General Wingate. The Japanese counterattacked in March, further to the south, and invaded Indian territory. At that time Chiang, under the pressure of a letter from Roosevelt on March 7, agreed to send two and later three divisions from Yunnan. These were transported by air over the Himalayas. It was absolutely necessary to enlist the other divisions in Yunnan also and this was finally accomplished, largely as a result of Roosevelt's constant and insistent appeals to Chiang.

The Americans played a decisive role. They had trained the Chinese troops in Assam and Yunnan. They supplied the engineering specialists and Chennault's air force bombed Rangoon and other cities in Burma. Finally, it was under American direction that, despite the monsoon, the new Burma Road was rapidly constructed. This road went from Ledo in Assam to North Burma and then to China. It was later called, quite aptly, the "Stilwell Road." It was not to be opened until January 24, 1945. Meanwhile, the Anglo-Indian forces were active on the maritime front and in South Burma.

Chiang's hesitation in taking part in the Burma war was justified by a powerful Japanese offensive in South China, which began in May. Since 1941 the situation there had been relatively stable. In 1944 the Japanese, threatened with the loss of their sea lanes by the American offensive in the Pacific, made a desperate effort to eliminate China from the war. Their aim was to connect North China, in which they were fairly well established, with Shanghai and Indochina. They gradually achieved this aim and took over a large part of South China —to the point where they endangered the northern end of the Burma Road, then under reconstruction.

Although the operation furnished Chiang with an excuse to avoid sending troops to Burma, Roosevelt and his advisers were, nevertheless, increasingly disturbed by the inertia of the Chinese. Having witnessed the excellent quality of Chinese soldiers in Burma, they could not help thinking that the weakness lay in the Chinese command and the Kuomintang government. The idea that the only solution was to enlist the Chinese Communists against Japan began to gain support. This would necessitate an agreement between Chiang and the Communists, in one way or another. Why should the United States not use its influence to bring about such an agreement? The first step was to send some American officers to Yenan, Mao Tse-tung's capital, to study the situation. This policy was first advocated in January 1944 by John Davies, political adviser to General Stilwell. Hopkins, after studying the Davies memorandum, persuaded the President, with the aid of Leahy and Marshall, that it was worthwhile. Roosevelt took it up with Chiang on February 9.

The generalissimo was profoundly disturbed by this move. He thought the Communists were strongly supported by the Soviet Union and that their only aim was to overthrow him and to make all of China Communist. The only basis on which he was willing to negotiate with them was their total dissolution as a political party. He wished to maintain the Kuomintang as the only political party, at least for the time being. He would admit Communist generals into a military council if their armies were under his command. On February 22, therefore, he sent an evasive answer to Roosevelt. The President did not dare to send a military mission to Yenan, as Stilwell, Stimson, Marshall, and the other military leaders wanted, and the matter dragged along with no results.

In May the Japanese offensive reopened the question. The Japanese posed a special threat to the American airfields under General Chennault's command. In the summer the Japanese advanced dangerously near to Kunming, the terminal point of the airlift, Hump. The matter became urgent. Roosevelt then decided to undertake two diplomatic initiatives. On the one hand, he asked Harriman to discuss with Stalin the question of Chiang and the Communists. The interview took place on June 10, four days after the landings in France. Stalin repeated what he had conceded at Teheran, namely, that Chiang alone could unify China, but he did not conceal his opinion that it was a weak solution. As for the Communists, he declared that they were not real Communists, and disclaimed them. He dismissed them with the bizarre expression "margarine Communists"—no doubt in contrast to the "real butter" of Soviet Communism. All summer long Stalin and Molotov, whether sincerely or not, cultivated the impression that they had given to the Americans, namely that the Soviet Union was not interested in what happened in China and felt no connection with Mao Tse-tung.

Roosevelt's second move was to send Vice President Henry Wallace on a special mission to Chiang. The Vice President traveled by way of eastern Siberia and Outer Mongolia, arriving in Chungking on June 21 with a team of experts, of whom the best known was Owen Lattimore. Wallace had a tendency, which later became clear, to minimize the ideological differences between the Soviets and the Americans. He therefore made an ardent plea for an understanding between the generalissimo and Mao Tse-tung. But he was knocking his head against a stone wall. Chiang told him that the Communists were satellites of Russia, that they would not be effective in the fight against Japan and that the United States had fallen victim to their propaganda. He gave in on three points, however. He agreed to the plan to send an American military mission to visit the Chinese Communists; he asked Roosevelt to mediate between him and the Communists in the name of the United States; and he suggested that Roosevelt arrange for him to meet Stalin, in order to clarify relations between the Soviet Union and China. The generalissimo also solicited an increase in American aid and took occasion to say that he "lacked confidence in General Stilwell." [34] Basically, he held it against Stilwell that the American general would not obey him, while Stilwell thought that China could not be saved by Chiang's passive policy of waiting. Wallace left via Kunming on January 26. In a telegram giving his impressions to Roosevelt, he suggested that the President send a personal representative to Chiang.

The situation in China continued to worsen after the Wallace mission and American anxiety became acute. Stimson and the military leaders constantly urged the President to take a stiffer line with Chiang. They thought that the only hope lay in making Stilwell commander-in-chief of the Chinese Army, including, if possible, the Communists. On July 6 Roosevelt gave in and for the first time he took a firm tone with Chiang. He sent him a memorandum, drawn up by the joint chiefs, that sounded like an ultimatum. In order to avoid total disaster, he asked the generalissimo to appoint Stilwell commander-in-chief of all operations against the Japanese, with the right to equip and use all the Chinese forces—this clearly meant that the Communists were to be included. On July 8 Chiang replied that he would study the question and asked again that the President send a personal envoy. He let it be known that he would not appoint Stilwell if the Communists were to be included. Finally, still trying to avoid Communist participation, he asked that the distribution of lend-lease supplies be entrusted to himself alone.

Roosevelt received this reply when he was about to meet Admiral Nimitz and General MacArthur at Pearl Harbor. He yielded to

Chiang's first wish and named General Patrick J. Hurley as his personal representative. For the rest, he continued his firm policy, which was opposed to the delaying tactics of the generalissimo.

Hurley went first to Moscow, where he also was told that the Soviet Union was not associated with the Chinese Communists, and then to Chungking, arriving on September 7, 1944. He immediately tried to convince Chiang of the necessity to appoint Stilwell as commander-in-chief. Stilwell, seeing the situation deteriorate from day to day, wrote to General Marshall on September 15 begging him to make a decision. Marshall was at the time in Quebec with the President. The combined chiefs were in the process of making final plans for the vast operations against Japan, that is, the attack on the Philippines and the increased effort to reopen the Burma Road. Chiang had just decided to withdraw the Chinese forces from North Burma—"a stupid decision" wrote Stilwell—and Marshall convinced Roosevelt that he should oppose it. On September 16 Roosevelt wrote to the generalissimo that he must absolutely (1) reinforce Chinese troops in Burma and (2) place Stilwell in command of all his forces with no restrictions. If he did not, all the immense effort of both Chinese and American armies in recent years would have been in vain.

When Stilwell received this message he enjoyed his triumph; he wanted to give it to Chiang in person. Chiang confined himself to the remark, "I understand." Chiang, according to Hurley, reacted "as if he had been hit in the solar plexus." Did this mean success for Stilwell? No. Chiang could not accept what he regarded as a personal humiliation. His representative in Washington, Kung, met with Hopkins and persuaded him that Stilwell's personality made the whole thing impossible. At that point pressure was brought on Roosevelt from two sources. One was that of the State Department, Hopkins, and, in the end, Hurley, all of whom thought that the most important thing was to support Chiang and that, therefore, the United States should defer to his desire to get rid of Stilwell. The other pressure was that of Stimson and Marshall, who thought that a strong stand was the only solution and that only Stilwell could save the military situation. They also thought the United States should threaten to cut off Chiang's supplies. Roosevelt chose the first solution. On October 18 he wrote to Chiang that he was replacing Stilwell by General

Wedemeyer, but that he did not wish him to take command of all the Chinese forces.

The following months saw continued success for the Japanese offensive. The decision taken at Pearl Harbor, not to land in China for the time being, combined with the decision to give up a Chinese counteroffensive under the only man capable of organizing it, would later have very important consequences. China was saved, but only by American successes in the Pacific. The Japanese began to withdraw in April 1945, but the Chinese Nationalists were not ready to re-occupy the territories evacuated, which allowed the Communists to extend their power greatly.

Obviously everything might have been different had there been an understanding betwen Chiang and the Communists. Hurley tried to bring this about by endless activity, but perhaps with too much optimism. Beginning in the autumn of 1944, in fact, the Soviet Union ceased to be "uninterested" in China. What would happen if Russia took a hand in the maneuvers of the Chinese Communists? It seemed certain that it would lead to a civil war in which Americans and Russians would fight through intermediaries. This would be the ruin of the great alliance, based on mutual confidence, in which Roosevelt thought the hope of the world lay. In Asia as in Europe, this alliance was already seriously compromised.

Chapter XV

Yalta and the Death of Roosevelt

American Hesitations and the Malta Meeting

Roosevelt wrote to Stalin on October 4, 1944, "I am sure you understand that in this total war there is literally not a single question, political or military, in which the United States is not interested. I am firmly convinced that we three and only we three can find solutions to questions that are still unresolved." [1]

He was expressing his apprehension. Churchill was about to meet Stalin in Moscow, after Stalin had turned down Roosevelt's suggestion to hold a Big Three meeting in the Hague, and the American President was kept at home by the election. Stalin, for his part, anticipated a final meeting on the Russian coast of the Black Sea and Roosevelt was worried that his two partners—too much inclined toward imperialism for his taste—would make some prior agreements. Only the obligation to deliver his annual message to Congress made him delay the Big Three meeting until early in the year 1945. Because of the elections in the United States and this delay, the autumn of 1944 was a period of little activity in United States foreign policy.

Churchill was in Moscow from October 9 to 18. At first Roosevelt had considered the possibility of his speaking for the United States also, but Hopkins warned him against it. He also refused to send Stettinius, acting Secretary of State during Hull's illness, or General Marshall. He asked only that Harriman be present at the talks, without the power to make decisions. Harriman was not present when Churchill and Stalin reached a rather vague agreement that after the war the Soviets would exert the chief influence in Rumania and Bulgaria, Great Britain would be dominant in Greece, and Yugoslavia and Hungary would be shared equally. Roosevelt, who heard of this without really being told, and who was opposed, as we have seen, to all spheres of influence, merely replied: "At the present time my active interest in the Balkan area is that there be taken such steps as are practicable to insure against the Balkans getting into an international war in the future." [2]

One of the reasons for the relative paralysis of American policy was the departure of Cordell Hull. When Roosevelt had accepted the nomination for a fourth term on July 20, he suggested that Hull run as vice president. Hull declined. He thought he could be more useful as Secretary of State. Moreover, his health was growing steadily worse. "On October 2, my seventy-second birthday, I left the Department of State, very ill," he wrote.[3] In spite of the President's protests he submitted his resignation, which was announced on November 27.

We have already been able to measure what was at the same time the merit and the weakness of this fine man—a legalistic idealism which always led him to prefer abstract principles to practical arrangements. From his active career there remain a number of successes to his credit, however. First, there is the fact that he had given American policy an integrity, a seriousness, which Roosevelt's volatile temperament sometimes jeopardized. Second, the planning agencies to deal with problems of the postwar period had been established. Finally, the fact that he had made possible a considerable degree of harmony between Congress and the Executive was greatly to his credit. In 1944 he began to secure the adherence and cooperation of Republicans; this is the origin of bipartisan policy. In August of that year the Republicans agreed not to argue about either the creation of the United Nations or the United States' participation in that organization during the election campaign. Roosevelt was skeptical but Hull succeeded.

A little more than a year earlier Undersecretary of State Welles had had to resign. The differences between him and Hull had become ever greater. He had direct contact with Roosevelt. "I found," writes Hull, "that Welles abused this privilege in sometimes going to see the President without my knowledge and he even tried to get a decision without my knowledge." [4] Hull adds that the good relations between Roosevelt and Welles were to be explained by the fact that their families were friends and that they had both gone to Groton. In fact, it was much more the result of the President's confidence in the undersecretary's judgment.

At the beginning of the summer of 1943 Roosevelt realized that the tension between the two men had reached the breaking point. As he left for Quebec he asked Welles for his resignation. On September 25 Edward R. Stettinius, Jr., was appointed undersecretary of state. When Hull resigned a year later it was natural to make Stettinius secretary of state. Roosevelt would have preferred Welles, but this would have been an insult to Hull. Judge James Byrnes would have been an acceptable secretary of state, because he had proved himself by defending future United States participation in the United Nations, but Roosevelt followed Hopkins' advice and chose Stettinius, who was devoted to Roosevelt personally and much interested in the establishment of the United Nations. Stettinius was efficient, but a bit colorless. More than ever the State Department disappeared behind the personality of the President. Roosevelt, said Hopkins, was "to be his own Secretary of State." [5]

The only two European problems with which American policy was actively concerned before the Crimea Conference were those of France and Poland.

As soon as Churchill left Moscow he was informed that the United States government had suddenly decided to grant de jure recognition to the Provisional Government of the French Republic. Stalin received a similar letter on October 21. As the delay in this recognition had been caused by the United States, Churchill and Stalin welcomed the news. The pretext for the American reversal of policy was that the French Advisory Assembly had been enlarged. It is possible that Hull's illness played a part in this change, although in his memoirs he claims that he agreed with the decision. Perhaps this sudden action resulted from some resentment on Roosevelt's part of the Churchill-Stalin meeting in Moscow. Perhaps it was influenced by Eisenhower's suggestion, although he does not mention it in his memoirs. The general expected to re-establish an "interior zone" in France as of October 23. Finally, there is General de Gaulle's explanation: "Franklin Roosevelt himself had to settle the matter to satisfy the American voters, from whom he was asking a new mandate and who were growing impatient with an unjustifiable attitude to the old friend, France." De Gaulle says that he did not thank the President and he declared at a press conference, "the French government is pleased to be called by its name." [6]

This certainly did not mean any significant improvement in relations between Roosevelt and De Gaulle. The general complained that the United States refused to increase substantially the flow of arms to France, because, he said, "the French army . . . would play a more influential role . . . and . . . France would have to be admitted to the armistice settlement, which Roosevelt wished to avoid." [7] When De Gaulle and Georges Bidault went to Moscow to state the French claims on the Rhineland and to sign a treaty of alliance, Stalin reported it faithfully to Roosevelt. Roosevelt replied on December 6 that he approved the treaty but remained faithful to the path he had chosen. He declared that any attempt to settle German frontiers should wait until the end of the war.

There were similar difficulties concerning the Crimea Conference. De Gaulle wanted passionately to take part and Churchill was not absolutely opposed. De Gaulle detected Roosevelt's influence in his exclusion—especially as Hopkins was sent to explain it to him. The conversation between De Gaulle and Hopkins was on a fundamental level. The two men argued about the underlying sources of Franco-American misunderstanding. De Gaulle examined the historical origins, Hopkins turned his attention to the future. The immediate future meant the Yalta Conference and on this point Hopkins' instructions did not permit him to give in.

The friction was to continue. It continued on the military level, for example, when, on January 3, 1945, De Gaulle told Eisenhower that he would not obey if ordered to evacuate Strasbourg. And it continued on the political level. On February 12 returning from Yalta, Roosevelt invited De Gaulle to meet him in Algiers. De Gaulle refused, saying "if it were for the good reason that Roosevelt wished to see De Gaulle, why had he not allowed him to go to the Crimea?" [8] Roosevelt was annoyed and called De Gaulle a capricious prima donna, but the general says, "if he had lived longer and we had had time to exchange mutual views at leisure after the war, I think he would have understood and appreciated the reasons which guided me in my action as the leader of France." [9]

In Moscow, Churchill and Stalin argued in vain about Poland. They kept Roosevelt informed of their disagreement, and, of course, Harriman was present. Mikolajczyk, summoned to the Soviet capital, still refused to accept the frontiers proposed by the Russians. Moreover the Soviets wanted Poland to be ruled by the Lublin Committee. Roosevelt defended himself against the charge of having accepted the Curzon Line at Teheran. Later, on December 18, Stettinius published a statement on Poland in which he said "A constant of United States government policy is that questions concerning frontiers must remain suspended until after the war." [10] The President sent this text on to Stalin the next day, insisting that the Russians should not go so far as to recognize the Lublin Committee as the government of Poland. No step forward had been taken.

For many reasons the conference planned at Yalta was necessary. Perhaps there was still a way to settle East-West difficulties, and the problem of Soviet intervention against Japan was increasingly thorny. First, however, an attempt must be made to improve Anglo-American relations, which since Churchill's visit to Moscow in October had become increasingly strained, in political matters as well as in military matters.

Stettinius' dry, harsh manner accounts for a good deal of the political tension, which had arisen from the clash of Churchill's royalist leanings and the republicanism of the Americans. The Prime Minister wanted to preserve the monarchies in Italy, Greece, and Belgium despite the opposition of a part of the population to their sovereigns. At the end of November, when Bonomi's cabinet resigned in Italy, Count Sforza was brought forward as Foreign Minister. Sforza, a man of the liberal Left and noted anti-Fascist, was well known in the United States where he had lived in exile, but deeply disliked by Churchill. On December 5 Stettinius announced that he would not oppose Sforza, invoking the principle of the right of the Italians to choose their own government. Churchill was furious and said publicly, in the House of Commons, that he had no confidence in Sforza. In the following weeks Churchill's anger was not appeased. The House of Commons had given him a vote of confidence by a large majority but United States Ambassador Winant did not think the Conservative House any longer represented the country.

Concerning Greece, the Americans refused to accept an order from British Admiral King to United States Admiral Hewitt which had not been cleared with the combined chiefs of staff. The order would have stopped supplies from going to Greece, where a Communist insurrection—accompanied by cries of "Vive Roosevelt!"—was in progress. The British Army was trying to maintain order in Athens. Here again Churchill was annoyed with his allies. On the strategic level, the combined chiefs, meeting in Malta, were in total disagreement.

It was therefore decided that Churchill and Roosevelt should meet in Malta, en route to Yalta, to eliminate differences before meeting Stalin. Roosevelt had with him Secretary Stettinius, Hopkins, James Byrnes, and the joint chiefs. He had come on the cruiser *Quincy* because his doctors advised against flying. The Malta Conference, begun on January 30 and 31 between the combined chiefs, continued on February 1 with a meeting of Stettinius and Eden and on February 2 with a meeting of Roosevelt and Churchill. The strategic problem was resolved first. The Americans advocated an intensive offensive up and down the Rhine, while the British preferred a concentrated offensive toward the Ruhr. The Americans protested that this was the most difficult point at which to cross the river. This was a transfer to the tactical level of the personal conflict between Eisenhower and Montgomery, his British assistant. A compromise solution was reached. The British resigned themselves to transfer some divisions in the Mediterranean to the German front, no doubt on Montgomery's insistence.

On the political level, Eden and Stettinius undertook a vast survey of the general situation. Churchill reproached Stettinius for his Italian policy. "Without mincing words he told me that I had made the Italian situation very difficult for him. He used very sarcastic language." [11] Churchill also complained of Stettinius in his conversation with Roosevelt, but that was as far as it went.

The only important agreement between the British and the Americans at Malta concerned the occupation zones in Germany. It is advisable to go back a bit and examine the development of American policy regarding the occupation zones. In Moscow on November 1, 1943, the European Advisory Commission had been created to work out the terms of German surrender and ways and means of the occupation. While the British wanted the European Advisory Commission to be a powerful organ, which could extend its jurisdiction in the future to other parts of Europe, "the opinion prevailing in United States Administration circles was that it would be unwise to try to resolve post-war problems during the war, except to bring into existence the United Nations organization." [12] The result was that United States Ambassador Winant in London played a minor role on the commission, owing to a lack of precise instructions.

Since the instructions could not come from the State Department alone, but also involved the War and Navy departments, a commission representing the three departments was established—the Working Security Commission, under Philip Mosely, a State Department expert. The War Department delegates belonged to the Civil Affairs Division. As they believed that only military men were qualified to work out the legal status and means of occupation for Germany they complicated the job of the Working Security Commission. For example, they were responsible for the failure to accept a suggestion of Mosely's to the effect that Berlin—which was to be placed under inter-Allied occupation—should be connected to the Western zone by a corridor. The American military men thought at the time that the Red Army would advance to the Rhine and that it was, therefore, futile to make an agreement about the zones, while Mosely thought that this very fact constituted one more reason to obtain commitments from the Soviet Union.

It was, therefore, on the basis of a British plan, presented on January 15, 1944, that the European Advisory Commission reopened its discussions. This plan included a Soviet zone which was exactly the one that later came into existence. The Soviets accepted it. The problem then was to divide the rest of Germany between the United States, Great Britain, and, eventually, France. The British claimed northwest Germany, the richest part of the country, leaving the south for the United States. Roosevelt refused because of the political difficulties between France and the United States. There was a risk that United States Army communications across France would be uncertain. As soon as Germany was defeated it would be necessary to transfer many troops to the Far East and rapid communications would be indispensable. Between April and September 1944 there was a complete impasse. By the end of July the European Advisory Commission had outlined three zones, but it was not decided whether the British or the Americans would have the northwest. Winant urged a prompt solution.

At the Quebec Conference in September, Roosevelt, under pressure from Stimson and Stettinius, resigned himself to accept the southern zone, on condition that United States troops could cross the British zone and that Americans would control the ports of Bremen and Bremerhaven. The conflict continued because the Americans understood by "control" much more extensive power than Churchill wished. Furthermore, during the autumn United States foreign policy had that floating, undefined character which we have mentioned.

Winant suggested the immediate elaboration of a plan on which the three Allies could agree: joint administration and reparations. He foresaw that Germany could become a pawn between East and West. The State Department thought, therefore, that Germany should not be harshly treated. Secretary of the Treasury Morgenthau, on the contrary, proposed a very severe plan which would practically have reduced Germany to an agricultural nation. The idea of dismembering Germany was adopted, but the State Department favored a sort of federation of the resulting German states while Morgenthau wanted them to be rigidly separate. Stimson more or less supported the opinion of Hull and opposed Morgenthau. Roosevelt seemed at first to accept Morgenthau's plan, then cooled and hesitated. On October 2 he wrote to Hull, "I don't like making detailed plans for a country we are not yet occupying." [13] Everything thus remained in the air.

It was the admission of France as a member of the European Advisory Commission which finally enabled a decision about zones to be made. Churchill and Stalin proposed in Moscow the admission of France and Roosevelt agreed. France was invited on November 11 and her delegate was to take his place on the twenty-seventh. Mosely, who had become Winant's assistant on the European Advisory Commission, thought that a solution should be reached before that date so as not to have the whole question reopened by the new partner. On November 14 the European Advisory Commission adopted the final protocol on occupation zones. At Malta, on February 1, 1945, the United States government finally accepted a document which spelled out in particular the right of American troops to cross the British zone.

At Malta, Stettinius, as he says himself, proposed to the British the idea of giving an occupation zone to France, to be taken out of the British and American zones. The British went even further and advocated the admission of France to the Inter-Allied Military Government, on an equal footing with the other three powers. Roosevelt did not accept this proposal, however.

Yalta

From Malta Roosevelt flew to Yalta—operation Argonaut, according to the code Churchill had invented. It was indeed to the Crimean coast—the Colchis of the ancients—that Jason had gone to seek the

Golden Fleece. The President arrived on February 3, as did Churchill. Stalin joined them the next morning. The American delegation stayed in the Livadia Palace, which had been hastily furnished, and the President slept in the tsar's bedroom. If his assistants, Byrnes, Hopkins, Harriman, Leahy, and the interpreter Bohlen were comfortably housed, the experts were piled in on top of each other. There were four types of meetings: plenary sessions, discussions at meal times between the Big Three or two of them, meetings of the foreign ministers, and military conferences. We obviously cannot follow the course of this complex conference, of which numerous accounts and a collection of official documents have been published. What interests us is to make clear United States policy at Yalta. Beyond the question of the international organization, discussed below, it can be said that three major problems were discussed at Yalta: the fate of Germany, the fate of the liberated countries of Eastern Europe, and the question of Russian participation in the war against Japan.

At Yalta very harsh decisions were made about Germany. The idea of competition in "softness" to "win over" German public opinion was conspicuous by its absence. The principle of dismembering Germany, already adopted at Teheran, was brought up again. It was decided to insert the word "dismemberment" in the plan for unconditional surrender which the European Advisory Commission had drawn up in July 1944. Churchill feared that this would arouse the Germans and stiffen their will to fight, but Roosevelt and Stalin favored it because they thought that the capacity for psychological reaction in Germany would be so weakened that anything could be imposed. The exact content of the word remained to be worked out. Roosevelt thought of the possibility of cutting up Germany into five or seven pieces, Churchill envisaged two or three. Stalin, who perhaps was already thinking of *not* dismembering Germany except in the East, proposed nothing. A committee was appointed to meet in London, consisting of Foreign Secretary Eden, United States Ambassador Winant and Soviet Ambassador Gusev.

The Soviets proposed heavy reparations, twenty billion dollars, to be paid half in capital payments—dismantling of factories and so forth —and half in annual payments. Fifty percent of the total would go to the Soviet Union and the rest would be apportioned among the other victorious nations. The apportionment would be based partly on the extent of damage suffered and partly on the basis of contribution to victory—which virtually excluded France. Only Churchill expressed doubts on the realism of such a policy and brought up the reparations of the First World War, which had been paid only up to 1932 and then only with the help of American loans.

Roosevelt said (1) that he would accept the figure of twenty billion dollars as a basis for discussion only; (2) that the United States, for its part, wanted neither the machinery nor the labor but only certain German holdings in the United States; (3) that the United States did not expect to give financial aid to Germany and hoped that Germany would be self-sufficient. The Russians had proposed that in principle the German standard of living should be reduced to that of Eastern Europe. There was no serious objection. A reparations commission of three members was to have its headquarters in Moscow. Roosevelt supported Stalin against Churchill when the Soviets proposed that France be excluded from the commission.

Concerning Germany, the problem most discussed was whether France should have an occupation zone. On the first day Stalin resigned himself to it, not without expressing some harsh judgments of France. The question was, should France be admitted to the Allied Control Council in Germany? Churchill pleaded the French cause energetically: France, Germany's immediate neighbor, could play an effective role and give solid support to the British when the Americans evacuated the country. Roosevelt declared that he "did not believe that American troops would stay in Europe more than two years," that Congress and public opinion would oppose it.[14] When Stalin showed opposition to the admission of France to the Control Council, Roosevelt appeared to support him. Churchill retorted that General de Gaulle would never accept an occupation zone without equal rights of control. Stalin then proposed the submission of the question to the European Advisory Commission—which would gain time—or that the question be postponed until after Yalta and then be handled through normal diplomatic channels. Roosevelt again supported Stalin against Churchill, who wished an immediate decision.

Only on February 10, five days later, did Roosevelt announce that he had changed his mind and that he favored French admission to the Control Council, in order to win De Gaulle's acceptance of other points. According to Stettinius, this change of mind was brought about through the influence of Freeman Mathews, who had been an adviser in the American embassy at Vichy, under Admiral Leahy. Stalin, who had gained advantages in Poland, said only "no objection." [15]

In all, Roosevelt had a harsh attitude toward Germany, stemming no doubt from the Morgenthau plan. When he met Stalin after his arrival on February 4 he said that "he had been very struck by the extent of German destruction in the Crimea, and that as a result he was more thirsty for German blood than he had been, and that he hoped that Marshal Stalin would again propose a toast to the execution of 50,000 officers of the German army." [16] It will be recalled that at Teheran Churchill had become angry when Stalin had made this barbarous suggestion. Of course Roosevelt was not serious. Nevertheless, we can understand his state of mind in the midst of the pitiless struggle. Otherwise the discussion about Germany was chiefly between Churchill and Stalin. Roosevelt accepted the idea of a great reduction in the German standard of living and strict inter-Allied control. On the whole, however, he avoided committing himself to a great extent, believing that United States troops would not remain long in Germany.

The problem of the nations of Eastern Europe was posed by the advance of the Red Army, which then had a superiority of 100 divisions over the Wehrmacht, according to Stalin. On February 1, 1945, the Soviets had reached a line just east of Stettin. Danzig and Königsberg were still held by the Germans. The Front then followed the Oder River in Silesia, cut Slovakia in half and reached to Lake Balaton in Hungary. Soviet troops had occupied Rumania and Bulgaria and invaded Yugoslavia.

At Yalta little attention was given to the southeastern states, Czechoslovakia, Hungary, Yugoslavia, Rumania, and Bulgaria. Poland, on the other hand, was a main subject of discussion. Roosevelt, for his part, tried to obtain a decision on the status of the liberated countries.

Each of the powers maintained its original position on Poland, Stalin more firmly than the British and Americans, who allowed some of their position to be worn down. On January 1, 1945, the Soviet Union had recognized the Lublin Committee—then transferred to Warsaw —as the Provisional Government of Poland. In London Mikolajczyk, more willing to compromise than the other members of the Polish government-in-exile, resigned and was replaced by Arciszewski, who was a Socialist and long a firm opponent of Communism. Roosevelt was much concerned with this situation and Stalin had paid no attention to the President's urgent request not to make it worse by premature recognition. In short, at Yalta the Polish problem became the test of East-West collaboration.

Roosevelt supported the plan to draw Poland's eastern frontier at the Curzon Line, although at the same time he proposed that the Soviet Union make the generous gesture of leaving Lvov to the Poles. Stalin was not the man to respond to sentimental appeals, however, and he refused. As to Poland's western frontier, the British and Americans learned with horror that the line proposed by the Russians was that of the Oder and the *western* branch of the Neisse, not the *eastern* branch. This meant that six million Germans would have to leave their homes. Stalin remarked that this was no problem as they had already fled before the Red Army. There was "little justification" for this frontier, said an American memorandum on February 8.[17] Roosevelt took refuge in a fairly feeble legal technicality. "I cannot now make a decision on frontiers; it will have to be decided later by the Senate." The United States, therefore, did not recognize the western frontier proposed by the Russians. But what else could it do?

The problem of the government of Poland was even more serious. It brought up a basic question: would the Soviets impose a Communist government on Poland as Churchill, more than Roosevelt, had always feared was actually being done? Roosevelt and Churchill both did their best to prevent it. They could not ask that the London and Warsaw Polish governments combine because the chasm between the two groups was too deep, but they insistently demanded the *replacement* of the Warsaw cabinet by a "government of national union." The Soviets, on the contrary, would accept only the *enlargement* of the Warsaw government by the addition of a few members suggested by Roosevelt. The Polish leaders could not be reached in time, however, and it proved impossible to bring them to the conference for consultation.

When Stalin declared that he expected general elections to be held in Poland within a month, hope revived. The British and Americans thought they could put up with the Lublin government until the election. Roosevelt and Churchill resigned themselves to the acceptance of a vague formula to the effect that "The Provisional Government which is now functioning in Poland should therefore be reorganized on a broader democratic basis with the inclusion of democratic leaders from Poland itself and from Poles abroad. This new

Government should then be called the Polish Provisional Government of National Unity." [18] This left the door open to Soviet initiative,
but it was less objectionable in the eyes of the West than the unquali-
fied continuation of the Lublin government. Could elections be guaranteed? Roosevelt proposed that Molotov and the ambassadors of the
Western powers in Moscow should constitute a commission which
would have among its responsibilities the assurance of free elections.
Molotov opposed the plan at first, under the pretext that it would
humiliate the Poles, and the President confined himself to the expression of a wish that he would like "to have some assurance for the six
million Poles in the United States that the elections would be free." [19]
Then the Soviet Union vaguely accepted a certain degree of control
and the creation of the Moscow committee.

Could a general safeguard be found? The State Department and
Roosevelt tried to do so through a Declaration on Liberated Europe.
The British and American members of the control commissions in
Rumania and Bulgaria were informing their governments that they
were not consulted, not even informed of what was happening, and
not allowed to travel freely in those countries. Churchill and Roosevelt could hardly demand equality with the Russians for their representatives in those countries. Not only had Churchill (in Moscow in
October) signed with Stalin an agreement which constituted a sort
of provisional division of Southeastern Europe into spheres of influence, but the Red Army was occupying Rumania and Bulgaria. Even
so, the Western Allies demanded equality for the period after Germany's defeat. They did the same for Hungary, which had signed
an armistice on January 19.

The State Department was very much disturbed. Would not the
United Nations be an illusion if the Soviet Union established Communist regimes everywhere its armies were in possession? Stettinius,
who shared his predecessor's inclination toward abstract principles,
prepared a declaration which was also signed by France. The three
heads of state "jointly declare their mutual agreement to concert, during the temporary period of instability in liberated Europe, the policies
of their three governments in assisting the peoples liberated from the
domination of Nazi Germany and the peoples of the former Axis
satellite states of Europe to solve by democratic means their pressing
political and economic problems." [20] The people of these states were
supposed to destroy the last vestiges of Nazism and Fascism and to

create democratic institutions of their own choice, as specified in the Atlantic Charter. The provisional governments would be largely representative of democratic elements in the country and should hold free elections as soon as possible.

There was little discussion of the principle, although Stettinius refused an amendment of Molotov's stating that "a large amount of aid should be given in these countries to those who had taken an active part in the fight against the German occupation." [21] Stettinius said that this would create great difficulties in the domestic affairs of the United States. Stalin then withdrew Molotov's amendment. Roosevelt did not propose, as Stettinius had suggested, that the Declaration on Liberated Europe be reinforced by the creation of a high commission for Europe. Thus the declaration remained up in the air.

The eventual participation of the Soviet Union in the war against Japan aroused no discussion, since both the Russians and the Americans thought it would be advantageous. It would be futile, on the basis of hindsight, to reproach Roosevelt for not having foreseen that Japan, whose fighting capacity was seriously weakened, would soon seek a way out of the war. Japanese soldiers were fighting to the death in the remote islands, almost to a man. Japan still had a fresh and well-equipped army in the home islands. What would happen if it resisted to the end? Lacking oil for their planes and with their fleet reduced to a skeleton, the Japanese had no chance of winning the war, but in fighting to the death at home they could kill hundreds of thousands of Americans. Also, would there be time to build the atomic bomb?

On November 8, 1941, Vannevar Bush, an expert in nuclear physics, proposed to Secretary Stimson that research on nuclear fission for military purposes be undertaken. Five weeks later a committee was established to advise the President on the matter. It consisted of Secretary Stimson, Vice President Wallace, James Bryant Conant, President of Harvard, and Vannevar Bush, with General Leslie B. Groves as director of the project at Los Alamos. It was difficult to get the necessary funds—600 million dollars in 1944—while keeping the matter secret.

The order to build the bomb "as fast as possible to hasten the end of the war" [22] was given in October 1942. At the beginning of 1945 the bomb was not yet ready and on May 9, a month after Roosevelt's death, an Advisory Commission consisting of physicists and high officials was created to discuss the eventual use of the bomb. It is, therefore, perfectly understandable that in February 1945, Roosevelt, in cooperation with Churchill, was seeking other means to hasten the end of the Japanese war. It is worth noting that in the military discussions at Yalta the American experts expected victory over Germany between July 1 and December 31, 1945, and anticipated that 18 months longer would be needed to defeat Japan.

Stalin made conditions for Russian entry into the war. These had been known ever since he had given them to Harriman on December 14, 1944: recognition of the independence of Outer Mongolia, annexation of the Kurils and southern Sakhalin, and the lease of Port Arthur and Dairen to Russia. Roosevelt himself had proposed at Teheran that Russia should have a warm-water port. Roosevelt argued about the latter point only, when he met Stalin on February 8. The President would have preferred the internationalization of Port Arthur. In fact, he hoped that the British would yield Hong Kong to China so that it could be a free international port. Stalin also wanted control of the South Manchurian Railway between Port Arthur and Harbin. Did this include the right of military occupation of the railroad zone which Russia had had before 1905? Stalin did not say so in so many words. Roosevelt suggested that the matter be settled by direct negotiation between Russia and China. He also proposed that Korea and Indochina be put under trusteeship and Stalin accepted the suggestion.

On the military plane, Stalin agreed that the establishment of American military bases in Kamchatka was necessary and it was decided that maritime intercourse between the United States and Siberia would be stepped up to transport matériel destined for the Red Army.

The Yalta Conference ended on February 11, after a final luncheon of the three leaders. The atmosphere was much more strained and less congenial than at Teheran. Roosevelt tried in vain to create a little warmth. For example, at dinner on February 8 he responded to Stalin's toast praising lend-lease by saying that the relations of the three countries were those of a family.

Roosevelt's conduct at Yalta has been much criticized because some people see in it the beginning of Western concessions to the Soviet Union. Stettinius defends him faithfully but with a certain naïveté. "At Yalta," he says, "the President showed extreme patience and firmness. At no moment did he flare up. He was pleasant and sympathetic, but determined." [23] Stettinius also says that Roosevelt often played the role of arbiter between Stalin and Churchill. In fact, at Yalta, the President, tired, even exhausted, played a less active and less brilliant role than at Teheran. Stettinius tries to prove that Roosevelt made no serious concessions. The Far East excepted, the problem which dominated discussion was what Stalin would do with the territories already occupied or soon to be occupied by the Red Army. The United States had no real means of exerting pressure in this matter.

The historian's task is not to judge, but if an opinion is permissible, we would say that Roosevelt managed well at Yalta. Granted that it was a retreating action, what else could he do? Roosevelt's real responsibility for the future of the world did not begin at Yalta but much earlier. It dates from the time when, because of his preoccupation with the war and his exclusive concentration on victory itself, he refused to subordinate and to relate military plans to political considerations. If he had accepted Churchill's plans for landing in the Balkans, or had followed the Italian campaign with a drive toward Vienna, perhaps the shape of postwar Europe would have been transformed. Here again, however, we do not know. Some experts, like Philip Mosely, believe that if the West had beaten the Russians to the Balkans the Soviets would have driven into the Scandinavian countries, Holland, Belgium, possibly even France. At any rate, by the time of the Yalta Conference it was too late.[24]

The Organization of the United Nations

In spite of increasing anxiety about Soviet plans in Eastern Europe, Roosevelt still had an important source of hope for the postwar period in the creation of the United Nations. The Declaration of Four, which Hull had proposed and had succeeded in getting accepted in Moscow in 1943, contained in one of its sections an agreement to create an international organization. The State Department had then gone to work and at the end of December 1943 Hull submitted a first plan, which the President approved in early February 1944. Hull immediately undertook two moves. On the one hand he redoubled his efforts in Congress. A special committee of eight senators, members of the Committee on Foreign Relations, met in April and May 1944. Democratic Senator Tom Connally and Republican Senator

Arthur Vandenberg were among them. Vandenberg saw the problem very clearly. "The new 'League' will defend this new *status
quo*. It is my position that the United States cannot subscribe to this
defense . . . unless and until we know more about what the new
status quo will be." [25]

Vandenberg did not want to delay the plan to create the United
Nations, however. Since 1944 was a presidential election year, it was
important not to have the question of the United Nations included in
the party platforms. Hull took the matter up with the Republican
candidate Thomas Dewey, who agreed that it should not be a partisan
issue. Dewey appointed John Foster Dulles to discuss the matter of
the international organization with the Secretary of State. On August
25 a statement was published assuring that the subject of the future
peace would be "kept out of politics." [26]

Hull's other move, which began in July 1944, was to send "provisional plans for a general organization" to Russia, Britain, and China.
A conference was held at Dumbarton Oaks, an estate near Washington. As the Soviet Union refused to associate with China, there were
two phases of the conference, a "Soviet" phase, between August 21
and September 28, and a "Chinese" phase, from September 29 to
October 7. On October 9 the decisions of Dumbarton Oaks were
published, as were recommendations to the participating governments.
Stettinius, then undersecretary of state, represented the United States;
Sir Alexander Cadogan, the United Kingdom; Andrei Gromyko,
the Soviet Union. China was represented by Wellington Koo, Chinese ambassador in London.

What interests us in the Dumbarton Oaks conference are the motives and attitudes of the United States government. The Americans,
says William McNeill, "tended to think that the establishment of an
international organization would be a sort of talisman possessing a
powerful magic—to stop quarrels between nations." [27] Herbert Feis
comments:

The concept of an association of free nations for common protection
and welfare had come to appear the most comfortable as well as the most
effective way to ward off future wars. We had tried isolation. We had
tried neutrality. We had tried exhortation. All had been found wanting.
We had no faith in balance-of-power arrangements, and did not want to
maintain large armies after the war . . . We sought to clear a new path
for the nations.[28]

Only a few experts on Russian affairs pointed out the dangers of the situation, in which the Soviet Union, while accepting an international organization in principle, sought at the same time to have a free hand in Eastern Europe. When Cordell Hull brought this matter up with Averell Harriman on September 18, Harriman was astounded to realize that the Secretary of State had not grasped the problem sooner. As George Kennan has said, "An international organization to keep peace and security is no substitute for a well thought out and realistic foreign policy." [29]

The United Nations Organization—the name Hull wanted to give it—as conceived by the Americans, did not solve the problem. It would include all nations—except for a short while the neutrals and the vanquished—but it was not established with supranational powers nor with an international police force. Its structure is well known. There are three main bodies: the General Assembly, the Security Council, and the Economic and Social Council, in addition to a number of specialized agencies. Walter Lippmann would have preferred the United Nations to be purely advisory, without real power. Policy-marking would then have remained in the hands of the large nations. At Teheran Roosevelt had anticipated that the great powers would constitute the police force, but the charter provided for the Security Council to have the police power. This meant the Big Five (France was invited to join although she had not been represented at the Dumbarton Oaks Conference). But what other forces could the Security Council use to police the world if not those of the great powers? It was decided to include six nonpermanent member nations on the Security Council. Roosevelt had also wanted Brazil to be a permanent member but he did not press the point.

Two serious problems were left up in the air at Dumbarton Oaks. One was the Russian claim to 16 seats in the General Assembly, one for each of the republics constituting the Soviet Union. Roosevelt opposed this energetically because he thought that the Senate would never accept it and it would thus risk reopening the questions of United States membership in the United Nations. The other problem concerned the extent to which the decisions of the Security Council implied unanimity of the great powers, in other words, the matter of the veto power. Would the veto apply in all cases, as the Soviets wished, or only, as Roosevelt wished, in cases in which the nation exercising the veto had no national interest in the question? Would it apply to procedural matters, such as the inclusion of a subject on the agenda of the Security Council? None of these matters were settled at Dumbarton Oaks, and it was understood that they would be taken up at the next meeting of the three heads of state.

The future international organization was also the subject of many of the talks at Yalta. The discussion concerned the very nature of the international organization. Did or did not the major powers have rights beyond the rights of the smaller nations? In the evening of February 4, during the first dinner attended by the three leaders, Stalin urged a preponderant role for those who had borne the chief weight of the war. He said that it was "ridiculous to think that a small nation like Albania could have an equal voice with the three Great Powers." He said that he was "ready to join with the United States and Great Britain to safeguard the rights of small nations, but he would never agree to submit the acts of the major powers to the judgment of the smaller ones." [30] Roosevelt conceded that the great powers had a responsibility to plan and maintain the peace but he agreed with Churchill that it was necessary to respect the rights of small nations. On February 6 Stettinius stated the American position on the method of voting: (1) For questions of procedure the Security Council would have to have a majority, that is, seven of the eleven members. (2) For other matters there should be a majority of seven including the five permanent members, except when one or more of them might be an interested party in the conflict under consideration. He stressed the necessity of allowing the smaller nations to make themselves heard. Stalin replied that "the main thing was to prevent any possible conflict among the Big Three and that, therefore, the problem was to assure their unity in the future." [31] He was disturbed by the possibility of the mobilization of world opinion against a great power. Roosevelt retorted that "full and friendly discussions in the Council would in no sense promote disunity, but on the contrary, would serve to demonstrate the mutual confidence of the Great Powers in each other." [32] The next day, February 7, to the general surprise, Molotov announced that the arguments of Stettinius and Roosevelt were satisfactory and that therefore, the Soviet Union would accept the American proposition for the system of voting.

Immediately afterwards Molotov abandoned the Soviet claim for 16 votes in the General Assembly, and asked only for 3 or 4, one for the Soviet Union and one each for the Ukraine, White Russia, and possibly Lithuania. This was a big step toward compromise. In a letter to Stalin Roosevelt asked for 3 votes for the United States, "to assure the wholehearted adherence of the Congress and people of the United States." [33] Stalin immediately agreed.

Stettinius proposed, finally, that the trusteeship system be studied in relation to certain dependent nations. Churchill protested energetically against this threat to the British Empire, and Roosevelt feared that the entire structure of the international organization would crumble. It was dangerous to bring up his idea about Hong Kong or even Indochina. Stettinius replied to Churchill that he was not at all thinking of the British Empire and that the vague formula of trusteeship (which was ultimately agreed upon) was to apply only to former League mandates, to territories which the Big Three were unwilling to leave under enemy sovereignty, and to territories which voluntarily submitted themselves to United Nations tutelage. It was finally decided to call a conference to establish the United Nations Organization in San Francisco on April 25 and to include France and China among the "inviting powers" along with the Big Three.

Roosevelt could take satisfaction on this point at least, for Russia had made concessions. The question was, what were these concessions worth? They in no way affected any possible differences between the United States and the Soviet Union. At Yalta Roosevelt could, perhaps, still believe that such difficulties would be avoided or resolved through diplomatic channels, but the coming months would show that this was a very optimistic view.

Even so, Roosevelt had another source of satisfaction. He had put through his plan for the United Nations and he was sure of wide support in public opinion. The objective Wilson had not been able to achieve, for which Roosevelt, then assistant secretary of the navy, had fought in vain, was now to be realized. What a change from the isolation of the 1930's! Even on May 20, 1941, to the question "Would you like to see the United States belong to a League of Nations after the war?" 49 percent had replied yes and 51 percent, no. On July 2, 1944, to a similar question about an organization "to take the place of the old League of Nations," 72 percent had replied yes; 13 percent, no; and 13 percent were undecided. Republicans had favored it almost as much as Democrats.[34] Besides, all signs pointed to Senate approval this time, by an enormous majority. As one senator said, "Isolation died at Pearl Harbor."

Latin America

Before studying the end of Roosevelt's career, let us make a brief survey of United States relations with Latin America in recent years. Though this subject received much space in the early chapters, I have seemingly neglected it since turning to World War II. This should surprise no one, for it reflects the facts. The truth is that, once plunged into the complexities of world politics, the United States was obliged to regard as very secondary what had formerly been its special diplomatic domain.

In December 1938 a regular Pan-American Conference met in Lima, with Cordell Hull heading the United States delegation. Since the Good Neighbor Policy was now an established fact, Hull directed his activity and his statements to the growing threat in Europe. "There must be no shadow of doubt whatever about the determination of the American nations not to permit an invasion of this hemisphere." [35] In fact, the activity of the Axis powers justified anxiety. Because of the German and Italian minorities in some of the South American countries, because of the movement encouraged by Franco known as Hispanism, and because of the presence of fifth columns, Latin American seemed threatened.

The Lima Conference achieved two results of unequal importance. A Declaration of Principles of Inter-American Solidarity and Co-operation was approved. This was proposed by Secretary Hull and was, characteristically, piously abstract in nature. More important was the Declaration of Principles of American Solidarity, or Declaration of Lima, as it is commonly called. This had been suggested as early as the Buenos Aires Conference of 1936, but it had been rejected by Argentina. It provided that in case of a threat to the peace, security, or territorial integrity of an American republic, the foreign ministers of all 21 republics would meet for consultation. The request of anyone of the 21 was sufficient for such a meeting to be called. As it was merely a declaration and not a treaty of alliance, the text did not have to be ratified. It was to provide a flexible and efficient instrument for the coordination of policies during the war.

The three main conferences of the foreign ministers were held in Panama after the outbreak of the European War (September 23–October 9, 1939), in Havana after the fall of France (July 21–30,

1940), and in Rio de Janeiro after Pearl Harbor and the Arcadia meeting of Roosevelt and Churchill (January 15–28, 1942). The decisions of these conferences had wide application.

In Panama it was decided that commercial ships of one American republic could be transferred to another. This allowed the United States to get around the "carry" clause of the neutrality law and place ships under the Panamanian flag. In 1928 it had been decided that armed ships could only be admitted into certain ports in American republics on the same basis as warships properly so called. This ruling had greatly hindered the movements of the British convoys and it was abolished in 1939. The Panama Conference set up a permanent Inter-American Neutrality Commission, which was to keep the member states in constant contact with each other. This commission took all sorts of measures against the subversive activities of the fifth columns and set up another body, the Inter-American Finance and Economic Advisory Commission, which would permit the United States to organize more effectively its purchases of raw materials. In this way the depression-born problem of meager United States purchases and consequent Latin American poverty was rapidly solved because of the United States' great need for strategic war materials.

At Havana in 1940, the main decision was not to tolerate any change of sovereignty in European colonies in the western hemisphere. This carried out a joint resolution of the United States Congress of June 8, 1940. After the conference many bilateral agreements were reached, both on strategic war materials and on common organization for defense.

At the Rio Conference in early 1942, a conference requested by the United States (and at which Sumner Welles headed the American delegation), the Latin republics were asked to break off diplomatic relations with the Axis. The nine small republics of Central America and the Caribbean had already declared war on Germany, Italy, and Japan and had thus been in a position to sign the United Nations Declaration. Subsequently the remaining Latin republics broke off relations, with the exception of the two farthest away, Argentina and Chile. In the summer of 1942, after the Germans had torpedoed some of their ships without warning, Mexico and Brazil declared war on the Axis and joined the United Nations. For the time being, the United States was not encouraging the other Latin American nations to declare war because of the purely symbolic value of such a declaration. We should also take note of the agreements by which the United States undertook to buy all surplus rubber in Latin America for five years. The United States had been suddenly cut off from the chief sources of rubber in Southeast Asia by the Japanese.

Chile decided to break off relations with the Axis on January 20, 1943, following upon new elections, but Argentina, which had become the refuge of the Nazis, refused to do so. Hull was much concerned with this situation but would not accept Morgenthau's proposition to freeze Argentine assets in the United States, because it would have been too serious a blow to the Good Neighbor Policy. He redoubled his efforts on the "bad neighbor" (the title of a chapter in his memoirs). On January 4, 1943, a coup d'état under General Ramirez took place in Argentina. The United States recognized him on the eleventh but not much was accomplished by the action.

In early 1944, on the basis of reports that Nazi activity was spreading from Argentina to neighboring countries, Roosevelt wrote to Hull, "We should take a firm line with Argentina." At this moment President Ramirez, who had finally broken with the Axis, was overthrown by an officers' junta under General Farrell and Colonel Juan Perón, who sympathized with Germany. This time the United States refused to recognize the new government and the American ambassador was recalled from Buenos Aires, with the full support of the other American Republics. Argentina was isolated. In November 1944, when the American foreign ministers met in Mexico, however, Argentina "submitted" and broke diplomatic relations with the Axis, whose defeat then appeared certain.

The other Latin nations were "good neighbors," unlike Argentina. Some, including Panama, Mexico, Ecuador, Peru, and Brazil, conceded bases to the United States for the duration of the war. Strategically most important were the Galápagos Islands southwest of the precious Panama Canal, put at the disposition of the United States by Ecuador on September 8, 1942. Brazil sent an expeditionary force to Europe, used its small navy for Atlantic patrols, and lost many commercial ships. Mexico—past differences forgiven and forgotten—actively collaborated with its northern neighbor, furnishing bases, raw materials, and 150,000 laborers. Roosevelt visited Mexico in 1943 and was enthusiastically received. At the end of 1944 only seven republics had not yet declared war on the Axis, Chile, Ecuador, Peru, Paraguay, Venezuela, Uruguay, and, of course, Argentina.

To do so was an urgent matter if they wished to take part in the conference at San Francisco whose task was to set up the United Nations. Stettinius kept urging them and, with the exception of Argentina, they all declared war on the Axis in February 1945. At first Stalin opposed their admission, saying that only those nations which were members of the United Nations at the close of the Yalta Conference should be allowed to attend the San Francisco Conference. Roosevelt defended them by recalling that three years before the State Department had advised them against entering the war. "Since these nations had followed the advice of the United States, they thought themselves to be in a good position . . . To tell the truth, our advice to the Latin-American nations was a mistake." [36]

Stalin gave in, but he spoke of "punishing" Argentina. Without going that far, Roosevelt agreed that she should not be invited to San Francisco. He was to change his mind, again with some reservations, on the very eve of his death. The last possible date for declarations of war was set for March 1, 1945, which allowed Turkey, Egypt, and Saudi Arabia also to be admitted to the United Nations.

In all, the Latin American policy of the United States during the war benefited greatly from the previous efforts to establish the Good Neighbor Policy. This was one of Hull's great diplomatic successes. In this sphere he was on home ground and he had the right to say, "In general the help of all kinds we received from Latin America during the Second World War was incomparably greater than that received in the First World War." [37]

The Break with the Soviet Union and the Death of Roosevelt

Roosevelt lived exactly two months after the end of the Crimean Conference. They were tragic months and Roosevelt was well aware of it although he died without revealing his consternation. Churchill, for his part, has shown how at the very moment he was being wildly acclaimed for the victory of the Allied armies, his mind was filled with anxiety aroused by the new attitude of the Soviet Union. Sherwood says, "It began to be feared that a monstrous fraud, of which Roosevelt and Churchill were the victims, had been perpetrated at Yalta." [38]

Roosevelt had flown from Yalta to Egypt, where, to Churchill's

great annoyance, he summoned three sovereigns to meet him aboard
the cruiser *Quincy*. They were King Farouk of Egypt, Ibn Saud of
Saudi Arabia, and Haile Selassie of Ethiopia. He intended to meet
De Gaulle afterwards, but the general did not cooperate. Roosevelt
returned to the United States in a state of extreme fatigue.

Immediately bad news began to come in. In the first place, Stalin's
tone changed. When Roosevelt asked permission, on March 3, for
ten American planes to land in Poland, planes bringing food and
medicine for American prisoners freed by the Red Army, Stalin immediately refused. On March 18 Roosevelt pressed the point and
Stalin replied that there were only seventeen American prisoners left
in the region. He added an unnecessary insult. "I must add . . . that
the former American prisoners of war freed by the Red Army are
living in good conditions in Soviet camps, better in any case than the
conditions provided for former Soviet prisoners of war in American
camps, where they are sometimes housed with German prisoners of
of war and where some of them are subject to unfair treatment and
illegal practical jokes." [39]

Then Roosevelt learned that the Soviet government was not planning to send Molotov to the San Francisco Conference, but only his
assistant, Gromyko. This was at a time when Roosevelt was having
Sherwood draft his great opening address. "All those people coming
from all over the world—it is a great honor for the country and I
want to tell them how much I appreciate it." [40] This was also the
time when, through an indiscretion, the press learned of the Yalta
negotiations on the possibility of giving the United States three votes
in the United Nations General Assembly. There was a strong reaction against this, as American public opinion disapproved such tortuous policy. Would the United Nations prove to be incapable of organizing their international organization? Roosevelt wrote to Stalin
on March 24 to express his concern. "I fear that Mr. Molotov's absence will be interpreted by the entire world as a sign of indifference
on the part of the Soviet government toward the great objectives of
this Conference." [41] Stalin did not change his mind.

Several much more serious things were also happening at the same
time. Between March 25 and April 12 Roosevelt addressed five letters
to Stalin, of which only the last—received by Stalin the day after
the President's death—had an optimistic tone.

The Rumanian problem arose first, two weeks after Yalta. The provisional government of the country, under General Radescu, was supported by a coalition of various parties. The Soviet intention was obviously to replace him by a virtually Communist government. On February 24 a Communist insurrection broke out in Bucharest. The Soviet commander took sides with the insurgents, in spite of Harriman's protests in Moscow on February 27. Vishinsky arrived in Bucharest on the twenty-eighth. He sent an ultimatum to the King demanding the dismissal of Radescu within two hours. In the following days Vishinsky notified the King that the Russians insisted on the nomination of the Communist Petro Groza as Prime Minister, which took place on March 16. In Rumania as well as in Bulgaria and Hungary, the British and American members of the Allied Control Commission were absolutely powerless.

The second problem was Poland. Even though he had yielded some ground at Yalta, Roosevelt could, nevertheless, expect that there would be a substantial change in the pro-Communist provisional government in Warsaw (formerly Lublin). Molotov, however, was insisting that the new members be chosen by the Warsaw government. The Committee on Poland created at Yalta, consisting of Molotov, Sir Archibald Clark-Kerr, and Harriman, was holding tense discussions, the British and Americans claiming the right to have a say in the choice of the Poles to be consulted and Molotov replying that this would be an odious interference in Poland's domestic affairs. Harriman and Clark-Kerr did not even have the right to go to Poland.

On April 1 Roosevelt wrote a long letter to Stalin:

I cannot conceal from you the anxiety I feel about the course events—in which our mutual interests are at stake—have taken since our fruitful meeting at Yalta. The decisions we made there were good ones, and most of them have been enthusiastically accepted by the peoples of the world, who see in our ability to find a basis of common understanding the best chance of obtaining a safe and peaceful world after the war . . . We have no right to disappoint them. Up to the present, there has been a discouraging lack of application, awaited by world opinion, of the political decisions of the Conference, especially concerning the Polish situation. I am frankly disturbed about the reasons for this state of affairs, and I must tell you that I do not wholly understand the apparently indifferent attitude of your Government in many respects.[42]

Roosevelt then reviewed the Rumanian question rapidly and the Polish question at great length. He reminded Stalin that it had been agreed that the Lublin government would be reorganized "in such a way as to constitute a new government" and he asked that the Committee of Three be immediately charged with the choice of Poles to be consulted. He also claimed the right of the British and American members to visit Poland. If the Polish question were not quickly settled, "all those threats to Allied unity—of which we were so conscious during our discussions in the Crimea—will face us in an even more acute form. You are not unaware, I am sure, that in the United States real popular support is indispensable to realize all government policy . . . the American people makes its own opinion and no government action can modify it." [43]

Stalin's reply of April 7 pretended that if the Polish problem were at an impasse it was because the British and American ambassadors in Moscow had introduced "new elements," unforeseen at Yalta. He suggested that new members simply be added to the Warsaw government in the proportion established for the Yugoslav government, which was twenty-one for Tito to six for the government-in-exile in London. Stalin obviously chose the communization of Poland rather than the continuation of the "family atmosphere" of Yalta. This disappointing letter arrived a few days before Roosevelt's death. The Polish problem was far from being solved.

The third difficulty arose over negotiations for the surrender of German troops in Italy. Contacts between Field Marshall Alexander and S.S. General Karl Wolff had begun in early March. United States General Lemnitzer and British General Airey then went together to Bern, not to *negotiate* with the Germans but to meet them. The negotiation was to take place in Allied Headquarters in Caserta. Molotov demanded that Soviet representatives in France should also go to Bern. Harriman did not favor this, as he did not believe the Soviets would invite American representatives to take part in any surrender on the Russian front. He, therefore, replied to Molotov on March 15 that at Bern there was to be a simple "contact," the Russian officers were only to be invited to Caserta. The next day Molotov sent an irritated reply and expressed the wish that the "negotiations" at Bern be immediately broken off. Harriman explained his attitude by saying that the Soviets were either defending their "prestige" (they claimed that the Wehrmacht had been defeated almost exclusively by the Red Army), or that the Soviets feared that the Germans would choose to surrender to the Western powers. There was perhaps also apprehension that the Western powers would encourage Germany to surrender to them and to mass their forces against the Soviet Union.

On March 25 Roosevelt wrote Stalin to explain courteously that there was no "negotiation," and that the Russians had not been invited because the Western powers wished to avoid delays which would mean further loss of lives. Stalin replied on March 29 that he did not approve of such talks unless the Germans were forbidden to transfer any divisions. He said that they had just moved three divisions from Italy to the Russian Front.

Roosevelt wrote again on April 1 to confirm what he had previously said, and remarked that there existed an unfortunate atmosphere of apprehension and suspicion. On April 3 Stalin's tone was much more violent. "You have told me that no negotiation has yet taken place. I have no choice but to suppose that your information is incomplete. As for my military colleagues, they have no doubt whatever . . . that talks have taken place." He added that the object of the maneuver was to permit the Anglo-American forces to "penetrate to the heart of Germany almost without resistance." He complained that the Germans had "in fact stopped fighting on the Western front," [44] at the same time that they continued to fight bitterly against Russia.

On April 5 Roosevelt could not but show his "astonishment" and he repeated that no negotiations had taken place in Bern.

Your information on this matter must come from German sources which have continually tried to create dissension between us . . . I would say, finally, that it would be one of the greatest tragedies in the history of the world if, in the very hour of victory—which is now in our grasp— such suspicion and lack of faith should compromise the whole undertaking . . . Frankly, I cannot help feeling a bitter resentment against your informants, whoever they are, for so basely distorting my actions.[45]

One could not get results from Stalin through emotional appeals, however. He said on April 7, "my informants are very honest, modest men who do their jobs conscientiously without meaning to offend anyone whatsoever." [46] Then he undertook to prove that Russian sources of information were superior to American sources. Roosevelt thought that this should be ignored. In a brief message which Stalin received on April 13, the day after the President's death, Roosevelt declared the incident closed. "In any case it is no cause for mutual suspicion, and minor misunderstandings of this sort should not arise in the future."

This was Roosevelt's last letter. To the end, in spite of all disillusionments, he tried not to cut the fragile thread that still held the alliance together. We will never know what his attitude would have been in the following weeks. His successor, President Truman, certainly made an effort to continue the same policy—that is, to increase gestures of appeasement in order to make the Russians feel confident. With General Eisenhower's full approval and in spite of Churchill, he opposed the eastward advance of Allied troops and the liberation of Prague by the Americans. Who knows if Roosevelt himself might not have chosen just this moment to make the key decision to take as much territory to the East as possible so as to have a solid basis on which to bargain with the Soviet Union?

The very suddenness of Roosevelt's death makes it impossible to know. Very tired, he went to Hyde Park and then to Warm Springs to rest. In the afternoon of Thursday, April 12, during a sitting for a portrait, he suddenly lost consciousness. He died several hours later without ever regaining it. Less than a month later Germany surrendered unconditionally. Roosevelt did not see this victory to which he had contributed so much, but when he died he had begun to realize that the postwar period would present problems just as difficult as the war itself. It can be said that it was a misfortune for his country and for all mankind that this extraordinarily able and intelligent man was not there to deal with them.

Conclusion

THIS study stops deliberately with Roosevelt's death and not with the end of the Second World War. This is not, of course, because the events between April and September 1945—such as President Truman's decision to use the atom bomb against Japan—are not of crucial importance, but rather because the death of Roosevelt seems to me to mark the end of an era in United States foreign policy. In the few pages to follow I shall summarize the dominant themes of the period we have covered and show how they affected the immediate future.

We must first ask whether, between 1913 and 1945, the United States had what is currently called—without precise definition—"a foreign policy." Every nation, even Japan before it was opened up by Commodore Perry, has relations with other nations and tries to exert influence beyond its frontiers. The particular acts of foreign policy which determine this influence may well be entirely separate and uncoordinated, however. It is correct to speak of "a foreign policy" only if one may discern, at least vaguely, certain characteristics of continuity and cohesion.

In a large democratic nation with a strong government and an articulate, powerful public opinion, the question must be approached in terms of the relationship between the exercise of power and the general public. There are reciprocal actions and reactions. Consequently a foreign policy can be said to exist if two conditions are met. The first is in the realm of *action*. One must determine if the responsible officers, in the United States the President or sometimes the Secretary of State, have a well-defined and continuing concept of the main national goals, in other words a "doctrine." It matters little whether they conceive such goals in terms of pure material interest or whether ideals also are involved, the main point is to determine whether there is an overall conception or whether the makers of policy are merely carried along on the tide of events.

The second condition is in the domain of *reaction*. Does that vague, but in the long run determining, factor called public opinion accept the views of the executive power, or does it not accept them? If the Executive succeeds in persuading public opinion, it really fulfills the function of *leadership*. To be a leader does not mean to make decisions all by oneself. Mussolini made an important decision on June, 1940, but he was not followed. Leadership consists in acting in advance of the amorphous reactions, but with every expectation of being followed. Let us review the phases of our study and attempt to assess them in terms of doctrine and leadership.

It was characteristic of Wilson that he had a doctrine in relation to foreign policy. It took him some time to work it out, to be sure, and his doctrine had variations in application. Moreover, he did not know how to adapt it to certain sections of the world—Central America in particular. But he had a doctrine. This could be stated as the aim to identify the supreme interest of the United States with the triumph of righteousness, as it is conceived in a true democracy. This view led him first to keep the country out of a war in which he did not see righteousness as being clearly on one side or the other, a war of rival imperialisms connected with the European balance of power. It led him to wish to play the role of mediator in this irrational war, even, after 1916, an armed mediator, because he thought that only the United States could guarantee the peace, and that peace was the essential condition for the triumph of a truly democratic conception of Right in the world. Wilson went to war because "Right is more precious than peace," and he wanted the war to end in a clear victory. He worked out a system which he hoped would guarantee the peace on just and lasting foundations, to create the world "safe for democracy" of which he dreamed. On a less exalted plane, he even tried to base his recognition of new governments on moral considerations. In this he met with doubtful success.

Wilson had the advantage of a doctrine—whether one accepts or rejects it—with the merits of coherence and continuity. But he was not really a leader. He imprudently advanced far ahead of public opinion. He did not understand that his great popularity was caused as much by military victory as by his ideas, which were too abstract to be grasped by the general public and thus left them somewhat unmoved. He made the mistake of pitting American opinion against Congress and the opinion of foreign peoples against their governments. He was too aloof, too isolated, too inaccessible, to assure a following. In the end he was not followed.

As a result the succeeding era, the era of nationalism in the 1920's, was a disconcerting, even deceptive period in American foreign policy. This period did not lack leaders in foreign policy, Hughes at first, then Hoover, and later, and above all, Stimson. But these were years torn by conflicts. The "nationalists" had won a decisive victory over the "internationalists," but this did not mean that they had a doctrine to oppose to Wilson's. Their position was essentially negative—"return to normalcy." Such return is not possible in history, and there is no "norm" for a major nation in the midst of great expansion followed by severe depression. In so far as nationalism consisted in acting without regard to foreign reactions it led to absurd situations, of which the best examples are the war debts and reparations. Since the conflict between the nationalists and the internationalists existed at the core of the government itself, between Harding and Hughes, and to a certain extent between Hoover and Stimson, the absence of coherence is striking. We have seen the extent to which Hughes, although he had many successes, was an empiricist.

As a result both of these conflicts and divisions and also of the effects of depression on the heels of prosperity, public opinion at its most naïve had exercised a virtually uncontrolled power. Reaction was stronger than action. There were *leaders* in this period, but no real *leadership*. From inertia or from conviction, the administrations were carried along on the major currents of popular opinion to solutions which bordered on absurdity. The badly conceived policy of disarmament, the unrealistic Kellogg-Briand Pact, and the policy of simple "moral condemnation" in Manchuria seemed at the time to be very successful. In fact, they diverted attention from the uniquely important matter of the defense of democracy and peace—that is, an effective defense of peace as distinct from mere verbal initiatives.

With Roosevelt the situation differed in at least one respect: for twelve years the United States had a great leader in the full sense of the word. Nobody was more capable than Roosevelt of measuring the authority which the people could give him; nobody knew better how to "educate" opinion in the way he thought necessary. His art of persuasion amounted to genius. Stimson, a man in a hurry, sometimes reproached Roosevelt for not using his capacity for leadership as much as he could, for instance, concerning the escort of convoys and the Second Front. In lend-lease, on the other hand, the President did everything; he was the originator, the guide, the man who recognized the necessity of daring, large-scale action.

The question arises, did this great leader have a "doctrine"? He is so complex, so basically enigmatic, that it is impossible to state flatly that he did not. We must recognize, however, that if he had such a doctrine it was uncertain, elusive, and that if it was consistent, the consistency was only in the secret of the man's mind—a mind which revealed everything but the most important matters.

Let us leave aside the period from 1933 to 1937, when Roosevelt thought that overcoming the depression was all-important and allowed reaction to dominate action in foreign policy. The neutrality laws were initiated by Congress and he did not choose to resist their pseudo policy whose essence was to prevent him, as President, from exerting any power in foreign affairs. Beginning in 1937, we can discern the development of more precise ideas and above all the determination to get them accepted by public opinion.

All told, a sort of neo-Wilsonism can be seen in Roosevelt's action. Wilson was at the same time the model to follow in the conception and the model not to follow in its execution. Roosevelt certainly shared Wilson's idea of the necessity of the triumph of Right, which he associated first with safety and then with victory of the democracies and the agreement of the Big Three. He thought he could accomplish what Wilson had failed to accomplish, a just and lasting peace, a League of Nations which would be accepted by the Senate.

Compared to Wilson's, however, all these views seem tortuous and stamped with the mark of empiricism. Sometimes there even seems to be a banal Machiavellianism combined with an excessive capacity to deceive himself. The policy toward Vichy up to 1942, the adoption of Darlan as the French protégé of the United States, is difficult to understand. Even more serious was the persistent illusion about Stalin's good intentions, at least until after Yalta, and the consistent over-estimation of Chiang Kai-shek. There was nothing Wilsonian in this. Wilson was extremely suspicious of foreign governments, even Allied governments.

In a word, Roosevelt seems to have been both more and less of a realist than Wilson. To call a spade a spade, it can be said that respon-sibility for the failure of the peace after the First World War falls more on the Senate than on Wilson. The failure of the peace—for this is what it really was—after the Second World War, with the Cold War and the victory of Communism in China, rests primarily on Roosevelt. On the other hand, since this man was extraordinarily quick to perceive change and to adapt to it, one cannot help thinking that, if he had not died at the critical moment, he would have quickly found a more appropriate formula for the situation. This formula was to some extent discovered later by his successor, but too late for the solution of many problems.

Leaving the separate phases, if we look at the period 1913 to 1945 as a whole and try to discern the main continuing threads of American foreign policy, we can express the pattern as follows: this large nation, far from the centers of power with little international power of its own, was faced with two new realities—the shortening of distances and the internal development of its human and economic potential. The problem first arose as early as the late nineteenth century. If we look only at the main cycles, the movement can be compared to great tides. A first wave coincides with the internationalist and expansionist phase of which Mahan was the theorist and Theodore Roosevelt the man of action. The European war at first caused a brief retreat, to be followed by a new rising tide of internationalism. Since this tide went too far, the next retreat was stronger than the first and public opinion irresistibly dragged the government into the nationalism of the 1920's and, after the depression, into the isolationism of the 1930's.

The failure of nationalism and isolationism was evident when Americans looked beyond their shores over the Great Wall of China they had built around themselves. Americans realized with horror that the world that suited them was about to collapse. As they felt perfectly capable of fixing the matter up, despite their reluctance to do so, the tide turned again and a new wave of internationalism led them first to aid the democracies "short of war," then to wage war so that they would triumph, and, finally, to decide to maintain their leading role in order to preserve the peace so dearly bought. Wilson triumphed after a delay of twenty-five years.

The American people have the virtue of always confusing their cause with the great cause of mankind. Throughout the period of this study, they clung to the deep conviction that they were right—whether the tide was high or low.

The feeling of satisfaction which dominated the history of the period 1913 to 1945 began to be mixed with anxiety and then with anguish in the spring of 1945. If the problem of victory was clearly resolved before Roosevelt's death, the problem of the peace presented a group of apparently insurmountable difficulties which kept increasing.

These difficulties arose from the discovery, made after Yalta, that Soviet Russia, which was Soviet as well as Russian, expected to create a zone of influence in Eastern Europe and perhaps also in Manchuria, Korea, and northern Iran. The problem was complicated for Americans by the fact that the Soviet rulers did not denounce the many declarations they had signed, but took advantage of them by giving the words meanings quite different from those understood in the West. "Democracy," "right of self-determination of peoples," "freedom," took on new meanings. In referring to the Yalta agreements, the Soviet rulers showed that their conception of those agreements was diametrically opposed to the American conception.

Moreover, Roosevelt was dead. The man who had inspired confidence, because he had met the most serious and complex situations masterfully, disappeared just when new situations, equally grave and complex, arose.What should be done? His successor, Harry Truman, although a strong man, was ill informed when he came to power and to some extent had to learn from the ground up. Nothing could be more natural than his initial reaction—to follow the trail blazed by Roosevelt.

The question was, what was this trail? If one could easily discern its main outlines, the man was too secretive for anyone to know his basic and ultimate aims. Roosevelt left no "political testament," so he was subject to interpretation. Quickly it was learned how difficult a task this was and how different the "glosses" were from each other. In a few months three main interpretations crystallized. It required more than a year and a half before President Truman could choose between them and work out his own policy.

The first interpretation was that of former Vice President Henry Wallace, Truman's Secretary of Commerce, strongly supported by various members of the Roosevelt family, notably by the President's son Elliott. President Roosevelt had understood that basic agreement between the Big Three was most important for the future peace. He had constantly tried to convince Stalin of this. But Stalin was not to be convinced by words and it was necessary to give him concrete proof of good faith or hostages. Roosevelt had certainly done so. He had voluntarily suggested that the Soviets should be given a warm-water port, should have friendly neighboring states the whole length of their frontiers, and should participate in the settlement of very varied problems all over the world.

Wallace concluded that this pattern should be continued, as he thought the President would have done. Since the Soviet Union seemed to be shutting itself up behind a barrier of suspicion, the suspicion must be removed at all costs. The price was to give the secret of the atom bomb to the Soviets, as well as further concessions in regard to trusteeships, the control of the Dardanelles, economic aid, and reparations. When this price had been paid, Wallace reasoned, confidence would be reborn and the Soviet domination of the satellites—a precautionary measure—would automatically be relinquished. Wallace's policy, to make every concession to gain confidence, was postulated on the assumption that once confidence was re-established the difficulties would disappear.

At the other extreme were those who did not trust the Soviets. In their eyes Roosevelt had modified his policy because of the increasing and really intolerable pressures of the Allies, who, once victorious, needed no further aid and suddenly brought out their undemocratic amibtions and claims. Secretary of the Navy James Forrestal, Dean Acheson, and the Soviet experts Bohlen and Kennan were the spokesmen of this interpretation. Their point of departure was Marxist-Leninist doctrine as Stalin seemed to interpret it. They did not think the Soviet Union had been converted to a flexible attitude by the war, but rather that, as in the past, she wanted to conquer the world for Communism, even if this were not the will of the majority of the people. They concluded, therefore, that it was futile to hope that the Soviet Union would let up in its efforts to dominate. On the contrary, it should be expected immediately to exploit any fissure in the non-Communist world. It followed that if some day war seemed to be the best way to spread Communism, the Soviet Union would go to war. The United States should, therefore, stand firm and remain strong, should not hasten to demobilize, should increase atomic armaments and be careful to keep its atomic secrets. This policy should be extended to all free countries, so that any cracks in the free world would be cemented over. Economic aid, military aid, psychological aid, and even alliances in peacetime were indispensable instruments of the policy of "containment."

Between these two interpretations lay that of James Byrnes, Secretary of State from July 1945 to January 1947. Contrary to Wallace,

Byrnes thought no concessions should be made, but contrary to Forrestal and Acheson, he did not think all negotiations with the Soviets were useless and futile. Somewhat naïvely he thought of negotiation on the world level not as bargaining, but as a sort of minuet in which each dancer would cut his own figure in turn. The Americans had started by making concessions, they should make no more, for it was Russia's turn. If one waited patiently the Russians would become conciliatory because of their desire for peace. The United States should, then, continue the interminable discussions in the hope that one day, suddenly, the Soviets would agree to go on with the minuet and make their own gesture.

President Truman eliminated Wallace in September 1946 and Byrnes in January 1947. General Marshall, who had spent the year 1946 in China and was convinced that China was lost to the West, became Secretary of State on January 9, 1947. He was strongly in favor of the views of Forrestal and Acheson and he was to launch the policy of containment and aid that the United States has maintained in various forms in the years which followed. Marshall was to add his own special mark. According to the theory of concentrated strategy, a diplomatic offensive should be brought to bear at the most important point. Since China was lost, the most important front was Europe. The Marshall Plan is the most striking instance of the theory of concentration as applied in diplomacy.

The "great debate" about the various directions of foreign policy was, therefore, won by the party which advocated a policy of strength. As a result, the United States continued to be concerned with the whole world and to give priority to foreign policy as it had done of necessity during the war against the Axis. Isolation was condemned not only by some currents of public opinion but also by the pressure of circumstances themselves. For reasons of security Americans did not withdraw into themselves. All traditions had been swept aside, even that of nonentanglement. Peacetime alliances were no longer shameful but welcomed. World responsibility, connected with power, imposed the necessity for the United States to make its presence felt everywhere outside the Iron Curtain.

We will never know if Roosevelt, with his extraordinary resources, had come to this point, whether he would not have found a way to avoid the hardening of policy, the absolute rigidity, which leaves the freedom of initiative to the adversary. Many things have changed, and the "great debate" today, in the 1960's, is no longer presented in the same terms as in 1945. Although I believe in the importance of individual actions in history—as this book proves—I cannot think that Roosevelt would have been able to transform the basic situation.

The basic situation is that the world is no longer based on a multilateral balance of power but on a bipolar system of power with each major power surrounding itself with satellites and dependents. Roosevelt had not foreseen this. Only one of his ideas has clearly triumphed: the colonial empires are destroyed. Even this destruction has taken place in a world dominated by the magnetic attraction of one or the other of the two major powers, however. Wilson had laid the foundations for the destruction of the European balance of power. Roosevelt, following an analogous line, contributed to the opening of a Pandora's Box. But who could have avoided it? To attribute to him personal responsibility for what has happened would be unjust and unworthy of the historian, who may merely observe facts and try to explain them. The task of the historian is not to draw so-called "lessons" for posterity.

Bibliography

In this bibliography I have tried to indicate, with a brief estimate of their value and importance, the source materials, the essential studies, and the various aids to research in the field. The scope of the subject and the number of works devoted to it have led me to adopt certain arbitrary rules: (1) To mention only works which are accessible. (2) To stress recent studies, especially those published since the *Harvard Guide to American History*, published in 1954. (3) To include only American memoirs. It is obvious that those of Churchill, Ciano, De Gaulle, and many others are essential to such a study. The reader who wants a complete list should consult bibliographies of books on foreign policy in general. (4) Translations are only mentioned if they are as valuable as the original. (5) Daggers indicate works of exceptional importance.

I. BIBLIOGRAPHIES

Every scholar working in American history should know the uniquely valuable *Harvard Guide to American History*, edited by Oscar Handlin, Arthur M. Schlesinger, Samuel Eliot Morison, Frederick Merk, Arthur M. Scheslinger, Jr., and Paul H. Buck, Cambridge, Mass., 1954. See especially chapters 26, "The Diplomacy of Expansion, 1900–1917," 27, "The World War," 28, "Decade of Prosperity, 1920-1929," 29, "Great Depression, 1930–1941," and 30, "War and Its Aftermath, 1941–1952."

To carry research a step further, the essential work is the series *Writings on American History*, published annually by the American Historical Association. (There are no volumes for the years 1904 and 1905, and 1941 through 1947; the latest published volume is that of 1955.) There is an index for the period 1906–1940. This collection lists virtually all the articles on American history, and is, therefore, indispensable.

To keep abreast of recent publications, the scholar should use the quarterly *American Historical Review*, which includes reviews of important books, bibliographical notices, and lists of recent magazine articles, as well as the quarterly *Foreign Affairs*, which publishes lists of recent works on foreign policy with short critical comments. *Foreign Affairs Bibliography* is a collection of book reviews from *Foreign Affairs* (vol. I: 1919–1932, ed. William L. Langer and H. F. Armstrong, 1953; vol. II: 1932–1942, ed. G. H. Woolbert, 1945; vol. III: 1942–1952, ed. Henry L. Roberts, assisted by John Gunther and Janis A. Kreslins, 1955.

II. Primary Sources

There are numerous manuscript sources available to the scholar. The State Department Archives are accessible at least up to 1941. Statesmen have also left their papers to university libraries or foundations; for example, the papers of Wilson, Bryan, Lansing, and Hughes are to be found in the Library of Congress; those of Hoover and Stimson at Yale; those of Lodge at the Massachusetts Historical Society in Boston; those of Kellogg in St. Paul. The papers of Franklin D. Roosevelt are in Hyde Park.

I have made use of the *printed* sources. The core of these is contained in the collection *Papers Relating to Foreign Relations of the United States.* This series, which begins in 1861, includes both annual volumes (several each year since 1919) and supplements. In the annual volumes the classification is, in general, as follows: General; Commonwealth and Europe; Near East; Africa; Far East; American republics. According to the importance and amount of material, there may be more than one volume to a category. For 1932, for example, two of five volumes deal with the Far East; for 1933, two of five deal with the American republics.

To mention only the volumes which have appeared since the *Harvard Guide*, in 1952 the materials covered include the year 1935. The publications of the years since then are:

1936: Vol. I, *General, The British Commonwealth* (1953). Vol. II, *Europe* (1954). Vol. III, *The Near East and Africa* (1954). Vol. IV, *The Far East* (1954). Vol. V, *The American Republics* (1954).

1937: Vol. I, *General* (1954). Vol. II, *The British Commonwealth, Europe, Near East, and Africa* (1954). Vol. III, *The Far East* (1954). Vol. IV, *The Far East* (1954). Vol. V, *The American Republics* (1954).

1938: Vol. I, *General* (1955). Vol. II, *The British Commonwealth, Europe, Near East, and Africa* (1955). Vol. III, *The Far East* (1955). Vol. IV, *The Far East* (1955). Vol. V, *The American Republics* (1956).

1939: Vol. I, *General* (1956). Vol. II, *General, the British Commonwealth, Europe* (1956). Vol. III, *The Far East* (1955). Vol. IV, *The Far East, the Near East, and Africa* (1955). Vol. V, *The American Republics.*

1940: Vol. I, *General* (1959). Vol. II, *General and Europe* (1957). Vol. III, *The British Commonwealth, the Soviet Union, the Near East, and Africa* (1958). Vol. IV, *The Far East* (1955).

1941: Vol. I, *General, the Soviet Union* (1958). Vol. II, *Europe* (1959). Vol. III, *The British Commonwealth, the Near East, and Africa* (1959). Vol. IV, *The Far East* (1956).

1942: *China* (1956). Only volume published.

There is unfortunately no index in some of the volumes. An index of the years 1900–1918 was published in 1941.

The supplements are often more useful than the annual volumes and usually well indexed. Those which relate to our study are: *The Lansing*

Papers, 1914–1920, 1940, 2 vols. *Diplomatic Correspondence relating to the World War, 1916–1918,* 2 vols. *Relations with Russia, 1918–1919,* 1937, 4 vols. *The Paris Peace Conference, 1919,* 1942–1947, 13 vols. *The Soviet Union, 1933–1939,* 1952, 1 vol. *Relations with Japan, 1931–1941,* 1943, 2 vols. *The Conferences at Malta and Yalta, 1945,* 1955, 1 vol.

To these must be added certain publications of the State Department: *United States Relations with China with Special Reference to the Period 1944–1949,* Washington, 1949. *A Decade of American Foreign Policy; Basic Documents, 1941–1949,* prepared at the request of the Senate Committee on Foreign Relations by the staff of the committee and the Department of State, Washington, 1950. *Postwar Foreign Policy Preparation, 1939–1945,* Washington, 1959.

The papers of the presidents are often very useful. For Wilson the following are important: ‡Ray Stannard Baker, *Woodrow Wilson, Life and Letters,* Garden City, N.Y., 1927–1939, 8 vols. ‡ Ray Stannard Baker and William Dodd, eds. *The Public Papers of Woodrow Wilson,* New York, 1925–1927, 6 vols. ‡Charles Seymour, ed., *The Intimate Papers of Colonel House,* London, 1926–1928, arranged as a narrative in four volumes: I, *Beyond the Political Curtain, 1912–1915;* II, *From Neutrality to War, 1915–1917;* III, *Into the World War, April 1917–June 1918;* IV, *The Ending of the War, June 1918–August 1919.*

For Hoover the chief collection is ‡William Starr Myers, ed., *The State Papers and Other Public Writings,* Garden City, N.Y., 1934, 2 vols. Hoover's speeches after 1933 are collected in 8 volumes under the title, *Addresses upon the American Road.* The volumes related to our subject are: I, *1933–1938* (1938); II, *1938–1940* (1940); III, *1940–1941* (1941); IV, *1941–1945* (1946). There is also Hoover's own book, *The Ordeal of Woodrow Wilson,* New York, 1958.

For Roosevelt there are two collections, not as good as Baker's on Wilson. ‡Samuel I. Rosenman, ed., *The Public Papers and Addresses of Franklin D. Roosevelt,* New York, 1938–1950, 13 vols. Judge Rosenman shared with Sherwood and Hopkins the task of drafting Roosevelt's speeches. He does not always reproduce them with absolute faithfulness. Elliott Roosevelt, ed., *F.D.R.: His Personal Letters,* New York, 1947–1950, 4 vols.

Also essential are the following: ‡Paul Mantoux, *Les Délibérations du Conseil des Quatre (24 mars–28 juin 1919),* Paris, 1955. Vol. I, *Jusqu'à la remise à la délégation allemande des conditions de paix;* vol. II, *Depuis la remise à la délégation allemande des conditions de paix jusqu' à la signature du traité de Versailles.* ‡David Hunter Miller, *My Diary at the Conference of Paris, with Documents,* New York, 1938, 21 vols. The minutes of the Supreme Council are contained in volumes XIV–XVI. There are also essential documents concerning the work of the experts.

On the Second World War, the Soviet Union has published the ‡*Correspondence between the Chairman of the Council of Ministers of the U.S.S.R. and the Presidents of the U.S.A. and the Prime Ministers of*

Great Britain, during the Great Patriotic War of 1941–1945, Moscow, 1957, 2 vols.

Finally, we should mention the printed hearings of the Senate Foreign Relations Committee and other committees, which are valuable, but very cumbersome and full of omissions. There is information important to our subject in the volume on the Treaty of Versailles, in the many volumes concerning the investigation of the Nye Committee, and in the *Hearings before the Joint Committee on the Investigation of the Pearl Harbor Attack*, Washington, 1946, 39 vols., combined with a *Report on the Investigation of the Pearl Harbor Attack*, Washington, 1946.

III. Memoirs

Only one statesman was in power before, during and after the period of our study: Henry L. Stimson. This makes his book, written in collaboration with McGeorge Bundy, of exceptional interest. Bundy is the son of Harvey Bundy, former aide of Stimson's in the State Department. ‡Henry L. Stimson and McGeorge Bundy, *On Active Service in Peace and War*, New York, 1948.

Two high-ranking diplomats kept diaries, virtually on a day-by-day basis: Joseph C. Grew, and J. Pierrepont Moffat (who married Grew's daughter). The two men exchanged notes and were able to take advantage of each other's observations. In both cases the published material represents only a fraction of the diaries. In his twenty-five years of service Moffat wrote fifty-two volumes of diaries, memoirs, speeches, and so forth, most of which are now in the Harvard College Library. Joseph C. Grew, *Turbulent Era: A Diplomatic Record of Forty Years, 1904–1945*, ed. Walter Johnson, Boston, 1952, 2 vols. This should be supplemented by his book on his ten years as ambassador to Japan: ‡Joseph C. Grew, *Ten Years in Japan*, New York, 1944. See also ‡Nancy H. Hooker, ed., *The Moffat Papers: Selections from the Diplomatic Journals of Jay Pierrepont Moffat, 1919–1943*, Cambridge, Mass., 1956.

To these sources of exceptional importance there should naturally be added innumerable other memoirs concerning international relations. We shall classify them chronologically as far as possible.

1. The Wilson Period

a) Works of Wilson's close collaborators

William Jennings Bryan (Secretary of State), *The Memoirs of William Jennings Bryan*, edited by Mary B. Bryan, Philadelphia, 1925.

‡Robert Lansing (Secretary of State), *War Memoirs*, Indianapolis, Ind., 1935, as well as ‡*The Peace Negotiations: A Personal Narrative*, Boston, 1921, and *The Big Four and Others of the Peace Conference*, Boston, 1921. A short work by Bainbridge Colby, Wilson's last Secretary of State: Bainbridge Colby, *The Close of Woodrow Wilson's Administra-*

tion and the Final Years: An Address Delivered before the Missouri Historical Society, Saint Louis, 28 April 1930, New York, 1930.

On Colonel House, in addition to his papers, cited above, see a collaborative work of many of the American experts at the peace conference: Edward Mandell House and Charles Seymour, *What Really Happened at Paris,* New York, 1921. (Contributors include: S. E. Mezes, C. Day, C. H. Haskins, R. H. Lord, C. Seymour, D. W. Johnson, I. Bowman, W. L. Westermann, M. O. Hudson, J. B. Scott, T. W. Lamont, A. A. Young, S. Gompers, H. Hoover, H. T. Mayo, T. H. Bliss, D. H. Miller, and E. M. House.)

W. G. McAdoo (Secretary of the Treasury, and Wilson's son-in-law), *Crowded Years,* Boston, 1931.

Josephus Daniels (Secretary of the Navy), *The Wilson Era, Years of War and After, 1917–1923,* Chapel Hill, N.C., 1946.

b) Works of experts or eye-witnesses at the peace conference

James Thomson Shotwell, *At the Paris Peace Conference,* New York, 1937. Charles Seymour, *Geography, Justice, and Politics at the Paris Peace Conference of 1919,* New York, 1951. Emile Joseph Dillon, *The Inside Story of the Peace Conference,* New York and London, 1920. Bernard M. Baruch, *The Making of the Reparation and Economic Sections of the Treaty,* New York, 1920. Philip Mason Burnett, *Reparations at the Paris Peace Conference from the Standpoint of the American Delegation,* New York, 1940, 2 vols. Charles Homer Haskins and Robert Howard Lord, *Some Problems of the Peace Conference,* Cambridge, Mass., 1920. ‡Ray Stannard Baker, *Woodrow Wilson and the World Settlement,* Garden City, N.Y., 1922, 3 vols. (by the editor of Wilson's papers). ‡Colonel Stephen Bonsal, *Unfinished Business,* Garden City, N.Y., 1944 (excerpts from his journal at the time he was Wilson's interpreter). Stephen Bonsal, *Suitors and Suppliants: The Little Nations at Versailles,* New York, 1946. Charles Thaddeus Thompson, *The Peace Conference Day by Day* (with an introductory letter by Colonel House), New York, 1920. Bernard Newman, *Secret Servant,* New York, 1936. Harris Henry Wilson, *The Peace in the Making,* New York, 1920. Harry Hansen, *The Adventures of the Fourteen Points: Vivid and Dramatic Episodes of the Peace Conference,* New York, 1919.

c) On the defeat of the treaty

The essential work is ‡Henry Cabot Lodge, *The Senate and the League of Nations,* New York, 1925. Wilson's secretary has published a work which Wilson's best biographer, Link, criticizes severely: Joseph P. Tumulty, *Woodrow Wilson as I know him,* Garden City, N.Y., 1921.

d) Works by members of Wilson's family

By his second wife: Mrs. Edith Bolling Wilson, *My Memoir,* Indianapolis, Ind., 1939.

By his daughter: Eleanor Wilson McAdoo, *The Woodrow Wilson's*, New York, 1937.

2. The Republican Period

Harding wrote no memoirs. There is, however, a short but extremely revealing autobiography by Coolidge: ‡Calvin Coolidge, *The Autobiography of Calvin Coolidge*, New York, 1929.

Hoover wrote a great deal. I refer specifically to: Herbert Hoover, *Memoirs: The Cabinet and the Presidency, 1920–1933*, New York, 1951–1952, 3 vols.

For Hughes, see Charles Evans Hughes, *The Pathway of Peace: Representative Addresses, 1921–1925*, New York, 1925.

For Kellogg, see an article in *Foreign Affairs:* Frank B. Kellogg, "Some Foreign Policies of the United States," *Foreign Affairs*, vol. IV (1926), no. 2.

Dawes, vice president under Coolidge, subsequently ambassador to England, has written three books: Charles Gates Dawes, *A Journal of Reparations*, London, 1939; *Notes as Vice President, 1928–1929*, Boston, 1935; *Journal as Ambassador to Great Britain*, New York, 1939 (important on the London Naval Conference and on the preparation of the Disarmament Conference).

Stimson has written a great deal. One should see especially: ‡Henry L. Stimson, *The Far Eastern Crisis*, New York, 1936.

3. Franklin Delano Roosevelt

Two works have been of primary importance in this study. ‡Cordell Hull, *The Memoirs of Cordell Hull*, New York, 1948, 2 vols., in which the Secretary of State gives a precise account of many details. The overall view of the situation is a bit distorted here by his personal illusions, but it is, nonetheless, an important work. ‡Robert Sherwood, *Roosevelt and Hopkins: An Intimate History*, New York, 1948.

For other works by Roosevelt's close collaborators see: James A. Farley, *Jim Farley's Story: The Roosevelt Years*, New York, 1948; Raymond Moley, *After Seven Years*, New York, 1939 (Moley indulges in several attacks, for he is an isolationist and Roosevelt had ceased to be one at the time this book was published); Samuel I. Rosenman, *Working with Roosevelt*, New York, 1952; ‡Fleet Admiral William D. Leahy, *I Was There: The Personal Story of the Chief of Staff to Presidents Roosevelt and Truman*, New York, 1950. Admiral Leahy played an extremely important role, both as ambassador to Vichy and as private adviser to Roosevelt.

There are several works of interest by members of the President's family: Eleanor Roosevelt, *This I Remember*, New York, 1949; James Roosevelt and Sydney Shalett, *Affectionately, F.D.R.*, New York, 1959, illustrated (not very useful for political history); Elliott Roosevelt, *As He Saw It*, New York, 1946 (in many places this seems too highly colored for reliability).

Among the works produced by members of Roosevelt's cabinet, the most important ones are: Frances Perkins (Secretary of Labor), *The Roosevelt I Knew*, New York, 1946; Harold C. Ickes (Secretary of the Interior), *The Secret Diary of Harold C. Ickes*, New York, 1953–1954, 3 vols.; Henry Morgenthau, Jr. (Secretary of the Treasury), "The Morgenthau Diaries," *Collier's*, September 27–November 1, 1947; ‡Sumner Welles, *The Time for Decision*, New York, 1944, *Where Are We Heading?* New York, 1946, and *Seven Decisions That Shaped History*, New York, 1951. By Cordell Hull's successor at the State Department: Edward R. Stettinius, Jr., *Lend-Lease, Weapon for Victory*, New York, 1944; ‡*Roosevelt and the Russians: The Yalta Conference*, ed. Walter Johnson, Garden City, N.Y., 1949. By Stettinius' successor, who was present at Yalta: James F. Byrnes, *Speaking Frankly*, New York, 1947. ‡Walter Millis and E. S. Duffield, eds., *The Forrestal Diaries*, New York, 1951.

There are numerous accounts by ambassadors or delegates of the President: Joseph E. Davies, *Mission to Moscow*, New York, 1941 (extremely favorable to the Soviet Union); William E. Dodd, Jr., and Martha Dodd, eds., *Ambassador Dodd's Diary, 1933–1938*, New York, 1941; John G. Winant, *A Letter from Grosvenor Square: An Account of a Stewardship*, Boston, 1947; Carlton J. H. Hayes, *Wartime Mission in Spain, 1942–1945*, New York, 1945 (Hayes is a professional historian); Herbert Feis, *The Spanish Story: Franco and the Nations at War*, New York, 1948 (a good supplement to Hayes); ‡General J. W. Stilwell, *The Stilwell Papers*, New York, 1948; C. F. Romanus and Riley Sunderland, *Stilwell's Mission to China*, Washington, Office of the Chief of Military History, Department of the Army, 1953; General C. L. Chennault, *Way of a Fighter*, New York, 1949. The books by Romanus and Sunderland and by Chennault, Stilwell's rival, supplement Stilwell's own account.

Among the innumerable accounts by military men, the following are the most important for what interests us here. ‡General Dwight D. Eisenhower, *Crusade in Europe*, Garden City, N.Y., 1948, and *Report by the Supreme Commander to the Combined Chiefs of Staff on the Operations in Europe of the Allied Expeditionary Force*, Washington, 1946; Harry C. Butcher (Eisenhower's naval aide), *My Three Years with Eisenhower*, New York, 1946; General Frederick E. Morgan, *Overture to Overlord*, Garden City, N.Y., 1950. On the three members of the joint chiefs of staff: Ernest J. King and Walter Muir Whitehill, *Fleet Admiral King: A Naval Record*, New York, 1952; General H. H. Arnold, *Global Mission*, New York, 1949; Walter Millis, ed., *War Reports of Marshall, Arnold, King*, Philadelphia, 1947. Marshall has not published, but see: Robert Payne, *The Marshall Story*, New York, 1951. Nor has MacArthur published, but see: James Kline Eyre, *Roosevelt-MacArthur Conflict*, Chambersburg, Pa., 1950; R. H. Rovere and A. M. Schlesinger, Jr., *The General and The President, and the Future of American Foreign Policy*, New York, 1951.

On the atomic bomb, see: Henry L. Stimson, "The Decision to Use the Atomic Bomb," *Harper's Magazine*, CXCIV (1947), 97.

Among other valuable memoirs, note: Husband E. Kimmel, *Admiral Kimmel's Story*, Chicago, 1955 (an opponent of Roosevelt, for he was the commander of the Pacific Fleet at the time of Pearl Harbor and was ousted); William Allen White, *Forty Years on Main Street*, New York, 1937 (valuable for the study of the peace movement, but biased in favor of the Democrats); *The Private Papers of Senator Vandenberg*, ed. by Arthur H. Vandenberg, Jr., and Joe Alex Morris, Boston, 1952 (deals with the period 1941–1951).

IV. WORKS ON THE MAJOR PROBLEMS

1. General Textbooks

The following are the most important. ‡Thomas A. Bailey, *A Diplomatic History of the American People*, 6th ed., New York, 1958. ‡ Samuel Flagg Bemis, *A Diplomatic History of the United States*, 3rd ed., New York, 1950. Especially important is Bemis' ‡*The United States as a World Power. A Diplomatic History. 1900–1955*, rev. ed., New York, 1955, which elaborates the second half of his earlier work. Bemis stresses, more than Bailey, relations with Latin America. See also ‡Julius W. Pratt, *A History of United States Foreign Policy*, New York, 1955; Robert H. Ferrell, *American Diplomacy. A History*, New York, 1959 (more analytical and less detailed than the others, but equally valuable).

Also useful are: Richard Van Alstyne, *American Crisis Diplomacy: The Quest for Collective Security, 1918–1952*, Stanford, Calif., 1952; Allan Nevins and Louis M. Hacker, eds., *The United States and Its Place in World Affairs, 1918–1943*, Boston, 1943; Louis B. Wehle, *Hidden Threads of History: Wilson through Roosevelt*, New York, 1953 (Wehle is a nephew of Louis Brandeis and worked for Newton D. Baker in the War Department).

And, finally, a particularly useful work: Samuel Flagg Bemis, ed., *The American Secretaries of State and Their Diplomacy*, New York, 1927–1929, 10 vols.

2. Fundamentals of American Foreign Policy

The best introductions to the study of these fundamentals seem to me to be: ‡Dexter Perkins, *The American Approach to Foreign Policy*, Cambridge, Mass., 1952 (rev. ed., 1962); ‡Gabriel A. Almond, *The American People and Foreign Policy*, New York, 1950; and, for an overall view of the "atmosphere," ‡Arthur M. Schlesinger, *The Rise of Modern America, 1865–1951*, New York, 1951, and ‡*Paths to the Present*, New York, 1949.

The following are also of interest. Daniel J. Boorstin, *The Genius of American Politics*, Chicago, 1953. Boorstin maintains that the essential characteristic of American policy is the rejection of all explicit theory. Geoffrey Gorer, *The American People: a Study in National Character*, New York, 1948. Gorer is a cultural anthropologist, of the school of Ruth Benedict and Margaret Mead.

It is necessary to give special consideration to the ideas of the historian Charles Beard. See especially: Charles A. Beard and William Beard, *The American Leviathan: The Republic in the Machine Age*, New York, 1930, and ‡Charles A. Beard, *The Idea of National Interest: An Analytical Study of American Foreign Policy*, New York, 1934. For details on Beard's approach see: Elias Berg, *The Historical Thinking of Charles A. Beard*, Stockholm, 1957, and, above all, ‡Gerald Stourzh, "Charles A. Beard's Interpretations of American Foreign Policy," *World Affairs Quarterly*, July 1957, pp. 111–148.

‡See also William T. R. Fox, "Interwar International Relations Research: The American Experience," *World Politics*, October 1949, pp. 67–79, and Fred Harvey Harrington, "Beard's Idea of National Interest and New Interpretations," *American Perspective*, Summer 1950, pp. 335–345.

On the "Great Debate," about idealism and realism in the foreign policy of the United States, the main works of the "realists" are: ‡Hans J. Morgenthau, *In Defense of the National Interest: A Critical Examination of American Foreign Policy*, New York, 1951; Hans J. Morgenthau, "The Mainsprings of American Foreign Policy," *American Political Science Review*, December 1950, pp. 833–854; George F. Kennan, *American Diplomacy, 1900–1950*, Chicago, 1951. The champion of the "idealists" is Frank Tannenbaum. See his *The American Tradition in Foreign Policy*, Norman, Okla., 1955, and "The American Tradition in Foreign Relations," *Foreign Affairs*, October 1951, pp. 31–50. Some syntheses have been attempted: Thomas I. Cook and Malcolm Moos, "Foreign Policy: The Realism of Idealism," *American Political Science Review*, June 1952, pp. 343–356, and, above all, ‡Robert E. Osgood, *Ideals and Self-Interest in America's Foreign Relations*, Chicago, 1953.

Frank L. Klingberg, "The Historical Alternation of Moods in American Foreign Policy," *World Politics*, January 1952, pp. 239–273, expounds the theory of cycles in United States foreign policy.

3. Population, Immigration, and the Frontier in Relation to Foreign Policy

On the evolution of the population, see especially: Warren S. Thompson and P. K. Whelpton, *Population Trends in the United States*, New York, 1933; Forrest E. Linder and Robert D. Grove, *Vital Statistics Rates in the United States, 1900–1940* (United States Department of Commerce. Bureau of the Census), Washington, 1943; Frank Lorimer, *et al.*, *Population Redistribution and Economic Growth, U.S., 1870–1950* (prepared under the direction of Simon Kuznets and Dorothy S. Thomas), Philadelphia, 1957.

On immigration, the following three books show well the evolution of attitudes: Henry Pratt Fairchild, *Immigration: A World Movement and Its American Significance*, New York, 1913, and *The Melting Pot Mistake*, Boston, 1926; Hannibal Gerald Duncan, *Immigration and Assimilation*,

New York, 1933. The most important works are those of Oscar Handlin, among which the most valuable for us are: ‡*The American People in the Twentieth Century*, Cambridge, Mass., 1954, ‡*Race and Nationality in American Life*, Garden City, N.Y., 1957, and ‡*Immigration as a Factor in American History*, Englewood Cliffs, N.J., 1959. On assimilation, see: E. P. Hutchinson, *Immigrants and Their Children, 1850–1950*, New York, 1956 (for the Social Sciences Research Council in cooperation with the United States Bureau of the Census). Finally, for the special case of the Oriental immigrants, see R. D. McKenzie, *Oriental Exclusion*, Chicago, 1928.

On the theory of the frontier, the essential article by Turner, written in 1893, is reprinted in ‡Frederick Jackson Turner, *The Frontier in American History*, New York, 1950 (1st edition, 1920). An interesting study with a copious bibliography is: ‡Robert E. Reigel, "American Frontier Theory," *Cahiers d'Histoire Mondiale*, Vol. III (1956), part 2, pp. 356–380. See also William Appleman Williams, "The Frontier Thesis and American Foreign Policy," *Pacific Historical Review*, November 1955, pp. 379–395, which, openly inspired by Marxist views, finds in Turner's theory a convenient justification for the aggressive, imperialist spirit. More moderate views are found in: L. S. Kaplan, "Frederick Jackson Turner and Imperialism," *Social Science*, January 1952, pp. 12–16; Merle E. Curti, *Frederick Jackson Turner: Life and Beliefs*, Mexico, 1949; G. R. Taylor, ed., *The Turner Thesis concerning the Role of the Frontier in American History*, Boston, 1949.

One must mention three important recent works on the evolution of the frontier: W. P. Webb, *The Great Frontier*, Boston, 1952, of which an extremely important review has been written by the British historian G. Barraclough ("Metropolis and Macrocosm," *Past and Present*, May 1954, pp. 77–90); Walker Demarquis Wyman and C. B. Kroeber, eds., *The Frontier in Perspective*, Madison, Wis., 1957; Thomas Dionysius Clark, *Frontier America: The Story of the Westward Movement*, New York, 1959, illustrated.

On the influence of Turner, see: Wilbur R. Jacobs, "Frederick Jackson Turner. Master Teacher," *Pacific Historical Review*, February 1934, pp. 49–58.

Finally, one must mention with Turner, another optimistic interpreter of the expansion, Brooks Adams, who had, as Turner did, a strong influence on Charles A. Beard. In Brooks Adams' view, only a policy of political expansion can preserve democracy. Brooks Adams, *The Law of Civilization and Decay: An Essay on History*, New York, 1897.

4. Strategic Theory and Imperialism

The main works of Mahan are: ‡*The Influence of Sea Power upon History, 1660–1783*, Boston, 1890; *The Influence of Sea Power upon the French Revolution and Empire, 1793–1812*, Boston, 1892, 2 vols.; *The*

Interest of America in Sea Power, Present and Future, Boston, 1897; *Lessons of the War with Spain and Other Articles*, Boston, 1899; *The Interest of America in International Conditions*, Boston, 1910.

There are two worthwhile biographies of Mahan, the first by a former British vice-consul in New York, Charles Carlisle Taylor, *The Life of Admiral Mahan*, London, 1920; the second, by an American Navy officer, Captain William Dilworth Puleston, *Mahan: The Life and Work of Captain Alfred Thayer Mahan, U.S.N.*, New Haven, 1939. But above all, see two remarkably fine studies of his doctrine and his influence: ‡William E. Levezey, *Mahan on Sea Power*, Norman, Okla., 1947; and ‡Margaret Sprout, "Mahan, Evangelist of Sea Power," in Edward Mead Earle, *Makers of Modern Strategy*, Princeton, 1943.

On American naval strength, see especially two books by Harold and Margaret Sprout, *The Rise of American Naval Power, 1776–1918*, rev. ed., Princeton, 1942, and *Toward a New Order of Sea Power: American Naval Policy and the World Scene, 1918–1922*, Princeton, 1946. See also: George Theron Davis, *A Navy Second to None*, New York, 1940; and D. W. Mitchell, *History of the Modern American Navy, from 1883 through Pearl Harbor*, New York, 1946.

On the history of the Army and of defense in general, see: William Addleman Ganoe, *The History of the United States Army*, New York, 1942 (1st ed., 1924); Merze Tate, *The United States and Armaments*, Cambridge, Mass., 1948; Walter Millis, *Arms and Men; A Study in American Military History*, New York, 1956.

5. Economic Factors in American Foreign Policy

‡Ernest L. Bogart and Donald L. Kemmerer, *Economic History of the American People*, rev. ed., New York, 1942. And by Bogart, volumes 7 and 8 of the *Economic History of the United States*, New York, 1942. See also: George Soule, *Prosperity Decade; From War to Depression: 1917–1929*, New York, 1947; Broadus Mitchell, *Depression Decade: From New Era through New Deal, 1929–1941*, New York, 1947; Louis Rosenstock-Franck, *Histoire économique et sociale des Etats-Unis de 1919 à 1949*, Paris, 1950.

On foreign economic policy, see: B. H. Williams, *Economic Foreign Policy of the United States*, New York, 1929, interesting because it was written at the end of the period of prosperity; George Soule, *Economic Forces in American History*, New York, 1952; W. Y. Elliott, ed., *The Political Economy of American Foreign Policy; Its Concepts, Strategy and Limits* (by a subsidiary group of the Woodrow Wilson Foundation and the National Planning Association), New York, 1955, which, although primarily concerned with immediate problems, contains many interesting ideas.

On the financial foreign policy of the United States, it is also worthwhile to compare two works written before the Second World War:

James W. Angell, *Financial Foreign Policy of the United States*, New York, 1933; James Watson Gantenbein, *Financial Questions in United States Foreign Policy*, New York, 1939.

The period of prosperity and the depression have stimulated some important studies: ‡William E. Leuchtenburg, *The Perils of Prosperity, 1914–1932* (in The Chicago History of American Civilization, ed. Daniel J. Boorstin), Chicago, 1958, extremely interesting on the concentration of power in a "business class" with little experience in social problems; James Warren Prothro, *The Dollar Decade. Business Ideas in the 1920's*, Baton Rouge, La., 1954; and, above all, a magnificent little book, ‡Herbert Feis, *The Diplomacy of the Dollar. First Era: 1919–1932*, Baltimore, 1950. Also by Feis, *The Investment of American Capital Abroad*, New York, 1945, and *The Changing Pattern of International Economic Affairs*, New York, 1940.

On the depression, the basic work is: ‡John Kenneth Galbraith, *The Great Crash, 1929*, Boston, 1955. On the interpretations of the situation by economists, see a recent volume of the monumental work by Joseph Dorfman of Columbia: Joseph Dorfman, *The Economic Mind in American Civilization, 1918–1933*, vol. 4, New York, 1959.

For the special relation of petroleum to foreign policy, see: Herbert Feis, *Petroleum and American Foreign Policy*, Stanford, Calif., 1944; John A. de Novo, "The Movement for an aggressive American Oil Policy Abroad, 1918–1920," *American Historical Review*, July 1956, pp. 854–876.

On dollar diplomacy, see: Juan Leets, *United States and Latin America: Dollar Diplomacy*, New Orleans, 1912; Scott Nearing and Joseph Freeman, *Dollar Diplomacy: A Study in American Imperialism*, New York, 1925.

6. Nationalism and Isolationism

The best study on American nationalism is: ‡Hans Kohn, *American Nationalism; An Interpretative Essay*, New York, 1957. The earliest masterful analysis of isolationism is: Perry Belmont, *National Isolation An Illusion; Political Independence Not Isolation*, New York, 1925.

In addition, there are two recent first-rate books on isolationism: one, by a professor at the University of Buffalo: ‡Selig Adler, *The Isolationist Impulse: Its Twentieth-Century Reaction*, New York, 1957; the other, published by a professor at Duke University, in collaboration with a brilliant team (William R. Allen, Richard N. Current, Robert H. Ferrell, William L. Neumann, Kenneth W. Thompson, and J. Chalmers Vinson): ‡Alexander De Conde, ed., *Isolation and Security; Ideas and Interests in Twentieth-Century American Foreign Policy*, Durham, N.C., 1957.

See also an extremely well-informed article, opposed to prevailing opinions: William Appleman Williams, "The Legend of Isolationism in the 1920's," *Science and Society*, Winter 1954; and a few other noteworthy articles: Victor L. Albjerg, "Isolationism and the Early New Deal, 1932–1937," *Current History*, October 1958; Ralph H. Smuckler, "The Region of Isolationism," *American Political Science Review,* June 1953, pp. 396–401; Samuel Lubell, "Who Votes Isolationist and Why?" *Harper's Magazine,* April 1951, pp. 29–36.

Finally, on several related movements, see: Arthur S. Link, "What Happened to the Progressive Movement in the 1920's," *American Historical Review,* July 1959, pp. 833–851; John M. Blum, "Nativism, Anti-Radicalism and the Foreign Scare, 1917–1920," *Midwest Journal,* Winter, 1950–1951; Sidney Warren, "Normalcy, Neutrality and Disillusion, 1920–1940," *Current History,* November 1951.

7. Public Opinion and Congress in Relation to Foreign Policy

Aside from the book by Gabriel Almond, cited above, the basic study is: ‡Thomas A. Bailey, *The Man in the Street; The Impact of American Public Opinion on Foreign Policy,* New York, 1948.

On various detailed points, see: Henry A. Turner, "Woodrow Wilson and Public Opinion," *Public Opinion Quarterly,* Winter 1957–1958, pp. 505–520; John Norman, "Influence of Pro-Fascist Propaganda on American Neutrality, 1935–1936," in Dwight E. Lee and George E. McReynolds, eds., *Essays in History and International Relations in Honor of George Hubbard Blakeslee,* Worcester, Mass., 1949, pp. 193–214; Fillmore H. Sanford, "Public Orientation to Roosevelt," *Public Opinion Quarterly,* Summer 1951, pp. 189–216; Ralph K. White, "Hitler, Roosevelt and the Nature of War Propaganda," *Journal of Abnormal and Social Psychology,* April 1949, pp. 157–174.

There is a large and valuable collection of polls taken between 1935 and 1946, easier to use for reference than the *Public Opinion Quarterly:* Hadley Cantril, ed., *Public Opinion, 1935–1946,* Princeton, N.J., 1951.

For the role of Congress as such, see: Mary E. Bradshaw, "Congress and Foreign Policy since 1900," *Annals of the American Academy of Political and Social Sciences,* September 1953; John C. Donovan, "Congressional Isolationists and the Roosevelt Foreign Policy," *World Politics,* April 1951, pp. 299–316; George L. Grassmuck, *Sectional Biases in Congress on Foreign Policy,* Baltimore, 1951; Roland Young, *Congressional Politics in the Second World War,* New York, 1956.

8. Early Stages of American Imperialism

Hobson's work is essential to this study. See ‡John Atkinson Hobson, *Imperialism, A Study,* New York, 1902; William L. Langer, "A Critique of Imperialism . . . by J. A. Hobson," *Foreign Affairs,* October 1935, pp. 102–119.

On imperialism properly so-called, the basic work is Howard K. Beale, *Theodore Roosevelt and the Rise of America to World Power,* Baltimore, 1956 (The Albert Shaw Lectures on Diplomatic History, 1953). To this one must add Julius W. Pratt, *America's Colonial Experiment; How the United States Gained, Governed, and in Part Gave Away a Colonial Empire,* New York, 1950; and George E. Mowry, *The Era of Theodore*

Roosevelt, 1900–1912 (The New American Nation series), New York, 1958.

Among the contemporary works reflecting moral scruples about imperialism, note the book by a professor at Harvard who lectured on this subject at the Sorbonne in 1906–1907: Archibald Cary Coolidge, *The United States as a World Power*, New York, 1908; and the work of an Englishman: J. M. Kennedy, *Imperial America*, London, 1914. In addition, see a study organized according to regions: William H. Haas, ed., *The American Empire*, Chicago, 1940; and William E. Leuchtenburg, "Progressivism and Imperialism: The Progressive Movement and American Foreign Policy, 1898–1916," *Mississippi Valley Historical Review*, 1952, pp. 483–504.

V. WORKS CLASSIFIED BY PERIOD

1. Wilson

a) General

Any study of Wilson should start with the two best biographies. One of these, in the process of being completed, is by Arthur S. Link, professor at Northwestern University. He has already published: ‡*Wilson: The Road to the White House*, Princeton, 1947, ‡*Wilson: The New Freedom*, Princeton, 1956, and ‡*Wilson: The Struggle for Neutrality, 1914–1915*, Princeton, 1960. See also Link's ‡*Woodrow Wilson and the Progressive Era, 1910–1917*, New York, 1954. The "Essay on Sources" in this last volume (pp. 283–313) is a fine summary of existing documentation on Wilson. Taking advantage of this essay, I will not stress publications which antedate it. The other notable biography is the work of a journalist. More anecdotal than Link's, it is nevertheless an extremely well-documented work: ‡Arthur Clarence Walworth, *Woodrow Wilson*, New York, 1958, 2 vols.

On Wilson's works, note also: Laura Shearer Turnbull, *Woodrow Wilson: a Selected Bibliography of His Published Writings, Addresses and Public Papers*, Princeton, 1948.

Wilson's career and writings have aroused many strong feelings. One must be familiar with the main pro-Wilson works written during the 1920's. Charles Seymour, the editor of Colonel House's papers, has published *Woodrow Wilson and the World War*, New Haven, 1921, *American Diplomacy during the World War*, Baltimore, 1942 (1st ed., 1933), and *American Neutrality: 1914–1917*, New Haven, 1935. Also in the same spirit, see the book by former Secretary of the Navy Josephus Daniels, *The Life of Woodrow Wilson, 1856–1924*, Philadelphia, 1924, and William Allen White, *Woodrow Wilson: The Man, His Times and His Task*, Boston and New York, 1924.

In opposition to these pro-Wilson writers, there arose a "revisionist" school, very active after 1935, when the threat of a new war appeared.

Its principal works are: Edwin M. Borchard and W. P. Lage, *Neutrality for the United States*, New Haven, 1937, which accuses Wilson of duplicity and a lack of a truly neutral attitude; and Charles C. Tansill, *America Goes to War*, Boston, 1938, strongly anti-British. More moderate from this same point of view is: Walter Millis, *Road to War; America 1914–1917*, Boston and New York, 1935. Millis, a revisionist during the First World War, was to become pro-Roosevelt during the Second World War.

The 1950's have produced a new flood of pro-Wilson literature because of the centenary of his birth in 1956. Two pertinent analyses of these publications have been made: Robert F. Durdan, "Woodrow Wilson and His New Biographers," *South Atlantic Quarterly*, Autumn 1957; Richard L. Watson, Jr., "Woodrow Wilson and His Interpreters, 1947–1957," *Mississippi Valley Historical Review*, September 1957. The main publications of the centenary are: Arthur P. Dudden, ed., *Woodrow Wilson and the World of Today* (essays by Arthur S. Link, W. L. Langer, Eric F. Goldman), Philadelphia, 1957; Edward H. Buehrig, ed., *Wilson's Foreign Policy in Perspective*, Bloomington, Ind., 1957 (contains articles by Charles Seymour, Buehrig, Vinacke, Bemis, Sir Lewellyn Woodward); Arthur S. Link, ed., *Wilson the Diplomatist: A Look at His Major Foreign Policies*, Baltimore, 1957; *Le Centenaire de Woodrow Wilson, 1856–1956*, Geneva (European Center of the Carnegie Foundation), [1957] (articles by Jacques Freymond, Maurice Bourquin, Paul Mantoux, William E. Rappart, J. B. Duroselle, and Herbert C. Nicholas.) There are other good, recent biographies of Wilson, aside from those by Link and by Walworth, mentioned above. One by a psychologist who is also author of a biography of Henry Cabot Lodge: John A. Garraty, *Woodrow Wilson: A Great Life in Brief*, New York, 1956; Garraty has summarized his conclusions in "Woodrow Wilson: A Study in Personality," *South Atlantic Quarterly*, April 1957, pp. 176–185; and a book with a deceptive title, since it actually treats the general policies of Wilson, and not the balance of power: Edward H. Buehrig, *Woodrow Wilson and the Balance of Power*, Bloomington, Ind., 1955.

b) Wilson's philosophy

The basic work is: ‡Harley Notter, *The Origins of the Foreign Policy of Woodrow Wilson*, Baltimore, 1937. Other publications are: James Kerney, *The Political Education of Woodrow Wilson*, New York and London, 1926, dealing more with biography than with ideas; John Morton Blum, *Woodrow Wilson and the Politics of Morality*, Boston, 1956; Earl Latham, ed., *The Philosophy and Policies of Woodrow Wilson*, Chicago, 1958 (with articles by Link, Langer, Seymour, Raymond Fosdick, Robert Osgood, and August Hecksher); Bernard Brodie, "A Psychoanalytic Interpretation of Woodrow Wilson," *World Politics*, April 1957; Merle Curti, "Woodrow Wilson's Concept of Human Nature," *Midwest Journal of Political Science*, May 1957; John M. Norris, "The Influence of British

Nineteenth Century Liberalism on Woodrow Wilson," *World Affairs Quarterly*, October 1957; James T. Shotwell (a former collaborator of Wilson), "The Leadership of Wilson," *Current History*, November 1951; and William Diamond, *The Economic Thought of Woodrow Wilson*, Baltimore, Md., 1943.

On the New Freedom, see Wilson himself: *The New Freedom: A Call for the Emancipation of the Generous Energies of a People*, New York, 1913; and especially the excellent biography of the author of this doctrine: A. T. Mason, *Brandeis: A Free Man's Life*, New York, 1946.

c) Wilson and his collaborators

In addition to the book cited above on Brandeis, there are several good studies on Lansing: ‡Daniel M. Smith, *Robert Lansing and American Neutrality, 1914–1917* (University of California Publications in History, vol. 59), Berkeley, Calif., 1958; Daniel M. Smith, "Robert Lansing and the Formulation of American Neutrality Policies, 1914–1915," *Mississippi Valley Historical Review*, June 1956, pp. 59–81 (using Lansing's papers, Smith shows that Lansing became a partisan of intervention very early); John Morton Blum, *Joe Tumulty and the Wilson Era*, Boston, 1951.

For an excellent work on House, see: ‡Alexander L. and Juliette George, *Woodrow Wilson and Colonel House: A Personality Study*, New York, 1956.

d) American neutrality, 1914–1917

‡Ernest R. May, *The World War and American Isolation, 1914–1917*, Cambridge, Mass., 1959 (Harvard Historical Studies, 71). Unfortunately, this excellent study does not include Franco-American relations. Other interesting publications are: Edward H. Buehrig, "Wilson's Neutrality Re-examined," *World Politics*, October 1950, pp. 1–19; Henry F. May, *The End of American Innocence: A Study of the First Years of Our Own Time, 1912–1917*, New York, 1959. H. F. May is the more controversial.

On the economic aspects, highly important since they made an impact on the very essence of political neutrality, see: Pierre Renouvin, "La politique des emprunts étrangers aux Etats-Unis de 1914 à 1917," *Annales*, July–September 1951.

e) The immediate causes of the war

Two good books are: Barbara W. Tuchman, *The Zimmermann Telegram*, New York, 1958; and ‡Samuel R. Spencer, Jr., *Decision for War, 1917; The Laconia Sinking and the Zimmermann Telegram as Key Factors in the Public Reaction against Germany*, Rindge, N.H., 1953, which is opposed to the revisionist school and extremely useful.

f) The United States at war

The best overall survey is: ‡Frederic L. Paxson, *America at War, 1917–1918*, Boston, 1939. On political policy toward the neutral countries during the war, see the fine book: ‡Thomas A. Bailey, *The Policy of the United States towards the Neutrals, 1917–1918*, Baltimore, 1942. On the peace movement, see: Horace C. Peterson and Gilbert C. Fite, *Opponents of War, 1917–1918*, Madison, Wis., 1957.

g) The New Diplomacy and the peace conference

An indispensable book, recently published by a young professor at Harvard, shows that Wilson's ideas had, in part, a European origin: ‡Arno Joseph Mayer, *Political Origins of the New Diplomacy, 1917–1918*, New Haven, 1959 (Yale Historical Publications, 18). A book which complements this is: Laurence W. Martin, *Peace without Victory; Woodrow Wilson and the British Liberals*, New Haven, 1958 (Yale Historical Publications, Miscellany 70).

On Wilson's role at the peace conference, the basic book is ‡Thomas A. Bailey, *Wilson and the Peacemakers*, which contains 2 volumes: I, *Woodrow Wilson and the Lost Peace*, New York, 1947, and II, *Woodrow Wilson and the Great Betrayal*, New York, 1947.

On the Covenant of the League of Nations, see: David Hunter Miller, *The Drafting of the Covenant*, London, 1928, 2 vols.; Florence Wilson, *The Origins of the League Covenant; Documentary History of its drafting* (introduction by P. J. Noel Baker), London, 1928.

On American public opinion see: William D. S. Witte, "American Quaker Pacifism and the Peace Settlement of World War I," *Bulletin of the Friends Historical Association*, Autumn 1957; Mary Misaela Zacharewicz, "The Attitude of the Catholic Press toward the League of Nations," *Records of American Historical Society of Philadelphia*, March–June, 1957.

On Wilson's candidacy in 1920 see: Wesley M. Bagby, "Woodrow Wilson, a Third Term, and the Solemn Referendum," *American Historical Review*, April 1955, pp. 567–575.

Finally, let us mention a worthwhile evaluation of the treaty, in moderate terms: Paul Birdsall, *Versailles Twenty Years After*, New York, 1941.

h) Wilson's policies, by country

FRANCE. There is no good overall study. See, however, chapters 21, 22, and 23 in Beckles Willson, *America's Ambassadors to France, 1777–1927*, New York, 1928; ‡George Bernard Noble, *Policies and Opinions at Paris, 1919; Wilsonian Diplomacy, the Versailles Peace, and French Public Opinion*, New York, 1935; Louis A. R. Yates, *United States and French Security, 1917–1921*, New York, 1957. (This last book is disappointing, because, although published in 1957, it does not refer to Paul Mantoux's papers.)

UNITED KINGDOM. Arthur Willert, *The Road to Safety: A Study in Anglo-American Relations*, London, 1952. This is an appealing work. The author was the *Times* correspondent and representative of the British Information Ministry in Washington.

BELGIUM. Suzanne Tassier, *La Belgique et l'entrée en guerre des Etats-Unis, 1914–1917*, Brussels, 1951. The author is the specialist on Belgium at the Hoover Library.

GERMANY. Nothing satisfactory has been written on espionage activities, notwithstanding two old books by Gabriel Alphaud: *L'action allemande aux Etats-Unis. De la mission Dernburg à l'incident Dumba (2 août 1914–25 septembre 1915)*, Paris, 1915; *Les Etats-Unis contre l'Allemagne. Du rappel de Dumba à la Déclaration de guerre (25 septembre 1915–4 avril 1917)*, Paris, 1917. The best synthesis is: H. L. Trefousse, *Germany and American Neutrality*, New York, 1951.

A Florida historian has done some noteworthy research on AUSTRIA-HUNGARY. ‡Victor S. Mamatey, *The United States and East Central Europe, 1914–1918; A Study in Wilsonian Diplomacy and Propaganda*, Princeton, 1957; "The U.S. and the Origins of the Adriatic Question of 1918," *Florida State University Studies*, IV (1951); "The Place of Germany's Satellites in Wilson's Psychological Warfare, 1917–1918," *Florida State University Studies*, XIV, (1954), pp. 71–84.

SOVIET RUSSIA AND THE FAR EAST. There is abundant literature in this realm. The basic work is by George F. Kennan, ‡*Soviet-American Relations, 1917–1920*, of which 2 volumes have been published: vol. 1, *Russia Leaves the War*, Princeton, 1956, and vol. 2, *The Decision to Intervene*, Princeton, 1958. Clearly presented and extremely interesting, although not using sources in the Russian language are: ‡Betty Miller Unterberger, *America's Siberian Expedition, 1918–1920: A Study of National Policy*, Durham, N.C., 1956, and "President Wilson and the Decision to Send American Troops to Siberia," *Pacific Historical Review*, February 1955. These works render less useful the fine research by John Albert White, *The Siberian Intervention*, Princeton, N.J., 1950, and make completely superfluous the superficial book by Clarence A. Manning, *The Siberian Fiasco*, New York, 1952.

On Far Eastern policy in general, see two informative books: Roy Watson Curry, *Woodrow Wilson and Far Eastern Policy, 1913–1921*, New York, 1957; and A. Whitney Griswold, *The Far Eastern Policy of the United States*, New York, 1938.

On relations with China, see: Tien-yi Li, *Woodrow Wilson's China Policy: 1913–1917*, New York, 1952.

On Japan, see: Ernest R. May, "American Policy and Japan's Entrance into World War I," *Mississippi Valley Historical Review*, September 1953; James William Morley, *The Japanese Thrust into Siberia*, New York, 1957; Russell H. Fifield, *Woodrow Wilson and the Far East: The Diplomacy of the Shantung Question*, New York, 1952. (Fifield, a former diplomat, deals essentially with the period of the peace conference.)

On LATIN AMERICA there are quite a number of publications. The essential work, which goes beyond this period, is: ‡Samuel Flagg Bemis, *The Latin American Policy of the United States: An Historical Interpretation*

(Yale Institute of International Studies), New York, 1943. This should be supplemented by: Wilfred H. Callcott, *The Caribbean Policy of the United States, 1890–1920*, Baltimore, 1942; and, especially, by an excellent article: Selig Adler, "Bryan and Wilsonian Caribbean Penetration," *Hispanic American Historical Review*, May 1940, pp. 198–226; and by Arthur P. Whitaker, *The Western Hemisphere Idea: Its Rise and Decline*, Ithaca, N.Y., 1954.

On the Monroe Doctrine the basic work is: ‡Dexter Perkins, *A History of the Monroe Doctrine*, rev. ed., Boston, 1955 (1st ed. in 1941). See also an interesting collection of documents by a Chilian journalist, Alejandro Alvarez, *The Monroe Doctrine, Its Importance in the International Life of the States of the New World*, New York, 1924 (Publication of the Carnegie Endowment); and Willy Feuerlein, *Dollars in Latin America*, New York, 1941.

There are numerous books on the Mexican affair, but none is truly satisfactory, and it is only in Link's work that the most precise information can be found. We should nevertheless mention: James Fred Rippy, *The United States and Mexico*, New York, 1926; Alfred Vagts, *Mexico, Europa und Amerika unter besonderer Berücksichtigung der Petroleumpolitik*, Berlin, 1928; Colonel Frank Tompkins, *Chasing Villa; The Story behind the Story of Pershing's Expedition into Mexico*, Harrisburg, Pa., 1934; Howard Francis Cline, *The United States and Mexico*, Cambridge, Mass., 1953. The basic Mexican work, written by a former collaborator of Carranza, is no more satisfactory than these others: Isidoro Fabela, *Historia Diplomática de la Revolución Mexicana* (vol. 1, 1912–1917), Mexico, 1958–59. Some information, though insufficient, is contained in the American Foreign Policy Library series, edited by Donald McKay and Sumner Welles, to which Cline's book, cited above, belongs. In this series are: Dexter Perkins, *The United States and the Caribbean*, Cambridge, Mass., 1947; Arthur P. Whitaker, *The United States and South America: The Northern Republics*, Cambridge, Mass., 1948, and *The United States and Argentina*, Cambridge, Mass., 1954. Finally, see Thomas F. McGann, *Argentina, the United States and the Inter-American System, 1880–1914* (Harvard Historical Studies, 70), Cambridge, Mass., 1957; Joseph O. Baylin, "American Intervention in Nicaragua, 1909–1933," *Southwestern Social Sciences Quarterly*, September 1954.

On the PHILIPPINES: Roy Watson Curry, "Woodrow Wilson and Philippine Policy," in *Mississippi Valley Historical Review*, December 1954; and, most important, Garel A. Grunder and William E. Livezey, *The Philippines and the United States*, Norman, Okla., 1951.

2. *The Republican Period, 1921–1923*

a) Biographies from 1921 to 1929

There is no entirely satisfactory work on any one of the following leaders.

On Harding, the most useful work is Samuel Hopkins Adams, *Incredible*

Era: The Life and Times of Warren Gamaliel Harding, Boston, 1939. This can be supplemented with: Frederick E. Schortemeier, *Redidicating America. Life and Recent Speeches of Warren G. Harding*, Indianapolis, Ind., 1920; Joe Mitchell Chapple, *Life and Times of Warren G. Harding, Our After-War President*, Boston, 1924. And the book, disheartening in its poor intellectual content, but significant by this very fact, by Harding's Attorney General, who had a difficult time clearing himself of accusations directed at the corruption of the regime: Harry M. Daugherty, *The Inside Story of the Harding Tragedy*, New York, 1932.

On Coolidge, see Claude M. Fuess, *Calvin Coolidge, the Man from Vermont*, Boston, 1940.

On Hughes, there fortunately is a very good book which, although not definitive, contains a good deal of information: ‡Merlo John Pusey, *Charles Evans Hughes*, New York, 1951, 2 vols. See also the interesting essay by ‡Dexter Perkins, *Charles Evans Hughes and American Democratic Statesmanship*, Boston, 1956 (the Library of American Biography); and Thomas T. Thalken, "The Papers of Charles Evans Hughes," *Library of Congress Quarterly Journal*, November 1953.

On Kellogg, see: David Bryn-Jones, *Frank B. Kellogg, A Biography*, New York, 1937.

There are biographies of other important persons of the era: Philip Jessup, *Elihu Root*, New York, 1933, 2 vols.; John A. Garraty, *Henry Cabot Lodge: A Biography*, New York, 1953; John Chalmers Vinson, *William E. Borah and the Outlawry of War*, Athens, Ga., 1957, to be supplemented by William Appleman Williams, "A Note on the Isolationism of Senator William E. Borah (1932)," *Pacific Historical Review*, November 1953; Belle C. La Follette and Fola La Follette, *Robert M. La Follette, June 14, 1855–June 18, 1925*, New York, 1953, 2 vols.

On the Democratic candidate for the presidency in 1928, see Oscar Handlin, *Al Smith and His America*, Boston, 1958.

b) The Washington Conference

There is no entirely satisfactory work. One must consult, in addition to Pusey and the historical accounts of the Navy (notably that by H. and M. Sprout, cited above): Raymond Leslie Buell, *The Washington Conference*, New York, 1922, and Yamato Ichihashi, *The Washington Conference and After*, Stanford, Calif., 1928 (by an interpreter for Baron Kato, who has become a professor at Stanford University). Certain particular points are clarified by: Herbert Osborn Yardley, *The American Black Chamber*, Indianapolis, Ind., 1931, which reveals how the Americans had learned of the Japanese intentions in advance; J. Chalmers Vinson, "The Drafting of the Four Power Treaty of the Washington Conference," *Journal of Modern History*, March 1953; Raymond O'Connor, "The 'Yardstick' and Naval Disarmament in the 1920's," *Mississippi Valley Historical Review*, December 1958, pp. 441–463; Russell H. Fifield, "Secretary Hughes and the Shantung Question," *Pacific Historical Review*, November 1954, pp.

373–385; Gerald E. Wheeler, "The U. S. Navy and the Japanese 'Enemy,' 1919–1931," *Military Affairs*, December 1957.

On the role of the Senate, an interesting work which reveals the illusions of nationalism is John Chalmers Vinson, *The Parchment Peace: The United States Senate and the Washington Conference, 1921–1922*, Athens, Ga., 1955.

c) Relations with Europe

On the Geneva Protocol, see David D. Burks, "The U. S. and the Geneva Protocol of 1924: A New Holy Alliance?" *American Historical Review*, July 1959, pp. 891–905.

On reparations, see Dieter Bruno Gescher, *Die Vereinigten Staaten von Nordamerika und die Reparationen, 1920–1924*, Bonn, 1956.

On the war debts, the article of P. Renouvin, cited above, traces developments up to 1917. If one excepts the general economic histories cited above, there is no good overall survey of the problem. Nevertheless, the contemporary works are often extremely revealing. Nearly all take a position in favor of canceling the debts. Harvey E. Fisk, *The Inter-Ally Debts*, New York, 1924; Philip Dexter and John Hunter Sedgwick, *The War Debts, An American View*, New York, 1928; Harold G. Moulton and Leo Pasvolsky, *War Debts and World Prosperity*, Washington, 1932 (for the Brookings Institution); William Withers, *The Retirement of National Debts: the Theory and History since the World War*, New York, 1932. These last works are by economists who advocate the cancellation of debts for technical reasons. Some other works raise the argument of sentiment, prized by the French. The best example is that of an American president of the Alliance Française in New York, author of an anthology, *France, Courageous and Indomitable* (Philadelphia, 1925): Oswald Chew, *The Stroke of the Moment: A Discussion of the Foreign Debts*, Philadelphia, 1928. See also: R. von Alstyne, "Private American Loans to the Allies," *Pacific Historical Review*, May 1933, pp. 180–183.

d) The Kellogg-Briand Pact

There are three essential works: ‡Robert H. Ferrell, *Peace in Their Time; The Origins of the Kellogg-Briand Pact*, New Haven, 1952, which must be supplemented by Ferrell's article in the work already cited published by A. De Conde, *Isolation and Security;* ‡John Edgar Stoner, *S. O. Levinson and the Pact of Paris: A Study in the Techniques of Influence*, Chicago, 1942; and the book already cited by John Chalmers Vinson on Borah.

On the conservative peace groups, see: Nicholas Murray Butler, *Across the Busy Years: Recollections and Reflections*, New York, 1933–1940, 2 vols.; James T. Shotwell, *The Pact of Paris*, Worcester, Mass., 1928 (Carnegie Endowment); James T. Shotwell, *War as an Instrument of National Policy and Its Renunciation in the Pact of Paris*, London, 1929.

On the radical peace groups: Marie L. Degen, *History of the Woman's*

Peace Party, Baltimore, 1939; Ruhl Jacob Bartlett, *The League to Enforce Peace*, Chapel Hill, N.C., 1944.

On Henry Ford as peacemaker: Louis P. Lochner, *Henry Ford: Don Quixote*, New York, 1925. (Lochner, secretary of the Chicago Peace Society, is the man who convinced Ford to participate in the peace movement.)

On the continuation of the peace movement, see Robert Edwin Bowers, *The American Peace Movement, 1933–1941.*

For an overall view of the illusions of the supporters of the peace movements, see a book with a revealing title, Isabel Leighton, ed., *The Aspirin Age, 1919–1941*, New York, 1949.

e) Hoover and Stimson

There is an excellent book covering this period: ‡Robert E. Ferrell, *American Diplomacy in the Great Depression; Hoover-Stimson Foreign Policy, 1929–1933*, New Haven, 1957. This should be supplemented by a book written by two journalists, superior to most books of this sort, both in the reliability of its information and in the shrewdness of its opinions: Drew Pearson and Constantine Brown, *The American Diplomatic Game*, New York, 1935.

No thoroughly comprehensive study of Hoover has been made. Nevertheless, certain books stand out: Harris Gaylord Warren, *Herbert Hoover and the Great Depression*, New York, 1959; William Starr Myers, *The Foreign Policies of Herbert Hoover, 1929–1933*, New York, 1940; Ray Lyman Wilbur and Arthur Mastick Hyde, *The Hoover Policies*, New York, 1937 (Wilbur was Hoover's Secretary of the Interior, later president of Stanford University; Hyde was Secretary of Agriculture); Harold Wolfe, *Herbert Hoover: Public Servant and Leader of the Loyal Opposition*, New York, 1956 (a bit too eulogistic); David Hinshaw, *Herbert Hoover: American Quaker*, New York, 1950. Hinshaw's thesis is not convincing. If Hoover is a militant Quaker today, he certainly was not during his presidency. See also Richard C. Watson, Jr., "Theodore Roosevelt and Herbert Hoover," *South Atlantic Quarterly*, January 1954.

On Hoover's Latin American policy, see an excellent work: ‡Alexander De Conde, *Herbert Hoover's Latin-American Policy*, Stanford, Calif., 1951.

On Stimson, in addition to the basic work by Stimson and McGeorge Bundy (cited above with the memoirs), and all of Stimson's works, one must mention the fairly critical biography by Richard N. Current, *Secretary Stimson; A Study in Statecraft*, New Brunswick, N.J., 1954. I was fortunate enough to be able to read the manuscript of the recently published biography by Elting Morison, *Turmoil and Tradition: A Study of the Life and Times of Henry L. Stimson*, Boston, 1960. This book is clearly the definitive work on Stimson.

No one work is satisfactory on the crisis in the Far East. But see: Sarah R. Smith, *The Manchurian Crisis, 1931–1932*, New York, 1948; Richard

N. Current, "The Stimson Doctrine and the Hoover Doctrine," *American Historical Review*, April 1954, pp. 513–542.

3. *Franklin Delano Roosevelt*

a) Biographies and general interpretations

The basic work, that of Frank Freidel, professor at Harvard, covers the period before 1933 in three volumes; the author plans to carry his study to 1945. See ‡Frank Freidel, *Franklin D. Roosevelt*, vol. I: *The Apprenticeship*, Boston, 1952; vol. II: *The Ordeal*, Boston, 1954; vol. III: *The Triumph*, Boston, 1956.

Among the many biographies which cover the whole period, three works stand out above the others, one written by an exceptionally gifted journalist, John Gunther, *Roosevelt in Retrospect: A Profile in History*, New York, 1950; a second, by a professor who is deeply involved in the activities of the Democratic party, James M. Burns, *Roosevelt: The Lion and the Fox*, New York, 1956; and finally, the work of a former collaborator of Roosevelt, a member of the "Brain Trust," who helped develop the New Deal, Rexford G. Tugwell, *The Democratic Roosevelt: A Biography of Franklin D. Roosevelt*, Garden City, N.Y., 1957.

On Roosevelt's development, see: Daniel R. Fusfeld, *The Economic Thought of Franklin D. Roosevelt and the Origins of the New Deal*, New York, 1956; and Thomas H. Greer, *What Roosevelt Thought: The Social and Political Ideas of Franklin D. Roosevelt*, East Lansing, Mich., 1958. Greer presents, in a slightly superficial way, the President's pragmatic philosophy.

On the spirit of the Age of Roosevelt, see ‡Arthur M. Schlesinger, Jr., *The Age of Roosevelt*, vol. I: *The Crisis of the Old Order*, Boston, 1957, vol. II: *The Coming of the New Deal*, Boston, 1959, vol. III: *The Politics of Upheaval*, Boston, 1962, vol. IV: *The Politics of Hope*, Boston, 1962.

Less detailed, but equally valuable, is ‡Dexter Perkins, *The New Age of Franklin Roosevelt: 1932–45*, Chicago, 1957. See also: Edgar Eugene Robinson, *The Roosevelt Leadership, 1933–1945*, Philadelphia, 1954; the work of a British scholar, Denis W. Brogan, *The Era of Franklin D. Roosevelt*, New Haven, 1951; a study by a German scholar, Waldemar Besson, *Die politische Terminologie des Präsidenten Franklin D. Roosevelt*, Tübingen, 1955, analyzes such coined phrases as "New Deal," "Arsenal of Democracy," and so forth.

On Roosevelt's anticolonial policy, see ‡Foster Rhea Dulles and Gerald T. Ridinger, "The Anti-colonial Policies of Franklin D. Roosevelt," *Political Science Quarterly*, March 1955.

b) Roosevelt's prewar administrations, 1933–1940

Until Robert Ferrell publishes his book on the period from 1933–1937 (the sequel to his works on the Kellogg period and on the Stimson period), the period from 1933–1937 will remain unsatisfactorily studied. There exists only the study by Charles A. Beard, which portrays Roosevelt as an isolationist up to 1937. Although prejudiced, Beard's is nevertheless an important work: ‡Charles A. Beard, *American Foreign Policy in the Making, 1932–1940*, New Haven, 1946.

On the recognition of the Soviet Union, see: William Appleman Williams, *American-Russian Relations, 1781–1947*, New York, 1952, with which the author, a Russophile—more especially Sovietophile—has aroused some controversy; R. P. Browder, *Origins of Soviet-American Diplomacy*, Princeton, N.J., 1953; Thomas A. Bailey, *America Faces Russia*, Ithaca, N.Y., 1950; Themistocles Clayton Rodis, "Russo-American Contacts during the Hoover Administration," *South Atlantic Quarterly*, April 1952; Robert P. Browder, "Soviet Far Eastern Policy and American Recognition, 1932–1934," *Pacific Historical Review*, August 1952; Paul F. Boller, "The 'Great Conspiracy' of 1933: A Study in Short Memories," *Southwest Review*, Spring 1954; Robert P. Browder, "The First Encounter, Roosevelt and the Russians, 1933," *U.S. Naval Institute Proceedings*, May 1957.

On neutrality, see the work by Selig Adler cited above. A good study on the Nye Committee has not yet been made.

On the Spanish Civil War, see a serious study: Foster Jay Taylor, *The United States and the Spanish Civil War*, New York, 1956. See also George V. Fagan, "F. D. R. and Naval Limitation," *United States Naval Institute Proceedings*, April 1955.

On the Quarantine Speech, see: Dorothy Borg, "Notes on Roosevelt's 'Quarantine Speech,'" *Political Science Quarterly*, September 1957.

On the Far East, in addition to the works cited above, see: William L. Newmann, "Franklin Roosevelt and Japan, 1913–1933," *Pacific Historical Review*, May 1953, pp. 143–153. See also John W. Masland, "Commercial Influence upon American Far Eastern Policy, 1937–1941," *Pacific Historical Review*, October 1942, pp. 281–299.

On the period 1937–1940, there is a work of the first rank, one of the masterpieces of American historiography: ‡William L. Langer and S. Everett Gleason, *The Challenge to Isolation: 1937–1940*, New York, 1952 (published for the Council on Foreign Relations).

On the 1940 election, see Paul H. Appleby, "Roosevelt's Third Term Decision," *American Political Science Review*, September 1952.

c) Pearl Harbor: Works favorable to Roosevelt

The origins of the Second World War have been the subject of an enormous number of publications. For a rather complete analysis, see: Richard L. Watson, Jr., "Franklin D. Roosevelt in Historical Writing, 1950–1957," *South Atlantic Quarterly*, Winter 1958; Louis Morton, "Pearl Harbor in Perspective," *United States Naval Institute Proceedings*, vol. 81 (1955), pp. 460–468; and, especially, the excellent study by ‡Wayne S. Cole, "American Entry into World War II; A Historiographical Appraisal," *Mississippi Valley Historical Review*, vol. 43 (1956–1957), pp. 595–617.

Of the authors who favor Roosevelt's policies, the two most important works are: ‡Herbert Feis, *The Road to Pearl Harbor: The Coming of the War between the United States and Japan*, Princeton, N.J., 1950; and ‡William L. Langer and S. Everett Gleason, *The Undeclared War, September 1940–December 1941*, New York, 1953 (Council on Foreign Relations).

There are other valuable works which we shall list according to their date of publication. A work by well-known journalists who had close ties with the government, Forrest Davis and Ernest K. Lindley, *How War Came, An American White Paper: from the Fall of France to Pearl Harbor*, New York, 1942; Dexter Perkins, *America and Two Wars*, Boston, 1944; Walter Millis, *This is Pearl! The United States and Japan—1941*, New York, 1947.

The career of Millis is rather unusual. Revisionist after the First World War, in 1935 he wrote the isolationist *Road to War* (cited above). His appointment as editorial writer for the New York *Herald Tribune* coincided with his own conversion to interventionism. In June 1940 he signed a petition asking for immediate American entry into the war. See his article, "1939 Is Not 1914," *Life*, November 6, 1939, pp. 60–75 and 94–98.

See also: Basil Rauch, *Roosevelt: from Munich to Pearl Harbor; A Study in the Creation of a Foreign Policy*, New York, 1950; Hans L. Trefousse, *Germany and American Neutrality, 1939–1941*, New York, 1951; Donald F. Drummond, *The Passing of American Neutrality, 1937–1941*, Ann Arbor, Mich., 1955; Paul W. Schroeder, *The Axis Alliance and Japanese-American Relations, 1941*, Ithaca, N.Y., 1958. (The last is a publication of the American Historical Association. Schroeder can also be classed with the moderate revisionists.)

There are also innumerable articles. Note especially the following: Norman L. Hill, "Was There an Ultimatum before Pearl Harbor?" *American Journal of International Law*, April 1948, pp. 355–367; Sherman Miles, "Pearl Harbor in Retrospect," *Atlantic Monthly*, July 1948, pp. 65–72; Joseph W. Ballantine, "Mukden to Pearl Harbor: The Foreign Policies of Japan," *Foreign Affairs*, July 1949, pp. 651–664; Immanuel C. Y. Hsu, "Kurusu's Mission to the U.S. and the Abortive *Modus Vivendi*," *Journal of Modern History*, September 1952, pp. 301–307; Richard N. Current, "How Stimson Meant to Maneuver 'the Japanese,' " *Mississippi Valley Historical Review*, June 1953, pp. 67–74; Dexter Perkins, "Was Roosevelt Wrong?" *Virginia Quarterly Review*, Summer 1954, pp. 359–364; Tracy B. Kittredge, "The Muddle before Pearl Harbor," *U.S. News and World Report*, December 3, 1954, pp. 52–63 and 110–139; Herbert Feis, "War came at Pearl Harbor: Suspicions Considered," *Yale Review*, Spring 1956, pp. 378–390; Fritz Wagner, "Geschichte und Zeitgeschichte: Pearl Harbor im Kreuzfeuer der Forschung," *Historische Zeitschrift*, April 1957.

Finally, see the opinion of one of the best experts on Roosevelt: Frank Freidel, "World War II: Before Pearl Harbor," *Current History*, October, 1958.

d) Pearl Harbor: The revisionists

We shall list the works of the revisionists in order of publication. One can consult the *Select Bibliography of Revisionist Books, Dealing with the Two World Wars and Their Aftermath*, Oxnard, Calif., 1957; John T. Flynn, *The Truth about Pearl Harbor*, New York, 1944; John T. Flynn, *The Final Secret of Pearl Harbor*, New York, 1945.

A very immoderate work by a journalist who became an editorial writer for the Chicago *Daily Tribune* in 1941, George Edward Morgenstern, *Pearl Harbor: The Story of the Secret War*, New York, 1947; Charles A. Beard, *President Roosevelt and the Coming of the War, 1941: A Study in Appearances and Realities*, New Haven, 1948 (a book in which the great historian, more emotional than ever, does not always maintain a balanced view of the situation); William Henry Chamberlin, *America's Second Crusade*, Chicago, 1950; Frederic R. Sanborn, *Design for War: A Study of Secret Power Politics, 1937–1941*, New York, 1951; Charles Callan Tansill, *Back Door to War: The Roosevelt Foreign Policy, 1933–1941*, Chicago, 1952. The work of Tansill, a professor at Georgetown University, is perhaps the best documented of the revisionist studies. Nonetheless, Tansill's strong anti-Roosevelt feeling is equaled only by that of Morgenstern and Chamberlin, cited above, and Barnes: Harry Elmer Barnes, ed., *Perpetual War for Perpetual Peace: A Critical Examination of the Foreign Policy of Franklin Delano Roosevelt and Its Aftermath,* Caldwell, Idaho, 1953. See also Rear Admiral Robert A. Theobald, *The Final Secret of Pearl Harbor: The Washington Contribution to the Japanese Attack*, New York, 1954.

e) Public opinion and United States entry into the war

The reference work for this entire period is the large collection already cited: Hadley Cantril, ed., assisted by Mildred Strunk, *Public Opinion, 1935–1946*, Princeton, 1951.

On the groups who favored increased aid to the Allies, the best works, largely based upon the William Allen White Papers, are: Walter Johnson, *The Battle against Isolation*, Chicago, 1944; and Walter Johnson, *William Allen White's America*, New York, 1947, which can be supplemented by another biography of White, written by a Quaker, David Hinshaw, *A Man from Kansas: The Story of William Allen White*, New York, 1945.

On the America First Committee, see a good study, Wayne S. Cole, *America First: The Battle against Intervention, 1940–1941*, Madison, Wis., 1953.

There are several studies on regional attitudes: Wayne S. Cole, "America First and the South, 1940–1941," *Journal of Southern History*, February 1956, pp. 36–47; Jeannette P. Nichols, "The Middle West and the Coming of World War II," *Ohio State Archaeological and Historical Quarterly,* April 1953, pp. 122–145. See also: Roscoe Baker, *The American Legion and American Foreign Policy,* New York, 1954.

On opinion in business circles, there is an excellent article by a professor at the University of Maryland, Roland N. Stromberg, "American Business and the Approach of War, 1935–1941," *Journal of Economic History,* Winter 1953.

f) Relations between the Allies during the war

The essential works are by Feis. ‡ Herbert Feis, *Churchill, Roosevelt, Stalin: The War They Waged and the Peace They Sought,* Princeton, 1957. This was unfortunately published before the Soviet publication of the correspondence. See his remarks on this subject: Herbert Feis, "The Three Who Led," *Foreign Affairs,* January 1959, pp. 282–292.

On the Far East, see ‡Herbert Feis, *The China Tangle: The American Effort in China from Pearl Harbor to the Marshall Mission,* Princeton, 1953. This should be supplemented by Ernest R. May, "The U.S., the Soviet Union and the Far Eastern War, 1941–1945," *Pacific Historical Review,* May 1955, pp. 153–174.

On France, see: William L. Langer, *Our Vichy Gamble,* New York, 1947; Marcel Vigneras, *Rearming the French,* Washington (Department of the Army, Office of Military History), 1957.

See also William Hard McNeill, *America, Britain and Russia, 1941–1946,* London and New York, 1953.

On Great Britain, see the conscientious work by Trumbull Higgins, *Winston Churchill and the Second Front, 1940–1943,* New York, 1957; Russell P. Strange, "Atlantic Conference. The First Roosevelt-Churchill Meeting, 1941," *U.S. Naval Institute Proceedings,* April 1953.

g) Problems of strategy

There are two comprehensive official histories, one of the Army (*United States Army in World War II*), which will eventually fill ninety-seven volumes, the other, of the Navy, by Admiral Samuel Eliot Morison (*History of United States Naval Operations in World War II*), of which twelve out of fourteen volumes have been published.

Of the official history of the Army, note especially these volumes: Mark S. Watson, *Chief of Staff: Prewar Plans and Preparations,* Washington, 1950; Maurice Matloff and Edwin M. Snell, *Strategic Planning for Coalition Warfare,* 2 vols., Washington, 1953–1959; Richard M. Leighton and Robert W. Coakley, *Global Logistics and Strategy, 1940–1943,* Washington, 1955. In connection with these works, see: Maurice Matloff, "Prewar Military Plans and Preparations, 1939–1941," *U.S. Naval Institute Proceedings,* July 1953; Jacques Néré, "Logistique et stratégie de l'alliance anglo-américaine," *Revue d'histoire de la deuxième guerre mondiale,* July 1957, pp. 1–18; Forrest C. Pogue, *The Supreme Command,* Washington (Department of the Army), 1954, to be supplemented by Forrest C. Pogue,

"S.H.A.E.F. A Retrospect on Coalition Command," *Journal of Modern History*, December 1951; Forrest C. Pogue, "Why Eisenhower's Forces Stopped at the Elbe," *World Politics*, April 1952.

Of Morison's *History of the United States Naval Operations*, note especially these volumes: I (1947): *The Battle of the Atlantic*, III (1948): *The Rising Sun in the Pacific*. See also Ashbrook Lincoln, "The U.S. Navy and the Rise of the Doctrine of Air Power," *Military Affairs*, Autumn 1951.

On Roosevelt's own strategy, see: William Emerson, "Franklin Roosevelt as Commander in Chief in World War II," *Military Affairs*, Winter 1958–1959; William L. Neumann, "F. D. Roosevelt: A Disciple of Admiral Mahan," *U.S. Naval Institute Proceedings*, July 1952.

h) Economic problems of the war

Eliot Janeway, *The Struggle for Survival; A Chronicle of Economic Mobilization in World War II*, New Haven, 1951; H. Duncan Hale, *North American Supply* (in *History of the Second World War, United Kingdom Civil Series*), London, 1955; Robert H. Connery, *The Navy and Industrial Mobilization in World War II*, Princeton, 1951; Tibor Scitovsky, Edward Shaw, and Lorie Tarshis, *Mobilizing Resources for War: The Economic Alternatives*, New York, 1951; Lester V. Chandler and Donald H. Wallace, *Economic Mobilization and Stabilization*, New York, 1951. These should be supplemented by the following two articles: Robert Mossé, "La mobilisation économique aux Etats-Unis pendant la seconde guerre mondiale," *Revue d'histoire de la deuxième guerre mondiale*, October 1953, pp. 1–24; Jacques Néré, "Points de vue sur l'économie de guerre aux Etats-Unis," *Revue d'histoire de la deuxième guere mondiale*, January 1955, pp. 37–46.

Notes

I. The Foundations of American Foreign Policy before the Election of Wilson

1. Dexter Perkins, *The American Approach to Foreign Policy* (Cambridge, Mass., 1952). See chapter 7, pp. 114–129, "A Cyclical Theory of American Foreign Policy."
2. Frank L. Klingberg, "The Historical Alternation of Moods in American Foreign Policy," *World Politics*, January 1952, pp. 239–273.
3. Howard K. Beale, *Theodore Roosevelt and the Rise of America to World Power* (Baltimore, 1956).
4. William H. Haas, ed., *The American Empire* (Chicago, 1940). At the time the historian Archibald Cary Coolidge gave a series of lectures at the Sorbonne, later published under a title new for the period, *The United States as a World Power* (New York, 1908). An Englishman, J. M. Kennedy, published a book entitled *Imperial America* (London, 1914).
5. William E. Livezey, *Mahan on Sea Power* (Norman, Okla., 1947), p. 51.
6. Alfred T. Mahan, *The Problem of Asia* (Boston, 1900), p. 97.
7. *Ibid.*, p. 187.
8. Alfred T. Mahan, "The Place of Force in International Relations," *North American Review*, January 1912.
9. Alfred T. Mahan, *The Interests of America in Sea Power* (Boston, 1897), p. 36.
10. *Ibid.*, p. 10.
11. George T. Davis, *A Navy Second to None* (New York, 1940), p. 87. Figures taken from the *Congressional Record*, 59th Congress, 1st Session, 6398, May 4, 1906.
12. This is the opinion of Harold and Margaret Sprout, *The Rise of American Naval Power, 1776–1918* (Princeton, 1939), pp. 207–209. See also, Margaret Sprout, "Mahan, Evangelist of Sea Power," in Edward Mead Earle, ed., *Makers of Modern Strategy* (Princeton, 1943), p. 436.
13. Livezey, *Mahan on Sea Power*, p. 235.
14. Davis, *A Navy Second to None*, pp. 171–173. It is true that the Navy was out of date in 1909. It had twenty-five battleships and ten heavy cruisers (compared to five and two respectively during the Spanish War) and no dreadnought. The two *Michigans*, the first American dreadnoughts, were commissioned at the end of 1909, as a result of the efforts of Admiral Fisher.
15. Brigadier General Dale O. Smith, *U.S. Military Doctrine* (New York, 1955), p. 73. William Addleman Ganoe, *History of the United States Army* (New York, 1924), calls the period 1865–1880, "the army's dark age."
16. Walter Millis, *Arms and Men: A Study in American Military History* (New York, 1956), p. 170.
17. Ganoe, *History of the United States Army*, p. 431.
18. See William Herbert Hobbs, *Leonard Wood* (New York, 1920), p. 117.
19. Millis, *Arms and Men*, p. 200.

20. See Seward W. Livermore, "The American Navy as a Factor in World Politics, 1903–1913," *American Historical Review*, July 1958, pp. 863–873.

21. New Orleans, 1912.

22. Benjamin H. Williams, *The Economic Foreign Policy of the United States* (New York, 1929), p. 17.

23. All these figures are from O. P. Austin, statistician of the National City Bank of New York, December 1924, cited in Scott Nearing and Joseph Freeman, *Dollar Diplomacy: A Study in American Imperialism* (New York, 1925), pp. 4–5.

24. Nearing and Freeman, *Dollar Diplomacy*, p. 18.

25. Coolidge, *The United States as a World Power*, p. 297.

26. Nearing and Freeman, *Dollar Diplomacy*, p. 262.

27. "The Economic Basis of Imperialism," *North American Review*, September 1898, pp. 326–340. See also William L. Langer, "A Critique of Imperialism," *Foreign Affairs*, October 1935, pp. 102–119.

28. Langer, "A Critique of Imperialism," pp. 102–105.

29. See also the opinion of Jacques Freymond, *Lenine et L'Imperialisme* (Lausanne, 1951).

30. Nearing and Freeman, *Dollar Diplomacy*, p. 265.

31. *Ibid.*, p. 266. See also A. Vialatte, *Economic Imperialism, and International Relations* (New York, 1923), p. 62.

32. New Haven, 1956.

33. Wolfers and Martin, *The Anglo-American Tradition in Foreign Affairs*, p. xv.

34. Oscar Handlin, *The Uprooted: The Epic Story of the Great Migrations That Made the American People* (Boston, 1951).

35. Geoffrey Gorer, *The American People; a Study in National Character* (New York, 1948).

36. Subsequently expanded into a book, Frederick Jackson Turner, *The Frontier in American History* (New York, 1920).

37. *Ibid.*, pp. 3–4.

38. *Ibid.*, p. 37.

39. See the excellent synthesis of Robert E. Riegel, "American Frontier Theory," *Cahiers d'Histoire mondiale*, vol. III (1956), part 2, pp. 356–380. There is an excellent bibliography.

40. Statistics from Henry Pratt Fairchild, *Immigration* (New York, 1913), especially chapter 7; and Hannibal Gerald Duncan, *Immigration and Assimilation* (New York, 1926), especially chapter 30.

41. Boston, 1926.

42. Fairchild, *The Melting Pot Mistake*, p. 261.

43. R. D. McKenzie, *Oriental Exclusion* (Chicago, 1928).

44. Hans J. Morgenthau, *In Defense of the National Interest: A Critical Examination of American Foreign Policy* (New York, 1951); see also George F. Kennan, *American Diplomacy, 1900–1950* (Chicago, 1951).

45. Frank Tannenbaum, *The American Tradition in Foreign Policy* (Norman, Okla., 1955).

46. *Ibid.*, p. 30.

47. Dexter Perkins, *The American Approach to Foreign Policy*, p. 32.

48. Robert Osgood, *Ideals and Self-Interest in America's Foreign Relations* (Chicago, 1953).

49. *Ibid.*, p. 17.

50. *Ibid.*, p. 18.

51. Beale, *Theodore Roosevelt*, p. 16.

52. Dexter Perkins, *Hands Off: A History of the Monroe Doctrine* (rev. ed., Boston, 1955), chapter 7, "The Policeman of the West. The Evolution of the Roosevelt Corollary."

53. *Ibid.*, pp. 238–239.

54. *Ibid.*, p. 241.

II. The Early Stages of President Wilson's Career

1. Cited by Alexander L. and Juliette George, *Woodrow Wilson and Colonel House* (New York, 1956), p. xvi.

2. Ellen Axson Wilson died in August 1914, when the President was 59 years old. On December 18, 1915, he married as his second wife, Mrs. Edith Bolling Galt, widow of a Washington jeweler.

3. Arthur Link, *Woodrow Wilson and the Progressive Era* (New York, 1947), p. 54.

4. *Ibid.*, p. 90.

5. Ray Stannard Baker, *Woodrow Wilson, Life and Letters*, (Garden City, N.Y., 1927–39, 8 vols.), III, 78–80.

6. *Ibid.*, III, 256.

7. Charles Seymour, ed., *Intimate Papers of Colonel House* (Boston, 1926–1928, 4 vols.), I, 114.

8. Cited by Link, *Woodrow Wilson and the Progressive Era*, pp. 20–21.

9. Baker, *Woodrow Wilson*, III, 274; see also p. 430.

10. *Ibid.*, III, 442.

11. James Kerney, *The Political Education of Woodrow Wilson* (New York, 1926), p. 316.

12. Thomas A. Bailey, *A Diplomatic History of the American People* (3rd ed., New York, 1947), p. 595.

13. Brandeis might have become Attorney General had he wished, but he did not want to and he had many enemies. Wilson, knowing this, eliminated him from the list, to the fury of the progressives. Brandeis continued to advise Wilson, however. He was appointed to the Supreme Court in 1916. See Alpheus T. Mason, *Brandeis, a Free Man's Life* (New York, 1946), p. 115.

14. Baker, *Woodrow Wilson*, IV, 55.

15. *Intimate Papers of Colonel House*, I, 177.

16. Baltimore, 1937.

17. Arthur S. Link, *Wilson the Diplomatist: A Look at His Major Foreign Policies* (Baltimore, 1957).

18. Notter, *Origins of the Foreign Policy of Woodrow Wilson*, p. 43.

19. Link, *Woodrow Wilson and the Progressive Era*, p. 11.

20. Notter, *Origins of the Foreign Policy of Woodrow Wilson*, p. 653.

21. *Ibid.*, p. 132.

22. Baker, *Woodrow Wilson*, IV, 67.

23. Link, *Woodrow Wilson and the Progressive Era*, p. 109.

24. Baker, *Woodrow Wilson*, IV, 284.

25. In his message to Sun Yat-sen, cited by Ray Watson Curry, *Woodrow Wilson and Far Eastern Policy* (New York, 1957), p. 16. See also Tien-yi Li, *Woodrow Wilson's China Policy, 1913–1917* (New York, 1952).

26. Curry, *Woodrow Wilson and Far Eastern Policy*, p. 23.
27. Cited by Link, *Woodrow Wilson and the Progressive Era*, p. 194.

III. The European War and American Neutrality

1. Suzanne Tassier, *La Belgique et l'entrée en guere des Etats-Unis, 1914–1917* (Brussels, 1950).
2. Cited by Curry, *Woodrow Wilson and Far Eastern Policy*, p. 44.
3. Figures taken from Bailey, *Diplomatic History of the American People* (New York, 1947), pp. 610f.
4. *Intimate Papers of Colonel House*, I, 264.
5. *Ibid.*, I, 280.
6. Bailey, *Diplomatic History*, p. 612.
7. The *Literary Digest* (November 14, 1914), on the other hand, estimated that 242 out of 367 newspapers claimed that they were not taking sides. Cited by Ernest R. May, *The World War and American Isolation, 1914–1917* (Cambridge, Mass., 1959), p. 36.
8. The British ship *Telconia* cut the German cables at the beginning of the war. From then on the Germans could have used a cable in American hands, via the Azores and South America, except that the owners, Eastern Telegraph, soon refused them its use. The only communications after this were via Radio Nauen near Berlin. See Barbara Tuchman, *The Zimmermann Telegram* (New York, 1958), p. 11. Later House made the courteous gesture of offering to the Wilhelmstrasse the use of the State Department's cable facilities.
9. *Intimate Papers of Colonel House*, I, 403.
10. Bailey, *Diplomatic History*, p. 627.
11. *Intimate Papers of Colonel House*, I, 434.
12. Samuel Flagg Bemis, ed., *The American Secretaries of State and their Diplomacy* (New York, 1927–29), X, 39.
13. *Intimate Papers of Colonel House*, I, 451.
14. Cited by May, *The World War*, p. 155.
15. *Intimate Papers of Colonel House*, II, 37.
16. May, *The World War*, p. 344.
17. According to Jusserand, *Le Sentiment Americain pendant la Guerre* (Paris, 1931), p. 82.
18. *Ibid.*, p. 83.
19. *Intimate Papers of Colonel House*, II, 85–86.
20. *Ibid.*, II, 131.
21. *Ibid.*, II, 164.
22. Sir Edward Grey, *Twenty-five Years, 1892–1916* (London, 1925), cited by May, *The World War*, p. 355. According to House, *Intimate Papers of Colonel House*, II, 196, it was on February 23. See also volume II, p. 201.
23. *Intimate Papers of Colonel House*, II, 282.
24. Cited by Link, *Woodrow Wilson and the Progressive Era*, p. 220.
25. On Hughes, see below, Part Two, Chapter VII.
26. See Link, *Woodrow Wilson and the Progressive Era*, p. 244.
27. Cited by May, *The World War*, p. 363.
28. Cited by Bailey, *Diplomatic History*, p. 618.
29. Estimated by P. Renouvin at $3 billion: $770 million for England and between $500 and $750 million for France. See P. Renouvin, "La politique des

emprunts étrangers aux Etats-Unis de 1914 à 1917," *Annales*, July–September 1951, pp. 289–305, especially p. 293.

30. One of his arguments was that after the British decision to add cotton to the list of contraband on August 20, the only solution was to accept the British proposition to buy *all* the South's cotton. This would necessitate granting credit to Britain. See also Baker, *Woodrow Wilson*, V, 383.

31. Bailey, *Diplomatic History*, p. 622.

32. Of this total more than 1 billion went to Great Britain, 694 million to France and 136 million to Russia. See Harold G. Moulton and Leo Pasvolsky, *War Debts and World Prosperity* (Washington, 1932), p. 35.

33. *Intimate Papers of Colonel House*, I, 285.

34. Millis, *Arms and Men*, p. 200. See also Hermann Hagedorn, *Leonard Wood* (New York, 1931).

35. Josephus Daniels, *The Wilson Era* (Chapel Hill, N.C., 1944), chapter 24, "A School on Every Ship."

36. *Ibid.*, I, 125.

37. According to Arthur P. Whitaker, *The Western Hemisphere Idea: Its Rise and Decline*, (Ithaca, N.Y., 1954), p. 74.

38. Link, *Woodrow Wilson and the Progressive Era*, p. 118.

39. *Ibid.*, p. 120.

40. J. Fred Rippy, *The United States and Mexico* (New York, 1931), pp. 356–357.

41. See the supplemental preface by James Brown Scott in Alessandro Alvarez, *The Monroe Doctrine* (New York, 1924), inserted between pages vi and vii.

42. Whitaker, *The Western Hemisphere Idea*, p. 121.

IV. Wilson and the War

1. *Intimate Papers of Colonel House*, II, 427.

2. *Ibid.*, II, 431–433.

3. Cited by Daniel M. Smith, *Robert Lansing and American Neutrality, 1914–1917*, Berkeley, Calif., 1958. See p. 146; p. 151 for the unsuccessful efforts of Lansing to have the expression "peace without victory" removed from the January 22 speech; and p. 154. In his *Diplomatic History*, Bailey points out the contradiction between Lansing's memoirs, published twenty years after the events, in which the author thinks that the war was necessary, and the papers of Lansing in American diplomatic documents, where he appears as a neutralist. Smith, using unpublished papers of Lansing's, shows, however, that Lansing had thought war against Germany inevitable since 1914. This text, among others, bears this out.

4. Smith, *Robert Lansing*, p. 157.

5. Baker, *Woodrow Wilson*, VI, 447; *Intimate Papers of Colonel House*, II, 442.

6. The telegram was also sent by two other routes. See Barbara Tuchman, *The Zimermannn Telegram*, p. 147. It will be noted that the cable was sent on January 17, before the break in diplomatic relations.

7. *Intimate Papers of Colonel House*, II, 469; Baker, *Woodrow Wilson*, VI, 425.

8. Victor S. Mamatey, "The Place of Germany's Satellites in Woodrow

Wilson's Psychological Warfare 1917–18," in *Florida State University Studies,* XIV (1954), 74.

9. *Intimate Papers of Colonel House,* II, 448; Henry Ford was also a self-avowed pacifist.

10. Opinion was also very inconsistent; compare what House says of the attitude in Kansas and Missouri, *Intimate Papers of Colonel House,* II, 469.

11. Osgood, *Ideals and Self-Interest in American Foreign Policy,* p. 273.

12. Walter Lippmann, *U.S. Foreign Policy: Shield of the Republic* (Boston, 1943), pp. 33–39, quoted by Link, *Woodrow Wilson and the Progressive Era,* p. 279.

13. H. C. Peterson and Gilbert C. Fite, *Opponents of the War, 1917–1918* (Madison, Wis., 1957).

14. Letter of March 7, 1915, in the Baker Papers, quoted by Henry A. Turner, "Woodrow Wilson and Public Opinion," in *Public Opinion Quarterly,* Winter 1957–58, p. 519. This is also the opinion of C. F. Bell, *Woodrow Wilson and the People* (Garden City, N.Y., 1945).

15. H. A. Turner, "Woodrow Wilson and Public Opinion," p. 510.

16. All these figures are to be found in Millis, *Arms and Men,* pp. 225, 236–237.

17. These figures are to be found in John Bach McMaster, *The United States in the World War (1918–1920)* (New York, 1920), chapter 2.

18. Baker, *Woodrow Wilson,* VII, 113.

19. Frederic L. Paxson, *America at War* (Boston, 1939), p. 11.

20. See also A. Tardieu, *Devant l'Obstacle, l'Amérique et Nous* (Paris, 1927), p. 224; quoting the report of Cromwell, Undersecretary of War, Tardieu estimates the arms furnished by France to the U.S. Army as follows: 4881 airplanes, 2150 75-millimeter guns, 1684 guns of other calibers, 260 tanks, and all kinds of artillery.

21. Paxson, *America at War,* p. 91.

22. Baker, *Woodrow Wilson,* VII, 317, 415, and elsewhere.

23. *Ibid.*

24. Arno Mayer, *Political Origins of the New Diplomacy, 1917–18* (New Haven, 1959), p. 235. See also Baker, *Woodrow Wilson,* V, 96.

25. Paris, 1919. See also Louis Aubert, *et al., André Tardieu* (Paris, 1957).

26. Briand, whom House met December 3, was in favor of such a declaration, but he was no longer in the government.

27. "The War Aims and the Peace Terms They Suggest," in *Papers Relating to Foreign Relations of the United States,* 1919, I, 41–53.

28. Quoted by Victor S. Mamatey, "The U.S. and the Origins of the Adriatic Question," *Florida State University Publications,* IV, (1951), pp. 49–50.

29. Baker, *Woodrow Wilson,* VII, 506.

30. Curry, *Woodrow Wilson and Far Eastern Policy, 1913–1921,* p. 176.

31. Quoted by Betty Miller Unterberger, *America's Siberian Expedition, 1918–1920* (Durham, N.C., 1956), p. 30–31.

32. *Ibid.,* 31–32.

33. Curry, *Woodrow Wilson and Far Eastern Policy,* p. 224.

34. George F. Kennan, *Soviet-American Relations, 1917–1920,* vol. II, *The Decision to Intervene* (Princeton, 1958), p. 428.

35. *Intimate Papers of Colonel House,* IV, 76–80.

36. Mamatey, "The U.S. and the Origins of the Adriatic Question," p. 56.

37. House to Lansing, October 29, 1918, in *Papers Relating to Foreign Rela-*

Isolationist Impulse, Its Twentieth Century Reaction (New York, 1957), especially pp. 137–239. Only after 1933 does he see what he calls "the isolationist tornado."

14. Philip Dexter and John Hunter Sedgwick, *The War Debts; An American View* (New York, 1928), p. 132.

15. Joe Mitchell Chapple, *Warren G. Harding, Our After-War President* (Boston, 1924), p. 122.

16. Frederick E. Schortemeier, *Rededicating America: Life and Recent Speeches of Warren G. Harding* (Indianapolis, Ind., 1920), p. 56.

17. Dexter Perkins, *Charles E. Hughes and American Democratic Statesmanship* (Boston, 1956), pp. xvi–xvii.

18. Cited by Merlo T. Pusey, *Charles E. Hughes* (New York, 1951), I, 215.

19. *Ibid.*, vol. I, p. 317.

20. *Ibid.*, p. 332.

21. *Ibid.*, p. 338.

22. Claude M. Fuess, *Calvin Coolidge, the Man from Vermont* (Boston, [194]0), p. 71.

23. *The Autobiography of Calvin Coolidge* (New York, 1929), p. 124.

24. *Ibid.*, p. 196.

25. Fuess, *Calvin Coolidge*, p. 316.

26. Bainbridge Colby, *The Close of Woodrow Wilson's Administration and Final Years* (New York, 1930), pp. 12–14.

[2]7. Cited by Pusey, *Charles E. Hughes*, II, 432.

[2]8. *Ibid.*, II, 600.

[2]9. *Ibid.*, II, 579.

[3]0. *Ibid.*, II, 582.

[ ]. Charles G. Dawes, *A Journal of Reparations* (London, 1939).

[ ]. According to Pusey, *Charles E. Hughes*, II, 591.

[ ]. Schlesinger, *Political and Social Growth*, p. 461.

[ ]. Cited by Williams, *Economic Foreign Policy*, p. 228.

[ ]. Cited by Roger Picard and Paul Hugon, *Le probleme des dettes inter-Nécessité d'une Revision*, Paris, 1934, pp. 204–205. [Oswald] Chew, President of the Alliance Française of New York, editor [of the] collection *France Courageous and Indomitable*, has published many texts [of this] kind in *The Stroke of the Moment: A Discussion of the Foreign Debts*, [Phila]delphia, 1928. Other authors at the same time supported the same point of [view,] stressing England: for instance, P. Dexter, and J. H. Sedgwick, *The War* [Debts, An American View*, New York, 1928.

[ ]. Williams, *Economic Foreign Policy*, p. 231.

[ ]. *Ib]id.*, pp. 241–242.

[ ]. [F]igures cited by Harold and Margaret Sprout, *Toward a New Order [of Sea] Power . . . 1918–1922* (Princeton, 1946).

[ ]. [A]nnual Report of the Navy Department, 1920, cited by Sprout, *Toward [a New] Order*, p. 80.

[ ]. [T]oward a New Order. This is the title of chapter 7, pp. 104–122.

[ ]. [Ibi]d., p. 118.

[ ]. [He]rbert O. Yardley, *The American Black Chamber* (New York, 1931). [Chap]ter 16, "The Washington Armament Conference." The Black Chamber [was] abolished by Stimson in 1929.

[ ]. [—], p. 313.

tions of the United States, suppl. 1, vol. I, p. 413. See also Charles Seymour, *American Diplomacy during the World War* (Baltimore, 1942), p. 367.

38. Wilson at first (Oct. 30) rejected this reservation, *Papers Relating to Foreign Relations of the United States*, suppl. 1, vol. I, p. 423; compare Seymour, *American Diplomacy*, p. 382. House suggested a compromise: the British would accept the principle but not its application. Wilson accepted the British reservation on November 4. Seymour, *American Diplomacy*, p. 389.

39. Arthur Clarence Walworth, *Woodrow Wilson, World Prophet* (New York, 1958), II, 197.

40. Seymour, *American Diplomacy*, p. 395.

V. Wilson and the Peace

1. *Intimate Papers of Colonel House*, IV, 206.

2. Arthur Willert, *The Road to Safety* (New York, 1953), p. 166.

3. Walworth, *Woodrow Wilson*, II, 207. Note that Hoover's preference for the Republican party was not yet known.

4. Quoted in *Le Centenaire de Woodrow Wilson* (Geneva, 1956).

5. These two texts quoted by George, *Woodrow Wilson and Colonel House*, p. 202.

6. *Ibid.*, p. 203; See also *Intimate Papers of Colonel House*, IV, 214.

7. *Ibid.*, p. 211.

8. Thomas Bailey, *Woodrow Wilson and The Lost Peace* (New York, 1944), p. 115.

9. *Intimate Papers of Colonel House*, IV, 280–288.

10. Walworth, *Woodrow Wilson*, II, 260.

11. *Ibid.*, II, 274.

12. *Ibid.*, p. 278.

13. Bailey, *The Lost Peace*, pp. 204–205.

14. George, *Woodrow Wilson and Colonel House*, p. 240. The Georges think Mrs. Wilson greatly dramatizes the situation.

15. R. S. Baker, *Woodrow Wilson and the World Settlement*, (Garden City, N.Y., 1922), I, 295–314. See also *Intimate Papers of Colonel House*, IV, 396f.

16. George, *Woodrow Wilson and Colonel House*, p. 246.

17. Paul Joseph Mantoux, *Les Deliberations du Conseil des Quatre* (Paris, 1955), I, 13.

18. *Ibid.*, I, 40 (March 27, 1919).

19. *Ibid.*, I, 60 (March 28, 1919). See also p. 90.

20. *Ibid.*, I, 28 (March 25).

21. *Ibid.*, I, 122 (April 2).

22. *Ibid.*, I, 68–69 (March 28, 1919).

23. *Ibid.*, I, 72.

24. *Ibid.*, I, 74.

25. *Ibid.*, I, 193–194.

26. *Ibid.*, I, 205 (April 9, 1919).

27. *Intimate Papers of Colonel House*, IV, 403.

28. In *The Lost Peace*, p. 232.

29. Mantoux, *Deliberations du Conseil des Quatre*, I, 237f. (April 13, 1919).

30. *Ibid.*, I, 278.

31. *Ibid.*, I, 282–285.
32. *Ibid.*, I, 293.
33. *Ibid.*, I, 338. See also p. 344 (April 23).
34. *Ibid.*, I, 255 (April 24).
35. *Ibid.*, I, 124.
36. Quoted by Curry, *Woodrow Wilson and Far Eastern Policy*, p. 241.
37. Mantoux, *Deliberations du Conseil des Quatre*, I, 20.
38. *Ibid.*, pp. 55–56 (March 27, 1919).
39. Quoted by Curry, *Woodrow Wilson and Far Eastern Policy*, p. 277.
40. Quoted by Walworth, *Woodrow Wilson*, II, 319.
41. Mantoux, *Deliberations du Conseil des Quatre*, II, 23 (May 10, 1919).
42. *Ibid.*, II, 69 (May 14, 1919).
43. *Ibid.*, II, 402–403. See also p. 456 (June 17, 1919).
44. *Ibid.*, II, 430–444.
45. *Ibid.*, II, 266–269.
46. *Intimate Papers of Colonel House*, IV, 474–476.
47. Mantoux, *Deliberations du Conseil des Quatre*, II, 280; see also p. 287.
48. *Ibid.*, II, 348 (June 7, 1919).
49. *Ibid.*, II, 356 (June 9, 1919).
50. *Ibid.*, II, 478 (June 22, 1919).
51. Quoted by Walworth, *Woodrow Wilson*, II, 330.
52. *Ibid.*, 332.

VI. The Defeat of Wilsonian Internationalism

1. Quoted by Thomas A. Bailey, *Woodrow Wilson and the Great Betrayal* (New York, 1947), p. 14. I make frequent use of this remarkable book in this section.
2. Henry Cabot Lodge, *The Senate and the League of Nations* (New York, 1925), p. 28.
3. *Ibid.*, p. 129–130.
4. *Ibid.*, p. 147.
5. The essential source is of course the volume *Treaty of Peace with Germany, Hearings before the Committee on Foreign Relations, United States Senate* (Washington, 1919).
6. See the text of the debates in Lodge, *The Senate and the League of Nations*, IV, pp. 296–379.
7. *Hearings*, pp. 1161f (September 12).
8. Robert Lansing, *The Peace Negotiations, a Personal Narrative* (Boston, 1921). See also Louis A. R. Yates, *The United States and French Security, 1917–1921* (New York, 1957), chapter 6, "The Guarantee Treaty—How the U.S. Reacted to It."
9. Lansing, *The Peace Negotiations*, p. 23.
10. See Russell H. Fifield, *Woodrow Wilson and the Far East* (New York, 1952), pp. 339f.
11. Lodge, *The Senate and the League of Nations*, pp. 175–176.
12. Wesley M. Bagby, "Woodrow Wilson, a Third Term and the Solemn Referendum," *American Historical Review*, April 1955, p. 568.
13. Lodge, *The Senate and the League of Nations*, p. 212.
14. *Ibid.*, p. 226.

VII. Hughes and the Postwar Problems

1. Arthur S. Link, "What Happened to the Progressive M 1920's," *American Historical Review*, July 1959, pp. 833–852.
2. Warren S. Thompson and P. K. Whelpton, *Populatio United States* (New York, 1933), p. 1.
3. *Ibid.*, p. 303.
4. Duncan, *Immigration and Assimilation*, pp. 482–484.
5. Arthur M. Schlesinger, *Political and Social Growth People* (New York, 1941), p. 459.
6. Nearing and Freeman, *Dollar Diplomacy*, p. 5. Sin reckoned in current dollar terms, the scale of the increase due to inflation.
7. *Ibid.*, p. 2.
8. *Ibid.*, pp. 15–16.
9. Benjamin H. Williams, *Economic Foreign Policy* (New York, 1929), p. 19.
10. Official figures of the Treasury Department, 193 *matic History*, p. 236.
11. *Congressional Record*, vol. 55, p. 760, cited in *eign Policy*, p. 219.
12. "The Legend of Isolationism in the 1920s," *Sci* 1954, pp. 1–20. The essence of this article, without important) has been reproduced in William App *Shaping of American Diplomacy. Readings and De eign Relations, 1750–1955* (Chicago, 1956), pp. 65
13. *National Isolation an Illusion, Political Indep* York, 1925). The word had not yet become fam hardly used by Charles A. Beard in *The Idea of I* 1934), and is not to be found in the index. Bear the leaders of isolationism after 1937, wrote in which used to be so convincing, can be used to the continuation of national security" (*The* 733). See Gerald Stourzh, "Charles A. Beard Foreign Policy," *World Affairs Quarterly*, J Appleman Williams challenges the word in a Note on the Isolationism of Senator Borah," *P* ber 1953, pp. 391–392. One gets the same imp Fola La Follette, *Robert M. La Follette, Ji* York, 1953), and John A. Garraty, *Henry* where the word *isolationism* is also not to be is that these men did not consider themselve ists." The word one often finds is "indep *and the League of Nations*. For Samuel American Defense and Diplomacy" in Reynolds, eds., *Essays in History and George Hubbard Blakeslee*, Worcester, concepts in the thinking of the 1920's: i neutrality, pacifism. See, finally, the c

45. Pusey, *Charles E. Hughes*, II, 489–490.

46. Cited by J. Chalmers Vinson, "The Drafting of the Four Power Treaty of the Washington Conference," in *Journal of Modern History*, March 1953, pp. 40–49, esp. p. 44.

47. Pusey, *Charles E. Hughes*, II, 499.

48. *Ibid.*, p. 500.

49. Cited by Russell H. Fifield, "Secretary Hughes and the Shantung Question," *Pacific Historical Review*, November 1954, pp. 373–385, esp. p. 374.

50. *Ibid.*, p. 385.

51. R. D. McKenzie, *Oriental Exclusion*, p. 37.

52. *Ibid.*, p. 45.

53. Pusey, *Charles E. Hughes*, II, 512.

54. S. F. Bemis, *The Latin American Policy of the United States* (New York, 1943), p. 203.

55. Perkins, *Monroe Doctrine*, 333.

56. *Ibid.*, p. 335.

57. David D. Burks, "The United States and the Geneva Protocol of 1924: A New Holy Alliance?" *American Historical Review*, July 1959, pp. 891–905.

VIII. Prosperity and the Great Illusion, 1925–1929

1. These figures come especially from George Soule, *Economic Forces in American History* (New York, 1952), especially pp. 468–481; and from Louis Rosenstock-Franck, *Histoire Économique et Sociale des États-Unis de 1919 à 1949* (Paris, 1950), especially pp. 58–66.

2. Arthur M. Schlesinger, Jr., *The Age of Roosevelt*, vol. I: *The Crisis of the Old Order* (Boston, 1957), pp. 71–76.

3. James Warren Prothro, *The Dollar Decade: Business in the 1920s* (Baton Rouge, La., 1954).

4. Joseph Dorfman, *The Economic Mind in American Civilization* (New York, 1959), IV, 44–85. (Volumes IV and V cover the period 1918–1933, vol. V deals particularly with the depression.)

5. Herbert Feis, *The Diplomacy of the Dollar, First Era, 1919–1932* (Baltimore, 1950).

6. Merle Thorpe, "An Editorial Article by Mr. Coolidge," *The Nation's Business*, January 1926, p. 30. Cited by Prothro, *The Dollar Decade*, p. 89.

7. Cited by Prothro, *The Dollar Decade*, p. 138.

8. *Ibid.*, p. 139.

9. Bruce Barton, *The Man Nobody Knows: A Discovery of the Real Jesus* (Indianapolis, Ind., 1924), p. 11. Cited by Schlesinger, *The Crisis of the Old Order*, p. 72, and Prothro, *The Dollar Decade*, p. 230.

10. Cited by Soule, *Economic Forces in American History*, p. 472.

11. Cited by Feis, *The Diplomacy of the Dollar*, p. 6.

12. These principles were "codified" as late as July 1929 in a note prepared by Undersecretary of State Joseph Cotton. See Feis, *The Diplomacy of the Dollar*, p. 18.

13. Cited by Feis, *The Diplomacy of the Dollar*, p. 22.

14. *Ibid.*, p. 42.

15. *Ibid.*, p. 46.

16. Cleona Lewis, *America's Stake in International Investments* (Washing-

ton, 1938), p. 392. See Rosenstock-Franck, *Histoire Economique et Sociale*, pp. 81–83.

17. Rosenstock-Franck, *Histoire Economique et Sociale*, pp. 82–85.

18. Cited by Feis, *The Diplomacy of the Dollar*, p. 14.

19. Cited by John E. Stoner, *S. O. Levinson and the Pact of Paris*, (Chicago, 1943), p. 45.

20. Cited by Robert Ferrell, "The Peace Movement" in Alexander De Conde, ed., *Isolation and Security* (Durham, N.C., 1957), p. 101.

21. Nicholas Murray Butler, *Across the Busy Years* (New York, 1939–1940), II, 202.

22. Robert Ferrell, *Peace in Their Time: The Origins of the Kellogg-Briand Pact* (New Haven, 1952), p. 71.

23. *Ibid.*, p. 265.

24. Cited by Feis, *The Diplomacy of the Dollar*, p. 26.

25. *Ibid.*, p. 29.

26. Pusey, *Charles E. Hughes*, II, 559–560.

27. Cited by Perkins, *Monroe Doctrine*, pp. 342–343; see also David Bryn-Jones, *Frank B. Kellogg* (New York, 1937), p. 179f.

28. Cited by Rippy, *The United States and Mexico*, p. 377.

IX. Hoover, Stimson, and the Great Depression

1. Schlesinger, *The Crisis of the Old Order*, p. 77.

2. *Ibid.*, p. 98.

3. David Hinshaw, *Herbert Hoover, American Quaker* (New York, 1950), p. 26. See also pp. 36–41, "Hoover Explained in American Terms."

4. Cited by Schlesinger, *Crisis of the Old Order*, p. 81.

5. Frank Freidel, *Franklin D. Roosevelt* (Boston, 1952), vol. II, p. 57.

6. Schlesinger, *Crisis of the Old Order*, p. 88.

7. Henry L. Stimson and McGeorge Bundy, *On Active Service in Peace and War* (New York, 1948), pp. 156–157.

8. *Ibid.*, p. 51.

9. *Ibid.*, p. 105.

10. Richard N. Current, *Secretary Stimson* (New Brunswick, N.J., 1954), p. 7.

11. Stimson and Bundy, *On Active Service*, p. 197.

12. Current, *Secretary Stimson*, p. 41.

13. According to John Kenneth Galbraith, *The Great Crash, 1929* (Boston, 1955), p. 7.

14. Rosenstock-Franck, *Histoire Economique et Sociale*, p. 84.

15. Galbraith, *The Great Crash*, p. 6.

16. Schlesinger, *Crisis of the Old Order*, p. 457.

17. *Ibid.*, p. 459.

18. Figures from Rosenstock-Franck, *Histoire Economique et Sociale*, pp. 54–55 and 94.

19. Harris Gaylord Warren, *Herbert Hoover and the Great Depression* (New York, 1959), p. 91.

20. *Ibid.*, p. 92.

21. Stimson and Bundy, *On Active Service*, p. 164.

22. Raymond G. O'Connor, "The 'Yardstick' and Naval Disarmament in the 1920's," *Mississippi Valley Historical Review*, December 1958, p. 442.

23. George T. Davis, *A Navy Second to None* (New York, 1940), pp. 335–337.

24. Stimson and Bundy, *On Active Service*, p. 171.

25. Millis, *Arms and Men*, p. 243.

26. Stimson and Bundy, *On Active Service*, p. 266.

27. *Ibid.*, p. 267.

28. *Ibid.*, p. 275.

29. Cited by William Starr Myers, *The Foreign Policies of Herbert Hoover* (New York, 1940), p. 140.

30. Stimson and Bundy, *On Active Service*, p. 213.

31. Castle, a personal friend of Hoover, had succeeded Joseph P. Cotton, a personal friend of Stimson, as undersecretary of state. Cotton died early in 1931.

32. Henry L. Stimson, *The Far Eastern Crisis* (New York, 1936), p. 41.

33. *Ibid.*, p. 44.

34. *Ibid.*, p. 50.

35. Cited by Current, *Secretary Stimson*, p. 76.

36. Cited by Current, *Secretary Stimson*, p. 79, according to Stimson's unpublished diary.

37. *Ibid.*, p. 81.

38. Current, *Secretary Stimson*, p. 93.

39. *Ibid.*, p. 116.

40. Alexander De Conde, *Herbert Hoover's Latin American Policy* (Stanford, Calif., 1951), p. 18.

41. *Ibid.*, pp. 21–22.

42. Cited by De Conde, *Herbert Hoover's Latin American Policy*, p. 79.

43. Sumner Welles, *The Time for Decision* (New York, 1944), p. 190f.

44. De Conde, *Herbert Hoover's Latin American Policy*, p. 127.

X. Roosevelt and Isolationism, 1933–1937

1. Frank Freidel, *Franklin D. Roosevelt*, vol. I: *The Apprenticeship* (Boston, 1952), p. 32.

2. *Ibid.*, p. 318.

3. *Ibid.*, vol. II., *The Ordeal* (1954), p. 178.

4. *Ibid.*, p. 183.

5. *Ibid.*, p. 235. See also Roosevelt's article in *Foreign Affairs*, July 1928.

6. Schlesinger, *The Crisis of the Old Order*, pp. 248–249.

7. *Ibid.*, p. 8.

8. *Ibid.*, p. 290.

9. New York *Times*, June 28, 1928, quoted by Charles A. Beard, *American Foreign Policy in the Making, 1923–1940* (New Haven, 1946), p. 58.

10. *Ibid.*, pp. 64–116.

11. *Ibid.*, p. 76.

12. Raymond Moley, *After Seven Years* (New York, 1939), p. 62.

13. Cordell Hull, *The Memoirs of Cordell Hull* (New York, 1948), 2 vols., I, 69.

14. *Ibid.*, p. 155.

15. *Ibid.*, p. 158.

16. *Ibid.*, p. 191.

17. *Ibid.*, p. 194.

18. Samuel I. Rosenman, ed., *The Public Papers and Addresses of Franklin D. Roosevelt* (New York, 1938–1950), 13 vols., II, 170.

19. Hull, *Memoirs*, I, 251.

20. The confiscation totaled $628,000,000. For the figure of $192,000,000 owed by the government see, *Papers Relating to Foreign Affairs of the United States, The Soviet Union*, July 27, 1933, p. 8.

21. Hull, *Memoirs*, II, 17 (October 4, 1933).

22. *Ibid.*, II, 59–60 (January 4, 1934).

23. *Ibid.*, I, 321.

24. *Public Papers of Franklin D. Roosevelt*, III, 11 (January 3, 1934, Annual Message to Congress).

25. *Ibid.*, IV, 410 (October 2, 1935. Address at San Diego Exposition).

26. Hull, *Memoirs*, I, 399.

27. Charles and Mary Beard, *The Rise of American Civilization*, vol I: *America in Mid Passage* (New York, 1939), pp. 429–430.

28. Elliott Roosevelt, ed., *F. D. R.: His Personal Letters* (New York, 1947–1950, 4 vols.), III, p. 352.

29. *Ibid.*, III, 701.

30. Hull, *Memoirs*, I, 435.

31. *Ibid.*, p. 461.

32. *Public Papers of Franklin D. Roosevelt*, V, 288 (August 14, 1936, Address at Chautauqua, N.Y.).

33. Hull, *Memoirs*, I, 564.

XI. Roosevelt Abandons Neutrality, October 1937–June 1940

1. *Public Papers of Franklin D. Roosevelt*, IV, 453 (letter to Bishop Aldham, Nov. 14, 1935).

2. *Ibid.*, V, 12 (Annual Message to Congress, Jan. 3, 1936).

3. *Ibid.*, VI, 408f. ("quarantine" speech), Chicago, Oct. 5, 1937.

4. Beard, *American Foreign Policy in the Making, 1932–1940* (New Haven, 1946), p. 187.

5. The part of the press conference which was "off the record" was reported to Beard by one of the newspapermen present. Quoted in *Ibid.*, pp. 188–190.

6. William L. Langer and S. Everett Gleason, *The Challenge to Isolation, 1937–1940* (New York, 1952), p. 20.

7. Hull, *Memoirs*, I, 539.

8. Beard, *American Foreign Policy in the Making*, p. 182.

9. Langer and Gleason, *The Challenge to Isolation*, p. 24.

10. Hull, *Memoirs*, I, 563.

11. *Ibid.*, p. 570.

12. Quoted by Beard, *American Foreign Policy in the Making*, p. 216.

13. *Public Papers of Franklin D. Roosevelt*, VIII, 1f (1939).

14. Langer and Gleason, *The Challenge to Isolation*, pp. 48–50.

15. Hull, *Memoirs*, I, 648–649.

16. *Ibid.*, p. 650.

17. *Ibid.*, p. 621–622.

18. Langer and Gleason, *The Challenge to Isolation*, p. 161.

19. *Public Papers of Franklin D. Roosevelt*, VIII, 463f.

20. Langer and Gleason, *The Challenge to Isolation*, p. 250.

21. Nancy H. Hooker, ed. *The Moffat Papers*, Selections from the Diplomatic Journals of *J. Pierrepont Moffat, 1919–1943* (Cambridge, Mass., 1956), p. 298.

22. Langer and Gleason, *The Challenge to Isolation*, p. 451.

23. *Ibid.*, p. 479.

24. *Ibid.*, pp. 489–490.

25. *Ibid.*, p. 491.

26. *Ibid.*, p. 516.

27. Paul Reynaud, *La France a sauvé l'Europe* (Paris, 1947), 2 vols., II, 331.

28. Langer and Gleason, *The Challenge to Isolation*, p. 539.

29. *Ibid.*, p. 551.

XII. The United States Entry into the War

1. See *Public Opinion Quarterly* and the voluminous collection edited by Hadley Cantril, *Public Opinion, 1935–1946* (Princeton, 1951), especially the chapter, "United States Neutrality," pp. 966–968.

2. David Hinshaw, *A Man from Kansas: The Story of William Allen White* (New York, 1945).

3. *Ibid.*, p. 286.

4. Walter C. Johnson, *The Battle against Isolation* (Chicago, 1944), also his *William Allen White's America* (New York, 1947).

5. Wayne S. Cole, *America First, The Battle against Intervention* (Madison, Wis., 1953).

6. *Public Papers of Franklin D. Roosevelt*, IX, 517f (1940).

7. Langer and Gleason, *Challenge to Isolation*, p. 755.

8. *Ibid.*, p. 756.

9. Stimson and Bundy, *On Active Service*, p. 348.

10. Langer and Gleason, *Challenge to Isolation*, p. 180.

11. *Ibid.*, p. 189.

12. *Public Papers of Franklin D. Roosevelt*, IX, 643 (Fireside Chat, December 29, 1940).

13. Quoted by Roland N. Stromberg, "American Business and the Approach of War," *Journal of Economic History*, Winter 1953, pp. 58–78.

14. Stimson and Bundy, *On Active Service*, p. 381.

15. Maurice Matloff and Edwin M. Snell, *Strategic Planning for Coalition Warfare, 1941–1942* (Washington, Department of the Army, 1953–59), p. 38.

16. *Ibid.*, p. 60.

17. Figures taken from Robert Mossé, "La Mobilisation économique aux Etats-Unis pendant la seconde guerre mondiale," *Revue d'histoire de la deuxième guerre mondiale*, October 1953, p. 4.

18. Robert Sherwood, *Roosevelt and Hopkins: An Intimate History* (New York, 1948), p. 225.

19. Langer and Gleason, *Challenge to Isolation*, p. 240.

20. *Public Papers of Franklin D. Roosevelt*, IX, 640 (1940).

21. *Ibid.*, p. 670 (Annual Message, January 6, 1941).

22. Quoted in Langer and Gleason, *The Undeclared War* (New York, 1953), p. 263.

23. *Ibid.*, p. 83.

24. Sherwood, *Roosevelt and Hopkins*, p. 231.

25. *Ibid.*, p. 242.

26. *Ibid.*, p. 257.

27. Stimson and Bundy, *On Active Service*, p. 371.

28. Quoted in Langer and Gleason, *The Undeclared War*, p. 503.

29. *Ibid.*, p. 510.

30. *Ibid.*, p. 442.

31. Sherwood, *Roosevelt and Hopkins*, p. 304.

32. *Ibid.*, p. 321–322.

33. *Ibid.*, p. 342.

34. Langer and Gleason, *The Undeclared War*, p. 691.

35. *Ibid.*, p. 734.

36. Herbert Feis, *The Road to Pearl Harbor* (Princeton, 1950), p. 41.

37. *Ibid.*, 237–238.

38. Sherwood *Roosevelt and Hopkins*, p. 316; Feis, *The Road to Pearl Harbor*, p. 241.

39. Feis, *The Road to Pearl Harbor*, p. 248.

40. Langer and Gleason, *The Undeclared War*, p. 695.

41. Feis, *The Road to Pearl Harbor*, p. 265.

42. *Papers Relating to Foreign Relations of the United States, Japan*, II, 792. See also Feis, *The Road to Pearl Harbor*, p. 339, and Langer and Gleason, *The Undeclared War*, p. 934.

43. Langer and Gleason, *The Undeclared War*, p. 936.

44. In the bibliography there is a more detailed analysis of works dealing with Pearl Harbor. See also the excellent study of Wayne S. Cole, "American Entry in World II, an Historiographical Appraisal," *Mississippi Valley Historical Review*, March 1957, pp. 595–617.

XIII. The United States at War: Initial Defeats and Recovery, 1942–1943

1. Hull, *Memoirs*, II, 1109–1110.

2. Sherwood, *Roosevelt and Hopkins*, p. 437.

3. *Ibid.*, p. 445.

4. Stimson and Bundy, *On Active Service*, p. 416.

5. Winston S. Churchill, *The Hinge of Fate* (Boston, 1950), p. 133.

6. Sherwood, *Roosevelt and Hopkins*, p. 474.

7. Elting Morison, *Turmoil and Tradition, A Study of the Life and Times of Henry L. Stimson* (Boston, 1960), p. 582.

8. *Ibid.*, p. 583.

9. George F. Horve, *Northwest Africa: Seizing the Initiative in the West* (United States Army in World War II, Washington, Department of the Army, 1957), p. 13.

10. Sherwood, *Roosevelt and Hopkins*, p. 485.

11. *Ibid.*, p. 482.

12. *Ibid.*, pp. 482–483.

13. William L. Langer, *Our Vichy Gamble* (New York, 1947), p. 221.

14. Charles de Gaulle, *Mémoires de Guerre*, vol. I: *L'Appel* (Paris, 1954), p. 531.
15. *Ibid.*, p. 193.
16. Langer, *Our Vichy Gamble*, 210–211.
17. *Ibid.*, p. 278.
18. *Ibid.*, p. 290.
19. *Ibid.*, p. 296.
20. De Gaulle, *Mémoires de Guerre*, vol. II, *L'Unité*, p. 9.
21. Langer, *Our Vichy Gamble*, p. 339.
22. *Ibid.*, p. 347.
23. *Ibid.*, p. 348.
24. *Ibid.*, p. 349.
25. *Ibid.*, p. 364.
26. Herbert Feis, *Churchill, Roosevelt and Stalin* (Princeton, 1957), p. 20.
27. *Ibid.*, p. 24, footnote.
28. *Ibid.*, p. 40.
29. *Ibid.*, p. 42.
30. *Ibid.*, p. 69.
31. *Ibid.*, p. 71.
32. *Correspondance secrète de Staline avec Roosevelt, Churchill, Truman, et Atlee* (Paris, 1959), I, 71–72.
33. *Ibid.*, I, 50.
34. Feis, *Churchill, Roosevelt and Stalin*, p. 80, and *Correspondance secrète de Staline*, I, 82.
35. *Correspondance secrète de Staline*, I, 107.
36. *Ibid.*, p. 113 (December 8).
37. Sherwood, *Roosevelt and Hopkins*, p. 511.
38. Hull, *Memoirs*, II 1482.
39. *Ibid.*, p. 1483.
40. Sherwood, *Roosevelt and Hopkins*, p. 524.
41. Hull, *Memoirs*, II, 1494.
42. Sherwood, *Roosevelt and Hopkins*, p. 404.
43. Herbert Feis, *The China Tangle* (Princeton, 1953), p. 62; and *United States Foreign Relations: China* (State Department, Washington, 1949), p. 519.
44. Feis, *The China Tangle*, p. 73.
45. Joseph W. Stilwell, *Stilwell Papers*, ed. Theodore H. White (New York, 1948), p. 232 (October 17, 1943).
46. Elliott Roosevelt, *As He Saw It* (New York, 1946), p. 117.
47. *Public Papers of Franklin D. Roosevelt*, XII, 39 (1943); see also Feis, *Churchill, Roosevelt and Stalin*, p. 109, and the comparison to Lee's unconditional surrender at Appomatox, pp. 111–112.
48. Sherwood, *Roosevelt and Hopkins*, p. 686.
49. Feis, *Churchill, Roosevelt and Stalin*, p. 117; see also *Correspondance secrète de Staline*, I, 152.
50. Churchill, *The Hinge of Fate*, p. 710.
51. Herbert Feis, "The Three Who Led," *Foreign Affairs*, January 1959, p. 291.
52. Feis, *Churchill, Roosevelt and Stalin*, p. 131, and *Correspondance secrète de Staline*, I, 181–182.

53. Feis, *Churchill, Roosevelt and Stalin*, pp. 134–135, and *Correspondance secrète de Staline*, I, 199–201.

54. Feis, *Churchill, Roosevelt and Stalin*, p. 139.

55. *Ibid.*, p. 142.

56. Trumbull Higgins, *Winston Churchill and the Second Front* (New York, 1957), p. 100.

57. Feis, *Churchill, Roosevelt and Stalin*, p. 147.

58. *Ibid.*, p. 167.

59. *Ibid.*, p. 169.

60. *Ibid.*, p. 172; see also *Correspondance secrète de Staline*, I, 215.

XIV. Victory in Sight, Spring 1943–Autumn 1944

1. *Postwar Foreign Policy Preparation, 1939–1945* (Washington, Department of State, 1949), p. 18.

2. *Ibid.*, p. 123.

3. Freidel, *The Ordeal*, p. 137; see also Foster Rhea Dulles and Gerald E. Ridinger, "The Anti-Colonial Policies of Franklin D. Roosevelt," *Political Science Quarterly*, March 1955, p. 2.

4. *Public Papers of Franklin D. Roosevelt*, XI, 437; see also Dulles and Ridinger, p. 8.

5. *Postwar Foreign Policy Preparation*, pp. 471–472.

6. Feis, *Churchill, Roosevelt and Stalin*, p. 123.

7. Hull, *Memoirs*, II, 1273.

8. Feis, *Churchill, Roosevelt and Stalin*, p. 206.

9. Hull, *Memoirs*, II, 1307.

10. Sherwood, *Roosevelt and Hopkins*, p. 770.

11. Hull, *Memoirs*, II, 1310; see also Feis, *The China Tangle*, p. 100.

12. Feis, *Churchill, Roosevelt and Stalin*, p. 277.

13. Winston S. Churchill, *Closing the Ring* (Boston, 1951), p. 346.

14. Sherwood, *Roosevelt and Hopkins*, p. 778.

15. *Ibid.*, p. 799.

16. *Ibid.*, p. 789.

17. Churchill, *Closing the Ring*, p. 548.

18. *Correspondance secrète de Staline*, I, 296.

19. *Ibid.*, II, 19.

20. Dwight D. Eisenhower, *Crusade in Europe* (Garden City, N.Y., 1948), p. 244.

21. Feis, *Churchill, Roosevelt and Stalin*, p. 306.

22. Eisenhower, *Crusade in Europe*, p. 250.

23. *Ibid.*, pp. 283–284.

24. Winston S. Churchill, *Triumph and Tragedy* (Boston, 1953), pp. 64, 65, and pp. 721–722 (Appendix D to Book I).

25. *Ibid.*, p. 100.

26. Feis, *Churchill, Roosevelt and Stalin*, p. 319.

27. Stimson and Bundy, *On Active Service*, p. 551; see also Feis, *Churchill, Roosevelt and Stalin*, p. 321.

28. Feis, *Churchill, Roosevelt and Stalin*, p. 332.

29. Hull, *Memoirs*, II, 1569.

30. Feis, *Churchill, Roosevelt and Stalin*, p. 343.

31. Churchill, *Triumph and Tragedy*, p. 140.
32. *Ibid.*, p. 155.
33. Feis, *The China Tangle*, p. 121.
34. *Ibid.*, p. 153.

XV. Yalta and the Death of Roosevelt

1. *Correspondance secrète de Staline*, II, 63.
2. Feis, *Roosevelt, Churchill and Stalin*, p. 450.
3. Hull, *Memoirs*, II, 1715.
4. *Ibid.*, p. 1227.
5. Sherwood, *Roosevelt and Hopkins*, p. 835.
6. De Gaulle, *Mémoires de Guerre*, vol. III, *Le Salut*, p. 44.
7. *Ibid.*, p. 32.
8. *Ibid.*, p. 88.
9. *Ibid.*, p. 89.
10. *Correspondance secrète de Staline*, II, 104.
11. Edward Stettinius, *Roosevelt and the Russians* (Garden City, N.Y., 1949), pp. 60–61.
12. Philip E. Mosely, "The Occupation of Germany: New Light on How the Zones Were Drawn," *Foreign Affairs*, July 1950, p. 581.
13. Hull, *Memoirs*, II, 1621.
14. *Yalta Documents* (Dept. of State, Washington, 1955), pp. 617 and 628.
15. *Ibid.*, p. 908.
16. *Ibid.*, p. 571.
17. *Ibid.*, p. 792.
18. *Ibid.*, p. 973.
19. *Ibid.*, p. 848.
20. *Ibid.*, p. 862.
21. *Ibid.*, p. 863.
22. Elting Morison, *Tradition and Turmoil*, p. 621.
23. Stettinius, *Roosevelt and the Russians*, p. 73.
24. Philip Mosely, "Hopes and Failures: American Policy toward East Central Europe, 1941–1947," in Stephen Kertesz, ed., *The Fate of East Central Europe* (Notre Dame, Ind., 1956), pp. 51–74.
25. Arthur H. Vandenberg, Jr., ed., *The Private Papers of Senator Vandenberg* (Boston, 1952), p. 96; see also Ruth Russell, *A History of the United Nations Charter, the Role of the United States, 1940–1945* (Washington, Brookings Institution, 1958), p. 194.
26. Russell, *History of the United Nations Charter*, p. 200.
27. William Hard McNeill, *America, Britain and Russia, 1941–1946* (London and New York, 1953), p. 501.
28. Feis, *Churchill, Roosevelt and Stalin*, p. 428.
29. Quoted in *ibid.*, p. 436.
30. Stettinius, *Roosevelt and the Russians*, p. 112, and *Yalta Documents*, p. 589.
31. *Yalta Documents*, p. 666.
32. *Ibid.*, p. 667.
33. *Correspondance secrète de Staline*, II, 135 (February 10, 1945).
34. Cantril, *Public Opinion*, pp. 372 and 908.

35. Samuel Flagg Bemis, *The United States as a World Power. A Diplomatic History, 1900–1955* (New York, 1955), p. 356.
36. Stettinius, *Roosevelt and the Russians*, p. 199.
37. Hull, *Memoirs*, II, 1422.
38. Sherwood, *Roosevelt and Hopkins*, p. 876.
39. *Correspondance secrète de Staline*, II, 144.
40. Sherwood, *Roosevelt and Hopkins*, p. 879.
41. *Correspondance secrète de Staline*, II, 147.
42. *Ibid.*, II, 151.
43. *Ibid.*, II, 153–154.
44. *Ibid.*, II, 157–158.
45. *Ibid.*, II, 159–160.
46. *Ibid.*, II, p. 163.

Index